EARLY HISTORY & RESEARCH DIGEST OF BEDFORD COUNTY TENNESSEE

by

TIMOTHY R. & HELEN C. MARSH

Southern Historical Press, Inc.
Greenville, South Carolina

Copyright © 2005 by:

Southern Historical Press, Inc.

All rights reserved. No part of this publication may be reproduced, stored in a retrieval system or transmitted in any form or by any means without the prior written permission of the author.

Please Direct All Correspondence and Book Orders to:

**Southern Historical Press, Inc.
PO Box 1267
375 West Broad Street
Greenville, S.C. 29602**

ISBN # 0-89308-702-5

Printed in the United States of America

Helen C. & Timothy R. Marsh

EARLY HISTORY AND RESEARCH DIGEST

OF

BEDFORD COUNTY TENNESSEE

By

Timothy R. and Helen C. Marsh

Introduction

This Book is intended as both an early Bedford County History and a historical facts research digest for the researcher that has an interest in Bedford County Tennessee. Much of the material in this publication was taken from the Marsh Collection and was compiled with the intent of sharing it with the readers.
Editors

CONTENTS

EARLY HISTORY SECTION...	1-155
RESEARCH DIGEST SECTION...	156-408
INDEX TO PLATS..	352
NAMES IN THE MASTER INDEX ARE TAKEN FROM PAGES...	1-248
NAMES IN LISTS ARRANGED IN ALPHABETICAL ORDER......	248-396

Timothy R. Marsh
Bedford County Historian
Archivist

Helen C. Marsh
Deputy Historian
Archivist

AN ABBREVIATED HISTORY OF EARLY BEDFORD COUNTY TENNESSEE
Written by

Timothy R. & Helen C. Marsh

This abridged history covering the brief span of years before and after the birth of Bedford County is included here to compliment this publication. It is not intended as a detailed in-depth treatment of the formative years of the county or its pioneer settlers. Some of the material presented herein may be repetitious and regrettably cannot be avoided. Hopefully much of the material will be virgin unpublished material of interest to the serious reader of Bedford County history.

BEFORE THE DAWN

Bedford County was part of North Caroline prior to statehood in 1796. For a brief period it was part of Washington, Greene, Davidson, Tennessee, Rutherford, Williamson and the short lived State of Franklin. Bedford was constituted as a county on December 3, 1807 by an Act of The Tennessee Legislature meeting at Knoxville. The parent county was Rutherford, a point of information not generally known is that from October 1799 until December 1807 a western strip of current Bedford was in Williamson County.

The eastern boundary of Williamson ran a short distance east of the village of Rover, once called Bylers, on the south near Unionville, once Union Campground crossing Duck River near the mouth of Sinking Creek, on southward to the Tennessee-Alabama State line, passing about two and one half miles west of where Fayetteville now stands. The boundaries of Bedford then ran from the Duck River Ridge situated between Murfreesboro and Shelbyville, being the dividing ridge between the waters of the Cumberland and the waters of Duck River, on south crossing Duck River, then Elk Ridge lying about nine miles south of Shelbyville, on southward crossing Elk River to the Alabama State Line, then the Mississippi Territory. For a brief time this included all of Lincoln and Moore Counties, part of Marshall County on the west and much of Coffee on the east. Bedford is located in the central basin of middle Tennessee. These grandiose boundaries would be short lived, as by November 14, 1809, the boundaries would be reduced to accommodate the formation of our neighbor Lincoln County to the south, and in 1835-36 the county was again reduced to its present size by the formation of Marshall and Coffee Counties.

Let us now examine the three "W's" of early Bedford County. The who's when and where, all three inter-connected. To find the name of the first who's in the county, we must first regress to a time in the early and mid 1700's, many years before the American Revolution, a time when this area was a wilderness of dense forests, canebrake and barrens, with no white settlers and still disputed territory claimed by the English, coveted by the French with the Spanish eagerly lurking near by to pick up the scraps. In 1714, a Frenchman by the name of Charles Charlesvillle set up a trading post at the French Lick on the Cumberland River. This was the site where French soldiers had established a fort on the bluff a few years before and was later to become Nashborough, still later Nashville, named for Colonel Francis Nash.

In 1748, Doctor Thomas Walker a prominent Virginian and explorer along with Colonel Patton and Major Charles Campbell made an expedition through the Cumberland Gap to a river that Doctor Walker named Cumberland. Years later he with Daniel Smith resurveyed the Virginia (now Kentucky) and North Carolina (now Tennessee) line that because of their not making proper allowances for variations of the needle or magnetic declination, resulted in the twelve miles error or jag at the Tennessee River referred to by some in that area as jag-start. The primary purpose of this expedition was to locate and take up land, which some of the party did. Some historians put them as far down as the French Lick, however, it should be noted that at this time in history Cumberland Country could have been anywhere west of the Cumberland Mountains or southern Kentucky. It is very unlikely that they came as far south as Duck River.

Another who came and stayed was Timothy Demonbreum, a Frenchman who settled at the lick in 1760, set up a trading post or store, lived and died there and left descendants to this day. The possibility exists that he may have challenged the wilderness and canebrakes as far south as Duck River on hunting and trapping expeditions. Still another possibility was Uriah Stone an explorer and hunter who came more than once to Cumberland Country, resulting in Stones River, a southern tributary of the Cumberland River being named for him. He in company with others in 1766 and 1767 explored on Stones River and its waters in present Wilson and Rutherford Counties and possibility as far south as Duck River Country. While it is possible that some of these early explorers and hunters viewed parts of the virgin lands in the central basin of Duck River, that is now Bedford County, Tennessee, this is at best an educated guess with no documented proof to substantiate this claim.

For many years before the first explorers came, the Duck River valley had experienced a period of relative calm and tranquility being disturbed only by Nomadic Tribes of American Indians as they traveled back and forth between the hunting grounds along the old Indian Traces, one being the War-Trace or trail that traversed the county in the area near the present town of Wartrace, which derived its name from the Wartrace Creek of fork that constitutes one of the three forks of Duck River. The trace also ran past the present town of Bell Buckle, that derived its name from the creek of the same name that is a fork of the Wartrace. The wartrace, path or trail was used in the distance past by warring tribes as they traveled through the area to the neighboring nations, from Georgia to the Ohio.

Another trace lying to the east of the war-trace was the Chichamauga trace later to become the Great Georgia Road and two hundred years later part of the Interstate 24. All of this area had been claimed by the Cherokees, the Chickamaugas, the Creeks and Chickasaws as their hunting grounds, as a consequence of the multiple claims each tribes was fearful of the other. This area was often sparsely inhibited except for a few nomadic who built temporary bark houses along traces, a few of these surviving and still standing as late as 1806 on the War-Trace, this is not to imply that this area was nor once Indian country, on the contrary centuries before, this area supported a thriving bustling civilization consisting of pre-historic Woodland Indians who had lived and died here from about 1000 BC to 1000AD. It was these people that are credited with building the ancient Stone Fort located at the fork of Duck River with Little Duck, once called Bark Creek, near Manchester, Tennessee. The Old Stone Fort is on a 5000 acre grant issued to Thomas and John Gray Blount and later became part of the vast land holdings of Andrew Erwin a Bedford County citizen of some prominence, who was a foe of General Andrew Jackson, having tangled with him over long land disputes. He is buried beside his wife Jane Patton, on their home place called "Rural Retreat," located south east of the town of Wartrace. The copena Tribe also occupied this area of Duck and Elk Rivers before the time of Columbus and large burial mounds have been found in Bedford and Lincoln Counties. The towns were often located at or near the mouth of major tributary of the rivers. This enhanced their defense as well as their ability to hunt and locate fresh game. Several large Indian towns uncovered in the county, one near Normandy, another on Weakley Creek and several other large camps in the bends of Duck River have produced excellent example of an early Indian culture, numerous Indian towns, burial grounds and artifacts adds credence to the fact that measured against the scale of time the early English, Scotch, Irish and German settlers who poured into the valley in the early 1800s were Johnnie-come-lately. Large civilizations having sprung up, flourished and died out centuries before the first white settlers came. Speaking of Indian burials presents an opportunity to set the record straight on a common misconception about such burials, one is the belief that old native rocks or fieldstones set at the head and foot of graves with no inscriptions on them, were used to mark "Old Indian Graves," this simply was not true. Marking graves with head and foot stones is an old and ancient practice not used by the early Indians. Those graces situated side by side with markers as described above are not Indian graveyards regardless of what some old timers say, rather they mark the final resting place of early Bedford County citizens who were not fortunate enough to have their graves marked with inscribed markers.

Near the end of the American Revolution, activity began to pick up in the Cumberland Country, then the western lands of North Carolina. The first major thrust towards permanent settlements in the area was made before December 1779 by three distinct and separate parties, not just one as we were often taught. Most often history dealt with the James Robertson-John Donaldson parties that left the Holston near Kingsport in east Tennessee about the same time, the younger able bodied men going overland with General Robertson, the older men, women and children and some younger men for various reasons not desiring to make the overland trip, left Ft. Patrick on December 22, 1779, going down river on a long and most remarkable journey that to this day demonstrates the adventurous and pioneer spirit these settlers exhibited. They made up the flotilla that was headed up by John Donaldson on his boat the "Adventure," with the destination of both parties to be the French Lick on the Cumberland.

The two other parties that were instrumental in bring civilization to this tint wilderness outpost on the Cumberland, were the Rains' Party headed by Captain John Rains, later to become a noted Indian fighter, and coming out from New River, Virginia, the other was the Mulherrin Party from South Carolina. These two parties were unique in that they contained women and children with their horses, cattle and personal possessions. They were coming to stay and not looking back. Their destination, unlike the Robertson Party, was Kentucky, not the French Lick, Rains having been there before. The three parties met in the wilderness above the Cumberland Gap in Kentucky and the amiable and persuasive Robertson, who would be later called the father of middle Tennessee, did a super selling job on the Rains and Mulherrin parties as he was later to do with the warring Indians and convinced them that it was in their best interest to alter their course and follow him to the French Lick on the Cumberland. The chance meeting in the wilderness undoubtedly speeded up the settling of the area.

Most of the Robertson group after the joyous reunion with their families on the bank of the Cumberland in April of 1780 settled down to the hazardous and hard frontier life in the fort at Nashborough, on the bluff, or in nearby stations opting to stay near civilization. Many of the Rains and Mulherrin parties not being all that enthusiastic about city life around Nashborough continued on into the wilderness and built their cabins and stations out of a radius of about 30 miles. One such station being the famed Buchanan Station on Mill Creek built by the Buchanans who came with the Mulherrin company. Another was Hickman Station built west of Nashville near Robertson Bend of the Cumberland River. Many of the stations and homes suffered severally from Indian raids and many of these first pioneer settlers were massacred. Some of these pioneers out of despair moved to Kentucky and at one time the entire settlement was threatened with complete extinction, but with the strong perseverance and guidance of Robertson and others, this tiny spark of civilization survived and grew and in so doing was the catalyst that brought civilization to the three forks of Duck River a quarter century later. It would be some twenty five years from the time of the settlement at the bluff that the Duck River Valley of Bedford County would began to be settled.

PASSING THROUGH

It was two hundred and twenty years ago at this writing , in 1783, that we find documented proof of the who, when and where relating to Bedford County. From old documents researched in the Tennessee State Archives many years ago by us and from information found in old land and court records in several middle counties of Tennessee, we have documented mush of the following.

In the struggle for American Independence from the haughty British in 1776-1783, the North Carolina fledgling government and people had suffered great privations. The struggle had been long and tiring having drained North Carolina of most of her resources. The treasury was bare, her gallant sons had suffered greatly in their fight for the cause. The North Carolina General Assembly in an attempt to show her gratitude to her sons and soldiers of the Continental Line and to recruit desperately needed man-power, took the following action. In the closing months of the American Revolution the North Carolina General Assembly passed an act for the relief of the officers and soldiers in the Continental Line and for other purposes. The act provided a specific amount of land for each soldier, depending on rank, provided they were then in service and should remain so until the end of the war. Each who met the above conditions was to have 640 acres, each non-commissioned officer 1000 acres, each Captain 3840 acres and etc. This act dictated that a large tract of western land, fifty five miles wide must be set aside for the purpose of honoring this promise, in addition to satisfying Bounty Land Warrants for military service. A commission was appointed consisting of Absalom Tatum, Isaac Shelby and Anthony Bledsoe to come to middle Tennessee, recruit a Commission Guard of nor more than one hundred men and to lay off the vast tract to be called the "Military Reservation," to satisfy the military claims and to examine the other claim of those people who held land titles by Pre-emption Rights granted to settlers on the Cumberland previous to May of 1780. This pre-emption right would include those settlers who were signers of the Cumberland Compact. Those settlers who had settled in this Military Reservation before it was reserved would be given Pre-emption Rights to 640 acres provided no salt lick or salt spring was included in the 640 acres.

The Compact of Government or usually called the Cumberland Compact was a loose cohesion of the citizens in the area into a primitive government or articles of agreement by two hundred and fifty settlers. In May 1780, apparently the area was in such turmoil by the constant agitation by the marauding Indians that no meetings were held and if so no minutes were kept until 1783, when Davidson, North Carolina was formed into a county that included all of middle Tennessee, north of Duck River, an examination of the signatures of the signers of the compact reveals a virtual who's who of the settlers in the wilderness of middle Tennessee in 1780.

An Additional duty of the commissioners was to locate and lay off a 25,000 acres or tract for General Greene. This tract was located near Columbia, Tennessee on Duck River. No list of the Commission Guards survived except for a few records in old court records. Each commissioner and guard were granted land for their service in this service and they were referred to as "Guard Right Grants." The writer while researching a fourth great grandfather William McGuaioch who was a guard and signer of the compact, discovered that the old Grant Books in the Tennessee State Archives, contained numerous Guard Right Grants. Some of these grants were issued for land inside the boundaries of the military reservation. By gleaning the names from the Grant Books, we have been able to construct a list of 146 men who meet the qualification of guard and claimed Guard Right Grants, considerably more than the 100 originally mentioned. There was one Guard Right Grant located in Bedford County. It was a grant for 3000 acres to Colonel Tilman Dixon, a Lieutenant in the commission and was located along Wartrace Creek north of Bell Buckle. Colonel Dixon was a Revolutionary Soldier, however, he never lived in Bedford County, having settled and died in Smith County. A brief description of the military reservation previously referred to has been researched by us as follows: "The south boundary line was to run 55 miles north of the 35th parallel or Tennessee-Alabama State Line, as determined by the commissioners at Latitude Hill. Major Daniel Smith's calculations of the parallel line were "off" several miles and the legislature rejected his findings and directed that the said line be laid off 55 miles south of the north boundary line of the state, the line to be run by General Rutherford in Spring of 1784, and it began at the point the Cumberland River crosses the north boundary line of the state, ran south passing a few miles of where Gainesboro now stands in Jackson County, the south east corner of the reservation being approximately 5 miles east of the Rock Island at the White and Van Buren County lines, the south boundary line ran about 2 miles south of Murfreesboro on westward to the Tennessee River, thence down the Tennessee to the north boundary line of the state, thence eastward with the line to the beginning. Encompassing a large area of North Carolina that is now north central Tennessee."

The first priority of the commissioners was to ascertain the 35th degree of north latitude, the line that later to become the Tennessee-Alabama State line. The southern boundary of the military reservation to be 55 miles north of the 35th parallel or later the southern boundary of the state. Middle Tennessee Counties now located inside the Old Military Reservation are: Cheatham, Davidson, Dickson, Dekalb, Houston, Humphrey, Montgomery, Macon, Robertson, Stewart, Smith, Sumner, Wilson and parts of Cannon, Clay, Hickman, Putman, Rutherford, Williamson and White. This group of men procured by the commissioners for their task set forth by the General Assembly were recruited from different regions, some from North Carolina, some from East Tennessee and some from those already at or near the French Lick on the Cumberland. This large contingency consisting of commissioners, surveyors, chain-carriers, hunters, doctors, teamsters, guards and their officers. They left the French Lick in the spring of 1783, set forth a southwardly course toward Elk River and began here to affix the 35th degree of north latitude, a requirement in locating the 55 mile point of the southern reservation line.

They left part of the group on the Harpeth in now Williamson County to do survey work, and to check out the validity of pre-emption grants, continued on a southwardly course crossed Duck River west to Holtland, continued on south to Duck River, here they crossed at the shallow ford west of Caney Spring in what was later to become Bedford County, still later part of Marshall County, on southward for some distance approximating the route of Interstate 65, on to Robertson Fork, named by General James Robertson who was one of the party, on south to Brashaw Creek following it down on the west side to near Dellrose, Tennessee, now in Lincoln County, here they camped for some days. Heavy spring rains caused Elk River to rise beyond fording and the commissioners intent to cross and proceed to the 35th parallel which they then estimated to be about two miles south, was changed because of the high waters in addition to the sighting of Indian signs, they decided to travel a short distance westward to a high hill on the north side of the river where the old McCutchin Trace crossed. Here they camped, made their observations and sightings and determined that they were two and three quarters miles north of the parallel or State Line. The Commissioners and guards made their marks, cutting initials and dates on the large trees covering the hill that was later known as "Latitude Hill." It was located at the Lincoln-Giles County line.

Some twenty years ago after searching old land deeds in Lincoln and Giles Counties, two old North Carolina entries disclosed detailed references to the "hill" where the commissioners made their marks in 1783. By plotting this information on USGS Maps, we were able to ascertain the exact location of Latitude Hill whose exact location had been unknown or questionable for years. An on-site inspection by us revealed only trees dating back some fifty or sixty years, with many old large stumps of earlier trees remaining. Signs of the old trace were still visible. In an interview with an elderly gentleman that had lived nearby all his life, he related a story that while still a young lad the large trees had been cut and sawed into lumber at a local sawmill and that he remembered seeing many blaze marks in the lumber that was a product of the trees, this very likely was the old commissioners marks made in February 1783. After determining the location of the south boundary of the State, the Commissioners and their guards traveled northward up Indian Creek to accomplish the second phase of the operation, that of laying off the 25,000 acres granted to General Greene, that was located near Columbia. After this task was accomplished they returned back to the Lick. These Commissioners with their associates were the first that we can positively identify by name as having penetrated the wilderness and cane-brakes of Duck River Valley and part of Bedford County. This event was to open the gate to the emigration that was to follow, for later that same year we find the first documented exploration of what is now Bedford County by one of the Commission Guards who later came, liked what he saw, stayed, died and is buried in Bedford County soil.

At the close of the American Revolution wealthy Land Speculators in the east, particularly North Carolina were eagerly acquiring large tracts of western land in what is now middle Tennessee. The Land Office in Hillsboro, North Carolina was issued by the State for Military Service performed in the Continental Line of North Caroline for the duration of the Revolution. If the original grant did not state "for Military Service" it was not a military grant, and you can write that in your book as absolute. There has been a great amount of misunderstanding about this point and it is not uncommon to hear of Land Grants of enormous tracts of land granted to an ancestor for his military service, when upon close examination, it becomes evident that the grant was not a military grant at all. If all the land had been granted to ancestors for military service that all their descendants have so indicated there would not be enough land available in the Continental United States to satisfy the claims and locate the grants. Perhaps this is partly because each of us would like to think our ancestors played an important role in the birth of our beloved country, and be justifiably proud of our contributing ancestor. Most of our fore-bearers played an important role in the struggle for independence, by they soldiers or patriots and most never received reimbursement for their efforts other than the satisfaction of being able to breathe the breath of freedom.

FIRST LAND LOCATIONS

The next documented record we have of the exploration of Bedford County began in August 1783 about six months after the commissioners' short visit to Latitude Hill. In this month, we find a group or land locators leaving the French Lick on horseback with the intention of going to Duck and Elk River Country for the express purpose of locating land for entry and to later apply to the land office of North Carolina then opening in Hillsboro for grants to same. Some of the locations were to be made for themselves, some to be located for others, with the locators to receive a third for their services. This group consisted of Jonathan Drake, Samuel Barton, Mathew Talbot, William Smith, Ambrose Mauldin, Julius Saunders and Alexander Greer. We have record that all these men were with the commissioners six months before at Latitude Hill with the exception of Smith.

Samuel Barton had been a surveyor and Saunders a Lieutenant in the commission guard. They left the French Lick, striking a course south, paralleling the one taken to Latitude Hill the fall before. Talbot and Smith lost their horses the first night out on the Harpeth. They turned back on foot and started the long trek back to the bluff. The remaining group camped the second night on the north side of Duck River at a spring later to be called "Venable Spring," that can be seen even today and is located a short distance west of the Village of Caney Spring in Marshall County. This camp was a short distance up river from where the commissioners had crossed. The next morning, with the coming of dawn, the party prepared to break camp, Alexander Greer and his pilots, Saunders and Mauldin stated that they were going to cross Duck River and go to Elk River and there make locations. Barton and Drake stated that they were going east on the north side of Duck River and make locations. This they preceded to do, going as far up as a creek they then named Falling (Fall) Creek. Here Barton made a 500 acre location for himself that he later sold in 1807 while living in Wilson County to Michael Fisher, who is listed as a Revolutionary Soldier. Fisher came here from Smith County as an early date and left many descendants. Barton pushed no further eastward but turned back to the French Lick.

Greer and his pilots crossed Duck River going south passing west of where Lewisburg now stands, on southward to the head of Richland Creek continuing on down Richland several miles then turning eastward traveling over rough terrain crossing several branches apparently arriving at a spot some three miles west of Fayetteville in Lincoln County, then a vast cane-brake along Elk River and Norris Creek. Here on the north side of Elk River near the mouth of a creek that Greer named Cane, he made a location of 2500 acres for his father Andrew Greer of East Tennessee. This appears to be the earliest location and grant issued south of Duck River. A location for 2625 acres was also made for his sister Ruth Talbot on both sides of Elk River, adjoining the 2500 acre grant. This is additionally verified by the fact that the writer has examined old land deeds that record old Greer boundary lines that crossed Elk River near "The Indian Crossing," where Julius Saunders and others crossed. This location is just below where the historical majestic "Old Stone Bridge" stood at Fayetteville, Tennessee. The Greer party then turned northward traveling up Cane Creek, called Little River, taking the east fork near Petersburg in north Lincoln County, here making a location for his brother Joseph Greer, remember as "The Kings Mountain Messenger," who located there in 1807 moving that year from Knoxville. He died there in 1831 and is buried in a cow pasture on his grant.

After making locations for family, Alexander Greer followed the east Cane Creek or its fork up to the head on Elk or Chestnut Ridge. On the north rim of the ridge, probably at or near Bledsoe's Gap, they looked northward and for the first time they saw the magnificent view of the virgin valley below. Greer liked what he saw for he made his location here, later returned, settled, lived out his allotted years and twenty seven years later died and was buried here on his grant. The party came down the north side of the ridge into the area that is now south central Bedford County, picking up the headwaters of a creek he named Greer's Lick or more often Lick Creek. The creek was to receive another name a few months later by another early explorer by the name of Amos Balch, who the next spring named the creek Sugar Creek after a creek by the same name located in his native Mecklenburg County, North Carolina. The same Sugar Creek stuck, Greer's did not. You win, you lose some.

While viewing the valley from the north side of the ridge Greer probably decided to mark the beginning corner of his 5000 acre grant. Said grant to run north then west. The old corner was located near Sugar Creek on Robinson Road some distance south east of the old Greer's Lick. While there were several licks on this large grant the one generally accepted as being the one they camped at is the Big Spring or Lick that was located on the dower tract a short distance east of Pleasant Grove. After making his location, the Greer party then followed the lick, or Sugar Creek to a lick and spring on the creek, this he called Greer's Lick. It was located about a mile east of the village of Pleasant Grove near the site of the old Big Spring

Baptist Church that once stood here. The Big Spring, once said to be Greer's Lick, has vanished by continuing spring flooding of Sugar Creek. Here they spent the night at his lick.

Greer made the location for 5000 acres for himself and his brother Thomas Greer. Alexander claimed the southern half, the half where the lick was located, brother Thomas to take the north and other half. Alexander Greer would be the first Justice of the fledgling Bedford County in 1807. He is thought to be buried in an unmarked grave in the old Dyer Graveyard that is located on the dower tract that his widow received at the settlement of his estate. She survived him many years. They were parents of several children. After making this location, Greer's party traveled north crossing Duck River at Thompson Ford near Halls Mill, going on north passing near where Unionville and Rover now stands, thence back to the Cumberland settlement. As far as can be determined Greer was the first to locate and receive a grant that he later lived on in Bedford County. This was not a military grant, rather it was a regular North Carolina grant. He was indeed eligible for military land as he like his brother Joseph was a Revolutionary Soldier. His half brother Thomas settled at a early date on his northern half of the joint grant, lived and died there and is buried in the old Sugar Creek Meeting House Burying Ground, that is situated on the west bank of Sugar Creek, at the Sugar Creek bridge on the Richmond Road. The site for the old Meeting House and graveyard were given by Thomas Greer to the Baptist at an early date. The graveyard now called Greer, contains a marker for a young daughter of Thomas Greer that has a death date of September 1805, the earliest death date found in Bedford County. It this is a marker for an actual interment, as it appears to be, then Thomas was indeed one of the earliest settlers here when this was still Rutherford County. He died in 1848. His wife, Catharine died in 1865 and they are both buried with other members of the family in the old graveyard. Alexander Greer was here at an early date, perhaps by 1806, and was a first Justice at the Old Mulberry or Bedford Court House at Widow Payne December 27, 1807. He is buried in Bedford County, not Texas as some have said. The one in Texas was a grandson. Alexander and wife

Jane are probably buried in the old Dyer, later called Big Spring Church Graveyard that is a very old graveyard located on the widow Greer's dower tract, east of Pleasant Grove. Alexander was the first to view traverse, settle, live and die in Bedford County.

EDMISTON COMPANY

It is possible that after the return of the Greer party to the fort at Nashborough, the sound of the English spoken word was not heard along Duck River during the winter of 1783-84. The next documented brief excursion into the county came during the early thaw in February of 1784 as Robert Weakley, later to become a United States Representative; Jonathan Drake, and old Indian fighter who later got his scalp lifted in Illinois; David Wilson, a Revolutionary Soldier formerly of Mecklenburg County, North Carolina and later of Sumner County, Tennessee; with chain carriers, left Nashborough came up Stones River to Jefferson Springs in Rutherford County, on to Duck River Ridge, fell upon the head of the North Fork, down it to the mouth at Duck River, on down said river to Caney Spring, where Weakley surveyed Wilson's 2000 acre Military Grant. Some other grants to Ezekiel and George Alexander, John Lock and John Wilson, all located near Unionville, may have been located on these expeditions.

About the first of March 1784, activity continued to pick up for it was this time that a large company of Land Locators called "The Edmiston Company" made its appearance upon the scene. This company of some twenty to twenty four men had been outfitted and directed by Colonel William Edmiston of Washington County, southwestern Virginia. Edmiston was a Virginian of the old school, a public spirited patriot who fought gallantly at Kings Mountain. He was a blue-stocking Presbyterian and was a member of the Glade Springs Presbyterian Church located east of Abingdon, Virginia. The writers, some years ago visited the old historic church still active and standing among the rolling hills of southwestern Virginia, an examination of the old session minutes show that this William Edmiston and General William Campbell while attending services were notified that a British spy had been captured nearby. Edmiston and Campbell excused themselves from the services, confronted the spy and upon searching him and finding hidden incriminating papers upon him, they hanged him and then promptly returned to the services. Having done what they felt was their duty to God and Country. Two of Edmiston's sons, William and G.W.C. (General William Campbell) Edmiston settled in Lincoln County, Tennessee. Son William, a Esquire and Surveyor, settled there in 1808. He was a first Justice of the county. Many years later he moved to west Tennessee and died there in 1853 at an advanced age.

This Edmiston Company had one purpose only. That was to locate large tracts of land that could be entered, surveyed and finally have grants issued by the Land Office at Hillsboro, North Carolina. As has been previously stated land locators often located, prepared entries and surveys the grants in exchange for a part of the grant. At this time the going rate was generally one third of the grant. We have gleamed the following names of some of those along on this expedition, Thomas Edmiston, Robert Edmondson, Joseph Thompson, Ezekiel Norris, Richard and George Martin, Patrick McCutchin, James McNit, Moses Buchanan, David Buchanan and Amos Balch. After this expedition Thomas and Robert and Robert Edmondson settled south of Nashville in Williamson County, Thomas came with Robertson in 1780. They were distantly related to Colonel William Edmiston of Virginia but consistently spelled their name Edmondson but the same often appeared in the records as Edmiston, Edmondson and Edmondson. Joseph Thompson settled in Williamson County, Ezekiel Norris made a 1280 acre location for himself on this expedition that included all of the town of Fayetteville, Tennessee. He was considered the first settler at Fayetteville and is buried to the rear of where his old log house stood in an unmarked grave, two blocks south of the Public Square. Norris Creek in Lincoln County bears his name. Richard Martin settled in Bedford County at an early date. We know little of him except that he was old enough to have been in the Revolution and in 1812 appeared to be living in

Captain Benjamin Hewitt's Militia Company which included the area west of Shelbyville, a fork of Powell Creek that crosses State Highway 64 about six miles west of Shelbyville, was once listed as Martin Branch. From deeds and description, George and Richard filed jointly with Amos Balch and James Bradshaw, for a large grant that lay about three miles southwest of Shelbyville. This was a 3294 acre grant. Balch had located while on this expedition, however he had located most of it in interference with the Alexander-Thomas Greer grant and lost the majority of it by action of the courts. Nothing else known of the Martin brothers except that George had applied for Revolutionary Pension in 1836 but could not prove six months service. Patrick McCutchin was listed as an early settlers in Williamson County. Of James McNit (McNatt?), nothing known. Moses Buchanan had come out of Washington County, Viriginia, a son of immigrant Samuel Buchanan. The Buchanans located several large grants in Lincoln County, Tennessee, some on this expedition. Moses was the uncle of young David Buchanan, then twenty years old. David located 1900 acres along Cane and Craighead Creeks, just south of the village of Howell, Tennessee. He moved to his grant from Nashville in about 1809 and lived out the balance of his life here and has an old sandstone marker at his grave, located beside the grave of his wife Margaret Steel.

A BEDFORD COUNTY PIONEER

Amos Balch (1758-1835), one of the Edmiston party, was born in Maryland, son of a Presbyterian Minister Reverend James and Ann Goodwin Balch. He was a Sergeant at the Battle of Camden in South Carolina. Enlisted from Mecklenburg County, North Carolina as a Mounted Volunteer, served eight months and was under Gates at Camden. He married Ann Patton, daughter of Samuel Patton, Senior, of Mecklenburg County, North Carolina. They had eight children. After the land location trip in 1784, he returned to Jefferson County, Tennessee, where he was listed as a Justice in 1792. He later moved to Kentucky, then to Bedford County, Tennessee in about 1808. He settled about two miles west of Shelbyville on the Lewisburg Highway, State Highway 64, at the junction of Naron Road. For many years Highway 64 would be called the Columbia Road. The Naron Road mentioned was first called the Old Base Line Road, later the Bledsoe Gap Road, the Gap being on Chestnut Ridge at the county line.

Balch settled on a small tract that had been granted to his father-in-law Samuel Patton. It has been said over the years that he was buried about two thousand feet south of his house on the brow of the hill adjoining a peach orchard on the south side of the Old Base Line. This was known for years as the Balch-Patton, later the Thompson Graveyard, it was old, dating back to the 1820's and contained graves covered by old box type vaults with old sand stone markers. Some of those buried were members of the Patton, Bradshaw, Doak, Thompson, McCarty and Balch families. It is a fact that Balch was teaching school in Henderson County, Tennessee a few years before his death. Did he come back to Bedford County and die here or was his body brought back? We have been unable to answer this question to our satisfaction but even if his grave was once marked the information would be forever lost as some years ago the vaults, markers and all visibly signs of this historic family burying ground were destroyed. Another part of history now gone forever. Another Revolutionary Soldier by the name of Theophilus Thompson is reported by descendants to have been buried in this same graveyard.

Having now briefly touched on the known participants of this expedition, let us now follow their course through the wilderness. The party came down the west fork of Stones River, by the future sites of Old Jefferson and Murfreesboro, picked up the middle fork and its headwaters, crossed over Duck River Ridge into the valley, on southward on a course on or near the Old Indian War-Trace, passing near where Bell Buckle and Wartrace would spring up more than a half century later.

According to Amos Balch's own words as found in old records by the writers years ago, the company crossed Duck River at the Three Forks of the river, said forks being the "Wartrace Fork," or "Garrison Fork" and the South or "Barren Fork."

The most direct and likely route after the crossing was to strike Thompson Creek follow it past the village of Raus on up the head of Thompson Creek, cross the Elk Ridge near Smith's Chapel, pick up Mulberry Creek and follow it to Mulberry Village, thence on to where Fayetteville is now located and proceeded to set up their base camps. An alternate route may have been after crossing at the forks, turn west on the south side of Duck River, continue past where Shelbyville would later be located on west to near Shelbyville Mills, then turn southward at Naron Road, down the Old Base Line or Bledsoe Gap Road, past where Balch would some years later live. Along this Base Line, Balch made locations for the Pattons, his father-in-law and brother-in-law and additionally located a 1000 acre grant for himself, which he later lost for taxes, in addition to a 3294 acre tract for himself, and the Martin brothers, most of this grant was to be lost later because of interference with the Alexander and Thomas Greer rant that lay to the west, this group having no knowledge of the Greer location made the fall before.

Balch located a 5000 acre grant south of his first one, for himself, James Bradshaw and others. Much of it overlapped the Greer grant, this later grant extended a short distance over the Elk Ridge into Lincoln County. After crossing the ridge, the Edmiston group followed either Mulberry or Norris Creeks down to Elk River at Fayetteville, where Ezekiel Norris made his 1280 acre location, here the company separated into three groups or camps. One going eastward up Elk River about two miles and made their Base Camp on a cedar bluff of the river near where Eldad Bridge now crosses the river. This group made their locations north and east along the river. The balance of the company went westward down the river for about two miles to the east side of a large creek they named Little River. This is the creek Alexander Greer had named Cane Creek the fall before. This name Little River did not stick for long but Cane Creek did, so Greer won one, this time. Here at the junction of Buchanan Creek with Cane Creek at a large spring called the Blue Spring. Another part of the company camped, they made locations north along Little River or Cane Creek. Balch and the Martins were in this group. The balance of the party continued on a short distance to the west, fixed their base camp on a bluff of the river and made their locations to the north and west. The camp at the Blue Spring, at the mouth of Buchanan Creek, was located about one half mile above the mouth of Cane Creek where first court of Lincoln County met at the log house of Brice Garner. Garner would become the first clerk of Lincoln County in 1809. Much of the land north of the river was located by this group. The Edmistons located large tracts around the Blue Spring, unfortunately as was the case in Bedford County, some was located on top of the Greer grants and litigation continued for years, all the way to the Supreme Court. In one hearing a letter from Colonel Edmiston in Virginia expressed his opinion that perhaps the Greers had in fact been there before them. David Buchanan who was with the Blue Spring Camp located his beginning corner of his 1900 acre tract about two miles up Cane Creek from the camp. His location was to run east and west from the beginning corner. The tree where Buchanan cut his initials to establish his corner has long ago rotted and fallen but the writer located the corner years ago and remains of the old stump had all but disappeared. It appears that Balch and Thompson located part of a grant for themselves or a client, on part of Buchanan's grant. Years later after court action, Buchanan retained his clear title.

The courts were busy for years trying to establish clear titles and reach compromise settlements. Vast acreages were involved in litigations and many early settlers did not live to see clear titles to their land. Many choice tracts had multiple locations made on them by some well meaning but uninformed locators and often by unscrupulous land hungry locators. Often the locators made vague or floating beginning corners and when surveyors came with their Jacob Staffs, compasses and chains carriers, they often spent hours and days thrashing around in the snake and mosquito infested wilderness trying to locate an elusive corner that sometimes never existed. Some locations were made on paper and the loctor never viewed the land in question. As previously stated a large part of Lincoln County, once Bedford, north of Elk River was located by this party much of the ridge land south of Elk River that included the barrens and craw-fishy land with scrub-oaks, was considered practically worthless to the early land speculators and no locations were made there by the first locators, but was later granted under the penny and twelve and one half cents law by the State of Tennessee.

After the Edmiston Company had completed their assigned tasks, they collected their notes, marshaled their forces and made the long journey back to Nashborough, then to prepare their entries for filing and await the surveys that would soon follow. At this writing, we have no definite information as to whether or not the Edmiston Company made locations north of Duck River on the trek south to Elk River in 1784. At this date, we have no absolute information as to whether or not the vast 85,000 acre Blount Grants were located by this group of not, but an educated guess would be no.

In the spring and summer of 1785, many of the early surveys were made of the lands that had been recently entered and located by Robert Weakley who had just arrived at the French Lick, by Henry Rutherford and by David Vance, most of the large surveys were made by these three parties, most of the land that had been located to satisfy the warrants were surveyed this year. The exception was the 85,000 acre Blount Grant on the Three Forks of Duck River, they were surveyed in late summer of 1792 by John Donelson, Jr., brother-in-law of General Jackson. These men, from the time of the commissioners in 1783 to the coming of the surveyors in 1785 to 1792 represented the first thrush of civilization into the Duck River Valley that was later Bedford County and later still Lincoln County.

THE BREAKING OF DAWN

For several years the settlers were slow in coming because this land was still protected by Indian Treaty and many were reluctant to settle in Indian Territory even though they held grants for the land. However, this changed on January 7, 1806 when the signing of the Dearborn Treaty with the Indians ceded the lands south of Duck River, the lands north of the river had been ceded three months before in October 1805. After this date the area around Bell Buckle and Wartrace began to be settled by those coming in from the northern parent counties. A petition filed before the State Legislature in 1812 states that at least 50 families were living on or adjoining the Old Wartrace school land 64 0 acre tract in 1806, this tract was located between Bell Buckle and the county line on the west side of the Old Liberty Pike. The tide of immigration began to pour into the basin and by December 3, 1807 the area was sufficiently populated to petition the Legislature, in session in Knoxville, to form a new county out of Rutherford County. This was done by Representative Joseph Dickson (Dixon) of Rutherford County, the parent county of Bedford County.

Dickson once had large land holdings in Bedford, between Murfreesboro and Shelbyville. The new county was to be named for Thomas Bedford, Jr., a Revolutionary Soldier who at an early date moved to Rutherford County, Tennessee and died there in 1804. Many earlier writings stated that Bedford was a Captain of the Continental Line during the Revolution and a Colonel in the War of 1812. This was not true as he died in 1804 near Old Jefferson in Rutherford County, Tennessee. His son Thomas was the 1812 veteran.

The legislature also directed that the first court was to meet at the recently erected house of Widow Payne who was living on the headwaters of the east fork of Mulberry Creek. The cabin was log and was situated on the south side of Elk Ridge about a half mile north east of the village of County Line in Moore County, Tennessee. The old cabin stood just east of the McClure home. It was near-by a short distance to the east that the noted David Crockett soon settled for a ehile before moving on to greater things and finally to a hero's death at the Alamo in Texas. It should be noted that the newly constituted county boundaries ran all the way to the Alabama State Line then the Mississippi Territory.

Thirteen Justices were appointed by the Legislature. They were John Atkinson, Abraham Byler, James Patton, Alexander Greer, William M. Quisenberry, William

Moody, William Norvill, David Robinson, Howel Dawdy, William Wilbourn, Joseph Walker, Joseph Ake and John Carter. These Justices assembled at the Widow Payne's house two days after Christmas in 1807 to convene the first court and give the people of Duck and Elk River, a belated Christmas present, a new county named Bedford.

Squire Atkinson probably had the longest ride as he was living near Holts Corner, now Holtland in what is now Marshall County, Tennessee. He probably rode by Abraham Byler's improvement where he was living on his 320 acres, half of 640 acre tract, he and Thomas Maxwell, his next neighbor, had purchased from Nathaniel Taylor of Carter County, Tennessee. This is the tract that the village of Rover, called Bylers until the early 1840's is located on. This 640 acre tract was located in the middle of the 3000 acre tract granted to George Daughtry who with the exception of the Blount brothers probably held more grant land in Bedford County than any other man. He died in Orange County, North Carolina but his widow and children came to Tennessee. Atkinson and Byler probably passed by where Shelbyville now stands, may have stopped in at Samuel Musgraves, a first settler at Shelbyville who was a squatter in the cane brakes at the Big Spring on land owned by Robert Smith of North Carolina, later to be purchased by Clement Cannon and deeded for the purpose of building a town named "Shelbyville." Musgrave, a man who savored his solitude in the wilderness, may have had a first glimpse of what he considered the fore-bidding clouds of approaching civilization. For we know that three years later his fears were realized when "horror of horrors" a town was to be built on top of him, in any event and for what ever purpose, by 1812, he had cast his eyes around him and selected a small tract of land on the headwaters of Flat Creek at the County Line where he lived until 1822, when once again perhaps creeping civilization caught up with him and he made the final move to Morgan County, Alabama. His claim to fame was that the small branch that runs from the spring to the river carried his name for a short time in history.

Squire Atkinson and Byler crossed Duck River, continued on south over Elk Ridge to the Widow Payne's house. In later old records the house was referred to as the "Old Bedford Court House" or the "Old Mulberry Court House."

Justice James Patton may have been one of several James Patton who were living in the county at that time. One James built an old double log house on Straight Creek below Fairfield and a short distance above where Kellertown once stood. The old log house built about 1808 is still standing today, but barely. This James Patton settled on a 484 acres tract he purchased from Patton and Erwin, part of Blount Grant No. 225, he married Sarah Cunningham in Buncombe County, North Carolina. They were parents of eleven children. He died in 1827 and is buried in the old Couch-Keller Graveyard located on the east bank of the Garrison Fork of Duck River. Two other James Pattons settled two miles south of Shelbyville, one or both being of the Samuel Patton family of Mecklenburg County, North Carolina and one other settled near Caney Spring in Marshall County.

William Norvill had settled on the Bell Buckle Fork of the Wartrace in 1806-7 where the town of Bell Buckle is now located, purchasing land from Alexander Outlaw out of a grant that had been one of the Blount Grants No. 222. The old Salem Camp Ground and Methodist Episcopal Meeting House was located on this tract. An old Norvill Burying Ground is located on the east side of the creek near Webb School that contains several graves. One grave has an old hand hewn field stone with the name of Mary Norvill, died 14 February 1813, in the 78 or 79 year of her age, which places her birth at about 1734. This may have been the mother of William.

Howel Dowdy often spelled Dawdy, with the corrupted spelling appearing as Doddy, according to North Carolina Revolutionary Army Accounts, he was a Revolutionary Soldier and residing in Washington or Sullivan County, Tennessee in 1781-83. We have no absolute fix on his residence in December 1807. We do know that in 1812, he was living near where Samuel Musgrave once lived near the spring, now the parking lot of the Big Spring Shopping Center, having purchased lots in 1810 when the first sale of town lots were held, he would, years later, give these lots to his son-in-law Thomas Blythe of Moore County, then Lincoln County, provided Blythe care for him and his wife Pheby in their old age. A street that ran by his lots was named for him and retained that name until sometimes after 1878 when the old Beer's Map still listed it as Dowdy. It is now Franklin Street or avenue. A branch that feeds Lake Bedford and empties into Duck River just below Cortners Old Mill north west of the town of Normandy was once named Dowdy and has been corrupted to Doddy Creek. Dowdy was appointed first County Ranger whose duties enclosed collecting and holding all strays, primary horses and to advertise their description and place of pick-up. By reading old newspapers, we find by his listings of strays that he was quite busy. In his infirmed years, he and his wife moved to Moore County to live with their daughter and son-in-law Thomas Blythe. According to the old ancient sandstone over their graves, he died in 1830, aged 84, Pheby died 1831, aged 81. They are buried on a hillside on Dogtail Creek exactly one mile west of the spot where he had attended the first Bedford County Court 22 years before. The 1830-31 death dates indicate that he may have died in the cholera epidemic that raged through the towns and countryside and leaving few families untouched.

Just above William Norvill's on up Bell Buckle Creek, Joseph Ake lived and appeared to have settled there about 1806 on land he had purchased from Tilman Dixon out of his Guard Right Grant or on a tract he, Ake, purchased of Alexander Outlaw. Two justices from this area indicate that this was perhaps one of the more densely populated areas at this time. Ake died at an early date and his heirs sold his land that touched Bell Buckle Creek and the Otter Fork of Bell Buckle Creek, to Burrell Featherston, also an early settler at Bell Buckle and brother-in-law of Doctor James B. Armstrong a prominent early doctor in Shelbyville and later at Fairfield, who had served as a surgeon on General Jackson
S Staff in the Creek Wars, but who later was an avid anti-Jackson man, a fact that was later to cause him great consternation and suffering. At this time, we had two Joseph Walkers, one lived in the area that is now Coffee County, the other around Fairfield on the upper Garrison. Quisenberry lived near Lynchburg. Moody has

been elusive and we have been unable to get a handle on him. Carter came from that area that is now Lincoln County, living near Elora at the foot of the Cumberland Mountain. John Atkinson was appointed chairman at the first sitting of the Court, finding no one with the proper credentials to open the court, Atkinson took the proverbial bull by the horns, duly swore himself in then with that preliminary out of the way, proceeded to swear in the remaining justices, a good example of the remarkable adaptability of our frontier statesmen and settlers.

William Wilburn had settled on Flat Creek near where the village of the same name is now located. He, of all the justices, had the shortest ride over the ridge to his neighbor the Widow Payne.

David Robinson, thought to be son of Michael Robinson, a Revolutionary Soldier of Orange County, North Carolina, had probably settled for a time on the 1500 acre grant of Michael Robinson that he willed to his sons, David, Joseph and John. The grant was located on the east side of Duck River about two and one half miles down river from Shelbyville on both side of the old road leading to the Fishing Ford, now called Warners Bridge Road of Duck River. Deeds show he sold his partition of the land to his brother at an early date. Asa Fonville, later of that area of the county around Caney Spring, purchased part of the tract in 1815. John Warner purchased a large tract that lay along the river where he settled, became the second Sheriff of Bedford County. The bridge across the river has been known as Warner Bridge for generations. Warner died in 1834 and is buried on his farm. The old Robinson Graveyard located on part of the old 1500 acre grant contains the remains of brother John and other members of the Robinson family. Brother Joseph moved to Marshall County at the Fishing Ford and died there. At least two sisters married and came to Bedford County, Tennessee. One married Henry Moore a Revolutionary Soldier, they settled about a mile above Richmond on Sinking Creek, the other sister married James Ray, they too settled on Sinking Creek, a neighbor to Moore.

Justice Alexander Greer of whom much has already been written probably saddled up, cut across country to the east, some seven or eight miles, crossed Flat Creek, and then south over the ridge to the Widow Payne. Here the business of fledgling county was conducted by the members of the County Court under the direction of the resourceful and dependable chairman John Atkinson for two years until the boundaries of the county were reduced by an Act of the Legislature on November 14, 1809 to accommodate the formation of a new county to the south of Bedford, named Lincoln. As the old Bedford or Mulberry Court House would then be located in the newly formed county of Lincoln, a new temporary site could be located. The act directed that John Atkinson, Howel Dawdy, Daniel McKissick, William Wood(Woods) and Barkley Martin be appointed commissioners to fix a permanent place on Duck River within two miles of the center of said county, on an east-west line and that they shall purchase one hundred acres and lay off a town to be known as Shelbyville, reserving near the center there of a Public Square of two acres on which the court house and stocks shall be built.

Barkley Martin had recently settled near his brother Matt Martin just above Fairfield. They had recently come down from Kentucky in about 1808. Matt immediately built a large brick house on the old Washington City Stage Road above Fairfield. The old house still stands today. Matt and Barkley were both Revolutionary Soldiers and had married the Clay sisters, relatives of Henry Clay. Barkley Martin died in 1815 while supervising the opening of the Georgia Road that ran to Chichamauga Town, or Ross Landing, now Chattanooga.

Of William Woods or Wood, we know nothing except in 1812 there was two William Woods in the county, one living near where the community of Flat Creek is now located, the other lived and is buried on the old Wartrace School land tract.

Daniel McKissick was a Captain in the American Revolution, was severely wounded at the Battle of Ramsours Mill in 1780 in Lincoln County, North Carolina. He came to Bedford County in the fall of 1807 from Lincoln County, North Carolina and settled on the 1000 acre grant of son James six miles south of Shelbyville on the Fayetteville Highway. He died in 1818 and is buried near where the old house once stood on the east side of the highway. A large box tomb with his epitaph inscribed covered his grave for many years, many years but unfortunately each generation produces a few deranged souls who have no sense of history and often destroy that which civilization strives to protect and preserve, in this case the tomb has long ago vanished at the hands of these thoughtless persons and only the approximate site of the grave remains today. Son, James, was Clerk of Bedford County Court for many years. James and Joseph, both sons of Daniel and his wife Jane Wilson, married daughters of near neighbor Alexander Greer. Mother Jane, son James and others in the family made the move westward to Arkansas in the eighteen thirties, selling much of the farm to George Waite who had recently moved here from Wartrace. Two other major purchasers of the McKissick land were Nathan Evans and Bluford Davidson. From 1788, James McKissick had claimed title to the land where he and his parents lived, running on south past where Waite later lived, to a line a short distance north of where the Hamlet of Hawthorn once stood.

These Commissioners went about the business of locating a site for a town abd began clearing, laying off and selling lots. By the time the site had been determined for the town the names of Sheriff Benjamin Bradford and John Lane had been added to this list to locate the town. They were additionally named with Barkley Martin and John Atkinson and to be known as Trustees of Dixon Academy named in honor of General Joseph Dickson then Speaker of the House. In 1811, Clement Cannon's name was added as Trustee and in 1817 he endowed the county and town with the gist of five acre lot on Jefferson Street to erect Dixon (Dickson) Academy. Sheriff Bradford acquired large acreage from Alexander Outlaw of Jefferson County, Tennessee, which was part of one of the old Blount grants on the Wartrace Fork. Anthony Branch situated between Wartrace and Bell Buckle once bore his name. In the interim, the temporary court met at the house of Amos Balch located as has been previously stated about two miles west of the future town of Shelbyville, at the junction of Naron Road and the Lewisburg Highway. The court would meet here from December 1809 to august 1810 at which time a small temporary log court house would be built on the north west corner of the town square. A permanent brick structure was advertised for bid in 1810 but all bids were rejected because some contractor's had bit without giving security. Specifications were redrawn and advertised April 1, 1811 to be completed by 1812, actually completed in 1813.

As the Legislature directed that one hundred acres be secured, the thirty acres that Mathew Cunningham, agent for the heirs of William Galbreath, Sr., deceased of Orange County, North Carolina and late of Pennsylvania, would not suffice. Goodspeed's history states that Galbreath and Balch each offered fifty acres. The deeds definitely say thirty acres was authorized by Cunningham, son-in-law William Galbreath and agent for his devises. This thirty acres was to be offered from a 1000 acre grant issued to Galbreath and was located a short distance south of Shelbyville on both sides of the Fayetteville Highway, the west boundary line was the old Base Line or Naron Road southwest of town. This grant had been issued jointly to Galbreath and Jeremiah Chamberland. Galbreath held title to another 1000 acre grant located immediately south of the first. Mathew Cunningham, a Revolutionary Soldier, with his wife, Elizabeth Galbreath, settled on this lower 1000 acre grant. In their old age, they sold out to Robert and William Reed and moved to the area of Flat Creek Village to be near their son Mathew, Jr.

Upon close examination of Balch's offer, we note that he had located 1000 acres for himself probably while on the Edmiston expedition, this was issued as Grant No. 23 issued in 1788. It included the mouth of Flat Creek and lay a little north and east of Balch's house. This tract was sold by Balch in 1797 while he was living in Logan County, Kentucky, to Thomas Love long before this was Bedford County. Later owners were R.C. Gordon, Samuel Thompson, William Orr, Samuel Doak who operated Doak's Mill at the mouth of Flat Creek, Henry Conway and Newton Cannon. Conway built a mill on Flat Creek at the south west corner of Shelbyville and was known as Conway's and later Newton Cannon's Mill. We also note that in January 1809, Amos Balch and wife Ann sold 122 acres, her remaining share of the land willed to her and the male heirs of her body by her father Samuel Patton, Sr., to Archibald Alexander. At this time we find no record of Balch owning other land in the area that would meet the qualifications set forth for location of the town.

This place where the second Seat of Justice was located at Amos Balch was part of a grant to Samuel Patton that was nearly erased by the overlapping of the Alexander Greer and Thomas Talbot Grants. The location on the rise above the old Balch Spring was the site of the house of Balch. A spacious and picturesque antebellum home was built here in the 1840's, probably by Samuel Doak, son of David and Jane Doak. Samuel and parents came here from Adair County, Kentucky. He, Samuel, became a slave trader, note shaver and land broker. The place was next owned by Doak's son-in-law Samuel B. Hays. The home fronting a large beautiful lake, was standing a short time before the Civil War and Doak had built a brick home across the turnpike with water from the lake piped under the turnpike to his house. An old access road lead from the turnpike through the river bottom to Doak's Mill near the mouth of Flat Creek. An abstract of this location lists first patent holder Samuel Patton, Sr., then Ann Balch's male heirs, James Gammill, William Orr, Jonathan Mosley, Newcome Thompson, Samuel Doak, Samuel Hay, James F. Cummings, William Little, Joseph O. Arnold, F.S. Landers, W.D. Wood and Murray Pickle. It was known as the old Pickle Place until a few years ago. One time Doak overextended himself financially, went bankrupt and moved to Texas before the Civil War. He was distantly related to Reverend Samuel Doak, first teacher and Presbyterian Preacher in Tennessee.

SHELBYVILLE THE TOWN

After Malcom Gilchrist had resurveyed the reduced county in 1809, the commissioners received an offer that must have been hard to resist from a young man from Williamson County by the name of Clement Cannon, a name recognized even today by long time residents of the town. Clement Cannon was son of Minos and Letitia Thompson Cannon and brother of Newton Cannon, two time Governor of Tennessee. Cannon is generally considered the "founder of Shelbyville." He married Susannah Lock in August 1810 just in time to bring his new bride to the new town he had just given to the county of Bedford. It appears that the couple soon set up a country home about a mile south of town in a grove of large tulip trees growing where the South Side School is now located on a part of his 1000 acres that he later sold to his brother Newton. This tract included most of the south side of Shelbyville. At an early date he would build large mills and factories on the river below the old ford that crossed at an island just above where the dam is now located. He also later had a mill that stood on the west bank of the river at Shelbyville. In 1825, William Galbreath and associates built a dam below Cannon's Dam and below the present bridge to power a carding factory. This resulted in court action brought by Cannon, who claiming that the new dam reduced water fall over his dam that resulted in insufficient power for his mills. Cannon and his wife had six children born to them. They soon relocated about one mile south east of the town square near Camp White. Their remains are interred in the Family Graveyard is now marked with a historical marker. The cemetery is still cared for by the town that was laid off in 1810.

Cannon was a surveyor and had been on Duck River earlier with survey parties. He had only recently purchased a one thousand acre tract along Duck River from Robert W. Smith of Cabarrus County, North Carolina and being a charitable but an enterprising young man, when the word reached him of the search for a site to build a new town from the ground up, he probably asked the obvious question "what if?' and after receiving an answer to his satisfaction and recognizing a once in a lifetime opportunity, he proceeded to offer as an outright gist to the commissioners one hundred acres out of his one thousand acre grant and being a man of vision could see a future thriving, bustling river town with fine homes, cotton gins, grist mills, spinning factories, shops, Doctor and Law Offices, Churches and Academies, wide streets and perhaps someday a street marked with his name, all of which came true. In May 1810, for and upon the receipt of one dollar to make the contract binding, he deeded the following 100 acres to the commissioners. 100 acres to and for the use of the County of Bedford and for then site of the "Town of Shelbyville," beginning at a stake two poles south of the mouth of Samuel Musgrave's Spring Branch, thence south 35 degrees east 85 5/10 poles to a small ash log and two cedars, thence east 48 poles to a white oak and dogwood, thence north 146 poles and 2/10 of a pole to a stake, thence west 120 poles to a stake, thence south to the beginning including Samuel Musgrave's improvement and spring, etc. The deed included all appurtenances, remainder, rents and profits of aforesaid land and every part thereof. Witnessed by James McKissick, Thomas Moore and Amos Balch. Moore was the first Court Clerk and McKissick probably Deputy Clerk as he later became County Court Clerk. From a close examination of the above deed, it would appear that Musgrave had received a diplomatic and polite eviction notice.

A brief examination of the deed will show that the south 55 degrees call started just below the river bridge on Cannon Boulevard 33 feet below the branch, thence up the river 1410.5 feet. The 48 pole south line ran just south of the power substation, crossing south Main Street. The east line ran through the eastern half of the old City Cemetery that is located to the rear of the First Baptist Church. The old cemetery was started shortly after the town was laid off. The eastern half of the cemetery as it is now was established in 1815 by Dr. James B. Armstrong with the burials of his young wife Sophia Smith Armstrong and their first born son Robert. This was on land he had purchased from Cannon in 1814. The land ran along the east boundary line of the town, on south past the south east corner of the town, then eastward to the Skull Camp of Duck River, a notorious ford of the river east of the town, that we find mention of as early as 1806.

Some years later, Dr. Armstrong moved to "Davis Mill," named for Henry Davis, purchased the mill on the Garrison with additional land where he built his home. Some years later the name of the Cross Roads was changed to Fairfield. Armstrong's Burying Ground at Shelbyville was soon incorporated into the old City

Cemetery which filled rapidly and particularly so during 1833, during the dark foreboding cholera epidemic in the town. By the 1840's, the old graveyard had reached capacity and the new Willow Mount Cemetery, located in the north west section of the town. The hundred acres donated by Cannon for the town had to be surveyed and staked, streets laid off, the two acre square cleared, trees cut, lots sold and the grounds prepared upon which to locate the permanent Seat of Justice, named Shelbyville.

The town was named in honor of rather Isaac or Evan Shelby. The jury is still out on this. Dr. Cogswell in earlier writings for the Bedford County Historical Quarterly wrote convincingly that it was Evan Shelby, not Isaac for whom Shelbyville was named.

The town had grown in nine years to a point where incorporation was sought and approved by the Legislature and was incorporated on October 7, 1819 and Thomas Davis elected the first mayor. In 1832, a bridge was constructed across the river below Cannon Mills and above Galbreath's Mills at Atkinson Street. The old town ford had served its purpose. Evidently as the town grew, reckless and sloppy parking became a problem with the gay blades as the following published ordinance will show that on February 21, 1818, "Be it Ordained, By the Board of Commissioners for the better regulations of the town of Shelbyville, that is any person or persons, shall from and after the passage of this ordinance, gallop, or strain any horse, mare, or gelding, thro' any street, or ally in the town of Shelbyville, he, she or they, shall forfeit and pay one dollar for every offence.

That if any person, shall hitch any horse, mare or gelding to the enclosure around the Court House in Shelbyville, he shall forfeit and pay the sum of dollar.

That is any person shall quarry, or cause to be quarried, any rocks in any of the streets or allys, in the town of Shelbyville, he shall for every such offense, forfeit and pay the sum of ten dollars. That if any person or persons, shall after the passage of this ordinance show any stud horse, within the town of Shelbyville, except on the 2nd day of each and every Court, such person or persons shall forfeit and pay for each and every offense the sum of ten dollars. Be it further ordained, that all by-laws and ordinances, this day passed, shall be published at the Court House in Shelbyville. Test: Geo. B. Balch, Clk. Signed: Howel Dawdy, Chm., February 6, 1818."

During the war between the states, Shelbyville was largely pro-union with large segments of the county being pro-rebel. Shelbyville's stand may partly be explained by the fact that many of the prominent and merchant families had ties to the north, and several years were Irish emigrants with strong pro-union feelings and throughout history many loyalties changed as the army's of occupation changed. Two notable events occurring during the war were the burning of the court house in 1863 and the charge at Skull Camp Bridge.

Early names of streets in the town were: Atkinson, Lane, Dawdy, Martin (changed to Main), Spring, Water, Deery, Britton and Jefferson. Of the above, Atkinson, Dawdy, Martin and Galbreath no longer exist as is the case of some of the names of the old county roads, "how soon we forget." Were one to have toured the town in the 1940's and again in the 1970's the change would have been astonishing. The face of the old town including slums and shanty had disappeared under the Big Spring Urban Renewal Programs, resulting in clean modern city, the first commissioners would have been proud of.

Several years ago while engaged in a historical project that entailed the copying and recording all tombstones standing in Marshall County, Tennessee, we observed from time to time as we traveled up and down Highway 31-A, a large standing object standing alone in a pasture some one hundred yards east of the highway, the distance prohibiting a determination as to whether or not the object was a tombstone or perhaps a weather beaten tree stump of fence post, curiosity getting the best of us, we investigated and found that indeed it was a tombstone of the old sandstone variety, standing tall on the west bank of the Old Fishing Ford Road that

General Jackson had traveled down on his way to the Creek Indian Wars in 1813-14. After cleaning the stone with special preparation we were able to read and photograph the following: "A Memorial for John Atkinson was bornd July the 19th, 1773 and dec'd this life March the 9, 1829." Surely he died with the personal satisfaction that a new county and town was born and all were doing well.

OWNERS OF FIRST TOWN LOTS
OF SHELBYVILLE

The town as laid off in 1810 consisted of 135 lots. The south boundary line ran immediately south of the city power sub-station. The east boundary line ran through the middle of the Old City Cemetery. The north boundary ran through the intersection of Cannon and North Main, and the west line ran south cornering at the beginning corner of the original 100 acre tract about where the flume discharge tube is located on the north bank of the river.

First lot owners as sold by the Commissioners in 1810-12:

1 & 2) Old City Cemetery
3) Baptist Church
4) Archibald Alexander
5) Jonathan Webster
6) Joseph Hastings
7) Levan Marshall
8) Levan Marshall
9) Benjamin Bradford
10) John Stone
11) John Stone
12) James Edde
13) James Edde
14) Moses Prewitt
15) Nathaniel Schooler

SEE PLAT SECTION, PAGE 392
FOR MAP OF FIRST TOWN LOTS

16) Thomas Collen

17) James S. Edde

18) Levi C. Roberts

19) William Cross

20) John Coats (Whitney Tavern here)

21) James Deery

22) Henry Conway (Old Cumberland Presbyterian Church here)

23) Thomas Loranore

24) Edmund Austin (to Presbyterian Church Elders in 1825)

25) John B. Hogg

26) Stephen Clark (Old W.B.M. Brame Lot)

27) Stephen Clark

28) John Stone

29) John Stone

30) John Stone

31) John Stone

32) Keeble Terry

33) Thomas Collins

34) Samuel Fleming

35) Newton Cannon

36) Robert Cannon

37) Clement Cannon (South east corner of Public Square)

38) Peter Chilcutt (Middle lot, east side of Public Square)

39) Samuel and John Porter (North east corner of Public Square)

40) Robert Cannon (Brick or Foreman's "Row," Holland Street)

41) Robert Cannon and Samuel Engram (North of Lot 40)

42) John Stone

43) James Patton (Old Stewart-Potts Building)

44) John Atkinson (now car lot)

45) John Snelling

46) James R. Terry

47) John Frazier to G. Burdett to Rev. Geo. Newton (M.E. Church here in 1878, C.P. Church here in 1888)

48 & 49) No early records found but the Shelbyville Post Office is located on 48 and Peoples Drive-In Bank on 49)

50) John Stone

51) John Stone (in 1845 Squire Thompson (a man of color) purchased lot. This lot was on north boundary line of the city)

52) George Bell

53) Keeble Terry (Fly's Old Manufacturing Company)

54) Minos Cannon (Shelbyville Public Library on south half)

55) John Atone (Old Globe Tavern, Dixie Hotel, now Peoples Bank, lot sold more that any other town lot)

56) Jesse Evans (Stables for Old Shelbyville Inn here)

57) Moses Yell

58) James McQuistion

59) John McBride (Old Black House stood here)

60) John Stone

61) Henry Windrow

62) Clement Cannon (Middle lot south side Square) (Old Cannon Tavern here was leased to county in 1861 to be used as Court House after the fire)

63) James McQuistion to James Deery (Deery's lot on north side of Square, Brickhouse stood here)

64) Old Jail Lot (Log Jail here, brick jail built here in 1837 on parts of Lots 64 & 71)

65) Ishmael Burrow

66) James McQuistion (Old M.E. Brick Church stood on part of Lot No. 66 and 58)

67) James McQuistion

68) John Stone

69) Clement Cannon (South west corner of Square, now Knox Pitts Hardware Store)

70) William Newsom (First M.E. Church on this Lot)

71) Joseph Walker (Old Jail built on part of this lot)

72) John Warner (Second Sheriff of Bedford County)

73) Benjamin Bradford

74) John T. Shanks

75) Benjamin McQuistion

76) James McKissick (Lots 76 & 77, known as "Council Row")

77) Samuel B. Harris (Gunter Building)

78) Nicholas Branch (Middle of block, west side of square)

79) Thomas Tolbot (Bank of Tennessee, now First National Bank)

80) Samuel Phillips

81) William Lock

82) Samuel Bell

83) David Lowe (Tan Yard)

84) James Holland

85) Joseph B. Howell (The Little spring was here)

86) Howel Dawdy (Big Spring Shopping Center)

87) For early city use (Big Spring located here)

88) Henry Horn, Jeremiah Dial

89) Daniel Dawdy

90) Benjamin Jordon

91) Benjamin Jordon

92) First record found shows Aldermen of Town to William Gilchrist

93) Registration not found

94) Benjamin Gambill

95) Sterling Newsome (on Old Bridge Street)

96) Abraham Thompson

97) Michael Fisher (Big Spring Shopping Center)

98) Howel Dawdy (Big Spring Shopping Center)

99) Henry Miller

100) John H. Anderson

101) Henry Murry

102) Newton Cannon

103) Joseph Woods

104) Daniel McCoy (Big Spring Shopping Center)

105) Howel Dawdy (Big Spring Shopping Center)

106) John B. Pinson

107) Alfed Dawdy

108) James Holland (Old Cannon Brick Mills, 2000 spindles)

109) Newton Cannon

110) Joseph Thompson

111) Amos Balch (Big Spring Shopping Center)

112) William Galbreath (Big Spring Shopping Center)

113) William A. Young

114) Nathaniel Schooler

115) Jos. Walker (William Galbreath's Wool Carding Factory and Dam)

116) James Walker (Yanyard)

117) James Russell

118) Jesse Evans

119) Jesse Evans

120) Francis Murry

121) Andrew Donaldson

122) James Walker

123) Edward Wade

124) 124) Jesse Evans

125) John Baird

126) Nathaniel E. Coldwell

127) Barkley Martin

128) Joseph Minafee

129) William Gore (Old Davidson Tanyard here)

130) Jesse Evans

131) Jesse Evans

132) Jesse Evans (Old Ray's Store Lot)

133) Howel Dawdy

134) Abner Chappel (Old Tennessee Power Lot)

135) Thomas Moore

THE LANDS OF BEDFORD

A detailed study of the land admittedly is a rather dry subject to most, but it is a subject that is generally dealt with rather lightly and without the land would be no history. It is interesting to note that if all land records were destroyed chaos would result in a short time. For a study of the lands of Bedford, it is imperative that we go back in time briefly to a period some years before the birth of the county in 1807.

As has been mentioned briefly before in this writing, large portions of Bedford County lands were entered by warrants held by land speculators, issued by the State of North Carolina for her western lands which included Bedford County. Over eight million acres were granted in this fashion, which included nearly two hundred thousand acres within the bounds of Bedford County, as first constituted in 1807.

The State of North Carolina was in dire financial strain at the beginning of the Revolutionary War and in order to recruit her citizens for Continental Service against the British and to meet other expenses related to the war, she issued script and made it legal tender. The script by continually rapid depreciation was almost worthless by 1782 at the close of the war. The State feeling that this unfortunate turn of events should not penalize her own soldiers who had in good faith fought and died for the state and county, directed that to make up the loss the soldiers had experienced by adopting a scale of depreciation based on the years 1777 to 1782. Samuel boards of auditors were established to audit all accounts for the depreciation and to issue certificates for the specific value, which might be exchanged for Land Warrants at fifty cents per acre. Anthony Bledsoe, Edmond Williams and Landon Carter were auditors for Washington and Sullivan Counties for 1781-1783. By the end of the war the Land Speculators had a well-organized lobby in the Legislature that included several powerful members of the Legislature who had more than a casual interest in the Land Grab Legislature. The speculators believed and correctly so that the soldiers after the long struggle with the British were often left improvised, deep in debt and with no stomach for following the long and tedious procedure to secure their grant. So the cash offered by the speculators were most often welcome. A bill favoring the speculators was passed that wound raise the amount of acres that could be purchased in one tract from 640 acres to 5000 acres, additionally the surveyors could piece several large tracts together, as was the case with the Blount Brother's Grants in Bedford County. William Blount, Governor of the Territory in 1790, was deeply involved in the western land deals and an examination of the Blount papers will show he was well aware of the personal advantage and financial gain the office held for him.

These early North Carolina grants normally show a price of ten pounds per hundred acres amounting to 40 to 50 cents per acre at that time. The Blount Brothers briefly held grants for the largest acreage in Bedford County, 85000 acres. George Daughtry came second. Most of these men who held these large grants never came to Bedford County. Some of their heirs did. Most often the land was sold off piece meal over the years to those who came and settled. Early Duck and Elk River and their waters embraced a vast extensive area diversified virgin country through which cold and inexperienced land locators and surveyors promiscuously appropriated land that resulted in a great conflict of titles particularly in places which were then notorious or well known. Locators often called the same creek and same fork by many different and un-appropriate names and locators, and surveyors had been extremely vague and indefinite often resulting in floating corners. All this resulted in grants issued in interference to others. Some located and surveyed on top of existing grants, which caused much litigation, and many times several surveys of the land in question. Many of the old grant lines were substantially changed from the first survey as an example of the questionable operations going on at this time, we will use the following example. By beginning at the south of Wartrace Fork as the beginning location and using imaginary floating corners on the adjoining grants, the 85,000 acre Blount Grants could have been located on paper without locators being on the scene. Some grantees in North Carolina that tried in vain to locate their grants in Middle Tennessee could find no corners called for in the entries and legal survey could not be made obviously if they could not find the land it could not be surveyed.

Henry Rutherford was one who had been accused by some of this practice. One such grant was a 1500 acre tract located at the mouth of Falling Creek, located for General William Lenoir of Wilkes County, North Carolina, who in June of 1806 sent his son Thomas to Duck River to try to locate the corner of his grant as surveyed by Rutherford in July 1785. The son contracted with Samuel Gentry of Williamson County, living near Eagleville then the southern outpost of civilization, to pilot him to Duck River to help find the corners. They came to Duck River and Falling (Fall) Creek. They made diligent search along the river and creeks but found no marks that had been given in the survey, after a fruitless search of two days in what he concluded was a God-forsaken dismal country, they concluded that no corners were then marked and in fact had never been so marked and in so concluding they abandoned the search. Apparently the corners were finally located or re-established and surveyed for in 1844, the son who was not all that enthused about this country, sold the 1500 acres of the late William Lenoir of Wilkes County, North Carolina to Newcum Thompson. The corner of this grant was located on the north side of Duck River just below Old Fisher's Mill, later Anchor Mills. To confuse the issue even more two different methods of surveying was used in the early days before the county was sectioned off into townships. The surveyor of the North Carolina Grants before 1806 ran out the lines to the needle of the compass, which was easier to do as no magnetic declination had to be allowed for. An examination of the early deeds reveal some rather vague and often humorous calls for old corners such as a stick stuck in the knot hole of a fallen beech tree. The corner of Widow Moore's hog pen an old rotten stump, a stake in an old field, an old ash root, five lynns growing from the same stump or a rock in the road. Vague calls of this nature often resulted in loss of old corners and difficulty in closing the survey. Often in Bedford County, particularly until after the Civil War, a type of survey called Processional Survey was practiced. This practice dated back to Scotland in the days when the populace was generally illiterate and deeds were not recorded. A common practice was for the Vicar of the local parish to lead a processional with all the children and older inhabitants of the area and to walk the lines stopping at each corner to announce it to all in the processional. Hereby the older and younger generations were all participants in establishing an oral deed history to the land in question, that would be handed down generation to generation. Many processional surveys were made in Bedford County immediately after the Civil War as several deed books had been burned in the Court House fire in 1863, and corners had to be established by mutual consent of all the effected neighbors.

In 1806, with the sectioning off of the counties of Middle Tennessee, the surveyors were directed to run the Range and Section Lines using the cardinal points of the compass which directed that the declination from true north must be accounted for or a north line to be run as true north, etc. This resulted in a hodge-podge of diagonal lines between late and older adjoining grants, with many small wedge shaped lines between the old and new grants. An aerial view of the county, even today, will show old fencerows and property lines that were originally surveyed using both methods.

On October 25, 1805, by the Tellico Treaty, the Cherokees relinquished all claims to all their lands north of a line that began at the mouth of Duck River, near New Johnsonville, on the Tennessee River up the main stream to the junction of the Garrison Fork with the main fork. This would be the Three Forks, thence up the main south or Barren Fork, thence in a direct line to opposite the mouth of the Hiwassee on the Tennessee. This would relinquish all land north of Duck River. Settlers would then have no qualms about Indian title to this area and early settlers would likely began to move in from the north and Rutherford County across the ridge into the area around what is now Wartrace and Bell Buckle as has been previously stated. The Treaty also stipulated that the government was to have free and unmolested use of two great roads, one to proceed from near the head of Stones River and fall into Georgia Road in a southwardly direction. This would be near the village of Beech Grove and near where Old Fort Nash once stood. The Georgia Road led to Ross Landing now Chattanooga.

On January 7, 1806, the Dearborn relinquished all Indian claims to land south of Duck River to the Alabama (then Mississippi Territory)-Tennessee State Line. This would clear any question of title to the lands in the southern part of Bedford, Marshall and Coffee and all lands in Moore and Lincoln. This Treaty resulted in an immediate and rapid flood of settlers into Duck River Valley.

In 1806, the curtain had been pulled and the show was on. As a result of a compact between the United States Government and the State of Tennessee, on April 18, 1806, an agreement was entered into settling a long running dispute of ownership of the lands in Tennessee and set in motion the practice of sectionalizing the southern half of Middle Tennessee.

Bedford was sectioned off into townships of sections, run to the true meridian of the compass at the direction of the Legislature by John Coffee, James Bright and others and the school land tracts were located and surveyed in August 1806. When one does land deed research on early Bedford County deeds and sections, ranges and school land terminology is encountered in the deeds the following information may be helpful. Before the area was sectioned off, surveys were made using metes and bounds descriptions and lines were run out following magnetic north. For a number of years after 1807 the range and section lines numbers were recorded in most deeds but after the mid-eighteen hundred's this practice died out. The locations of the old range and section lines in the county are generally unknown today. No plat, or map of the township lines exist today, except the one compiled by this writer.

As the section and range lines were surveyed in 1807, a tree was marked along all lines at each point and was referred to in deeds as one-mile tree, two-mile tree, etc. Each section was six miles square. The section started at the south boundary line of the Military Reservation and was to run south to the old Tennessee-Alabama State Line, then west to the east boundary line of the Congressional Reservation in Giles County. The middle section of the Tennessee-Alabama State Line was ran in preparation for the section surveys and congressional line in 1806 by James Bright, late of Lincoln County. James Bright was appointed by his uncle, William Anderson, surveyor of the Second Surveyors District. The line as run out by Bright fell two miles and 242 poles short of the true State Line and was rejected by the Legislature in October 1807. General John Strother, William P. Anderson and Colonel Meigs met near the Taft Community is now located in Lincoln County, Tennessee to ascertain the true State Line which was two miles and 4002.57 feet south of the first line. The Old State Line Road, or Bright's State Line was referred to in deeds for many years after the line was resurveyed. Because of the mix-up in establishing the true State Line a small strip in southern middle Tennessee fell into a fractional section of Section One. A copy of Bright's Old Survey is in the writer's possession. Signs of the Old State Line Road were well visible during the writer's youth, running about a mile above the old home-place at Lincoln, Tennessee. It was etched in my mind not because of any historical significance but rather because of the abundance of huckleberries along the old road or trail. Bright ran the Congressional Line as part of the compromise settlement with the Federal Government in 1806. This line began where Elk River crosses the south boundary of the State, then run north to Duck River, thence down said river to south boundary line of the Military Reservation. For this compromise, the Federal Government ceded all rights to land north and east of the reservation. This included the lands of Bedford, one condition being that 640 acres be set aside in each six square acre for the express use of schools, hence the name School Land Tracts. The school land tracts that were surveyed and set aside for then use of the Common Schools by Action of the Legislature were often located on unproductive land the large grantees did not want. Some had 320 acres, most had 630 acres, as there were fourteen tracts in all in the county. Their names and locations are as follows:

Richmond Tract located on Sinking Creek near the village of Richmond.

Sinking Creek Tract located at the village of Wheel, which derived its name from and Agriculture Grange or Wheel that flourished in the county in the 1870's.

Powell Creek Tract located on the east side of Comstock Road about seven miles west of Shelbyville.

North Fork Tract located north of Halls Mill.

Clem's Creek Tract located between Rover and Unionville.

Wartrace Creek Tract located north of the village of Wartrace near the Rutherford County Line.

El Bethel Tract located on Unionville Highway at El Bethel Baptist Church.

Sulphur Spring Tract located on old Nashville Dirt Road north west of Shelbyville.

Flat Creek Tract located at village of Flat Creek.

Waters of Flat Creek located south of center Church and Center Church Road.

Upper Thompson Creek Tract located at the village of Raus.

Lower Thompson Creek Tract located east of Shofners Lutheran Church, this grant was swallowed up by later surveys of some of the Blount Grants.

South Side Duck River Tract located on Sulphur Spring Road.

University of North Carolina 1000 Acre Tract located in south west corner of the county.

Commissioners were appointed to oversee the renting and collections of the monies of the tracts. Often the tracts were rented out for cultivation and some never had schools built on them. In 1846, with the approval of the Legislature, the various School Districts were allowed to hold referendum to approve the sale of the tracts in lots, to the highest bidder. By 1855, all the tracts had been sold and State Grants issued to the Grantees. Few of the grants are recorded in the Bedford County Court House, but all are in the Tennessee State Archives in Nashville, Tennessee.

THE THREE FORKS

The Three Forks of Duck River, often mentioned in early records was the confluence of the Garrison Fork, The Wartrace Fork and The Barren or South Fork. The Garrison Fork starts in what is now Cannon County, Tennessee, flows by Fairfield paralleling the Old Crawford Trace, and on down to the fork. Straight and Knob Creeks are tributaries of the Garrison which probably got its name for the Old Garrison, once located north east of Beech Grove, at the edge of Coffee and Cannon Counties but until the formation of Coffee County in 1835, was located in Bedford County. The Wartrace Fork of Duck River starts on Duck River Ridge at the Rutherford County Line, north of Bell Buckle Post Office, past where Old Wartrace Post Office once stood at the Timothy Sugg place, on southward flowing east of Bell Buckle where it receives the waters of Bell Buckle Creek and its tributaries, the Otter and Cedar Forks, continuing on southeastwardly, just east of the old Salem Methodist Camp Ground, picking up the waters of a branch called Muse Branch named for an early family of that name that lived on the branch, on south passing Wartrace once called Wartrace Depot, on the west through the grant once owned by General Andrew Jackson and later by Rice Coffey and Kinchen Stokes, then picking up a branch entering from the west once called Little Wartrace now Stokes Branch, and immediately emptying into the Garrison. It was here at the mouth of the Wartrace Fork with the Garrison that one of the beginning corners for four of the 5000 acre grants of the Blount brothers was located and the surveys of their 85,000 acre empire began here in August of 1792 by surveyor John Donelson, Jr., of Nashborough with chain carriers, John Castleman, Terry Poe and John Peyton and others. From the function with the Wartrace Fork, the Garrison flows on south for two miles and there it junctions with the Barren or South Fork. This location is the actual "Three Forks" and it was here that the Reverend Samuel King and William McGee, two of the founders of The Cumberland Presbyterian denomination settled, built a mill on the river and a church near by in 1812, called The Three Forks Meeting House. Over the years quite a complex of races, holding ponds, saw mills, grist mills and carding factories sprang up here. Brother McGee died here in 1817 and later members of his family moved westward to Arkansas. Brother King fathered other churches in the county, one being Hastings Camp Ground. He moved to Arkansas in the late 1820's and lived the remainder of his days there. The mills changed hands many times, being owned by Burdett, Maupin, Shofner, Timmons and Bernard. It was nearly destroyed as a result of the Civil War, and never regained the prominence it once enjoyed. At this point the Barren Fork runs to the east and main Duck River continues on its westward course to Shelbyville and westward. The Barren of South Fork flows on eastward by the Gabriel and Blan Maupin place, picking up the waters of Shipman Creek named for pioneer Daniel Shipman, on north of Rowesville and the old John Ewell grant, passing south of the old Allen Knights, later William Culley farm, picking up the water from Russell Branch once called Sinking Creek, not to be confused with another Sinking Creek in the western part of the county, on eastward where it once turned the waterwheel of the old Cortner Mill, passing to the north of Jacob Troxler's land, all this area being part of the Blount Grant No. 231. The river then turns eastwardly and south past the village of Normandy leaving the old Peter Huffman land on the north, here at the TVA dam that Normandy Lake is now located, then on up the lake reservoir past the mouth of Riley Creek and immediately the mouth of Davidson Branch where John Davidson, a Revolutionary Soldier, once lived near his brother Hugh and near the old Davidson Post Office site, on eastwardly on winding course through Coffee County past the old Stone Fort at Manchester. Here the river takes a northerly and north westerly direction and starts about one half mile south of the Cannon County Line about four miles east of the course of the Garrison and a short distance east of the site of the old Fort Nash at Purdy's Garrrison, that was located east of Beech Grove in 1794, and may have given the Garrison Fork its name.

THE BLOUNT GRANTS

Through the years much has been written and published locally, some documented, some not, about the Blount Grants and Colonel Andrew Erwin's brick house, located on one of the grants, namely No. 221. I will give here a brief chronology of the Blount Grants of the Three Forks of Duck River. The seventeen grants consisting of 5000 acre each or a total of 85,000 acres, were all touched by one or more of the Three Forks of Duck River. They encompassed an area along and on both sides of Duck River, running from about two and one half miles east of Shelbyville to north east of Beech Grove in Coffee County on the Garrison or sometimes called the Middle Fork and to Manchester once called Mitchelville, including the ancient Indian Fort in Coffee County on the south or Barren Fork of Duck River.

This masterful stroke of land locating was strategically engineered by the Blount agents, Stokly Donalson being one, as it in essence controlled the waters of Duck River from its headwaters of its Three Forks to near the center of the County of Bedford as well as much of Coffee County to the east. The grants were surveyed in August and September of 1792 by surveyor John Donalson, Jr., son of Captain John Donalson who in 1779 piloted the Adventure from the Holston in East Tennessee, down the Tennessee to the Ohio and then up the Cumberland arriving at the Bluffs on the Cumberland at French Lick in April 1780 with his precious cargo of pioneer settlers and their families, as well as the families of the Robertson Party who eagerly awaited them at the bluff.

After the initial survey in late summer of 1792, grants were issued to John Gray and Thomas Blount on June 27, 1793 by the State of North Carolina, these were not military grants but rather North Carolina General Grants so sought after by the hoards of land speculators who were clamoring for the western lands in Cumberland Country. The Blount brothers in the following year after the grants were issued, to be exact on October 9, 1794 sold vast wilderness empire on Duck River to David Allison, merchant and land speculator of Philadelphia. As can best be determined the Blounts never saw this Duck River land as the holding here were small indeed in comparison to their vast holding east of the Alleghenies and they were most certainly to preoccupied with their numerous land, mercantile and shipping interest on the east coast, to build a spacious brick house in the wilderness of Duck River where even they questioned the clear title, due to prior and existing Indian claims to the land. Ten months later on August 1795, David Allison being financially embarrassed mortgaged the Duck River lands to Norton Pryor of Philadelphia. Allison defaulted on payment to Pryor and was thrown in Debtors Prison in Philadelphia where he wrote many pleading letters to his old business associates the Blounts. Praying for relief but to no avail and he died in prison in 1798, sick and destitute. His heirs later settled in Georgia. Norton Pryor in an attempt to regain his losses at Allison, resorted to the Federal Courts and the Federal Marshall advertised for sale in the Knoxville Gazette. The mortgaged lands (85,000) sale to be held at the "Court House" in Nashville April 19, 1802 and not at the "brick house" on Duck River as has been reported in the past.

At the Marshall's sale, Andrew Jackson purchased two grants and as agent for Joseph Anderson of Jefferson County, Tennessee, purchased four grants for him. Pryor retained the remaining eleven grants. Jackson sold one Grant No. 235 that lay to the west of the Three Forks to John Overton and Jenkin Whiteside. They then sold the 5000 acres off in various tracts to early settlers who settled on the tracts, some being the Dickersons, Kings, Dodds, Gibsons, Youngs and Mullins. He sold his purchased Grant No. 234 that lay west of the town of Wartrace and east of Horse Mountain. Early purchasers of this tract were Nathaniel Hayes, Moses Yell, Charles Harryman, John Shelby, William Waite, William Ditto, Timothy O'Neal, William and Thomas McGuire, Michael Holt, William Sharp, Kinchen Stokes, Rice Coffey, Thompsons and Gannaways and Butlers. The old original east boundary line of this grant ran north and south through part of the town of Wartrace. Part of the old Indian War Trace ran through this grant and old Indian Bark Houses still stood here as late as 1806. The grants, General Jackson purchased for Joseph Anderson were 218, 220, 222 and 230. Anderson sold parts of some of these grants to Alexander Outlaw of Jefferson, West Tennessee. He then sold various tracts to early settlers. Patton and Erwin later acquired the remainder of these four grants from Anderson No. 218 and 230 were in what is now Coffee County.

Fairfield is located on Grant No. 220. Some early purchasers were Matt Martin, a Revolutionary Soldier, William Finch, Walkers, Scotts, Sheltons, Davis, Muse, Armstrongs, Crutchers, Slaytons, Tillmans, Hords and Smallings, the Garrison Flows through this grant as well as Noah's Fork and Straight, tributaries of the Garrison. Andrew Jackson and John Donelson each had a 640 acre grant on the north of this grant. Grant No. 222 sold to Joseph Anderson and part later sold to Outlaw, lay immediately south and south east of the Town of Bell Buckle and included the Wartrace Fork and the junction of the Bell Buckle Creek, with the Wartrace. Anthony Branch once called Bradford Creek also junctions with the Wartrace on this grant. The most westward line of the grants ran about one and a half miles east of Horse Mountain. The Blount Grants were surveyed and resurveyed numerous times in the early years with the lines shifting back and forth until the 1820's when with the compromise settlement they finally were stabilized.

COLONEL ANDREW ERWIN

James Patton, a native of County Derry, Ireland, came south from Pennsylvania as a peddler, first to Wilkesboro, North Carolina and later to Buncombe County at Ashville. There he died years later. He took as a partner young Andrew Erwin, age 17, a Virginian who later married Patton's sister, Jane. Patton and Erwin were to become joint owners of a vast empire of land and other interests in North Carolina and Tennessee.

In 1800, Erwin was a member of the North Carolina House of Commons from Wilkes County, North Carolina. He was Post Master at Ashville, North Carolina from 1809 to 1807. James Patton had brothers, Thomas who with wife Jane Shaw settled on the Noah's Fork in Bedford County, later Coffee, and Daniel who also came to Bedford County. Patton and Erwin dissolved partnership in March 1814, Patton taking the North Carolina lands and Erwin all their lands in Tennessee, this included the remainder of the 85,000 acre Blount Grants in addition to many smaller Tennessee Grants and assignees land in Middle Tennessee. In 1814, Erwin removed to Augusta County, Georgia, owning numerous business enterprises in Georgia, Charleston, Nashville, New Orleans and Bedford County, Tennessee, where he died in 1834. His widow Jane died in 1859. They are buried in the family graveyard at "Rural Retreat." Their old country home located one and one half mile south east of Wartrace.

John Donelson made the first survey in 1792 of the lands later owned by Erwin. Resurveys made by John Drake in 1807. Seven tracts again in September 1814 by processional survey, being Grant No. 217, 220, 222, 224, 225, 232 and 234. There is no documented evidence that Erwin ever lived in Bedford County before 1818 at which time he appears to have removed from Georgia to Bedford County, Tennessee. He probably made short visits here while still living in Georgia to protect his interests. His son James who died in Fayette County, Kentucky in the early years acted as Power of Attorney for his father in disposing of his lands in Middle Tennessee.

Colonel Andrew Erwin was an anti-Jackson man having a long running dispute with Jackson about the disposition of the clear title for the lands Patton and Erwin had acquired from the sale of the Blount Grants and it involved Jackson's method of obtaining clear title to the lands that Erwin later owned. This dispute became so heated that violence was narrowly averted by the intervention of Colonel Erwin's wife Jane or so the story has been handed down numerous versions to meet various occasions. Erwin was later plagued with financial reverses and that his creditors bounded him is evident by reading the land deeds of Bedford County. The brick house tract called "Rural Retreat" along with most of his other holdings in Tennessee, Georgia and South Carolina were advertised for sale to satisfy judgments against him time after time but he managed to hold on to the brick house or home tract on Grant No. 22 1 and passed it to his children at his death. His son Andrew Erwin, Jr., lived in the brick house during the Civil War, later selling it to relatives and then moving to Alabama. There has been much conjecture as to the exact date that the old brick house was built, such as the late 1700's by the Blounts to oversee their holdings on Duck River. Of course the Blounts never came to Bedford County as they had plenty of troubles of their own fighting land fraud proceedings against their vast holdings in North Carolina. They only kept the Duck River land a short time before David Allison purchased the lands on credit and failing to pay, died in a Debtor's Prison in Philadelphia, and the holdings were sold at a Marshall's sale at the Court House in Nashville in 1802. Having checked all claims to the construction date before 1800 and finding absolutely no documentation to such claims, rather much evidence to the contrary, the conclusion points to a construction date of 1814-1817. This has been presented here not because of any great significance the date of the brick house may have on the course of history, but simply at this late date to attempt to set the record straight. Colonel Erwin with his vast holdings had a great influence, both directly and indirectly on the early growth and development of Bedford County, Tennessee. Erwin represented Bedford County in the 14th General Assembly 1821-1823.

OUR GALLANT MEN

We would be amiss in closing this paper if we neglected to mention those gallant men and women who not only contributed greatly to the growth and development of the county but also the birth and freedom of our nation. Bedford County's sons and daughters have ever been willing to come to our country's defense in all wars and many have made the supreme sacrifice. Their names are no less important that those listed below but their names are more readily accessible than those who fought in this Nations War of Independence. Most of the first settlers in Bedford County in 1807 were then in their 40's or older, had been involved in the struggle for freedom.

IN THE REVOLUTIONARY WAR

NAMES TAKEN FROM A REVISED PLAQUE
LOCATED IN THE BEDFORD COUNTY COURTHOUSE
Researched by Helen C. and Timothy R. Marsh, 1988

James Anderson
Kenneth Anderson
James Andes
W.D. Ashby
Amos Balch
John Bearden
Samuel Bigham
Jacob Bledsoe (Bletcher)
Jacob Bletcher
Charles Brandon
Brechen, William, Senr.
Philip Brown
Thomas Buchanan
John Burns, Sr.
"Daddy" Call
Solomon Campbell
Robert Caruthers
Abner Chappell
Anthony Clark
Rachel Clay
Sallie Clay
Nicholas Coble
John Connelly
Horatio Coop

Hugh McCrory (McCarey)
James McCuistion
William McGuire
Daniel McKisick
Francis McKaimy
George McLain
David McRoberts
Robert Majors
John F. Marion
George Martin
Josiah Martin
Matt Martin
Richard Martin
Daniel Meadors
James Miller
Peter Miller
Henry Moore
James Moore
John Moore, Sr.
Randolph Moore
John Morrison
James Mosely
Joseph Mullins
James Murray, Sr.

Abraham Cooper	James Norsworthy
James Coursey	David Osteen
John Culver	James Orr
George Cunningham	James Patton
Matthew Cunningham	John Patton
William Cunningham	William Pearson
Tigney Damron	Baxter Ragsdale
Andrew Davidson	John Rainey
John Davidson	Anthony Reagor
Jesse Davis	David Reavis
Howel Dawdy	John Reed
Jeremiah Dial	Ezekiel Reynolds
Thomas Drake	John Robinson (Robison)
William Eakin	Joseph Rogers
Richard Elkins	John Sack
Alexander Ewing	John Sark
Charles Fane	Samuel Sarrett
Michael Fisher	Christopher Shaw
David Floyd, Sr.	Martin Shofner
Charles Garmon	Thomas Aldridge Sikes
John Gibby	James Slaton
John Gibbs	George Smith. Sr.
Thomas Gore	William Smith
Samuel Gray	Samuel Spears
Elijah Green	Josiah J. Stafford
Alexander Greer	John Stone
James Haley	John Tacke
Barzilla Harrison	Thomas Talbot
William Harrison	Thomas Rollins Talbot
Joseph Hastings	Charles Taylor
Abraham Helton	John Theophillis Thompson

Joshua Holt	Thomas Thompson
Shadrack Holt	William Tipper
Joseph Jacobs	John Towson
Nathaniel Johnson	David Tucker
Nelson Kelly	Samuel A. Turrentine
Edward King	Joseph Walker
Samuel Knox	Matthew Wallis
Benjamin Lentz	Matthew Wallis
Jackson Lile	Jacob Wilhoit
Nicholas Loyd	John Williams
	John Wood
	Zadoc Wood
	Nicholas Woodfin
	Aaron Woosley

HISTORICAL MARKERS

3 A 47 – Bedford-Rutherford County Line.

3 G 24 – Church of the Redeemer – Bedford County, in Shelbyville, at corner of North Jefferson and East Lanes Streets. This was Lot No. 44 (24) of the original town plan. A log church was built here in 1815. The Presbyterians used it, and built the present church in 1817. In 1856, a Catholic Congregation bought the building, selling to the Northern Methodist in 1894. These sold the building at auction in 1934. The Protestant Episcopal Diocese of Tennessee bought it in 1935 and consecrated it in 1936.

3 G 31 – Prentice Cooper – 1895-1969 – Bedford County, in Shelbyville, at 413 East Lane Street. Governor of Tennessee for three successive terms 1939-1945. A native of Bedford County and graduate of Webb School, Princeton and Harvard Law

School, he was Attorney General of the 8th Judicial Circuit, a member of the 63rd and 70th General Assembly, U.S. Ambassador to Peru 1946-1948, President of the 1953 Tennessee Constitutional Convention, Veteran of WWI and State Commander of the American Legion. He reactivated the Tennessee Historical Commission and was a member 1941-1969.

3 G 8 – Army of Tennessee – June 27, 1863 – Bedford County, U.S. 41A, west outskirts of Shelbyville. Polk's Corps took up strong defensive positions in this area in early January 1863. Direct pressure by Stanley's Cavalry Corps and Grainger's Reserve Corps, plus flanking operations by Rosecran's Armu at Manchester, forced its withdrawal to Tullahoma, and later to Chattanooga.

2 G 27 – Webb School – (State 82) Bedford County, in Bell Buckle. Founded 1870, at Culleoka, by William R. ('Sawney") Webb, whose brother, John M. ("Old Jack") Webb joined him in 1874. It moved here in 1886. Its curriculum, embracing chiefly Latin, Greek and Mathematics, was designed to give a sound preparatory education. Many of its early graduates have conducted schools of the same type, which were once prominent in the South's educational system.

3 G 6 – Army of the Cumberland – June 27, 1863 – Bedford County, at Guys Gap. The reserve Corps (Granger) moved south along this road, screened by the Army's Cavalry (D.S. Slantey). Taking Guy's Gap against minor resistance, they pushed rapidly into Shelbyville, evacuated the same morning by the Corps of Maj. Gen. Leonidas Polk, which withdraw to Tullahoma.

3 G 28 – Henry Brevard Davidson – January 28, 1831-March 4, 1899. U.S. 231, Bedford County, in Shelbyville, on North Main Street. Born in a house, which stood here. Enlisted in the 1st Tennessee Volunteers for the Mexican War; on graduation from U.S. Military Academy in 1853, commissioned in Dragoons. Resigning for the Confederacy and rapidly promoted to Colonel, he was captured at Island No. 10;

promoted on exchange and given a brigade in Wheeler's Cavalry Corps. Surrendering at Greensboro, North Carolina, he moved to California, where he was once Deputy Secretary of State. He is buried in Oakland, California.

3 G 29 – Clement Cannon, Sr., Bedford County, in Shelbyville, at the intersection of Brittain Street and Lynchburg Road. Born in North Carolina 1783; veteran of the War of 1812; early Bedford County manufacturer; Whig political leader. In 1810, Cannon provided 100 acres of land for the site of the "Town of Shelbyville" and in 1817 donated 5 acres to Dickson Academy and a lot to a local church. He died in 1860 and is buried in the Cannon Cemetery 400 feet southwest.

3 G 7 – Army of Tennessee – State 64 – Bedford County, near Fairfield. Hardee's Corps retired to the Wartrace-Fairfield defensive line, January 1863. Here they remained until late June, when Rosecrans, moving the bulk of the Federal Army of the Cumberland around the right flank to Manchester, made Bragg withdraw from his strong positions to Chattanooga.

3 G 16 – Andrew's Raiders – State 64 – Bedford County, 1.8 miles east of Shelbyville. On this knoll, members of the Federal Party attempted to destroy the Western and Atlantic RR in 1862, assembled before starting their foray. It started with seizure of the engine "General" and ended with recapture of the engine at the Georgia State line the same day. Several of the party was subsequently hanged.

3 G 22 – Confederate Cemetery – Bedford County, Shelbyville, entrance to Willow Mount Cemetery. In the cemetery north of the road are buried Confederate soldiers of the Army of Tennessee, who fell while opposing the advance of Rosecrans' Army of the Cumberland through Liberty Gap and Guy's Gap, in late June 1863. Also buried here are soldiers of the Forrest's Cavalry, killed in minor operations.
Editor's Note: Moved to entrance of Willow Mount Cemetery March 2003, formerly stood Route 64 at Farmington.

Bedford County – Established 1807 in honor of Thomas Bedford, Jr.

Thomas Bedford was a native of Virginia, a member of the Virginia Assembly, and an officer in the Revolutionary War. He moved to Tennessee around 1795 where he had obtained large tracts of land around Nashville. He later moved from Davidson to Rutherford County where he settled at Jefferson Springs, and contributed to settlement and development of Rutherford County. He died in 1804.

BEDFORD COUNTY TOWNS AND VILLAGES

Shelbyville

The County Seat of Bedford County was established in 1810 on land provided by Clement Cannon, an early settler. The town was named for Evan Shelby. Incorporated in 1819. First settler at the town spring was Samuel Musgrove. In 1890, Shelbyville became a major manufacture of cedar products that evolved into the major pencil industry now supported here. The Walking Horse Capitol of the World. Located on Duck River, a tributary of the Tennessee, 55 miles south of Nashville.

Bedford

Established as a Post Office after the Civil War. Located on the old Michael Marsh estate, one time affectionately known as "Fleaburg," 6 miles west of Shelbyville on State Road 64.

Bell Buckle

Established in 1850's, unique name, only one in United States. Many theories as to the origin of the name. Actually the village assumed the name of the creek that runs through the town. The name Bell Buckle Creek is documented as early as 1806. Famous Webb School located there in 1886. Located 8 miles north east of Shelbyville on State Road 82 off Highway 231.

Deason

Established first as "Bellmount." Located between the Matthew Locke and Caleb Phifer North Carolina Grants. Named for John Deason who lived here on the turnpike in the 1830's. Location: 8 miles north of Shelbyville on U.S. Highway 231.

Fairfield

This early village has carried many names, most of them prompted by the rapid exchange and ownership of the fine mill located there on the Garrison, namely Parrs in 1810, Crutchers, Hickman in 1816, and Davis in 1819. It carried the name Davis Mill for many years. Later in the 1820's Dr. James Armstrong, a surgeon under Jackson, moved here, purchased the mill and tried to establish the name of Petersburg, but this name was short lived. The Old Stage Road ran through this village eastward to Washington City. Location: 10 miles north of Shelbyville on State Road 64.

Flat Creek

Established in 1850's. Located on the north boundary of 640 acre School Land Grant. Named for the creek. James Gage, William Hazlett and Michael Prewitt (later Hix) operated mills here early. Primitive Baptist Church here on the hill in 1820's. Located: 6 miles south southwest of Shelbyville on State Road 82.

Haley

First named "Maupin" for R.B. Maupin who owned the land. Sprang up with the coming of the railroad, later name changed to Haley, for a family by that name. Located: 8 miles east of Shelbyville, on Haley Road, off State Road 64.

Halls Mill

First name in the early 1800's was "Thompson's Ford," a major ford on the north-south road. First land locators crossed here in 1783. Old Halls Mill was located below the bridge. Lutheran Church established her in early 1800's. Located: 8 miles north west of Shelbyville on Halls Mill Road, off U.S. Highway 41-A.

Himesville

Derived its name from a German family named Himes who came from Maryland in 1810 or 1822 with a related family named Keyser. Name changed to Belmont in 1902 when a Post Office was located there, reverting back to Himesville after the demise of the Post Office. Located: 4 miles south east of Shelbyville on State Road 82.

Longview

Established first as "Center Grove" in 1870's. The name Longview is obvious if one views the area. It is on the northeast corner of an Old Land Grant of Ebenezer Alexander. Located: 10 miles north east of Shelbyville on Longview Road off U.S. Highway 41-A.

New Herman

First known as "Deans." A Post Office by that name operated there for several years in the late 1800's. The name 'New Herman" evolved from the church that was established there in the 1830's. Located: 9 miles south of Shelbyville on the New Herman Road, off State Road 82.

Normandy

Established in 1852 with the arrival of the railroad. Town named for Norman Creek. John Gage was living here and operating a mill in 1812. Located: 1 mile southeast of Normandy TVA Lake and 10 miles east of Shelbyville on State Road 16.

Pleasant Grove

Established in 1830's as "Robertsons Store." In 1850's assumed the name of "Cottage Grove," located on west boundary line of Alexander and Thomas Greer's 5000 acre North Carolina Grant. Early Big Spring Baptist Church once stood nearby. First land locators camped here in August 1783. Located: 5 miles south west of Shelbyville on State Road 130.

Raus

Established first as "Thompson Creek," located on a School Land Grant. First establishment was Thompson Creek Baptist Meeting House built in early 1800's. In 1892, Frederick Raus ran a store and Post Office there. A first citizen, Elijah Parker settled here in 1807. Located: 8 miles south east of Shelbyville on State Road 130.

Richmond

Established in 1830's on separate land grants issued to John Phillips and John Smith, Sr. Once a thriving village, on the old North-South Fishingford-Hannah Gap Road. Located: 9 miles south west of Shelbyville on State Road 130.

Roseville (Rowesville)

Established in the 1830's when Dr. Joseph Rowe laid off and sold lots, was on the Malcom Gilchrist Tennessee Land Grant. The main Pond Spring (Hillsboro, Coffee County) Road ran through the village. Daniel Shipman who named the creek, settled immediately south of this grant in 1806. Located: 8 miles east of Shelbyville on State Road 16.

Rover

Established in early 1800's by Abraham Byler, a first Justice of the Peace, known as "Bylers" until the 1840's when the name Rover first appeared in print. Located: 13 miles north west of Shelbyville on U.S. Highway 41-A.

Singleton

Derived its name from a family of that name who once ran a general store there. Peter Singleton, a native of Virginia, once owned the land. A Post Office was established in 1881. Other names were Bismark and Fair Play. Located: 5 miles south east of Shelbyville on State Road 130.

Wartrace

Established about 1853 with the coming of the railroad. First known as Wartrace Depot. The Wartrace Post Office was located in the 1830's above Bell Buckle on the Liberty Pike, located on Wartrace Creek, near the ancient Indian War-Trace. Located: 7 miles east-northeast of Shelbyville on State Road 64.

Wheel

Established in the 1870's. This unusual name was derived from a State Agricultural and Mechanical Organization known as "Wheelers" who located a lodge at then Liggett's Chapel, now "Wheel." Joshua Musgrave an early settler here. Located: 9 miles west of Shelbyville on State Road 64.

EARLY HISTORICAL SITES

First County Court

First County Court in present Bedford County Court. In 1810, the County Court met at the house of Amos Balch, before moving to the permanent location of Shelbyville. Located: 2 miles west of Shelbyville, on the hill in the west corner of the intersection of Naron Road and Highway 64.

Amos Balch Spring and Tannery

Balch settled here in 1801 on land willed to his wife Ann Patton. A large magnificent spring gushed from the side of the hill where his house stood. The spring supplied the water for an early tannery that was located across the old Columbia Road, now Highway No. 64. Balch was buried in the Old Patton Graveyard a short distance south of the house. Graveyard now destroyed. Location: Same as above.

Old Town Ford at Shelbyville

Crossed the river immediately above the dam where a large island was then located.

Thompson's Ford

An old ford located on Duck River at Halls Mill. This was an early crossing of the river of a north-south route. The Greer Expedition crossed here in the Fall of 1783. Located: At Halls Mill, 8 miles down river from Shelbyville.

Greer's Lick

A large Spring or lick where Alexander Greer and others camped in August 1783. Greer located his 5000 acre grant here at this time, a first settler. He later built his home west of the lick. A first Justice of the Peace of the county. Location: South west of Pleasant Grove near the site of the Old Big Spring Baptist Church.

Old Base Line Road

A Base Surveyors North-South Line set up by Robert Weakley in 1785, when he surveyed large North Carolina Grants North and South and East and West along this base line. It began on Duck River near Sylvan Mills and ran south into Lincoln County. It has been called Base Line Road, Bledsoe Gap Road and presently Naron Road. Location: Naron Road off Highway 64.

First Mill On Sinking Creek

Before 1812, Nathaniel Porter had constructed a mill on Sinking Creek, that ran through his property. The mill has had many named. For many years, known as Ray's, then Cunningham's Mill. Porter died in 1813 and is buried on his place. Located: 2 miles north of Richmond on old Meredith Gentry farm.

Meredith Gentry

One time Congressman from Tennessee, candidate for Governor against Andrew Johnson, had a tumultuous political career. Built a fine home named "Hillside," that was part of the old Nathaniel Porter estate on Sinking Creek above Richmond. Gentry died in 1866 in Nashville. Located: 2 miles north of Richmond on Sinking Creek.

Early Town Mills

The first was Clement Cannon's Mill at the Town Ford. Mill located on west side of river. Newton Cannon owned mill on Flat Creek, near the corner of Kaden Street and Linda Drive. Sharp's Mill located on the river off Coney Island Road. This mill was later Sanders', Burdett then Marbury. On up the river was an early mill named Sims Mill. After the Civil War, it was Holt's Mill.

Cannon's Tavern

General Robert Cannon owned Town Lot No. 62, located on the south side of the Public Square, now Knox Pitts Hardware. Before the war, a tavern was operating here. After the Courthouse burned in 1863, this tavern was used as a temporary Court House.

The Three Forks Crossing

In the Spring of 1784, a group of about 20 land locators, known as the Edmiston Company, came down by Old Jefferson in Rutherford County and crossed Duck River at the Three Forks, probably below the old bridge and continued on southward to Elk River Country where they made many locations of land for filing with the Secretary of State of North Carolina. This is the first documentation of a group of men traversing the county from border to border. The Three Forks Mill operated here about 1812. First owners were McGee and King. Location: 1 mile south west of Haley.

Skull Camp Ford and Bridge

As early as 1806, the Skull Camp Ford of Duck River is mentioned. When the first bridge was constructed across the river in 1848, large collections of skulls were uncovered. It was here in 1863, that the skirmish of Skull Camp Bridge took place, with Wheeler's Retreat across the river towards Tullahoma. Location: At the end of Belmont Avenue.

Guy's Plantation

Major William Guy came from North Carolina about 1816 and settled on the northeast corner of a 5000 acre tract granted to Mathew Locke. Guy soon became a large landowner, and with the building of the turnpike in 1832, he built a fine brick home called "Roseland," after his death his son-in-law Dr. Preston Frazier lived there. McFerrin Chapel was built north of the house in later years be a descendant. A fine Race Tract was constructed here also. A Regiment of Braggs Army camped here on the Frazier land during the winter of 1863. Dr. John McFerrin of early Methodism fame was a Chaplain with the regiment that winter. William Guy died in 1847, was buried across the pike from Roseland. Location: 2 ½ miles north of Deason, on U.S. Highway 231.

Old Mills West Of Shelbyville on Duck River

Early mills located down Duck River from Shelbyville: 1st Doak's, 2nd Wilhoite's, 3rd Sims', Temple's and Fisher's.

Martin House

The oldest standing brick house in Bedford County, is the Matthew Martin house built in 1809 by Martin, a Revolutionary Soldier. Brother Barkley Martin was also a Soldier of the Revolution. The Martin brothers married the Clay sisters. They are buried on the knoll to the rear of the house. Located: Between Fairfield and Beech Grove on State Road 64.

Dr. Armstrong's Stone House

Dr. James Armstrong, a physician and surgeon with Jackson in the Creek Wars, removed from Shelbyville and settled here in the 1820's. His old stone house stood on the bank of the Garrison in the south east corner of the cross roads of Fairfield, then called Davis Store. He held strong anti-Jackson feelings. Location: Fairfield.

Rural Retreat

Home of Colonel Andrew Erwin, who at one time was the largest landowner in Bedford County. In about 1817, he made his final move from Augusta, Georgia, built a large brick house named "Rural Retreat." He endeavored to establish a profitable hemp business here, but was not successful. His early partner was his brother-in-law, James Patton of Ashville, North Carolina. Erwin was an out-spoken foe of Andrew Jackson. He and his wife Jane are buried on the old plantation. Location: 2 miles south east of Wartrace.

Oldest Standing Brick In Shelbyville

The Church of the Redeemer, Episcopal, was built ca 1825 by the Presbyterians, on Town Lot No. 24, not No. 44 as is stated on the Historical Marker. The Presbyterians sold the structure and built the present First Presbyterian Church, located nearby in 1854. Location: East Lane and North Brittain.

Old Town Spring

The Old Town Spring that quenched the thirst of the fledgling town, but later spread deadly disease, is now covered by the parking lot of the Big Spring Shopping Center. Samuel Musgrove was living here before the town was laid off. Location: Big Spring Shopping Center, Shelbyville.

Old Stage Road

Known as the Old Washington City Stage Road. It ran from Huntsville through Fayetteville, over Chestnut Ridge, stopping on the ridge at Glidewell's, on by Hawthorn and McKissick's on Highway 231 to Shelbyville, on to Davis Store, now Fairfield, thence on to McMinnville, Crab Orchard and eastwardly. A early mail and stage route.

Oldest Burying Ground In The County

The oldest marked grave in the county is that of a child of Thomas Greer, brother of Alexander. The marker shows a death date of 1805, which means, if this is a good date, that this burial took place while this area was still Rutherford County. This Greer graveyard stands on Thomas Greer's land beside the site of the Old Sugar

Creek Baptist Meeting House. Location: At the Sugar Creek Bridge and State Highway 130.

Old City Cemetery

Lots 1 and 2 were reserved in the original town plan for a community burial ground. Dr. James Armstrong owned property on the east boundary of the cemetery lots. His own family graveyard was started in 1815 with the death of his wife. She and other members of the family are buried in an area that is now included in the present Old City Cemetery. These Armstrong graves are the first marked burials in the cemetery. Located: In Shelbyville, to the rear of the First Baptist Church on Depot Street.

A Lost Corner

On Monday June 30, 1806, Thomas Lenoir with Samuel Gentry, pitched camp at the mouth of Fall Creek, up river from Hall's Mill, to locate a beginning corner of 1500 acre grant of William Lenoir, after searching up and down the river, they were unsuccessful in locating the corner. Lenoir concluded he would leave this dismal and deserted place and return to Nashboro, which he did. This area at this time was still uninhabited.

Horse Mountain

The highest point near Shelbyville has an elevation of 1197 feet, served as a Signal Station for the Confederate Forces during the Civil War. Now supports a maze of broadcast and communication systems. Located: 3 miles north east of Shelbyville.

Old County Jail

Built in 1867. Unique in its rock construction, now used for storage. Located: Behind the New Brick Jail, Shelbyville.

Unknown Soldiers

In Willow Mount Cemetery, in the shadow of a large marble inscribed shaft, erected by the Daughters of the Confederacy, are located numbered graves that mark the final resting place of about 600 unknown Soldiers of the Confederacy whose bodies were moved and placed here in 1867. Located: Willow Mount Cemetery, north - west Shelbyville.

ORGIN OF THE NAME BELL BUCKLE

The Creek and The Town
By
Timothy R. Marsh

Having researched, authored and published numerous books and papers on middle Tennessee historical records and being county historians of Bedford County, Tennessee, it is the inborn tendency of the writers to be cautious and slow to accept fiction and myth as fact, myth often makes good reading and may titillate ones literary fancy and will if repeated long and often enough be accepted as fact.

The historiån must be judicious and ever on guard resisting the temptation to accept or hearsay as fact without first having explored all possibilities to document the subject under study regardless of how logical it may sound. Having said this, let us now examine a fascinating subject that has long been a confusing mixture of fact and fiction, being the origin of the name Bell Buckle.

An attempt to find the true origin of this unusual name Bell Buckle, the only one of its kind in the country, as far as we have been able to determine, prompted a detailed search of early Middle Tennessee histories, court records, land records, and grant books in Davidson County, North Carolina, now Tennessee, Rutherford, Williamson and later the earliest Bedford County, Tennessee records.

Perhaps this is much ado about nothing but as this has been a subject of some interest since the beginning of the county, I feel it worthy and presentation.

By 1784, all major creeks of the Three Forks of Duck River had been named by the early land explorers who by that date had traversed this area. The names of the Wartrace Fork, Garrison or Middle Fork and South or Barren Fork of Duck River appear in old land or historical writing by this time. The names of the creek by the name of Bell Buckle had not yet surfaced.

Any documented origin of the name Bell Buckle is lost in antiquity. We will state up front that we have concluded after intensive research on the subject that as of the origin cannon be absolutely documented nor can it be disproved, we have no choice but to accept the long circulated story of the carving of a bell and buckle on a beech tree found on the headwaters of the creek, now known as Bell Buckle by a person or persons unknown as an early date.

From our research, it appears that in the year 1806, the Bell Buckle was first mentioned in Old Rutherford County records simply as a fork of the Wartrace Fork of Duck River. By the spring of 1808, it appears in Old Bedford County records as the Bell Buckle Fork of the Wartrace.

The account of the Bell Buckle carved on a beech tree has been repeated by word of mouth for over a hundred years and appeared in historical writings shortly after the Civil War. Since that time the story has been refined, polished, misquoted and given that extra literary touch over the years by moving the beech tree with its reported carving around from tree to tree, up and down the Bell Buckle, even down the wrong creek, the Wartrace Fork, as far down as the town of Wartrace. Some early supporters of General Jackson bestowed upon the General the honor of carving the symbols on the beech while he was visiting his close friend General John Coffee, which was quite a fete as Coffee never lived in Bedford County, but rather in Rutherford County above where Murfreesboro now stands. Other versions of the origin, a roguish cow with a bell and its buckle was found wondering in the wilderness along the creek, and another, the supposition that the first explorers or pioneers may have found an abundance of some exotic wild flowers, now extinct, growing along the creek. These versions are pure speculation.

While in a speculative mood, what was a bell and buckle carved on a tree? Certainly not a marked corner for land tracts or grants, as they were marked by blazing or tomahawking the corners with initials of locators and the date the location was made. Perhaps it may have been placed there by some early traveler, as a marker, as he traversed the ancient War-Trace that paralleled the creek for some distance. It was not named for other creeks in other parts of the state or country, as was often the custom in that day, when as unexplored area was opened up, no other creeks by this name exists, then or now. Why would a creek be given this unusual name? It may have been prompted by some visual sighting not the figment of some early settlers imagination.

To summarize after weighing all the facts, which are few, we will go with the over one hundred year old written account, be it fact or fiction, until proven otherwise, that the name of the creek was indeed prompted by the sighting of a carved bell and buckle or facsimile thereof, before 1807-08. Absence of documented evidence leaves us little choice.

While researching the origin of the name of the creek we recovered other facts about the little creek with the famous and unusual name that we will put down here. The names of the various waters of the Bell Buckle of the old Bell Buckle differ from those of today. Research done by the writers with input by the late Mr. W.H. Bomar, uncovered a little known fact, the creek called Bell Buckle in the early eighteen hundreds ran north west from where the two bridges now stand on Highway 82, just west of the Railroad for a short distance where it makes a wide lazy loop to the south west continuing on in that direction until it crosses Highway 82, then turns west and parallels the highway for about two miles where it rises near

MENTION OF BELL BUCKLE & THE OTTER FORK
Bedford County, Tennessee Deed Book "AA", page 421
1829

W.P. Sample to Richard Cardwell - 75 acres.
Beginning at the center of the Otter Fork of Bell Buckle, east with Featherston 128 poles to John Norvell's north west corner, south with same 164 poles to center of Bell Buckle, up middle to mouth of the Otter Fork, up said fork 207 poles to beginning.
Reduced to straight line.

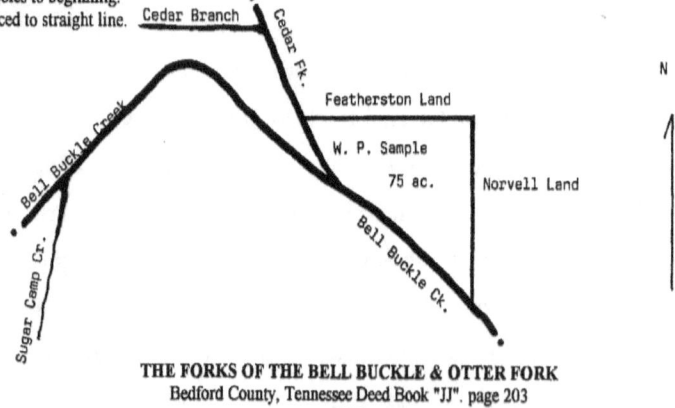

THE FORKS OF THE BELL BUCKLE & OTTER FORK
Bedford County, Tennessee Deed Book "JJ", page 203
1837

This fork is located in the Town of Bell Buckle at the two bridges on Highway 82.
In 1806, The Otter Fork, now called Bell Buckle, was called a Fork of the Wartrace.

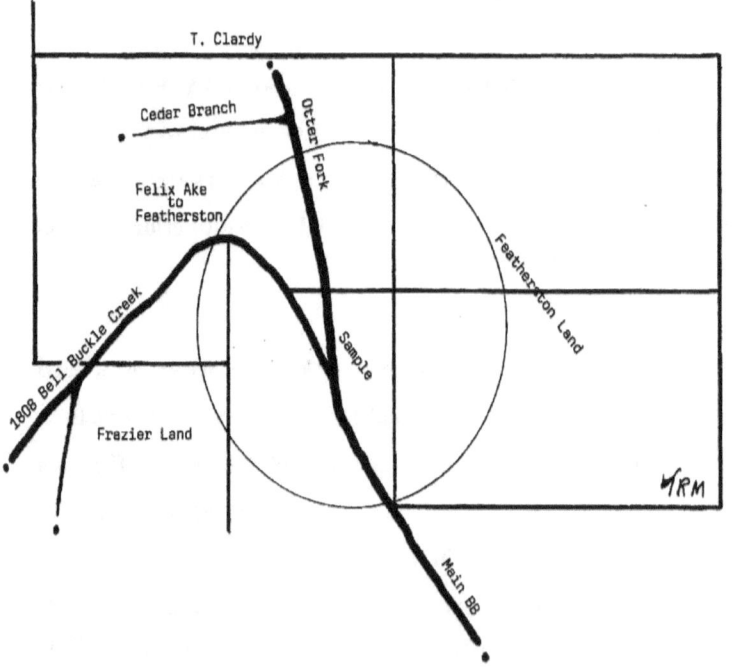

the highway. The early records always referred to this creek as The Bell Buckle. The channels are substantially the same but the names differ.

The other creek that runs up the railroad from the fork near the two bridges is now called Bell Buckle but was first always referred to in early records as the Otter Fork of the Bell Buckle. A small branch entering the Otter Fork on the west side about a mile up the railroad from the forks was called the Cedar Branch. The earliest Bell Buckle of record was the westward fork of the creek.

The Town of Bell Buckle adopted the name of the creek in 1852 with the coming of the railroad.

EARLY LAND ALONG THE BELL BUCKLE

By the spring of 1808, the name Bell Buckle was known and recorded in several documents by that name. One of the first records that deals with the Bell Buckle in the years 106-1808 when Alexander Outlaw of Jefferson County, Tennessee sold several large tracts of land he had acquired out of the old Blount brother's North Carolina Grants No. 219 and No. 222, to John Whitehead, William Norvell, William Knott, Joseph Ake and Jesse Davis.

The two aforesaid grants were two of seventeen, five thousand acre North Carolina Grants that Andrew Jackson, acting as agent for Senator Joseph Anderson of East Tennessee purchased at the U.S. Marshall's foreclosure sale at the courthouse in Nashville in April 1802. Anderson then conveyed said to his son-in-law Outlaw. These grants were located and entered in the mid 1780's, and granted to John G. and Thomas Blount, half brothers of Gov. Willie Blount and surveyed by John Donelson, Jr. in August of 1792. No mention was made of the Bell Buckle in these detailed surveys but the Wartrace Fork was referred to often and was known as early as 1784,when in the Spring of that year, a party of about twenty land locators, outfitted by Col. William Edmiston of Abbington, Virginia came down from Nashboro by way of old Jefferson, on Stones River, followed it to the head of one of its most southern branches at Duck River ridge, the ridge separates the waters of the Cumberland and Duck River. It appears that they passed near old Fosterville, on southward striking the Otter Fork of Bell Buckle, on down the creek likely passing near where the Town of Bell Buckle now stands, on to the Three Forks, where they crossed Duck River and continued on up Thompson Creek to Elk Ridge, on down Mulberry Creek to near where Fayetteville is now located, where they ranged up and down the river making locations for eastern clients some who later became large land barons, owning large North Carolina Grants in what is now Middle Tennessee. This probably dates the approximate time that the dawn of civilization penetrated the thick canebrakes of the Bell Buckle area.

The early settlement of this area was influenced by two Indian Treaties signed in 1805-1806, the first the Tellico Treaty signed October 25, 1805 ceded all Indian Lands and extended north of Duck River to the Duck River ridge. About three months later, in January 1806, all lands south of Duck River were ceded by treaty. Bu the signing of these two treaties all the land in what is now Bedford County, Tennessee now had clear title and could be sold without fear of conflict. This was the incentive needed to open up the area for rapid settlement. Bu the Fall of 1806, the area along Bell Buckle and the Wartrace Fork had numerous settlers, clearing, building cabins and starting a new life on the waters of Duck River.

As previously stated, the first land owners who purchased land where the Town of Bell Buckle now stands were John Whitehead, Joseph Ake, James and William Norvell, Jesse Davis, Tillman Dixon, William Knott and George Strong. It appears that Whitehead settled on his 400 acres that he purchased in 1806 from Alexander Outlaw but soon sold off much of his land to Jesse Featherston, James Norvell and George Norvell. The main business section of Bell Buckle is located on the tract he sold to Featherston and Norvell.

In a pasture south of Webb School and Webb Road in the fork between the road and railroad, on the old James Norvell, Sr.', 262 acre tract that he purchased of Outlaw in March 1808. The writers copied in 1975 from an old hand hewn stone the inscription: "Here lies Mary Norvell, died the 14th day of Feb 1813, in the 78 or 79 year of her age." Old family records show Mary Knott Norvell as wife of James Norvell. This must have been the matriarch of this pioneer Bell Buckle family as the dates on the stone would place, her birth in 1734 or 1735 and she was probably in her seventies when she first saw the waters of the Bell Buckle in about 1806 as records list the Norvells as being here at that date. This area was first Norvell's Settlement, later Old Salem Camp Ground, and Bell Buckle.

The Joseph Ake tract was located north of Highway 82 up the Otter Fork of the creek. It joined the Tillman Dixon 3000 acre North Carolina Grant No. 381 that was entered January 1786, as stated in the grants on the waters of the Wartrace Fork, no mention of the Bell Buckle Creek found in the grant but it is known that the creek ran through part of the grant. This grant was issued 1801 in this area that was then called part of Green County, Tennessee. For a few months the middle Tennessee area of Duck and Elk Rivers was listed as part of Green County. This Dixon grant was called a "Guardright Grant," the only one of its kind in Bedford County. It was granted to Commissioners and Soldiers of the Commission Guard, a contingent of guards, surveyors, hunters and woodsman who were commissioned by the State of North Carolina in 1783 to ascertain the true 35th parallel or the south boundary of the then western lands of North Carolina and to lay off a vast area of land in Middle Tennessee called the Military Reservation, that included all land that lay within the boundary lines that ran from Duck River, near Columbia in a easterly direction passing immediately south of where Murfreesboro now stands, on to near Rock Island, then north to where Cumberland River crosses the Kentucky State Line, then westward with the state line to Duck River, thence south to the beginning. All this land was set aside by the State of North Carolina to locate and grant the land set aside for the Soldiers of the Revolution that had served the State of North Caroline in the Continental Line. Dixon was one of the commissioners of the party but never lived in Bedford County, Tennessee, having settled in Smith County, Tennessee, he sold off his tract to numerous early pioneers who settled on his grant up and down the Otter Fork of Bell Buckle and up the head of the Wartrace Fork. Some of the first settlers on this land were Ake, Suggs, Brooks, Coops and others.

The Norvells, Knott and Davis families settled on part of Grant No. 222, on the south side of Bell Buckle extending down as far as Cascade School. The Old Salem Camp Ground was located on this grant. This grant included land on both sides of the ancient Indian Wartrace sometimes written the Indian War Road in earliest records but never War Trail. This trace was one of several that ran through Bedford County as well as other parts of Middle Tennessee. Other counties also have war traces and creeks by that name.

It is obvious that the long lived myth that the Wartrace Creek was named by General Andrew Jackson by his carving on a tree, this is not acceptable as the creek and trail were named long before Jackson arrived on the scene in Middle Tennessee.

A documented record naming many of the first settlers living between the head waters of the Otter Fork of Bell Buckle and the Wartrace, north of Bell Buckle in 1806 was uncovered by the writers in an old petition found lying forgotten in the Tennessee State Archives some years ago. A copy of the petition is reprinted here to speed the names of these pioneers upon the pages of this brief history.

FIRST SETTLERS
Petition To The Legislature
Wartrace School land Petition

State of Tennessee
Bedford County

To the Honorable General Assembly of the State aforesaid now sitting

The petition of the inhabitants of one of the School Tracts of Land (Wartrace Tract) in said county, lying on the head waters of the War-trace fork of Duck River, with a number of other citizens of this county, humbly sheweth to your Honorable Body, that your petitioners, or part thereof, settled on said tract prior to the Legislature passing an act relative to School Tracts in 1806.

When settling on the land we believe it to be vacant and un-appropriated land, (which it was in reality), at the time of it being settled, and we fully intended complying with the requisitions of the law in respect to securing the land, but was prevented, by reason of it being appropriated to the use of schools before we had an opportunity of securing the land, for which the surveyors refused to survey for us. We further state to your Honorable Body that the land when laid off was not done according to law, for it was not laid off near the center of the section, where it is demonstrated the land was vacant, but it was laid off over our heads and one side of the section, wherein less than three quarters of a mile of the Sectional Line. On this ground, we humbly hope and trust that your Honorable Body will take our situation under your paternal consideration, and grant us yet an opportunity of securing our land by warrants, as we settled with no other intention but to procure the land, for the maintenance of our family's and at the time laboring under very difficulty and disadvantage that a people could so settling in new country, where the sword was not against them. Therefore we put confidence enough in your beneficence to rely wholly upon your wisdom, justice, patriotism and benevolence, that you will address our grievance and grant our petition, for which we, as in duty bound will ever pray &c.

Persons living on land in 1806

William Fowler	Reuben Manly	Noble Magers
William Matlock	Richard Coop	John Magers
James Wood	C. Jacob Rigs	Thomas Rushing
Doak Nicks	William Brooks	Thomas Smith
George Nicks	William Weaver	(Lizney) Booth

William Wood	We-tman Gullett	Stephen Booth
Robert Chapman	Harbert Sugg	Benjerman Booth
Ballard Colewell	George Roberts	Abraham Cooper
(William) Cooper	Jno. Knott	John H. Sugg
James Norvell, Esq.	George Beard	Thomas Sugg
Edward Cage	Tazey Prince	Laban G. McClendon
Timothy Sugg	John Williams	James Coop
Edmund Sugg	Thomas Kelley	James Frizel
Wm. Sugg	Joel M. Goode	Abraham Frizel
John Williams	William Hill	Wm. Frizel
Abraham Frizel	Nathan Frizel	John C. Coldwell
	Peter Rushing	Martin Hoover
		William McMahan
		David Fain

(Names spelled as written)
Sworn September 18, 1812

SCHOOL LAND TRACTS

The school land tract referred to in the above petition was only one of thirteen school land tracts in Bedford County that had located and surveyed in 1806 when the State Legislature directed that the area from the south boundary of the Military Reservation to the southern boundary of the State be sectioned off into six mile Sections or Townships and that they be located as near the center of each section as possible, depending upon existing grants. The surveyor should survey and set aside an area of six hundred and forty acres more or less, to be used by the Public Schools. The location of the aforementioned tracts were as follows, one near Richmond, Wheel, Comstock Road, Flat Creek Village, south of Center Church Road, Raus, Lower Thompson Creek east of Shofner Lutheran Church, south of Duck River near the Narrows, two tracts between El Bethel and Highway No. 231, one east of Poplin Cross Roads, Clem Creek tract and finally the above Wartrace tract that is referred to in this petition. This tract is located at the county line between Liberty Pike and the Otter Fork of the Bell Buckle. It lay north of the Tillman Dixon 300 acre Guard Right Grant. In the late 1840's, by vote of the populace, these grants were divided into sellable lots, auctioned off to the highest bidder and Tennessee Grants issued to the buyer. It may be of interest to note that

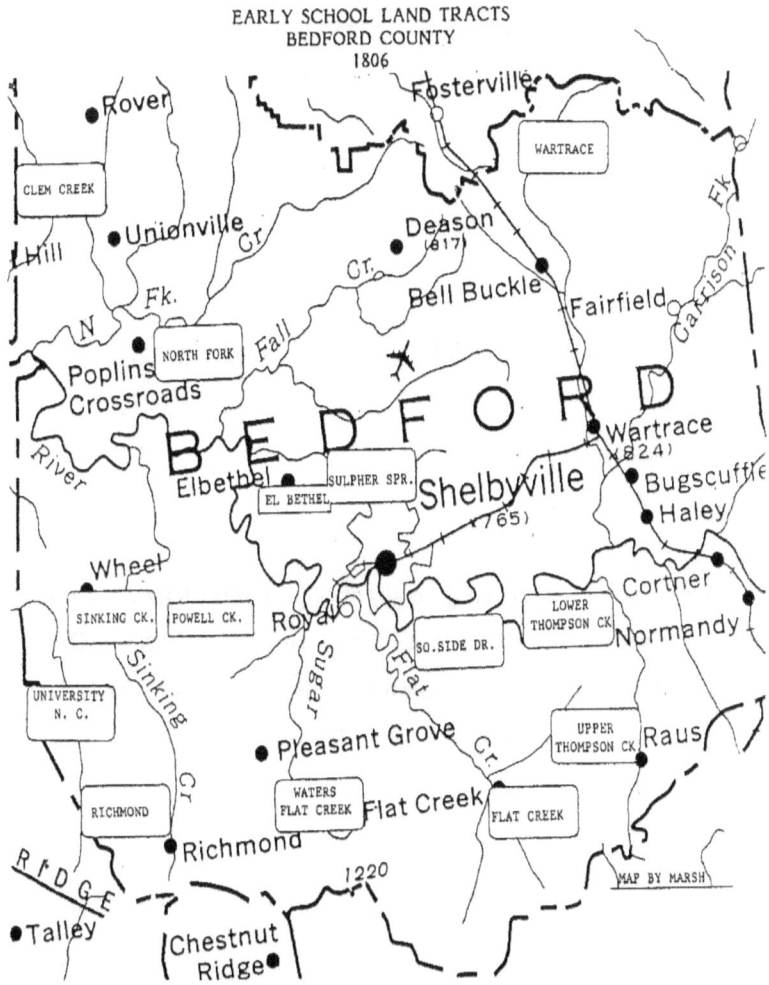

In 1806, the legislature directed the Surveyor General of the Second Surveyors District, including South Central Tennessee, south of the old Military Reservation, to section off that area into sections and townships of six miles square each and in each section to lay off as near the center of each section as pre-existing entries would permit, a tract of six hundred and fifty acres to be set aside for the purpose of the common schools. This land was known as school land and was mentioned in the calls of early land surveys. By about 1850, all these tracts were auctioned off to the highest bidder and Tennessee grants were issued.   Marsh

the first Wartrace Post Office was located near the Wartrace School Land Grant, on the Liberty Pike at the home of William Sugg.

By Helen C. Marsh
Contributing Editor
1994

TWO KINDS OF EARLY TENNESSEE GRANTS

1) Regular purchased grants
2) Military Bounty Grants

Purchased Grants were paid for generally at 10 pounds per hundred acres. Military Bounty Grants were awarded for military service in North Carolina Line of the Continental Army and were given according to the following schedule:
All ranks suppose 48 months service from 1776 to 1783.
Private 640 acres.
Non-Com. 1000 acres
Below Captain 2560 acres.
Captain 3840 acres.
Major 4800 acres.
Lt. Colonel 5760 acres.
Colonel 7200 acres.

BOUNTY LAND WARRANTS

North Caroline used Bounties to entice volunteers in the Revolution. She offered Privates approximately 7.6 acres for each month spent in the Continental Line provided they served at least a total of 2 years. Militiamen even if they were detached to service with the Continental Line were not entitled.

Military Warrants were issued to entitled soldiers for the amount of land they were entitled to.

In 1783, a great tract near Nashville was reserved and laid off for fulfilling the Bounty Land promise, eventually all this land was exhausted and Bounty Land Warrants were issued for land elsewhere. All this Bounty Land was in Tennessee.

If a Deed or Warrant does not specify <u>Continental Line Service to the State of North Carolina, it is not a Revolutionary War Land Grant.</u> <u>This you can trust and believe.</u>

The only exception is Guard Right Grants.

POTPOURRI OF GENERAL TERMS

e.g. – for example (this is or in other words)

NE or N.E. etc

abstracted – removed or separate from accessible ready available

Legatees – one to whom a legacy is bequeathed

Genealogy

Alphabetical order

Executor – Executrix

Pole – P or p

Acre – A or a

illegible

circa – ca

Addendum or appendix or appendices – to be added

Devices – to whom something has been bequeathed

collection

Jurat – a person legally sworn – certification by proper person

Reference

Ibid – "There the same"

──── FIRST COURT ────

X marks the spot where the first Court of Bedford County, Tennessee was held in December 1807. It convened at the log house of widow Ann Payne. The house stood a short distance north east of the Village of County Line, now in Moore County. It was located on what was later known as the Billy Stone farm.

After 1809, when Lincoln County was formed out of Bedford, the court met at the house of Amos Balch located on the west side of Naron Road and the Lewisburg Highway. It met there until late 1810 when town lots were sold and a temporary log courthouse was erected.

──── SECOND COURT ────
1809

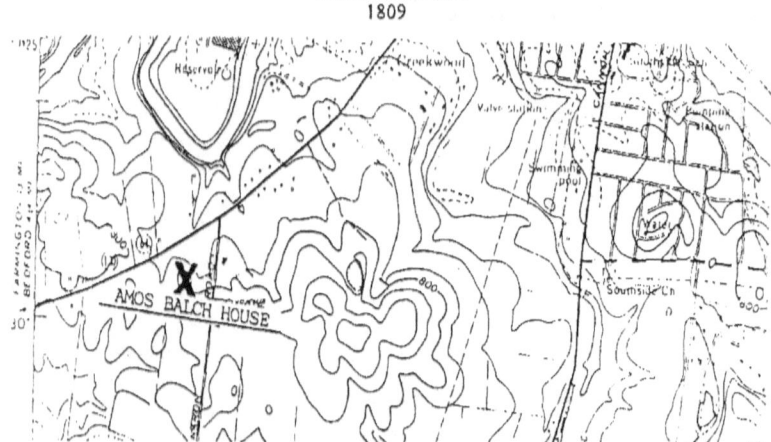

CREATION OF BEDFORD COUNTY TENNESSEE
ACTS OF 1807 CHAPTER NO. 37

Section 1. That a new county be, and the same is hereby established south and south-west of, and adjoining the said County of Rutherford, by the name of BEDFORD, in memory of Thomas Bedford, deceased; which said county shall begin at the south west corner of Rutherford, and south east corner of Williamson County on the Duck River ridge, and run thence with said Williamson County line, to the line of the County of Maury, thence along the same southwardly to the south boundary of the state; thence eastwardly to the east boundary of Rutherford County, thence along the same to the ridge that divides the waters of Duck River from those of Cumberland; thence along the same westerly, to the south east corner of Williamson County, leaving Rutherford County its constitutional limits; and all that tract included in the above described lines, shall be included within the said County of Bedford, and all the lands north of the first described line on Duck River ridge where the said line intersects White County line, thence north with said line until it strikes the corner of Rutherford and Wilson County line at a place known by the name of Rush Spring, then to follow the old line of Rutherford County, as by law established, shall be and remain the County of Rutherford.

Section 2. That for the due administration of justice, the first court, and all subsequent courts shall be held in said County of Bedford, until the end of the next General Assembly, at the improvement lately made and occupied by Mrs. Payne, near the head of Mulberry Creek, and all courts held in and for said County of Bedford shall be held by commission of the said justices, in the same manner, and under the same rules and restrictions, and shall have and exercise the same powers and jurisdiction as are or shall be prescribed for the courts of the several counties in this state.

Section 3. That the courts of Bedford shall be held regularly by the justices of said county, on the fourth Monday of December, March, June and September, annually.

Section 4. That it shall be the duty of the sheriff of said county of Bedford, to hold an election at the place of holding courts in said county of Bedford, on the first Thursday and succeeding day in March next, for the purpose of electing one colonel and two majors for the said county of Bedford, under the same rules and regulations as are prescribed by law in similar cases; and the militia of said county of Bedford shall constitute the twenty-eight regiment, and be attached to the fifth brigade.

Section 5. That the elections for company officers for the county of Bedford, shall be held as such places as the commandant of said county may think proper to appoint; which said elections shall be held on the fourth Monday in June next, under the rules, regulations, and restrictions as are prescribed in like cases.

Section 6. That said county of Bedford, be a part of the district for electing a governor, representative or representatives to congress, electors to elect a president and vice-president of the United States, and members of the general assembly, to which it hath here-to-ford belonged, and that the elections be held at the place of holding courts in said county; at the time and in the manner by law directed, and that the sheriff or returning officer, made a return of polls at the court-house in the town of Jefferson, on the day next succeeding each election of the sheriff or returning officer for the county of Rutherford, and upon comparing the votes, they shall declare the candidate for the representation of said Counties of Rutherford and Bedford, who may have the highest number of votes duly elected, and give a certificate accordingly; and it shall be the duty of the sheriff of Rutherford County, to make the return for senator of said district, as here-to-fore directed by law.

Section 7. That the sheriff or collector of public taxes for the county of Rutherford, shall have full power, and authority to collect any taxes that are yet unpaid, from any person or persons in said county of Bedford, and to collect any money that may be due on writ of Fieri Facias, that is at this time in the hands of said sheriff or Rutherford County, in as full and ample a manner as it the said county had remained a part of Rutherford County.

Section 8. That said county of Bedford shall in all cases, be considered and remain part of Mero District and send two jurors to Mero Superior Court; and Rutherford County shall send two jurors less than formerly compelled by law to do.

Passed: December 3, 1807

Thirteen justices were named in the first court. They were John Atkinson, chairman, Abraham Byler, James Patton, Alexander Greer, William M. Quisenberry, Alexander Moody, William Norvell, David Robertson, Howel Dawdy, William Wilbourn, Joseph Walker, Joseph Ake, and John Carter.

Benjamin Bradford was elected sheriff, Thomas Moore County Court Clerk, Daniel McKisick Circuit Court Clerk, Joseph Ake, Register, Howel Dawdy County Ranger.

ACTS OF 1809
November 14, 1809

An act to reduce the limits of Bedford County to establish its permanent boundaries.

Section 1. Be it enacted by the General Assembly of the State of Tennessee that the lines and boundaries of Bedford County shall be as follows, to wit, Beginning on the north east corner of Maury County and running south with the eastern boundary thereof to the extreme height of the ridge dividing the waters of Duck River from the waters of Elk River, thence eastwardly on the extreme height of said ridge to the present eastern boundary line of the said county of Bedford, thence north to the southern boundary line of Rutherford County, thence westerly with the said line to the southern boundary line of Williamson County and thence with the said line of Williamson to the beginning.

Section 2. Be it enacted that John Atkinson, William Wood, Bartlett (Barkely) Martin, Howel Dawdy, Daniel McKisick be and they are hereby appointed Commissioners to fix on a place on Duck River within two miles of the center of said County on a line east and west at the father-most, and the said Commissioners shall purchase one hundred acres of land at the place which they may fix upon as aforesaid and shall receive a title to the same in fee simple to themselves and their successors in office and shall lay off the said hundred acres of land into a Town to be known by the name of Shelbyville reserving near the center thereof a Public Square of two acres on which a Courthouse and stocks shall be built likewise reserving any other lot they may think proper for the purpose of having a Jail built thereon for the use of the said County of Bedford.

Section 3. Be it enacted that the said Commissioners shall sell the lots of said town at public sale, on a credit of twelve months serving due notice thereof in one of the public newspapers printed in Nashville and shall take bond with sufficient securities from the purchasers of said lots payable to themselves and successors in office and shall make title in fee simple to the respective purchasers of said lots.

Section 4. Be it enacted that the proceeds of the sale of the lots aforesaid shall be a fund in the hands of the said Commissioners for defraying the expenses incurred in the purchase of the tract of land on which the Town abode mentioned is directed to be laid off for defraying the expense of building a Courthouse, prison and stocks.

Section 5. Be it enacted that the said Commissioners shall superintended the building of the said Courthouse, prison and stocks, and shall let the Courthouse to the lowest bidder advertising the same sixty days in one of the newspapers printed in Nashville, setting forth the dimensions of which it is to consist and the materials of which it is to be built and shall take a bond with sufficient securities from the person to whom the said Courthouse is let payable to themselves and successors in office in the sum of ten thousand dollars conditioned for the faithful performance of his contract and it the proceeds of the sale of said lots is not sufficient for the purpose above mentioned it shall be the duty of the County Court of Bedford to lay a tax not exceeding the amount of State Tax levied in said County be applied to the subjects aforesaid and be continued until all arrearages are paid off.

Section 6. Be it enacted that the said Commissioners before they enter on the duties of their appointment shall give a bond in the sum of five thousand dollars each payable to the chairman of the County Court of Bedford and his successors in office for the use of said County conditioned for the faithful performance of the trust reposed in them and shall likewise take the following oath. I, A.B., do solemnly swear or affirm that as a Commissioner to act for the County of Bedford, I will do equal and impartial justice to the citizens of said County to the best of my skill and ability, so help me God, and the said bond shall be filed in the Clerk's Office for the County of Bedford and shall not be so construed as to make any one of the Commissioners security for another.

Section 7. Be it enacted that until the Town above mentioned is laid off the Court of Bedford County shall be held at the dwelling house of Amos Balch and all matters, causes and things now depending in the County Court of Bedford shall be tried and determined at the house of Amos Balch in the manner as they had been originally, returnable to said place.

Section 8. Be it enacted that a majority of the successors by this Act appointed shall in all cases be competent to perform the duties assigned them and if any one neglects or refuses to act, a majority of the Justices of said County of Bedford may appoint another in his place and when the said Commissioners shall have performed the duties above enjoined upon them, they shall lay the County Court of Bedford County a full statement of all their proceedings and the said County Court shall make them a reasonable compensation for their services.

Section 9. Be it enacted that this Act shall be in force from and after the first day in January in the year one thousand eight hundred and ten.

14 Nov. 1809   Joseph Ake, Speaker of the
                                        House of Representatives

EDITORIAL REVIEW AND COMMENTARY
ON
CREATION OF BEDFORD COUNTY, TENNESSEE

COMMISSIONERS

John Atkinson lived about one mile south of Holtland, now Marshall County, near the Williamson County line. The Old Fishingford Road ran by his house. He died in 1829 and is buried beside the road in a well-marked grave. He was the first Chairman of the County Court of Bedford County. He owned one lot in Shelbyville, Lot No. 44, which he purchased in 1815 and sold to Gideon Rigg in 1828, the year before his death. This Lot No. 44 was located at the northeast corner of North Main Street and East Lane Street. A car lot is now erected on the southern fraction of this lot. NOT the Episcopal Church, as is commonly believed and so marked.

Abraham Byler settled on Clem Creek in the northwest corner of the county, where the community of Rover now stands. Up until about 1840, the community was called Bylers. Abraham's son John was a Captain in the Militia in 1812.

James Patton, several James Pattons in the county. Two where around the Town of Shelbyville was to be laid off, one near the north east corner of the Town of Shelbyville near McKissicks, and one near Caney Springs in Marshall County, Take your pick.

Alexander Greer, a first settler, settled at Greers Lick, now Pleasant Grove on Sugar Creek.

William A. Quisenberry, settled below Lynchburg.

Alexander Moody, nothing known.

William Norvell, first settler at Bell Buckle.

David Robertson, settled west of Shelbyville on Duck River.

Howel Dawdy, (Dowdy, Doddy) was born about 1746 and according to a folio of North Carolina Revolutionary Army Accounts in the North Carolina State

Archives, he submitted several claims for services performed. He first purchased Lot No. 86 and lived on this lot for many years. This lot located immediately west of the Big Spring now Big Spring Shopping Center, and adjoining the improvements of Samuel Musgrove, Shelbyville's first resident. Dawdy owned several lots in this area, also Lot No. 133, the most northwest lot in the Town in 1810. He was the first County Ranger and in the early 1820s, he and his wife Pheobe moved to Lincoln County, now Moore County, to live with their son-in-law Thomas Blythe. Howel Dawdy died in December 1830, aged 84 years. Phoebe Dawdy died December 1831, both have native limestone hewn marker in the Blythe graveyard on Dogtail Branch near the community of County Line.

William Wilbourn, lived near the mouth of Thompson Creek.

Joseph Walker, first settler east of Fairfield, erected first mill on Noah Fork.

Joseph Ake, a first settler at Bell Buckle.

(Mad) John Carter, by 1807, living above Elora in Lincoln County, then a part of Bedford.

William Woods (Wood), there were at least three William Wood, sometimes spelled Woods, living in Bedford County at this time in history. One living at Flat Creek, soon moved to Arkansas. Another lived near Old Belfast, now in Marshall County, Tennessee. And the William Wood who was living above Bell Buckle as early as 1806 and a member of the Old Liberty Meeting House (Union) on Liberty Pike near the Gap, and whose ancient broken sandstone grave marker was recently uncovered in the Beachboard graveyard off Liberty Pike, by Middle Tennessee Civil War historians Leslie Marsh and Jim Knight. A skirmish between the north and south was fought in and around this family cemetery resulting in some casualties. No absolute identity of this Commissioner that helped to locate the Seat of Justice on Duck River has been found. This early William Wood is a possibility.

Barclay (Barkley) Martin, a Soldier of the Revolution, member of the 10th General Assembly of Tennessee, settles between Bell Buckle and Fairfield, died in 1815, buried in the Martin family graveyard on his brother, Mathew Martin's farm near Fairfield. Time has made his grave marker nearly illegible.

Daniel McKisick (McKissick), was born 1755 in North Carolina, died 1818 in Bedford County. He was a Soldier of the Revolution. He married Jane Wilson and lived and died on his farm located about eight miles south of Shelbyville on the Fayetteville Highway. Two of his sons, James and Daniel, held County Offices or note. His wife along with other members of the family moved to Arkansas in the 1830s. There was once a fine vault and marker covering his grave, that has long ago fallen victim to the ravages of time and man.

The Widow Ann Payne's log house, where the first Bedford County Court met, was located at the head of the east fork of Mulberry Creek about a half mile north of the community of County Line in Moore County, in the forks of Highway 82 and 55. The first minutes if Lincoln County, Tennessee, this location was referred to as "The Old Bedford Courthouse."

The Widow Payne soon had neighbors James Gowen, an early settler about two or three miles west, and the noted David Crockett about the same distance to the east.

Goodspeed, in his history, said 50 acres offered by William Galbreath and Amos Balch, however, note the excerpt from Bedford County Deed Book "B", page 211. Also, Amos Balch was loving at this time about two miles west of Shelbyville on the land inherited by his wife, Ann Patton, from her father, Samuel Patton, Sr. The 1000 acres that Balch had owned by Grant No. 23, joined Patton on the north east and included the mouth of Flat Creek. In 1787, Balch, while residing in Logan

County, Kentucky, sold the 1000 acres to Thomas Love and seven years later in January 1808, Love conveyed the same to George Gordon of Greene County, Tennessee. Gordon began to sell the tract to numerous purchasers in 1811.

There is some question with reasonable justification as for which Shelby, Isaac or Evan, the Town of Shelbyville was named. The Legislature, which named and charged the Commissioners with the responsibility of location the town, to be named Shelbyville did not specify after whom the town was to be named. Our research agrees with Dr. Robert E. Cogswell, who did extensive research on the subject about twenty years ago while a resident of Bedford County, concluded that the little river town was probably named for Evan Shelby a long time Tennessean, not Isaac Shelby, the son.

The Commissioners were expressly directed to construct the Court'House and Stocks on the two acres set aside as Public Square. If the directions of the General Assembly were followed, the first log Court House erected in the new Town of Shelbyville would have been located on said Public Square. Tradition and public opinion insists the north west corner of the square, some say the site of the Methodist Episcopal Church, some say on Lot No. 64. To this date there is no absolute proof in writing to substantiate any of the claims. The lot that the First Methodist Church is located on, Lot No. 70, was sold at the sale of the Town Lots in July 1810, to a private citizen, William C. Newman. Lot No. 80, was located immediately across Spring Street and the Methodist Church was purchased on the 3rd day of the sale of lots, July 14, 1810, by Samuel B. Phillips, his lot was later owned by Edward Wade. As directed by the by the General Assembly, a lot was set aside for the purpose of erecting a jail. This lot was No. 64, the present Rock Jail stands on part of this lot. In 1817, a log jail was on this lot. In 1837, a new brick jail was erected on Lot No. 64 and the eastern half of Lot No. 71. The eastern half of Lot No. 71 was purchased from Daniel McKissick, Jr. The brick jail was replaces by the present rock jail. So if the Court House, the jail and the stocks (erected later) were all built on this lot, with a frontage of 96 feet, our first Justices would have en-cantered rather crowded conditions but perhaps no more crowded that at Amos Balch's house or Widow Payne's cabin. However, the Commissioners and Justices could have done as their neighbors to the south in Lincoln County did, simply locate the temporary Court House in the corner of the Public Square, so as not to interfere with normal traffic of the erection of the permanent Court House. There was ample room to do this at this time in the development of the town. We may be assured the problem was solved, for on July 4, 1810, eight days before the sale of the Town Lots, the Tennessee Gazette reports the Celebration of the American Independence at the Court House, a large number of citizens assembled to listen to an oration by George B. Balch, then seventeen toasts were drank. So as to the exact location of the first Court House in Shelbyville, you may simply check A, B, C, or none of the above.

Lots for Sale, advertised in the Democratic Clarion and Tennessee Gazette, June 1, 1810. Lots were sold on July 12, 13, and 14, 1810 and on April 1, 1811.

The specifications for the first permanent Court House were advertised in the Tennessee Gazette, August 12, 1810 and stated bid to be let October 22, 1810. However, some bids were turned in without security being posted by the contractors and the specifications were changed and more detailed. The building proposed to be slighter larger and advertised in January 1811, in the Tennessee Gazette, specifically requesting that all contractors bidding name his security. The building is to be delivered by October 1, 1812. Bid to be let April 1, 1811.

> "The Building of a court House, Prison and Stocks,
> will be let to the Highest Bidder"
> Bedford County, January 25, 1811

The dimension of the Court House as follows, viz, 42 by 38 feet in the clear, the walls to be built of brick upon a foundation of stone, 2 ½ feet thick, sunk two feet under ground and raised two feet above; the brick walls to be two stories high, the first story 16 feet high in the clear, the second story to be 11 feet high in the clear, the walls to be substantial and of a thickness, to be well painted outside, the second story to be well painted inside also. The floor be laid with brick the edge up; the lower story to be wainscoted as high as the bottom of the windows and well painted a marble color, from the wainscoting to the ceiling, the walls to be plastered white, and ceiling above, the second floor to be supported by a girder 12 inches square, the girder be supported by two walnut or black locust posts, neatly turned and of equal diameter with the girder, to be set upon stone pedestals which are not to appear above the floor, the posts to be painted the same color as the wainscoting, the joist of the second floor to be 12 by 5 inches and laid two feet asunder from center to center, the joist to be of yellow popular, the floor to be laid of good yellow popular quarter plank 1 ½ inch thick, well planed on the upper side, tongued and grooved; 8 windows in the lower story of 24 lights each, the glass 10 by 12 inches, the windows shutters to be paneled and lined, and secured inside by good bolts. Three doors in the lower story, good stone steps to each. The shutters to be paneled and lines, a row of lights above each door, the front door, to be furnished with a good and sufficient double lock, one spring bolt and one bolt to turn by key. The other two doors to be secured by good and sufficient bolts. The Judges seat, the Bar, the Clerks seat and table, to be elevated a proportion-able height above the floor. The Sheriffs seat, within the Bar, the criminals box behind the Bar and immediately fronting the Judges seat. The jury boxes to be the right and left of the Clerks table, the Bench, the Bar and Jury Boxes to be of circular form. The upper tier of joists to be 8 by 4 inches, ceiling underneath the yellow popular quarter planed and beeded, an 8 feet passage from wall on the second floor, on each side of which the house to be divided by partition, the passage and partitions to be of yellow polular quarter plank 1 ½ inches thick, well planed tongued grooved and beeded. The doors of the several rooms to open into the passage, the fire place of common size in each corner of the second story; 6 windows in the second story of 24 lights each, glass 10 by 12 inches. The roof to be hipped and on the top to have a cupola and to be covered with yellow popular or chestnut joint shingles, good and sufficient well framed rafters, sheated with good yellow polular inch plank, the roof to be painted red or brown as soon as practicable after it is covered, in a flight of stairs to ascend from the jury boxes to the right and left of the Judges seat, to lead to and meet in the passage on the second floor, which are to be put up with banisters and railing, the cornices and Medallions of the roof, the facings of the doors and windows, the sash and ceiling above in under story, the front side of the window shutters, to be well painted white, the shutters of the lower doors to be painted a mahogany color, the bench, the Bar, and Banisters and railing of both stair cases to be painted green, the doors of the several rooms to open into the passage to be light panel doors and furnished with good double locks. The whole of the building to be composed of good and durable materials; the work to be well executed and finished in a workman like manner, to be completed and done ready to be delivered to the Commissioners before the first day of October, 1812. In order to prevent men who cannon give security bidding, as was the case before, no person will be permitted to bid who does not before the letting, inform the Commissioners who his security will be, that they may know whether they ought to permit him to bid.

The plan of the jail will be made known as the time of the letting, so will that of the stocks.

The Commissioners reserve to themselves the right of altering or amending of the aove plan at the time of completing the work, at the time of letting.

Commissioners: Dan. McKissick
Barclay Martin
Wm. Wood
John Atkinson
Howel Dawdy
Benj. Bradford

DEED FROM CLEMENT CANNON TO THE COMMISSIONERS
FOR 100 ACRES

C. Cannon to Commissioners

This indenture made this second day of May in the year of our Lord one thousand eight hundred and ten. Between Clement Cannon of the County of Williamson, in the State of Tennessee, of the one part and John Atkinson, William Woods, Bartley (Barkley) Martin, Howel Dawdy, Daniel McKissick, Benjamin Bradford and John Lane of the County of Bedford on the other part, Commissioners appointed by the General Assembly of the State of Tennessee aforesaid for the County of Bedford aforesaid authorized to purchase one hundred acres of land for the site of the Town of Shelbyville &c &c which indenture witnesseth that the said Clement Cannon for and in consideration of the sum of one dollar to him in hand aid before the ensealing and delivery of these presence, the receipt whereof is hereby acknowledged and himself therewith fully satisfied hath given granted, bargained and sold aliened and confirmed and by these present doth give grant bargain, sell alien convey and confirm unto the said John Atkinson, William Woods, Bartley (Barkley) Martin, Howel Dawdy, Daniel McKissick, Benjamin Bradford and John Lane, Commissioners as aforesaid and their successors in office in fee simple forever one hundred acres of land to and for the use of the County of Bedford and for the site of the "Town of Shelbyville." Situated lying and being in the said County of Bedford on the north side of Duck River. Beginning at a stake in said River, two poles south of the mouth of Samuel Musgroves' Spring Branch, running thence south fifty five degrees east 85 5/10 poles to a small ash log and two cedars, thence east forty eight poles to a white oak and dogwood, thence north one hundred and forty six poles and two tenths of a pole to a stake, thence west one hundred and twenty poles to a stake, thence south to the beginning, including Samuel Musgroves' improvement and spring and containing one hundred acres being part of a tract of land granted to Robert Smith, late of the County of Caswell in the State of North Carolina by Grant No. 15 from the State of North Carolina and by Robert Washington Smith of the County of Caswell and State of North Carolina, heir of the said Robert Smith, dec'd, conveyed to Clement Cannon reference to the several records had will more fully and at large appears, also all the woods, ways, waters and waters courses and all the appurtenances hereunto belonging or in any wise appertaining and the revisions and versions and remainders, rents issues and profits of the aforesaid land and premises and every part thereof, and all the Estate right title interest claim property and demand whatever of the said Clement Cannon of in and to the same and every part or parcel thereof to have and to hold the said hundred acres with the appurtenances unto the said John Atkinson, William Woods, Bartley (Barkley) Martin, Howel Dawdy, Daniel McKissick, Benjamin Bradford and John Lane, Commissioners as aforesaid their successors in office forever expressly for the site of the Town of Shelbyville and the said Clement Cannon for himself his heirs and assignees the lawful rights, title or claim free from any in-cumbrances whatever by these presents. In witness whereof the said Clement Cannon hath hereunto set his hand and Seal the day and year above written, signed, sealed and delivered in the presence of   Clement Cannon

Jas. McKissick, Thos. Moore
Amos Balch.

Ref: Bedford County Registers Office, Deed Book "C", page 275
Note: Beginning corner near mouth of the "flume at the river.

1832
SHELBYVILLE
X- Beginning corner of the 100 acres

CLEMENT CANNON LAND AT SHELBYVILLE

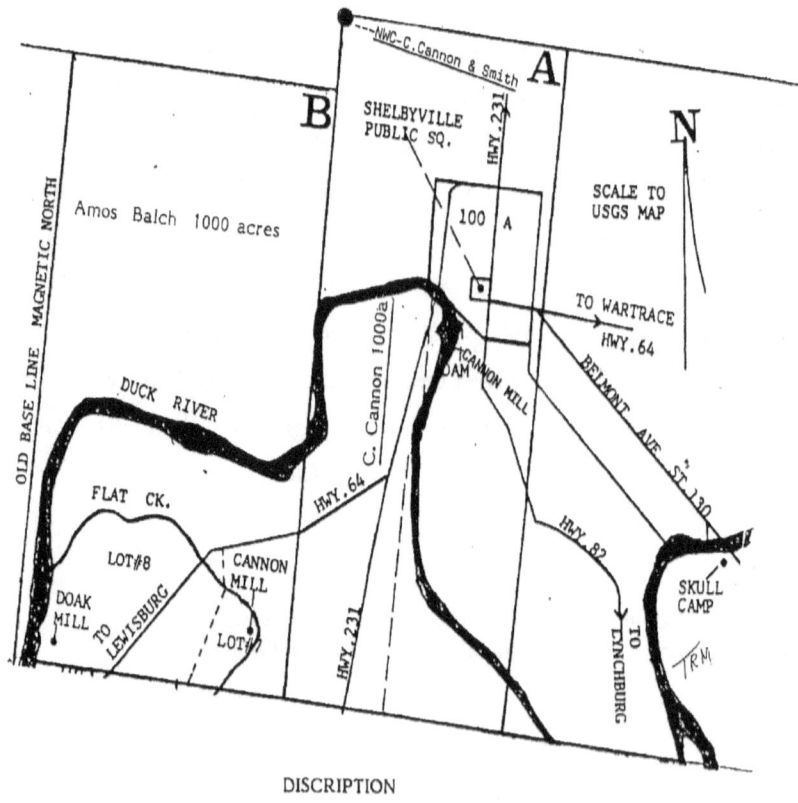

DISCRIPTION

Tract A – This 1000 acres was purchased from Robert W. Smith of Cabarrus County, North Carolina by Clement Cannon, March 23, 1810 and Cannon deeded to the Commissioners of Bedford County, Tennessee 1000 acres, to locate the Town of Shelbyville. Clement Cannon deeded 300 acres, the south western part of the 1000 acres that lay south of the river to Newton Cannon, much of the north side, Shelbyville is now located on this tract. The part of the south side, located east of South Cannon Boulevard or the Fayetteville Highway and north of Davis Street, is located on the part of the 1000 acres that Clement Cannon retained.

Tract B – This 1000 acre, Grant No. 23, was granted to Amos Balch who sold to Thomas Love. Love, in 1808, conveyed to George Gordon. In 1811, Gordon sold all this tract south of Duck River, including the mouth of Flat Creek. The north boundary is Dover Street.

Marsh

ESQR
JOHN ATKINSON
1773 - 1829
FIRET CHAIRMAN OF THE BEDFORD COUNTY COURT - 1807

Marker, One Mile South Of Holtland
On West Side Of Old Fishing Ford Road

THE SHELBYVILLE TORNADO
Of May 31, 1830

BANNER AND WHIG – EXTRA
Saturday June 5, 1830

PARTICULARS OF THE STORM

Extract from a letter to the editor, dated
SHELBYVILE, TEN., June 2, 1830

Dear Sir – Shelbyville is in ruin. On Monday night 31st May, about 12 o'clock, it pleased an all-wise Providence to visit this place with a most devastating hurricane. The Court House, Market-house, Methodist Church, the Brick Hotel, the Bank, and many other valuable buildings were prostrated in an instant. Five young men were killed and many others bruised and wounded. Mr. Newton, editor of the Shelbyville Intelligencer, was carried amidst the ruins of his house 100 yards, and instantly killed and dreadfully mangled, the other men who were killed were Mr. David Whitson, Mr. Caldwell, saddlers, Mr. Rideout, and Mr. Arnold, clerk in Mr. James Reid's store. Messers Blackman, Dodson, Solomon Dews, and many others were badly hurt. About thirty-eight stores and shops, and ten or fifteen houses were overthrown.

I shall not attempt to describe the scene. Those who have seen most of such scenes, I imagine, attempt the least to describe them. No one heard the fall of a tree, or fence, or house. It was one constant monotonous, shrill roar, the voice of the Tempest. The lightning was one constant flash, rendering every thing visible. The earth was covered with a sheet of water. From the Public Square east, all is one undistinguished mass of ruins. The very foundations on many houses were blown up, and scarcely one store left upon another. The preservation of lives amid such destruction of habitants, seem almost miraculous. Many found them-selves lying on their floors without a roof over them or walls around them, others were extricated by their own exertions, or that of their friends, from the midst of rafters, beams and rubbish. Some were carried to a distance between masses of timber and brick bats. The storm began to subside, and the cry of distress was heard. People half naked were seen running through the streets to extricate their friends, or convey them to a place of safety. Mr. Arnold's case was very pitiable. In passing from the store to the street, where he was picked up and carried into unroofed house and laid during that night and the next day in the greatest agony, which he bore with remarkable fortitude, and at length, died, giving his friends the most consolatory evidence of his unshaken and triumphant faith.

The damage is variously estimated, from fifty to a hundred thousand dollars. Some have lost their all, and are without houses, furniture, or food. Mr. Turrentine's Jewelry shop was literally torn to pieces, and his whole stock scattered in every direction. The goods in most of the stores sustained a good deal of injury.

Writer unknown

COURT IN SESSION AT CANNON'S TAVERN

This 26th day of July 1866

Minos Cannon Lease To Bedford County, House for Court House.

"Minos T. Cannon has leased to Jos. Thompson, Thomas H. Coldwell and Edmond Cooper, Commissioners, on the part of Bedford County and appointed by the County Court of said County at the January Term 1866 to lease Court House and offices for the consideration of four hundred and eighty dollars per year for and during the term of three years and five months, said lease to terminate on the first day of January 1870, the following property to wit, the house known as Cannons Old Tavern house and the grounds in the rear of said building. Said building is on the south of the Public Square (Lot 62) in the Town of Shelbyville and adjoining the frame house of Henry Yancy on the east and running back to an ally or street (now McGrew) that runs east to the Baptist Church Lot and running west to Spring Street, near the cotton house of the factory. We are to have the possession of all the building except the two rooms now occupied by John W. Ruth as a Jewelry Store and he agrees to take warrants on the County of Bedford in payment of the said rent, said rent is to be paid semi-annually at the rate of four hundred and eighty dollars per annum, that being forty dollars per month. The fixtures, platform, shelves, benches &c that are put in said house for the use of the court and offices are to be done at the expense of the county and the Commissioners are to have the right to remove at the expiration of the lease.

This the 26th day of July 1866

Minos T. Cannon (Seal)

Ack. August 3rd 1866

Joseph H. Thompson, Clerk

Noted Oct 25, 1866 at 9 o'clock A.M.

H.H. Holt, Register BC"

SECOND BEDFORD COUNTY COURTHOUSE
1833-1863

We are fortunate to have a detailed description of the first permanent brick courthouse (1812) as it was advertised for bid in a Nashville newspaper in 1810 and later re-bid. A photograph of this edifice never existed, despite an account to the contrary. It was completely destroyed by a devastating tornado that struck Shelbyville on the evening of May 31, 1830, as described separately in this publication. This pre-dated the development of the Art of Photography by Lewis Deguerra in 1839, and its marketing in the mid 1840's, however because of the detail description of the structure, as supplied by the Commission in preparing for bid, the writers with the aid of the late Dr. Herbert Cooper, an accomplished draftsman, were able to draw a reasonable accurate reproduction of the courthouse as advertised.

It is generally accepted that the Second Courthouse was completed in 1833, this was also before the birth of photography and to our knowledge no photography of this structure was ever made, though one could have been made in later years as it stood until 1863, when it was destroyed by fire.

Some time ago a photograph was circulated and reported to be of the first permanent Bedford County Courthouse, as taken in 1833, we find two problems with this. One, the first permanent courthouse was erected in 1812, not 1833 as had been stated. Two, because of the date of the development of photography could not have been taken of either courthouse in 1812 or 1833. A lengthy search has failed to turn up a detailed description of the second courthouse of 1833-63, as it was advertised for bid. We were forced to rely on newspaper accounts as the early court records were destroyed in the 1863 fire and to complicate the matter the newspapers are silent on this subject.

The appearance and description of the Second Permanent Courthouse is quite an enigma and we were fortunate to find a back door approach to this problem. A document in our possession, originating from neighboring Marshall County, sheds an interesting light upon the subject. Follows a copy of said document as it was drafted by the Commissioners of The Marshall County Court in session at Lewisburg, relating in the building of their first permanent Courthouse in 1838. Marshall County Minutes, January 2, 1837, page 61.

"To The Worshipfuls:

The County Court of Marshall County, we, a part of the committee appointed by your worshipfuls, to digest and report a plan for a Court House and Jail for Marshall County in obedience thereto report as follows, viz, after collecting all the information within our power with regard to the structure of such building, both for cheapness, neatness, convenience and durability and after given the subject its due consideration in every other respect, have come to the direct conclusion that the Court House and Jail in Bedford County are the best models we can select for said buildings in Marshall County and accordingly recommended them to your worships as such with the following alternations therein, viz, we recommend that the Court House be of the same width as the Court House in the Town of Shelbyville and two feet longer that said Court House so as to admit of a passage of ten feet between the Clerk's rooms and the Court Room. The partition between the Court Room and passage to be of plank and the partition between the Clerk's Rooms and the passage be of brick, between the Clerk's rooms there shall be a passage of ten feet leading through the aforesaid passage into the Court Room at each end of which passages there shall be an arched door with folding shutters. All the rooms below to be as near the same size of those in the Bedford County House as practicable after allowing the passage of ten feet aforesaid and all the rooms above to be of the same dimensions as those in the Shelbyville Court House as near as practicable. The Court House to be finished off in the same manner in every other respect like the Shelbyville Court House as modified according to the last or discretion of the Commissioners, the full and true dimensions of which we will be able to lay before your worships at the next term of your worshipful court, as we have the promise of a gentleman of Shelbyville who can be relied on that the same shall be forwarded as soon as General Robert Cannon shall return from Mississippi with all the costs and expenses attached therein. We further recommend that the Jail be constructed of the same materials and of the same dimensions as the jail in Shelbyville as set forth in papers marked "A" and made a part of this report in every respect the dungeon windows which may be only twelve lights each, eight by ten inch glass with four different sets of iron grates in each window, a little larger and stronger that those in the Shelbyville jail. We cannot at present suggest or recommend any other alternations or additions to either the Court House or Jail that those already offered unless it might be a picketing wall of cedar logs around the jail about fifteen feet high with one end sharpened and the other let into the ground and made fast which we leave as a matter altogether discretionary with the court and County Commissioners. All of which is respectfully submitted &c.

BY FIRE 1863
SECOND PERMANENT COURT HOUSE
———1833-1863———

2 January 1837   G.W. Haywood
                                  Joel Yowell

We, the balance of the Commissioners as a majority of them having read the above report concur therein. 2 January 1837

James C. Record, Thos. Ross and William Williams.

Editors Note: The Jail in Shelbyville mentioned in the Marshall County Minutes was a new Jail constructed of brick on Lot 64 & 71. (50 X 26 feet)

From an article appearing in an old Marshall County Historical Paper, we gleaned the following description of the First Permanent Marshall County, Tennessee Courthouse. From this description the Second Bedford County Permanent Courthouse, 1833-163, was drawn as it appears on the Picture Page of Bedford County Courthouses.

Marshall County's first courthouse stood in the center of the public square on land deeded by Abner Houston to the Commissioners on October 18, 1836. A committee was appointed on December 7, 1836, to draft plans and specifications for the building. They were William Williams, Joel Yowell, Aaron Boyd, and James C. Record. The building was modeled after the one in Shelbyville, Bedford County, Tennessee. It was built to the cost of $8,750 and was completed, received, and occupied by October 1, 1838.

The Courthouse was a two-story building about sixty feet square with cross halls; one large office located in each corner of the ground floor. The stairway went up the north side of the east and west wall. All of the north side of the second floor was in the courtroom. On each side of the upper south hall were two small offices.

The building was of Georgian design with eight windows, four downstairs and four upstairs, on each side. The top of each window was arched; each sash was made up of four glass panes. The lower sash could be raised.

RECORDS OF THE BURNING OF THE BEDFORD COUNTY COURT HOUSE
March 1863

MARCH WINDS OF DESPAIR

Minutes: Bedford County Court, January Tern A.D., 1863

(page 1) Monday 5th January 1863

Be it remembered that at a County Court began and held for the County of Bedford at the Court House in Shelbyville on the first Monday in January 1863, the same being the 5th day of said month and of American Independence the 86th year. Present and presiding, William Galbreath, Chairman, and Justices, Phillips & Davidson, members of the Quorum Court.

Proclamation being made, Court was opened and the same being a Quarterly Court, but a quorum not being present the Quarterly Court is adjourned until court in course and therefore because of the excitement incident to the military movements as also on because of the absence of several of the attornies of this court, the Quorum Court is also adjourned until Court in Course.

William Galbreath
Rich'd Phillips

February Term, 1863

Be it remembered that a County Court began and held for the County of Bedford on the first Monday in February 1863 at the Court House in Shelbyville, present and presiding William Galbreath, chairman, and Justices Phillips and Davidson, members of the Quorum Court. Proclamation being made Court was opened and thereupon because of the occupancy of the Court House by the Confederate Military Authorities, Court adjourned until Court in Course.

William Galbreath
Rich'd Phillips

Minutes Bedford County Court.   March and April Term, A.D. 1863.

Be it remembered that a County Court began and held for the County of Bedford at the Court House in Shelbyville on the first Monday of March 1863, the same being the 2nd day of said month and of American Independence the 86th year. Present and presiding Wm. Galbreath, chairman and Justices Phillips and Davidson, members of the Quorum Court.

Proclamation being made Court was opened and because of the occupancy of the Court House by the Military Authorities, Court adjourned until Court in Course.

William Galbreath
Rich'd Phillips

Editors Note: The Court House was standing on March the 2nd 1863.

April Term

(page 2) Be it remembered that at a County Court, began and held for the County of Bedford at the Court House in Shelbyville on the first Monday in April the same being the 6th day of said month and of American Independence in the 86th year. Present and presiding William Galbreath, Chairman. Justices: Phillips and Davidson of the Quorum, and the same being a Quarterly Court. The following Justices appeared and took their seats upon the bench viz, H.F. Holt, Jas. K. Martin, G.W. Gregory, Jas. P. Taylor, James Dillard, William Wood, Jas. H. Harrison, Payton S. Dean, E.J. Halsey, and Robt. L. Landers.

The Court being called to order, the chairman attention of the Justices to the fact that the Court House of Bedford County while occupied by the military authorities was recently destroyed by fire, that many valuable records had been lost and that it was now incumbent upon the Court to take some steps necessary for the safety of the records, by procuring a temporary place of meeting until a new Court House could be erected.

Editors Note: The following Clerks notation was written in the left margin of the minutes on page 2.

Clerk's Note: Instead of meeting at the Court House at the April Term 1863, as the caption shows, he should have said, the Court met in the store room of Robert Mathews, which was kindly tendered by him for this purpose, the Court House being destroyed. (The Mathews storehouse was located on Town Lot No. 78, in the middle of the west side of the Public Square.)

On motion, it is therefore, ordered by the Court that Joseph M. Thompson, James H. Neil and Robert B. Davidson be and are hereby appointed a committee to make inquiry (page 3) upon what terms a suitable building can be rented and also upon what terms such a building can be purchased and that they report to this Court on the third Monday in this inst.

It is also ordered by the Court that, Thomas C. Whiteside, George W. Buchanan, Joseph H. Thompson, , James J. Neil (Neal), and Robert B. Blackwell be and are hereby appointed a committee with free and discretionary powers to confer with the Confederate Authorities and to respectfully demand payment of them for the loss that the County has sustained by the destruction of its Court House whilst in the hands and under the control of their officers and troops. It is therefore ordered that said committee shall have full power to receive and receipt for whatever amount may be agreed upon between them and the Confederate Authorities and that the amount they recommend shall be considered final settlement of all damages that the County of Bedford claims for the loss aforesaid.

It is also ordered by this Court that, Charles A. Warren, William Little, W.A. Allen, James S. Scudder and F.F. Fonville are hereby appointed a committee to superintend the removal of the old Court House walls and other rubbish now in the court yard, that in performing this duty they shall have full power to sell or otherwise dispose of the brick in said walls as well as any other material belonging to said Court House, that they shall also have full power to employ all necessary hands or workman and that that they report to the Court, as soon as practicable, their action on the premises, the foundation excepted.

-1871-

BEDFORD COUNTY COURTHOUSES

-1935-

OLD ROCK JAIL
1867

LANE PARKWAY & N. SPRING
SHELBYVILLE

THE BIG SPRING IN SHELBYVILLE

The notorious Town Spring, once a landmark in the town, was located 550 feet north at a spot now paved over, once the south west corner of Franklin (Dawdy) and Spring Streets. Samuel Musgrove and Howel Dawdy, first settlers, used this spring before the Town of Shelbyville was established in 1810, on the 100 acres given to the Commissioners by Clement Cannon for that purpose.

The spring provided fresh water, comfort and a public meeting place for the early pioneer families for the town. Unfortunately it is said to have also contributed to the deadly fever and cholera epidemic of 1833 and 1873. The controversial spring was finally closed to the public in 1922.

cession of her share of the western lands and continued to promote the land rush in Middle Tennessee. In December 1789, North Carolina finally ceded its western lands, now Middle Tennessee, to the Federal Government, to be called the Territory South of the Ohio River.

The Blount Grants

Bedford County was well acquainted with the enormous land deals that were promoted by the post war government of North Carolina. A major recipient of large North Carolina grants were, the Blount brothers, Caleb and Martin Phifer, William Polk, George Doughtry, Stokley Donelson, Robert Smith, Joseph Dixon, Alexander and Thomas Greer, and Anthony Newman, all the above named held grants of five thousand acres or more in Bedford County, Tennessee.

By far the largest holder of these North Carolina grants were Thomas and John G. Blount, they held locations of eighty five thousand acres in seventeen separate five thousand acre tracts that were strategically located on the Three Forks of Duck River, entered so as to have title to both sides of the forks of the river. The grants began a short distance east of Shelbyville, running to the Old Stone Fort at Manchester. John Donelson surveyed these grants in August of 1792. The Blount brothers never lived on this land and kept it only a short time after it was surveyed.

In 1808, Patton and Erwin, a partnership of Ashville, North Carolina, purchased fifty five thousand acres out of the seventeen grants, from Norton Pryor of Philadelphia. James Patton and Andrew Erwin dissolved partnership in 1814. Andrew Erwin, the partner, taking all of the Duck River land in the settlement. Erwin came to the Three Forks in 1814 to oversee survey changes in his vast holdings. His place of residence was in Augusta, Georgia until 1817 when he moved from Georgia to Bedford County, Tennessee, settling on his now famous brick house tract, east of Wartrace, where he died in 1834. He was a one time member of the Tennessee State Legislature.

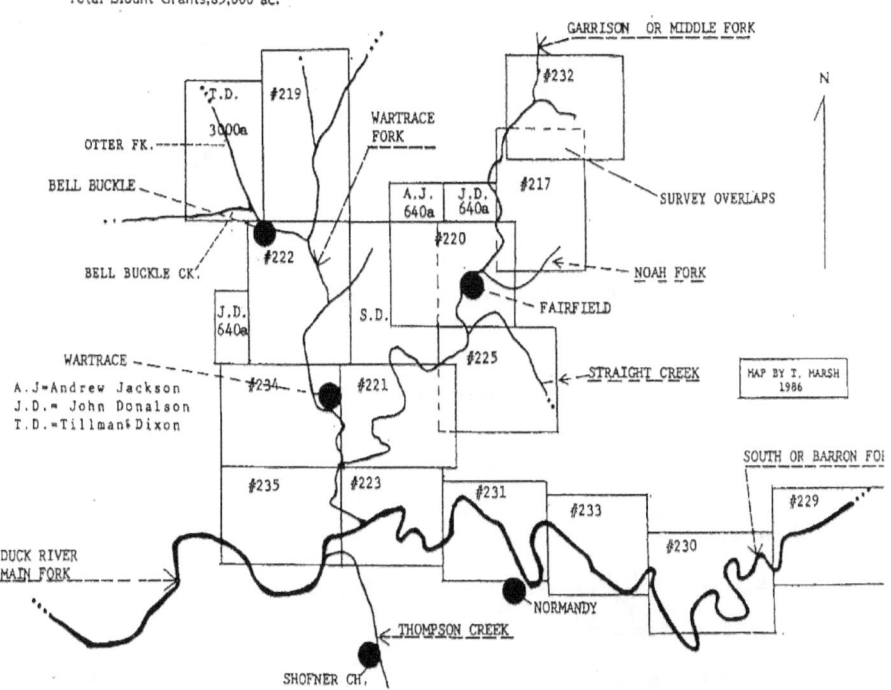

THE TENNESSEE GAZETTE, KNOXVILLE, TENNESSEE

Vol. 2, No. 89 Wednesday March 17, 1802

Benjamin J. Bradford, Editor

Pursuant to a decree of the Honorable Circuit Court of the United States for the District of West Tennessee passed at the October Term 1801, will be sworn to the highest bidder for cash at the Court House in the Town of Nashville on Monday 19 day of April next, 85,000 acres of land in 17 different tracts adjoining, on the Three Forks of Duck River in the Middle District as per Grant Numbered 216, 217, 218, 219, 220, 221, 222, 223, 229, 230, 232, 234, and 235. The property of the heirs and devises of David Allison, deceased, to satisfy the aforesaid decree obtained by Norton Pryor against the said heirs and devises. Sale will begin about 12 o'clock.

Robert Hays, M.D. W.T.

February 9, 1802

EARLY GRANTS IN BEDFORD COUNTY

Blount Grants and others

Page 252

Grant No. 225

Entry No. 1160 Middle District   June 27, 1793

5,000 acres located on both sides of Duck River.

Beginning on the north bank of said fork where the upper line of a survey made for Blount of an Entry No. 1670, crosses said fork, running north 220 poles to a beech, east 952 poles crossing said fork, south 840 poles, west 952 to a stake, north 620 poles crossing said fork to beginning.

Page 253

Grant No. 217

Entry No. 1668   June 27, 1793

5,000 acres located on both sides of Middle Fork.

Beginning on north bank of said fork where upper line of Grant No. 1661, (Grant No. 221) crosses said fork, thence north 640 poles to white oak, east 833 poles to walnut and beech, south 960 poles said fork to stake, west 833 poles to stake, north 320 poles crossing said fork to beginning.

Page 254

Grant No. 219

Entry No. 1165   June 27, 1793

5,000 acres located on both sides of Wartrace Fork.

Beginning at a hickory and dogwood, north east corner of Entry No. 1677, north 1250 poles to ash, west 640 poles crossing said fork to stake, south 1250 poles to stake in the upper boundary of said entry, east 640 poles to beginning.

Page 255

Grant No. 231

Entry No. 1675   June 27, 1793

5,000 acres located on both sides of the South Fork of Duck River.

Beginning on south bank of said fork where upper line of Entry No. 1667 crosses same, south 320 poles to a beech, east 894 poles to a white oak, north 894 poles crossing said fork to a stake, west 894 poles to a stake, south 574 poles crossing said fork to beginning.

Page 256

Grant No. 221

Entry No. 1670   June 27, 1793

5,000 acres located on both sides of Midfork of Duck River.

Beginning on south bank of said fork opposite the mouth of the Wartrace Fork at a black walnut, hickory and plum trees and a flat stone set up against the walnut, marked: G.B., J.C., T.P., and J.D., running north 840 poles crossing Wartrace Fork four times to a forked cherry, box elder and walnut, east 952 poles to a stake, south 840 poles crossing the Midfork to a stake, west 952 poles to beginning. (Chain carriers: John Castleman, Terry Poe, and John Peyton, M. and John Donnelson, Surveyors)

Page 257
Grant No. 229
Entry No. 1659   June 27, 1793
5,000 acres located on both sides of South Fork of Duck River.
Beginning on north bank of said fork where the upper line of Entry No. 1658(3) crosses said fork, north 480 poles to a small walnut, east 960 to beech, south 830 poles crossing said fork to a strake, west 960 poles to a stake, north 350 poles crossing said fork to beginning.

Page 259
Grant No. 233
Entry No. 1656   June 27, 1793
5,000 acres located on both sides of South Fork of Duck River.
Beginning on the south bank of said fork where upper line of Entry No. 1675 crosses said fork, south 420 poles to white oak, east 894 poles to a beech, north 894 poles crossing said fork to a stake, west 894 poles to a stake, south 474 poles crossing fork to beginning.

Page 260
Grant No. 390
Entry No. ___ State of North Carolina to Robert Alexander December 19, 1794.
2,000 acres, located on both sides of Duck River, about 1 mile above the mouth of Fall Creek. Beginning at elm on south bank of river opposite Samuel Barton's southeast corner, south 340 poles to a stake, east 800 poles, north 460 poles to a stake on river bank, down river to beginning. (John Wilson and Ebenezer Alexander, CC and David Wilson, Surveyor)

Page 266

Grant No. 234

Entry No. 1676   June 27, 1793

5,000 acres located on both sides of Wartrace Fork.

Beginning on south side of the Mid-Fork on the bank opposite the mouth of the Wartrace Fork at a black walnut, hickory and plum tree and a stone set up against the walnut marked: G.B., J.C., T.P., and J.D., south 840 poles crossing Wartrace Fork four times to a forked cherry and walnut, west 952 poles to a stake, south 840 poles to a stake, east 952 poles to beginning.

Also,

Grant No. 235

Entry No. 1657

Beginning at mouth of Wartrace Fork, west 894 (actual measurement 920 poles), south 920, etc.

Page 293

Grant No. 222

Entry No. 1677

5,000 acres located on both sides of Wartrace Fork of Duck River.

Beginning at a mulberry, walnut and dogwood, 40 poles east of the north east corner of Entry No. 1676, north 960 poles to hickory and 2 dogwoods, west 833 poles to a stake, south 960 poles to a stake, east 833 poles to beginning.

Page 300

Grant No. 232

Entry No. 1669

5,000 acres located on Middle Fork of Duck River.

Beginning on north bank of said river where upper line of Entry No. 1668 (Grant No. 217) crosses said fork, north 480 poles to black walnut and ash, east 960 poles to a beech, south 833 poles to a stake, west 960 poles to a stake, north 353 poles crossing said fork to beginning. (Does not plot)

Page 301

Grant No. 230

Entry No. 1658 June 27, 1793

5,000 acres located on both sides of the South Fork of Duck River.

Beginning on north bank of said fork where upper line of Entry No. 1656 crosses said fork, north 480 poles to ash, east 960 poles to a small walnut, south 833 poles crossing said fork to stake, west 960 poles to a stake, north 353 poles crossing river to beginning.

Page 302

Grant No. 224

Entry No. 1671 June 27, 1793

5,000 acres located on both sides of Middle Fork of Duck River.

Beginning on north bank of said fork where upper line of Entry No. 1669 (Grant No. 232) crosses said fork, north 480 poles to red oak and ash, east 960 poles to dogwood and hickory, south 833 poles crossing said fork to stake, west 960 poles to stake, north 353 poles crossing said fork to beginning. (Does not plot)

Page 305

Grant No. 220

Entry No. 1661 June 27, 1793

Original location Grant No. 1788, surveyed on August 29, 1792.

5,000 acres located on both sides of Middle Fork of Duck River.

Beginning on the north side of said fork where upper line of Entry No. 1660 crosses said fork, west 340 poles to a mulberry and ash, north 833 poles to a black walnut, east 960 poles to a stake, south 833 poles crossing said fork to stake, west 620 poles crossing said fork to beginning.

Page 307

Grant No. 1663   June 27, 1793   Surveyed August 30, 1792

5,000 acres located on both sides of the South Fork of Duck River.

Beginning on the north bank of said fork where upper line of Entry No. 1678 crosses said fork, north 320 poles to a white oak and beech, east 960 poles to a white oak, south 833 poles crossing said fork to a stake, west 960 poles to a stake, north 513 poles crossing said fork to the beginning.

Page 326

Grant No. 223

Entry No. 1667   June 27, 1793   Surveyed August 26, 1792

5,000 acres located on both sides of South Fork of Duck River.

Beginning on the bank of the Middle Fork opposite the mouth of Wartrace Fork at a black walnut, hickory, plum tree and stone marked: G.P., J.C., J.P., J.D., running east 894 poles to white oak, south 894 poles crossing said fork to a stake, west 894 poles to a stake, south east corner of an Entry No. 1657, north with the upper boundary of said Entry 894 poles crossing said fork to the beginning.

Page 354

Grant No. 216

Entry No. 1678   June 27, 1793   Surveyed August 31, 1792

5,000 acres located on both sides of South Fork of Duck River.

Beginning on north bank of said fork where upper line of Entry No. 1659 (Grant No. 229) crosses said fork, north 480 poles to ash, east 960 poles to beech, south 833 poles crossing said fork to stake, west 960 poles to a stake, north 353 poles crossing river to the beginning.

Page 312

Grant No. 1223   November 18, 1793   North Carolina to William Hill

2,000 acres, Green County, located on south side of Elk River on a small creek empting in a small distance above the Three Forks (Cane).

Beginning at a beech east 640 poles to a black oak, north crossing creek at 200 poles (in all 500 poles) to a buckeye, west 640 poles to a stake, south 500 poles to beginning.

Page 382

Pryor to Erwin   Processional Survey

5,000 acres   June 22, 1807

No. 233

Beginning on Entry Line No. 1675, with line (south) crossing the corner in all 420 poles to white oak near top of a ridge having crossed a branch running to the right at 258 poles, ___ east striking the south bank of the South Fork at 660 poles, keeping in it about 18 poles and crossing out on the same side at the mouth of a creek, running in on the south side, crossed the South Fork of Duck River at 822 poles, in all 894 poles, to a beech and 2 chestnuts, the beech marked N.P., P. & E., north 894 poles to 2 red oaks, the white oak marked as above, west 894 poles crossing several branches to an ash and 2 hickories on a ridge near a path, south 474 poles crossing the South Fork of Duck River to the beginning.

Page 383

Grant No. 219

Entry No. 1665   June 28, 1807

5,000 acres located in 2 District Rutherford, on Wartrace Fork.

Beginning at 2 dogwoods and hickory, the north east corner of Grant No. 222, Warrant No. 1677, north crossing several branches of the Wartrace Fork 1250 poles to an ash on the south side of a ridge, west 640 poles crossing the heads of the Wartrace Fork 4 times to a large beech, ash and poplar on the west side of a hill, south crossing the Wartrace Fork 4 times to a white oak, ash, and gum standing in a marsh, east 640 poles crossing the Wartrace Fork at 250 poles to beginning.

Page 383

Grant No. 299

Patent No. 1659   June 25, 1807

5,000 acres.

Beginning at 2 chestnuts on a bluff standing on the north bank of the South Fork of Duck River in the upper line of a 5,000 acre tract Warrant No. 1658, running north 480 poles crossing South Fork at 254 poles and again at 355 poles and struck and kept up some distance came out on north side to 2 gums and dogwood by a trace standing near a red oak marked N.P., east crossing a branch near its junction with a south fork at 100 poles, cross the South Fork at 300 poles crossing a large fork empting into the South Fork at 358 poles and again at 772 poles in all 960 poles to a red oak, south crossing 2 bogs, forks or creeks 833 poles to 2 post oaks in the Barren, 40 poles east of which is a red oak marked as corners at the intersection of the eastern boundary line of the 3rd 5,000 acre tract by virtue of Warrant No. 1658, north 353 poles crossing the south Fork of Duck River to the beginning.

Page 384

Grant No. 231

Warrant No. 1675   (no date)

5,000 acres.

Beginning at a white and black oak on a bluff on bank of a south fork where the upper line of a 5,000 acre tract No. 1667 crosses, running with same south passing the corner thereof 320 poles to a beech and white oak, marked N.P., east crossing a creek near its mouth 566 poles crossing the South Fork of Duck River at 600 poles crossing at 700 poles, in all 894 poles to a white oak on a ridge, north crossing a branch and the south Fork of Duck River 894 poles to a beech standing on the north side and near the top. The beech marked N.P., P. & E., standing on the north side of a ridge, south 574 poles crossing the South Fork to the beginning.

Page 385

Warrant No. 1668

5,000 acres.

Beginning where the upper line of No. 1661 (Grant No. 220) crosses Mid-Fork of Duck River, at 2 beeches, one of which is marked N.P., P. & E., standing on the north side of a ridge, south 574 poles crossing the south fork to the beginning.

Page 385

Warrant No. 1668

5,000 acres.

Beginning where the upper line of No. 1661 (Grant No. 220) crosses Mid-Fork of Duck River, at 2 beeches, one of which is marked N.P., P. & E., standing on the north bank of Mid-Fork of Duck River a small distance above the mouth of Puncheon Camp Creek, north 640 poles crossing Mid-Fork of Duck River at 180 poles and again at 268 poles to 2 sugar trees and beech, the beech marked N.P., P. & E., east crossing Mid-Fork of Duck River at 98 poles, crossing several branches and ridge, in all 833 poles to large white walnut near top of the ridge, south crossing a large fork of the Mid-Fork at 880 poles, 960 poles to a large poplar 2 small beeches standing on a ridge, one of the beeches marked N.P., P. & E., west crossing 2 creeks the 1st of which Nall (John) lives on, in all 833 poles to a stake east of which 2 hickories and pin-oak, marked as a corner in the eastern boundary line of 5,000 acre tract of Warrant No. 1661 (Grant No. 220), north 320 poles crossing the Mid-Fork of Duck River to the beginning.

Page 385

Grant No. 221

Warrant No. 1670   June 13, 1807

5,000 acres.

Beginning at a black walnut, hickory and plum tree and a stone marked: B.G., J.C., T.P., J.D., standing on east bank of the Mid-Fork of Duck River, opposite the mouth of the Wartrace Fork, north crossing Mid-Fork of Duck River at the end of 5 poles and crossing the Wartrace Fork 4 times, in all 840 poles to 2 beeches and a hickory, one of the beeches marked N.P., P. & E. and sundry other letters, east crossing the dividing ridge between the Wartrace and Mid-Fork, crossing the Mid-Fork 3 times, in all 952 poles, to 2 dogwoods and ash standing near large beech tree marked N.P. & P. & E., near head of a valley, south crossing a branch at 160 poles, in all 840 poles to 2 large beeches on west side of Knobb 30 poles, east of a branch, the beeches marked N.P. and P. & E., west 952 poles to beginning.

Page 386
Grant No. 225
Warrant No. 1660
5,000 acres.

Beginning on the north bank of Mid-Fork of Duck River where upper line of Warrant No. 1670 crosses it, north 220 poles to ash, white oak and mulberry, standing near some rocky ground, east to north bank of Mid-Fork at 56 poles opposite to an ____, crossing Straight Creek at poles and again at 410 poles, in all 952 poles to a stake in a hurricane, 112 poles west of which is an elm tree marked N.P., P. & E. 1807, standing near a large red oak, blazed and marked "D," south running through the hurricane 840 poles, west crossing 2 branches, the 1st at 20 poles, in all 952 poles to a stake having crossed the eastern boundary of Warrant No. 1670 at a distance of 600 poles, where there are 3 lynns growing from same root, marked as a corner, north 620 poles crossing Mid-Fork to the beginning.

Page 386
Grant No. 223
Warrant No. 1667
5,000 acres.

Beginning at black walnut, hickory, plum tree and stone (marked) opposite the mouth of Wartrace Fork, east 894 poles to large sugar tree and elm standing on the east side of a ridge 28 poles west of a branch, the sugar tree marked N.P., P. & E., south crossing the south fork of Duck River at a bluff on south side thereof in all 894 poles to a large white oak and 2 sugar trees on the top of a ridge, west crossing several branches and 2 creeks, one of which is called Thompson's Creek, in all 894 poles to a red oak, mulberry and white oak, the mulberry marked N.P., P. & E., north 894 poles crossing Thompson's Creek and South-Fork to the beginning.

Court House, Nashville, Tennessee   19 April 1802

Andrew Jackson, Esq.

85,000 acres (to be auctioned)

10,000 acres   17 Grants

Grant 234 & 235

Grant 234, located on both sides of Wartrace Fork, beginning on bank opposite mouth of Wartrace Fork at black walnut, hickory, plum tree and marked stone, north crossing Wartrace Fork 4 times 840 poles to forked cherry tree, west 952 poles, etc.

WARTRACE SCHOOL SECTION
1806

717+ ACRES

[Plat map showing the Wartrace School Section with the following labeled tracts and features:]

- N. Chaffin Land — 300 poles
- I.J. MILLER, 63 A., # 24436, Ju. 1857 — 78 poles
- RICHARD S. THOMAS, 208 A., # 24435, Apr. 1857 — 252 poles
- RIDGE — 107 poles
- ELNATHAN DAVIS, 108 A., # 24453, Apr. 1857
- JOHN NELSON, 145 A., # 24434, Apr. 1857 (Later Beechboard)
- JOSHUA MILLER, 193 A., # 24437, Ju. 1857
- WARTRACE FORK — 142 poles
- 88 poles; 88 poles; 166 poles; 188 poles
- Graveyard X
- LIBERTY PK.
- 40p, 199 poles, 85 poles 2 KM
- William Sugg
- Brooks Mill X
- ROAD
- Plat: T. R. Marsh
- N (compass)

This plat of the old controversial <u>WARTRACE SCHOOL SECTION</u> was surveyed out at 717+ acres in 1806. It was rented out by the County Common School Commission until 1857, when it was divided into lots and sold to the highest bidder to those listed on the plat. A Tennessee Grant was then issued to each owner. It appears that <u>JOHN NELSON</u> had lived on his 145 acre purchase long enough before the division in 1857. Nelson, his wife and daughter, were probably the first to be buried in the old graveyard. The first division and owners of the school land was finally un-covered by us in May 1997 in the Tennessee State Archives. Records could not be found locally.   Tim & Helen Marsh, 1997

TENNESSEE GRANT # 24434 OCCUPANT GRANT TO JOHN NELSON
Book 9, page 436 Microfilm Roll # 109

The State of Tennessee to all whom these presents shall come –

Greetings: Know ye, That in consideration of the sum of seventeen hundred and seventy dollars and twenty five cents paid into the Treasury of the State for the use of Common Schools, which payment appears by the receipt of R.N. Wallace, cashier of the Bank at Shelbyville dated April 6th 1857 there is granted by the State of Tennessee, unto JOHN NELSON, a certain Tract or Parcel of Land, containing One hundred forty five acres and eight poles lying in Bedford County in Range 8, Section 5, and bounded as follows. Beginning on a beech and lynn stump the original south east corner of the original tract, running north 1+ degrees East 32+ poles to a sugar tree stump SE of a large chinquapin; thence North 9 degrees West 31+ poles to a flat rock; thence North 2 degrees 30' East 124+ poles to a beech and sugar tree in the east boundary; thence North 68+ West 86+ poles to the center of the Wartrace Creek above where a small spring breaks out on the east bank, with beech and ironwood pointers; thence South with the meanders of the creek as follows South 54 degrees 30' West 22+ poles; thence South 35 degrees West 12+ poles; thence South 58+ degrees West 10+ poles; thence South 17+ degrees West 9+ poles; thence South 49+ degrees West 24+ poles; thence 51+ degrees East 12+ poles, thence South 19 degrees 7' West 12+ poles; thence South 39 degrees 30' West 10+ poles; thence South 9+ degrees East 6+ poles; thence South 59+ East 4+ poles, thence South 7+ East 3+ poles to the center of the creek with beech pointers on the east bank; thence North 79+ degrees East 21+ poles to the center of the Murfreesboro and Shelbyville road; thence South with the same 9+ degrees East 92 poles to a stake in the center of the road; thence South 24+ degrees East 34+ poles to the south boundary line of the original tract crossing where the above named road crosses the said boundary; thence 89 degrees East 85+ poles to the beginning.

To JOHN NELSON   Signed by ANDREW JOHNSON

10TH Sept. 1857

This Grant was part of the Wartrace School Land Tract and surveyed out at 717+ acres. It was laid out in 1806 by order of the General Assembly.

It was known as the Wartrace School Section and was rented out by the Common School Commissioners and the revenue deposited into the school fund. This was voted out by, the citizens before 1860. The land sold for the highest and best bid and a Tennessee Grant issued. Others that received grants out of this 717+ acre tract in the 1850's were Elnathan Davis, Isaac J. Miller, Joshua Miller and Richard S. Thomas. John Nelson was probably renting this 145 (147)-acre tract in the 1830's when his daughter was buried there. It appears that after the elderly Nelsons died, L.P. Fields purchased the tract at a Sheriff's sale.

This School Land Grant, was found in the Tennessee State Archives and Library in the Land Grant Sections by us (Tim and Helen Marsh) in May 1997 when we uncovered it following a long trail of research. There is no early records available in Bedford County relating to this School Land Tract or if so could not be found by us.
Tim and Helen Marsh
June 1997

EARLY MILLS IN BEDFORD COUNTY, TENNESSEE

ANTHONY MILL – Thompson Creek near Midway

DAVID BLEDSOE MILL – Sinking Creek

CANNON MILL – Duck River at Shelbyville

CANNON – CONWAY MILL – Flat Creek near Higgins' home, south side of Shelbyville.

CORTNER MILL – Duck River, above Normandy

COX – WATSON MILL – Lake Elaine

PETER CROWELL MILL – Duck River below Halls Mill

DOAK MILL – near Flat Creek Village

SAMUEL DOAK MILL – Duck River at Rubber Mill

DOWDY MILL – Thompson Creek near Raus

DAVID DRYDEN MILL – Headwaters of Sugar Creek

EARNHART MILL – Duck River at Warner Bridge, Fishingford Road

EDWARDS – BURDETT – SANDERS – MARBURY MILL – Duck River above the town of Coney Island

FALL CREEK MILL – At the mouth of Fall Creek

FISHER – ANCHOR MILL – Duck River

JAMES GAGE MILL – Bobo Creek, east of Flat Creek – First in area

GREGORY MILL – North Fork

IVIE'S MILL – Flat Creek, south of Shelbyville

McGEE – KING MILL – Garrison-Three Forks

MICHAEL MOORE'S MILL – Sinking Creek

MULLINS MILL – Duck River above bridge, Tullahoma Highway 41-A South

NEELEY'S MILL – Sinking Creek

NATHANIEL PORTER – CUNNINGHAM MILL – Sinking Creek above Richmond

PRESGROVE MILL – North Fork

PREWETT – HIX MILL – Flat Creek

ROSEWILL – ROWESVILLE MILL – Shipman Creek

SHARP MILL – Mouth of Thompson Creek

DANIEL SHIPMAN MILL – South of Rowesville on Shipman Creek

JAMES SHARP MILL – 1812 – East of Shelbyvile

SIMS MILL – Duck River above Shelbyville

SIMS MILL – Sims Spring Branch

SMITH MILL – Wartrace Fork at Suggs

TEMPLE – JOHN SIMS MILL – Duck River, Temple Ford

WILHOITE'S MILL – Duck River, west of Shelbyville

WILSON'S MILL – Near Greer's estate, Sugar Creek

EARLY MILLS AT FAIRFIELD

The first travelers along the upper Garrison traversed the old trail that ran along then called the Crawford Trace. As travel increased the roads up the Garrison or Middle Fork became known as the Winchester City Stage Road. When the county seat of Shelbyville was established in 1810 and eager settlers began to take roots, grist mills, a necessity of the time, began to appear throughout the county.

In the year 1810, Alexander Outlaw of upper East Tennessee sold Jonathan Parr of Rutherford County, 655 acres, part of Blount Grant No. 220. Parr moved on to his purchase and soon erected a mill on the Garrison where Fairfield now stands. Joseph Walker had just erected his mill on the Noah Fork, a mile to the east. In 1814, Thomas Crutcher purchased the mill and adjoining land. For three years the road from the fledgling Village of Shelbyville to the north east and was known as Crutchers Mill Road, changing to Hickmans Mill Road in 1817 with the purchase of the mill by William Hickman, changing again in 1819 to Davis Mill when Thomas Davis of Shelbyville purchased the mill. In 1822, Dr. James Armstrong, late of Shelbyville, purchased a substantial tract of land along the Garrison including the mill. The Community continued to be called Davis Mill for some years. Later Dr. Armstrong attempted to change the name to Petersburg but the name never caught on. The pleasant smell of warm stone ground meal experienced in ones childhood, as it produced by the mill, by the mill stones was an experience, one will not soon forget.

INCORPORATION OF THE TOWN OF WARTRACE DEPOT
OCT 3, 1853

This day a petition of the citizens of the town of Wartrace Depot in Bedford County was filed in court which petition is in the words and figures following, to wit,

State of Tennessee
Bedford County

To the Worshipful County Court of Bedford County.

"The undersigned petitioners of the town of Wartrace Depot in said county, petition your worship to grant us the privilege of incorporating said village, running one quarter of a mile in every direction from the center of said Depot ground so as to elect officers to carry into effect the laws provided in such cases, and for the benefit of the good citizens of said village for which your petitioners will ever pray. This the 3 day of October 1853.

Daniel Stephens	B. Z. Gannaway	J. D. Payne
Robert Buchanan	John R. Coffee	A. E. Mullins
John Stephens	W. T. Green	Joseph Sherwood
N. C. Harris	Willis Pruett	Robert Erwin
W. H. Clark	T. A. Prince	M. Payne
W. B. Norville	R. E. Coffee	A. T. Garrett
G. W. Martin	T. C. Mills	H. M. Keller
R. P. Gannaway	Wm. H. Sims	J. W. Tilford
T. P. Gannaway	C. M. Norville	

and on motion it war ordered by said court that said town be incorporated as the town of Wartrace Depot with all the privileges and liabilities prescribed by the General Assembly of the State of Tennessee Chapter No. 17 passed January 7th 1850 and that the corporation of said town extended one quarter of a mile in every direction from the center of the Depot grounds.

And it was ordered by the court that said petition be spread upon the minutes and that a copy of this entry properly certified be given for registration and that the same be registered in the Registers office in Bedford County, twelve acting Justices being present and voting in the affirmative.

P. C. Steele
Jos. Hastings
Wm. Galbreath

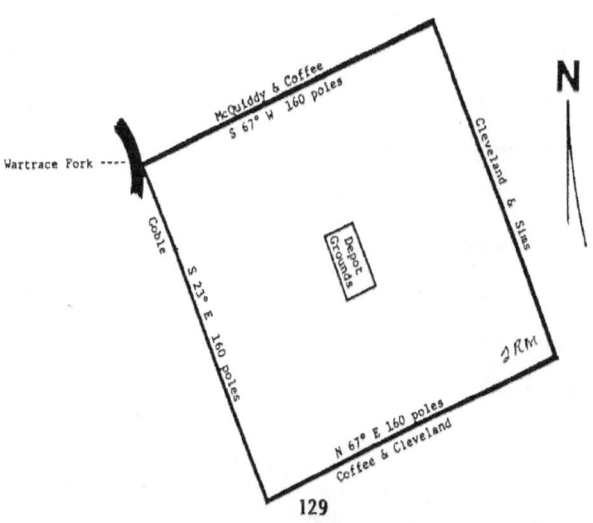

DEASON

By the year 1836, the name "JOHN DEASON'S" was well known as a place on the Shelbyville-Murfreesboro-Nashville Turnpike where the Deason's had lived for many years and were the voters in the 5th District went to vote, at the house of John Deason. Prior to this date this cross roads was in the old Militia Company of James Yell, a brother of Archibald Yell, later Governor of Arkansas.

The new macadamized turnpike that was chartered in 1831, was now completed with toll gates up and operating. Deason's was at the cross roads of the turnpike and the Byler's (Rover) – Davis Mill (Fairfield) Road. The stagecoaches now made good time on their regular schedules by John Deason's. John, son of Enoch Deason, late of Anson County, North Carolina, now found that this was becoming a place of some significance, on the "Big" road.

Enoch and Rebecca Deason had settled here by 1812, on a 270 acre Tennessee Grant that was then open land, later in possession of General Andrew Jackson, the man of the hour and an acquaintance of Deason. In 1818, Deason secured title to the 270 acres for one dollar and other considerations. This small grant ran along the road leading to Widow Byler's and was located at the cross roads. It lay between two major North Carolina Grants. On the north was the 5000-acre North Carolina Grant No. 34 of Mathew Lock, surveyed in 1785, and extending northward to the Rutherford County line, it included the Captain Guy's plantation (later Dr. Frazier) and Guy's Gap. On the south lay the 5000-acre North Carolina Grant No. 102, granted to Caleb Phifer. This large grant extended southward including the old Dr. Houston Plantation, to Hurricane Creek at Whiteside.

In 1840, Benjamin C. Ransom, member of a prominent Rutherford County family, purchased Lot No. 5 of the division of the Mathew Lock grant, this lot was surveyed out at 1814 and ran west along the Unionville Road for a mile plus and northward along the west side of the turnpike (231) cornering at the cedar knob (Ransom Hill) in the gap.

By about 1844, Benjamin C. Ransom having died that year, sons W.K. (William King) and Benjamin F. moved into their inheritance. By 1852, John Deason had died and with the final purchase of Deason land from Widow Sarah (Arnold) Deason, W.K. and B.J. Ransom owned all the land west of the turnpike from Deason's to Guys Gap. B.J. Ransom later acquired a strip along the east side of the turnpike.

In 1839-40, with the division and sale of the Lock Grant land, G.W. Bell and Joseph Loyd purchased land on the east side of the crossroads. Bell gave land to the Cumberland Presbyterians for a church to be called Bell Mount, a name that the village carried for many years.

Deason's first church of record was the United Baptist Meeting House erected about 1835 on land located on the east side of the pike, that was given by John Deason.

In 1894, W.K. Ransom gave the land and support for the building of Ransom Methodist Church that stands today. The deed is recorded in Deed Book 2, located in the Register of Deeds Office in Shelbyville, Tennessee.

The name "Deason" was officially given to the village in 1895 at the suggestion and prompting of Squire W.K. Ransom, with the establishment of the Post Office in the village. Squire Ransom's son was appointed Postmaster.

In 1905, The Deason Church of Christ was established in the village on the east side of 231.

ABOUT THE LAND

In the formative years of the early 1800s, the Phifer Grants, on the south, the Mathew Lock and Thomas Dougan Grants on the north and east and strip that lay between them, were surveyed and resurveyed resulting in corners that changed or floating from year to year, probably causing frustration for the early settlers, not knowing from day to day where their property line actually ran.

The strip of 1188 acres that was finally agreed upon was surveyed as follows, Andrew Jackson 270 acres, William Caswell 278 acres, Malcum Gilchrist 640 acres.

Sometimes thee strips of open land that occurred frequently, intentional or not, minimized overlapping locations and surveys. It apparently also gave the early entry takers a shot at acquiring large personal holdings of cheap land. Many early land locators operating independently of each other had located grants on top of grants never aware that the other had been there.

The land grab act frequently produced great abuse. Locations were often locations on paper only. Some surveys were paper surveys only. In early Bedford County, Tennessee, overlapping surveys were quite common. The courts were clogged for years with interference land lawsuits.

Marsh

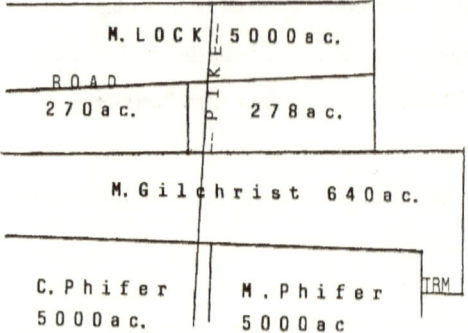

TAXABLE PERSONS LIVING OR OWNING PROPERTY IN OR AROUND SHELBYVILLE IN 1812

Baired, John
Balch, George B.
Bingham, William
Branch, Nicholas
Brown, Shedrick
Burns, Saml.

Cannon, Clement
Cannon, Minos
Cates, William
Chilcut, Peter
Claxton, John
Coats, John
Coats, Wilson
Cockrill, John
Culp, Henry

Damorah, Sam'l T.
Davis, Daniel
Davis, Henry
Davis, Thomas
Dawdy, Alfred
Dawdy, Danl.
Dawdy, Howell (2)
Deery, James
Dempsey, John B.
Denison, Robert
Donnalson, Andrew

Ganeway, Burrel
Gibson, Jeremiah
Gilchrist, Daniel
Gilchrist, Malcom
Gore, William
Gleaves, Therman
Green, Daniel
Green, William

Hamm, Joshua
Harman, Gedian
Harman, Lewis
Harris, James
Harris, Mosebey
Henderson, Wm. F.
Hogg, John B.
Holland, Thomas
Hopkins, William
Hudson, Jessee

Ingram, Samuel

Larimore, Hance
Lee, John
Locke, David

Mason, Michael
McAdams, Amos

Murray, Francis

Nance, Reuben
Neile, Nicholas
Newsom, William

O'Mehundro, Wm.
Oaks, Hezekiah
Owens, David

Parson, George
Parson, Thomas
Patton, James (2)
Phillips, Matthew
Price, Reece

Ragsdale, Edward
Rawling, Hosey
Read, William

Sebastian, Saml.
Shote, Arthur
Snell, Charles
Sark, Thomas
Stone, John
Stone, William
Stringer, James
Summer, Samuel

Drake, Zachariah
Dungan, Jacob

Edde, James
Ellis, John
Evans, Jesse

Fisher, Michael
Flenn, James
Fugit, Moses
Fuller, Isaac
Fuller, Jacob

McAdams, James
McCuestion, Benj.
McCuestion, John
McCuestion, Saml.
McFarling, Robert
McKisick, James
Miller, Henry
Mitchell, Marmaduke
Moore, Thomas
Morgan, James
Murkison, Murdock
Murphry, Stephen

Temple, Robert
Tucker, James

Wade, Edw. Jr.
Wall, John
Westmoreland, Vincent
Whitworth, Jacob
Williams, Elisha
Williams, Isaac
Williams, Nathl.

Young, Edward

EARLY LAND GRANTS & TITLES

IN

THE OLD TENTH DISTRICT

From the Marsh Collection

Description
1980

George Doherty – 3000 acre Tennessee Grant No. 603, surveyed May 28, 1808, Warrant No. 1503. Doherty was a large land speculator and died in North Carolina. John Strother and Willliam P. Anderson had located, filed and surveyed most of Doherty's thousands of acres in several Middle Tennessee Counties. At his death, they received a division of his land holdings as payment for their services. The above 3000 acres, being part of the settlement, the eastern half of the grant was sold by Strother and Anderson in 1815 to Malcum Gilchrist, a Bedford County Deputy Surveyor who sold it to numerous settlers in the area. After Strother's death, James Lockhart, his Executor, sold the western part of the grant in 1826 to Alfred Balch, a Bedford County and later Davidson County Attorney. Balch, over the next several years disposed of the land by sale to purchasers. This 3000 acre Grant was located in Range 3 and Section 7, of the Second Surveyors District, which included all of Bedford County, Tennessee. Bedford County was sectioned off in 1806-07 by Act of the Legislature but the system was never completely adopted as it has been in the flat land states.

Nathaniel Taylor – 640 acre Tennessee Grant No. 1639, Entry No. 61, 1807. Nathaniel Taylor of Carter County, Tennessee, was assignee of Benjamin Skipper who held North Carolina Military Warrants No. 4778, surveyed April 18, 1808. Taylor sold the entire tract to Abraham Byler and Thomas Maxwell, Byler taking the upper or north half and Maxwell the lower half. A Deed of Division by Byler and Maxwell was not recorded until 1822. The Old Nashville-Shelbyville Road was the approximate dividing line. In 1807, Abraham Byler and Thomas Maxwell were listed in the Williamson County Tax List as owning no land. In the 1808 list, Byler and Maxwell are listed on Clems Creek, each owning 320 acres. This was the 640 acres they had purchased from Taylor. The Taylors Fork of Clems Creek runs the entire length of the 640 acre tract, Byler lived on this tract and was living on it in 1815 and the widow Nancy still on it in 1836-39. See Deed Books BB, page 150, GG, page 323 and 1836 Tax List. Abraham Byler, Sr. had numerous grants in Bedford County, Williamson County and in some West Tennessee Counties. He was issued Tennessee Grant No. 8151 at the county line in Bylers Bottom. He never sold this grant. He had small grants to the west and northwest of Rover, also a grant adjoining his son, John, north of Enon Church. Early Rover was called "Bylers." By 1842, land Deeds called it "Rover." Abrahan Byler, Jr. t his death owned 150 acres at "Byler Bottons" at the county line.

Thomas Thompson – 93 acre Tennessee Grant. This small grant was issued by 1807, and was granted before Nathaniel Taylor and George Doherty grants were entered. The exact date and grant number is recorded in the Old Grant Books in the Tennessee State Archives. In 1830, Thompson was in Hardeman County, Tennessee and the land was sold to Lewis Anthony who sold to James Lile and Lile sold to Christopher S. Dudley and Sheriff's Sale in 1844 to Thomas C. Rankin, and changed hands numerous times before the Civil War.

Clems Creek School Land Tract – 640 acres. This was one of several tracts in Bedford County, Tennessee, set aside by an Act of the Legislature in 1806 to be used for the support of Public Education. Most often the land was rented out under the supervision of a local School Commissioner and the revenue appropriated for the Common School Fund. In the late 1840s as the result of a public referendum, the land was sold in lots at auction to the highest bidder. Not shown on the Grant Map is a narrow strip running along the south boundary line of the School Tract, this was the result of a resurvey of some of the Old Grants. This, thirty six by two hundred and twenty two pole strip was entered by John Cooper, who sold it to Asa

Stem in 1823, it adjoined the Old Charles Brandon home tract. Brandon was a Soldier of the American Revolution and was living here when he died.

William Clark – 247 acre Tennessee Grant No. 3238, surveyed 1809 on the waters of Clem Creek, joins the south boundary line of the School Land 640 acre tract. This tract was later divided and sold to Kimbro and Thomas Allison, then to Curtis Snell. In 1818, the Clark heirs of Orange County, North Carolina sold the 247 acres to Major Samuel Turrentine and the same year sold 110 acres lying to the northeast of the William Hill 320 acre tract to Samuel and Alexander Turrentine, who sold to John Cooper in 1825.

William Hill – of Wake County, North Carolina, 320 acres. In 1815, Hill sold the 320 acres to Mark Hardin of Rockingham County, North Carolina and Hardin sold tract to Robert Allison in 1823. Early small grant owners in this area between this William Hill grant and the Captain John Byler grant to the east at Enon were: Amos McLemore, Job Cooper, John Cooper, Charles Brandon and Elijah Rutledge.

Jonathan Graves – 3000 acre North Carolina Grant, 1797. On Duck River and Wilson Creek, early division of this tract, Jonathan Graves of Rutherford County, Tennessee, sold to Z. Daniel 600 acres in 1809, sold to Joseph D. Graves 480 acres in 1812, to James Dickson 810 acres in 1811, smaller tracts to Walter Sims, William Meeks, Giles Burditt, Littlebury Green, Joshua White (now Dr. Albert Cooper).

Robert Allison – 240 acre Tennessee Grant No. 368, surveyed September 28, 1809. This tract was located along the west boundary line of the Old John Wilson North Carolina Grant at Unionville. Allison lives and died on this grant. In 1823, he purchased the adjoining 320 acre tract patented to William Hill. Allison was one of the larger landowners in the area.

Abraham Byler – 100 acre Tennessee Grant No. 319, 1809. This grant was located south of Taylor Cross Roads, north of Enon Church and was located between the two large grants of Ebenezer Alexander and George Doherty. John Harris held a small grant immediately to the north.

John Byler – 200 acre Tennessee Grant No. 2439, surveyed March 1810. This was an Occupant Grant and Captain John Byler, who was a Captain in the Militia in 1812, lived on this tract until 1819 when he sold to William Wheeler of Rutherford County, Tennessee, reserving forever from sale one acre whereon a Meetinghouse and Burying Ground are located (Enon). The branch that runs through the tract carried Bylers name, he also owned a 100 acre tract to the south and another small tract to the east in the wedge shaped strip of un-appropriated land between Byler and Ebenezer Alexander.

John Wilson – 3000 acre North Carolina Grant No. 323, Warrant No. 1802, surveyed 1792 by David Wilson. John Wilson of Mecklenburg County, North Carolina. This tract was an overlapping grant and about two thirds of it was lost by interference with the 2000 acre North Carolina Grant No. 1063 issued to John Lock. Part of the western end of this Wilson Grant was sold to James Ray and Union Camp-ground, later "Unionville" is located on this part of the grant. The heirs of John Wilson sold 890 acres to Burton Jordan who then sold to William Ogilvie 225 acres in 1815, to James Ray of Williamson County, Tennessee 247 acres in 1817, and to James Williams 388 acres in 1814.

Ebenezer Alexander -- 3000 acre North Carolina Grant No. 43, Warrant No. 2081, surveyed 1785 by Henry Rutherford. Longview is located in the northeast corner of the grant. The Joseph Dickson 3000 acre grant is located to the east of this grant with a narrow strip of un-appropriated land located between the two grants. Much of this grant was sold to Newton Cannon, Ezekiel Norris of Lincoln County, Tennessee, Samuel Bell, John, Samuel B., and Evan Harris, Joseph Wallace, William Allison and Robert Morrison father of John Morrison a Revolutionary Soldier who lives on this land.

George Alexander – 1650 acre Tennessee Grant No. 1689, entered 1808. George Alexander of Cabarrus County, North Carolina. This grant was located to the north and adjoining the Ebenezer Alexander 3000 acre grant. In 1808, Newton Cannon purchased 825 acres of this grant and in 1820 the heirs of George Alexander sold 687 acres of this tract to James Cooper of Bedford County, Tennessee. George Alexander also owned a 1000 acre grant at the mouth of Alexander Creek. These early surveys were run to the needle of the compass (magnetic reading) and the grants at Rover were surveyed and lines run to true north, therefore in this area as well as other parts of the county, we find many small wedge or pie shaped tracts of land between the larger grants, many of these small tracts of un-appropriated land were not known to exist until most of the larger tracts were surveyed in the 1820s. Much of this land was then entered by Malcum Gilchrist, a Deputy Surveyor of the Second Surveyors District with headquarters in Shelbyville. This land sold at from one to twelve and one half cents per acre as set by the State Legislature. ———— SELECTED GRANTS AROUND ROVER ————

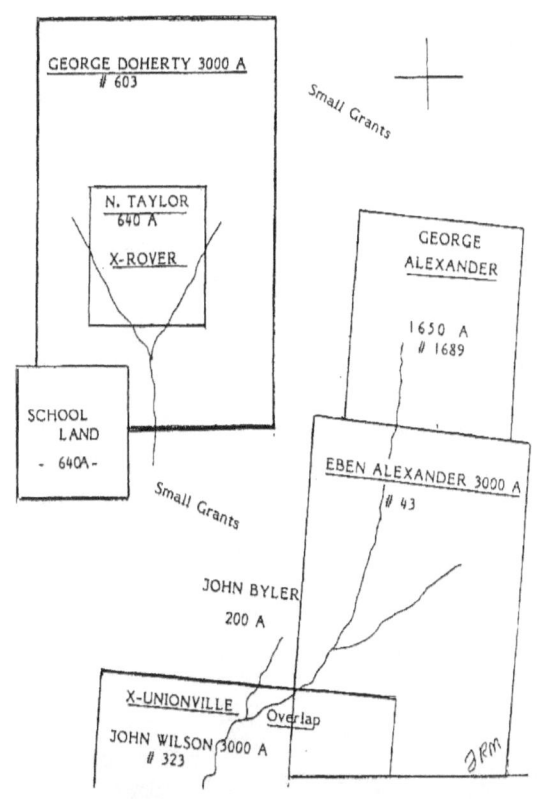

LOTS IN SHELBYVILLE, FOR SALE

On the first Monday in April next the sale of the Lots in Shelbyville, the County Town of Bedford County, elegantly situated on the banks of Duck River, and surrounded by a very rich body of land, on which a number of wealthy farmers have already settled, tradesmen and merchants are invited to attend and judge for themselves. A credit of twelve months will be given to those who enter into bond and give approved security. Sale to continue from day to day until finished.

Bedford County, Jan. 25, 1811.

Apparently the Court met twice at the house of Amos Balch, March 1810, and June 1810. If so the Tennessee Gazette indicated, the Celebration of the 4th was held at the Bedford Court House and not the place of holding Court at the house of Amos Balch. Then the Court would have been held the first Quarter Session in the new temporary Court House in Shelbyville in August 1810.

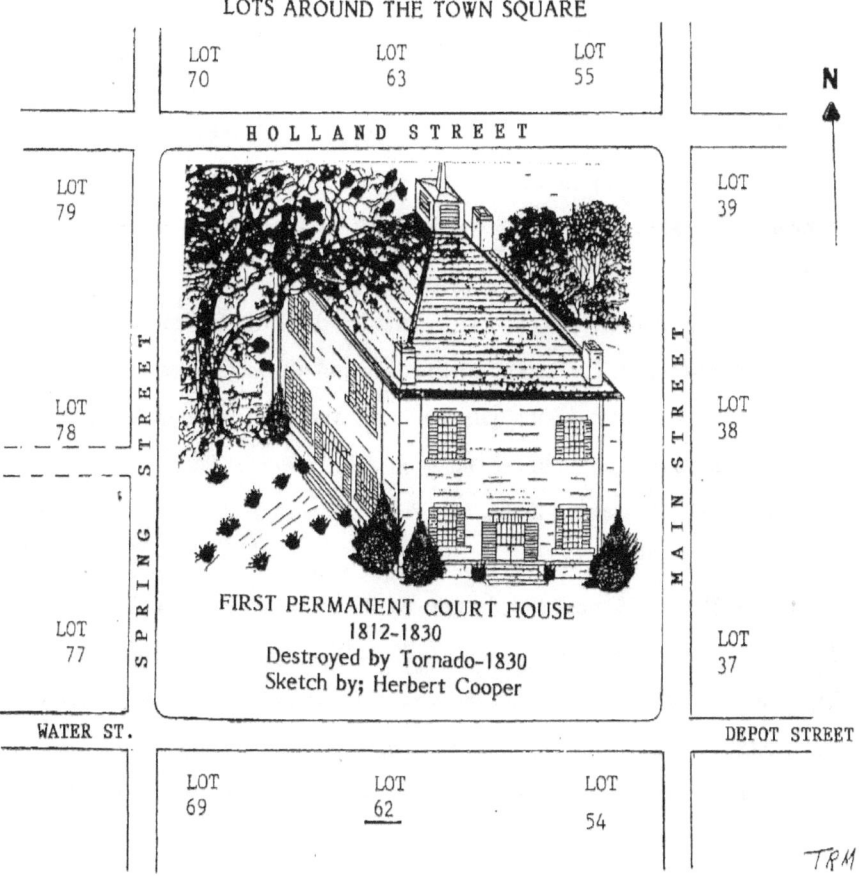

LOTS AROUND THE TOWN SQUARE

| LOT 70 | LOT 63 | LOT 55 |

HOLLAND STREET

LOT 79

LOT 78

LOT 77

SPRING STREET

MAIN STREET

LOT 39

LOT 38

LOT 37

FIRST PERMANENT COURT HOUSE
1812-1830
Destroyed by Tornado-1830
Sketch by; Herbert Cooper

WATER ST.

DEPOT STREET

| LOT 69 | LOT 62 | LOT 54 |

Editors Note: Lot 62, the lot on which the Cannon Tavern once stood was the middle town lot, situated on the south side of the public square. This lot was purchased, July 1810 by Clement Cannon, at the public town lot sale for $17.00.

In the beginning it was a valuable town lot, often sold. By 1819, the lot was owned by Minos Cannon and his brother, General Robert Cannon, brothers of Clement. In 1866, the Cannon Tavern was owned by Minos Thompson, the only son of Gen. Robert Cannon.

EARLY LOTS AROUND THE SQUARE

ORIGINAL TOWN LOTS FRONTING ON THE SQUARE WERE:

EAST SIDE: Lot 37, was on the south east corner, original purchaser was Clement Cannon (July 1810), Cannon to Francis Murry, to Thomas and Henry Davis, to James Edde.

Lot 38, original purchaser was Peter Chilcutt, July 12, 1819, Chilcutt to William J. Whitthorne and Daniel Turrentine, later to John and Alexander Eakin, and others.

Lot 39, northeast corner, original purchaser was Andrew Erwin and James Patton. In 1815, Patton and Erwin sold to Samuel and John N. Porter, Porter to George and Hezekiah Balch. Later sold to J.C. and N.C. Coldwell, and Levi C. Roberts and others.

NORTH SIDE: Lot 55, was located on the northeast corner, original purchaser was John Stone, July 12, 1810. Stone sold to William West and M.D. Mitchell and a long list of others. Through the years, this was the most bought and sold lot in town. The Globe Tavern, Shelbyville Inn, Evans House and Dixie Hotel were located on this lot. The stables were located on Lot 56, the lot located to the north of Lot 55. The New Peoples National Bank is now on this lot.

Lot 63, original purchaser was James McQuistion, July 1810. McQuistion sold to James Deery, a native of Ireland, and a first settler and merchant in Shelbyville.

Lot 70, located on the northwest corner, original purchaser was William Newsom, July 1810. Newsom sold to John Marbury, Marbury sold to William Deery, Deery sold to William S. Eakin, later purchased by the Methodist Church. The present beautiful Shelbyville Methodist Episcopal Church now stands on this lot.

WEST SIDE: Lot 79, was located on the northwest corner, original purchaser was Thomas Talbot, July 14, 1810. Talbot's estate of Davidson County, Tennessee, to Benjamin Strickler, to Bank of Tennessee, to Robert Mathews (a native of Ireland), to Branch Bank of Tennessee and others. The First National Bank is now located on this lot. The old Fire Hall and City Hall was once located on this lot.

Lot 78, original purchaser was Nicholas Branch, July 1810, later to A. Donaldson, to Henry Conway, to William Gilchrist, to James Frazier, to Dr. Preston Frazier, to Mrs. Jane Frazier, to E.J. Frierson, to Robert Mathews and others. This lot changed hands many times and fronted on Bridge Street and the Square.

Lot 77, was located on the southwest corner, original purchaser was Samuel B. Harris, July 1810. Harris sold to Henry Conway and James McKissick. Part of lot sold to Malcolm Gilchrist, to E.J. Frierson, to Thomas C. Whiteside and others. The Gunter Building is now on this lot.

SOUTH SIDE: Lot 69, was located on the southwest corner, original purchaser was Clement Cannon, July 23, 1810. Lot was sold in 1817 to Andrew Erwin, to Robert Cannon, to William Hickman, to C. Cannon and A.B. Morton and others.

Lot 62, the original owner was Clement Cannon, July 1810. Cannon sold to John Drake, Drake to James McClure, to A.B. Morton, to Minos and C. Cannon (Old Cannon Tavern was on this lot), later owned by Joseph D. Wilhoite and J.C. Coldwell and Company, and others.

Lot 54, located on the southeast corner, original purchaser was Minos Cannon, July 13, 1810. Cannon sold to Robert Cannon, to Thomas Yeatman, to Dr. James L. Armstrong, to Thomas Davis and George Davidson (in 1827, Major Thomas Davis was residing on this lot), to James Britton, and others.

This list of Lots and Owners is a sample of the owners of these lots in the early dte of the town and is not an absolute abstract, as time and space would not permit, even if the records were available and complete.

OVER THE MOUNTAIN TO CUMBERLAND COUNTRY
The Beginning

The first explorers and settlers that came to stay in what is now the new world were the Lost Colony on the outer banks of North Carolina, at Roanoke Island and the Jamestown settlement on the James in 1607.

Who Claimed What

First the mound builders, then the native Americans, Cherokees and Chickasaws, then the French, then the English. From the time of the English settlement at Jamestown in 1607 until the closing days of the Revolution, Middle Tennessee, then called the Cumberland Country was inhibited primarily by the native American although some accounts mention a settlement of Welch from the British Isles, as being on the waters of the Tennessee in the mid 1600's. The wilderness area, now Tennessee, was first claimed by the English Crown as Virginia, still later by North Carolina. The south boundary line of North Carolina was supposed to be the 35th parallel, a line common to North Carolina and later Tennessee, called Cut-Ta-Wa, by the Cherokees. Surveyors struggled with this line for years trying to accurately a-fix, an exact location without success until late 1807.

1708

In 1708, French traders were at the Muscle Shoals, the suck or whirl of the Tennessee River. In 1779, before Nashborough was settled, Robertson, Rains and Donelson knew of the shoals and how to get there from the French Lick.

1714

By 1714, French traders were at the French Lick, a salt lick on the Cumberland where the buffalo and deer had watered from ancient times. First man known there by name, as a Frenchman named Charleville, who trapped, hunted and traded there. Timothe (Timothy) Demunbreun, from the Illinois Territory, was there by the time the long hunters began to arrive in 1763. In 1819, the line between North and South Carolina was agreed on.

1728
Lords Proprietors Grants

About 1600, certain grants were issued by James I and Charles II, sometime called Crown Grants. They were issued to noblemen that held favor with the crown. The lands were in the new world of Virginia and North Carolina. By 1728, the proprietors frustrated by the revolt of early settlers that had lately settled on the land with the expectation of occupying and entering on the lands but instead being evicted or charged Quit Rent, were beginning to resist the tactics of the Lords. Proprietors, most often had the Governor in their pockets. Most of the Proprietors buckled under and sold their land back to King George. In 1728, The Earl of Granville opted to keep his huge grant that encompassed a trip of sixty-six miles wide then extending southward along the Atlantic, and westward to the Mississippi River. This Granville Grant included all of the northern half of now Tennessee, then North Carolina. To this date accurate surveys had not been made. Rivers, lakes and mountains and other natural boundaries were used as lines or markers.

Anson County, North Carolina
1728

All of the land south of the sixty-six mile strip of the Granville, Lords Grant, fell in Anson County, North Carolina, then a vast county that ran all the way to the Mississippi River. The south boundary of the Earl of Granville Grant (1728-1782) ran east to west near or at the Rutherford-Bedford County lines.

1750

Dr. Thomas Walker, an early surveyor of Virginia, was surveying at the junction of East Tennessee and North Carolina. Some years later, Walker would help survey the northern boundary line of Tennessee. The accuracy of the line as surveyed was disputed for many years after Tennessee became a State in 1796.

The Real Beginning On The Cumberland

1760

In 1760, Pioneer Daniel Boone, out of North Carolina, passed by Boon, North Carolina, on through Johnson County, Tennessee, on along the Wilderness Road, through the Cumberland Gap into Kentucky.

The Long Hunters

1766-67

In June 1766, we find documented accounts of long hunters, explorers that ranged long distance from home base, exploring down the Cumberland to its mouth at the Tennessee. Uriah Stone, one of the parties reported, no white men found. Stones (Stone) River was named by and for Uriah Stone on this expedition. It is said that Stone and a Frenchman, probably Demunbreun from the lick, traveled up the Stone River to the head. If this is true, it is likely that the explorers, curious as they were, likely peeped over the Duck River Divide at or near Liberty Gap, perhaps a first look at now Bedford County.

Research discloses that in 1769, ten years before the Robertson-Rains parties arrived at the Great Salt Lick in December 1779, a contention of twenty hunters our of Western Virginia traveled the wilderness trail that Boone had traveled, some going on the Kentucky, some on west to the famous lick. Uriah Stone once again was in the middle of the excitement, along to share in it was Isaac Bledsoe and Captain John Rains who later in the key year of 1779, led a party of men, women and children, out of western Virginia, planning to settle in Kentucky, going out by way of the Cumberland Gap. Their plans changed when they chanced to meet up with the Robertson party, out of Fort Patrick Henry on the Holston, who were on the way to settle at the French Lick. Robertson, persuasive fellow that he was, talked Rains and his party into following him to the French Lick.

Commerce On The Cumberland

By 1769, Commerce had developed in the Cumberland Country, with the birth of the meat processing and packing business, promoted by the processing of buffalo and other wild game then in abundance on the French Lick and the waters of the Cumberland. The meat products were furnished by the hunters, boats built locally, loaded for the long journey to Natchez and New Orleans, where the meat and boats were sold and the long overland trip back up the Natchez Trace to the Lick began. This was the beginning of a long and prosperous business that developed between Middle Tennessee and the gulf coast, lasting into the 1830's this included such commodities, exported from Bedford County as Tennessee pork, corn and red cedar, all in great demand on the gulf coast.

1770

In 1770, James Robertson, often considered the father of Middle Tennessee, made his appearance in Watauga, on the Holston near where Kingsport now stands. He, Daniel Boone and many others were disgusted with the oppression of the citizens by Governor Tyron of North Carolina and his political cronies and were moving westward to escape graft, high taxation, without representation. Over the mountains new lands were there for the taking, most of the good land in the Carolinas was already taken by the favored land grabbers, and the Lords Proprietors.

1780

On September 25th, 1780, in Carter County, the wilderness area now Tennessee, the citizens made their contributions to the American cause against the haughty British, when several hundred mountain men marshaled while the Rev. Samuel Doak, pioneer Presbyterian minister, asked for the Devine guidance and aid for those valiant men as they prepared to march to King's Mountain, where on October 7th 1780 Ferguson was defeated in a decisive battle at the little mountain. Joseph Greer, brother of Alexander Greer, a first explorer, early settler, Justice of Bedford County, and son of Andrew Greer, a first settler in Carter County, Tennessee, was chosen to carry the message of the defeat of the British, at King's Mountain, to the Continental Congress in Philadelphia. Joseph Greer settled in Lincoln County, Tennessee on Cane Creek in 1806/7 and is buried on his plantation east of Petersburg, Tennessee.

Cumberland Country Calling

1779-1780

In the spring of 1779, Col. James Robertson and a party of seven others once again made the overland trip from Virginia to the French Lick on the Cumberland and began clearing, planting and building crude cabins for their families whom they planned to bring out in the Fall or Spring of that year.

In the fall, the corn was gathered and the party returned to Fort Patrick Henry by the long way around, going by way of Vincennes, an outpost on the Wabash in

Illinois. Here Robertson met with George Rogers Clark, noted frontiersman and friend of Jefferson, consulting with him about cabin rights on the Cumberland, thinking that the bend of the Cumberland, at the lick was in Virginia. Robertson, John Donnelson and others of the party made plans that included Robertson meeting the Donnelson flotilla at the Muscle Shoals of the Tennessee, where they would then go overland to the French Lick. This obviously did not happen, as a long bitter winter and threats of Indian activities caused Col. Robertson to abandon this plan and the flat boat "The Adventure" was forced to continue the long water route down the Tennessee and up the Cumberland to the bluffs, arriving on April 24th 1780. Captain Donnelson, boats-man and a few older men and the women and children departed the fort December 22nd 1779, destination, the French Lick. Col. Robertson and his party having already departed westward by way of the Cumberland Gap, destination the French Lick. At the Lick they would unite with their families and began a new life in the Cumberland Country. One should note that this venture was in the midst of the Revolution and these pioneers were isolated from the war much more that those on the other side of the mountain. They were on a mission that literally consuming their lives.

The Arrival and Crossing

December 25th, 1779

The Robertson-Rains parties arrived at the lick and crossed the river, then frozen over, to their destination on the bluff. In 1780, the name of Nashborough is given to the new settlement.

Land Deals and Dirty Tricks

1783-1784

At the close of the Revolution the State of North Carolina was destitute, owing a huge debt to her own soldiers of the Continental Line, for their services, in addition her share of the expenses in supporting the late war. All she had was vast lands in the western frontier, west of the mountains and westward to the Mississippi. Much of this land was held by treaty with the Chickasaws in West Tennessee, and the Cherokees in extreme Eastern Tennessee. The Continental Congress began to call in her debts, pressuring the states for a cession (surrender) of her western lands. Gen. Martin of North Carolina resisted this pressure from the Congress with all vigor and simply marked time and chose to postpone or ignore a settlement with the government. The exception of this action, or lack of it, was a promise the State had made to her soldiers, for land in payment for their services during the Revolution. In 1783, a large tract of land on the waters of the Cumberland was sat aside for survey. It began where the Cumberland intersected the southern boundary line of Virginia, now Kentucky, running southwest fifty miles to near Rock Island, then west passing near the south city limits of where Murfreesboro now stands, continuing westward to the Tennessee River, thence down said river to the Virginia line, thence along said line, eastward to the beginning. This vast tract was called the "Military Reservation" being reserved for the North Carolina Soldiers of the Continental Line. The remainder of the western lands were then opened for entry to land jobbers that were eagerly awaiting the go signal. A land office was opened in Hillsboro, North Carolina and the rush was on. Land locators poured into the western lands in force to gobble up the millions of acres, by entry for ten pounds per one hundred acres. Questions were raised about the questionable activities in the Hillsboro Land Office, charges were made that some in favor were given first choice at the trough.

General Caswell, John and Stokley Donelson, the Blount brothers, William Polk and George Doherty, to name a few, seized the opportunity, and began to feverishly make locations in Middle Tennessee. Others locating in the area were Alexander Greer, later of Bedford County, Tennessee and the William Edmiston party out of Abbington, Virginia. North Carolina still resisted the call of the Congress

MAJOR WILLIAM GUY & GUYS GAP
Major William Guy (1788-1847)

Major William Guy came to Bedford County, Tennessee before August 1815 (Deed Book "Y", page 123), from North Carolina and was living on his 210-acre holdings on the North Fork at the Bedford-Rutherford County line at that time, being part of the Mathew Lock 5000 acre, North Carolina Grant No. 34. By 1836, the 210-acre tract had grown to 1260 acres, and extended south to the Cedar Knobs (Guys Gap) that carried Major Guys name. He was also agent for the large Alexander Worke holdings in Bedford County, Tennessee. Guy's land holdings were purchased, by deed, not granted for military services.

Bedford County Deed Book "G", page 248, "We, Alexander Guy, John, Samuel, Sally and Margaret wife of Joseph Lawrance and Ann Guy, all of Iredell County, North Carolina appoint our beloved brother William Guy of Bedford County, Tennessee."

Major Guy first built a log house beside a spring and trace about one mile west of where, in 1837 he would build his Roseland, beside the Shelbyville-Murfreesboro Turnpike near the Rutherford County line.

There is a record of only one child born to William and Margaret Guy, the child was a daughter, Elizabeth who was probably born in North Carolina. She apparently stayed with her father until his death in 1847. The mother Margaret died before 1820. We find by 1850 daughter Elizabeth Guy had married a prominent local Doctor by the name of Preston Frazier. They with Dr. Frazier's nephew, William Temple, were living at Roseland at that time.

Dr. Frazier was a son of Hugh and Jane Frazier. The widow, Jane having settled south of Bell Buckle on Bradfords Branch. His siblings were James, Granville, John S., and Mary who married Dempsey P. Temple. Mary and Dempsey had a son

William A. Temple who studied under his uncle, Dr. Preston Frazier, and became a country doctor. He married Mary Ann Davis. Anne Elizabeth, a daughter, was born in 1854 at Roseland. William A. Temple's father, Dr. William P. Temple, died in 1859. Anne Elizabeth Temple was raised by her great uncle, Dr. Preston Frazier and his wife, Elizabeth Guy Frazier, a daughter of Major William Guy and wife Margaret. Anne Elizabeth Temple married Rev. Thomas S. McFerrin, a country Methodist preacher and race horse, owner and trainer. Thomas was a nephew of Rev. J.B. McFerrin, a noted Methodist preacher and publisher, who was commissioned a Chaplain in Hood's Army of Tennessee in 1863. A Confederate Regiment of the Army of Tennessee camped on the Frazier (Guy) farm in the winter of 1863. The Rev. Thomas S. McFerrin of Roseland served the southern cause in Robinson's Second Infantry, and died at Roseland in 1888, leaving his widow Anne Elizabeth Temple McFerrin as the heir to the Major Guy estate. She remarried a Mr. Wilkinson some years later.

The wife of Major William Guy, Margaret Ann, died before 1820. Major Guy died in 1847. Dr. Temple died in 1859. Dr. Preston Frazier died in 1865, his wife, Elizabeth died April 25, 1881. It is not definitely known how Major Guy acquired his military title, perhaps War of 1812, Seminole War Militia or Honorary.

According to previously written accounts, after the turn of the century, the widow of Rev. Thomas McFerrin, finding the upkeep of Roseland too much of a chore, decided to erect a small house across the turnpike from Roseland, near the site of the family graveyard. It is reported she arranges to have the grave markers removed and neatly stacked to the rear of the barn, where they eventually wound up in a large ditch to the rear of the barn-house, where in 1974 the writers found the original markers of Major William Guy and Dr. Frazier and had them restored and placed in the corner of the yard near the Old Guy Graveyard to honor the memory of these pioneer settlers.

At this writing, the spot where Roseland once stood is now the right-of-way of the new four lane divided Highway US 231 North, once the Shelbyville-Murfreesboro Turnpike, and the monuments of Major Guy and Dr. Frazier still stand on the property.

****

Pound - $2.40 in early 1800's

Fee Simple – absolute owner

Feme Sole – a single woman or a married woman whose marriage ended in death of divorce

Feme Covert – a married woman could not in her own name sign or sell

Entry – First step in acquiring a grant

Floating Entry – left deliberately vague

Moiety – The half or equal part of anything

Appurtenance – thing attached to or belonging to

Venire facias – "You cause to come" command sheriff to summon jury

Metes – Angles in degrees

Bounds – Boundary lines with terminal points

John (Proper) – Jack (nickname)

Joseph – Joe

Alexander – Sandy

Ann – Nan, Nancy

Christopher – Cris, Kit

Elizabeth – Liz, Lizzie, Lib, Betty

Henry – Hank, Harry

Margaret – Maggie, Peggy

Martha – Mattie, Pattie, Patsy

Mary – Molly, Polly

Richard – Dick, Rick

Sarah – Sallie

Gerald – Jerry

Robert – Rob, Bob

Raymond – Ray

END OF HISTORY SECTION

RESEARCH DIGEST SECTION

CONTENTS

EARLY HISTORY OF BEDFORD COUNTY, TENNESSEE	1-154
RESEARCH DIGEST SECTION	155-396
1836 TAX LIST	155-248

NOTE: ALL NAMES IN THIS TAX LIST APPEAR IN THE MASTER INDEX

THE FOLLOWING LISTS APPEARING BELOW IN THIS DIGEST SECTION ARE ARRANGED IN ALPHABETICAL ORDER AND ARE **NOT** INCLUDED IN THE MASTER INDEX IN THE BACK OF THIS BOOK.

1812 TAX LIST	249-285
EARLY LAND DEED INDEX	286-316
WILL INDEX OF BEDFORD COUNTY	317-324
CEMETERY INDEX AND MAPS	325-350
PLATS AND DEEDS	351-396

The fonts and structure of some of this research digest section may vary from the history section of this book as some of this material was taken from earlier transcripts of the Marsh Collection that was compiled many years ago.

****** INDEX INCLUDED IN THE MASTER INDEX ******

1836 TAX LIST
OF
BEDFORD COUNTY, TENNESSEE

The following is a list of taxables residing in the Civil Districts that made up Bedford County, immediately after its reduction in 1836, with the formation of Marshall and Coffee Counties. Until December 1835, the county was sectioned off into Militia Companies, known as Captain's Companies (see 1812 Bedford County Tax List). In early 1836 commissioners were appointed by the Tennessee State Legislature to lay off Civil Districts in the county. On January 8, 1836, the State Legislature passed an act creating a new county named Coffee, located immediately to the east of Bedford. The boundaries to the new districts of Bedford were laid off by February 10, 1836. By February 26, a new county of Marshall was erected, to be located west of Bedford.

This tax list was transcribed from the original tax book, now located in the Tennessee State Archives, by the editors in 1980. In the list, the lots, when listed, are by both lot number and number of lots.

Abbreviations:

DL: Deeded Land

SL: School Land (Tennessee Land Grants)

S: Slaves

( ): Insert by the Editors.

This tax list includes an eastern part of Marshall County
and a western strip of Coffee County

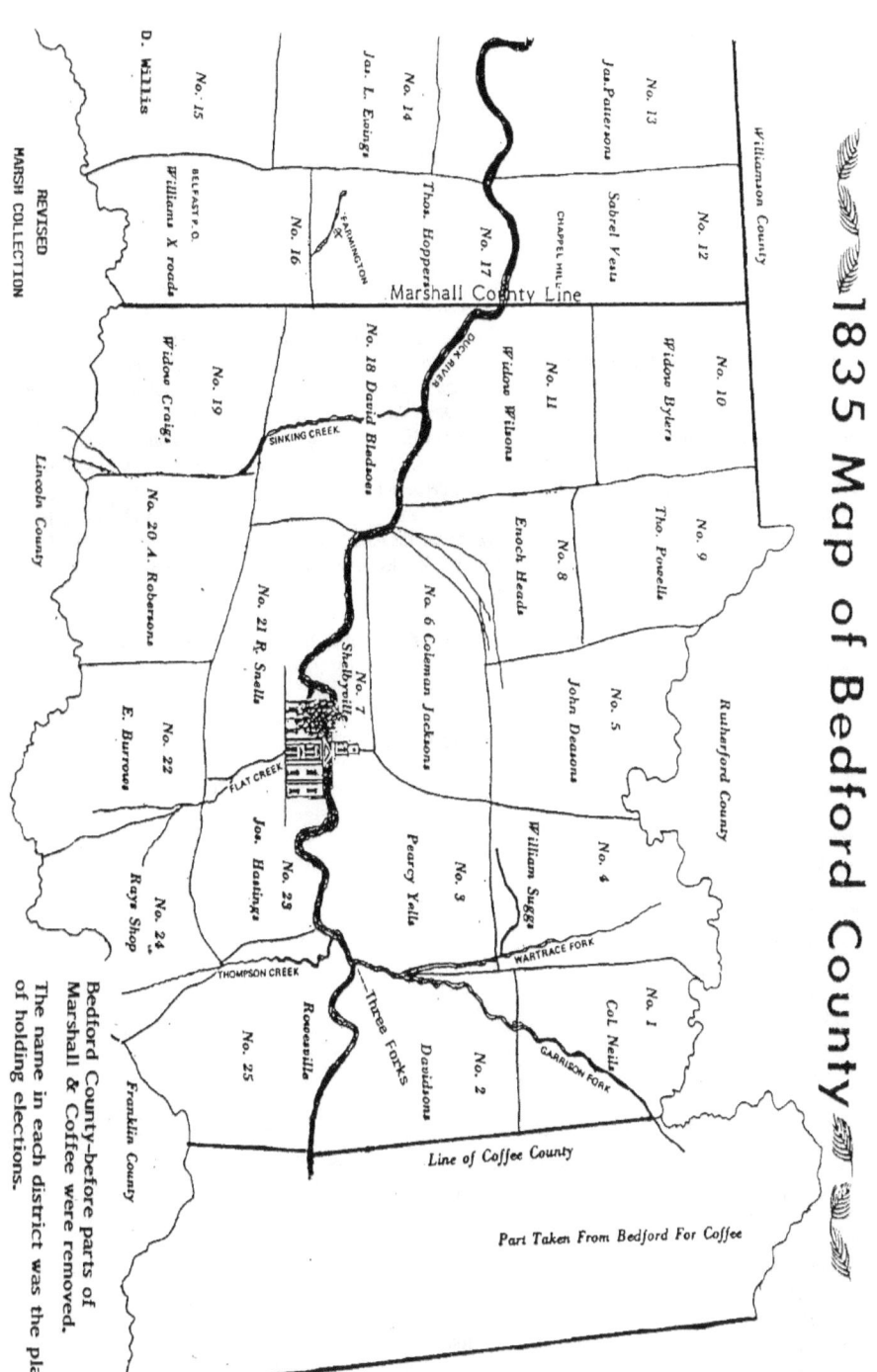

BOUNDARIES OF CIVIL DISTRICTS

1835

BEDFORD COUNTY - DISTRICT NO. 1

Beginning at Doctor Norton's Storehouse (Beech Grove) being the north west corner of Coffee County, thence running south with the line of Coffee County to the top of the ridge, dividing Noah's Fork and Straight Creek waters, thence westwardly with said dividing ridge to the forks of the road by the hemp field, and with the Shelbyville Road crossing the Garrison Fork below Davis' Mill (Fairfield) - and with the Bradford or Sutton Roads, to a cross lane about 80 poles west of Maj. John Bradford's house, near George Muse's house, thence north with Wm. Merritt's east boundary line, to Sam'l Mirchell's south east corner of his Keesee tract of land, and with the east boundary of his Horton tract, and with the same between his and A. Caruther's land - with the lane west of Anthony Thomas' - with the lane between Elijah Dyer's and _____ Thomas, thence northwardly to the lane running between Robert Majors and E.A. Mosley's and from the north end of said lane, due north to the top of the first ridge, and northwardly with the extreme heights of said ridge to the Stones River ridge on Rutherford County line and eastwardly with said line to the beginning.

The place appointed for holding elections in said district to be at the house of Col. John L. Neill. (East of Fairfield).

1836 TAX LIST

NAME	DL	SL	WP	S
Brookshire, Benjamin			1	
Brookshire, Josiah			1	
Bird, John			1	1
Bird, Sharel			1	
Bird, Samuel	173			4
Burditt, Patience	120			4
Burditt, Sarah	5			
Brewer, James			1	
Bailey, John			1	
Baker, James			1	1
Campbell, Wm. P.			1	
Coffman, Jacob	34		1	
Cavin, Joseph	100	40	1	
Cooper, William	10			
Coalton, Thomas	50		1	
Crews, Elisha			1	
Caruthers, Archibald	150		1	2
Crossland, Elijah			1	
Cook, Stephen			1	1
Dyer, Elijah	100			
Denneston, Thos. L.			1	
Denniston, Robert	174	16	1	
Drake, Thomas	40	65	1	
Davis, Henry	300			7
Eoff, William	250	250	1	3

NAME	DL	SL	WP	S
Eoff,John	41	129	1	
Eaton,John			1	
Ford,Simon T.			1	
Finch,Matt S.			1	2
Ferrill,Robert			1	
Fields,James			1	
Gill,George	32		1	
Green,B. Green			1	
Gaston,William			1	
Gregory, Thomas			1	
Gregory, Henry	10		1	
Haile,Alexander			1	
Hord,Edmund	169			2
Haile,William G.			1	
Harmon, Leonard	60		1	
Hall,James			1	
Haile,Meade	158	45		3
Haile,John			1	
Haile,Meade Jr.			1	
Harris,L.B.			1	
Hailey, Tauner			1	
Jones,Elizabeth	10			3
Jones,Benjamin	140			
Jakes,John	75		1	1
Jones,Samuel	35	12	1	
Jones,Jonathan			1	
Jones,Joseph	40	40	1	
Jones,Robert, Sen.	130	37.5		
Keele,James	49			
Keele,William	110	25		
Kindle,Thomas	148			
King,JAmes			1	
King,John				1
Knox,William	63	46	1	
Knox,John			1	
Lingan,Archibald	118			1
Lawry, John			1	
Lee, Alexander		62.5	1	
Mason, John E.			1	
McMahan, James			1	
Mosley, Edwd. A.	217			
Mosley,Thomas .	230	16.25	1	8
Mosley, Thomas B.	179			
Manning, Mark			1	
Morrow, James	438	70	1	

NAME	DL	SL	WP	S
McGuire, John B.		30	1	
McGuire, Polly		28		
Mason, Thomas W.			1	1
McMahan, Joel B.	100		1	
McMahan, Abraham			1	1
McMahan, Mary S.				2
Martin, Elizabeth	200			2
Martin, Matt Jr.	320		1	5
Martin & Mosley Exr. of H.B. Martin	343.75			9
Martin, Matt	809.5			8
Majors, Robert	140		1	1
Majors, Alexander			1	
Majors, Noble L.	64	86	1	
McMahan, James			1	
Nichols, Jacob	100			4
Norton, William	80		1	1
Neill, John S.	948		1	5
Robenett, Jesse Jr.			1	
Robenett, Alfred			1	
Robenett, Jesse Sen.	230		1	
Ragsdale, John W.	37.50		1	
Robeson, John Esq.	27.50	268.50	1	
Robeson, James Jr.			1	
Robeson, John Sen.		9	1	
Routen, Abram	190		1	2
Rucker, Saml. R.	186			
Ragsdale, D.M.			1	
Shaw, R.C.C.P.	175	151		7
Shaw, Mary	350			7
Shaw, C.G.W.B.	300		1	6
Sharp, William	385		1	1
Stephens, Richard			1	
Sutton, John			1	
Stephens, William	37		1	
Sutton, James	125	50	1	
Stephenson, Sarah	65	30		2
Smith, Thomas			1	
Taylor, Winston			1	
Thomas, William	122	18		
Thomas, Anthony	100		1	
Tolliver, William			1	
Tolliver, Charles			1	
Tedrow, John C.			1	
Tilman, John	200	60		17
Tilman, John	509			

NAME	DL	SL	WP	S
Vanderow, Francis			1	1
Walker, P.M.	160		1	
Wood, Abslwm			1	1
Wood, William	75		1	
Walker, John G.	62			

BEDFORD COUNTY - DISTRICT NO. 2

Beginning on the west boundary line of Coffee County on the top of the ridge between Noah's Fork and Straight Creek the south east corner of District No. 1, thence running west with said ridge to the forks of the road by the hemp fields, and with the Shelbyville Road by Bradford's and Sutton's to a cross lane near George Muse's, thence west of John Bradford, thence south with the lines of Grants No. 219 & 220 to the Bald Knob east of Mrs. Waits, thence south with the dividing ridge between the Garrison and Wartrace Forks, and down the Garrison Fork to it's mouth into the Barren Fork of Duck River, thence up said Barren Fork to the line of Coffee County, thence with said county line to the beginning.

Place of holding elections at John Davidson's old place on Knob Creek. (East of Wartrace).

NAME	DL	SL	WP	S
Anderson, John			1	
Arnold, Richard			1	
Allen, John W.			1	
Anderson, Jacob	100		1	
Armstrong, Jas. L.	578			6
Ditto for the heirs of Wm. B. Sutton				2
Ayers, Payne			1	
Bates, Randolph			1	
Blendill, William			1	
Bates, John B.	100		1	1
Black, James M.	100		1	
Blendill, Henry			1	
Blank			1	1
Bates, Matthew			1	
Bramlett, John	133		1	
Burrow,			1	
Bradford, John	100			2
Cully, William	128		1	
Cleveland, Jeremiah	1431		1	10
Couch, James				
Couch, Isaac	100		1	1
Couch, Reuben	126		1	
Cortner, Matthias	100			6
Cortner, Daniel			1	
Couch, Joseph	266		1	1

NAME	DL	SL	WP	S
Cully, Thos. J. & Bennett	90		2	
Cole, Levi			1	
Cully, Zachary	165		1	
Davidson, John	500			7
Davidson, Andrew M.			1	
Drake, Catharine	40			
Davidson, John Q.	233		1	3
Dean, John			1	
Daniel, Martin C.			1	
Erwin, James	3450			17
Erwin & Myers	400			12
Ferguson, H.C.	128		1	2
Ferrill, Richard	100		1	
Finch, William P.	1415			5
Floyd, John			1	
Franklin, Jackson			1	
Garrett, Elijah			1	
Griggs, Ferrill			1	
Green, James	70	70	1	
Green, Robert	40	40	1	
Green, Elijah	85		1	
Green, Willis	462		1	
Gallagly, Stephen	116	25	1	
Holt, Joseph	163		1	
Holt, Jesse			1	
Holt, Larkin			1	
Hall, Fergus	245			3
Holt, William			1	
Haggard, James			1	
Haggard, Rector			1	
Haggard, Squire			1	
Hooser, William	120			
Holt, Elijah	294		1	
Hall, John			1	
Hatchett, James			1	
Haggard, Samuel	115			
Hord, Edmond	550			9
Hord, Edwin			1	
Haynes, Enoch	100	60	1	
Houfman, Alfred	36		1	
Hall, L.W.	205			1
Harris, John			1	
Jones, Samuel	45	55		
Johnson, Nathan	112		1	
Jones, Levi			1	
Johnson, William	85		1	
Johnson, Stephen			1	

NAME	DL	SL	WP	S
Jolly, William			1	
Knight, Allen	345		1	
Knight, John	63		1	
Kimbro, Jeremiah	100			
Keller, Francis	250		1	
Keller, Jacob			1	
Keller, John M.			1	
Keller, Joseph	350		1	
Keek, John			1	
Kimbro, Powell			1	
Lewis, John			1	
Ledbetter, Alfred			1	
Meadows, William			1	
Muse, Isaac	271			1
Muse, George P.			1	
Muse, Orvill			1	
Muse, Richard	151		1	1
Muse, John			1	
McClure, Jacob			1	
Myers, Abraham			1	
Myers, Jonas			1	
Myers, John			1	
Moore, Harmon			1	
Maupin, Robert B.	550		1	4
McLean, C.C.	166		1	1
Osburn, G.G.	490		1	6
Osburn, R.T.	60		1	1
Payne, Moses	220		1	
Rayburn, Jos. M.			1	
Roberts, William			1	
Rose, William			1	
Scott, Elijah G.			1	
Slaton, Martha	48	23		2
Scott, William			1	
Smith, John			1	
Stroud, Hodge			1	
Suggs, Thomas	162		1	
Stroud, Bethel			1	
Smith, George			1	
Stephen, John	300			4
Stephen, Thomas			1	
Scruggs, John E.	90		1	4
Scruggs, Mary	300			3
Stephens, Daniel	97		1	1
Scott, John Esq.	275			14
Scott, Joshua P.			1	

NAME	DL	SL	WP	S
Thompson, James	102		1	
Thompson, John			1	
Tindall, James			1	
Throgmorton, Wm.	96		1	
Truslove, Zepaniah			1	
Throgmorton, B.	100		1	1
Throneberry, Benjamin				1
Trammill, David	177		1	
Vannoy, Andrew				2
Walls, William			1	
Williams, John			1	
Welch, John James B.	182		1	2
Walker, James	90			
Walker, William			1	
Williams, Patrick W.	10			
Waxter, David			1	
Yates, Samuel	90		1	
Yates, Elias	221			

BEDFORD COUNTY - DISTRICT NO. 3. or WARTRACE DISTRICT

Beginning at the mouth of the Barren and Garrison Forks, thence up the Garrison to the mouth of the Wartrace, thence with the ridge between the Garrison and Wartrace Forks to the Bald Knob, thence north with the lines of Grant No. 219 and 220 to where the same crosses the branch on which Isaac Muse lives, thence west leaving Curry McGrew, W.P. Goodwin, Col. Arnold, D.S. Evans & Q.T. Mayfield on the north in the Salem District - to John Sutton's Jr., leaving him on the south, thence south leaving the Widow Cooper on the west, thence to include Elijah Arnold, thence with the ridge southwardly to intersect the McMinnville Road east of the place where Thomas Norville once lived and west of the 3 mile post on the said road, thence westerly to where the same crosses the south boundary line of the Polk survey, thence west with the said line to Gilchrist corner, due north of the mouth of the lane west of Levin Marshall's old place, thence south with Gilchrist's line to his southeast corner, thence a direct line to Marbury's Mill, thence up Duck River to the beginning.

Place of holding elections, etc., (District No. 3), appointed as the house of Pearcy Yell. (Mt. Moriah).

NAME	DL	SL	WP	S
Allbritton, John			1	
Anglin, Adrain Sr.	57.50			
Anglin, Peyton			1	
Anglin, Adrain Jr.			1	
Anderson, Zachariah V.			1	
Ault, James H.			1	
Ault, Margaret	81			
Arnold, Elijah	198		1	2

NAME	DL	SL	WP	S
Arnold, D.D.			1	
Abbott, Wilson	140		1	
Arnold, Willie			1	
Arnold, Smith	100			2
Arnold, Alsey			1	
Bradford, Jno.				
heirs of G. Waite	78			
Bradford, Theodrick F.	300			19
Bradford, Henry C.	252			1
Bomar, Elijah	779.50			4
Bomar, William			1	
Bomar, B.B.			1	
Bomar, James			1	
Bruco, William			1	
Bradford, James			1	
Brown, James			1	
Burnett, Jas. M.			1	
Bower, John	142			8
Bryant, Thomas			1	
Bradford, Barkley			1	
Brown, Nathan'l	300			
by Adrain Anglin				
Cox, Martha	23			
Cardwell, John B.			1	
Coopes, Joseph H.			1	
Coble, Phillip	111		1	
Chambers, Robert	240			3
Chambers, Wm. L.			1	
Clagett, Horatio	360			13
Cothern, John			1	
Chandler, Allen				1
Chandler, Wm. C.			1	
Chandler, John A.			1	
Cothern, Jesse			1	
Cobbett, Jesse	35		1	
Clardy, Peter			1	
Coble, Neeley	55		1	1
Coffee, Rice	528			1
Coffey, Alex H.			1	2
Coffey, Henry B.	100		1	
Cross, Uriah	151.50		1	1
Claiborn, W. Coats	50		1	
Ditto, William	270			8
Dickinsin, Jas. W.	170			1
Dickinsin, Letitia C.	100			
Dalby, Polly	84			1
Davis, Henry				2
Dunnaway, Sam'l.			1	
Edwards, James			1	
Franklin, Peter	118			

NAME	DL	SL	WP	S
Frazer, Jane	107			6
Frazer, John			1	2
Foster, James	20		1	
Frizzell, A.D.			1	
Gordon, Sam'l B.			1	
Gunn, Judith	24			2
Gordon, Jonathan			1	
George, Redding	186		1	2
Garrett, Stephen			1	
Gilchrist, Daniel	1670			
Horsley, William S.	112			
Haggard, Richard			1	
Heathcoat, William			1	
Hooser, Josiah			1	
Humphries, Larkin			1	
Hooser, William Esq.	1350			11
Harman, George			1	1
Holder, Thomas			1	
Holland, James	30		1	
Hurt, John			1	
Hastings, John H.			1	
Holland, Thos. Sen.	150			7
Holt, Michael	200			
Harris, Moseby	100			
Hunter, David			1	
Harris, Newton			1	
Holt, Henry	100		1	1
Hooser, Wm.				
Wm. Dickinson				2
Isley, Benjamin			1	
Johnson, Manchester			1	
King, R.J.	229		1	
Kent, Thomas			1	
Lee, William			1	
Lee, Peter	200			1
Lacy, Ebenezer			1	
Lacy, Robert				
Meadows. William	107		1	
Meadows, Henderson			1	
Moore, Green M.	35		1	
Miller, James Jr.			1	
Mays, Lazarus			1	
Marbury, Josiah H.	127		1	
Moore, Carlos			1	
McGuire, William	30		1	1

NAME	DL	SL	WP	S
Meadows, John			1	
Miller, Arnold			1	
Morgan, James			1	
Mullins, William			1	
Miller, Peter	80			2
Moore, John A.	223.50		1	5
McGuire, John	200		1	
Manning, W.D.			1	
Meadows, Jane				2
Mullins, Matthew	140			
Mullins, James			1	
Moore, John	35			1
Norville, E.M.B.			1	1
Nelson, Moses	100			
Norville, David Sr.	708			9
Norville, David Jun.			1	
Norville, Thomas			1	
Norville, James			1	
Overton heirs by J. Young	400			
Pace, Richmond			1	
Patterson, Isaac			1	
Phillips, Samuel	300		1	4
Phillips, James			1	
Patterson, Elijah			1	
Patterson, William W.			1	
Rippy, John			1	
Robeson, Margaret	50			
Ragsdale, David A.B.			1	
Robeson, Nancy	81			
Ragsdale, Henry M.			1	
Sharpe, Anderson	170		1	
Sharp, William Jun.	65		1	
Snelling, Hugh	1041			10
Sharp, John	100		1	
Suiter, William E.	48		1	
Shofner, John	318			3
Shofner, Loton			1	
Snelling, Lemuel	150			1
Shofner, Austin	161		1	
Stokes, Kinchen	220			6
Stokes, John			1	
Sriver, Abraham	187		1	1
Sriver, John J.			1	
Sharp, William Esq.	250			1
Sutten, Samuel	100		1	1
Smith, Edward	93		1	

NAME	DL	SL	WP	S
Taylor, John	325			
Thorn, James				
Thornsberry, Lewis	86.50		1	
Thornberry, Levi			1	
Trammell, W.T.			1	
Waite, Magdalena	280			
Whiteside, Thos.				
by T.C. Whiteside	1200			
Wood, Zadock	50			
Warren, Rebecca	91			3
West, Isaac	100		1	
Wood, William G.	150		1	2
Wood, R.W.			1	
Younger, John B.	120			
Yell, Pearcy	100			
Young, Acton	76		1	
Young, James Esq.	716		1	5
Yell, Alex C.			1	1

BEDFORD COUNTY - DISTRICT NO. 4 or SALEM DISTRICT

Beginning at the northeast corner of District No. 3 where the west boundary line of Blounts 5000 acre tract crossed the branch on which Isaac Muse lives, thence to the cross lane near George Muse's, west of John Bradford's and north westwardly with the east boundary of Mrs. Merritt's lands and Col. Mitchell's land and with the lane between him and A. Caruther's - with the lane west of Anthony Thomas and with the lane between Thomas and Elijah Dyer's and north to the lane running between Robert Major's and E.A. Mosley's and north to the top of the first ridge, and with the main top of the said ridge to the Rutherford County line and westwardly with said county line to the middle of the Murfreesboro Road, thence south leaving Daniel Morris' on the west, thence to William Rogers' leavig him on the west, thence to Cader Murphree's, leaving him on the west, thence to Edward Freeman's, leaving him on the west, thence running between James Coop's and John Marsh's, thence southwardly leaving John Culver on the west, thence southwardly including Thos. A. Peacock, thence to include John Sutton's, Junior, thence eastwardly to include Q.T. Mayfield, D.S. Evans, Col. Arnold, thence to include W.P. Goodwin and Curry McGrew and to the beginning.

The place of holding elections, etc., the house of William Suggs, Wartrace. (Old Wartrace Post Office, north of Bell Buckle, on Liberty Pike).

NAME	DL	SL	WP	S
Armstrong, George C.	60		1	
Arnold, James	102.75			2
Arnold, Thomas			1	
Bingham, Saml. M.	312		1	
Bingham, William	207	69		
Bingham, William G.	92		1	
Biggars, Anderson			1	

168

NAME	DL	SL	WP	S
Bowling, James			1	
Bradford, Absalem			1	
Cage, Alford			1	
Cage, Wilson			1	
Cardwell, Richard W.	75			
Cardwell, Hosea G.			1	
Chaffine, Nathan	583		1	9
Clark, Robert	273			1
Clark, James H.	109.50		1	
Clay, Samuel	436		1	4
Coop, Horatio	134			
Creicy, Calvin	122.50		1	
Culver, John	99.50			
Cunningham, James T.	100			1
Davis, Elnathan	146		1	3
Davis, John	106		1	4
Daniel, Drury	67.50		1	
Elkins, William	100			4
Elkins, Robert			1	
Evans, David S.			1	
Elliott, Simon P.	36		1	
Elliott, Thomas			1	
Featherstone, Burrell	205.50			
Featherstone, Burrell	262.50		1	3
Frazer, Farwick	144		1	
Frizle, David			1	
Frizle, James	338		1	
Frizle, James M.				3
Frizle, Abram			1	
Fugate, Alfred D.	127.50		1	
Fugate, Benjamin	295		1	5
Fugate, Townsend	265			6
Giles, Milton Esq.	120		1	
Gilmore, Elizabeth	37			
Gilmore, heirs	74			
Goodwin, W.P.			1	
Gregerie heirs	69.50			
Haile, Thomas	30	70		
Haile, James			1	
Hill, George			1	
Hoover, Martin	540		1	3
Henslee, Franklin				
Harp, Jefferson			1	
Hatehill, Thomas			1	
Hartless, James			1	

NAME	DL	SL	WP	S
Hugle, Mary				2
Hays, Hezekiah	196			
Hays, Henry			1	
Hays, Hiram			1	
James, John			1	
James, Isaac	140		1	
Knott, Sarah	30			
Keith, John	78		1	
Lane, John			1	
Lynch, Arden			1	
Lynch, Gray	200		1	2
Loyd, Anderson			1	
Lynch, William			1	
Loyd, Lee			1	
Manly, Absalom	102			1
Manly, James			1	
Manly, Reuben	219.50			1
Manly, Nathan	1125		1	
Marr, Alfred			1	
Marr, John	100		1	
Marr, Nimrod			1	
Marr, Samuel			1	
Majors, R.H.				
for Richard Clardy heirs	200			2
Majors, Robert H.	270		1	3
Miller, Isaac J.	82.50		1	
Mitchel, Saml.	1674		1	18
Mitchel, Saml.	95.50			
Merritt, Benjn.	147.75		1	1
Mosley, Ed. A.	315		1	
Mosley, Ed. A.	62		1	10
Mosley, Thos. B.	177			
Mayfield, Q.T.	307		1	2
Mayfield, Q.T.	121			
Montgomery, Thomas			11	
Martin, Rachel	656.75			9
McCowan, William			1	
McElroy, Andr. M.			1	
McClure, John	166			3
McClure, Jno.				
for Cooper heirs	27			
McCrory, John	100		1	
McCrory, Hugh (Estate)	100			
McFearson, Vincent			1	
McGrew, Curry	100		1	
McGrew, William	227			5
Mash, John W. (Marsh)	50		1	
Mash, Stires A.	50		1	

NAME	DL	SL	WP	S
Narran, Francis E.			1	
Nelson, John				5
Norvile, John H.	122		1	2
Nichols, Thomas			1	
Nichols, Coleman			1	
Nicholes, Larry			1	
Norville, John Sen.	266.75		1	5
Norville, Henry J.H.			1	
Norville, Sefaney S.			1	
Norville, Jno. W.	52.50		1	1
Norville, William	1.125		1	
Norville, David	52.50			
Norville, John T.	51.50		1	
Norville, James			1	
Peacock, William J.			1	
Peacock, Tho. A.	135			
Peacock, John Jun.	258 (Est.)			
Peacock, Thomas J.			1	
Parker, Timothy	72.50		1	
Pitts, Isaac			1	
Powell, John			1	
Ragsdale, Baxter	40			2
Reid, Thomas C.			1	1
Robert, Alexander	115			
Rodgers, Drury	60			
Rushing, Thomas	125			
Rushing, Wilson E.	85		1	
Smithson, Benjamin W.	10		1	
Smith, Thomas	3.25 (Mill)			
Smith James	50		1	
Smalling, Elizabeth				1
Sutton, John Sen.	707	93		4
Sutton, John Jun.	531		1	3
Sutton, Charles F.	474		1	3
Stovall, J.A.			1	
Stovall, Saml. Jr.			1	
Sugg, Aquilla			1	
Sugg, Nehemiah	89.25		1	
Sugg, William Sen.	89.50			
Sugg, William Jun.			1	
Sugg, Micajah			1	
Sugg, Davidson			1	
Sugg, James			1	
Scraggs, Jas. & Matt	281		2	3
Thomas Winne	22		1	
Thomas, David	187			
Thomas, R.S.			1	
Thomas, William			1	

NAME	DL	SL	WP	S
Vaugh, Willis			1	2
Vancleave, Thomas	60		1	
Williams, William	80			
Waite, William	177.25		1	1
Warren, William	31		1	
Warren, John	200	46		
West, Joshua F.			1	
Wallis, Allen	260		1	
White, B.G.	2			
White, Augustus H.			1	
Whitworth, Samuel			1	

BEDFORD COUNTY - DISTRICT NO. 5 or TURNPIKE DISTRICT

Beginning where the middle Murfreesboro Road crosses the Rutherford County line, thence southwardly to include Daniel Morris and William Rodgers & Cader Murphree, leaving Ed Freeman on the west to include James Coop and John Culver, thence to Thos. A. Peacock's, leaving him on the east, thence to John Sutton's Jr., leaving him on the east, thence west to where the middle Murfreesboro Road crosses the dry fork of Falling Creek near Charles Cooper's old place, thence in a direct line to the north end of Biedleman's and the south end of Peacock's contracts of the Turnpike Road, thence west including Mysenhemmer's to the lower of Middleton Road, on the ridge north of Phifer's place at the graveyard, thence with said road to the Rutherford County line and with said county line eastwardly to the beginning.

Place of holding elections, etc., at John Deason's on the Turnpike Road. (Deason) (Nashville, Murfreesboro & Shelbyville Turnpike was chartered in 1831).

NAME	DL	SL	WP	S
Anderson, Samuel	469			
Anglin, David W.			1	
Blankinship, Benj.	89			2
Barber, Thomas	50			
Bigham, Oliver H.			1	
Brame, William C.	107		1	3
Bingham, Robert heirs of	631			
Barber, Ira	150		1	
Blakeley, William	127.50			2
Coop, George			1	
Clark, Walter	63.75		1	
Coop, John F.J.			1	
Claxton, Hiram			1	
Clinkingbeard, Robt.	96		1	
Cooper, Elizabeth	214			3
Cooper, Jonathan	40		1	1
Connel, John W.			1	

NAME	DL	SL	WP	S
Chumley, Jas. E.			1	
Coop, James	100		1	
Coop, Horatio			1	
Damron, Edmond	84		1	
Dearing, Wm. W.			1	
Dunlap, John C.			1	
Deason, Jesse			1	
Dillard, Joel	135			
Deason, Joel			1	
Deason, John	152		1	3
Edward, Amos				
Elley, Josiah	100.75		1	
Gabrille, ISaac			1	
Freeman, Alexander			1	
Freeman, Edward			1	
Guy, William	1260			18
Gibbs, E.F.	55.50		1	
Hart, Stephen	49		1	
Hamilton, Volney M.			1	
Hale, Green B.			1	
Hart, Thomas	43		1	
Hart, James	200		1	
Henley, Elmore			1	
Hoover, William	119		1	
Houston, William	833.50		1	12
Hutton, John	400			
John, James A.			1	1
John, Levi C.			1	
Kent, John	46			
Leah, Marcus H.	120.50		1	1
Lowrance, A.S.			1	
Lowrance, Alex			1	
Loyd, Joseph	116		1	
Lingo, J.C.			1	
Leverette, Johnson P.			1	
Lowrance, Joseph A.			1	
Lannons, William B.	50		1	
Lowrance, A.D.A.			1	
Murphree, William	460		2	4
Morris, Daniel			1	
McMinn, Robert	160		1	
McRee, Wm. C.	60			

NAME	DL	SL	WP	S
Moran, Samuel H.			1	
Morris, James			1	
McKinley by Jos. Steele, Agt.	130			
McKenzee by Wm. Houston, Agt.	833.33			
McRee, Margaret E.	229			
Means, Robert S.	180			
Nash, Travis C.				6
Nichols, Isaac			1	
Nailor, John	100			
Nash, James C.			1	
Nailor, Woodfin			1	
Owen, Ephraim			1	
Overcast, John			1	
Price, Mathis			1	3
Price, Thomas			1	
Price, Franklin B.			1	
Roane, William by Agt.	344		1	
Rogers, William			1	
Ricketts, James H.			1	
Rowland, Harrison S.			1	
Russell, William B.	50		1	
Robey, H.			1	
Stollard, Joseph P.	126		1	
Sharpe, Alexander			1	
Scott, Jesse	50		1	
Scott, Jeremiah			1	
Scott, John W.			1	
Smith, Meredith			1	
Springer, Josiah	100			
Searse, David	134			
Steele, Price C.	67.50			
Steele, Joseph	36			
Tucker, Jesse P.			1	
Tucker, David			1	
Wilkes, Miner	200		1	
Webb, Isiah	150		1	1
Work, Ann by Agt.	198			
Watson, D.			1	
Webb, William	98		1	
Walker, William	70		1	
Watson, Jesse	1000		1	
Work, May by Agt.	190		2	3
Williams, Phillip			1	

NAME	DL	SL	WP	S
Williams, Elijah			1	
Woodfin, Hannah by Agt.	200			1
Work, Alex. heirs				
by Guy in five tracts	1905			
by Guy for Tucker heirs in 9 tracts	1393			
Weaver, William			1	

BEDFORD COUNTY - DISTRICT NO. 6 or SULPHUR SPRINGS DISTRICT

Beginning at the McMillville Road at the corner of the fence where Thomas Norville once lived and west of the 3 mile post, thence northwardly with the Horse Mountain Ridge leaving Elijah Arnold on the east, thence north to John Sutton's Junior, leaving the Widow Cooper on the west, thence west with the line of District No. 5 to where the Middle Murfreesboro Road crosses the Hurricane of Dry Fork of Falling Creek, a small distance north of Charles Cooper's old place, thence to the end of Peacock's and Beidleman's contract on the Turnpike Road, and westerly leaving Mysenhammer on the north passing the corner of the said District No. 5 at the graveyard and to include John Orr's and the Widow McElreath's to Parch Corn Creek and with the same to its mouth into the Dry or Hurricane Fork of Falling Creek, thence to include Thomas Parson's old place and on to the mouth of Hurricane Creek above John Frazer's, thence up Duck River to a point east of George Earnhart's, thence east running east with the ridge north of the Widow Warner's and Asa Fonville's, leaving James and John Roberson on the south and to the end of a lane running east and west, north of John C. Coldwell's house, leaving him on the south, thence to the lane passing between John McQuistain's and S.S. Brown's, thence to the southwest corner of the Polk survey and with the south boundary of the Polk survey to the McMillville Road and withthe road to the beginning.

The place of holding the elections, etc., at Dr. Coleman Jackson's. (North of Shelbyville-Murfreesboro Highway at Peacock Lane).

NAME	DL	SL	WP	S
Arnold, Jesse			1	
Alexander, Nathl.	633.33			
Brown, Harris C.			1	
Brown, Solomon			1	
Brown, Spencer			1	
Brown, Henry	280		1	2
Brown, Benj.	500			5
Burns, Thos. P.	110		1	
Brothers, John			1	
Bell, S.A.	170		1	1
Burton, David	63.75		1	
Burton, Nathl.			1	
Brown, Shad. S.	280			8
Brown, G.W.			1	
Brown, William			1	
Clardy, Joseph				2
Coats, Payton H.	134.75		1	
Cooper, John B.	174		1	6

NAME	DL	SL	WP	S
Clardy, James	352			3
Claxton, Solomn	52.50		1	
Davidson, George	152			8
Davidson, H.M.			1	
Davidson, George N.			1	
Davidson, John P.			1	
Davidson, McClain A.			1	
Dwyer, Daniel	103			1
Dickson, Michael	115		1	
Eakin, John Esq.	588		1	10
Edwards, Thomas			1	
Epps, Daniel	100		1	
Farrar, John	225			1
Foster, Jacob	50			
Freeman, Hartwell			1	
Green, Joseph	100		1	2
Goodrum, A.J.			1	
Hester, James			1	
Hutton, John	200		1	
Haley, Wm. T.			1	
Hickman, Jos.			1	
Haley, Edward T.	80			
Knott, Blackman L.	145		1	
Knott, William S.			1	
Kelton, John	50		1	
Knott, John				1
Loyd, John			1	
Lindley, James			1	
Morton, Jacob	173		1	7
McClung, Isham			1	
Mallard, Thornton	57			
Mallard, Alfred			1	
Madox, Notley	280		1	3
Madox, Charles S.	89		1	2
McCuistion S.B.	107			
McCuistion, John C.	97			
McCuistion, Benj. F.			·1	
Mccuistion, Benjamin	287			4
McAdams, Amos	297.50			2
McAdams, Thomas			1	
McFarland, Thomas	216			1
McFarland, N.P.			1	2
McAdams, James			1	
Nowlin, James R.	230		1	3

NAME	DL	SL	WP	S
Nowlin, Thomas	118		1	1
Nowlin, Benjamin	214		1	
Orr, John	50		1	
Orr, David	112.50		1	4
Orr, Wm. N.	62		1	
Orr, L.B. for				
McElrath heirs	313			
Phillips, Matthew Esq.	114			4
Phillips, Garrett			1	1
Phifer, Martin	5000			
Phifer, Martin	1600 (Esq. Steele has this tract on his Revenue Book in District No. 8)			
Purdy, Thomas J.	234			3
Paulden, William			1	
Phillips, Jesse			1	
Roane, William	321			
Reach, Willie			1	
Rowland, A.	111			
Rushing, Elijah				
Schooler, Nathan H.	100			1
Stone, Willie B.			1	
Smith, Hardy S.			1	
Smith, Morgan	188		1	
Saunders, Alex.	198		1	
Stewart, Grayson	1		1	
Tullop, _____	87		1	1
Tune, John	164		1	
Tune, Thomas			1	
Tune, Demarcus	100		1	
Turpin, Matthew			1	
Taylor, Charles	23			
Winsett, Jarman	192			2
Wynne, Ridley B.	226		1	4
Winsett, Robert			1	
White, Moses			1	
Williams, Wallis			1	
Williams, Moses			1	
Watson, Nathan			1	
Watkins, Thos. G.	140		1	1
Watson, William	160			

BEDFORD COUNTY - DISTRICT NO. 7 or SHELBYVILLE DISTRICT

Beginning at L.W. Marbury's Mills, thence running north including the mills, to the southeast corner of Gilchrist tract of land and with his east boundary line passing the end of the lane of Levin Marshall's old place, and north to the south boundary of the Polk survey, thence west with the south boundary of said survey to the end of lans, passing between John McQuistain's and Shadrick A. Brown's, thence with J.C. Coldwell's lane including John and James Roberson's and with the ridge north of Asa Fonville's and Mrs. Warner's to a point on Duck River, east with Duck River to the mouth of Flat Creek, thence up said creek to the Fayetteville Road, thence east to include John B. Cummings' and to the extreme south bend of Duck River, south of A. Dobson's house, thence up the river to the place of beginning.

Place of holding the elections, etc., at the Court House in Shelbyville.

NAME	DL-Lot	SL	WP	S
Anderson, Jon, H.	100 & 104			
Arrington, R.S.			1	
Anderson, R.L.	40		1	2
Buffalow, W.E.			1	
Blakemore, J.A.			1	
Blanton, Wilkins			1	
Balch, Alfred	3			
Brame, Wm. B.M.			1	
Black, C.W.			1	
Barksdale, J.G.	14, 15, 35		1	2
Burnett, William	33. 34			11
Blessing, John	127.50		1	
Brown, Benjamin	100			
Burditt, Joel H.			1	
Burditt, Williamson R.			1	
Brassfield, Isiah C.			1	
Blessing, David			1	
Brown, William	56		1	1
Britain, James heirs	75.75, 54			
Brooks, Phillip			1	
Bowles, Samuel B.			1	
Buckingham, Nathaniel			1	3
Cooper, Abram	4		1	
Cannon, Minos	5		1	
Coldwell, John C.	565, 3		1	3
Coldwell's Nathl. heirs of	2			
Cannon, Newton	300, 4			11
Coats, S. Mrs.	160			3
Cunningham, Jeremiah			1	
Cannon, Clement	500, 2			6
Cannon, Charles L.			1	
Cook, Grenville			1	
Cummings, J.B.	167			2
Cochrane, Cha.			1	
Cummins, Edward	230			4
Cannon, Robert Gen.	205, 3		1	4

NAME	DL & Lot	SL	WP	S
Cannon & Marbury	4			
Coats, Wilson heirs	60.75			1
Cannon, R.T.	18			
Cannon, Minos heirs	54			
Cannon, Henry	15		1	1
Cowan, William G.			1	
Cathey, H.R.			1	
Coldwell, Ballard	76			
Deery, James	30, 2			1
Davis, Thomas	2.75, 2		1	
Davidson	1 part of 3	(1 carriage)	1	5
Dobson, A.	156, 1		1	7
Dobson, B.C.	1	(1 carriage)	1	1
Deery, William	2			
Davidson, Geo. for C.C. McGempsy part of 30				
Davidson, G. for C. Davidson				3
Epps, Irby			1	
Eakin, John	4			
Eakin, J. & S.	4			3
Eakin, Spencer	2			
Ervin, James	1			
Eakin, Alexander	3, 2		1	
Eakin, William			1	
Escue, Samuel	1		1	4
Elliott, William			1	
Frazier, John S.			1	
Frazier, Preston	5, 1			
Fonville, Asa	250			7
Fuqua, John J.			1	
Fogleman, G.W.	129		1	
Fulten, Shirly & Grown	1			
Frierson, E.J.	45, 2		1	3
Flack, Rufus K.			1	
Greer, Henry Harmon			1	
Gutteridge, Dawson			1	
Galbreath, John			1	
Galbreath, William			1	
Gilchrist, Malcom	50			
Green, James			1	
Gilchrist, William	44, 5	(1 carriage)		1
	8			
Greer, Thomas Sen.	8			
Gray, M.J.			1	
Green, W.D.	2		1	
Graham, J.H.			1	
Green, T.C. heirs	4			
Green, Isaac			1	

NAME	DL & Lot	SL	WP	S
Green, U. Jun.			1	
Green, U.M.			1	
Green, Wm. Sr.			1	
Gibson, Jesse	4, 3			
Gowan, Wm. B.			1	
Green, Joseph			1	
Hall, John & Watts heirs	1			
Holland, Thos. Jun.	24, 3	(1 carroiage)	1	1
Horsley, William	2			
Harris, J.W.			1	
Harris, Jo. M.	172		1	
Heaslett, Wm. Esq.	4.50			
Hamlin, Arthur			1	
Heath, John			1	
Hooker, John			1	
Harrison, R.P.	13		1	1
Hooker, Joseph			1	
Haggard, W.			1	
Jones, James W.			1	3
Jacobs, John	2			1
Jarrett, David	1			
Kincaid, Joseph	part of 30		2	1
Kincaid, Joseph & McGempsy	part of 30		2	
Knott, Thomas			1	
Kindell, John			1	
Kindell, William			1	
Lipscomb, Thomas			1	
Long, William F.	40	1 carriage	1	2
Lipscomb, Dabney			1	
Laird, John H.	4		1	
Matthews, Robt.			1	
Morton, Jacob	1			
Morgan, M.A.	1			
Morgan, John			1	
Morton, A.B. heirs	32, 54			2
McClintock, E.Mrs.	60			1
McClintock, Geo.			1	
McAdams, J.N.	300		1	
Marshall, Moses	50		1	
Morgan, Mrs. S.	2			
Marbury, L.W.	75		1	1
McChristian, John	224			5
Moore, Serad			1	
Martin, Jas. C.			1	
McCarty, W.			1	
Neil, John T.			1	

NAME	DL & Lot	SL	WP	S
Neeley, Samuel				2
Newson, Thomas			1	2
Newton, Geo. Rev.	5, 2			4
Newsom, Sterling	105			5
Norman, David			1	
Neadlett & others by Agt.	2			
Orr, L.B.			1	
Pettis, Thomas	118			
Patton, S.M.			1	
Philpot, C.T.			1	
Pinson, Jno. B.	25, 3		1	
Phillips, Thomas			1	
Parker, J.C. Rev.			1	
Proby, James			1	2
Robinson, James	285		1	4
Roberson, David			1	1
Ringstaff, Jno.	1, 1		1	
Robinson, John	377			4
Roberson, Joseph	250		1	
Ruth, G.W.			1	
Stewart. G.H.			1	
Spoffard & Tillamon	18			
Story & Frierson	50			
Story, James	4		1	3
Shapard, ___ part of 1			1	
Shanks, Charles			1	
Shanks, Jos. S.			1	
Sandford, Joseph			1	
Swift, Jacob			1	
Strong, Joseph C. Jun.	3		1	
Shapard, Booker	1			
Stephens, Augustine			1	
Sutton, M.B. heirs of 350	4			
Swift, Flower	200			3
Swift, Thomaa W.			1	
Schooler, Nathan H. part of 2				
Sutton, John Sen. part of 2				
Terry, Dorothy M.				2
Thompson, H.L.			1	
Temple, D.P. heirs	95			
Thompson, N. Sen.	200			6
Temple, Robert			1	
Thompson, Saml.	180			
Terry, Jas. R.			1	1
Temple, L.C.	356		1	8
Temple, Eliza				3

NAME	DL & Lot	SL	WP	S
Vanwee, Isaac			1	
Wilcox, J.R.	10		1	
Wortham, James	73		1	1
Wisner, W.H.			1	
Watterson, Wm. L.	2			
Wilhoite, William			1	
Whiteside, Thos. C.			1	
Wade, Martin F.			1	
Wilhoite, Willis W.	1		1	
Wilhoite,			1	
Williams, T.T.			1	
Wardlow, Hugh			1	
Walker, Robert			1	
Wade, Nathan	1		1	
Warner, Eunice Mrs.	250, 1			13
Watkins, Williw B.	3.50, 3		1	1
Wade, William	1			
Williams, D.M.			1	1
Whitney, James G.			1	
White, John R.			1	
Yancy, Kavanaugh				4
Young, Alexr.			1	
Young, Wm. A.	1		1	1
Yancy, A.W.			1	
Delinequents:				
Moffatt, Robert			1	
McClelland, Wm.			1	

NOTE: Some of the town lots are listed by lot number, others by the number of lots.

BEDFORD COUNTY - DISTRICT NO. 8 or FALLING CREEK

Beginning at the graveyard on the Middleton Road north of the Phifer place, the southwest corner of District No. 5, thence running north with the Middleton Road to the Section Line between Sections No. 6 and 7, in Range 4 known as the School Section, that crosses said road between the Widow Cooper's and Dudley Clanton's, thence west with said school section to the Nashville and with the road to the end of the lane between John Hudgins and John Rushing and west with the said lane to the Range line or west boundary of said school section, thence south with said line to where it crosses Duck River between the mouth of Falling Creek and James Turrentine's, thence up the river to the mouth of Hurricane Creek, thence to Thos. Parson's old place including Parsons and to the mouth of Parch Corn Creek and up the same leaving Mrs. McElrath's on the south to John Orr's, leaving him on the south and from there east to the beginning.

Elections to be held at the dwelling of Enoch Head's. (West of El Bethel).

NAME	DL	SL	WP	S
Allison, Robert	310			10
Allison, Robert	91.75	50		
Adcock, Henderson			1	
Brown, N.M.			1	
Boothe, John S.			1	
Boothe, J.B.			1	
Burrow, Wm.			1	
Barnhill, Benj.			1	
Burnett, Wm.	75			
Crutchfield, L.S.	106		1	
Claxton, John Jr.			1	
Claxton, John Sen.	59			
Claxton, George	50			
Claxton, James	266		1	
Clark, James D.	50		1	
Claxton, David			1	
Claxton, Jonathan H.			1	
Chester, John			1	
Cooper, Jonathan	60			
Claxton, Wesley			1	
Clark, Elbert			1	
Donaldson, Arthur	180.50			
Donaldson, William A.			1	
Damron, Sion	116		1	
Deason, Joel R.			1	
Daniel, Obadiah			1	
Deason, Gilbert			1	
Ervin, Adolphis	200			
Frizle, David	100			
Foster, Thomas			1	
Featherston, John			1	
Fisher, Jacob Esq.	100		1	
Fisher, John	100		1	3
Frazer. John			1	
Frizle, Nathld.			1	
Frizer, John Extor	100			
Frizele, John			1	
Farmer, Amos			1	
Gaither, Reason	85			
Gregory, Thomas	200			1
Gowan, Shadrick			1	
Gilley, Simeon	44.25			
Goodman, Cynthia	40			
Gregory, James			1	
Harris, George T.			1	
Hudgins, John			1	

NAME	DL	SL	WP	S
Head, Enoch	418		1	
Head, Enoch	35			
Haynes, Elizabeth	36			
Head, James W.			1	
Head, John A.			1	
Harris, John			1	
Harris, James	100			5
Hutson, William			1	
Harston, Robert			1	
Holden, Dennis, Guard.	112			
Harris, Hiram	32.25		1	
Larimore, John	80		1	
Leverett, Jas. W.			1	
Lively, James			1	
Morris, Austin P.			1	
Morgan, John	49		1	
Meadows, E. Jr.	100		1	
Meadows, Henderson			1	
Moore, Samuel H.			1	
McClintock, John			1	
Morgan, Ridley			1	
Moxfred, Hiram	54			
McLoy, William	73.50		1	
Nichols, Nathan	145			
Nichols, Alfred				1
Neeley, James G.	175			1
Nichols, Jeremmiah B.	106			1
Nash, Travis C.	429			
Omohundro, James Y.				1
Parker, Elizabeth	190			
Pressgrove, Andrew	200			
Presgrove, William			1	
Parsons, George W.	121		1	
Parsons, Abijah			1	
Parkason, Joab	31.50		1	
Parkason, Alfred	31.25		1	
Parsons, Michael H.			1	
Phifer, Martin	1600 (this tract listed in the 6th District)			
Rackley, Jackson	17		1	
Steele, Carlos D.	180		1	
Springer, Zadock			1	
Steele, John P.	136		1	
Springer, Dennis	268		1	
Saunders, George	51		1	
Steele, Joseph	240			2
Steele, Joseph	69.50			

NAME	DL	SL	WP	S
Saunders, Nathan	20			
Saunders, Susannah	46			
Saunders, John			1	
Steele, Wilson heirs	168		1	
Steele, Price C.	352		1	
Springer, N.W.	45			
Turrentine, Wilson	193.75		1	2
Thompson, Christiana	204	19		7
Thompson, John	69.50			
Turrentine, Charles	150		1	
Willes, William N.	100		1	
Woods, James			1	
Wilson, James	40		1	1
Whelman, Edward	200		1	1
Walbanks, Bazel			1	
Wilson, H.S.			1	
Wheeler, Thomas	150		1	
Wheeler, William			1	
Wheeler, Martin			1	
Wilson, Mary	69.50			
Wilson, Ebenezer	65			
Wilson, Fordic	65		1	
Wilson, Fordic	40			
Wilson, Jas. S.	69			
Wood, John	149		1	1
Wood, John				
Wheeler, ___	300			4

BEDFORD COUNTY - DISTRICT NO. 9

Beginning on the north east corner of District No. 8, where the section line crosses said road between Mrs. Cooper's and Springer's, thence west with said section line to the Nashville Road and with the same to end of the lane between John Hudgens and John Rushing, thence west to Range Line or corner of District No. 8, thence north including Abel Rushing, striking the Nashville Road at the end of the lane west of Isaiah Atkinson's and with the road to Weakley Creek, thence up the creek to the road leading from Middleton to Byler's, thence north leaving Major Thomas Black on the west, thence north to the Williamson County line, at a large pond, east of Barnaby Haley's, east and north with Williamson County to the Rutherford County line and with said county line eastwardly to the Middleton Road and with said road to the beginning.

Elections to be held at the house of Thomas Powell's. (Near Rutherford County, line, Midland Road).

NAME	DL	SL	WP	S
Alexander, James	100	12	1	
Adcock, Harmon			1	
Alford, John C.			1	
Allen, William R.	77		1	

NAME	DL	SL	WP	S
Atkinson, Josiah	106		1	1
Anglin, Zephat	145		1	
Bette, Rebecca	84			1
Barnes, D.J.			1	
Batte, Robt. C.	85	68	1	1
Blythe, Andrew			1	
Bullion, John			1	
Berryman, William			1	
Barnes, Gabriel				1
Bulling, Solomon			1	
Batte, Frederick	140		1	
Bandy, Richard	494		1	2
Callen, Thomas	340	68		2
Cooper, John L. Esq.	87	1 carriage	1	4
Clark, Moses B.			1	
Clanton, Dudley			1	
Cousey, Charles	133		?	
Crutchfield, Gideon	85		1	
Clark, James K.			1	
Culberhouse, Thomas	107			
Culberhouse, Moses	73		1	
Culberhouse, Jesse			1	
Culberhouse, Jeremiah	73		1	1
Coursey, William	18	82	1	
Cooper, Belinda	143			
Dunn, William	200			
Dunlap, John C.			1	
Dwiggins, Daniel	250		1	
Damron, James			1	
Dunn, John	79	21	1	
Dudley, C.S.			1	
Evans, Henry			1	
Frizle, Nathan			1	
Foster, James	235		1	1
Guest, William			1	
Guest, Moses	150			
Guy, Ann	175			3
Grininage, Wm. M.			1	1
Grininage, John R.			1	
Garner, Hezekiah			1	
Hosking, John E.	139		1	
Harris, James	162		1	
Hutton, John W.	45		1	
Haggard, Wm.			1	
Housten, Wm.	311			

NAME	DL	SL	WP	S
Haley, JAmes	122		1	
Haley, Charles	65		1	
Harrison, Edward C.			1	
Hite, Nancy	52			
Hoover, Christopher	50			
Harrison, Wm. H.	62	25	1	1
Harris, Hiram	104			
Hill, Spencer			1	
Hooper, Elisha M.	89			
Jones, George	140		1	
Jones, Robert T.P.	114		1	1
Jackson, John	184		1	2
Jordan, Wm. B.	314		1	
Johnson, Thomas	48			
Lane, Isham H.	196	22	1	1
Lane, Drury	64		1	
Lane, H.G. Esq.	50		1	1
Low, Gabriel	140		1	
Landers, Richard	50		1	
Landers, Elijah			1	
Landers, Frances			1	
Landers, George T.	81			3
Landers, Alexander			1	
Landers, Rowland			1	
Landers, Thos. G.			1	
Landers, George S.	140			
Landers, Anderson	76		1	
Locke, Martha A.	190			
Lamb, Barram			1	
Lile, Jackson	257			1
Leathers, William	40			
Lovorn, Edmund C.			1	
Lane, John R.	86		1	1
McLean, Eph B.	42			
McLean, Judiah A.	100		1	
McLean, Josiah T.	140		1	
McLean, David V.		82		
McGowan, James	205			3
McGowan, Jas.			1	
McGowan, William			1	
Morrison, Jas. W.	55		1	
Nance, Richard	75		1	
Primrose, Thomas	175		1	
Primrose, William	105		1	
Powell, Thos. P.	231		1	4
Presgrove, Jno. M.	100		1	
Pinkerton, Hugh	132		1	

NAME	DL	SL	WP	S
Powell, Robert	85			3
Parkson, Richd.	111		1	
Puckett, William S.	84		1	1
Puckett, Elam	75		1	
Primrose, Geo. W.			1	
Rushing, Jno.	303		1	
Rushing, Abel			1	
Rucker, Jesse			1	
Rankin, Thos. C.	367		1	1
Rucker, William	65		1	
Rodgers, Erwin		74	1	
Rucker, Elliott	335			1
Stovall, Jackson W.			1	
Spence, Rencher	100		1	
Steel, Volney H.	311		1	1
Spruce, Phillip			1	
Sims, Swepson	200		1	3
Simpson, John W.	50		1	
Smitherman, Sarah	80	50		
Smitherman, Thos.			1	
Smothers, James	75		1	
Turner, Littleberry			1	
Taylor, Wm. G.	122		1	
Taylor, Robert	104		1	
Tucker, Kinchen	100		1	
Tarpley, Edward	180			
Thompson, L.C.	150			
Wheeler, America			1	
Webb, Bushrod	200	35		4
Watkins, John M.			1	
Webb, John A.	70		1	4
Wheelhouse, Dennis			1	1
Woods, Edmond	98		1	
Wade, William			1	
Walls, Anderson			1	
Wade, Benjamin	95			
Wallace, Evan	380		1	
Wade, Maslin			1	
Wheeler, Nathan	50			
Work, Alexander	146			
Work, Alexander	226			
Williams, William	187		1	

BEDFORD COUNTY - DISTRICT NO. 10

Beginning on the Nashville Road, at the end of the lane west of Isaiah Atkinson's house, the northeast corner of District No. 11, thence running north with said road to Weakley's Creek, thence up the creek to the road leading from Middleton to Byler's, thence to include Major Thomas Black and north to Williamson County line at a large pond east of Barnaby Haley's, thence west with the Williamson County line to the line run by George Cotner, called the New County Line, cornering near Throneberry, thence south with the New County Line to a point due east of Martin Adam's house, thence east to Jonas Sykes' lane, leaving John Ray on the south and with Sykes' lane and east to the north boundary of Thomas Allison's lands and with same east leaving Adam Strator on the south and to the north west corner of the old Lock Survey and with the north boundary of said survey to the beginning.

Place of holding elections, etc., at the Widow Byler's. (Now Rover).

NAME	DL	SL	WP	S
Atkinson, Jas. M.			1	
Atkinson, Jesse	130			
Arnold, Joseph A.	150	12		1
Arnold, John W.	50		1	
Arnold, Elisha	48		1	
Arnold, Joseph			1	
Adams, William			1	
Allison, William	951			12
Allison, Robt. Jun.	96			
Atkinson, Wm.			1	
Bullock, William			1	
Briant, David O.	100			
Briant, Frederick O.			1	
Byler, John	192		1	
Byler, James J.			1	
Briant, David P.			1	
Benford, Anderson A.			1	
Bird, Spirell			1	
Byler, Nancy	274	16		1
Brown, Willliam			1	
Braden, James			1	
Brandon, Charles	283	40		
Brandon, Elias			1	
Black, Thomas	352	6	1	1
Bullock, Olive	70		1	
Blackburn, Elijah	43	60		
Blackburn, Leroy			1	
Biggers, James	295		1	
Balch, Alfred	424			
Boyce, Jno.	50		1	
Barringer, D.L. Genl.	500			
Balls, Henry	192			
Blackburn, William			1	
Carlton, Wm. C.			1	
Call, Uriah			1	
Corbitt, Meredith			1	
Carlton, Thos. B.			1	

NAME	DL	SL	WP	S
Calhoun, J.P.			1	
Cox, Caleb	175		1	
Corbitt, Richard			1	
Cooper, Joel			1	
Cooper, Dayton	53		1	
Cook, William C.			1	
Carlton, Thomas	212	34	1	2
Coats, Charles	2		1	
Carlton, Crawford	82		1	
Clements, Willis			1	
Cooper, Job	38			
Cooper, John	263			
Cooper,			1	
Cathey, James			1	
Corbett, William	74		1	
Cheatham, Thomas	150		1	4
Clinton, heirs of J.	200			
Chambers, Jno. A.	63		1	
Clark, George			1	1
Davis, J.M.	132			
Denny, Lucy	80			
Demet, Charley			1	
Dixon, Jno.		40	1	
Dixon, Harry			1	
Daisey, Jasper	260			1
Daisey, Kindall			1	
Dawson, Nelson			1	
Dowson, Robert			1	
Deason, William			1	
Eperson, L.B.			1	
Eperson, William	140		1	
Elmore, William	90		1	
Fann, Charles			1	
Freymon, Jno. S.	152		1	
Fulmore, Andrew J.			1	
Fulmore, George			1	
Garrett, James	300			6
Gault, Renwick A.			1	
Gault, Hugh M.	120		1	
Hooper, George			1	
Haley, Barnaba	30	15		
Haile, Meshack			1	
Heathe, Lewis Rev.			1	
Hooper, Willliam			1	
Haile, Joel			1	
Hays, Wm. T.			1	
Hill, William D.	74		1	

NAME	DL	SL	WP	S
Hoskins, James	45	12	1	
Hoskins, Alfred			1	
Hobbs, John			1	
Harris, Jno. S.	140	12		
Hendricks, Elisha		68		
Harris, Jno. T.	100			
Halbrooks, Jno.			1	
Hooper, James	186			3
Johnson, Saml.			1	1
Jackson, Saml.	100		1	
John, J. heirs	350			
Jackson, Gilliam			1	
Lannders, Wm.			1	
Lile, James H.			1	
Lytle, William	108		1	
Lytle, Abel	174		1	
Lawrence, James			1	
Morrison, Jno.	100			
Morrison, Zenor C.			1	
McCall, Thomas	174			
Maxwell, Anna	75			
Marchant, Willie			1	
McCuistion, Thos.	60		1	
Moore, Jennings	100		1	
Mankins, James	124		1	
McLean, Vance			1	
Moore, J.A.			1	
McCuistion, Robt.	307			
Nunn, Thomas	400		1	1
Nunn, Wm. R.	150			
Osteen, Benjamin			1	
Osteen, Edward	86		1	
Putman, Michal			1	
Pinkerton, Wm.			1	
Phillips, Ivey	86		1	
Pope, Quinn			1	
Pope, Hardy	90			2
Pinkerton, Wm. Sen.	45			
Poplin, Wm.	80			
Pounds, Wm.			1	
Phillips, Charlott	89			2
Perry, Willie Esq.	36		1	4
Rushing, Keziah	45			1
Ray, John	200			
Ransom, Alford	180		1	2

NAME	DL	SL	WP	S
Rucker, James	175			
Rushing, E.D.	100		1	
Rodgers, Thos. D.			1	
Stem, Asa	50	30	1	
Simpson, Jno. W.	83			
Simpson, _____	100			
Smith, James	133	40		
Stuckart, Absalom	63		1	
Sherwood, Hugh	84		1	
Stephenson, Geo. W.	96		1	
Stratten, William			1	
Smith, James P.	50		1	
Simar, John			1	
Shuffield, Arthur	100			
Thomason, Wm. T.	110		1	
Taylor, Stephen	90		1	1
Terry, Vincent			1	
Thompson, James			1	
Taylor, William	145		1	
Vickory, Andw.	100		1	
Vickory, Jonathan			1	
Wilson, Joseph			1	
Ward, Spias			1	
Wilson, Thomas	61			
Williams, Alfred			1	
Winters, Joh. W.			1	
Walls, John			1	
Ward, Ezekiel			1	
Whitehead, Mansfield	400		1	2
Winsett, Elijah D.			1	
Wheeler, Smauel	79		1	
Wheeler, Jesse	68		1	
Ward, Burwell	268			2

BEDFORD COUNTY - DISTRICT NO. 11

Beginning where the School Section or Range Line crosses Duck River below the mouth of Fall Creek and above James Turrentine's the lower corner of District No. 8, thence north with the said Range Line to the corner of the section westwardly from Esq. Evan Harris, thence to the southwest corner of the 9th District, thence north leaving Abel Rushing's on the east, and to the southeast corner of the 10th District on the Nashville Road, at the end of a lane west of Isiah Atkinson's house, thence west with the old Lock Survey to the northwest corner, thence to include Adam Strator and to Thomas Allison's northeast corner and west with his lands and to the end of Jonas Sykes' land and west to a point east of Martin Adams' house including John Ray on the New County Line run by Cotner, thence south with said New County Line to Duck River, thence up the river to the beginning.

Place of holding elections, etc., (District No. 11), at the Widow Wilson"s or Walnut Grove. (2 1/2 miles south of Unionville).

NAME	DL	SL	WP	S
Allison, Kimbro	633	285	1	3
Allison, James P.	659		1	5
Anderson, William	85		1	2
Anderson, Richard			1	
Anderson, Joseph	58		1	
Anderson, David	146			3
Allison, Thomas	350			5
Allison, Robt. J.			1	
Allison, Robt. heirs of	200			
Allison, Robt. Sen.	225			
Armstrong, William heirs	160			
Brown, Tho. E.	(1 Lot)		1	
Blanton, Meredith	16	60	1	
Bell, James A.			1	
Boyd, Eli			1	
Bulling, Wm.			1	
Barkley, heirs	240			
Brintle, Solomon			1	
Covington, Lavisa	64			1
Clark, Henry			1	
Capley, George			1	
Capley, David			1	
Capley, Martin			1	
Crowell, Saml.	124	62	1	
Crowell, Samuel[s]			1	
Crowell, Benjamin			1	
Crowel, William			1	
Capley, Peter Senr.	159			
Clardy, Richardson	100			
Cook, Joseph			1	
Cook, John			1	
Cook, Jefferson			1	
Church, Robert			1	
Carlton, William	58 (3 Lots)		1	
Capley, John	150		1	
Crowell, Joshua			1	
Dickins, Daniel			1	
Dickins, Stephen			1	
Davis, Jonah G.			1	
Dollar, Reuben			1	
Doud, Charles			1	
Daniel Graves heirs	400			
Eakin, John			1	
Fain, Richd.	150.75		1	

NAME	DL	SL	WP	S
Fain, William	100		1	
Fain, John			1	
Farmer, Margaret	116			
Farmer, John			1	
Farmer, Benjamin			1	
Garner, John			1	
Horton, Elijah			1	
Hineman, Jonathan			1	
Hoover, Christopher	50			
Henley, John J.			1	
Jackson, John Sen.	78			
Jackson, Avery			1	
Jeffress, Thos. B.			1	3
Kimmery, Thomas	(1 Lot)		1	
Keele, David	63		1	
Keener, William			1	
Locke, Matthew P.	170.50			
Locke, James H.	80			
Locke, Wm. H.	88.50			
Lowrence, Merrett				
Lentz, John T.	388.75		1	
Lile & Bond by				
Peter Singleton, Agt.	554		1	
Locke, Robt. W.	90		1	
Landers, Henry			1	
Lillard, A.F.			1	
Lenior, Wm. by J. Harris	1500			
Mayfield, Haram			1	
Miller, Adam	50			
Marian, John F. heirs	40			
Moon, John P.	34		1	
Martindale, Thomas			1	
Morris, Jesse			1	
Mitchell, Richd.			1	
McDaniel, Hiram			1	
Moon, Alex. B.	477		1	5
Mayfield, Jno. W.			1	5
Mayfield, Abraham	611			8
Mangum, Samuel			1	
Nichols, Jackson	141	1		
Owens, Travis W.	38.50		1	
Oglevie, William	400	32		2
Oglevie, James	124			2

NAME	DL	SL	WP	S
Prince, Hosea			1	
Prince, Thomas			1	
Prince, Cary	200		1	
Putman, Hiram	67		1	
Prince, Ranson			1	
Prince, Lytleton			1	
Prince, Miles			1	
Pollock, Jno. M.			1	
Pounds, John	30			
Putman, Danl.	154		1	2
Pinkston, Wm. heirs of	232			
Prince, Simeon			1	
Prince, Asa			1	
Rogers, Elijah			1	
Rodgers, John M.			1	
Ray, Thomas	106		1	2
Rodgers, David R.	17.50		1	
Rodgers, John	113			
Rodgers, Bedford			1	
Rodgers, James	94			
Rodgers, Saml.			1	
Rushing, Asa	52		1	
Reeves, Absalum	751			
Ray, David	60		1	
Reynolds, Ezekiel	131			
Reynolds, John	56			
Rodgers, Joseph	58		1	
Ray, Robt.	332		1	12
Ray, Sarah	80			
Shearin, Wm. heirs of	778.50			
Smith, Jno. E.	1000		1	7
Shaw, William M.	81	51	1	
Shaw, John		71		
Smith, George Sen.	213			4
Smith, George Jun.	1000		1	3
Shearin, Matthew			1	1
Saxon, Benjamin			1	
Smith, Amon			1	
Stong, Thomas			1	
Smith, Barry			1	
Sykes, Jonas	102		1	
Strator, Adam	45	68		
Short, William	344		1	3
Sugg, Edmund				1
Turrentine, James Sen.	112			
Turrentine, Felix	55		1	
Tilford, David			1	
Thompson, Calvin	52			

NAME	DL	SL	WP	S
Thompson, Jas. Esq.	145	25	1	5
Thompson, John Sen.	174	30		5
Thompson, & Sims		315		
Thompson, Pinckney H.	25	45	1	
Thompson, Jas. P.		100	1	
Turrentine, Archelaus	1000		1	7
Tucker, Wm. E.	100		1	2
Thompson, Jos. heirs of	77			2
Thompson, Jno. A.	25		1	1
Thompson, Martha				2
Thompson, Elizabeth	106			
Turrentine, James Jun.	200		1	5
Vincent, Jacob			1	
Wade, William	99		1	1
Wade, Charles E.			1	
Wilson, Nancy	125			4
Wilson, William			1	1
Wilson, Augustine			1	
Wilson, John C.	120		1	
White, Thomas			1	
Wood, Jonathan	79			1
Wood, Jno. P.			1	
Wood, Jas. B.			1	
Walker, James	(1 Lot)		1	
Wadley, Geo. W.	100		1	
Willliams, Joseph	254		1	1
Wortham, William	340.75	50		3
Wortham, Edward			1	

BEDFORD COUNTY - DISTRICT NO. 12

Beginning where the line run by Cotner crosses Duck River, a short distance below Esq. Kimmon's late residence, thence north with said line to the corner made by Cotner on the Williamson County line near Mr. Throneberry's, thence west with the Williamson County line to a point near the Widow Rigg's being the corner of the companies commanded by Captain Holt and Captain Marshall, thence southwardly with the dividing line of said companies to the corner of Captain Rainey's and Captain Wilson's companies, and with line of said companies to the old Warner Road on Duck River, thence up the river to the place of beginning.

Place of holding elections, etx., at the house of Samuel Vest's. (Now Marshall County).

NAME	DL	SL	WP	S
Atkinson, Nancy	183			2
Adams, Martin	275			1
Alexander, Wm.			1	
Alford, Wm. H.	140		1	
Alexander, David			1	

NAME	DL	SL	WP	S
Billington, Samuel			1	
Briant, Jeremiah			1	
Braden, Saml.			1	
Briant, John P.			1	
Bruce, Geo. W.			1	
Ballard, Baxter			1	
Brunce, John P.	2.25		1	
Billington, Elias	117		1	
Baker, William			1	
Burns, Cunningham			1	
Cathey, George	100		1	2
Collins, Augustine			1	
Clark, Joseph			1	
Corbitt, Needham			1	
Collier, William	50		1	
Caruthers, Robert	50			2
Crockett, Samuel	55		1	
Cook, Henry	300			
Dooley, Andrew J.			1	
Davidson, John D.			1	
Davis, Saml.			1	
Davis, Hillard			1	
Davour, Jackson C.	25		1	
Ezell, Joseph D.	100		1	1
Edmonds, Bartlett			1	
Fleming, Wm. A.			1	
Fulten, James C.	102			1
Forrest, Nathan heirs	100			
Favour, Thos. B.	105		1	
Faver, Jas. E.	100		1	
Falwell, Elisha	100			
Falwell, John			1	
Falwell, Moses	75		1	
Falwell, William	65		1	
Forrest, Jonathan	100		1	
Forrest, James N.			1	
Faver, William B.	16		1	
Forrest, Brittain H.			1	
Gibson, Nathan			1	
Graves, Samuel	140			
Graves, Aaron W.			1	1
Garret, Darrington	129		1	1
Gilberth, Robert			1	
Gambill, Bradley K.	125		1	
Graves, James N.			1	
Graham, David B.			1	
Graham, Richard	168			1

NAME	DL	SL	WP	S
Good, John			1	
Hamilton, Frances	171		1	
Hughes, Madison R.	634		1	10
Hughes, Reuben	210		1	7
Hughs, Joseph			1	
Hart, Calvin R.			1	
Henley, John	50		1	
Higgs, Susannah	85			
Henley, Micjah			1	
Harris, Andrew	66		1	
Haddock, John G.	96		1	1
Hall, Jno. G.	98.50		1	
Hunter, Thos. O.	5			
Henley, William	60		1	
Hamilton, Wm.			1	
Haddock, Thos. B.	106		1	
Jones, William S.	61			1
Joice, James	100			
Jones, Presley	75		1	
Keys, Hugh	75			
Lile & Bond	800			
Lee, John	78			1
Ledbetter, Jesse M.			1	
Ledbetter, William	183			2
Ledbetter, Madison			1	
Little, John L.			1	
Little, William	50		1	1
Lavender, Bird B.	123		1	
Little, John	176.50		1	
Long, Benjamin			1	
Little, Daniel	50		1	
Laws, John			1	
Miller, Adam	115			
Miller, Thos. C.H.	80		1	2
McLean, Ephraim H.	295		1	3
Marshall, Joseph	51		1	2
Moseley, Jas. heirs	30			
Minton, Zachariah	100		1	
Mayberry, Geo.			1	
Mayberry, Joseph			1	
Montgomery, John A.			1	
Martin, Henry	83		1	
Montgomery, Stewart			1	
Montgomery, William			1	
Mabin, Azariah			1	
Mabin, William			1	
Marshall, Stephen			1	

NAME	DL	SL	WP	S
Manier, Phillip	100			
Manier, John A.	36.50		1	
Murdock, Hiram	153		1	1
Morris, Willis J.			1	
Marshall, Robert E.			1	
Marshall, Peter W.			1	
Mayfield, Wm. S.	4		1	1
Mangum, James			1	
Neese, Susannah	156			1
Nickens, Calvin	50		1	
Nickens, Samuel	88		1	
Nickens, Andrew			1	
Nickens, Lamb			1	
Oglevie, Jason W.	335		1	1
Oakley, Stanford T.			1	
Price, Jno. H.	80		1	
Prince, Elijah			1	
Prince, Owen			1	
Patterson, Fitzeller			1	
Patterson, Robert Sen.	367.50			1
Patterson, Housten			1	
Patterson, Robert Jun.			1	
Perry, Isaac			1	
Patterson, Robt.S.	100		1	
Pannell, L.D.			1	
Prince, Joshua			1	
Putman, James W.			1	
Patterson, Andrew	400			6
Patterson, Andrew	70			
Patterson, Wm. L.	.50		1	
Patten, Elisha A.	2		1	1
Putman, Bazil			1	
Riggs, James M.	1		1	
Roberts, Bright heirs of	130			
Roberts, John H.	2		1	1
Rickman, John A.			1	
Rickman, Jno.	150			3
Rickman, Lawson			1	
Rumsey, James	175		1	
Reynolds, John			1	
Rickman, Len A.			1	
Rodgers, George	75		1	1
Rodgers, Peter	75		1	
Ramsey, Robert			1	
Scudder, Elizabeth S.	315			
Scudder, Elizabeth	600			
Shuffield, John			1	1

NAME	DL	SL	WP	S
Spears, Saml. F.	68			
Shuffield, Arthur heirs	150			3
Spears, Saml. T.				
Shuffield, Jason B.	643			2
Scott, Elias			1	
Scott, Jno.	60			
Scott, James			1	
Smith, Andrew			1	
Stanley, John			1	
Smith, Benjamin	63			1
Stegall, Ralph	175		1	3
Stephens, Redding			1	
Shuffield, John A.			1	
Scott, George R.	168		1	4
Siles, Mary	170			2
Sims, Walter	420			
Sims, Walter	150			
Turner, William			1	
Thornborough, Allen	50		1	
Taylor, James	96		1	
Terry, Vincent S.			1	
Terry, Henry B.	250		1	1
Vest, Samuel	146		1	1
Wilson, Joseph W.	50		1	
Whitworth, B.F.			1	
Whitworth, Edw.	296			5
Wilson, Saml.	240			
Wilson, John	320			
Wilson, Samuel	100		1	
White, 618				4
Williams, James	856			7
Wall, David	40		1	
Westmoreland, Robt.			1	
Warren, William 112				4
Wilson, Josiah	45			
Wilhoite, Pearce	107			
Wilson, Jas. C. heirs	263			
Warrener, Joseph			1	
Wilson, James heirs	696			
Winston, Wm. D.			1	
Wilson, Robt. heirs of	21			
Wilson, Jno. H.	392		1	1
Wilson, Moses	133			1
Wilson, James	126			2
Wilson, Robert			1	
Walker, James	147.50		1	

BEDFORD COUNTY - DISTRICT NO. 13

Beginning at Warner's old ford on Duck River, the lower corner of District No. 12, thence running northwardly with the company lines between Capt. Rainey's and Capt. Wilson's companies and between Capt. Holt's and Marshall's companies to the Williamson County line near Widow Rigg's, thence west with Williamson County to the northeast corner of Maury County, thence south with the Maury County line to Duck River, thence up the river to the beginning.

Place of holding elections, etx., at the residence of James Patterson's, in the forks of Caney Spring Creek. (Now Marshall County).

NAME	DL	SL	WP	S
Atkins, Thomas			1	
Atkinson, John			1	
Atkinson, Nancy	238			
Allen, George H.	248	20		2
Aldridge, Flower	160		1	
Bullock, Leonard	175		1	
Butler, John G.			1	
Butler, B.D.			1	
Brittain, S.B.			1	
Bedwell, ___			1	
Boyd, Aaron	225			
Boyd, Aaron	108		1	
Boyd, J.B.	17.75		1	1
Boyd, Rebecca	200			2
Brittain, Thomas			1	
Boyd, John			1	
Billington, James	80			
Billington, James	90			
Bass, John			1	
Bass, Willis			1	
Billington, Ezekiel	231			2
Bankston, Elliott			1	
Burns, John	532			6
Braden, William			1	
Bedwell, Archibald	350		1	
Beck, A.H.			1	
Bass, Lemuel	110	108	1	
Beck, Jeffrey	250		1	5
Brittain, Joseph H.	750			
Brittain, Joseph	120		1	5
Bass, James Sen.	188	67		
Carrington, C.D.			1	
Caps, Daniel	2		1	
Calton, Howard	78.50		1	
Calhoun, George	181			
Calhoun, J.J.	130		1	
Cathey, Charles			1	
Cook, Marcellus	172		1	1

NAME	DL	SL	WP	S
Cathey, James			1	
Calton, Lewis			1	
Chadwell, David			1	
Cathey, John Sen.	284			
Cathey, John Sen.	20			3
Cathey, John Jun.	60		1	
Christman, David		160		
Carter, J. Carter	65		1	
Cherry, Jane	116			
Dowdy, William	191		1	
Doss, Phillip			1	
Doxey, Daniel			1	
Dixon, Josiah	212		1	
Dunnagin, Shad.	188			
Dunnagin, Shad.	166		1	2
Ezell, Jepthah	131.50		1	
Ellington, D.T.			1	1
Ezell, Calvin			1	
Fergusen, John F.	709		1	2
Fisher, Reuben	69.25		1	
Gillam, Harrison			1	
Gonan, Jacob	30		1	
Greer, Edmund			1	
Gammill, Moses	147		1	
Gilman, Hariah J.	62.50		1	
Holt, John H.	576.50		1	2
Holt, Jno. H. Guard.				
for H.F. Fulton	141			
and for J.B. Fulton	149			
Harris, Ephraim	217		1	
Hatchell, Willis			1	
Hill, William			1	
Hogg, J.F.			1	
Houston, William			1	
Hall, Thomas			1	
Hall, James			1	
Howard, William			1	
James, Rylie			1	
Jacob, Solomon			1	
Kirk, E.F.			1	
Lovins, P.H.			1	
Laird, Agnes	96			
Lavender, Charles	39.50			1
Laird, John	10	226		

NAME	DL	SL	WP	S
Lavender, B.B.	81			
Lavender, John	78.50		1	
Manier, J.W.	174			3
McClellan, Hugh			1	
McClellan, S.K.			1	
Murdock, Thomas Sen.	353	51		6
Murdock, Thomas Jun.				
McCall, Samuel	87			
Morris, Henry				
May, George	328			
Morton, John	150			2
Moses, Phillip	73		1	
Martin, P.D.			1	
McCall, Thomas	100			
Neil, C.R.			1	1
Neatherly, John			1	
Neil, William	470			4
Neil, W.L.			1	
Neil, J.H.S.			1	
Neil, John C.			1	
Neatherly, Robert			1	
Neatherly, William			1	
Oglevie, Archibald	100		1	
Oglevie, Elizabeth				1
Patton, Jane	240			1
Patterson, James	55		1	
Patterson, Jno.			1	
Patterson, James Sen.	214			1
Patterson, John	240		1	1
Patterson, James	122.50	130		
Patterson, George				
Powell, Thomas	310			6
Rosson, Joseph	443	67	1	2
Rosson, Jos. Agt for Kivet	35			
Rosson, Jos. Guardian				
Kivet heirs	129			
Rosson, Osburn			1	
Rainey, Stephen	173.50		1	
Robinson, James			1	
Reed, Samuel D.			1	
Radford, J.W.			1	
Riley, J.A.			1	
Riley, J.W.			1	
Reed, Hannah	73.25	8.25		1
Riggs, Gideon	130			
Robeson, Michael	401			10
Rainey, Isaac N.	156	56	1	3
Rainey, Isaac Sen.				2

NAME	DL	SL	WP	S
Rainey, B.G.	426	46	1	1
Robinson, William	100		1	
Rosson, John	100		1	
Ring, Lewis	72			
Robinson, John	150		1	
Riley, John	50			
Radford, Saml.	361			
Rue, Jefferson			1	
Rainey, Jesse G.	125			
Robeson, John	100		1	
Ragsdale, John	110		1	
Stephens, James Sen.	80	118		
Stephens, James Jun.	32		1	
Stephens, Jeremiah	109		1	
Smith, Samuel	55		1	
Smith, Thomas			1	
Smith, Henry	235			
Street, Mary	100			1
Shepard, James	136		1	
Saunders, Wm. J.			1	
Smith, E.D.	645		1	2
Smith, John			1	
Tull, Josiah B.			1	
Taylor, Henry	109.50		1	
Taylor, Frederick	147		1	1
Turner, Joseph R.	125	25		
Thompson, James	250		1	
Venable, John			1	
Venable, Richard			1	
Vanable, Simeon				1
Venable, Andw.	239			1
Vanable, Larkin			1	
Weldon, William			1	
Wallace, Matthew	96			2
Wallace, William	112		1	
Wilson, Marcus	150		1	
Wilson, Marcus	35			
Williams, William F.	50		1	
Wills, James M.			1	
Walker, Edward			1	
Wilson, Hiram	195		1	
Wilson, Jonathan	150			
Wells, Mary	203	22		
Wells, W.R.			1	
Wells, J.B.	20			
Walker, John			1	
Wilson, Josiah	127.50			1
Wilson, Josiah Jun.			1	

NAME	DL	SL	WP	S
Wallis, John	482			
Williams, D. Wm.			1	
Wilson, John H.	62			
Wilson, Aaron C.	150		1	
Williams, James	436			
Wilson, Thos, heirs	125			

BEDFORD COUNTY - DISTRICT NO. 14

Beginning where the Maury County line crosses Duck River, thence south with the Maury line to a point due west of the northeast corner of Esq. Hugh Houston's field north of his dwelling house, thence east in a direct line to Elias Stilwell's springhouse on the west fork of Rock Creek, thence crossing said creek between Peter Woods and Osburn's mill, thence in a direct line to include George Finley's old place and east to a point south of Ezl. Vernon's on the line of District No. 16, thence north to E.E. Vernon's well, thence north to the southwest corner of the first processioning survey of the Cathy claim including the old Joe Thompson place and leaving the Saunders place on the east and with the west boundary of the Cathey survey to the northwest corner, thence north to include John Denny, thence to include Robert Houston's old place and E.W. Hunter, thence in a direct line to Blair's old mill, thence a direct line to Hamilton's old ford on Duck River and down the river to the beginning. (Now Marshall County).

NAME	DL	SL	WP	S
Appleby, Samuel B.	100		1	
Appleby, Benj.			1	
Appleby, William			1	
Appleby, John Sen.	157	57		1
Appleby, John Jun.			1	
Alexander, Memnon	53	25	1	
Beckett, Susannah	40	66		
Burrow, Henry			1	
Beaty, Sherwood W.	95	50	1	1
Burrow, Ephraim			1	
Bills, William	100	150	1	
Bills, Jonathan	85		1	
Bills, Danl. B.		180		
Bolton, Seth			1	
Buchannon, James			1	
Bell, Mary	63	50		
Beaty, John H.			1	2
Brewer, Nathaniel			1	
Brewer, Asa			1	
Batt, James N.			1	
Brooks, Loyall			1	
Criswell, Henry	34	61		
Cowden, Robert Sen.	40			
Criswell, Andrew			1	
Clapp, Henry			1.	

NAME	DL	SL	WP	S
Caid, Isaac			1	
Cowden, Joseph		21.50		
Cook, John			1	
Cowden, Robt. Jun.	56.25		1	
Criswell, David	35		1	
Collins, Adam	45	40	1	
Cummings, Thos. E.B.				
by Jno. Orr, Guardian	100			
Devin, John	100	60	1	1
Doyle, Edward			1	
Denny, John	313	155		
Denny, Alexander			1	
Daniel, Ezekiel			1	
Dysart, Francis heirs	235.25			
Ewing, James Esq.	652	176		3
Ewing, Mary	50 (1 carriage)			2
Ewing, George	200			7
Ewing, Jas. L. Esq.	567.50	150	1	7
Ewing, William D.	20	18		
Ewing, Lile A.	117.50			
Ewing, James V.	520		1	6
Ewing, Jas.P. heirs of	40			
Ewing, James D.	96		1	2
Fisher, George W.	37.50		1	
Fisher, James K.			1	
Fisher, Jacob	64			
Fisher, Frederick	81.75			
Fisher, Joh.	60	115	1	
Fisher, James F.			1	
Fisher, George	127	50	1	1
Farrar, Peter	30	50	1	
Green, Ephraim	673.75	18.75		
Green, David	184	26		
Giles, Matthew H.	40	45	1	
Green, Thomas			1	
Green, Eph R.			1	
Helm, Moses W.			1	
Helm, Thomas			1	
Hall, William			1	
Headlee, Joseph	20		1	
Headlee, David	16	60	1	1
Hubbard, Daniel			1	
Hopper, James			1	
Hooper, Jackson			1	
Hogge, Ezekiel	20		1	
Hunter, Elihu W.	250		1	2
Helm, William			1	
Hooten, John	80			

NAME	DL	SL	WP	S
Hugh, Houston Sen.		50	1	
Hunter, Robert heirs	1000			
Hunter, Edwin C.	89.50	282.50		
Helmich, John			1	
Hightower, Joh. A.T.	65	45	1	
Jennings, Thomas			1	
Jennings, John N.			1	
Jones, John C.			1	
John, John R.	1144		1	10
Jones, Fanning M.	1086		1	8
Jones, Luton			1	
King, John			1	
Legget, James			1	
Leggett, Holden W.			1	
Leggett, F.F.			1	
Leeper, Allen (1 carriage)	1817	165		6
Lane, Joseph			1	
Little, Jackson			1	
Leavill, Benjn.	250			
McCleary, W.D.	744	294	1	2
McCleary, John	50			
Malcom, John			1	
Morten, John O.	100		1	1
Morten, Joseph	100		1	1
Morten, Charles P.			1	
McNease, Washington			1	
McCordy, Samuel	65	25	1	
McClean, Andrew M.	250			
McClure, William	188			11
McCord, Joseph	60	140	1	
Morris, Henry			1	
Miller, John H.	50		1	
Nix, William			1	
Osburn, John		90		
Owen, Robert			1	
Orr, John	366	84		
Orr, W.D.		40		
Roane, Henry	137		1	
Roane, Levi			1	
Stephenson, Jos.			1	
Stuart, Oth'l	120		1	
Stokes, David			1	
Stilwell, Elias	157	53		
Smith, Work			1	

NAME	DL	SL	WP	S
Tilman, Saml. T.	73.50		1	
Tankersly, David			1	
Tankersly, John			1	
Verner, Ezl. E.	50	25	1	
Vincent, Susannah	40			
Vance, David by Agent W.D. Orr	1000			
Vincent, William			1	
Wood, William			1	
Wood, William H.			1	
Watson, Saml. M.	125		1	
Williams, James	200			
Wilkorison, John			1	
Wiggs, Needham			1	
Yarborough, H.D.			1	
Yarborough, Reuben			1	
Yarborough, Samuel	20	12.50	1	

BEDFORD COUNTY - DISTRICT NO. 15

Beginning on the Elk Ridge or Lincoln County line at the point of the ridge between the McCerley's Creek waters and the fork on which Esq. Reed lives, thence northwardly with the dividing ridge west of McCerley Creek (now Snake) including Shadrick Mustain, thence to Elisha Garrett's and Benjn. Bingerman's and John Christopher's leaving them on the east, thence the southeast corner of District No. 14, south of E.E. Vernor's, thence west leaving George Finley's old place on the north, thence in a direct line to the west fork of Rock Creek between Osburn's mills and Peter Woods and by Elias Stilwell's spring, thence in a direct line to the north boundary of Esq. Hugh Houston;s farm and west to the Maury County line at the corner of District No. 14, thence south with Maury line to the southwest corner of Bedford County, thence east withthe Lincoln County line to the beginning.

Elections appointed to be held at the house of David Willis on the Pulaski Road. (Now Marshall County).

NAME	DL	SL	WP	S
Ausley, Wesley			1	
Allen, John			1	
Beck, John	80		1	
Bickett, John			1	
Bigham, H.B.	80.50		1	1
Boyt, Catharine	63			
Boyt, James	67		1	1
Bevins, Wm. S.	312			
Bigham, William	140			6
Bills, Garsham	155		1	

NAME	DL	SL	WP	S
Bills, John H.	215		1	2
Birmingham, Elijah			1	
Bevins, Abraham			1	
Birmingham, John Jun.			1	
Bryant, Russel	156		1	
Birmingham, John Sen.	149.75	24		
Birmingham, George W.			1	
Bradley, Edward	110.50		1	
Beck, Ebenezer			1	
Bevins, Daniel	310		1	
Boyt, Priscilla	117.75			
Boyt, Elizabeth	50			
Boyt, Bethena	50			
Boyt, John F.			1	
Boyt, Jesse J.			1	
Bills, John heirs of	72			
Cochrane, Jas. Sen.	60			
Collins, Henry	124		1	1
Cochrane, Levi	350		1	1
Charlton, Elijah			1	
Cochrane, James Jun.			1	
Cunningham, John	200		1	1
Callahan, Wm. S.	53.50	67.50	1	
Cheek, Benjn. R.			1	
Caple, Sarah	71			
Cochrane, Ezra	75		1	
Cochrane, Silas M.			1	
Cheek, Thomas D.	180		1	1
Cloud, Joseph	66.25	14	1	1
Devin, Elizabeth				6
Davis, Robert			1	1
Davis, Samuel			1	
Davis, William	200			
Davis, Reuben J.			1	
Elliott, Samuel J.	98		1	
Elliott, Sarah	103.25			
Elliott, Cornelius A.			1	
Edwards, James	32.50		1	
Elliott, John			1	
Elliott, Eli			1	
Fowler, John B.	302.25			7
Fowler, Jacob B.			1	
Fleming, Henry			1	
Fowler, P.W.			1	
Finley, John			1	
Giles, Wesley A.	75		1	
Garrett, William	98.50		1	

NAME	DL	SL	WP	S
Glenn, James	369.75		1	
Goodwin, Peter G.W.			1	
Garrett, Elisha	100	86		
Gifford, William			1	
Graham, William			1	
Glover, James			1	
Gray, Jarman			1	
Glenn, Wm. A.			1	
Glenn, Joseph			1	
Haywood, Geo. W.	570		1	5
Hardin, Mary				2
Houston, Abner (1 carriage)	452	137	1	6
Houston, Christopher, 200				8
Houston, James G.			1	
Houston, Hugh Jun.			1	
Houston, Hugh Sen.	212	61		
Houston, John M.			1	1
Hopwood, Clark	50		1	
Hardin, John L.	192		1	1
Hardin, Burgess	246			1
Hopwood, Willis Sen.	323			4
Hopwood, Thomas			1	
Hackney, Allen			1	
Halbrooks, Wm. C.			1	
Hardin, Henry			1	
Hardin, Jno. L.	140			
Houston, Jno. W.			1	
Kenier, Joseph	119		1	
Kenier, John			1	
Lincoln, Elijah			1	
London, William	261			2
London, Thomas A.			1	
McKnight, Thomas	13.50		1	
McClure, William	111			
McKnight, Ezekiel	87.50		1	2
Mustain, Shadrock			1	
McDaniel, Francis	93	95		
Malone, Murdock	25		1	
McCrory, Robt.	333		1	4
Nowlin, Eliz by Exr.	157	93		2
Nowlin, David			1	1
Nix, Thomas S.			1	
Nash, George w.	102	33	1	
Odum & Orr	50			
Osburn, John	283	143	1	1
Orr, Wm. D.		40		

NAME	DL	SL	WP	S
Panton, John	227			1
Phelps, Amos	87		1	
Patterson, Thomas	136			
Purdam, George			1	
Pettis, Garrison			1	
Paxton, Jno. F.			1	
Ross, Thomas Esq.	94		1	2
Rambow, Elias	187	56		1
Rambow, F.K.	142		1	
Ruston, Elijah			1	
Ramsey, Solomon	65.50			
Record, James C.	300		1	9
Reed, John H.			1	
Reed, John H.			1	
Reed, James Esq.	94	130		
Stilwell, Eleazor	247		1	
Stilwell, Elias	232		1	
Swan, Alex H.	18			
Snell, John A.	60		1	
Sharp, Andw. D.			1	1
Turner, James	140.75			
Tally, Berry			1	
Turner, William			1	
Thompson, Benjamin	137	28		
Thompson, Abraham	117			3
Thompson, Hugh			1	
Tally, Abram			1	
Thompson, Henry			1	
Thompson, Moses			1	
Tally, William			1	
Turner, Spratley	226			
Twitty, Leonard	118.50		1	
Willis, Davis	212.50		1	1
Williams, William	45	425		
Williams, Bayer	292		1	
Welch, H.B.	183	36	1	
Wilder, David W.	46		1	
Welch, Charles			1	
Welch, William			1	
Weaver, Jno. S.			1	

BEDFORD COUNTY - DISTRICT NO. 16

Beginning at the southeast corner of District No. 15 on the Elk Ridge or Lincoln County line at the point of the ridge that divides the waters of McCerleys Creek (now Shake) from the creek that Esq. James Reed lives on, thence northwardly with said ridge leaving Shadrick Mustain on the west, thence to include Elisha Garrett and Benj. Bengarman and John Christopher and passing the corners of District No. 14 & 15 and on the E.E. Vernor's well, thence north to the old procession corner of the Cathey Survey including the old Saunders place and with the west boundary of the Cathey Survey to Alex. B. Reed corner, thence east with the dividing line between John Reed and Violet Cathey to their eastern corner leaving A.B. Reed, Isaac W. and Jas. Walker on the north and G. and A.L. Bills on the south, thence eastwardly including John and Andrew Dysart and John's son to the east fork of Rock Creek below the Widow Logan's field, thence up said creek to the New County line to the Lincoln County line at the lane between Josiah Blackwell and Mary Endsley's, thence west to the Lincoln County line to the beginning.

Place of holding elections, etc., at Williams Cross Roads or Belfast Post Office. (Old Belfast).

NAME	DL	SL	WP	S
Adams, James Esq.	944	100		
Adams, James Jun.	300		1	1
Adams, Alex. D.	100		1	1
Adams, A.C.	195.50	103.50		2
Adams, William W.			1	
Armstrong, Geo. A.	115		1	1
Anderson, William	82		1	
Brown, Caleb			1	
Bigger, Joseph Jr.			1	
Brown, James		44		
Bills, Amos L.	220		1	
Bingarman, Benj.	100			
Brown, Jonathan	110			
Brecheen, Elizabeth	72			4
Brecheen, Josiah	244	36.50	1	1
Brown, Brazilla	7	50	1	
Bishop, Henry	176			3
Beckham, Willie			1	
Bingarman, H.G.	80			
Burgess, Willie	100		1	
Bell, James W.	83.50		1	
Bethane, William	55		1	
Cumings, George Esq.	262	81.50		3
Christopher, John	55		1	
Coffey, Allen	47.50		1	
Cannon, Elizabeth	750			3
Carpenter, Peter	185.50	8.50	1	5
Carpenter, John	135			4
Cannon, Robt. Genl.	275			
Chilton, James Sen.	112			
Christenberry, Thos.			1	
Cummings, John			1	
Chilton, Richard			1	
Chilton, James Jun.			1	
Cummings, Thos. A.			1	
Cummings, Milton			1	
Cummings, Thos. Jr.			1	
Cheek, James			1	

NAME	DL	SL	WP	S
Cummings, Virgil			1	
Cummings, Benjamin			1	
Campbell, David S.			1	
Chilton, John			1	
Cummings, Newton			1	
Dysart, James P.	115		1	2
Dysart, Robert C.	113.50		1	
Dysart, Robert heirs of	115			1
Dysart, Robert	343			
Dysart, Alexander	116		1	2
Dysart, Andrew	433	130	1	
Dysart, John	100			
Dysart, John heirs	50			
Dysart, Cary A.			1	
Dysart, Gideon B.			1	
Endsley, Mary	438	36		4
Endsley, Bedford			1	1
Ervin, Henry B.	84		1	1
Ervin, John R.	317		1	
Ervin, Wm. P.			1	
Garrett, Elisha	144		1	
Glenn, David			1	
Hardin, Tho. H.	337.50			2
Hunter, Edwin C.	270		1	
Henly, Peter			1	
Kidd, James Sen.	60	34.50		
Kidd, James Jun.			1	
Larue, John	92			
Logan, Mary		150		4
Larue, Squire	136			
Logan, Jane	140	40		
McAdams, Ervin	309	59		
McCuistion, Elizabeth				1
McLean, Henry	50			1
McLean, Jesse	47			
Miller, James Sen.	102	21		4
Miller, Andrew	110		1	
Martin, William	67	45		
Montgomery, Esther		50		
Martin, Vincent B.			1	
Miller, John	173	6	1	1
Miller, James	94		1	
McLean, John	80		1	
Morphis, David			1	

NAME	DL	SL	WP	S
Montgomery, Robt.			1	
McAdams, John			1	
Neil, Geo. C.	150	50		1
Neil, Jno. L. Jun.			1	
Newton, Ebenezer	100			
Orr, Robert Sen.	321			
Orr, Robt. J.				
Orr, Robt. Jun.	143		1	
Orr, John Sen.	150			3
Orr, Samuel			1	
Orr, Joseph C.			1	
Orr, William D.	233	212.50		
Orr, Alexr.			1	
Patterson, James			1	
Patterson, Robt. A.	195.50	65.50	1	
Ramsey, David	505		1	1
Ramsey, Samuel	124		1	1
Rankin, Richd. D.	97.75		1	
Riddle, Samuel			1	
Rodgers, James			1	
Rambow, Samuel			1	
Sides, Henry	75			4
Stewart, William			1	
Stockden, L.D.	54		1	
Seaton, Ryan			1	
Twitty, Whitfield			1	
Woods, Francis H.	195			2
Woods, F.H.				
for F. Dysart heirs	50			
Woods, James Sen.	130			
Woods, Francis B.	100		1	
Woods, Samuel	108.50		1	
Woods, James L.	155		1	
Woods, Saml. W.			1	
Williams, William	457	75		4
Williams, Robt.			1	3
Worley, Moses	200			
Wright, John O.			1	
Wilson, Robt.			1	
Wisener, Martin	85		1	4

BEDFORD COUNTY - DISTRICT NO. 17 or FARMINGTON DISTRICT

Beginning at Hamilton's old ford on Duck River, thence south including John Lane, Esq., to Blair's old mill, thence to the northeast corner of the Cathey claim, leaving Robert Hunter's place, E.W. Hunter's and John Denny on the west and south with west boundary line of the Cathey claim to the division corner of John Reed's and Violet Cathey's lands, thence with their line, (including A.R. Reed, J.W. and James Walker) to their eastern corner, thence to the east fork of Rock Creek below Widow Logan's field - then leaving H.A. Dysart and Johnson on the south, thence up said creek up to the New County line run by Webster above A.C. Adam's house, the northeast corner of the 16th District, thence north with said line to a point opposite Lemmon's old cabins on Duck River below Smith's mills, thence to said cabins down the river to the beginning.

Place of holding the elections at the house of Thomas Hopper. (Now Marshall County).

NAME	DL	SL	WP	S
Alvis, Wm. C.			1	
Bullock, John			1	
Bullock, Nathan	162.50		1	
Ballard, Joel			1	
Ballard, Thomas			1	
Ballard, James			1	
Batton, James			1	
Boren, James	135	55		
Brantley, Benjamin C (3 Lots).	745			
Bright, John M.			1	
Burrow, Duvaney W.			1	
Boren, Saml. H.			1	
Bookes, Elijah			1	
Burrow, Jeffrey W.			1	
Chapman, William	140			
Chapman, Robert	100	28		1
Cheek, Edmund R.			1	
Cotner, David	164			
Cathey, George	350	150		
Criswell, David C.	572	88.25	1	
Cleek, Joseph	99		1	
Chapman, K.O.			1	
Cleek, Ezekiel	75		1	1
Cleek, William	130	65		
Collins, Hollin	125			
Chilton, William			1	
Crawford, John			1	
Collins, Henry			1	
Cathey, Violet	350			
Chandler & Hoozer	103			
Claxton, Jeremiah			1	
Dysart, Saml. D.	42.50			
Dysart, E.B.			1	1
Dryden, Robert M. (1 Lot)				1
Davis, H.L.			1	
Deveraus, Thos. P.	1107		1	

NAME	DL	SL	WP	S
Dysart, John Jn.	100		1	
Dysart, Jno. heirs of	205			
Eakin, James	65		1	
Eakin, Ewell			1	
Ewing, Lile A. (3 Lots)			1	1
Ellison, John Esq.	540		1	2
Ellison, John for the heirs of Jno. Ellison				1
Ervin, James P.			1	
Ewing, Saml. W.	180		1	
Ewing, Wn. A.D.	179			
Eakin, J. & S.				1
Eures, Mills			1	
Fuller, Edmond			1	
Fulton, James			1	
Fisher, William D. (1.50 Lots)			1	
Glascock, Richd.	77		1	1
Glasscock, Peter N.	52	25	1	
Harkness, Jno. Sen.	35			
Harber, Henry	81		1	
Harris, Hiram	45		1	
Hopper, Thomas	156		1	
Hooten, Thomas	110		1	
Hays, Anderson S.	87		1	
Harkness, Jas. for Ellison heirs	144			
Harkness, James			1	
Hopper, Uriah			1	
Harber, Christian	322			
Harris, Lawson	105		1	
Harris, Ruth				4
Hopkins, Eli			1	
Hay, John B.			1	
Hopper, Charles	450		1	1
Harbour, George A.	100	25	1	
Hays, John M.			1	
Harkness, John Jr.	62	5	1	
Harkness, Benjamin			1	
Harkness, Samuel			1	
Hall, Thomas J.	336	50		
Hall, Thomas A.			1	
Harris, John T.	170			
Hunter, Thomas O. (1 carriage)	1710		1	9
Hays, Jeremiah	109			
Hunter, Ephraim (2 Lots)	502	25	1	3
Hay, Martha				1
Jones, Aquilla	120		1	
Jones, Lewis B.			1	
Jones, James G.			1	

NAME	DL	SP	WP	S
Jones, Elias			1	
Josse, Michael C. (2 Lots)				
Lunn, Alfred			1	
Lane, John M.	300	100	1	6
Lane, John M. for heirs of Thos. Lane	186			
Lane, John	1050			12
Long, Thomas	93	31	1	
Lunn, Nathan	107			
Lunn for Powdille				
Long, Rick			1	
Long, Richard	308			6
Long, Mary				
heirs of B. Long	100			1
Lunn, Nathaniel A.			1	
Lunn, Felix G			1	
Lunn, Elbert J.			1	
Morris, John			1	
McMorris, Alexander	65	18		
Morris, Allen	30		1	
Mason, William	87		1	
McDowell, Joseph C. (5 Lots)				
McDowell, William K.			1	
Meek, Mary	95			1
McClure, A.E.			1	
Morton, Josiah			1	
Miller, David H.	137	66		
McClelland, Samuel			1	
Neil, James H.			1	1
Nowlin, Armstead			1	
Noblin, Samuel J.		12	1	
Neeley, Thomas	50		1	
Neill, George		50	1	
Neill, Ann	165	18		
Neill, A. for Algernon Crawford	9			
Neeley, George			1	
Neeley, Elias			1	
Oakley, M.W.	275		1	
O'Neal, Isham	125	43		2
O'Neal, Moses	30	36	1	
O'Neal, James H.			1	
O'Neal, Wiley J.	100		1	
Orr, John Col.	100	60	1	6
Oglevie, Geo. W.	296		1	4
O'Neal, Jno.				
for Wilkerson heirs	9			
Powdrill, Thomas		175	1	1
Pyland, Cullin			1	

NAME	DL	SL	WP	S
Parnell, Gideon	200			
Parnell, Henry	196		1	
Pyland, William		91	1	
Pyland, James			1	
Parnell, Reiley			1	
Pyland, Bennett			1	
Pardee, Miles (1 Town Lot)			1	
Pyland, Bluford			1	
Parnell, ____			1	
Putman, John	150			1
Penn, John	187		1	
Reed, John	250			
Rodgers, John	75			
Ray, Hugh	150		1	1
Reed, Alex. B.	129		1	1
Ramsy, John (1 Town Lot)			1	
Russell, John (3 Town Lots)	309		1	
Saunders, Gabriel			1	
Sims, Robert W.	196.50		1	
Sims, Briggs G.	100		1	
Shaw, Richard L. (Part of 1 Lot)			1	
Stone, William S.			1	
Shaw, James	50			
Stephens, Dabs. G. (4 Lots)				
Stegall, Jesse			1	
Stallions, William		25		
Tucker, William	636			5
Tucker, John W.	112		1	
Tucker, George W.			1	
Taylor, Lewis			1	
Thompson, Joseph P.	41			
Thomas, Jonathan	197		1	
White, Sorrell	100			
Williams, Richard			1	
Walker, James T.			1	
Walker, Isaac W.	131		1	
same for Nathl. Dryden heirs	194			1
Williamson, Mary				
same for Jno. Williamson heirs	106			
Woods, Thomas			1	
Wood, Peter			1	
Webb, Jesse			1	
Warren, William			1	
Wilkerson, Debarry			1	
Winstead, Samuel	680		1	
Wilson, John (2 Lots)		25	1	
Whitthorne, Wm. J. (2 Lots)		150	1	
Warner, Richard	180		1	3

NAME	DL	SL	WP	S
Warner, Richard for Jas. F. Meeks	136			
Wood, James			1	
White, James G.			1	
Wood, Hugh			1	
Walter, Robt. W.	140		1	
Woods, Allen N.			1	
Yarboro, George			1	

BEDFORD COUNTY - DISTRICT NO. 18

Beginning at what is known as Lemmon's old cabins on Duck River below Smith's mill, thence west to the New County line run by Webster and Cotner, thence south with line to a point opposite the Widow of Robert Montgomery's on the east boundary of District No. 16, thence to include Jabus Nowlin and in a direct line to where the Pulaski Road crosses Sinking Creek below Michael Moore's, thence to the northeast corner of Samuel Harper's land, thence to include John H. Gambell, R. and S. Anderson and Jesse Muse, thence to Campbell and Phillips' stillhouse on the upper Pulaski Road, thence with said road east to the first branch east of George Campbell's at the Range line, being the southwest corner of District No. 21, thence north with the Range line to the Thompson Ford Road, thence in a direct line to Henry Earnhart's still house on Duck River and down the river to the beginning.

Place to hold the elections, etc., at the house of David Bledsoe. (1.5 miles southeast of Sim's Spring, Pisgah).

NAME	DL	SL	WP	S
Anderson, Saml.	75		1	
Aaron, James	100		1	
Aaron, William			1	
Anderson, Livingston			1	
Anderson, Elizabeth	50			
Anderson, Richard	75		1	
Aaron, Moses	50	150		
Anderson, John H.	222		1	
Bledsoe, David			1	
Buchanan, Jane C.	63			
Braughton, Benjamin	150		1	
Bell, Feilding	108	92	1	
Bell, James W.		75		
Bledsoe, Jacob	195	288		
Bryant, Edward	300			3
Bryant, Peter L.			1	
Brown, John M.	84.50		1	
Burten, David			1	
Bryant, John	210			
Bryant, Elbert			1	
Bussey, Daniel			1	

NAME	DL	SL	WP	S
Brown, Neal	100		1	
___ Bright per Turnage heirs	61.25			
Chapman, Robert		100		
Camples, Asa	49	67		
Christenberry, Wm.			1	
Calhoun, George	181			
Camples, Willis			1	
Cook, William			1	
Crowell, Henry			1	
Campbell, James	151		1	
Culp, Adam	107.50			
Cleeks, M. heirs	200			
Chappel, Robert			1	
Cheeves, ___	50		1	
Card, Samuel H.	50	100	1	
Clift, John	50			
Clift, James	50		1	
Cheeves, Calvin			1	1
Cheeves, Jacob		193.50	1	
Coffey, Benjamin	63	100	1	
Coffey, Thomas			1	
Crowel, Peter Sen.	200	350		4
Crowel, Samuel Jun.	105		1	
Campbell, Redmond			1	
Davis, James			1	
Dobbs, Lindsey	50		1	
Dobbs, Willliam		100	1	
Doty, Preston L.	100		1	
Dougal, John	100			
Darnell, Joel Jun.	80	58.50	1	
Dobbs, Jeremiah	58	50		
Dryden, David	148.50		1	
Ewing, Jas. for G. Haines heirs				
Earnhart, Benj.	226.50		1	
Ellison, Jno. for Davis heirs	88	75		
Evans, Zebellon			1	
Earnhart, Henry	176.25		1	2
Evans, Daniel	135			
Evans, David B.			1	
Earnhart, Daniel	168		1	
Evans, Joseph			1	
Ellis, James			1	
Evans, Willie			1	
Evans, William		114		
Forbs, Jeremiah			1	
Freeman, Russell	115.50			
Freeman, Wilson			1	
Freeman, Hartwell	31.50	35		

NAME	DL	SL	WP	S
Freeman, Nile			1	
Freeman, Joel	41.50		1	
Fisher, Michael	55		1	
Fisher, George	70.50		1	
Fugett, Benjamin			1	
Fugett, Nancy	165.25			
Glascock, Charnel	65		1	
Glascock, George	15			
Gambill, John H.	104		1	
Gambill, James C.	50		1	1
Garren, Peter	140	232		
Grames, John		50	1	
Gibson, John	235			
Gambill, Aaron	286.50			1
Gibson, Asa			1	
Green, Lewis			1	
Goodwin, Peter			1	
Gaunt, Lewis	538		1	5
Gaunt, Willliam A.	220		1	7
Gaunt, Jon. heirs	487			
Gibson, John Jun.			1	
Gambill, Thomas			1	
Guest, David			1	
Hughes, John			1	
Hammil, William	338			1
Holly, William				3
Harris, Nicholas			1	
Harrison, John	25	115	1	
Hammond, Mary	118	225		
Hughes, Agnes	61	50		
Harrison, Tyre		75	1	
Harris, James	84.50		1	1
Hix, James	23		1	
Hanby, George W.			1	
Henderson, Logan	446			
Irvin, Samuel		50	1	
Jones, Napoleon B.			1	
Jones, Lawrence E.			1	
Jones, William B. Esq.	5	250	1	
Jones, James B.	30	77	1	
Jordan, Tabitha	200			
Jordan Jefferson			1	
King, John			1	
Liggett, Jonathan		90	1	
Lentz, Thomas W.	77		1	
Lentz, Jacob	80			

NAME	DL	SL	WP	S
Lentz, John J.			1	
Lentz, John	58		1	
Lentz, Valentine			1	
Lentz, Benjamin	40	50	1	
same for heirs of Benj. Lentz	117	50		
Leach, Elisha		55	1	
Moore, James			1	
Moore, Thomas	182		1	
Moss, Samuel				2
Musgrave, Joshua	150	25		
Musgrave, Thomas			1	
Molder, Jacob	10	43	1	
Morgan, William			1	
Morgan, Jacob			1	
Muse, Jesse	100		1	
Muse, Joseph C.			1	
Murphy, John	300		1	
Murphy, Neil			1	
Moss, James			1	
Neil, John T.		333		
Neil, Joseph heirs	100	100		
Neill, James D.	60		1	
Neeley, Green T.			1	
Neill, James	60		1	
Neill, Andrew	170		1	1
Nowlin, Jabus			1	6
same for A. Burford's heirs				1
Neil, Newton F.	300		1	
Nicholas, Jno. T.			1	
O'Neal, Wm. Sen.	212.50	174		4
Oliver, Wright			1	1
O'Neal, Jno. P.	73		1	
O'Neal, William Jr.			1	
O'Neal, Willie Sen.			1	
O'Neal, Isham	219			
O'Neal, Jno.	429	32	1	2
Pearson, James			1	
Pickle, James	50		1	
Pickle, Major			1	
Pickle, Henry	104.25	25		
Paschal, James		100	1	
Pearson, John			1	
Pickle, John			1	
Roberts, Minton			1	
Reynolds, Michael			1	
Ray, Charles			1	

NAME	DL	SL	WP	S
Sims, William			1	
Stamps, Wm. D.			1	
Stephenson, John	55		1	
Shearin, Thomas	40	25	1	14
Stephenson, Edward	427			1
same for Susan Parker	90			
Sims, Martin	141		1	
Stephenson, D.G.			1	
Stephenson, Wm. H.			1	
Stephenson, Richard P.			1	
Stephenson, Geo. W.			1	1
Sharp, Joseph P.			1	
Stewart, John			1	
Stephens, Redding	52.50	50		
Stallings, Wm.	100	31	1	1
Stallings, Wm.	63.50			
Stallings, John			1	
Thompson, John		76		
Temple, D.P. heirs		150		
Thorn, William Jr.			1	
Thompson, Balaim			1	
Trollinger, Jacob			1	
Trollinger, Joseph			1	
Thorn, Harbert			1	
Thorn, William Sen.	75	25		1
Thompson, John F.	139		1	3
Wilson, Samuel			1	
White, Sion	70		1	
White, Aden			1	
Westerman, William			1	
Westerman, Clifford	36		1	
Warner, John Sen. heirs	200			
Williams, Jesse E. heirs	280.50			

Lands and Polls not reported before the first Monday in July, 1836 to Commissioners:

Gilchrist, Malcum	250			
Gilchrist, Malcum	100	60		
Gilchrist, Wm. & Arch B.	600	600		
Wheat, Josiah				1

BEDFORD COUNTY - DISTRICT NO. 19

Beginning at the southeast corner of the 16th District on the Lincoln County line between Joseph Blackwell's and the Widow Endsleys, thence running north with the New County line to the corner of District No.

18 opposite the Widow of Robert Montgomery's house, thence east leaving Jabus Nowlin's on the north and John Jabus on the south and a direct line to the ford of Sinking Creek on the Pulaski Road below Michael Moore's, thence to Samuel Harper's northeast corner, thence south to Sinking Creek and up said creek opposite Richmond, thence southeastwardly to the ridge above Phillip's spring including Phillips and with the ridge dividing Sugar Creek and Sinking Creek to the Lincoln County line, thence with said line west to the beginning.

Appointed elections to be held at the house of the Widow Craig's. (Pickle Road).

NAME	DL	SL	WP	S
Anderson, Alfred	100		1	
Adams, Robert W.			1	
Adams, Mary	184			
Allison, Thomas H.	107		1	2
Adams, Archibald			1	1
Adams, James	339			
Allison, James	384.50			8
Armstrong, Nathan			1	
Armstrong, John	100		1	?
Anderson, Amzi D.			1	
Anderson, James D.	110			
Brown, William			1	
Bowden, Jas. M.			1	
Bradley, Joel	117		1	
Blackwell, Gabriel	497	150	1	1
Blackwell, John Sen.	660			
Blackwell, S.B.			1	
Blackwell, James			1	
Bradley, Jefferson C.			1	
Blackwell, B.M.G.	223		1	
Blackwell, J.W.H.			1	
Blackwell, Elizabeth	200			
Bryant, John			1	
Blackwell, James G.			1	
Blackwell, Josiah	114		1	
Brown, Archibald			1	
Barksdale, Wm. W.			1	
Bryant, Thos. W.			1	
Cummings, Thos.	259			1
Craig, Wm. heirs	200			
Cummings, Hugh			1	
Cook, Henry			1	
Curtis, Jas. H.			1	
Catowell, Robert			1	
Craig, John	101		1	
Cunningham, Wm.				5
Collins, Alex H.			1	
Coffey, Jas. L.	80		1	1
Cunningham, Thos. P.			1	
Cummings, A.E.	95		1	
Coffey, Thos. Esq.	172		1	

NAME	DL	SL	WP	S
Coffey, Thos. Esq.	119.75			
Cummings, G.W.	57.25		1	
Cook, Elizabeth	152			
Coffey, James W.			1	
Craig, Robert			1	
Darnall, Moses			1	
Davis, James	113		1	
Davis, Gabriel			1	
Davis, Timothy			1	
Davis, Zachariah	410		1	4
Dawdy, John Sen.	200	50		3
Durrett, Solomon	100		1	3
Davis, Mary	454			1
Dillard, James	300		1	
Dunham, Hardy	114		1	
Davidson, Thomas	450			1
Dobbs, John			1	
Dawdy, John W.			1	
Delk, John			1	
Darnall, Joel Sen.	100			
Dryden, Thomas	211		1	
Endsley, Isaac N.	150		1	1
Endsley, Jno. M.	199		1	1
Endsley, Bedford	195			
Endsley, Mary	180			
Epps, Joshua			1	
England, John	150			
Fisher, Mary	60			
Garrin, Peter		65		
Gibson, John M.	160		1	
Goodwin, Geo. W.			1	
Gaunt, John	3			
Hill, Green			1	
Harper, Jno. M.			1	
Harrison, Mary	182.50			
Hart, John N.	181			
Harper, Thos. W.	109	30	1	
Heamiller, Thomas	160		1	
Harper, Samuel	192			
Hall, Hugh A.			1	
Harrison, William			1	
Harrison, C.H.			1	
Heaslett, E.H.			1	
Hill, James			1	
Helton, James	49			
Hill, Gillam			1	

NAME	DL	SL	WP	S
Jeanes, Thos. C.	56		1	
Jones, JAmes			1	
Johnson, Edward	70		1	
Killingsworth, H.	10		1	
Looney, P.D.			1	
Looney, Wm. B.			1	
Looney, Hugh			1	
Lovett, Kitty	180			1
Loyd, A.M.	.75		1	
Larue, Isaac B.	100		1	1
Larue, John	615		1	6
Lovett, Enoch			1	
Lowry, Jas. B.	230		1	1
Love, Martha	379			3
McCool, Benjn.			1	
Musgrave, Jas.			1	1
Moore, Henry	116.25		1	
McAdams, Joseph	130		1	
Moore, Michael	175	110	1	1
Moore, Charles R.			1	1
Marr, John	40			
Mays, Willie			1	
Moore, Margaret	42.50			
Medearis, W.D.	800			7
Marcum, W.B.M.			1	
McLaughlin, J.H.	150			
Norman, Robert	100			
Osteen, Samuel			1	
Osburn, daniel			1	
Price, Jesse	50	25		
Payne, Harrison			1	
Price, James K.	37.50		1	
Parrish, Abraham			1	
Phillips, John	317			
Patton, B.F.			1	
Privit, Berys			1	
Putman, Sarah	229			1
Porter, Stephen	500			
Patterson, John			1	
Robertson, William	356		1	
Roberts, Peter	111	48	1	
Roberts, Rezin	90		1	
Roberts, John	160			1
Ray, Alexander	116		1	
Ray, Jas. heirs	270			

NAME	DL	SL	WP	S
Ray, George M.			1	
Ray, John	745		1	2
Ray, Jennet				2
Revis, David	50			
Russell, William			1	
Russell, Jno. M.			1	
Revis, Johnson			1	
Russell, Thomas			1	
Smiley, Hugh B.	231		1	3
Swanson, William C.	400			
Smith, Thomas	629		1	12
Smith, Reizen	311			4
Simmons, Cyrus	175			
Sullivan, Alfred			1	
Towell, Jesse F.			1	
Venabile, Thomas			1	
Webb, John			1	
Whitfield, Travis			1	
Woodard, Garman	100		1	
Woodard, John			1	
Yancy, David	100		1	2

BEDFORD COUNTY - DISTRICT NO. 20

Beginning on the Lincoln County line on the dividing ridge east of Hanna's Gap on the Sinking Creek and Sugar Creek waters and with the ridge east of John Phillips' house striking Sinking Creek opposite Richmond and down Sinking Creek to a point south of Samuel Harper's northeast corner, thence to said corner on the line of the 19th District, thence east to Jesse Muse's, leaving him on the north and thence to Campbell and Phillips' still house on the upper Pulaski Road, thence with said road to the Range line at the first branch east of George Campbell's, being the corner of Districts 18 and 21, thence with the line of the 21st District leaving Gab'l Knight's on the north, thence to Trice, leaving him also on the south, thence to Sugar Creek Meeting House and with the Winchester Road (Snell) to the top of the dividing ridge between Sugar Creek and Flat Creek, west of Jordan C. Holt's, thence south with the main ridge dividing the waters of said creeks, to a point north of Templeton's old house, on Col. McKisick's old farm, thence with the ridge south of said house and with the same, dividing the branches on which the Widow Dryden lives, to the Lincoln County line, thence westwardly with the said line to the beginning.

Place of holding the elections, etc., at Alexander Roberson's. (Ed Note: Pleasant Grove)

NAME	DL	SL	WP	S
Allen, John	60			
Allen, Josiah			1	

NAME	DL	SL	WP	S
Adams, Joseph	151		1	
Adams, Cophas			1	
Adams, Elizabeth	150			1
Adams, Benjamin			1	
Andrews, Benj.			1	
Brantley, Joseph A.			1	
Bradshaw, Elijah			1	
Bradshaw, Jno. W.			1	
Bradshaw, Jas. N.			1	
Bradshaw, James E.			1	
Bradshaw, O.W.			1	
Brown, Solomon			1	
Brown, Thos. heirs	100			
Brown, John S.	112		1	1
Brown, Mary				1
Baker, Lewis			1	
Bain, Andrew	75		1	
Bradshaw, Robt. E.	425		1	1
Barrett, John	280		1	1
Brassfield, Jas. H.			1	
Blagg, Jehu			1	
Balch, Saml. P.	250		1	
Barringer, D.L. Genl.	700		1	
Brown, Thomas			1	
Brown, Jesse Sen.				3
Craig, Wm. H.			1	
Carliles, William	100			
Carlton, James			1	
Campbell, Charles	101		1	
Cunningham, J.W.C.			1	
Campbell, John			1	
Campbell, George	140			2
Combs, John	266			2
Comb, John T.			1	
Cunningham, G.W.	275		1	
Cunningham, Humphrey	302			
Cotner, Daniel	194			
Cotner, John			1	
Dyer, Martha	200			
Dyer, Samuel			1	
Dyer, Joseph G.			1	
Dyer, Gibson J.			1	
Dyer, John	30		1	
Davis, Frederick			1	
Davis, George			1	
Davis, William	133		1	
Davidson, Andrew	274			6
Dryden, Thomas	130	50	1	1
Delk, Benjamin			1	

NAME	DL	SL	WP	S
Delk, Geo. W.			1	
Delk, William			1	
Davidson, Carlton	195			
Evans, Nathan	900		1	7
Evans, Theophilus			1	
Elliott, L.B.			1	
Ewens, James P.			1	
Ewens, Robert	54.75			
Ellis, George			1	
Ellis, B.F.	100		1	
Ellis, Wm. M.			1	
Frazier, Bryson			1	
Farrar, Jno. H.			1	
Fields, Henry		56	1	
Fonville, Frederick	50		1	
Freeman, Christian			1	
Freeman, Stephen			1	
Greer, Thomas Sen.	445			
Greer, Robert J.			1	
Greer, David			1	
Gambill, George			1	
Gambill, John			1	
Gambill, Benjamin	135			1
Garrison, Samuel	146			
Gaunt, John Sen.	580		1	1
Gaunt, James Sen.	628			3
Gaunt, James Jun.			1	
Gaunt, John Jun.			1	
Greer, Alexander			1	
Glidwell, Barrister			1	
Gambill, Newton C.	150		1	
Gambill, William	85		1	
Greer, Frances	445			4
Harrison, John			1	
Hall, John Sen.				
Hall, B.M.			1	
Hainey, Jno. P.			1	
Holland, Nelson	100		1	
Hyde, Gray M.			1	
Johnson, John A.	100			
James, John P.			1	
Killingsworth, Henry	57			
King, Nathaniel			1	
Logan, Robert	117		1	

NAME	DL	SL	WP	S
Morton, Joseph	80		1	
Morrison, Jane H.	170			1
Moore, Mary	96			
Moore, James			1	
McClure, Willliam			1	
McClure, Houston	147		1	2
Morrison, A.W.			1	
Muse, Thomas			1	
Moore, David			1	1
Nelson, Robert	100		1	
Nance, Hon.	100		1	
Newson, Allen	200		1	
Patten, James	150			
Patten, Joseph	87		1	
Phillips, Miles	138		1	
Phillips, Jesse	129.50		1	
Phillips, John Sen.	372		1	2
Phillips, John Jun.			1	
Phillips, Calvin			1	
Phillips, James			1	
Pickens, Wm. M.			1	
Parks, John			1	
Parks, Robert	337		1	
Potter, Wm.			1	1
Porter, John N.	200			9
Russell, Chas. B.	52		1	
Russell, Wm. M.	50			3
Russell, Jas. R.			1	
Radford, Henry			1	
Robinson, Alexr.	326		1	1
Randall, Griffin				1
Ray, James M.	201		1	
Riley, Robert	79			
Richards, David			1	
Richards, William			1	
Robinson, John	150		1	
Scales, Noah	290		1	
Stephens, Wilson			1	
Staggs, Unity	40	47		
Snell, Roger	363			
Stewart, John	280		2	
Shaddy, Jacob Sen.	73			
Shaddy, JAcob Jun.			1	
Shaddy, Peter			1	
Staggs, James			1	
Thompson, Samuel				6
Terry, Henry			1	

NAME	DL	SL	WP	S
Thomas, James			1	
Thompson, Newcum			1	1
Thomas, Mark			1	
Trice, John	80		1	1
Turpin, Henry	60			
Thompson, Wm.			1	
Talleafairo, Charles			1	
Whitsell, G.W.	50		1	
Whitsell, John Sen.	250			1
Whitsell, Jno. Jr.			1	
Williams, John Jr.			1	
Wilson, John			1	
Wiggins, Harrell	254		1	2
Wiggins, Jno. W.	35		1	
White, Nathaniel	250		1	
White, Wm. S. heirs	50			
Yeates, William	212		1	

BEDFORD COUNTY - DISTRICT NO. 21

Beginning at Henry Earnhart's still house on Duck River, upper corner of District No. 18, thence southwesterly to where the Range line crosses the Thompson Ford Road and with said Range line to the upper Pulaski Road, east of George Campbell's, thence eastwardly to include Gab'l Knight and Trice and to Sugar Creek Meeting House; and with the Winchester Road to the first creek east of the Widow Hasting's house, thence down the said creek to its mouth into Big Flat Creek and down the said creek to Andrew Reed's lower lot, thence north to the extreme south bend of Duck River, south of A.C. Dodson's house, thence west to where the Fayetteville Road crosses Big Flat Creek, leaving John B. Cummings on the north, thence down the creek to its mouth into Duck River and down the river to the beginning.

Place to hold elections at the house of Roger Snell. (Naron Road).

NAME	DL	SL	WP	S
Alexander, Joseph	100		1	
Blackwell, John	275			6
Baker, John			1	
Brame, Melch.	310			5
Boyd, Lewis A.	732		1	5
Burnett, John T.	200		1	
Byram, Elijah			1	
Bryam, Jesse			1	
Brame, John I.			1	2
Brown, Jesse W.			1	
Bryam, Joseph			1	

NAME	DL	SL	WP	S
Cates, John S.			1	
Doak, Samuel	75		1	6
Dixon, James	609		1	8
Delk, Jacob B.			1	
Ellis, Michael	150		1	
Fonville, William			1	
Greer, Thomas	2511		1	12
Gray, Joseph	118.50		1	3
Gammill, James	200		1	
Galbreath, Kezia	311			4
Gibson, George B.			1	
Gambill, Alfred H.			1	
Greer, Jacob	74			4
Hughs, William L.			1	
Holt, Jordan C.	733		1	5
Holt, Michael	530		1	6
Hall, John Sen.	111		1	9
Hix, Joshua M.	50		1	
Hix, John S.			1	
Holt, Hiram	230			
Hartsfield, Wm.	285	300		
Hartsfield, Andw.	200		1	5
Hastie, Joseph	75			1
Hubbard, John H.	124		1	
Hall, John Jr.			1	
Head, David W.			1	
Head, Calvin H.			1	
Heaslett, Henry E.	50			
Harman, Lowe	139.25		1	
King, Wm. C.			1	
Knight, Gabriel			1	2
Knight, Obadiah W.			1	1
Knight, William	648			8
King, Isaiah	50		1	
Kizer, Jacob	26			
Kirk, Eli			1	
King, Charles			1	
Moseley, Jonathan	400		1	7
Moseley, Isham	256		1	1
McCarver, James	50			2
Moseley, John			1	2
Muse, John T.	534.75		1	2
Morton, William	50		1	
Morrison, Ziza			1	
Moseley, William	101		1	4

NAME	DL	SL	WP	S
Newsom, Randolph	107		1	3
Orr, William D.	30		1	1
Olive, Sarah				2
Osburn, Willie W.			1	
Osburn, Abner			1	
Parks, Joshua	90			2
Patton, James W.	140			2
same for McKamys heirs	90			
Patton, John	160		1	2
Parrish, Isaac			1	
Parks, Jefferson,			1	
Riggs, Adams	85.50			1
Reeves, John H.			1	1
Roane, William			1	
Smith, Alexander			1	
Solomon, Willie			1	
Sims, John	450	85		12
Streeter, John	246		1	9
Sims, Richard H.	243		1	7
Smiley, Matthew A.	50			
Snell, Roger	267			10
Smith, Harbert	142			
Stephens, Willie heirs	153.50			
Smith, Allen J.			1	
Stephens, Ransom			1	
Smith, D.M.			1	
Smiley, Willis H.			1	
Stephenson, William			1	
Stephens, Martha	350			3
Stinson, William			1	
Tribble, Michael			1	2
Tribble, William			1	
Thompson, John			1	
Temple, L.C.	405			
Wiggns, Hundley	500			12
Wilhoite, John	200		1	4
Whiteside, for Wm. Phillips	202			
Whiteside, Lewis			1	
Warner, Eunice		250		
Warren, Montgomery			1	
Whorley, Joel			1	
Wilhoite, William	200		1	5
Yeates, Joshua	201		1	3

BEDFORD COUNTY - DISTRICT NO. 22

Beginning on the northeast corner of District No. 20 on the south boundary of the 21st District where the Winchester and Columbia Road crossed the dividing ridge between the waters of Sugar Creek and Flat Creek, west of JOrdan C. Holt's, thence east with said road to a point due west of Robert Snoddy's house, thence east to Big Flat Creek, thence up said creek to a point of a ridge lying between main Flat Creek and the fork coming down from Watson's old tanyard and with the main dividing ridges between the creeks to the Lincoln County line at the western corner of what is called New Bedford, near Novillle, thence west with the Lincoln County line to the corner of District No. 20 at the end of the ridge dividing the branches on which the Widow Dryden and the Widow Bradshaw and John McNatt live, thence north with said ridge to Templeton's old house inclusive, thence north to a large hill and with the same dividing ridge between Sugar Creek and Flat Creek tothe beginning.

Place of holding elections appointed at the Widow Eve Burrows. (Goose Creek at Pleasant Garden).

NAME	DL	SL	WP	S
Appleby, Saml.			1	
Anthony, Alfred	51			
Allbright, Jacob	135	90		
Butler, James S.			1	
Boon, William	237.50	237.50	1	5
Bateman, Wm.			1	
Bruton, Amilia	11	171		
Bennett, John			1	
Bennett, Mary	77	100		
Burrow, Banks M.D.	4	58.50	1	
Bartlett, William			1	
Brown, Hezekiah	133	144		
Black, George	77		1	
Burgess, Richard	200			
Burgess, Wilsy				
Burrow, Eve	205			2
Burrow, Mary	130			
Burrow, James			1	
Burrow, Phillip			1	
Broadway, Lemuel	75		1	
Brown, Miles			1	
Bartlett, Joel			1	
Brown, Hezekiah Jun.			1	
Brown, Jesse	50		1	
Brown, John			1	
Burrow, Jesse		100		
Brown, Thomas S.	67		1	
Burrow, John			1	
Campbell, Arthur	104	24		1
Campbell, William			1	
Cochran, Willis			1	
Conwell, Thomas	60	320	1	2
Collins, Martin	50	125	1	
Casteel, John	34.50	182	1	
Cooper, John B.			1	

NAME	DL	SL	WP	S
Cotes, James	24	116	1	
Driver, Jordan		75		
Dryden, Jonathan B.	75	160	1	
Davidson, Bluford	119.75		1	
Dean, Thomas	184	74	1	8
Dean, Henry	316	198	1	3
Davis, William	97	156	1	2
Evans, Sarah	33.33		1	
Friddle, Martin	179		1	
Fulgram, John			1	
Freeman, A. Manier	77		1	
Fuller, William			1	
Grammar, Peterson	12.50	122.50	1	
Gossage, Washington			1	
Gossage, Walker			1	
Garrett, Elijah	17		1	
Grammer, John Jun.			1	
Gossage, Patten	24	81		
Grammer, William			1	
Grammer, Leonard			1	
Hart, Henry	68	191		
Hawkins, Samuel			1	
Hix, John	60		1	1
Hix, Sarah	205			2
Hix, James			1	
Hastings, William			1	
Holt, H.F.			1	3
Hurst, William			1	
Hasting, Wm.	85		1	
Hasting, Josiah Jun.	49		1	
Hasting, Josiah Sen.	133			
Hart, John H.			1	
Hudlow, George	73		1	
Holt, Joshua Sen.	900			6
Hurst, William Sen.	137.50			1
Holt, Joshua Jr.	280		1	
Jones, James	80	25	1	
Long, Andrew			1	
Lacy, Elijah	95			2
Morris, James B.			1	
Morris, Thomas			1	
McLaughlin, William			1	
Mullins, Jordan	66.75		1	
Mullins, Richd.	50		1	

NAME	DL	SL	WP	S
McNatt, Levin	225	25		
McNatt, William			1	
McNatt, John			1	
McLaughlin, Samuel		50	1	
Mullins, David			1	
McMillian, John	2		1	1
Morgan, Andw.			1	
Muse, Saml.			1	
Norman, John F.			1	
Norman, Jonathan	232	18		2
Noblett, Wm.	47	272		
Noblett, Sarah	63	108.75		
Noblett, Isaac			1	
Noblett, Abraham		50	1	
Neece, Sampson	240		1	
Ortner, Jesse			1	
Ortner, Phebe	25	36		
Phillips, William	40	38		
Phillips, Jefferson			1	
Phillips, Allen			1	
Parker, Joseph	96		1	1
Polk, John		75		
Phillips, Benjamin	200		1	
Phillips, Lemuel			1	
Patton, Joseph			1	
Parks, James P.			1	
Phillips, Jesse	50			
Patton, David	40	155	1	
Raney, Peter	58	33.50		
Reager, A.W.	108	42	1	2
Rozer, David		100		
Reeves, Archibald	128			4
Raney, John W.		73	1	
Raney, Henry K.	125		1	
Raney, Thomas			1	
Reager, Abraham	75		1	
Rotrammel, John			1	
Roberts, Nathanl.			1	
Robertson, John	100			
Ross, John P.	118		1	
Reynolds, Richd.			1	
Reynolds, Jane	181			2
Rotrammel, Abraham			1	
Rager, James	65	38.74	1	
Stewart, Saml.	60	19		
Sutton, John	76			
Sutton, Thomas			1	
Sent, John			1	

NAME	DL	SL	WP	S
Word, William	252		1	2
Word, Thomas	130		1	1
Word, Edmund	68.25	42	1	
Whinning, Joshua			1	
Wilson, Archibald			1	
Wilson, Elizabeth		53		
Wilson, James			1	
Wilson, Samuel			1	
Wilhoite, Pearce	125	93	1	2
Wilhoite, Willie, ded	121			
Wilhoite, Mary	82	13		2
Warren, Benjamin			1	
Woodard, John	150	420	1	
Waite, George	536		1	6
Wommack, Hawkins	100		1	
Willis, Phillip			1	
Williams, Isaac	60	50	1	
Watson, John			1	
Walker, William		80	1	
Walker, John			1	
Wommack, Michael	130		1	
Woodard, George			1	
Wilkes, Jesse M.			1	

BEDFORD COUNTY - DISTRICT NO. 23

Beginning at the southeast corner of the 21st District at the south bend of Duck River, south of A.C. Dodson's house, thence up the river to the mouth of Nease's branch below the mouth of Thompsons Creek, thence up said branch to its head excluding Freeman Burrow, Jr. and H. Anthony, thence in a direct line to Henry Greason's old place where Elkins now Lives, leaving Elkins on the east, thence to Thompsons Creek in a direct line from Elkins to the point of the ridge between Peter Shofner's and Andertons Branch, thence from Thompsons Creek below Thomas Roberts a direct line to the top of the ridge near Penland's old storehouse, thence westerly with the extreme height of the ridge dividing the western branches of Thompsons Creek and the waters of Little Flat Creek and with the old Regimental line between the regiments to the point of the ridge leading down by Robert Snoddy's house, leaving him on the south to a point on Big Flat Creek west of his house, thence due west to the Winchester Road and with the road to the first creek east of the Widow Hastings' house, thence down said creek to its mouth into Big Flat Creek and down said creek to And. Reed's lower lot, thence due north to the extreme bend of Duck River of A.C. Dodson's house.

Place of appointed for holding elections, etc., atthe house of Joseph Hastings, Esq.

NAME	DL	SL	WP	S
Anderton, Wm.	102		1	
Andrews, B.G.	140		1	
Arnold, Nancy				1
Arnold, Wiseman			1	

NAME	DL	SL	WP	S
Butler, John			1	
Bobo, Franklin D.	100		1	
Bryan, Nathl. C.			1	
Brunfield, David			1	
Brumfield, Anna	50			
Bearden, Willis			1	
Burrow, Numrod			1	
Bobo, Weldon W.	220		1	
Brown, Paschal			1	
Buckingham, Nathl.			1	
Cross, Sarah	4			
Cannon, Letitia (1 carriage)	417			4
Cheshire, Nathaniel				
Caruthers, Stewart S.	49		1	
Cates, Willliam H.			1	
Campbell, Alfred	100		1	1
Cobbs, John W.			1	2
Claunch, James H.			1	
Claunch, Jeremiah	142		1	
Cates, John			1	
Cheshire, Zacheus			1	
Cates, Jos. S.			1	
Cheshire, William			1	
Cunningham, Matthew	60		1	
Cunningham, Wm. G.	112			
Chamberlin, Thos.			1	
Cheshire, James	50		1	
Cannon, Elijah			1	
Cannon, Almon			1	
Carter, William	263			4
Cross, Joshua			1	
Crews, William			1	
Cannon, Newton Gov.	20			
Crews, George			1	
Coats, James			1	
Daniel, Frances W.				2
Drummond, William	77.50		1	
Darnaby, Edward			1	
Davis, Matthis			1	
Daniel, Willie	1000		1	10
Dunnaway, John	102		1	
Escue, Samuel	86			
Edmondson, Phillip				2
Elkins, James			1	
Floyd, William H.			1	
Ferguson, John A.	100		1	
Grooms, John			1	

NAME	DL	SL	WP	S
Gardner, John W.	100	28.75	1	
Green, Jesse			1	
Green, Daniel			1	
Hime, John W.			1	
Hix, Demarcus D.	263.50		1	5
Hime, Mary Ann	119			
Hime, Nathaniel			1	
Hime, William	62		1	
Hime, M.A. for J. Himes heirs				
Hime, Daniel K.			1	
Hastings, Susannah				1
Himeman, Robt. A.			1	
Hopkins, Thos. by R.P. Harrison, Agt.	60			
Huff, Ann	163			
Hyles, Joseph	275	25	1	
Hastings, Henry F.	94	32		
Haley, James			1	
Heaslett, William	126.25	8		
Hastings, Joseph Esq.	179.50	45.75		1
Harrison, Jacob	81		1	
Holder, Joseph			1	
Hastings, John	129		1	
Johnson, James M.	105		1	
Johnson, John B.	105		1	
King, Franklin			1	
Koonce, Jesse	50		1	
Kirley, John	69.75		1	
Kimery, Turley	156.25			
Kizer, Enoch				2
Koonce, John Sen.	212			
Koonce, John Jun.			1	
Kizer, Jacob	186		1	4
Kirley, James			1	
Kizer, Nancy	197			3
Kizer, David			1	
Koonce, Blackman			1	
Loyd, William A.			1	
Loyd, Thos. J.			1	
Loyd, Lemuel	86			
Loyd, Wm. A.			1	
Lurin, Henry	141.50		1	
Lacy, John			1	
Miles, James H.	75.25		1	
Miles, John H.	50.25		1	
Miles, Wm. H.	75.25	13	1	
Maxwell, Edward			1	
Murphree, Davis			1	

NAME	DL	SL	WP	S
Martin, Lyttleton			1	
Morgan, Robert G.			1	
Morgan, Benjamin B.			1	
Murphree, William	60		1	
Pratt, Henry	200			
Prewitt, P.H.	117			1
Pratt, James			1	
Raney, John	170			1
Russell, Lewis			1	
Reeves, William			1	
Reeves, Benjamin	40			2
Rogers, John J.			1	
Reeves, Isham	120		1	
Rogers & Snell Adm. for A. Cross	100			
Rice, Claiburne			1	
Rogers, Jesse	176		1	
Rice, John	173		1	
Rodgers, Dennis	126 (2 tracts)		1	
Reid, Robert	100		1	
Reid, Robert	237			
Reed, Andrew	220		1	
Snell, Willie B.	63	13	1	
Singleton, Peter	225			13
same for Lile & Bond	1200			
same for Eliz. S. Scudder	600			
same for Kibble T. Wynn	100			
Smiley, Matt. A.			1	
Stevens, Ervin	50			
Sutton, John	126			
Stewart, William	100	12	1	
Singleton, Allen			1	
Suiter, William			1	
Ship, Elizabeth	60	50		
Trot, Enoch			1	
Tribble, Melches.			1	
Terry, Kibble	371	46		12
Trollinger, John	41		1	
Troxler, Jacob	86			
Towsend, Joshua	237	30	1	
Wilson, William W.	38		1	
Woosley, Joshua			1	
Wommack, Michael	15			
Walker, L.D.	73		1	
Woosley, William			1	
Wallace, John	27		1	
Woosley, Elijah	50	10		
Walker, Callaway			1	

NAME	DL	SL	WP	S
Walsh, Elizabeth	136	25		
Williams, Stephens	65	25	1	
Williams, Wm.	180			
Whitman, Robert			1	
Young, Asa			1	
Young, Abijah	64	1		

BEDFORD COUNTY - DISTRICT NO. 24

Beginning at Flat Creek, west of Robert Shoddy's house, thence east including said Snoddy and with the ridge or Regimental line between the 28th and 103rd Regiments and with the dividing ridges between Little Flat Creek, Big Flat Creek and Thompsons Creek to the top of the ridge near Penland's old store house, thence in a direct line to where the Rowesville District line crosses Thompsons Creek between Shofne's and Elkins' the southeast corner of the 23rd District below Thomas Roberts, thence with the line of the Rowesville District or from the creek to the point of the ridge between Peter Shofner and Anderton's Branch, thence with the main ridge between said branches to the Franklin County line, thence westwardly with the south boundary of Bedford County to the western corner of New Bedford near Merrill's being the corner of the 22nd District, thence northwardly along the dividing ridge between the main fork of Big Flat Creek and the fork running down from the tanyard once owned by Watson, to the junction of said creek, thence down the creek to the beginning.

Elections appointed to be held at Ray's Shop. (Above Raus).

NAME	DL	SL	WP	S
Anderton, Thomas	100	200	1	
Anderton, John			1	
Anderton, James Esq.			1	
Adkins, Margaret	104			
Bennett, Hezekiah		185	1	
Bearden, Nimrod	20	51	1	
Bobo, Washington P.		88		
Bobo, Elisha	306	234	1	4
Bobo, Elijah		60	1	
Brown, Daniel			1	
Bateman, Tilman			1	
Bomar, Mary	28.75	171.25		
Bennett, William	100		1	
Bearden, Nancy	190.50	128.25		
Blankinship, Jas.			1	
Cook, Henry & Elz, heirs	31	60		
Carpenter, John H.			1	
Crisco, William		76	1	
Chandler, Henry S.	75		1	2
Crolley, John				1
Crisco, Daniel	50	285		

NAME	DL	SL	WP	S
Crawford, Thomas			1	
Caldwell, Samuel	151.75	219.25		1
Cates, Timothy	55			
Cox, Thomas	75		1	
Chandler, Joel			1	
Driver, Noel		100		
Daniel, Plummer		60	1	
Driver, Benjamin		250		
Dean, John		100		
Dean, Jeremiah		125	1	
Duckworth, Hezekiah			1	
Dillingham, Joshua			1	
Dean, William			1	
Dean, Martin			1	
Dillingham, Jackson			1	
Dillingham, William			1	
Daniel, Hiram	20	80	1	
Daniel, Robert	25	475	1	
Dean, John Esq.	40	85	1	
Elkins, Alexander		92		
Evans, William M.	124	74	1	
Floyd, Elijah	117	10	1	
Floyd, Samuel				
Floyd, Saml. & Anthony		147.50		
Floyd, David	127	202	1	
Fulkerson, James			1	
Finney, James			1	
Frost, Ebenezer	191	120	1	
Finney, Norman			1	
Fuller, Jacob	38	26		1
Gobble, John	15	159	1	
Gore, Amos	59	117	1	
Gowen, Matthew P.			1	
Gowen, James B.	139.50	202		2
Gore, Thomas	43	43	1	
Garrett, Wilson			1	
Hutson, Cuthbert C.	62.50	80	1	
Hubbard, Sally	86			1
Holt, Hiram	30		1	3
Heaslett, William Esq.	153	10		1
Huffman, Jarrett B.			1	
Hill, Lewis A.	50		1	
Hammack, Willouby			1	
Hix, William	78			
Hodge, Hugh R.	200			
Howard, Daniel			1	
Holt, Eve	70			

NAME	DL	SL	WP	S
Hutson, William	63			
Holt, Jeremiah			1	
Hawkins, John	54	35		
Hornedy, Solomon	132			
Hodge, John		115		
Henderson, Rice			1	
Heathcock, Allen C.			1	
Hornady, Christopher			1	
Jones, Jonathan N.			1	
Jones, Rebecca	100			1
Jones, Rebecca, Guardian	178			
Jones, Hix				
Jones, Willie B.	100			2
Ivey, James	20	122.50		
Kimbro, Levi		195	1	
King, Henry A.	27			
Knight, Charles			1	
Long, John, Adm. Jno. Gore		320		
Mullins, Thomas R.		80		
McElvaney, Robert			1	
Martin, Thomas	3.50	158		
Massey, John			1	
Martin, Asa			1	
Merrill, Jonathan	30	51		
Mitchell & Welch		150		
Martin, William	20	243		
Martin, John		123.50		
Newton, Nicholas			1	
Nicholas, John		144	1	
Newton, John	60	50	1	
Nelson, William			1	
Neeley, Moses			1	
Neeley, Elijah	110	30	1	
Neeley, William			1	
Nelson, Adam		50	1	
Orrick, James	181.25	100		
Parker, Elijah, Esq.	269.75	140		3
Parker, Charles H.	130	40	1	1
Parker, James H.			1	
Pearson, William	119	120		4
Prince, Thomas			1	
Prince, Jeremiah			1	
Prince, William			1	
Prince, Asa		112	1	

NAME	DL	SL	WP	S
Prince, Presley	40	100	1	
Pearson, Sarah	108.50			
Pollock, Zachariah			1	
Parker, Jonathan	170	32	1	5
Powell, John	45	450	1	
Pearson, Kindred Esq.	100	36	1	
Pollock, William			1	
Riddle, Stephen			1	
Reed, Wilson C.			1	
Reese, James R.	75		1	
Ray, William			1	
Russell, William	20	70	1	
Ray, Thomas			1	
Ray, Jason	230		1	
Raney, Bennett C.	20	70	1	
Ray, hezekiah	64	127		
Roberts, Thomas	165	11.50	1	3
Reese, William			1	
Shofner, Martin	50			
Stewart, Chas. E.	50			
Stone, James	150		1	
Shook, William	90	103		
Shook, John			1	
Shook, Jonathan			1	
Shook, Levi	12	88	1	
Shook, Abram	38	17.50		
Spand, Robt. L.			1	
Sexton, Jesse	15	30		
Snoddy, Robert	85			1
Shofner, Austin	50	139		
Sexton, Robert B.			1	
Tribble, James C.	80	26	1	
Turman, John C.	50	89	1	
Turner, Henry		75		
Turner, Rebecca		200		
Turner, Wesley			1	
Word, William			1	
Watson, Walter,			1	
Walker, James		100		
White, William			1	
Wood, Andrew C.			1	
Walsh, Elizabeth		50		
Williams, Charles	67	50	1	

BEDFORD COUNTY - DISTRICT NO. 25

Beginning on Duck River at the upper corner of the 23rd District at the mouth of Nease's Branch below the mouth of Thompsons Creek, thence up said branch including said Nease, F. Burrow and Henry Anthony, thence to include Harrison Elkins, crossing Thompsons Creek to Peter Shofner's peach orchard, and with the ridge between Peter Shofner's and Anderton's branches and with the main ridge leading to the Franklin County line so as to leave the waters of Thompsons Creek only on the west, thence with the Franklin County line to the corner of Coffee County, thence north with the said county line to the Barren Fork of Duck River, thence down the river to the beginning.

Elections appointed to be held at Rowesville.

NAME	DL	SL	WP	S
Anthony, Nicholas	198.50			
Anthony, Nicholas	120		1	
Ayers, Garland			1	
Anthony, Adam	15	100		
Ayers, Moses		300	1	
Arnold, Robert F.			1	
Arnold, Absalom			1	
Ayler, Anthony			1	
Anthony, Henry			1	
Amix, James			1	
Adams, Thomas			1	
Bateman, Thomas E.			1	
Bridges, George W.			1	
Bonds, John (2 town lots)				
Burt, Frederick			1	
Boon, Jesse			1	
Barnett, Isaac (1 town lot)	75		1	
Burrow, JAcob C.	30	61	1	1
Brooks, John Rev.			1	2
Brooks & Mitchell	160			
Burrow, Nimrod			1	
Burrow, Phillip J.			1	
Blanton, Sarah	150			2
Burrow, Freeman				1
Burrow, Freeman H.			1	
Burrow, Joshua			1	
Barnett, John	100	25	1	3
Calahan, Moses P. (2 town lots)			1	
Clapp, John			1	
Carr, William	41			
Chamberlain, Wm. P.		125		
Couser, Robert M. (part of lot)	30		1	
Coble, Jacob	392.50		1	2
Duncan, Laudin				
Edwards. Sterling			1	
Ewell, Mary	634	417		5

NAME	DL	SL	WP	S
Elkins, Harrison			1	
Elkins, David Jr.			1	17
Evans, John			1	
Euless, Adam	200			1
Fowler, James (4 town lots)	68.50		1	2
Fowler, Harrison N.			1	
Gann, Iverson			1	
Gilly, John			1	
Graves, Peter		25		
Gilbert, Cynthia	13.75			
Heard, George W.			1	4
House, Thomas			1	
Haithcoat, Barney			1	
Height, John T.			1	
Howe, John W.	30		1	
Howe, Joseph M.			1	
Ham, James			1	
Hemby, Dennis	65	1048.50		
House, D.P.T.	161		1	1
Harrison, Robert	260			1
Hendrix, John		65		
Hemby, Pherebe		50		
Huffman, George	48	251.50		
Howard, Oliver			1	
Hooser, Daniel	60		1	
Harrison, John			1	
Holt, Lodwick	100			
Iseley, John			1	
Iseley, Benjamin			1	
Johnson, John B.		100		
Jenkins, William Rev.	85			
Jameson, John	286			
Jameson, Samuel			1	
Jolly, John			1	
Kerby, William			1	
Keck, John	124			
Keck, Isaac			1	
Kimbro, Benjamin		171	1	
Kortner, George	350		1	
Kimbro, John	50			1
Kimsey, Ham P.			1	
Kimbro, Allen			1	
Kimbro, George	172.25			2
Kelly, Benjn. D.	145		1	
Kelly, Nathan T.	145		1	
Kimbro, James			1	

NAME	DL	SL	WP	S
Lindley, Thomas I.			1	
Latemor, Anderson			1	
Landis, R.L. & A/	26		1	
Landis, Abel	179	23		
Landis, Abel	50		1	2
Landis, A. (guardian)	75.50	50		
Landis, John	73	50	1	
Low, David	160	100		
Low, Iredell J.			1	
Lucas, Charles	130		1	
Moss, Eli (4 town lots)				
Moss, Matthew			1	
Maupin, Blan & Gabriel	243		2	1
Moss, Felix	50			
Moss, Matthew Sen.	52	50		
Martin, Andw. J.			1	
Nicholas, Arthur			1	
Nutt, Murphy			1	
Nutt, David	42	25	1	
Nutt, Jesse			1	
Neese, William	92		1	
Puryear, Robert	100	60		
Parker, Elijah	210		1	5
Roberts, Zachariah			1	
Riggins, Willie			1	
Ross, James		50		
Robertson, Thomas			1	
Shofner, Martin	378			6
Shipman, Wm.	167	50	1	
Still & Lindley	10			
Still, Joel H.			1	
Shofner, William	50	50	1	
Scruggs, Samuel			1	
Shofner, Frederick	206.50		1	
Sherrill, George			1	
Shipman, Reuben			1	
Simpler, Andrew J. (1 town lot)				
Scott, John H.			1	
Stanfield, John	112	90	1	
Spears, Nathan			1	
Scruggs, David,		400	1	
Smith, John	106.50			3
Shipman, James	29		1	
Shofner, P.L.	100		1	
Shipman, Danl.	15	115	1	
Shofner, Gabriel	87.25		1	
Spears, James			1	

NAME	DL	SL	WP	S
Stevens, John	100			
Truman, Willliam (1 town lot)				
Troxler, Anthony	49.50		1	
Timmons, Ambrose	63		1	
Troxler, Nicholas	110.50		1	1
Troxler, Jacob	70			
Turner, Henry		100	1	
Timmons, Charles		30		
Turner, John	84	50		
Troxler, Isaac	114		1	
Weaver, Zephaniah		142.75		
Williams, Patrick	17			
Williams, John			1	
Whitfield, F.M.			1	
Weaver, David	127	138		
Weaver, Sarah		92.50		
Ward, Wyatt			1	
Watkins, Willliam A.			1	
Webster, Henry	70			

TOTALS FOR DISTRICTS 1 THROUGH 25

ACRES - 341,823+
SCHOOL LAND - 41,485+
LOTS - 200
SLAVES - 2,345
CARRIAGES - 14

CARRAIGE OWNERSHIP :
Andrew M. Davidson
James Erwin
William Houston
John Eakin, Esq.
George Davidson
E.C. Dobson
William Gilchrist
Thomas Holland, Jr.
William F. Long
John L. Cooper, Esq.
Mary Ewing
Allen Leeper
Thomas Q. Hunter

END OF 1836 TAX LIST

BEDFORD AFTER THE REMOVAL
OF
LINCOLN-COFFEE & MARSHALL
1836

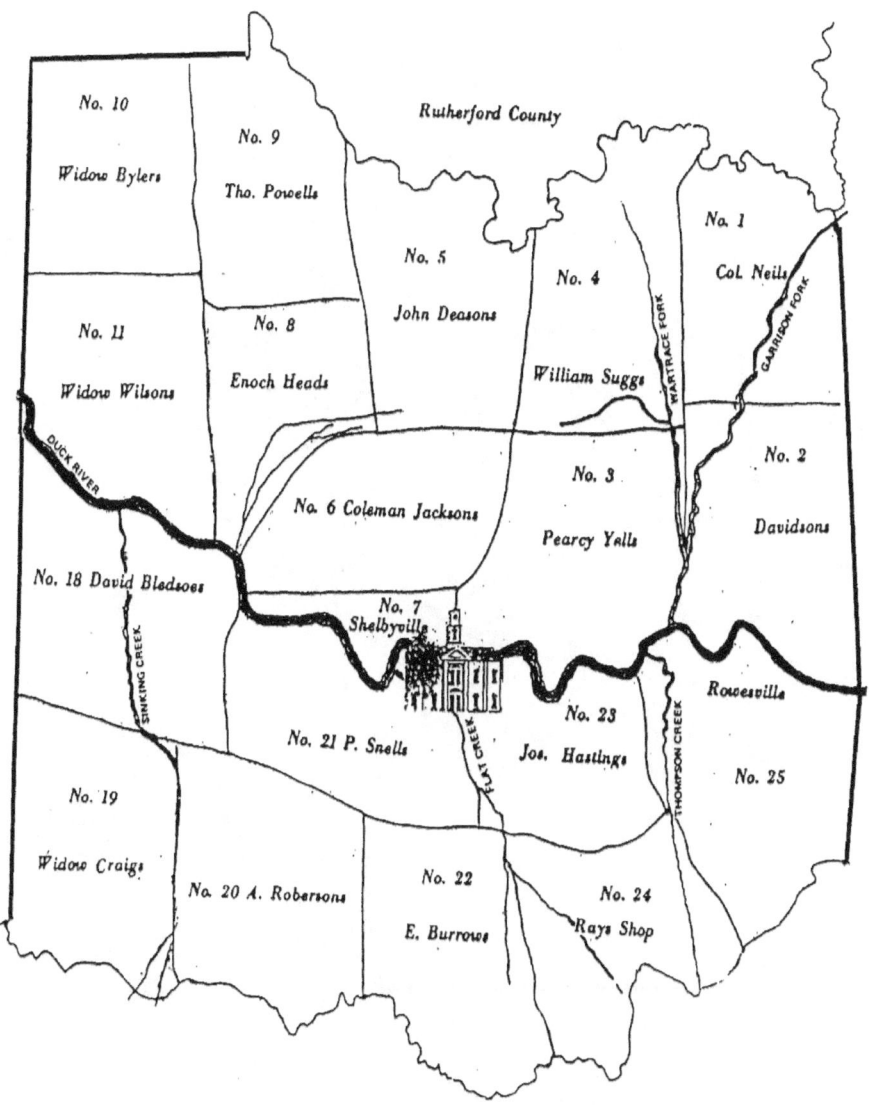

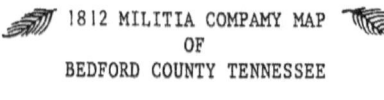

1812 MILITIA COMPAMY MAP
OF
BEDFORD COUNTY TENNESSEE

BY
TIMOTHY R. MARSH

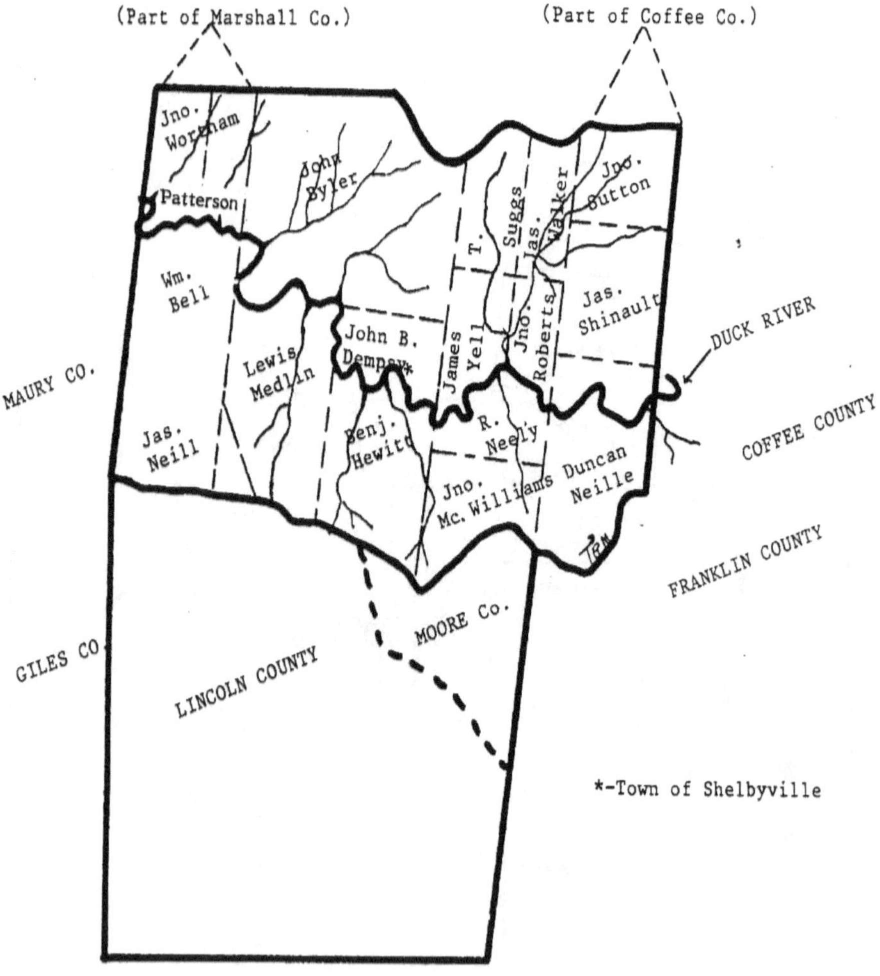

*-Town of Shelbyville

1812 TAX LIST OF BEDFORD COUNTY, TENNESSEE

This Tax List is the next best substitute to an 1812 Census of Bedford County, Tennessee, and gives a reasonably good list of the early settlers who were here in Bedford and the eastern half of Marshall in 1812. It can be used as a good substitute for the 1810 census which was destroyed during the War of 1812. See the Captain's Company Map accompanying this list, it is an original that was researched and drawn by the authors to help in locating that part of the county the taxables were located in. Some did not make the list for various reasons, some due to age. Prior to 1836, the parent county was made up of Captain's Companies that served as an early substitute for the Civil Districts that were established in 1835-1836. Inserts in parenthesizes were added by the authors. The original Tax List is in the Tennessee State Archives in Nashville, Tennessee.

Timothy R. & Helen C. Marsh

ALPHABETICAL ORDER

LIST

NAME	CAPTAIN'S COMPANY	PAGE NUMBER
Aaron, Moses	Richard Neely	30
Abbott, William	John McWilliams	30
Ables, William	James Yell	19
Abner, Paul	Richard Neely	30
Adams, Archibald	Lewis Medlin	4
Adams, David	Duncan Neille	7
Adams, Edwin	John Wortham	1
Adams, George	Patterson (Andrew)	12
Adams, James	Lewis Medlin	4
Adams, Robert	James Neill	2
Adams, William	Patterson (Andrew)	12
Ake, Joseph	Timothy Sugg	20
Adkin, John	Lewis Medlin	4
Akles, Moses	John McWilliams	28
Aldridge, John	Benjamin Hewitt	10
Aldridge, Nathan'l	Benjamin Hewitt	10
Alexander, Archibald	Benjamin Hewitt	11
Alexander, Archibald	John B. Dempsey	17
Alexander, Joseph	John McWilliams	28
Alexander, Joseph	Benjamin Hewitt	11
Alexander, William	John McWilliams	29
Allen, John	James Yell	19
Allen, Valentine	John B. Dempsey	16
Allen, William	John B. Dempsey	16
Allison, John	William Bell	9
Allison, John	John McWilliams	28
Allison, Thos.	Lewis Medlin	4
Allred, Isaac	William Bell	8
Allred, James	William Bell	8
Allred, William	William Bell	8
Allred, William Jur.	William Bell	8
Alvis, Zacharias	Benjamin Hewitt	10
Anderson, Gabriel	James Yell	18
Anderson, Holmes	James Neill	3
Anderson, Isaac	Benjamin Hewitt	11

1812 TAX LIST

NAME	CAPTAIN'S COMPANY	PAGE NUMBER
Anderson, John	James Neill	3
Anderson, Peter	John McWilliams	28
Anderson, William	James Neill	3
Andrews, James	John Wortham	1
Angle, Reuben	John Sutton	26
Angle, Reuben	John Sutton	26
Anthony, Jacob	Richard Neely	30
Anthony, Nicholas	Richard Neely	30
Appleby, John	William Bell	8
Arenton, Jacob	Richard Neely	31
Armstrong, George	Patterson (Andrew)	13
Armstrong, James	John Wortham	1
Armstrong, William	Lewis Medlin	4
Arnold, Robert	Richard Neely	31
Arnold, Smith	James Yell	19
Aronton, Charles	Richard Neely	30
Ashbrooks, Moses	James Yell	18
Ashbrooks, William	James Yell	18
Ashworth, Moses	Duncan Neille	7
Atkins, Robert	Richard Neely	30
Atkinson, John (Esq)	Patterson (Andrew)	13
Ault, John	John McWilliams	28
Au<u>ph</u>, Henry	James Walker	24
Ausamus, John	Duncan Neille	8
Ausamus, Phillip	Duncan Neille	7
Auston, William	John Byler	14
Balch, Amos	Benjamin Hewitt	11
Bailey, Thomas	Lewis Medlin	5
Bailey, Thos.	James Neill	3
Baily, John	James Neill	3
Baird, George	Lewis Medlin	5
Baird, George	Timothy Sugg	20
Baird, John	John B. Dempsey	17
Baker, George	John McWilliams	29
Baker, John	John McWilliams	29
Baker, Robert	James Shinault	6
Baker, Robert	John McWilliams	29
Balch, George B.	John B. Dempsey	17
Bankston, Washington	James Yell	18
Barnet, Hugh	Benjamin Hewitt	10
Barnet, John	Benjamin Hewitt	10
Barnett, James	Benjamin Hewitt	10
Barratt, Isaac	John McWilliams	29
Barratt, Jonathan	John McWilliams	28
Barton, Benjamin	James Yell	19
Baskins, Walter	James Shinault	6
Bates, George	John Sutton	26
Bates, James	John Sutton	26
Beaird, John	James Walker	24

1812 TAX LIST

NAME	CAPTAIN'S COMPANY	PAGE NUMBER
Beans, James	Benjamin Hewitt	11
Beasley, Willie	Richard Neely	30
Beck, John	John Wortham	1
Bedwell, James	John Wortham	1
Bedwell, Reuben	John Wortham	2
Bell, David	John Byler	14
Bell, John	John Byler	14
Bell, Sam'l	John Byler	14
Belt, Thos.	John Sutton	26
Benjamin, Henry	John Roberts	22
Benson, Daniel	James Shinault	6
Benson, John	James Neill	3
Benson, Leaben	James Neill	3
Berrett, John	James Walker	24
Berry, Enoch	John McWilliams	28
Berryman, John	Patterson (Andrew)	13
Bevins, Stephen	James Neill	3
Billington, Ezekiel	Patterson (Andrew)	13
Billow, John	John McWilliams	29
Bingham, William	John B. Dempsey	16
Bishop, Henry	Lewis Medlin	5
Blackburn, James	James Walker	24
Blackburn, John	James Yell	19
Blackburn, Samuel	James Yell	18
Blackman, Elijah	John Byler	14
Blackwell, John	Lewis Medlin	4
Blackwell, Nathan	Lewis Medlin	5
Blair, Thos.	John Sutton	26
Blanton, Alexander	John Sutton	26
Blessing, Henry	James Yell	18
Bloodworth, Thomas	William Bell	8
Bloyd, Tubby	Benjamin Hewitt	11
Bloyth, James	Duncan Neille	7
Bolt, James	Patterson (Andrew)	13
Bolt, John	Patterson (Andrew)	13
Boon, Henry	James Neill	3
Booth, Henry	Timothy Sugg	20
Booth, Stephen	Timothy Sugg	20
Botts, John	William Bell	9
Box, William	James Shinault	6
Boyd, Alexander	Duncan Neille	8
Boyd, John	John Wortham	1
Boyd, Joseph	James Yell	18
Boyd, William	Duncan Neille	7
Boyd, William	Duncan Neille	8
Boyet, Ethrildred	Lewis Medlin	4
Boyet, Jehu	Lewis Medlin	4
Boyett, James	Lewis Medlin	4
Boyett, Jesse	James Neill	3

1812 TAX LIST

NAME	CAPTAIN'S COMPANY	PAGE NUMBER
Brock, George A.	John McWilliams	29
Bracken, Henry	Benjamin Hewitt	11
Bradaway, John Junr.	John McWilliams	30
Bradford, Benjamin	John Roberts	22
Bradford, Hamilton	John Roberts	22
Bradford, John	John Roberts	22
Brains, John	Lewis Medlin	4
Branch, Jno.	Timothy Sugg	20
Branch, Nicholas	John B. Dempsey	17
Brandon, Charles	John Byler	15
Brandon, John	John Roberts	22
Breedon, Mason	John Roberts	22
Brittain, Benjamin	Duncan Neille	7
Brittain, Joseph	John Wortham	1
Brodaway, John	John McWilliams	30
Brodaway, John	Benjamin Hewitt	11
Brookes, William	Timothy Sugg	20
Brooks, John	Timothy Sugg	20
Brown, Absolom	John Byler	15
Brown, Hezekiah	John McWilliams	30
Brown, Hugh	James Walker	24
Brown, Jonathan	Lewis Medlin	4
Brown, Joseph	John McWilliams	29
Brown, Robert	James Walker	25
Brown, Samuel	Timothy Sugg	20
Brown, Samuel	Richard Neely	30
Brown, Shedrick	John B. Dempsey	16
Brown, Solomon	John McWilliams	29
Browning, Beedy	Benjamin Hewitt	10
Browning, Caleb	Benjamin Hewitt	10
Browning, George	Benjamin Hewitt	11
Browning, Joshua	Benjamin Hewitt	10
Bruce, Edward	Patterson (Andrew)	12
Bruce, John	James Walker	25
Brumfield, Joseph	John McWilliams	29
Bryans, Edward	Lewis Medlin	4
Buchannon, Thos.	William Bell	8
Buckham, Willie	Lewis Medlin	4
Buckhannon, Benjamin	William Bell	8
Buckhannon, James	William Bell	9
Buckhannon, John	William Bell	8
Buckhannon, John Senr.	William Bell	9
Buckhannon, Thos. Jr.	William Bell	8
Buckley, James	John McWilliams	29
Balla, Isaac	John Sutton	27
Balla, James	John Sutton	27
Burdett, Jesse	John McWilliams	28
Burdett, Jiles	John McWilliams	28
Burdett, William	John McWilliams	28

1812 TAX LIST

NAME	CAPTAIN'S COMPANY	PAGE NUMBER
Burges, John	Benjamin Hewitt	11
Burges, Richard	Benjamin Hewitt	11
Burnet, William	John Byler	14
Burnham, Thomas	John Roberts	22
Burns, Jeremiah	Timothy Sugg	20
Burns, John Junr.	Patterson (Andrew)	12
Burns, John Senr.	Patterson (Andrew)	12
Burns, Josiah	Patterson (Andrew)	13
Burns, Robert	Timothy Sugg	20
Burns, Saml.	John B. Dempsey	16
Burrham, Richardson	James Shinault	6
Burrham, Saml.	James Shinault	6
Burrham, William	James Shinault	6
Burrough, Freeman	Richard Neely	30
Burrough, Ishmael	Richard Neely	30
Burrough, Jarald	Richard Neely	30
Burrow, Philip Junr.	John McWilliams	28
Burrow, Philip Senr.	John McWilliams	29
Burrow, William	John McWilliams	28
Burrows, Boas	James Yell	19
Busby, Thos.	Duncan Neille	8
Bussey, Elliot	William Bell	8
Bussey, George	William Bell	8
Bussey, George Sen.	William Bell	8
Bussey, Washington	William Bell	8
Butler, John	Richard Neely	30
Byler, Abraham	John Byler	15
Byler, John	John Byler	14
Bynom, Benjamin	John Sutton	27
Bynom, Humphrey	John Sutton	27
Bynom, John	John Sutton	27
Bynom, William	John Sutton	26
Byrom, Benjamin	Duncan Neille	7
Byrom, James	Duncan Neille	8
Cable, Adam	John McWilliams	29
Cagburn, Zachariah	Duncan Neille	8
Cage, Edward	John Roberts	23
Caisey, William	John McWilliams	30
Calhoon, George Senr.	Patterson (Andrew)	13
Calhoon, George W.	Patterson (Andrew)	12
Calhoon, William	John Sutton	27
Campbell, Alexander	Patterson (Andrew)	13
Campbell, George	Benjamin Hewitt	10
Canal, Thomas	Duncan Neille	8
Cannon, Andrew	John Roberts	22
Cannon, Clement	John B. Dempsey	17
Cannon, Minos	John B. Dempsey	16
Campbell, William	Benjamin Hewitt	10

1812 TAX LIST

NAME	CAPTAIN'S COMPANY	PAGE NUMBER
Caplen, John	Lewis Medlin	4
Capley, John	John Byler	15
Caps, Allsey	James Neill	2
Carman, Skipper	James Yell	18
Carney, ____ (Joseph)	John Sutton	27
Carothers, William	John Roberts	22
Carpenter, John	Lewis Medlin	4
Carr, James	William Bell	8
Carr, Robert	John McWilliams	29
Carrons, David	Lewis Medlin	4
Carson, Andrew	John Wortham	1
Carson, David	John Wortham	2
Carter, James	Richard Neely	30
Carter, Jesse	Richard Neely	30
Cartmel, John	Duncan Neille	8
Cartmel, Thomas	Duncan Neille	8
Cartmell, John	Duncan Neille	7
Caruthers, Thomas	James Walker	24
Cates, John	Richard Neely	30
Cates, Wm.	John B. Dempsey	16
Cathey, George	James Neill	3
Cathy, Hugh	James Neill	3
Cathy, John	John Wortham	1
Cathy, John	William Bell	9
Chaepen, Nathan	Timothy Sugg	20
Chapel, Abner	Richard Neely	30
Chapen, Jesse	Timothy Sugg	20
Chilcut, Peter	John B. Dempsey	17
Childress, Joseph	James Shinault	6
Churchhill, Richard	John Sutton	27
Clardy, Richard	Timothy Sugg	20
Clark, James	Patterson (Andrew)	12
Claxton, John	John B. Dempsey	16
Clemens, Ham	James Yell	18
Clemens, John	Patterson (Andrew)	12
Clemons, Thomas	Richard Neely	30
Clerk, James	Duncan Neille	7
Clift, John	Benjamin Hewitt	10
Clinton, James	John Byler	15
Coats, Benjamin	Benjamin Hewitt	11
Coats, John	John B. Dempsey	16
Coats, William	Benjamin Hewitt	11
Coats, Wilson	John B. Dempsey	17
Cockrill, John	James Neill	2
Cockrill, John	John B. Dempsey	16
Coffee, Benjamin	John Roberts	23
Coffee, James	Lewis Medlin	5
Coffee, John	John Roberts	23

1812 TAX LIST

NAME	CAPTAIN'S COMPAMY	PAGE NUMBER
Coffee, Thomas	Lewis Medlin	5
Coffey, William	John Roberts	22
Coffy, Rice	John Roberts	22
Coldwell, Ballard	Timothy Sugg	20
Coldwell, James	James Yell	18
Cole, Abraham	John Wortham	1
Cole, Dixon	John Wortham	1
Cole, Neri	John Wortham	1
Cole, William	Duncan Neille	7
Collings, Durham	James Neill	3
Collins, Joseph	John McWilliams	29
Colvert, John	William Bell	8
Colvert, Joseph	William Bell	8
Colvert, William	Benjamin Hewitt	10
Condiff, Frail	James Yell	18
Conway, Henry	John Roberts	23
Conwell, Jesse	John McWilliams	28
Conwell, John	John Sutton	27
Conwell, Thos.	John McWilliams	28
Cook, Charles	James Neill	3
Cook, Charles Junr.	James Neill	3
Cook, George	John McWilliams	30
Cook, John	Richard Neely	30
Cook, John Junr.	Richard Neely	30
Cook, Robert	James Neill	3
Cook, Stephen	James Neill	3
Coonse, John	John McWilliams	28
Coop, Horatio	Timothy Sugg	20
Coop, James	Timothy Sugg	20
Coop, Richard	Timothy Sugg	20
Cooper, Abraham	Timothy Sugg	20
Cooper, Charles	James Yell	18
Cooper, Christopher	Richard Neely	30
Cooper, Edward	John Byler	15
Cooper, Job	John Byler	15
Cooper, John	John Byler	15
Cooper, William	James Shinault	6
Cooper, William	Richard Neely	30
Cooper, William	Timothy Sugg	20
Cooper, William	John Byler	15
Cople, William	James Neill	2
Carliles, William	John Sutton	26
Cotton, Daniel	Lewis Medlin	4
Couch, Thomas	James Walker	25
Courts, William	Duncan Neille	7
Cowden, Elijah	John Roberts	22
Cowden, Robert	John Roberts	22
Cowden, William	John Roberts	22
Cox, Caleb	John Byler	15

1812 TAX LIST

NAME	CAPTAIN'S COMPANY	PAGE NUMBER
Cox, David	James Walker	24
Cox, James	James Yell	18
Cox, Thomas	John McWilliams	29
Crain, Ambrose	John McWilliams	30
Crain, Joel	John McWilliams	30
Craig, Crozier	William Bell	9
Craig, John	James Yell	19
Craig, John	William Bell	9
Crawford, James	Benjamin Hewitt	11
Crawford, William	John Roberts	22
Crawley, Michael	John Roberts	22
Crig, Alexander	James Yell	18
Crisp, William	William Bell	8
Crite, William	Duncan Neille	8
Croff, Jacob (Cross)	James Walker	24
Croft, Danl. Berry	Benjamin Hewitt	11
Crook, John	Benjamin Hewitt	11
Cross, Asel	John McWilliams	30
Cross, David	James Walker	25
Cross, Gibson	James Shinault	6
Cross, William	John Sutton	26
Crosslin, Thomas	James Shinault	6
Crow, Levi	Benjamin Hewitt	11
Crowel, Samuel	John Byler	15
Crowel, William	John Byler	15
Crump, George	James Shinault	7
Cry, John	John Byler	14
Culp, Henry	John B. Dempsey	16
Cummins, John	James Neill	3
Cummins, Thomas	Benjamin Hewitt	10
Cunningham, Humphrey	Benjamin Hewitt	10
Cunningham, Jno.	Richard Neely	30
Cunningham, Paul M.	Richard Neely	30
Curtis, Henry	Lewis Medlin	5
Damorah, Samuel T.	John B. Dempsey	17
Daniel, Wats	Duncan Neille	7
Dankin, John	Duncan Neille	7
Darden, ____	Richard Neely	31
Davidson, Lewis	Richard Neely	31
Davidson, Thomas	Lewis Medlin	5
Davidson, William	Benjamin Hewitt	10
Davis, Daniel	Lewis Medlin	5
Davis, Daniel	John B. Dempsey	17
Davis, Henry	John B. Dempsey	17
Davis, Isaac	William Bell	9
Davis, Jesse	John Roberts	22
Davis, John	Lewis Medlin	5
Davis, John	William Bell	22

1812 TAX LIST

NAME	CAPTAIN'S COMPANY	PAGE NUMBER
Davis, Sherod	Lewis Medlin	5
Davis, Thomas	John B. Dempsey	17
Davis, Zachr.	Lewis Medlin	5
Dawdy, Alfred	John B. Dempsey	17
Dawdy, Danl.	John B. Dempsey	17
Dawdy, Howel	John B. Dempsey	17
Dawdy, Howel	John B. Dempsey	17
Dawson, Jonathan	William Bell	22
Day, Danl.	Duncan Neille	7
Day, Hugh	James Shinault	6
Days, John C.	James Walker	24
Deal, Charles	Richard Neely	31
Deal, Henry	James Yell	18
Dial, Jeremiah	James Yell	18
Dial, Jeremiah Junr.	James Yell	18
Dial, Larkin	James Walker	24
Dean, Greenberry	Patterson (Andrew)	12
Deason, Abraham	James Yell	18
Deason, Absolom	James Yell	18
Deason, Enoch	James Yell	18
Deason, William	James Yell	18
Deery, James	John B. Dempsey	17
Dempsey, John B.	John B. Dempsey	17
Denison, Robert	John B. Dempsey	17
Denny, John	William Bell	22
Depriest, William	Benjamin Hewitt	10
Dewall, Bailey	William Bell	22
Dickson, Ephraim	Patterson (Andrew)	12
Dickson, Ephraim D.	Patterson (Andrew)	12
Dickson, James	Patterson (Andrew)	12
Dickson, John	Patterson (Andrew)	12
Dickson, Matthew	Patterson (Andrew)	12
Die, Martin	Timothy Sugg	20
Ditto, William	James Yell	18
Dobbs, David	James Shinault	6
Dobbs, Fortunatus	Lewis Medlin	5
Dobbs, Henry	James Neill	3
Dobbs, James	Lewis Medlin	5
Dobbs, Joseph	James Yell	18
Dobbs, Joseph	Richard Neely	31
Dobbs, William	Lewis Medlin	5
Dobb, Mark	John Wortham	2
Doddy, Anson	James Yell	18
Doherty, Joseph	John Wortham	2
Doherty, Robert	Benjamin Hewitt	10
Doherty, William (Esq)	John Robert	22
Donnalson, Andrew	John B. Dempsey	17
Doogan, Saml.	John Sutton	27
Dorman, Joseph	James Walker	24

1812 TAX LIST

NAME	CAPTAIN'S COMPANY	PAGE NUMBER
Dormand, Jesse	James Yell	18
Dorment, Benjamin	James Yell	18
Dorty, Tyler	John Sutton	27
Doty, Isaac	Benjamin Hewitt	10
Douglass, Rhodeham	John Sutton	27
Douglass, Thomas	John Sutton	27
Dowdy, John	Duncan Neille	7
Dowdy, Micaijah	John Wortham	2
Dowdy, Thomas	John Wortham	2
Downen, William	Patterson	12
Drake, Thomas	James Walker	24
Drake, Zachariah	John B. Dempsey	17
Driskill, Obediah	John McWilliams	28
Dryden, John	Lewis Medlin	5
Dryden, Jonathan	Benjamin Hewitt	10
Dryden, Nathanl.	Lewis Medlin	5
Duckery, Matthew	John McWilliams	28
Duckery, Matthew	John McWilliams	28
Duens, Thomas (Deans)	James Yell	18
Dugh, William	James Walker	24
Duncan, Josiah	James Neill	3
Dungan, Jacob	Benjamin Hewitt	10
Dungan, Jacob	John B. Dempsey	17
Dungan, Jonathan	Benjamin Hewitt	10
Dungan, William	Benjamin Hewitt	10
Dunn, John C.	Patterson	12
Dunham, John	John Roberts	22
Dunham, Joseph[s]	Lewis Medlin	5
Dwiggins, Daniel	John B. Dempsey	17
Dyzard, William	William Bell	9
Dyzert, Francis	James Neill	4
Elam, Jonathan	James Walker	23
East, Jno. W.	Timothy Sugg	20
Edde, James	John B. Dempsey	16
Edward, Andrew	Benjamin Hewitt	10
Edwards, Andrews	James Yell	19
Edward, Riggs	John Wortham	2
Elam, William	James Shinault	6
Elim, Jesse (Elam)	James Walker	25
Elim, William (Elam)	James Walker	25
Elliott, Simon	James Walker	24
Elliott, William	John Wortham	2
Ellis, John	John B. Dempsey	16
Ellis, John	John McWilliams	30
Ellison, Robert	John Byler	14
Elord, William	Timothy Sugg	20
Emanuel, Cuthbert	James Neill	3
Emanuel, Poston	James Neill	3

1812 TAX LIST

NAME	CAPTAIN'S COMPANY	PAGE NUMBER
Eoff, Isaac	James Walker	25
Eoff, Joseph	James Walker	24
Eoff, William	James Walker	24
Epps, John	Richard Neely	31
Enoch, Robert H.	James Walker	24
Evans, Jesse	John B. Dempsey	16
Ewell, John	Duncan Neille	7
Erwin, Josephus	James Walker	24
Ewing, James	James Neill	2
Ewing, George	James Neill	3
Ewing, Robert	James Neill	3
Ewing, William	William Bell	9
Fain, Charles	Timothy Sugg	20
Fain, David	James Walker	24
Fallwell, Elisha	John Byler	15
Farlor, Clay	John Roberts	22
Farlor, Jesse	John Roberts	22
Farmer, Joseph	James Yell	18
Farriar, George	Patterson	12
Ferguson, John	John Roberts	22
Ferguson, William	James Yell	18
Ferrel, Charles Jun.	John Sutton	27
Ferrel, Charles Senr.	John Sutton	27
Ferrel, Harrison	John Sutton	27
Ferrel, John	John Sutton	27
Ferrel, John	John Sutton	27
Ferrel, John Junr.	John Sutton	27
Ferrel, William	John Sutton	27
Finch, William	James Walker	24
Findley, Alexander	Richard Neely	31
Findley, John	Richard Neely	31
Finley, George	James Neill	3
Fisher, Jacob	John Byler	15
Fisher, John	James Neill	3
Fisher, John	William Bell	9
Fisher, Michael	William Bell	9
Fisher, Michael	John B. Dempsey	17
Fisher, Thomas	John Wortham	2
Fisher, William	William Bell	9
Fitch, William	John Roberts	22
Fleming, David	Patterson	12
Fleming, John	Patterson	12
Fleming, Juliss	William Bell	9
Fleming, Saml.	Patterson	12
Fleming, Saml.	John McWilliams	28
Flenn, James	John B. Dempsey	17
Floyd, David	John McWilliams	28
Floyd, David Senr.	John McWilliams	28

1812 TAX LIST

NAME	CAPTAIN'S COMPANY	PAGE NUMBER
Fonville, Asa	John Wortham	2
Forrest, Nathan	John Wortham	2
Forrest, Shedrick	John Wortham	2
Forrest, Shedrick Junr.	John Wortham	2
Foster, George	James Shinault	6
Fowler, James	James Shinault	6
Fowler, Obediah	James Shinault	6
Fowler, William	Timothy Sugg	20
Fox, Titus	Timothy Sugg	20
Francis, Leaden	Lewis Medlin	5
Frazier, John	John Roberts	22
Frazier, John	John McWilliams	28
Freeman, Amos	Duncan Neille	7
Frizzel, Abraham	Timothy Sugg	20
Frizzel, James	Timothy Sugg	20
Frizzel, William	Timothy Sugg	20
Fry, Absolom	William Bell	9
Fryer, James	Duncan Neille	7
Fugit, Moses	John B. Dempsey	17
Fuller, Darling	James Yell	18
Fuller, Darling	Richard Neely	31
Fuller, Isaac	John B. Dempsey	17
Fuller, Jacob	John B. Dempsey	17
Fulton, James	John Wortham	2
Gage, James	John McWilliams	30
Gage, James Junr.	John McWilliams	29
Gage, Jonathan	James Walker	25
Galeway, Robert	John Sutton	27
Galigla, Garner	James Walker	25
Gamble, Aaron	Benjamin Hewitt	10
Gammell, James	John Wortham	1
Gammell, Joseph	John Wortham	1
Gandy, Edmond	James Walker	24
Ganeway, Burrel	John B. Dempsey	17
Gant, James	Benjamin Hewitt	10
Gant, Lewis	Benjamin Hewitt	10
Gardner, John	John Wortham	1
Gardner, Thomas	John Wortham	2
Garmon, John	Benjamin Hewitt	10
Garner, Parish	Lewis Medlin	5
Garner, Parish	Benjamin Hewitt	12
Garner, Thomas	Lewis Medlin	5
Garratt, Isaac	John McWilliams	30
Garret, Hozea	John Roberts	22
Garrett, Moses	John McWilliams	29
Gates, Allen	William Bell	9
Gates, Alexr.	William Bell	9
Gates, Benjamin	William Bell	9

1812 TAX LIST

NAME	CAPTAIN'S COMPANY	PAGE NUMBER
Gibson, Isham	Duncan Neille	7
Gibson, James	Lewis Medlin	4
Gibson, James	John Sutton	26
Gibson, Jeremiah	John B. Dempsey	17
Gibson, John	John McWilliams	28
Gibson, Neely	James Shinault	6
Gibson, William	Lewis Medlin	4
Gideon, Isaac Jr.	Benjamin Hewitt	10
Gideon, Isaac Sr.	Benjamin Hewitt	11
Gideon, James	Benjamin Hewitt	10
Gideon, John	Benjamin Hewitt	10
Gilbert, Edward	William Bell	9
Gilbert, James	Richard Neely	31
Gilbert, Joseph	William Bell	9
Gilchrist, Daniel	John B. Dempsey	17
Gilchrist, Malcom	John B. Dempsey	17
Gipson, John	Benjamin Hewitt	10
Glover, Joseph	John McWilliams	28
Gochen, Henry	Lewis Medlin	5
Gochen, James	Lewis Medlin	5
Good, Joel	Timothy Sugg	20
Goodson, John	Benjamin Hewitt	10
Gordon, David	Richard Neely	31
Gore, William	John B. Dempsey	16
Garren, Peter	Timothy Sugg	20
Goss, Jacob	Duncan Neille	7
Gragg, John	John Roberts	22
Gragg, Robert	John Roberts	22
Graham, James	John Wortham	2
Graham, John	John Wortham	2
Graham, John	James Walker	24
Gray, John	Duncan Neille	7
Gray, Samuel	Lewis Medlin	4
Greaves, Jonathan	Patterson	12
Greaves, Joseph	Patterson	12
Greaves, Samuel	Patterson	13
Greaves, Therman	John B. Dempsey	16
Greer, Andrew	Benjamin Hewitt	11
Green, Archibald	James Shinault	6
Green, Daniel	John B. Dempsey	16
Green, Elopan	John Sutton	26
Greer, Isaac	John Roberts	22
Green, James B. (Greer)	Benjamin Hewitt	10
Green, William	John B. Dempsey	16
Green, Willis	John Roberts	22
Greer, Thos.	Benjamin Hewitt	10
Gregory, ___	John Sutton	27
Griffath, John	James Shinault	6

1812 TAX LIST

NAME	CAPTAIN'S COMPANY	PAGE NUMBER
Grimes, Joshua	Timothy Sugg	20
Grooms, James	Richard Neely	31
Gross, Frederick	James Yell	18
Garron, James	Timothy Sugg	20
Hagan, John	John Sutton	27
Haggard, James	John Roberts	22
Hail, Dudley	Timothy Sugg	20
Hail, Mead	James Walker	25
Hains, Henry	John Byler	15
Haistings, Henry	John McWilliams	29
Haistings, John Junr.	John McWilliams	30
Haistings, Joseph	John McWilliams	29
Haistings, Joseph Junr.	John McWilliams	29
Haistings, Richard	John McWilliams	29
Haistings, Robert	John McWilliams	29
Haistings, Stephen	John McWilliams	29
Hale, Asa	Patterson	13
Hale, Jesse	James Walker	25
Hale, William	Patterson	13
Hale, William	James Walker	25
Hall, Elisha	Benjamin Hewitt	10
Hall, Elisha	James Walker	25
Hall, James	Lewis Medlin	5
Hall, James	Benjamin Hewitt	12
Hall, Jeremiah	Benjamin Hewitt	11
Hall, Joel	James Shinault	6
Hall, Joseph	Lewis Medlin	5
Hall, Joseph	Benjamin Hewitt	12
Hall, Levi	Patterson	13
Hall, Simon	Patterson	13
Hall, Thomas	Lewis Medlin	5
Hall, Thomas	Benjamin Hewitt	12
Hall, William	Lewis Medlin	5
Hall, William	James Shinault	6
Hall, William	Benjamin Hewitt	12
Ham, John	John McWilliams	30
Hamby, Isaac	Timothy Sugg	20
Hamill, Andrew	Benjamin Hewitt	10
Hamill, William	Benjamin Hewitt	10
Hamilton, John	James Yell	19
Hamilton, Joseph	James Yell	19
Hamm, Joshua	John B. Dempsey	17
Hanbacks, Mitchell	James Shinault	6
Hemby, Dennis	Richard Neely	31
Hanes, John S.	John Sutton	26
Hannah, Robert	Lewis Medlin	5
Hannah, Robert	James Walker	24
Hannah, Samuel	James Walker	24
Hannah, William	James Walker	25

1812 TAX LIST

NAME	CAPTAIN'S COMPANY	PAGE NUMBER
Harbeson, James	James Neill	3
Harden, Burgis	James Neill	3
Harden, Mark	James Neill	3
Harden, Martin	James Neill	3
Harden, Thomas H.	James Neill	2
Harkness, John	John Wortham	1
Harman, Esaiah	John Byler	14
Harman, Gedian	John B. Dempsey	16
Harman, Jonathan	Timothy Sugg	20
Harman, Lewis	John B. Dempsey	16
Harmon, Henry	William Bell	9
Harmon, John	Benjamin Hewitt	10
Harmon, Lewis	Benjamin Hewitt	10
Harper, Samuel	Lewis Medlin	4
Hart, David	James Walker	24
Hart, Moses	James Walker	24
Harrel, David	John Sutton	26
Harrel, William	John Sutton	26
Harrel, William	John Sutton	27
Harrice, Saml. B.	John Byler	15
Harris, Evan	John Byler	15
Harris, Isham	Richard Neely	31
Harris, James	John Byler	14
Harris, James	John B. Dempsey	16
Harris, John	John Byler	14
Harris, John	John Byler	14
Harris, Mosebey	John Roberts	23
Harris, Nathaniel	John McWilliams	29
Harris, Shadrick	James Yell	18
Harrison, Jonathan	Timothy Sugg	20
Harrison, John	John Byler	14
Harrison, John	John McWilliams	28
Harrison, Robert	Richard Neely	31
Harrison, Thomas	Timothy Sugg	20
Harryman, Charles	John Roberts	22
Harryman, John	John Roberts	22
Haskins, Jesse	James Neill	3
Hatchet, Herod	Patterson	13
Hathcock, Auston	John Sutton	26
Hathcock, Charles	Richard Neely	31
Hathcock, Elisha	Richard Neely	31
Hathcock, Howell	John Sutton	26
Hathcock, Howell	Richard Neely	31
Hathcock, John	Richard Neely	31
Hathcock, John	Richard Neely	31
Hathcock, Philip	Richard Neely	31
Hatley, Henry	Benjamin Hewitt	12
Hatley, John	Lewis Medlin	5
Hatley, Robert	Lewis Medlin	5

1812 TAX LIST

NAME	CAPTAIN'S COMPANY	PAGE NUMBER
Hatley, Robert	Benjamin Hewitt	12
Haynes, Joseph	John Sutton	25
Hayns, Joseph Senr.	John Sutton	27
Hays, Charles	John Sutton	27
Hays, Thomas	Lewis Medlin	4
Hayslet, William	John McWilliams	28
Heart, Henry	John McWilliams	28
Helton, Abraham	Lewis Medlin	4
Helton, Abraham Junr.	Lewis Medlin	4
Henderson, Wm. F.	John B. Dempsey	16
Henry, Isaac	James Walker	24
Hewitt, Benjamin	Benjamin Hewitt	10
Hickney, Preston	Richard Neely	31
Hicks, Benjamin	John McWilliams	28
Hicks, John	John McWilliams	29
Hicks, William	John McWilliams	28
Higgenbotham, Wm.	Duncan Neille	7
Higgenbotham, Wm.	Duncan Neille	7
Higginbottom, Wm.	John McWilliams	29
Higs, John	Patterson	12
Hile, Benj. H.	Lewis Medlin	4
Hile, George	Timothy Sugg	20
Hile, William	Timothy Sugg	20
Hill, James	Benjamin Hewitt	10
Hill, Jesse	Benjamin Hewitt	10
Hill, Richard	John Roberts	22
Hill, Robert	Benjamin Hewitt	11
Hill, Spencer	John Byler	14
Hill, William	John Byler	14
Hobbs, James	James Shinault	6
Hodge, William	John Roberts	22
Hodges, Charles	John Sutton	26
Hodges, Edmond Junr.	John Sutton	26
Hodges, Edmond Senr.	John Sutton	26
Hogg, John B.	John B. Dempsey	16
Holden, James	James Neill	2
Holden, John	James Neill	2
Holebrook, Ezekiel	Patterson	13
Holebrook, Henry	Benjamin Hewitt	11
Holebrook, Henry	James Walker	24
Holebrook, George	James Shinault	6
Holland, Harphrey	John Byler	15
Holland, Thos.	John B. Dempsey	16
Holland, Thos.	James Yell	18
Hollon, Martin	James Walker	25
Holmes, Isaac	John Roberts	22
Holmes, James	James Neill	3
Holmes, John	Lewis Medlin	5
Holmes, Pheneas	James Neill	3

1812 TAX LIST

NAME	CAPTAIN'S COMPANY	PAGE NUMBER
Holpan, Joseph	James Walker	25
Holt, Edmond	Richard Neely	31
Holt, James	Richard Neely	31
Holt, John	James Walker	25
Holt, Nicholas	Richard Neely	31
Holt, Shedrick	Richard Neely	31
Holt, William	Richard Neely	31
Hooker, Nathan	William Bell	8
Hooker, Richard	William Bell	8
Hooper, John	William Bell	9
Hooper, Obediah	William Bell	8
Hooper, Richard	James Neill	3
Hoover, Martin	Timothy Sugg	20
Hopkins, William	John B. Dempsey	17
Hopwood, William	James Neill	3
Hopwood, Willis	James Neill	3
Horn, George	Lewis Medlin	4
Hornaday, Solomon	Richard Neely	31
Hotsen, Isaac	James Walker	25
Houben, Christian	William Bell	8
Houben, Jacob	William Bell	8
Holt, Joshua	John McWilliams	30
Holt, Michael	John McWilliams	29
House, Joseph	John Wortham	1
Houston, James	Benjamin Hewitt	10
Houston, John	Benjamin Hewitt	10
Howell, Joseph B.	John McWilliams	29
Hubard, Edward	John McWilliams	28
Hubert, Nathaniel	John McWilliiams	28
Hucker, Normand	Richard Neely	31
Hudson, Jessee	Benjamin Hewitt	11
Hudson, Jessee	John B. Dempsey	17
Huffman, John	John Sutton	26
Hugh, George	James Walker	25
Hugh, Joel	James Walker	25
Hughs, Goodman	Patterson	12
Hughs, Jesse	James Neill	2
Hughs, John	James Neill	2
Hughs, Josiah	James Shinault	6
Hughs, Rice	James Shinault	7
Hughs, Robert	James Shinault	6
Hughs, Samuel	James Shinault	6
Hughs, William S.	James Shinault	6
Hughston, Hugh	James Neill	2
Hunter, Theophilus	James Yell	19
Hurst, John	John McWilliams	29
Hurst, William	John Williams	28
Hutchings, Christopher	James Yell	19
Hutchings, John	James Yell	19

1812 TAX LIST

NAME	CAPTAIN'S COMPANY	PAGE NUMBER
Hutchings, Lemuel	Richard Neely	31
Hynds, John	John McWilliams	29
Ingam, John	Lewis Medlin	4
Ingrum, Samuel	John B. Dempsey	16
Ivey, Henry	Benjamin Hewitt	10
Ivey, Joseph	Benjamin Hewitt	11
Ivie, Anderson	William Bell	8
Jackson, David	James Neill	2
Jackson, Graham	James Neill	2
Jackson, James	James Neill	2
Jackson, Jeremiah	John Byler	15
Jackson, Joel	James Walker	24
Jackson, John	John Byler	15
Jackson, Robert	James Neill	2
Jacobs, John	John Sutton	26
Jacobs, William	John Sutton	27
James, Hugh	James Walker	24
Jarves, William	James Yell	18
Jeans, Hardy	Benjamin Hewitt	11
Jenkins, John	Duncan Neille	8
Jenkins, Thomas	James Yell	19
Johnston, Chapman	John Wortham	2
Johnston, Elisha	John Wortham	1
Johnston, James	John Roberts	22
Johnston, James	John McWilliams	28
Johnston, Stephen	John Byler	15
Johnston, Thos.	John McWilliams	28
Jones, Andrew	James Shinault	6
Jones, John	John Byler	14
Jones, John	James Yell	19
Jones, John	John Roberts	22
Jones, Jno.	Timothy Sugg	20
Jones, Morton	James Walker	24
Jones, Robert	John Sutton	26
Jones, Wood	Richard Neely	31
Julin, George E.	John Wortham	2
Jurnigan, Felix	John McWilliams	29
Jurnigan, Lewis	John Sutton	26
Keener, John	John Byler	14
Kener, Martin	John Byler	14
Kelley, ___	James Walker	25
Kelley, Alfred	Patterson	12
Kelley, John	John Roberts	22
Kelley, Joshua	James Walker	24
Kelley, Thos.	Timothy Sugg	20
Kelley, William	James Walker	24

1812 TAX LIST

NAME	CAPTAIN'S COMPANY	PAGE NUMBER
Kelly, Reuben	James Walker	25
Kembro, George	Richard Neely	30
Kenedy, Joseph	James Yell	18
Kenny, Daniel	Benjamin Hewitt	12
Kerr, William	Duncan Neille	7
Kerr, William	John McWilliams	29
Keyser, Philip	John McWilliams	28
Keyser, Valentine	John McWilliams	29
Kidd, James	Lewis Medlin	4
Kiddy, Jacob	John McWilliams	29
Killer, Robert	Duncan Neille	8
Killingsworth, Freeman	Duncan Neille	8
Kimmons, Joseph	John Byler	15
Kinard, Philip	John Sutton	26
Kindal, Thomas	James Walker	25
King, Alxr.	Richard Neely	31
King, Benjamin	John Roberts	22
King, Edward	Benjamin Hewitt	11
King, George	John McWilliams	28
King, Jacob	Benjamin Hewitt	10
King, Jeremiah	Richard Neely	31
King, Nathaniel	Benjamin Hewitt	11
King, Samuel	Richard Neely	31
King, William	James Shinault	6
Kirkland, Moses	James Shinault	7
Kirkman, Elijah	Lewis Medlin	4
Kristtle, Frederick	James Yell	18
Knott, David	John Roberts	22
Knott, John	John Roberts	22
Knott, Jno.	Timothy Sugg	20
Knott, William	John Roberts	22
Knox, Saml.	John Sutton	27
Knox, William	John Sutton	26
Kunsley, Samuel	Richard Neely	31
Lacy, Elijah	John McWilliams	29
Lacy, Matthew	Richard Neely	31
Ladd, Amos	Timothy Sugg	20
Laden, George	Benjamin Hewitt	10
Landcaster, Aaron	Patterson	13
Landers, Henry	Richard Neely	31
Landers, Isaac	Richard Neely	31
Landers, William	Richard Neely	31
Lane, Joel	William Bell	8
Lane, John	William Bell	8
Lankester, William	Patterson	13
Larimore, Hance	John B. Dempsey	16
Larrimore, James	James Yell	19
Larken, Edward	John Byler	15

1812 TAX LIST

NAME	CAPTAIN'S COMPANY	PAGE NUMBER
Lawrance, David	James Neill	2
Lawrance, Joseph	James Yell	19
Leaky, Eli	James Walker	25
Lee, John	John B. Dempsey	16
Lee, Peter	John Sutton	27
Lee, Peter	James Walker	25
Lee, Robert	Duncan Neille	7
Lee, William	James Sutton	27
Leeper, Allen	James Neill	2
Leeper, Hugh B.	Lewis Medlin	5
Leeper, James	James Neill	2
Leeper, John	William Bell	9
Lemarr, Benjamin	John Byler	15
Lemean, William	William Bell	9
Lidon, Josiah	Patterson	12
Little, Benjamin	Patterson	12
Little, George	Patterson	12
Little, John	Patterson	12
Locke, David	John B. Dempsey	17
Locke, Jacob	John Sutton	27
Locke, Jonas	James Walker	25
Locke, William	John Byler	14
Logan, William	Richard Neely	31
Lohorn, John	Benjamin Hewitt	12
Long, James	James Neill	3
Long, John	Patterson	13
Long, Richard	William Bell	8
Long, William	John McWilliams	29
Long, William	John Wortham	2
Lord, John	John Wortham	1
Lord, William	John Sutton	26
Low, David	Richard Neely	31
Lovelady, Levy	Benjamin Hewitt	10
Lovelady, Simeon	Benjamin Hewitt	10
Lovens, Hough L.	John Wortham	1
Lowrey, Greenberry	John Roberts	22
Loyd, Howell	James Yell	19
Loyd, Joseph	James Yell	18
Loyd, Nathan	John Wortham	2
Loyd, Nicholas	James Yell	19
Loyd, Wilson	James Yell	18
Luther, George	James Shinault	6
Lynas, George	John McWilliams	29
Maben, Stephen	John Byler	14
Madairas, Washington D.	Lewis Medlin	4
Medlin, William	James Neill	3
Medlin, Lewis	Lewis Medlin	4
Majors, John	John Roberts	23

1812 TAX LIST

NAME	CAPTAIN'S COMPANY	PAGE NUMBER
Majors, John	Timothy Sugg	20
Majors, Noble	Timothy Sugg	20
Majors, Robert	Timothy Sugg	21
Mallard, John	John Byler	14
Mallard, Thornton	John Byler	14
Manley, Reuben	Timothy Sugg	21
Marberry, Isaac	James Yell	19
Marberry, John	James Yell	19
Marchbanks, Jonathan	John Sutton	27
Marshall, Jarrel	James Yell	19
Marshall, John	James Walker	24
Martin, Barkley	James Walker	25
Martin, Benjamin	Timothy Sugg	21
Martin, John	James Walker	25
Martin, Matt	James Walker	25
Martin, Richard Junr.	Benjamin Hewitt	11
Martin, Richard Senr.	Benjamin Hewitt	11
Martin, William	James Walker	24
Martin, William	James Neill	3
Martin, William	Benjamin Hewitt	12
Mason, John	John Byler	14
Mason, Michael	John B. Dempsey	17
Matthews, Thomas	Duncan Neille	8
Maxwell, Danl.	John Byler	15
Maxwell, John	John Byler	15
Maxwell, Solomon	John Byler	15
Maxwell, Thomas	John Byler	15
Maxwell, Thomas Junr.	John Byler	14
Mayfield, Abraham	John Byler	15
Mayfield, William	John Byler	15
McAdams, Amos	John B. Dempsey	17
McAdams, James	John B. Dempsey	16
McAlister, Barnabas	Patterson	13
McBride, Hugh	John Byler	14
McBride, James	John Byler	14
McBride, John	John Sutton	27
McBride, William	John Sutton	26
McCall, James	John Wortham	1
McCardy, David	James Neill	2
McCardy, James	James Neill	2
McCardy, James Junr.	James Neill	2
McCardy, William	James Neill	2
McCleren, Reuben	Patterson	13
McClaren, Daniel	John Wortham	1
McClaren, Daniel Junr.	John Wortham	1
McCleardy, James	James Neill	3
McCleary, James A.	James Neill	3
McCleary, John	James Neill	3
McClerdy, David	James Neill	3

1812 TAX LIST

NAME	CAPTAIN'S COMPANY	PAGE NUMBER
McClerdy, John	James Neill	3
McClern, Hugh	John Wortham	1
McCleren, John	John Wortham	2
McClure, William	John Wortham	2
McClure, William Junr.	John Wortham	2
McCory, John	John Wortham	1
McCory, John Junr.	John Wortham	2
McCrory, Hugh	John Wortham	1
McCrory, Hugh	Lewis Medlin	5
McCrory, Robert	Lewis Medlin	5
McCuestian, Benjamin	John B. Dempsey	17
McCuestian, James	John B. Dempsey	17
McCuestian, John	John B. Dempsey	17
McCuestian, Saml.	John B. Dempsey	16
McDaniel, Alexr.	Benjamin Hewitt	10
McDaniel, James	James Neill	3
McDonald, Daniel	John Roberts	22
McDonald, Henry	James Yell	18
McEleroy, William	John McWilliams	29
McEntosh, Anguish	John Sutton	27
McFadden, Elias	James Yell	18
McFadden, Elias	James Yell	18
McFarling, Robert	John B. Dempsey	16
McFinn, Samuel	James Yell	18
McGee, William	Richard Neely	31
McGill, David	John Sutton	26
McGill, James	John Sutton	26
McGin, David	James Walker	24
McGuire, Elijah	James Yell	18
McGuire, John	James Yell	18
McKimsey, William	James Walker	25
McKisick, Daniel	John Byler	14
McKisick, Daniel	Benjamin Hewitt	11
McKisick, Daniel Junr.	Benjamin Hewitt	11
McKisick, David	Benjamin Hewitt	11
McKisick, James	John B. Dempsey	17
McKisick, John	John Byler	15
McKisick, Joseph	Benjamin Hewitt	11
McLane, James	James Walker	24
McLure, Matthew	John Byler	15
McMahon, William	James Walker	25
McMain, James	James Yell	18
McMears, Jonathan	Duncan Neille	3
McMiller, Rolly	John McWilliams	28
McMillin, Andrew	Benjamin Hewitt	10
McMillin, John	Benjamin Hewitt	10
McMorris, Alan	William Bell	9
McMorris, James	Lewis Medlin	4
McMurtrey, John	Benjamin Hewitt	11

1812 TAX LIST

NAME	CAPTAIN'S COMPANY	PAGE NUMBER
McMurtrey, William	Benjamin Hewitt	11
McNatt, Leven	John McWilliams	28
McQuistian, Robert	John Byler	15
McRaynolds, James	Patterson	13
McRaynolds, Thomas	Patterson	13
McRory, Hugh	William Bell	9
McRory, Robert	William Bell	9
McWilliams, John	John McWilliams	28
Meadlock, William	Timothy Sugg	20
Mears, Griffin	Benjamin Hewitt	11
Mears, William	Benjamin Hewitt	11
Medairas, John	Lewis Medlin	4
Meek, James	William Bell	9
Meek, William	William Bell	9
Merryfield, John	John Sutton	27
Mileham, Drury	Lewis Medlin	5
Miles, John	John McWilliams	30
Milikan, Isaac	John McWilliams	28
Miller, George	James Walker	24
Miller, Henry	John B. Dempsey	16
Miller, Jacob	James Walker	25
Miller, James	James Neill	2
Miller, Jesse	James Walker	24
Miller, John	James Yell	18
Miller, Nathaniel	Richard Neely	31
Miller, Nathaniel	James Yell	18
Mitchell, George	John Roberts	22
Mitchell, Marmaduke	John B. Dempsey	16
Mize, Jesse	Lewis Medlin	4
Montgomery, David	Richard Neely	31
Moody, Samuel	John Roberts	22
Mooney, John Senr.	Patterson	12
Mooney, John Junr.	Patterson	12
Moore, George	Richard Neely	31
Moore, George L.	John Sutton	27
Moore, James	Duncan Neille	8
Moore, John	James Yell	19
Moore, Levy	James Yell	19
Moore, Levi Junr.	John McWilliams	30
Moore, Levi Senr.	John McWilliams	30
Moore, Perry	James Yell	19
Moore, Robert	Benjamin Hewitt	11
Moore, Samuel	James Yell	18
Moore, Thomas	John B. Dempsey	16
Moreland, Vinson	John McWilliams	28
Morgan, Enous	Richard Neely	31
Morgan, James	John B. Dempsey	16
Morgan, Martin	Richard Neely	31
Morris, Charles	William Bell	9

1812 TAX LIST

NAME	CAPTAIN'S COMPANY	PAGE NUMBER
Morris, Joseph P.	John Byler	15
Morrison, Andrew	Benjamin Hewitt	11
Morrison, William	John Sutton	26
Morrow, James	James Walker	24
Morrow, John	James Walker	24
Moseley, Archibald	John Wortham	1
Moss, John	Duncan Neille	7
Moss, Matthew	Duncan Neille	7
Moses, Solomon	John McWilliams	29
Murkison, Kennuth	John Sutton	26
Murkison, Murdock	John B. Dempsey	16
Murphree, Isah	James Yell	18
Murphree, John	James Yell	19
Murphree, William	James Yell	19
Murphrey, Nimrod	James Yell	18
Murphry, Stephen	James Yell	18
Murray, Francis	John B. Dempsey	16
Murray, Robert	John B. Dempsey	16
Muse, Isaac	James Walker	24
Musgrave, Samuel	John McWilliams	29
Musgrave, Thomas	John Byler	14
Napper, Rone	William Bell	9
Nailer, John	James Yell	19
Nance, Reuben	John B. Dempsey	16
Neely, Clement	Richard Neely	31
Neely, John	John Byler	14
Neely, Richard	Richard Neely	31
Neil, Joseph	John Byler	14
Neile, Alexr.	William Bell	9
Neile, Andrew	William Bell	9
Neile, Geo. C.	James Neill	3
Neill, James C.	James Neill	3
Neile, James	William Bell	9
Neile, John	William Bell	9
Neile, John	James Yell	18
Neile, Nicholas	John B. Dempsey	17
Neille, Duncan	Duncan Neille	7
Nelson, Moses	James Yell	18
Newsom, ____	Richard Neely	31
Newson, Sterling	Richard Neely	31
Newsom, Sterling	James Yell	18
Newsom, William	John B. Dempsey	16
Nicholas, Coleman	Timothy Sugg	20
Nicholds, Jacob	James Shinault	6
Nicholds, William	James Shinault	6
Nichols, Benjamin	Timothy Sugg	21
Nichols, Jesse	Timothy Sugg	21
Nichols, Nathan	Timothy Sugg	21

1812 TAX LIST

NAME	CAPTAIN'S COMPANY	PAGE NUMBER
Nicholson, Elijah	John McWilliams	29
Nickes, John	Timothy Sugg	20
Nicks, Doke	Timothy Sugg	21
Nicks, Jno. Senr.	Timothy Sugg	21
Nicks, William	Timothy Sugg	21
Noham, John	Duncan Neille	8
Nokes, Euriah	Duncan Neille	8
Nole, James	James Shinault	6
Nole, John	James Shinault	6
Nole, William	James Shinault	6
Norman, Robert	John McWilliams	29
Norvile, Clinton	John Roberts	22
Norvile, James	John Roberts	22
Norvile, John	John Roberts	22
Norsworthy, James	Benjamin Hewitt	11
Norvell, John	John Roberts	22
Norvell, William	John Roberts	22
Nowlan, Bryan W.	James Neill	2
Nowlan, John	Patterson	13
Nowlan, John	William Bell	9
Nowlan, Peyton	Lewis Medlin	5
Nowlan, Tobias	James Neill	2
Oaks, Hezekiah	John Sutton	26
O'Mehundro, William	John B. Dempsey	16
O'Neal, Isham	William Bell	9
O'Neal, John	John Sutton	26
Orr, John	Lewis Medlin	5
Orr, Robert	Lewis Medlin	5
Orr, Robert Junr.	Lewis Medlin	5
Osten, William	James Walker	24
Owens, David	John B. Dempsey	17
Owens, James	William Bell	9
Owens, Samuel	James Yell	19
Page, John	Richard Neely	31
Parker, Elijah	Richard Neely	31
Parker, James	John Sutton	26
Parker, Winburn	John Byler	15
Parmer, Samuel	Duncan Neille	7
Parry, Bartley	James Yell	18
Parry, Thomas	John Sutton	26
Parsons, George	John B. Dempsey	16
Parsons, Thomas	John B. Dempsey	16
Pascal, Asa	John Byler	15
Pascal, Eli	John Byler	15
Pascal, James	John Byler	14
Patrick, John	James Shinault	6
Patterson, Andrew	Patterson	12

1812 TAX LIST

NAME	CAPTAIN'S COMPANY	PAGE NUMBER
Patterson, James	Lewis Medlin	5
Patterson, James	John Wortham	1
Patterson, John	John Wortham	1
Patterson, Robert	Patterson	12
Patterson, Robert	John Sutton	26
Patterson, Thomas	Duncan Neille	2
Patterson, Thomas	John Wortham	2
Patterson, William	John Byler	15
Patten, Joshua	Richard Neely	31
Patton, James	John B. Dempsey	16
Patton, James	John B. Dempsey	17
Patton, James	James Walker	25
Patton, James	John Wortham	1
Patton, James	Benjamin Hewitt	11
Patton, James W.	Benjamin Hewitt	11
Patton, John	Benjamin Hewitt	11
Patton, John	James Walker	24
Patton, John	John Wortham	1
Patton, John Jr.	Benjamin Hewitt	11
Patton, John Sr.	Benjamin Hewitt	11
Patton, Neely	James Shinault	6
Patton, Saml.	Benjamin Hewitt	11
Patton, Thomas	James Shinault	6
Patton, William	John Roberts	22
Patton, William	John Wortham	2
Paxton, John	James Neill	2
Paxton, John	James Neill	3
Payne, Moses	Timothy Sugg	21
Payne, Sylvester	James Yell	18
Peace, John	Benjamin Hewitt	11
Peacock, John Junr.	James Yell	19
Peacock, John Senr.	James Yell	19
Peacock, Thomas A.	James Yell	19
Peacock, William	James Yell	19
Pennington, Elijah	James Shinault	6
Perry, Dempsey	John Byler	15
Perry, Joseph	John Byler	15
Perry, Lemuel	Patterson	13
Perry, Martin	John Byler	15
Perry, Martin	John Byler	14
Perryman, John	Benjamin Hewitt	10
Peters, Saml.	John Byler	15
Perry, Theophilus	William Bell	9
Pew, Jacob	John Byler	14
Pharr, Jonathan	James Walker	24
Philips, Bennett	Benjamin Hewitt	10
Philips, David	Lewis Medlin	4
Philips, Isaac	John Byler	15
Philips, John	Lewis Medlin	4

1812 TAX LIST

NAME	CAPTAIN'S COMPANY	PAGE NUMBER
Philips, Josiah	Lewis Medlin	4
Philips, Matthew	John B. Dempsey	17
Philips, Nathan B.	Richard Neely	31
Philips, Samuel	James Yell	19
Pickens, Cornelius	Duncan Neille	7
Pickens, Thomas	Duncan Neille	7
Pickle, Henry	John Byler	14
Pinkerton, Matthew	James Yell	18
Pittman, Thomas	John McWilliams	29
Plumley, Samuel	John Byler	15
Plumley, Thos.	John Byler	15
Plumley, Jonathan	John Byler	15
Plumley, Jonathan	John Byler	14
Plumley, Solomon	John Byler	14
Pogue, William	James Shinault	7
Pole, Peter	John McWilliams	28
Polk, John	John Wortham	1
Pollard, John	John Byler	14
Pollard, William	John Byler	14
Pool, William	John Sutton	26
Pool, William	Timothy Sugg	21
Pope, John	James Yell	18
Poteet, Thomas	Duncan Neille	7
Potts, John	John Wortham	1
Pouge, Samuel	James Yell	18
Pratt, George	John McWilliams	30
Presgrove, Andrew	John Byler	14
Presgrove, Andrew	John Byler	15
Prewitt, Michael	John McWilliams	30
Price, Isaac	James Walker	25
Price, James	Benjamin Hewitt	10
Price, Jonathan	Benjamin Hewitt	10
Price, Jonathan	Benjamin Hewitt	12
Price, Reece	John B. Dempsey	17
Price, Richard	James Yell	19
Price, Simon	Benjamin Hewitt	10
Price, William	James Yell	19
Prince, Aaron	Timothy Sugg	21
Prince, Eli	Timothy Sugg	21
Prince, Gilbert	Timothy Suggg	20
Prince, Nathan	Timothy Sugg	21
Purnell, Esau	John McWilliams	29
Putt, William	Patterson	13
Rades, Ephraim	Duncan Neille	7
Radford, Samuel	James Neill	3
Raggsdale, Baxter	John Roberts	22
Raggsdale, Daniel	Patterson	13
Raggsdale, Edward	John B. Dempsey	17

1812 TAX LIST

NAME	CAPTAIN'S COMPANY	PAGE NUMBER
Raggsdale, John	John Roberts	23
Ragsdale, John	John Roberts	23
Raiger, Anthony (Reagor)	John McWilliams	29
Rambo, Elias	James Neill	3
Ramsey, Samuel	Lewis Medlin	4
Raney, John	James Walker	24
Rawling, Hosey	John B. Dempsey	17
Rawlings, Roderick	James Yell	19
Ray, Thomas	Timothy Sugg	21
Rayburn, Henry	John Sutton	26
Rayburn, James	Richard Neely	31
Rayburn, John	John Sutton	27
Read, William	John B. Dempsey	16
Read, William	John McWilliams	30
Reaves, William	Timothy Sugg	20
Reece, Samuel	John Sutton	26
Reed, Abraham	James Walker	25
Reed, James	James Neill	3
Reed, John	James Neill	3
Reed, Thomas	Patterson	12
Reid, Ezekiel	Duncan Neille	8
Renfrow, Bartlett	Duncan Neille	8
Rhey, William	John Byler	15
Rice, Dangerfield	Lewis Medlin	4
Richards, John	James Walker	25
Richardson, Shadrack	John McWilliams	28
Rickman, John	John Wortham	2
Ridgway, James	John McWilliams	29
Ridgway, James	John McWilliams	29
Ridgway, Jonathan	John Byler	14
Ridgway, Samuel	John McWilliams	29
Riggs, Jacob	Timothy Sugg	21
Riggs, Reuben	Lewis Medlin	4
Right, James	James Yell	18
Riley, Abrm.	James Neill	8
Riley, Edward	James Neill	7
Riley, William	James Neill	8
Roach, Pharo	Timothy Sugg	21
Roach, Stephen	Timothy Sugg	21
Roan, George	James Neill	2
Roberts, Graham	John Roberts	23
Roberts, John	John Roberts	23
Roberts, Solomon	Patterson	12
Roberts, Thomas	Richard Neely	31
Roberts, William	Duncan Neille	7
Roberts, William	John Roberts	23
Roberts, Willis	Timothy Sugg	20
Robertson, Burrell	Richard Neely	31

1812 TAX LIST

NAME	CAPTAIN'S COMPANY	PAGE NUMBER
Robertson, Elisha	Richard Neely	31
Robertson, James	James Walker	24
Robertson, James	John Roberts	22
Robertson, John	Benjamin Hewitt	10
Robertson, Moore	Benjamin Hewitt	10
Robinson, Nathaniel	James Yell	18
Roden, William	James Walker	24
Rodgers, Joseph	Lewis Medlin	5
Rogers, Joseph	Benjamin Hewitt	12
Rogers, Josiah	John McWilliams	28
Rogers, Stephen	John McWilliams	29
Rogers, William	John McWilliams	29
Rollins, Hance	James Yell	18
Ronan, David	John Sutton	26
Rossen, David	Benjamin Hewitt	11
Ross, Elijah	James Shinault	7
Ross, Isaac	Benjamin Hewitt	11
Ross, James	Benjamin Hewitt	10
Ross, James	James Shinault	7
Ross, John	Benjamin Hewitt	11
Ross, John	James Shinault	7
Ross, William	James Shinault	7
Ross, William T.	Benjamin Hewitt	10
Runion, Freeman	John Roberts	23
Rushman, John	James Yell	19
Rushing, Thomas	Timothy Sugg	21
Russel, Jo	Timothy Sugg	20
Russel, Matthew	John Wortham	2
Russel, Solomon	John Wortham	2
Rutledge, Robert	John Byler	14
Sailing, Henry	Benjamin Hewitt	12
Sailing, Peter	James Walker	25
Sanders, George	John Byler	14
Sanders, George	John Byler	14
Sanders, John	John Byler	14
Sanders, Peter	John Byler	14
Sanders, David	William Bell	8
Sawyers, Sampson	John McWilliams	30
Say, William	William Bell	7
Schooler, John	John McWilliams	28
Schooler, Nathan	John McWilliams	28
Scisco, Simion	John McWilliams	30
Scott, Eli	James Neill	3
Scott, James	John Wortham	1
Scott, Jesse	James Yell	18
Scott, John	James Walker	24
Scott, John	William Bell	9
Scott, Patrick	Lewis Medlin	4

1812 TAX LIST

NAME	CAPTAIN'S COMPANY	PAGE NUMBER
Sebastian, Saml.	John B. Dempsey	16
Segrist, William	John Wortham	2
Selman, John	Timothy Sugg	20
Shaddey, Jacob	Lewis Medlin	4
Shannon, John	Duncan Neille	8
Sharpe, James	Richard Neely	32
Sharpe, Josiah	John Roberts	23
Sharpe, William	John Roberts	23
Shaw, James	William Bell	8
Shaw, Christopher	James Walker	25
Shelphen, Michael	James Neill	2
Sheron, Jeread	John Byler	14
Sheron, Thomas	John Byler	14
Shinault, James	James Shinault	7
Shinault, William	James Shinault	7
Shipman, Christopher	Richard Neely	31
Shipman, Daniel	Richard Neely	31
Shipman, David	Richard Neely	32
Shipman, James	John McWilliams	28
Shoffner, Martin	Richard Neely	31
Shoffner, Peter	Richard Neely	32
Shook, Abraham	John McWilliams	28
Shook, William	John McWilliams	28
Shook, William Sr.	John McWilliams	29
Short, Enus	Timothy Sugg	21
Shote, Arthur	John B. Dempsey	16
Shuffield, Arthur	Patterson	12
Shuffield, Arthur Junr.	Patterson	12
Shuffield, Ephraim	Patterson	12
Shuffield, Jason B.	Patterson	12
Shuffield, William	Patterson	12
Sibley, John Junr.	James Neill	3
Sibley, John Senr.	James Neill	3
Sienaller, John	James Walker	25
Smily, Hugh	James Neill	2
Simmons, Benjamin	Lewis Medlin	5
Simmons, Jacob	Lewis Medlin	4
Simmons, Jesse	Lewis Medlin	4
Sims, Martin	Lewis Medlin	4
Simpson, Elisha	Richard Neely	32
Sing, William	John Roberts	23
Sing, William	Timothy Sugg	21
Singleton, Aphi	James Neill	3
Singleton, John	James Walker	25
Singleton, Lewis	James Walker	24
Singleton, Peter	Richard Neely	32
Slayton, James	James Shinault	6
Sloss, Joseph	William Bell	9
Smedley, John	John McWilliams	28

1812 TAX LIST

NAME	CAPTAIN'S COMPANY	PAGE NUMBER
Smedley, William	John McWilliams	28
Smith, Anderson	John Roberts	23
Smith, Anderson	John Roberts	23
Smith, Caleb	James Yell	19
Smith, Elijah	John Roberts	23
Smith, George	John Byler	15
Smith, Isaac	James Walker	24
Smith, James	James Walker	25
Smith, James	John Byler	14
Smith, John	James Walker	24
Smith, John	James Shinault	6
Smith, John	Lewis Medlin	4
Smith, Joseph	Richard Neely	31
Smith, Thomas	James Walker	25
Smith, Vincent	John Roberts	23
Smith, William	John McWilliams	29
Smith, Zachariah	Richard Neely	31
Snell, Charles	John B. Dempsey	16
Snell, Charles	Benjamin Hewitt	11
Snell, Roger	Benjamin Hewitt	11
Srivere, Abraham	James Yell	18
Snow, Jacob	James Walker	25
Solomon, Auston	Benjamin Hewitt	11
Sorrels, David	John Sutton	26
Sorrel, Walter	John Sutton	26
South, Philip	James Yell	18
Sowell, Lewis	Benjamin Hewitt	11
Sowell, William	Benjamin Hewitt	11
Speckman, William	Timothy Sugg	20
Springer, Josiah	John Byler	14
Spraggin, William	James Walker	24
Stags, William	William Bell	9
Standley, Jeptha	James Yell	18
Standy, Henry	Richard Neely	32
Starks, Thomas	John B. Dempsey	16
Starrett, John	Richard Neely	32
Steele, George	James Walker	25
Steele, Joseph	John Byler	15
Stephens, John	John Sutton	26
Stephenson, Edward	Benjamin Hewitt	12
Stewart, John	James Neill	3
Stinson, James	Lewis Medlin	4
Stokes, Kinchen	James Yell	18
Stone, John	John B. Dempsey	17
Stone, William	John B. Dempsey	17
Stone, William	Timothy Sugg	20
Stringer, James	John B. Dempsey	17
Strong, John C.	John Byler	14
Stuard, William	John McWilliams	29

1812 TAX LIST

NAME	CAPTAIN'S COMPANY	PAGE NUMBER
Stuart, Alexander	James Walker	25
Sugg, Edward	Timothy Sugg	21
Sugg, Harbert	Timothy Sugg	21
Sugg, Thomas	Timothy Sugg	20
Sugg, William	Timothy Sugg	21
Suggs, Jno. H.	Timothy Sugg	21
Sugg, Timothy	Timothy Sugg	21
Summer, Samuel	John B. Dempsey	16
Summers, Samuel	Benjamin Hewitt	11
Summers, William	Benjamin Hewitt	11
Sutton, Jacob	James Walker	25
Sutton, John	John Sutton	26
Sutton, William Junr.	John Sutton	27
Sutton, William Senr.	John Sutton	27
Swift, Flower	John McWilliams	29
Talley, Richard	Timothy Sugg	21
Tankersley, Charles	Duncan Neille	7
Tankersley, Richard	James Neill	3
Taylor, John	John Roberts	23
Teal, Edward	James Shinault	6
Teal, Timothy	James Shinault	6
Temple, Robert	John B. Dempsey	17
Templeton, John	Benjamin Hewitt	10
Templeton, Saml.	Benjamin Hewitt	10
Terry, Kebble	Richard Neely	32
Terry, Thompson	Richard Neely	32
Thomas, William	Lewis Medlin	4
Thompson, Abraham	John Byler	15
Thompson, Ginnins	James Neill	3
Thompson, John	John Byler	15
Thompson, Joseph	John Byler	15
Thompson, Philips	Benjamin Hewitt	11
Thompson, Reuben	John Byler	15
Thompson, Thompson	John Byler	15
Thornton, Richard	John McWilliams	28
Thrasher, John	Richard Neely	32
Tilly, John	Richard Neely	32
Tilford, Samuel	Richard Neely	32
Tilford, William	Richard Neely	32
Tilford, John	James Walker	24
Todd, Daniel	John Wortham	1
Toliver, Charles	James Shinault	7
Tribble, Peter	John McWilliams	28
Trip, John	John McWilliams	29
Tucker, Edward	James Yell	18
Tucker, James	John B. Dempsey	16
Tucker, John	John Roberts	23
Tucker, John	John Wortham	1

1812 TAX LIST

NAME	CAPTAIN'S COMPANY	PAGE NUMBER
Turman, John	Duncan Neille	7
Turner, James	Lewis Medlin	5
Turner, James	James Neill	3
Turner, John	Richard Neely	32
Turner, Spratley	James Neill	3
Turner, William	James Shinault	7
Turner, Zachariah	John Roberts	23
Turrentine, James	John Byler	14
Twitty, Willie	James Yell	19
Uless, Adam	Richard Neely	32
Vance, David	John Roberts	23
Vancleave, Ebenezer	John McWilliams	29
Vanoy, Elijah	James Shinault	6
Vanoy, Joel	James Shinault	6
Venable, Richard	John Wortham	2
Venable, Richard Junr.	John Wortham	2
Venable, Samuel	John Wortham	2
Venable, Thomas	John Wortham	2
Vincent, David	James Neill	3
Vincent, Drewry	James Neill	3
Vincent, Jordan	James Neill	3
Waddle, Saml. D.	John Byler	15
Wade, Edward	John B. Dempsey	16
Waggoner, Joseph	James Shinault	6
Waggoner, Samuel	James Shinault	6
Waggoner, Thomas	James Shinault	6
Waggoner, Willliam	James Shinault	6
Wagner, Joseph	James Walker	25
Walker, James	James Walker	24
Walker, John B.	James Walker	24
Walker, Joseph	James Walker	25
Walker, Joseph	Duncan Neille	8
Walker, Nathaniel	John Byler	15
Walker, Philip	Patterson	13
Walker, Robert	Patterson	13
Walker, William	James Yell	18
Wall, John	John B. Dempsey	17
Word, Cuttbirth	John McWilliams	29
Word, Thomas	John McWilliams	29
Ware, William	Richard Neely	32
Ware, William	James Yell	19
Warmick, David	John McWilliams	29
Warmick, David Junr.	John McWilliams	29
Warmick, William	John McWilliams	29
Warmith, Henry	John Byler	14
Warnell, Natty	John McWilliams	28

1812 TAX LIST

NAME	CAPTAIN'S COMPANY	PAGE NUMBER
Warnick, Alexander	John McWilliams	29
Warner, John	William Bell	9
Warner, John	John Wortham	1
Warner, William	John Wortham	2
Warren, Jno.	Timothy Sugg	20
Watterson, Wm.	John Sutton	26
Watley, Walter	James Shinault	6
Watson, Benjamin	James Walker	24
Weatherford, Money	James Walker	25
Weaver, Benjamin	James Neill	3
Weaver, David	Duncan Neille	7
Weaver, John	Duncan Neille	7
Weaver, Joseph	James Neill	3
Weaver, Joshua	James Yell	18
Weaver, William	Timothy Sugg	21
Weaver, William Senr.	Timothy Sugg	21
Webster, Jonathan	James Walker	25
Welch, John	John Roberts	23
Wellburn, Eliott	James Shinault	6
Wembsly, Isaac	John Sutton	27
Werstmel, Charles	John McWilliams	30
West, Berry	Benjamin Hewitt	11
West, Elijah	John Byler	14
West, James	Patterson	13
West, Jeremiah	Duncan Neille	7
Westmoreland, Vincent	John B. Dempsey	17
Wheeler, Nath.	John Byler	14
White, James	John Byler	15
White, James	James Neill	3
White, John	Lewis Medlin	4
White, John	Richard Neely	32
White, Sorrell	William Bell	9
White, Scion	William Bell	9
Whitehead, John	Timothy Sugg	21
Whitehead, Lazareth	Timothy Sugg	21
Whitehead, William	James Walker	24
Whitworth, Edward	Patterson	13
Whitworth, Isaac	James Shinault	6
Whitworth, Jacob	John B. Dempsey	17
Whitworth, Macob	Timothy Sugg	21
Whitworth, Saml. J.	Patterson	13
Whitney, William O.	Richard Neely	32
Whitson, Thos.	James Shinault	6
Wilkerson, Charles	James Walker	24
Willaford, Samuel	Lewis Medlin	5
Williams, Reavis	James Shinault	7
Williams, Daniel	John Byler	14
Williams, David	James Neill	3

1812 TAX LIST

NAME	CAPTAIN'S COMPANY	PAGE NUMBER
Williams, Elijah	John McWilliams	28
Williams, Elisha	John B. Dempsey	16
Willliams, Hamill	Benjamin Hewitt	12
Williams, Isaac	John McWilliams	29
Williams, Isaac	John B. Dempsey	16
Williams, Isaac Junr.	John McWilliams	29
Williams, James	John Byler	14
Williams, John	Timothy Sugg	21
Williams, Jno. T.	Timothy Sugg	20
Williams, Joseph	John Byler	15
Williams, Nathanl.	John B. Dempsey	16
Williams, Nathaniel	John Byler	14
Williams, Owen	Patterson	13
Williams, Terry	James Neill	2
Williams, William	Lewis Medlin	4
Williamson, Thomas	James Neill	7
Willingham, Elijah	John Roberts	23
Willis, Davis	Lewis Medlin	5
Willis, Thomas	James Neill	3
Wilmouth, James	James Yell	18
Wilson, Aaron Junr.	Patterson	13
Wilson, Aaron Senr.	Patterson	13
Wilson, Eben	John Byler	14
Wilson, George	John Byler	14
Wilson, James	William Bell	9
Wilson, James Junr.	Patterson	13
Wilson, James Senr.	Patterson	13
Wilson, James	James Neill	2
Wilson, James A.	John Wortham	1
Wilson, John	Duncan Neille	8
Wilson, John	Patterson	13
Wilson, John	Duncan Neille	7
Wilson, Mark	John Byler	14
Wilson, Michael	John McWilliams	30
Wilson, Moses	Patterson	13
Wilson, Samuel	John McWilliams	30
Wilson, Zacheus	John Wortham	2
Windsor, Benjamin	James Yell	18
Winston, John	James Yell	19
Winston, Nathaniel	James Yell	19
Winters, Samuel	Benjamin Hewitt	11
Wintoth, John	John Sutton	27
Wise, Henry	Benjamin Hewitt	10
Wise, John	Benjamin Hewitt	10
Wise, Stephens	Benjamin Hewitt	11
Wise, William	Benjamin Hewitt	10
Wiser, John	James Shinault	7
Wisner, Martin	Lewis Medlin	4
Wolf, Jacob	William Bell	8

1812 TAX LIST

NAME	CAPTAIN'S COMPANY	PAGE NUMBER
Wood, William	John McWilliams	28
Woodard, William	John McWilliams	30
Woodfin, Nicholas	James Yell	18
Woodram, James	James Shinault	6
Woodram, Joel	James Shinault	6
Woods, Abraham Junr.	John McWilliams	28
Woods, Abraham Senr.	John McWilliams	28
Woods, Francis H.	Lewis Medlin	5
Woods, James	Lewis Medlin	4
Woods, John	William Bell	9
Woods, Joseph	John Byler	15
Wooldridge, John	John McWilliams	30
Wooten, John	John Neill	2
Word, Jonathan	James Yell	19
Wortham, Charles	John Byler	15
Wortham, James	Patterson	13
Wortham, John	John Wortham	1
Wortham, William	John Wortham	2
Wright, George	John Roberts	23
Wright, Henry	John Roberts	23
Wright, James	John Byler	14
Wright, Jeremiah	James Walker	24
Wright, John	John Sutton	26
Wright, Peter	Richard Neely	32
Wright, Thos.	John Sutton	27
Wright, William	John Roberts	23
Wyatt, William	John McWilliams	30
Yates, Absolem	John McWilliams	28
Yates, Jesse	John Roberts	23
Yates, John	John McWilliams	30
Yates, Jonathan	John Roberts	23
Yates, Joshua	John McWilliams	29
Yates, Samuel	John McWilliams	28
Yates, Thomas	John Roberts	23
Yell, James	James Yell	18
Yell, Moses	James Yell	19
Young, Edward	John B. Dempsey	17
Young, William	James Yell	18
York, Daniel	John Roberts	23
York, Jonathan	John Roberts	23
Young, David	James Yell	18
Young, James	James Yell	18
Young, John	James Yell	19

August 30th 1812
Signed by
Thomas Moore, Clerk
John Atkinson, Presiding Justice
Bedford County, Tennessee

EARLY LAND DEED INDEX ******

Bedford County, Tennessee

1788- 1815

Most "assigners" listed in this index appear to have performed Military Service in the North Carolina Line during the American Revolution and were issued land warrants for their services to the mother state. These warrants were frequently assigned, or signed over, to hungry settlers or land speculators who upon the filing, followed by approval of the proper entry, were then issued Tennessee Land Grants. Few assignors ever settled in Bedford County.

ALPHABETICAL ORDER

This index represents a time in the young county's history when it was a buyers market.

****** GRANT BOOK INDEX ******

This Grant Index included land that was granted in an area that now includes Bedford, Lincoln and Moore Counties.

GRANTEE	GRANTOR	DATE	PAGE
Ake, Joseph	Alexander Outlaw	1806	10
Allbright, Simon	Assignor	1808	91
Allison, David	John Gray Blount et al	1808	136
Anderson, Wm. P. et al	State of Tennessee	1808	66
Armstrong, Martin	Assignor	1808	37
Armstrong, Martin	Assignor	1808	180
Armstrong, Martin	Assignor	1808	220
Armstrong, Martin	Assignor	1808	223
Armstrong, Martin	Assignor	1808	225
Armstrong, Martin	Assignor	1808	226
Ayers, Moses	Alexander Outlaw	1806	14
Balch, Amos	State of North Carolina	1788	18
Balch, Amos	State of North Carolina	1788	26
Balch, Amos	State of North carolina	1788	248
Beard, John	State of Tennessee	1808	131
Beard, John	State of Tennessee	1808	132
Bell, William	Assignor	1808	57
Bell, Robert	Robert Bean	1808	240
Blount, Tho. & Jno. G.	Procession Survey	1808	5
Blount, Thomas et al	State of North Carolina	1807	42
Blount, John Gray	State of Tennessee	1808	57
Blount, John Gray	State of Tennessee	1808	64
Blount, John Gray	State of Tennessee	1808	89
Blount, John Gray	State of Tennessee	1808	98
Blount, John Gray	State of Tennessee	1808	178
Bradford, Benjamin	Alexander Outlaw	1808	7
Brahan, John et al	State of Tennessee	1808	59
Brahan, John	State of Tennessee	1808	134
Brandon, James	State of North Carolina	1798	45

GRANTEE	GRANTOR	DATE	PAGE
Bright, James	State of Tennessee	1808	73
Bright, James	State of Tennessee	1808	85
Brown, Emanuel	Assignor	1808	88
Buckannan, John	Robert Buckannon	1808	1
Burke, Francis	Assignor	1808	177
Campbell, Collins	State of Tennessee	1808	91
Campbell, George W.	State of Tennessee	1808	173
Campbell, George W.	State of Tennessee	1808	174
Campbell, George W.	State of Tennessee	1808	184
Carmical, Dugald	Assignor	1809	199
Cathey, George, Sr.	State of North Carolina	1788	107
Chamberlin, Jeremiah	State of Tennessee	1808	70
Coffee, John	State of Tennessee	1808	228
Cuningham, Robert	William Edmiston	1808	217
Cunningham, Aron	State of Tennessee	1808	257
Dalton, William	Assignor	1808	134
Davis, Jessee	Alexander Outlaw	1808	12
Davis, Micajah	Assignor	1808	79
Dickey, Matthew	Robert Bean	1808	235
Dixon, Tilman	State of Tennessee	1808	79
Doherty, George	State of Tennessee	1808	58
Doherty, George	State of Tennessee	1808	63
Doherty, George	State of Tennessee	1808	67
Doherty, George	State of Tennessee	1808	77
Doherty, George	State of Tennessee	1808	80
Doherty, George	State of Tennessee	1808	82
Doherty, George	State of Tennessee	1808	83
Doherty, George	State of Tennessee	1808	86
Doherty, George	State of Tennessee	1808	92
Doherty, George	State of Tennessee	1808	94
Doherty, George	State of Tennessee	1808	95
Doherty, George	State of Tennessee	1808	100
Doherty, George	State of Tennessee	1808	101
Doherty, George	State of Tennessee	1808	179
Doherty, George	State of Tennessee	1808	182
Doherty, George	State of Tennessee	1808	190
Donelson, Stokely	State of North Carolina	1807	43
Doneldson, John	State of Tennessee	1808	229
Donelson, Jo. & Samuel	State of Tennessee	1807	260
Drake, Ephraim	State of Tennessee	1808	188
Dunn, John	Spencer Griffin	1808	246
Eastland, Thomas et al	State of Tennessee	1807	29
Edmonson, John	State of North Carolina	1807	20
Edmonson, John	State of North Carolina	1794	22
Edwards, Jonathan B.	Robert Bean	1808	237
Erwin, Andrew et al	State of Tennessee	1808	103
Erwin, Andrew et al	State of Tennessee	1808	106
Erwin, Andrew et al	Norton Prior	1808	192

GRANTEE	GRANTOR	DATE	PAGE
Erwin, Andrew et al	State of Tennessee	1809	199
Erwin, Andrew et al	State of Tennessee	1809	202
Erwin, Andrew et al	State of Tennessee	1809	203
Erwin, Andrew et al	State of Tennessee	1808	205
Erwin, Andrew et al	State of Tennessee	1808	207
Erwin, Andrew et al	State of Tennessee	1809	210
Exum, Phillip	Assignor	1808	207
Flood, William	State of Tennessee	1808	184
Gilbreathm William et al	State of Tennessee	1808	70
Gilbreath, William	State of Tennessee	1808	72
Gilchrist, Malcolm	State of Tennessee	1808	69
Gilchrist, William et al	State of Tennessee	1808	70
Gilchrist, Malcolm	State of Tennessee	1808	104
Gordon, George	Thomas Love	1808	129
Grant, James	State of North Carolina	1793	112
Grant, James	State of North Carolina	1793	115
Greenlee, James	State of Tennessee	1808	75
Greenlee, James	State of Tennessee	1808	189
Greer, Ruth (Talbot)	State of North Carolina	1794	48
Hargett, Frederick et al	Assignor	1808	186
Harris, Edward	State of Tennessee	1808	177
Harris, Edward	State of Tennessee	1808	231
Harryman, Charles	Andrew Jackson	1806	22
Hartley, John	Assignor	1808	231
Henderson, Robert	Assignor	1808	106
Henry, William et al	State of Tennessee	1807	29
Holly, Benjamin	Assignor	1808	66
Holman, Hardy	Thomas Eastland et al	1808	252
Jackson, Andrew	State of Tennessee	1808	36
Jackson, Andrew	State of Tennessee	1808	37
Jackson, Andrew	State of Tennessee	1808	219
Jackson, Andrew	State of Tennessee	1808	220
Jackson, Andrew	State of Tennessee	1808	222
Jackson, Andrew	State of Tennessee	1808	223
Jackson, Andrew	State of Tennessee	1808	225
Jackson, Andrew	State of Tennessee	1808	226
Justin (Justice), David	State of North Carolina	1802	27
Kirkingdall, Matthew	Assignor	1808	205
Kirkingdall, James	Assignor	1808	205
Kirkingdall, James	Assignor	1809	210
Kirkingdall, Matthew	Assignor	1809	210
Knott, William	Alexander Outlaw	1808	9
Lewis, Micajah Green	Assignor	1808	85
Lewis, James	State of Tennessee	1808	97
Lewis, Micajah Green	Assignor	1808	104
Lewis, James	State of Tennessee	1808	175

GRANTEE	GRANTOR	DATE	PAGE
Love, Thomas	Amos Balch	1797	16
Love, Thomas	Amos Balch	1797	250
Martin, George et al	State of North Carolina	1788	26
Martin, Richard et al	State of North Carolina	1788	26
Martin, William	State of Tennessee	1808	185
Maxwell, Samuel	State of Tennessee	1808	259
Meek, Alexander	Robert Cunningham	1808	216
Mitchel, James et al	James Patton et al	1808	212
Montfort, Henry	State of Tennessee	1808	61
McCorrey (McCrory), Thos.	State of Tennessee	1808	180
McQuillan, Walker	Assignor	1808	257
Nelson, John	Assignor	1808	228
Norvill, James	Alexander Outlaw	1808	233
Norvill, William	Alexander Outlaw	1808	254
Outlaw, Alexander	Assignor	1808	222
Overton, Thomas et al	State of Tennessee	1808	59
Overton, John et al	Robert Hayes, (Marshal)	1808	140
Overton, John et al	Robert Hayes, (Marshal)	1808	165
Overton, John	Jenkin Whiteside	1808	168
Overton, James	Assignor	1808	188
Patterson, Samuel	State of North Carolina	1794	214
Patton, James et al	State of Tennessee	1808	103
Patton, James et al	State of Tennessee	1808	106
Patton, James et al	Norton Prior	1808	192
Patton, James et al	State of Tennessee	1809	199
Patton, James et al	State of Tennessee	1809	202
Patton, James et al	State of Tennessee	1809	203
Patton, James et al	State of Tennessee	1808	205
Patton, James et al	State of Tennessee	1808	207
Patton, James et al	State of Tennessee	1809	210
Patton, James et al	James Patton et al	1808	212
Perkins, Thomas H.	Assignor	1808	110
Prior, Norton	Joseph Anderson	1808	52
Prior, Norton	David Allison	1808	147
Prior, Norton	Robert Hayes, (Marshall)	1808	155
Ramey, Peter	Assignor	1809	203
Randal, William et al	Assignor	1808	186
Rawlings, James	Assignor	1808	36
Robinson, Charles et al	Assignor	1808	186
Shelby, John	Andrew Jackson	1806	55
Ship, Daniel	State of Tennessee	1808	110
Sims, Walter	Gideon Denison	1798	119
Sloan, John	State of North Carolina	1794	34
Smith, George	State of Tennessee	1808	88
Smith, Tob	Assignor	1808	98

GRANTEE	GRANTOR	DATE	PAGE
Smith, John	State of Tennessee	1808	186
Strong, George	Alexander Outlaw	1807	30
Talbot, Ruth Greer	State of North Carolina	1794	48
Talbot, Thomas	State of North Carolina	1788	50
Taylor, Isaac	John Armstrong	1785	43
Taylor, Joseph	Nathaniel Hays	1808	243
Temple, E.	Henry Ivy	1825	82-A
Thompson, Robert	Assignor	1808	59
Tilghman, William	Assignor	1808	103
Tilly, Jenny	Robert Bean	1808	238
Trimble, James	Assignor	1808	173
Trimble, James	Assignor	1808	174
Verner, Robert	Assignor	1809	202
Wadsworth, Obedance	John Warner	1808	32
Waggoner, John	Thomas Eastland et ux	1808	39
Walker, Robert	State of North Carolina	1809	198
Whaley, Ezekiel	Assignor	1808	256
Whitaker, John	Thomas Eastland et ux	1808	241
White, Robert	State of Tennessee	1808	256
Whitehead, John	Alexander Outlaw	1806	31
Whiteside, Jenkin et al	Robert Hayes, (Marshal)	1808	140
Whiteside, Jenkin et al	Robert Hayes, (Marshal)	1808	165
Whiteside, Jenkin	John Overton	1808	168
Williams, Oliver et al	State of Tennessee	1808	66
Willson, Thomas	Spencer Griffin	1807	41
Wilson, Thomas	Spencer Griffin	1807	245

BEDFORD COUNTY DEED BOOK "A" GRANTEE INDEX

GRANTEE	GRANTOR	DATE	PAGE
Ake, Joseph	Alexander Outlaw	1806	9
Alexander, Walter	State of Tennessee	1809	369
Allison, David	John Gray & Thomas Blount	1808	186
Anderson, Wm. P. et al	State of Tennessee	1808	76
Ayers, Moses	Alexander Outlaw	1806	13
Balch, Amos	State of North Carolina	1788	18
Balch, Amos et al	State of North Carolina	1788	26
Beard, John	State of Tennessee	1808	180
Beard, John	State of Tennessee	1808	182
Blount, John Gray & Thomas	Processional Survey	1808	3
Blount, John Gray & Thomas	State of North Carolina	1807	49
Blount, John Gray	State of Tennessee	1808	65
Blount, John Gray & Thomas	State of Tennessee	1808	75
Blount, John Gray	State of Tennessee	1808	102
Blount, John Gray	State of Tennessee	1808	114
Blount, John Gray	State of Tennessee	1808	238
Bradford, Benj.	Alexander Outlaw	1808	4
Braham, John et al	State of Tennessee	1808	69
Braham, John	State of Tennessee	1808	184
Brandon, James	State of North Carolina	1788	53
Bright, James	State of Tennessee	1808	84
Bright, James	State of Tennessee	1808	98
Buckhannon, John	Robert Buckhannon	1808	1
Cage, Wm.	State of North Carolina	1794	362
Campbell, Collin	State of Tennessee	1808	104
Campbell, George W.	State of Tennessee	1808	230
Campbell, George W.	State of Tennessee	1808	232
Campbell, George W.	State of Tennessee	1808	246
Cannon, Clement	Wm. Wilbiurn et al	1809	367
Cannon, Newton	Wm. Wilbourn et al	1809	352
Cathey, George, Sr.	State of North Carolina	1788	126
Chamberland, Jeremiah et al	State of Tennessee	1808	80
Clay, Stephen	John Coffee	1809	354
Coffee, John	State of Tennessee	1809	300
Cunningham, Aron	State of Tennessee	1809	395
Cunningham, Robert	Wm. Edmiston	1808	287
Davis, Jessee	Alexander Outlaw	1818	11
Davis, John	David Buckhannon	1809	363
Dickey, Mathew	Robert Bean	1808	377
Dixon, Tilman	State of Tennessee	1808	90
Doherty, George	State of Tennessee	1808	67
Doherty, George	State of Tennessee	1808	73
Doherty, George	State of Tennessee	1808	78
Doherty, George	State of Tennessee	1808	88
Doherty, George	State of Tennessee	1808	90
Doherty, George	State of Tennessee	1808	92
Doherty, George	State of Tennessee	1808	94

GRANTEE	GRANTOR	DATE	PAGE
Doherty, George	State of Tennessee	1808	96
Doherty, George	State of Tennessee	1808	106
Doherty, George	State of Tennessee	1808	108
Doherty, George	State of Tennessee	1808	110
Doherty, George	State of Tennessee	1808	116
Doherty, George	State of Tennessee	1808	118
Doherty, George	State of Tennessee	1808	240
Doherty, George	State of Tennessee	1808	244
Doherty, George	State of Tennessee	1808	256
Doherty, George	State of Tennessee	1809	371
Doherty, George	State of Tennessee	1809	373
Doherty, George	State of Tennessee	1809	375
Donaldson, Stokley	State of North Carolina	1793	52
Donalson, John	State of Tennessee	1809	302
Donalson, John	State of Tennessee	1809	348
Donalson, John & Samuel	State of Tennessee	1808	399
Drake, Ephraim	State of Tennessee	1808	252
Dunn, John	Spencer Griffin	1808	387
Eastland, Thomas et al	State of Tennessee	1808	31
Edmunson, John	Partition	1807	20
Edmondson, John	State of North Carolina	1792	22
Edwards, Jonathan B.	Robert Bean	1808	379
Enochs, Enoch	Andrew Jackson	1809	343
Erwin, Andrew et al	State of Tennessee	1808	120
Erwin, Andrew et al	State of Tennessee	1808	124
Erwin, Andrew et al	Norton Pryor	1808	258
Erwin, Andrew et al	State of Tennessee	1809	267
Erwin, Andrew et al	State of Tennessee	1809	269
Erwin, Andrew et al	State of Tennessee	1809	271
Erwin, Andrew et al	State of Tennessee	1809	273
Erwin, Andrew et al	State of Tennessee	1809	275
Erwin, Andrew et al	State of Tennessee	1809	278
Erwin, Andrew et al	State of Tennessee	1808	310
Gilbreath, Wm.	State of Tennessee	1808	82
Gilcrest, Malcom	State of Tennessee	1808	79
Gilcrest, Malcom	State of Tennessee	1808	122
Gilcrest, Wm. et al	State of Tennessee	1808	80
Gordon, George	Thomas Love	1808	148
Greer, Alexander	John Stone	1809	332
Greer, Alexander	John Stone	1809	334
Greenlee, James	State of Tennessee	1808	86
Greenlee, James	State of Tennessee	1808	254
Greer, Andrew	State of Tennessee	1808	339
Greer, Joseph	State of Tennessee	1808	335
Greer, Joseph	State of Tennessee	1809	341
Greer, Ruth	State of North Carolina	1794	56
Greer, Thomas	Wm. Nichols	1809	358
Grant, Jas.	State of North Carolina	1793	132
Grant, Jas.	State of North Carolina	1793	135

GRANTEE	GRANTOR	DATE	PAGE
Harris, Edward	State of Tennessee	1808	236
Harris, Edward	State of Tennessee	1809	304
Harryman, Charles	Andrew Jackson	1806	23
Henry, Wm. et al	State of Tennessee	1808	31
Holman, Hardy	Thomas Eastland et ux	1808	389
Jackson, Andrew	State of Tennessee	1807	42
Jackson, Andrew	State of Tennessee	1807	44
Jackson, Andrew	State of Tennessee	1809	289
Jackson, Andrew	State of Tennessee	1809	291
Jackson, Andrew	State of Tennessee	1809	293
Jackson, Andrew	State of Tennessee	1809	294
Jackson, Andrew	State of Tennessee	1809	296
Jackson, Andrew	State of Tennessee	1809	298
Jackson, Andrew	John Donalson	1809	326
Justice, David	State of North Carolina	1802	29
Knott, Wm.	Alexander Outlaw	1808	7
Lewis, James	State of Tennessee	1808	112
Lewis, James	State of Tennessee	1808	234
Love, Thomas	Amos Balch	1797	15
Martin, George & Richard et al	State of North Carolina	1788	26
Martin, Matt	Andrew Jackson	1809	328
Martin, Matt	Andrew Jackson	1809	330
Martin, Wm.	State of Tennessee	1808	248
Maxwell, Jessee	State of Tennessee	1808	346
Maxwell, Samuel	State of Tennessee	1809	397
Meek, Alexander	Robert Cunningham	1808	285
Mitchell, James et al	James Patton et al	1808	280
Munfort, Henry	State of Tennessee	1808	71
McCiustian, John	Howell Tatum	1809	315
McCrory, Thomas	State of Tennessee	1808	242
McGhee, Wm.	State of Tennessee	1809	308
Norvell, James	Alexander Outlaw	1808	306
Norvell, Wm.	Alexander Outlaw	1808	391
Overton, John et al	Robert Hays, (Marshal)	1808	191
Overton, John et al	Robert Hays, (Marshal)	1808	219
Overton, John et al	Partition Deed	1808	224
Overton, Thomas et al	State of Tennessee	1808	69
Patterson, Samuel	State of North Carolina	1794	282
Patton, James et al	State of Tennessee	1808	120
Patton, James et al	State of Tennessee	1808	124
Patton, James et al	Norton Pryor	1808	258
Patton, James et al	State of Tennessee	1809	267
Patton, James et al	State of Tennessee	1809	269
Patton, James et al	State of Tennessee	1809	271

GRANTEE	GRANTOR	DATE	PAGE
Patton, James et al	State of Tennessee	1809	273
Patton, James et al	State of Tennessee	1809	275
Patton, James et al	State of Tennessee	1809	278
Patton, James et al	James Patton et al	1808	280
Patton, James et al	State of Tennessee	1808	310
Pryor, Norton	Joseph Anderson	1808	60
Pryor, Norton	David Allison	1808	199
Pryor, Norton	Robert Hays, (Marshal)	1808	209
Pryor, Norton	State of North Carolina	1809	313
Robison, Felix	John Jackson	1809	364
Rosebrough, Wm.	David Buckhannon	1809	356
Ross, James	Amos Balch	1808	360
Shelby, John	Andrew Jackson	1806	63
Ship, Daniel	State of Tennessee	1808	129
Sims, Walter	Gideon Dineson	1808	138
Sloan, John	State of North Carolina	1794	39
Smith, George	State of Tennessee	1808	100
Smith, John	State of Tennessee	1808	250
Stone, John	Stokley Donalson	1807	319
Strong, George	Alexander Outlaw	1807	33
Sorrels, David	James Patton et al	1809	322
Talbot, Thomas	State of North Carolina	1788	58
Talbot, Thomas	State of Tennessee	1808	337
Taylor, Joseph	Nathaniel Hays	1808	385
Tilley, Jenny	Robert Bean	1808	381
Thompson, James	Robert Buckhannon	1809	350
Townsend, Wm.	Andrew Boyd	1809	317
Wadsworth, Obedance	John Warner	1808	37
Waggoner, John	Thomas Eastland et ux	1807	46
Walker, Robert	State of North Carolina	1809	265
White, Robert	State of Tennessee	1809	393
Whitehead, John	Alexander Outlaw	1806	35
Whiteside, Jenkin et al	Robert Hays, (Marshal)	1808	191
Whiteside, Jenkin et al	Robert Hays, (Marshal)	1808	219
Whiteside, Jenkin et al	Partition Deed	1808	224
Whittaker, John	Thomas Eastland et ux	1808	383
Williams, Oliver et al	State of Tennessee	1808	76
Williams, Oliver	State of Tennessee	1809	324
Wilson, Thomas	Spencer Griffin	1807	48

DEED BOOK "A" ASSIGNOR'S INDEX

ASSIGNOR	DATE	PAGE
David Brown	1808, 1809	235, 241
Francis Burk	1808	236
Dugald Carmicael	1808	269
Philip Exum	1809	275
John Hartley	1809	304
Robert Henderson	1808	124
Daniel McKissick	1808	310
Walter McQuillon	1809	395
Jas. Overton	1808	252
Peter Rayney	1809	271
Michael Shipman	1809	348
John Smith	1808	114
Robert Verner	1809	269
Ezekiel Whaley	1809	393

****

BEDFORD COUNTY DEED BOOK "B" GRANTEE INDEX

GRANTEES	GRANTORS	DATE	PAGE
Aldridge, Nathaniel	Malcom Gilchrist	1810	325
Alexander, Archabald	Commissioners	1811	461
Alexander, Archabald	Commissioners	1811	473
Alexander, Ezekeel	State of North Carolina	1810	242
Allison, David	James Grant	1810	213
Allison, John	Newton Cannon	1809	13
Allison, William et al	John Harris	1809	33
Anderson, William P.	State of Tennessee	1810	200
Anderson, Jos.	Plat of Procession	1810	323
Bags, Robert	Jacob Meleham	1811	451
Baird, Lewis	State of Tennessee	1809	1
Bell, Samuel	Commissioners	1811	485
Blair, Hays	William Wilborn	1809	56
Blair, Hays et al	State of Tennessee	1809	64
Bond, Joshua B.	David Allison	1811	503
Boyd, John	State of Tennessee	1809	179
Boyd, John	State of Tennessee	1808	181
Bradford, Benjamin	Baxter Ragsdale	1809	168
Bradford, Benjamin, Sheriff	John Griffin	1810	334
Bradford, Benjamin	Commissioners	1810	370
Brahan, John	Thomas Overton	1809	125
Brandon, James	State of Tennessee	1809	145
Bright, James	William Galbreath Heirs	1811	453
Brown, Shadrack	Howel Tatum	1809	26
Bryant, Edward	State of Tennessee	1810	402
Bryant, Edward	State of Tennessee	1810	404
Bryant, Edward	State of Tennessee	1810	406
Bryant, John	State of Tennessee	1811	520
Burnam, Thomas	Joseph Walker	1810	280
Campbell, William	Alexander Campbell	1809	164
Cannon, Clement	State of Tennessee	1810	373
Cannon, Clement	Robert Smith	1811	481
Cannon, Minos	State of Tennessee	1810	271
Cannon, Minos	Commissioners	1811	540
Cannon, Newton	Samuel Maxwell et al	1810	313
Cannon, Newton	State of Tennessee	1810	340
Cannon, Newton	State of Tennessee	1810	341
Cannon, Newton	State of Tennessee	1810	342
Cannon, Newton	State of Tennessee	1810	343
Cannon, Newton	State of Tennessee	1810	345
Cannon, Newton	State of Tennessee	1810	347
Cannon, Newton	State of Tennessee	1810	349
Cannon, Newton	State of Tennessee	1810	351
Cannon, Newton	State of Tennessee	1810	353
Cannon, Newton	State of Tennessee	1810	355
Cannon, Newton	State of Tennessee	1811	511
Cannon, Newton	State of Tennessee	1811	522

GRANTEES	GRANTORS	DATE	PAGE
Carr, Benjamin	John Thompson	1811	436
Couser, John	Aaron Cunningham	1809	4
Chapman, Robert	Stephen Hubbert & John Harris	1810	299
Chapman, Robert	Alexander Rutledge	1810	305
Clift, Sarah	George Martin	1810	286
Cockran, James	David Buckhanan	1809	120
Coffey, James	Minos & Clement Cannon	1810	311
Coleman, Joseph	State of Tennessee	1810	414
Cook, Joseph	Andrew Jackson	1810	282
Cooper, Job	William Wilbourn	1809	66
Cox, Thomas	Newton Cannon	1809	11
Cummings, Thomas	Clement Cannon	1810	388
Cuningham, George	Robert Cuningham	1810	357
Davidson, Ephrim	State of North Carolina	1811	514
Davis, John	David Buckhanan	1809	108
Dawdy, Howel	Commissioners	1810	372
Dixion, William et al	Mathew Cunningham	1810	202
Dixon, James	Jonathan Graves	1811	512
Dixon, Robert	Francis McKimie	1810	183
Deneson, Gideon	David Allison	1810	422
Deneson, Gideon	Joshua Bond et ux	1811	496
Drake, John	Alexander Outlaw	1810	278
Drake, John	Joseph Coleman	1810	418
Edde, James	Commissioners	1811	479
Elam, William	James Patton et al	1810	386
Enochs, John	State of Tennessee	1809	127
Enochs, John	State of Tennessee	1809	129
Erwin, Andrew et al	State of Tennessee	1809	131
Erwin, Andrew et al	State of Tennessee	1809	133
Erwin, Andrew et al	State of Tennessee	1809	135
Erwin, Andrew et al	State of Tennessee	1809	139
Erwin, Andrew et al	State of Tennessee	1809	141
Erwin, Andrew et al	State of Tennessee	1809	143
Erwin, Andrew et al	James Patton	1810	366
Ewin, James	Martin Phifer	1810	321
Farley, Jessie	Jonathan Pharr	1810	284
Fauts, Jacob & Lewis	William Bell et al	1809	103
Finch, William P.	Alexander Outlaw	1809	147
Fisher, Michael	Samuel Barton	1811	444
Fisher, Michael	Commissioners	1811	465
Fisher, William	State of Tennessee	1811	530
Fleming, Samuel	Commissioners	1810	400
Floyd, David	Newton Cannon	1809	20
Ford, John	John Griffin, Sheriff	1810	332
Ford, John et al	Benjamin Bradford	1810	336
Galbreath, William et al	Mathew Cunningham	1810	202
Gambell, Aaron	Newton Cannon	1809	37
Gambill, Benjamin	Newton Cannon	1809	35

GRANTEES	GRANTORS	DATE	PAGE
Gamble, Benjamin	Commissioners	1810	378
Garren, James	Alexander Outlaw	1810	293
Gilbert, James	Clement Cannon	1809	110
Gibson, Patrick	Robert Chapman	1810	316
Gibson, William	State of Tennessee	1810	264
Gibson, William	Malcom Gilchrist	1810	328
Gilchrist, Malcom	State of Tennessee	1810	266
Gilchrist, Malcom	State of Tennessee	1810	408
Gilchrist, Malcom	State of Tennessee	1810	410
Gilchrist, Malcom	State of Tennessee	1810	412
Gilchrist, Malcom	State of Tennessee	1811	528
Gilchrist, Malcom, Sr.	Malcom Gilchrist, Jr.	1810	186
Glaves, Michael	Andrew Jackson	1809	16
Gloneger, John	John Stone	1809	154
Graham, James	William Graham	1811	456
Grant, James	State of North Carolina	1810	194
Grant, Lewis	Malcom Gilchrist & William Gibson	1810	330
Gray, Benjah	Zachaes Wilson	1810	240
Greer, Alexander	John Stone	1810	197
Griffin, Samuel	William P. Anderson	1809	60
Griffin, Samuel	William P. Anderson	1809	62
Greenlee, James	State of Tennessee	1809	97
Gunn, William	John Maclin	1809	166
Hail, Mead	Alexander Outlaw	1810	303
Hanna, William	James Patton et al	1810	380
Harris, Samuel B. et al	John Harris	1809	33
Harris, Samuel B.	Newton Cannon	1809	118
Hawkins, Henry	Alexander Outlaw	1809	156
Hays, Patsy	Robert Butler et ux	1810	246
Hays, Rachel & Patsy	Andrew Jackson	1810	244
Higginbottom, William	John Boyd	1810	275
Hodges, Philliman	State of Tennessee	1809	137
Holland, James	Commissioners	1810	368
Holland, James	Commissioners	1810	374
Holt, Joshua	Mary Parker	1811	446
Houston, John	James McKisick	1809	19
Hughs, Robert	Thomas Burnam	1809	106
Hughs, Samuel	Thomas Burnam	1809	101
Hunter, Ruben	David Buckhanan	1809	113
Hutchins, Lemuel	Timothy O'Neal	1809	54
Irwin, Josephas	Thomas Burnam et al	1810	382
Jackson, Andrew	Alexander Ewing	1810	359
Jackson, David John	Alexander Outlaw	1810	307
Jackson, David John	David John Jackson et al	1810	320
Jones, Ezra	James Hill	1809	39

GRANTEES	GRANTORS	DATE	PAGE
Kennedy, Joseph	Moses Yell	1810	292
Kindale, Thomas	James Patton er al	1810	363
Laramore, Thomas	Commissioners	1811	475
Leeper, Allen	William Wood	1810	398
Leeper, James	John Rogers	1810	309
Leeper, James	Clement Cannon et al	1810	392
Lamare, Benjamin	Newton Cannon	1811	438
Lock, John	State of Tennessee	1810	258
Lock, William	Commissioners	1811	483
Love, Joseph	Stephen Childress	1809	160
Legrand, Peter	Ben. Bradford	1810	427
Lytle, William	John Maclin	1809	74
Macklin, Polly	Christopher Taylor	1809	13
Marshal, Leven	Commissioners	1811	469,471
Martin, Matt	Alexander Outlaw	1809	149
Meleham, Jacob et al	Joseph Branch et al	1811	442
Menafee, Jonas	Commissioners	1811	487
McNairy, John	State of Tennessee	1809	81
McNairy, John	State of Tennessee	1809	83
McNairy, John	State of Tennessee	1809	85
McNairy, John	State of Tennessee	1809	87
McNairy, John	State of Tennessee	1809	89
McNairy, John	State of Tennessee	1809	91
McNairy, John	State of Tennessee	1809	93
McNairy, John	State of Tennessee	1809	95
Moore, David	State of Tennessee	1809	68
Moore, David	State of Tennessee	1809	70
Moore, David	State of Tennessee	1809	72
Moore, David	State of Tennessee	1809	77
Moore, David	State of Tennessee	1809	79
Moore, David	William P. Anderson	1808	99
Murry, Robert	Commissioners	1811	477
McCuistion, James	State of Tennessee	1811	492
McCuistion, James	State of Tennessee	1811	493
McDaniel, Samuel	David Justice	1810	394
McKamee, William et al	Mathew Cunningham	1810	202
McLemore, Amos	State of Tennessee	1810	362
Newsom, William et al	John Southgate et ux	1809	22
Newsom, William	Commissioners	1811	455
Nixon, H.	William Arnold	1809	172
Null, Nicholas	Thomas Learmore	1811	450
O'Neal, Timothy et al	Benjamin Bradford	1810	336
Orr, Robert	Minos Cannon	1810	290
Outlaw, Alexander	Joseph Anderson	1809	151
Outlaw, Alexander	Joseph Anderson	1809	158
Outlaw, Alexander	Joseph Anderson	1809	169

GRANTEES	GRANTORS	DATE	PAGE
Overton, John et al	Return of Processional & Division	1808	41
Overton, John et al	Deed of Partition	1809	48
Patrick, John	State of Tennessee	1811	490
Patton, James et al	State of Tennessee	1809	131
Patton, James et al	State of Tennessee	1809	133
Patton, James et al	State of Tennessee	1809	135
Patton, James et al	State of Tennessee	1809	139
Patton, James et al	State of Tennessee	1809	141
Patton, James et al	State of Tennessee	1809	143
Patton, James et al	James Patton	1810	366
Patton, James	James Patton & Andrew Erwin	1810	262
Patton, John	James A. Wilson	1810	396
Patton, William	Joseph Walker	1810	295
Pharr, George	Jonathan Pharr	1810	327
Philips, Bennett	Roger Snell	1811	459
Philips, Josiah	Michael Campbell	1810	188
Philips, John	Michael Campbell	1810	191
Philips, Mathew	Howel Tatum	1809	58
Philips, Samuel	Commissioners	1810	376
Poland, Moses et al	Benjamin Bradford	1810	326
Robertson, David, Joseph & John	Michael Robertson	1810	253
Robertson, James	William Henry	1810	255
Rager, Anthony	Job Cooper	1809	173
Rogers, John	Newton Cannon	1809	31
Ross, David	State of Tennessee	1810	198
Ross, James	Roger Snell	1811	489
Rowsey, Samuel	Minos Cannon	1810	318
Rutledge, Elijah	State of Tennessee	1811	518
Saunders, Ruben	State of Tennessee	1809	116
Saunders, Ruben	State of Tennessee	1809	122
Simpson, William et al	Joseph Branch er al	1811	442
Sims, Walter	Gidion Dineson	1810	224
Smith, Robert	State of Tennessee	1810	268
Smith, Thomas	James Patton & Andrew Erwin	1810	384
Smith, Thomas	Jonathan Pharr	1811	463
Smith, William	Newton Cannon	1809	8
Stuart, Duncan	Benjamin Fitzrandolph	1809	3
Talbot, Thos.	Survey	1808	7
Talbot, Eli et al	Benjamin Bradford, Sheriff	1810	236
Taylor, Green B.	John Maclin	1810	237
Taylor, Joseph	Andrew Jackson	1809	114
Taylor, Nathaniel	State of Tennessee	1810	239
Templeton, John & James	Amos Balch	1809	29
Thompson, Abraham	Commissioners	1811	534
Thompson, Jason	State of Tennessee	1810	390
Torrentine, Alexander	State of Tennessee	1810	416
Torrentine, Alexander	State of Tennessee	1810	420

GRANTEES	GRANTORS	DATE	PAGE
Townsen, William	Jessie McCarty	1809	124
Trotter, Richard	James Brandon	1811	430
Trotter, Richard	James Brandon	1811	432
Vinzart, Jacob	Ruben Saunders	1809	175
Waggoner, George	Newton Cannon	1809	177
Waite, William	Andrew Jackson	1811	440
Walker, James	William Henry	1810	222
Walker, Joseph	Commissioners	1811	536
Webster, Jonathan	Commissioners	1811	467
White, William et al	Benjamin Bradford, Sheriff	1810	236
Whiteside, Jenkin et al	Return of Processional & Division	1808	41
Whiteside, Jenkin et al	Deed of Partition	1809	48
Wilborn, William	State of Tennessee	1809	64
Williams, Christopher	Jacob Melcham et al	1811	495
Williams, William	Minos Cannon	1810	297
Wenro, Henry	Commissioners	1811	538
Wilson, Aaron	Samuel Patterson	1810	260
Wood, Frances	Minos Cannon et al	1810	288
Wood, Joseph	Commissioners	1811	532
Woods, James	James Cummins	1811	516
Wortham, Charles	Felix Robertson	1810	301
Wrights, Thompson	State of Tennessee	1811	524
Wrights, Thompson	State of Tennessee	1811	526
Yell, Moses	Robert Butler et ux	1810	250

DEED BOOK "B" ASSIGNOR'S INDEX

ASSIGNOR	DATE	PAGES
John Barcoe	1809	68, 70, 83
Robt. Carmicle	1809	139
Benj. Davidson	1809	520
John Edwards	1808	264
Thomas Hays	1809	137
John Jordan	1808	524, 526
Hugh Kilpatrick	1809	1
Jeremiah Letteral	1808	490
Dan'l McKissick	1809	133, 135, 143
Solomon Overton	1809	89, 91, 93, 95
Amos Paramore	1808	351, 355
Andrew Philips	1808	518
Joseph Richards	1809	343, 347
John Roundtree	1808	402, 404, 406
William Rowland	1809	349, 390
Benjamin Shepperd	1809	339
James Sullivant	1809	530
Robt. Verner	1808	131
James Woodward	1807	81, 85, 87

BEDFORD COUNTY DEED BOOK "C" GRANTEE INDEX

GRANTEE	GRANTOR	DATE	PAGE
Adams, John	Benjamin McCuistion	1811	331
Aldridge, Nathaniel	Malcom Gilchrist	1811	287
Alexander, Archabald	Commissioners	1811	130
Alexander, Archabald	Commissioners	1811	142
Alexander, Archabald	Robert C. Gordon	1812	498
Alexander, George	State of Tennessee	1811	369
Alison, Robert, assignee of Benjamin McCullock	State of Tennessee	1812	463
Allison, David	Gideon Dineson	1810	95
Allison, David	John Blount et al	1812	561
Alsop, William	Robert C. Gordon	1812	474
Anderson, Patton	Alexander Outlaw	1811	309
Anderson, William P.	John Drake	1812	616
Atkinson, John	State of Tennessee	1812	606
Bags, Robert	Joseph Meleham	1811	120
Baker, Martha, assignee of Abraham Ray	State of Tennessee	1812	614
Barton, Benjamin	Lemuel Hutchings	1811	274
Bell, Samuel	Commissioners	1811	154
Bernard, George	Benjamin Bradford	1812	634
Blackwell, John	John Blair	1811	286
Blackwell, John, assignee of John Flinthon	State of Tennessee	1811	299
Bond, Joshua B.	David Allison	1811	173
Booth, Stephan	Andrew Erwin et al	1812	542
Bradford, Benjamin	Commissioners	1810	41
Bradford, Benjamin, Sheriff	Marlin Jones	1811	357
Bradford, Benjamin	Meade Hail	1811	401
Branch, Nicholas	Commissioners	1811	230
Branch, Nicholas	James Russell	1811	365
Brandon, Charles, assignee of William Reams	State of Tennessee	1811	405
Brandon, Charles	Alexander Rutledge	1811	436
Brooks, John	Tilmon Dixon	1811	335
Brooks, William	Tilmon Dixon	1811	359
Brown, Samuel	Clement Cannon et al	1812	630
Bright, James	William Gilbreath Heirs	1811	122
Bryans, Edward, assignee of John Roundtree	State of Tennessee	1810	76
Bryans, Edward, assignee of John Roundtree	State of Tennessee	1810	78
Bryans, Edward, assignee of John Roundtree	State of Tennessee	1810	80
Bryant, John, assignee of Benjamin Davidson	State of Tennessee	1811	191
Bullington, Ezekiel	William House	1811	339
Burns, Jeremiah	James Patton et al	1812	550
Burrow, Philip et al	Mathew Dockery	1812	576

GRANTEE	GRANTOR	DATE	PAGE
Burrow, Philip et al	Mathre Dockery	1812	576
Butler, Peirce	Joseph Anderson	1812	523
Byler, John	State of Tennessee	1811	371
Calhoon, George	James McReynold et al	1811	438
Callen, Thomas	Newton Cannon	1811	349
Campbell, George	Newton Cannon	1811	244
Cannon, Clement & Newton	State of Tennessee	1810	14
Cannon, Clement	Robert Smith	1811	150
Cannon, Clement	Robert Smith	1812	467
Cannon, Clement	Thomas Moore	1812	566
Cannon, Minos	George Alexander	1811	248
Cannon, Minos	Commissioners	1811	214
Cannon, Minos	Commissioners	1811	216
Cannon, Newton, Assignee of John Floss	State of Tennessee	1810	12
Cannon, Newton, Assignee of John Stross	State of Tennessee	1810	13
Cannon, Newton, Assignee of Joseph Richards	State of Tennessee	1810	16
Cannon, Newton, Assignee of John Stoss	State of Tennessee	1810	17
Cannon, Newton, Assignee of Joseph Richards	State of Tennessee	1810	18
Cannon, Newton, Assignee of William Rowland	State of Tennessee	1810	20
Cannon, Newton, Assignee of John Stoss	State of Tennessee	1810	22
Cannon, Newton, Assignee of John Rowland	State of Tennessee	1810	25
Cannon, Newton, Assignee of William Polk	State of Tennessee	1811	182
Cannon, Newton, Assignee of John Sloss	State of Tennessee	1811	194
Cannon, Newton	George Alexander	1811	258
Cannon, Newton	Elizabeth Giles	1811	296
Cannon, Robert et al	Commissioners	1811	218
Cannon, Robert et al	Commissioners	1811	301
Carothers, William	Joseph Walker	1812	629
Carr, Ben	John Thompson	1811	106
Cates, John	Newton Cannon	1812	477
Chappel, Abner	Commissioners	1811	327
Church of Christ	James Torrentine	1811	279
Clinton, James	State of Tennessee	1811	391
Coats, John	Commissioners	1811	226
Coleman, Joseph, Assignee of John Gray & Thomas Blount	State of Tennessee	1810	86
Commissioners	Clement Cannon	1811	275
Conway, Henry	Benjamin Bradford	1812	444
Conway, Joseph	Patton & Erwin	1812	520
Cooper, Job	Amos McLemore	1811	105
Copper, John	Elizah Rutledge	1811	289
Creenk, Richard	James Brown	1812	559
Culp, Henry	Michael Fisher	1811	283
Cummins, Thomas	Clement Cannon	1810	62
Cummins, Thomas	William Bond	1812	633

GRANTEE	GRANTOR	DATE	PAGE
Cunningham, George	Robert Cunningham	1810	26
Cunningham, Humprey	Daniel Kinny	1812	598
Davidson, Ephraim	State of North Carolina	1811	186
Davidson, Thomas	James Hart	1811	451
Davis, Archibald, Assignee of			
Samuel Shannon	State of Tennessee	1811	395
Dawdy, Howel	Commissioners	1810	44
Dickson, James	Jonathan Graves	1811	184
Dickinson, William	John Overton	1811	387
Dineson, Gidion	Joshua B. Bond et ux	1811	165
Dobs, William	Malcom Gilchrist	1811	240
Doherty, George	State of Tennessee	1811	291
Drake, John	Joseph Coleman	1810	89
Drake, Zachariah	Nicholas Branch	1812	612
Edde, James	Commissioners	1811	148
Edde, James	Commissioners	1812	507
Elem, William	James Patton et al	1810	60
Ellison, William	Samuel B. Harris	1811	337
Erwin, Andrew et al	James Patton	1810	37
Evans, Jessee	Robert C. Gordon	1812	544
Evans, Loverance	Henry Saling	1812	472
Evans, Loverance	Alexander Outlaw	1812	479
Farley, Jesse	Jonathan Pharr	1812	540
Fergerson, John	James Robertson	1811	246
Fisher, Michael	Samuel Barton	1811	114
Fisher, Michael	Commissioners	1811	134
Fleming, Samuel	Commissioners	1810	74
Fonville, Asa	David Wilson	1811	446
Ford, John et al	John Griffin, Sheriff	1810	4
Ford, John et al	Benjamin Bradford	1810	8
Forester, Nathan	Joseph Brittain	1812	486
Foster, William	State of Tennessee	1811	204
Foster, William	State of Tennessee	1811	385
Foster, William	State of Tennessee	1811	393
Fugat, Moses	William Alsop	1812	574
Gage, James, Assignee of John Melves			
& William P. Anderson	State of Tennessee	1812	502
Gamble, Benjamin	Commissioners	1810	50
Gant, James	Newton Cannon	1811	266
Gant, Lewis	William Gibson et al	1810	3
Gardner, Thomas	James A. Wilson	1812	632
Gibson, James	Malcom Gilchrist	1812	552
Gibson, Samuel	Andrew Jackson	1811	341
Gibson, William	Malcom Gilchrist	1810	1
Gilchrist, Malcom, Assignee of			
Benjamin McCullock	State of Tennessee	1810	82
Gilchrist, Malcom	Edward Bryan	1810	93
Gilchrist, Malcom	State of Tennessee	1811	202

GRANTEE	GRANTOR	DATE	PAGE
Glover, Joseph	Clement Cannon	1812	600
Gordon, Robert	George Gordon	1811	356
Graham, James	William Graham	1811	126
Graves, Samuel	Aaron Wilson	1811	353
Gray, Benajah	Thomas Wilson Sr.	1812	470
Gray, John et al	Newton Cannon et al	1811	315
Griffin, Spencer et al	William Sasser	1811	389
Hail, Mead	Benjamin Bradford	1811	401
Hall, John	George Martin	1811	419
Hanna, William	James Patton	1810	52
Harden, Martin	Thomas Parker	1812	604
Harper, Samuel	Newton Cannon	1811	259
Harris, Mosby	Henry Conway	1811	444
Harris, Samuel B.	Commissioners	1811	224
Harrison, Robert	Clement Cannon	1812	590
Hastings, Joseph	Commissioners	1811	234
Hael, Dudly	James Garren	1812	608
Hay, Oliver B.	William White	1811	448
Heggs, John	Minos Cannon	1812	483
Higginbottom, William	Benjamin Bradford	1811	401
Holland, James	Commissioners	1810	39
Holland, James	Commissioners	1810	46
Holland, Thomas	Benjamin McCuistion	1811	311
Holt, Abner et al	Newton Cannon	1811	315
Holt, Joshua	Mary Parker	1811	115
Howel, Joseph B.	Commissioners	1811	222
Hughes, Jesse	John Redford	1811	417
Hughes, Jesse	Henry Rutherford	1812	594
Hughes, Robert	James Mitchell	1812	485
Hunter, Elisha, Assignee of Daniel Smith	State of Tennessee	1812	460
Hunter, James	State of Tennessee	1811	429
Ingram, Samuel et al	Commissioners	1811	218
Ingram, Samuel et al	Commissioners	1811	301
Irvine, Josephas	Thomas Burnam et al	1810	54
Jackson, Andrew	Alexander Erwing	1810	29
Jordon, Barton	Newton Cannon	1811	254
Jordon, Johnston	Newton Cannon	1811	264
Kelley, Reuben	Patton & Erwin	1811	383
Kennaday, Joseph	Moses Yell	1812	481
Kenny, Daniel	Amos Johnston	1811	252
Kimbro, Jeremiah & Phillip Burrow	Mathew Dockery	1812	576
Kindale, Thomas	Patton & Erwin	1810	34
Kiser, Valentine	Clement Cannon	1812	493
Kiser, Valentine	John Strother	1812	571
Knott, William	Benjamin Bradford	1811	363
Krowell, William, Guardian of Jane & Anne, daughters of Anthony Newman	John Newman	1811	281

GRANTEE	GRANTOR	DATE	PAGE
Lamare, Benjamin	Newton Cannon	1811	108
Laramore, Thomas	Commissioners	1811	144
Lacy, Elisha	James McCuistion	1812	580
Leeper, Allen	William Woods	1810	72
Leeper, James	Minos Cannon et al	1810	66
Leeper, John	Adley Alexander	1811	440
Le Grande, Peter	Benjamin Bradford	1810	99
Locke, William	Commissioners	1811	152
Locke, William, George & James	Agreement	1811	367
Locke, William	Joseph Steel	1811	450
Madaris, William D.	John Blackwell	1811	286
Marshal, John & Elizah et al	Benjamin McCuistion	1811	313
Marshal, Lavin	Commissioners	1811	138
Marshal, Lavin	Commissioners	1811	140
Martin, Barkley	Walker & Caruthers	1812	522
Martin, Matt	James Patton et al	1811	431
Mayfield, Abraham	John Parker	1812	496
Meleham, Jacob et al	Joseph Branch et al	1811	112
Menafee, Jonas	Commissioners	1811	156
Morris, Joseph P.	George G. Black	1811	409
Mosley, Thomas P.	Matt Martin	1811	411
Mosley, Thomas B.	Patton & Erwin	1812	516
Murry, Robert	Commissioners	1811	146
McBride, Hugh	William Lock	1811	270
McClenhen, Hugh	David Wilson	1811	343
McClentuk, John et al	Robert C. Gordon	1812	557
McCoy, Daniel	Commissioners	1811	228
McCuistion, Benjamin, Assignee of Abel Sutton	State of Tennessee	1811	373
McCuistion, Benjamin, Assignee of David Ross	State of Tennessee	1811	374
McCuistion, Benjamin, Assignee of James McCuistion	State of Tennessee	1811	376
McCuistion, Benjamin, Assignee of Abel Sutton	State of Tennessee	1811	377
McCuistion, Benjamin, Assignee of James McCuistion	State of Tennessee	1811	379
McCuistion, Benjamin, Assignee of Abel Sutton	State of Tennessee	1811	381
McCuistion, James, Assignee of Alexander McCall	State of Tennessee	1811	161
McCuistion, James, Assignee of Robert McCuistion	State of Tennessee	1811	162
McCuistion, James	Commissioners	1811	220
McCuistion, Robert	Clement Cannon et al	1811	256
McCuistion, Samuel	State of Tennessee	1812	453
McDaniel, Samuel	David Justice	1810	68
McKisick, James	Commissioners	1811	323
McLemore, Amos, Assignee of John Kennedy	State of Tennessee	1810	32

GRANTEE	GRANTOR	DATE	PAGE
McMahan, William	Jonathan Pharr	1812	602
Neely, Clement	Newton Cannon et al	1811	361
Newsom, William	Commissioners	1811	125
Nowlin, Bryan W.	Henry Rutherford	1812	582
Null, Nicholas	Thomas Learamore	1811	119
Oliver, George	George Alexander	1811	333
O'Neal, Timothy et al	John Griffin, Sheriff	1810	4
O'Neal, Timothy et al	Benjamin Bradford	1810	8
Patrick, John	State of Tennessee	1811	159
Patton, James et al	James Patton	1810	37
Patton, James	David Wilson	1811	345
Patterson, Alexander	Samuel Patterson	1811	427
Patterson, Andrew	Samuel Patterson	1811	421
Patterson, John	James A. Wilson	1810	70
Patterson, Thomas	Samuel Patterson	1811	423
Patterson, William	Samuel Patterson	1811	425
Peacock, William	Alexander Outlaw	1811	261
Pewett, Michael	Commissioners	1812	510
Pewett, Moses	Commissioners	1812	508
Pharr, Jonathan	Alexander Outlaw	1811	278
Pharr, Jonathan	Alexander Outlaw	1812	568
Pharr, Jonathan	Thomas Smith	1812	588
Philips, Bennett	Roger Snell	1811	129
Philips, Isaac	William Wood	1811	434
Philips, Samuel	Commissioners	1810	48
Pinkston, Hugh	John Strother	1811	442
Plumlee, Solomon, Assignee of Philip Newton	State of Tennessee	1811	295
Poland, Moses et al	John Griffin, Sheriff	1810	4
Poland, Moses et al	Benjamin Bradford	1810	8
Polk, William	State of Tennessee	1811	293
Rambow, Elias	Henry Rutherford	1812	584
Reid, James	Isaac Crowe	1812	592
Reynolds, Richard et al	William Sasser	1811	389
Ridgeway, James	William Woods	1812	596
Roberts, Thomas	Newton Cannon	1812	637
Ross, James	Roger Snell	1811	158
Rutledge, Alexander	State of Tennessee	1811	403
Rutledge, Elijah, Assignee of Andrew Philips	State of Tennessee	1811	189
Saling, Peter	Alexander Outlaw	1811	272
Sanders, William	Clement Cannon	1812	578
Schooles, Nathaniel H.	Commissioners	1811	325
Schooles, Nathaniel H.	Commissioners	1811	329
Scott, John	Patton & Erwin	1812	512
Shaw, Christopher	Patton & Erwin	1812	518
Shook, William	State of Tennessee	1812	504

GRANTEE	GRANTOR	DATE	PAGE
Simmons, Benjamin	Robert Elliott	1811	268
Simpson, William et al	Joseph Branch et al	1811	112
Smith, James, Assignee of Burwell Smith	State of Tennessee	1812	454
Smith, James, Assignee of George Blackmore	State of Tennessee	1812	456
Smith, James, Assignee of Burwell Smith	State of Tennessee	1812	457
Smith, James	State of Tennessee	1812	459
Smith, John	Malcom Gilchrist et al	1812	556
Smith, Thomas	Jonathan Pharr	1811	132
Smith, Thomas	Andrew Erwin et al	1810	57
Smith, Vincent	James Patton et al	1812	554
Steel, Joseph	William Lock	1811	397
Stone, John	Stephen Clark	1812	495
Stone, John	Commissioners	1812	500
Stone, John	Commissioners	1812	534
Stone, John	Robert C. Gordon	1812	546
Stone, John	Commissioners	1812	536
Stone, John	Commissioners	1812	538
Suggs, Timothy	Tilmon Dixon	1812	490
Suggs, William	Tilmon Dixon	1812	491
Talbot, Thomas	Commissioners	1812	586
Taylor, Green B.	John Marlin	1810	7
Taylor, Nathaniel, Assignee of Benjamin Skipper	State of Tennessee	1810	11
Terry, Kebble	Commissioners	1811	319
Terry, Kebble	Commissioners	1811	321
Tilmon, John	Matt Martin	1811	414
Thompson, Abraham	Commissioners	1811	208
Thompson, Anny	Thompson Thompson	1811	285
Thompson, Jason, Assignee of William Rowland	State of Tennessee	1810	64
Thompson, John, Assignee of Edmund Dodd	State of Tennessee	1811	305
Thompson, Joseph	Commissioners	1811	232
Thompson, Thomas, Assignee of Thomas Taylor	State of Tennessee	1811	307
Torrentine, Alexander, Assignee of William P. Anderson	State of Tennessee	1810	88
Torrentine, Alexander, Assignee of Malaikie Russell	State of Tennessee	1810	92
Trotter, Richard	James Brandon	1811	101
Trotter, Richard	James Brandon	1811	103
Vinzant, Jacob	Rueben Sanders	1811	242
Wade, Edward	Alexander Outlaw	1812	513
Wade, Edward, Assignee of Tilmon Dixon	State of Tennessee	1812	639
Waite, William	Andrew Jackson	1811	110
Walker, James	Commissioners	1812	569
Walker, James	Commissioners	1812	610

GRANTEE	GRANTOR	DATE	PAGE
Walker, Joseph	Commissioners	1811	210
Ward, James et al	Robert C. Gordon	1812	557
Webster, Jonathan	Commissioners	1811	136
Wilkins, John, Assignee of Daniel Smith	State of Tennessee	1812	462
Willhoite, Jacob	John Stone	1812	548
Williams, Christian	Jacob Meleham et al	1811	164
Williams, James	Robert Allison	1812	476
Williams, Joseph	Thomas Thompson	1811	317
Wilson, James	Zacheas Wilson	1811	347
Wilson, John	Samuel Wilson	1811	407
Wineson, Martin	Newton Cannon	1811	303
Wenro, Henry	Commissioners	1811	212
Woods, James	Thomas Cummins	1811	188
Woods, Joseph	Commissioners	1811	206
Woods, William	Perry Moore	1811	469
Wright, Jeremiah	Abraham Simpson	1811	250
Wright, Thompson, Assignee of John Jordon	State of Tennessee	1811	196
Wright, Thompson, Assignee of John Jordon	State of Tennessee	1811	198
Wright, Thompson, Assignee of John Jordon	State of Tennessee	1811	200

****

BEDFORD COUNTY DEED BOOK "D" GRANTEE INDEX
1812 - 1814

GRANTEE	GRANTOR	PAGE
Adams, James	Grant No. 4305	547
Adams, Archibald, Assignee of Archibald Clanton	Grant No. 3533	549
Adams, James	Grant No. 4306	551
Ake, Joseph (Heirs)	John Gage	136
Allen, Vallentine	William Alsop	121
Allison, Robert	Grant No. 368	72
Allison, John & Thos. Cox for William Brown services	Grant No. 2570	298
Allison, John & Thos. Cox for William Brown services	Grant No. 4129	300
Allison, John & Thos. Cox for William Brown services	Grant No. 2577	302
Allison, John & Thos. Cox	Grant No. 2578	306
Allison, John	Thomas Cox	343
Allison, John	John Neill	357
Allison, Robert	Robert Lock	398
Allison, Thomas	William Williams	466
Anderson, Gabriel	Tilmon Dixon	402
Appleby, Agnes	David Sanders	394
Atkinson, John, for William Cochran services	Grant	363
Baird, John	Commissioners	326
Barrett, Jonathan	Elisha Hall	493
Beavers, James	Samuel Harper	322
Bell, David	Samuel Bell	436
Bernard, Walter	Grant	257
Boyd, Etherald	John Record	141
Boyles, Chas. & Andrew Campbell	Daniel Kinny	592
Bradford, John	Benjamin Bradford	588
Brandon, Charles	Amos McLemore	3
Branch, John	Sheriff Bradford	193
Branch, Nicholas	John Warren	209
Branch, William	North Carolina Grant No. 855	253
Brandon, Charles	Grant	199
Byler, John	Archibald Adams	276
Byler, Abraham	Grant	328
Byler, Abraham for John Kennedy services	Grant No. 4822	332
Byler, Abraham for John Kennedy services	Grant No. 4823	361
Burns, John	Benjamin McQuiston	23
Burrow, Freeman	Benjamin Bradford, Sheriff	1
Burrow, Freeman	Benjamin Bradford, Sheriff	62
Cage, Edward	Benjamin Ragsdale	43
Campbell, Thomas	Joseph Allison et al	69
Campbell, George	Richard Martin	242
Campbell, Andrew et al	Daniel Kinny	592
Cannon, Clement	Commissioners	15
Cannon, Clement	Commissioners	17
Cannon, Minos	Clement Cannon	57

GRANTEE	GRANTOR	PAGE
Cannon, Thompson	Minos Cannon	149
Carr, Benjamin, Assignee form Wm. T. Lewis	Grant No. 4264	545
Carr, Benjamin, Assignee of Joe West	Grant No. 4263	482
Caswell, William	Grant No. 1522	369
Casewell, William for Wm. Casewell services	Grant No. 1523	284
Casewell, William for Joseph Handle services	Grant No. 4590	430
Chafin, Jesse	Joel Dyer et al	33
Cherry, Jeremiah for Benj. Kennedy services	Grant No. 469	280
Cherry, Daniel	Jeremiah Cherry	387
Clardy, James	James Torentine	355
Clark, William for Moses Leathers services	Grant No. 3238	297(6)
Clark, James Heirs	David Justice	444
Coats, Wilson	Clement Cannon	227
Coats, Jno. for Edward Dodd services	Grant	385
Coats, John	Samuel Sebastian	412
Colwell, James	Gabriel Anderson	400
Conway, Henry	Samuel B. Harris	104
Conway, H.	Robert C. Gordon	181
Cooper, William	Patton & Erwin	132
Cox, Thomas	John Allison	438
Cox, Thos. & John Allison for Wm. Brown services	Grant No. 2570	298
Cox, Thos. & John Allison for Wm. Brown services	Grant No. 4129	300
Cox, Thos. & John Allison for Wm. Brown services	Grant No. 2577	302
Cox, Thos. & Jno. Allison for Wm. Brown services	Grant No. 2578	306
Crage, John PA	Alexander Crage et ux	590
Crane, Giles B.[5]	William Polk	472
Crutcher, Thomas	Jonathan Pharr	53
Cummins, Thomas	Barton Jordan	29
Cummins, Thomas	William Bond	49
Cunningham, Hance & Jane	Burton Jordon	27
Davis, Thos. & Henry	Benj. Bradford, Sheriff	165
Davis, Thos. & Henry	Frances Murray	177
Davis, Thos. & Henry	James Edde	270
Davis, John L.	William Nash	499
Deery, James	Clement Cannon	486
Deason, Enoch	Joseph Ake	418
Dennison, Robert	Joseph B. Howell	112
Dixon, William	John Higgs	183
Dixon, Robert	Wm. Gilbreath et al	223
Dobbs, James, Assignee for Sampson Williams	Grant No. 3132	424
Dowdy, Howell	Clement Cannon	221
Dyer, Jock	Wm. Walker et al	203
Dysart, John	Violet Cathey	82
Edmonston, David	John Boyd et al	515
Enoch, John	Benj. Bradford, Sheriff	447

GRANTEE	GRANTOR	PAGE
Enoch, John	Benj. Bradford	449
Erwin, Andrew	James Patton	572
Ewell, John	Jas. Patton et al	416
Ewing, W.A. David	William Woods	35
Ewing, George	Adley Alexander	347
Ewing, James	Allen Leeper	543
Finch, William	Benj. Bradford, Sheriff	187
Floyd, David	Grant No. 2511	74
Floyd, David	Mathew Duckery	531
Fogleman, Samuel & Michael	James A. Wilson	539
Fonville, Asa	Charles Sanders	455
Forley, Jessee	Benj. Bradford	375
Frazer, John	Malcom Gilchrist	336
Frazer, Jane	Edw. Cage	495
Gamble, Aaron	William Bond	31
Gant, Lewis	John Phillips	191
Gibson, Patrick	Mark Wilson	219
Gilbert, John	James Gilbert	47
Gilchrist, M.	Samuel B. Harris	114
Giles, Eli	Archibald Johnston et al	148
Gilmore, Nathaniel	J.A. Wilson & Steele	143
Gilmore, Nathaniel Heirs	J.A. Wilson & Steele	145
Givins, James et al	Grant No. 3836	474
Gore, William	Commissioners	225
Graves, Elizabeth	Jonathan Graves	127
Graves, Joseph & Thos. Smith	Jonathan Graves	98
Graves, Joseph	Jonathan Graves	100
Graves, Adaline R.	Jonathan Graves	125
Graves, Isabella	Jonathan Graves	126
Greer, Thos.	Samuel Patton	303
Greer, Thos.	Lewis Harmon	490
Gunn, Elias	James Robertson	263
Hall, Elisha	William Bond	116
Hall, Fergus	James Patton et al	334
Hall, Elisha	Thos. Greer	537
Hamilton, William	Ephraim Davidson et al	470
Hammel, Andrew	Burton Jordan	13
Harrington, Jacob	James Shriver	130
Harrison, William	James Ridgeway	249
Harrison, William	James M. Smith	314
Harrison, John & L. McNatt, Assignee of Robt. Kirkpatrick	Grant No. 4069	318
Henry, William	Stokely Donalson	288
Hix, John	Elisha Hall	535
Holt, Joshua	David Low	214
Hoover, Martin	Nicholas Branch	76
Hopkins, William	John Huff	196
Hopwood, Willis	Abner Pillow	353
Hord, Edmund	Jas. Patton et al	102

GRANTEE	GRANTOR	PAGE
Howell, Joseph B.	Daniel McCoy	383
Howell, Joseph B.	David Pinkston	586
Hughes, Samuel	Stephen Johnston	491
Hunter, Robert	Benj. Bradford, Sheriff	528
Hutchings, John	John Donalson	468
Hutchings, John	Benj. Bradford, Sheriff	514
Irven, Josephas	Loverance Evans	92
Jackson, John	Benj. Bradford, Sheriff	292
Jackson, John	Patton & Erwin	511
Jetton, John L., Assignee of Dan'l Williams	Grant No. 3857	153
Jetton, John L., Assignee of Jonas Cosgrove	Grant No. 3856	155
Johnston, Stephen	Newton Cannon	390
Jones, Mathew & Labon	Patton & Erwin	175
Jordan, Burton	Eli Giles	396
Julen, James for Jeremiah Litteral services	Grant	373
Kemzee, Samuel	Daniel Cherry	476
Kedd, James	James Smith	7
Kapley, John	John Newman	163
Kerr, James	David Kerr	324
Kingree, Samuel	Daniel Cherry	476
King, Benjamin et al	William McGuire	501
Lane, John	Nathaniel Jones	558
Lawrence, David	Jeremiah M. Smith	478
Lay, William	Allen Leeper	503
Leeper, Allen	William Laye	530
Lince, Jacob	Charles Fisher	420
Little, William	Grant	426
Locke, Wm. & Edw. Wade	James Locke (PA)	330
Loden, Frances	Washington Medearis	518
Lovins, Hugh H.	Shadrack Forrest	520
Lytle, William	Grant No. 3237	367
Lytle, William	Grant No. 1521	432
Majors, Robert	Grant No. 3943	404
Marberry, John	William Newsom	188
Martin, Matt	Patton & Erwin	80
Martin, Matt	Jas. Patton & Erwin	123
Martin, Barkley	Matt Martin	311
Martin, George M. et al	Robert C. Kennedy	388
Maupin, Blan	Patton & Erwin	497
Medearis, Washington D.	James Gibson	488
Medearis, Washington	Frances Loden	522
Medearis, Washington Davis	John Medearis	524
Miller, Henry	Grant No. 263	61
Mitchell, Marmaduke	Clement Cannon	5
Morris, William	John E. Dunn	106
Muckelroy, William	William Smith	456

GRANTEE	GRANTOR	PAGE
Neely, Richard	Abner Chappell	51
Neely, Richard	Keeble Terry	246
Neely, Jacob	John Jackson	507
Neill, John, Assignee of Elisha Waling	Grant No. 4421	440
Neill, Nicholas	Benjamin Bradford	25
Neill, Andrew	Alexander Neill et al	138
Neill, John, Assignee of Elisha Waling	Grant No. 3343	151
Neill, Robert	John Neill	215
Newsom, Sterling	Commissioners	21
Norvell, David	James Norvell	19
Ore, John	Thos. Gleaves	251
Parsons, Thos. & George	Freeman Burrow	45
Patterson, Thomas	Abner Pillow	340
Patton, Samuel	Thos. Greer	118
Patton & Erwin	Norton Pryor 85,000 A.	569
Payne, Shrewsberry	Patton & Erwin	253
Payne, Zedekiah	Patton & Erwin	259
Peacock, William	Conway & McKissack	78
Pearson, William	John Allison	458
Phillips, Isaac	Newton Cannon	345
Pressgrove, Andrew	William Neely	526
Ragsdale, Baxter	Benjamin Bradford	90
Ragsdale, Baxter	William Knott	108
Ramsey, Samuel	Clement Cannon	235
Ray, Sarah	Charles Wortham	169
Ray, Sarah	John Jackson	171
Ray, William	John Jackson	173
Ray, James	Mary Doherty	349
Rayburn, John	Patton & Erwin	41
Reynolds, Jane	John Strother	359
Ridgeway, Jonathan for Martin Armstrong services	Grant No. 793	304
Robertson, Michael & Joseph	David Robertson	480
Roland, Hosey	Samuel McQuiston	39
Roseborough, Joseph	James B. Porter	351
Ross, Thomas	Charles Fisher et al	422
Rushing, Joseph	Benjamin Lamar	96
Russell, James	Commissioners	110
Russell, Armistead	Andrew Tonnehill	207
Scott, John	William Woods	11
Scott, John, Assignee of Robert Reed	Grant	563
Sebastian, Samuel	John Coats	414
Speekman, William	Nicholas Branch	94
Sheffield, William	John Atkinson	240
Sheffield, Jason for Roger Helton services	Grant No. 4367	365
Shofner, Peter	Jacob & Wm. Harrington	244
Shofner, Peter	Thomas Roberts	320
Shook, William, Assignee of John Owen	Grant No. 3383	59
Shook, William	James Gage	68
Smith, Thomas & Jas. Graves	Jonathan Graves	98

GRANTEE	GRANTOR	PAGE
Smith, George	John Newman	179
Smith, John Jr.	John Smith Sr.	338
Taylor, John	Benjamin Bradford, Sheriff	84
Taylor, John	Benjamin Bradford, Sheriff	87
Terry, Keeble	Abner Chappell	9
Thompson, Elizabeth & Zelphia	Martha Thompson	442
Thompson, Thomas F.	John NEwman	451
Thompson, John (Heir of Moses Powell)	Grant No. 2200	66
Thompson, Jason	Grant No. 1883	157
Thompson, Jason	Grant No. 2113	159
Thompson, Joseph for Moses Powell services	Grant	371
Tilman, George	Wm. & John Payton	336
Tilman, George	David Green	580
Townson, John	Jeremiah Cherry	134
Torrentine, Alexander for Malachi Russell services	Grant No. 3234	282
Ulas, Adam	Clement Cannon	217
Vanoy, Joel	Thomas Patton	161
Wade, Edward et al	Samuel Locke (PA)	330
Ward, Jonathan	Samuel B. Harris	278
Waterson, Barnabas	William Morrison	554
Webster, Jonathan	Archibald Alexander	205
White, nancy et al	Benajah White et al	378
Whitworth, Samuel S.	John C. Dunn	565
Wilson, William S.	John Parker	341
Wilson, David	Zachariah Wilson	408
Wilson, Thomas	David Edmonson	516
Wood, Josiah	George Oliver	392
Wood, John for John Punavy services	Grant No. 4333	462
Woods, John for Abraham Key Kendall services	Grant No. 1553	464
Wright, James	James Turrentine	406
Yell, Moses	Percy Yell	377
Yell, Moses	Percy Yell	567
York, Jonathan	James Walker	255

(Out of order)

McBride, John	Commissioners	272
McClerin, Ruben	Grant No. 3969	64
McConnell, John P. et al	Robert C. Kennedy	388
McCammick, Robert	Grant	434
McCammick, Robert	Grant	560
McKissick, James	Alexander Outlaw by Thos. Moore	265
McKissick, James	Thos. Moore, atty. for Alexander Outlaw	267
McLemore, Amos	Grant	201
McLemore, John C. et al	Grant	474
McMahan, William	Benjamin Bradford, Sheriff	533
McNatt, L. & Jno. Harrison	Grant No. 4069	318

GRANTEE	GRANTOR	PAGE
McGuire, William	Willliam Ditto et al	501
McCuistion, Benjamin	Daniel Dwyer	237
McCuistion, Benj.	Commissioners	261
McCuistion, Robert for Jeremiah Litteral services	Grant	410
McCuistion, Robert for Alexander Gammill services	Grant No. 3304	453

****

***** BEDFORD COUNTY WILL INDEX *****
BOOKS I & II
1863-1910
ALPHABETICAL ORDER
BOOK I

ANDERSON, ALBERT
ARMSTRONG, JAS. L., SR.
ANDERTON, THOMAS
ANDERSON, JOSEPH
ALEXANDER, JAMES
ADAMS, A.L.
ARNOLD, CHESLEY
ALLISON, ROBERT
ADAMS, JNO. W.
ALLISON, KIMBRO
ANTHONY, POLLY
ALLISON, MARY
ADAMS, FAMEY A.
ATKINSON, A.E.
ALLEN, MARTHA

BOONE, AB. S.
BROWN, JOHN W.
BROWN, TABITHA
BIVINS, SILAS A.
BINGHAM, A.J.
BURTON, DAVID
BURT, SUSAN E.
BROWN, JOHN WESLEY
BATTE, FREDRICK
BOOTH, J.B.
BATES, L.T.
BROADAWAY, LEMUEL
BROWN, M.A.
BROWN, HENRY
BURT, SUSAN
BRITTAIN, DANIEL
BENNETT, JAMES M.
BURROW, BANKS A.
BLANTON, MEREDITH
BROWN, WILLIAM
BATTE, EDWIN
BROWN, MRS. JANE G.
BURT, W.C.
BUCHANAN, THOMAS W.
BROWN, THOMAS J.
BELL, GEORGE W.
BENNETT, JOHN
BENNETT, NANCY
BINGHAM, REBECCA
BURROW, NIMROD
BURROW, MRS. JEMIMA
BUMPUS, HENRY MARTIN
BEACHBOARD, B.N.
BROWN, WILLIAM B.
BOUNDS, G.W.
BLAIR, J.
BLACKBURN, WILLIAM
BENNETT, NANCY
BRADLEY, J.C.
BURNETT, PARTHENIA
BARRETT, ELIZABETH

BRAME, WM. B.M.

CANNON, LETITIA
COBB, SARAH
COGGINS, JOEL
CLARK, ROBERT
CANNON, ROBERT
CARUTHERS, SARAH S.
COBLE, BENJAMIN K.
CARLTON, THOMAS
CLARDY, JAMES
CALL, LEMUEL
CURTISS, JAMES H.
COVINGTON, LEVICY
COFFEY, ALEXANDER H.
CHAMBERS, GEORGE W.
CHAMBERS, R. JUDAH
CASTEEL, NANCY
CAMPBELL, ARTHUR
CANNON, CLEMENT, SR.
CLARK, HENRY
CULLEY, WILLIAM, SR.
CUNNINGHAM, MATHEW T.
CHAFFIN, NATHAN
COOPER, FANNIE G.
CULBERHOUSE, JEREMIAH
CANNON, WILLIS 25
CLEVELAND, ROBERT M.
COBLE, NELLIE
CRUTCHER, GEORGE
CHRISMAN, SARAH
COWAN, JOHN W., SR.
COATS, PEYTON H.
COWAN, WILLIAM G.
CLARDY, PETER E.
COOK, WILLIAM C.
CHAMBERS, JOHN G.
CONNELL, LURANCY
CROWELL, JOSHUA
COLLINS, WILLIAM
CALL, JAMES E.
CROWELL, WILLIAM
COUCH, CATHERINE
CROWELL, SAMUEL
CANNON, ROBERT T.
CORTNER, MATTHEW
CHAMBERS, ROBERT G.
COWAN, WILLIAM B.
CAMPBELL, JAMES H.
CLARY, JOHN W.
CUNNINGHAM, MARY A.
COOP, HORATIO
CHOCKLEY, JESSE C.
COUCH, MARY J.
COLDWELL, THOMAS H.
CARD, SAMUEL H.
CUMMINGS, MRS. NANCY J.

317

CHAMBERS, JOHN A.
CHAMBERS, PARTHENIA F.
CLARK, R.S.
CASTLEMAN, ALCY
COFFEE, JAMES WALTON
CLARK, JNO. S.
COLEMAN, WILAFORD E.
COFFET, SALLY R.
CRUNK, J.W.
COOPER, JOHN L.
CHAMBERS, HARRIET C.
CLEVELAND, ANN

DAVIS, GEORGE
DAVIS, JOHN S.
DAVIS, ZACHARIAH
DOZIER, ZACHARIAH
DANIEL, ROBERT C.
DOBBS, RACHAEL
DAMRON, NANCY E.
DAVIS, W.J.
DAVIS, ZORAH M.
DYER, SAMUEL G.
DIXON, CYNTHA
DAVIS, BENJAMIN F.
DYER, ESTHER G.
DAVIS, J.H.
DARNELL, JOEL
DAVIS, JOHN E.
DAMRON, ELIZABETH
DUNNAWAY, J.A.
DAVIDSON, I.S.
DAVIS, JESSIE E.
DRUMRIGHT, A.J.
DIXON, R.B.
DEARING, F.M.

EDMONDSON, W. SCOTT
ELKINS, MARY S.
EVINS, DAVID S.
EAKIN, ALEX
EVANS, ELIZABETH P.
EARNHART, BENJAMIN
ERWIN, MARTIN P.
EARNHART, DANIEL
EVANS, ROBERT F.

FOREMAN, RICHARD
FRIZZELL, DAVID
FRAZIER, PRESTON
FRAZIER, GRANVILLE H.
FREEMAN, MARY E.
FEATHERSTON, BURRELL
FREEMAN, FANNY R.
FLOYD, GEORGE W.
FINNEY, JAMES
FLOYD, JAS. K.
FUGITT, TOWNSEND
FRIZZELL, JAS.
FLOYD, ELIJAH
FOSTER, GUYNN
FARMER, B.F.
FRAZER, MRS. ELIZA

FONVILLE, ASA
FLETCHER, MRS. JANE M.
FOSTER, MRS. SARAH R.
FLETCHER, JOHN R.
FRIERSON, ROBERT P.
FRIERSON, JOHN W.
FIELDS, L.P.
FRIDDLE, MARTIN
FREEMAN, J.H.
FRIERSON, FELICIA C.

GREEN, EDMOND
GUY, ANN
GREER, JACOB
GREER, CATHERINE R.
GABBERT, WILLIAM
GREGORY, THOMAS
GAMBILL, MINERVA
GAMBILL, NEWTON C.
GUTHERIE, ELIZA
GANT, ELIZABETH
GOWAN, WILLIAM P.
GALBREATH, WILLIAM E.
GORDON, WILLIAM J.
GOSLING, WILLIAM
GOODRUM, A.J.
GALBREATH, WILLIAM
GALBREATH, JAMES H.
GREER, BENJAMIN F.
GOWEN, JAMES B.
GREEN, JASON
GILL, HENRIETTA B.
GRAVES, H.L.
GREER, NANCY M.
GREER, A.J.
GALBREATH, MARY L.
GIBSON, ELIZABETH
GREER, GEORGE W.
GREER, GARTHA VANCE
GILL, ARMSTEAD
GIBSON, GEORGE W.
GORDON, SAMUEL B., SR.
GREEN, MRS. A.P.
GREGORY, GEORGE W.
GANT, ABRAM
GREGORY, MAHALA
GREEN, LUCINDA
GAMBILL, WILLIAM HENRY
GEORGE, W.F.

HARRIS, JAMES
HOOSER, DANIEL
HOLT, HENRY
HARRISON, THOMAS
HARRISON, ELIZA W.
HILE, JOSEPH
HUFFMAN, ALFRED S.S.
HALL, JNO. F.
HIX, JOHN C.
HARRIS, JOHN T.
HAGGARD, SAMUEL
HELTON, JAMES
HOLT, ELIZA

HORNADY, MARGARET
HIX, D.D.
HEMBY, DANIEL
HOUSTON, WILLIAM
HARRIS, MARY J.
HOSKINS, JOHN E.
HUFFMAN, MARTHA J.
HOLT, JEREMIAH
HIX, WILLIAM C.
HUFFMAN, JNO.
HOLT, MRS. MARY C.
HASTY, JOSEPH
HASKINS, J.R.
HEARD, ELIZABETH
HAGGARD, WILLIAMSON
HUFFMAN, GEORGE
HORNADAY, J.A.
HOPKINS, WILLIAM H.
HOLDER, HENRY
HILES, WILBURN
HARRIS, NANCY T.
HENLEY, AMANDA C.
HALL, JOHN E.
HINES, THOMAS A.
HARRISON, ALBERT M.
HAYNES, RACHAEL
HALEY, MARY B.
HARRIS, NANCY T.
HARRIS, ALFRED

JONES, JOHN R.
JEFFRESS, THOMAS B.
JONES, JNO. B.
JENKINS, WILLIAM
JONES, SEABORN
JONES, JOSEPH
JOYCE, ANDERSON
JAKES, JOHN
JENKINS, DANIEL M.

KIMBRO, JNO.
KINCAID, W.H.
KNOTT, WILLIAM S.
KINGSTON, MARY
KINGSTON, SALLIE
KOONCE, ELIZA ELLEN
KIMERY, JOHN J.
KELLER, JOSEPH
KNOTT, A.F.
KERK, EDWIN F.
KIMERY, EDWIN
KING, R.J.
KEY, LUCY
KIMMONS, JOSHUA
KING, C.B.
KINCAID, C.M.

LANDERS, ABRAHAM
LAMB, THOMAS
LENTZ, VOLENTINE
LAIRD, THOMAS B.
LEHR, JOHN F.
LOW, DAVID

LINCH, GREY
LOKEY, M.H.
LANDERS, ROBERT L.
LANDERS, THOMAS
LYTLE, JAMES K.P.
LINCH, ANNIE S.
LOCKE, JAMES H.
LITTLE, VIRGINIA C.
LIPSCOMB, THOMAS
LANDIS, BRYANT
LANDESS, HARMAN H.
LAWRENCE, A.S.

MOODY, SAMUEL SHAW
MOSELEY, THOMAS
MAUPIN, ROBERT B.
MILLER, JAMES J.
MEADOWS, WILLIAM
MORGAN, L.B.
MOORE, MICHAEL
MUSE, THOMAS W.
MOORE, MRS. M.F.
MONTGOMERY, T.A.
MAUPIN, GABRIEL

McKINLEY, JAS. R.
McGREW, WILLIAM
McCLURE, WILLIAM M.
McCRORY, JOHN
McREE, J.V.
McREE, MRS. C. ANNIE
McFARLAN, BENJAMIN
McFERRIN, T.S.
McLAIN, G.W.
McGREW, JOSEPH H.
McCORD, T.N.
McCLAIN, MRS. ADRIANAH L.
McCLAIN, J.A.

NASH, W.T.
NOWLIN, BRYAN W.
NEIL, JOHN T.
NANCE, JOHN
NEWTON, JAMES S.
NOBLETT, JNO.
NEIL, MRS. ELIZABETH P.
NUTT, JESSE
NELSON, ELIZA M.
NEIL, MRS. EVALINE M.
NORMAN, MRS. E.C.
NORTH, H.B.
NUCKOLLS, EXINE WYCHE

OWENS, BERRY C.
O'CONNELL, PATRICK
ONEAL, JOHN
OGILVIE, JANE G.
OTEY, MRS. FANNIE LOU
OSBORNE, R.T.

PHILLIPS, SAMUEL
PATRICK, J.T.
PROBY, JAMES M.

PRICE, SARAH B.
POWELL, JNO.
PETTUS, THOMAS
PERRY, WILLIE
PARKER, JOEL H.
PHILLIPS, RICHARD
POWELL, WILLIAM J.
PHILLIPS, GARRETT
PURVIS, MARGARET M.
PARKER, NEHEMIAH
PHILLIPS, WILLIAM
PYLAND, BLUFORD
PATE, DOOLEY
PARSONS, JACOB M.
PATE, JULIETTE R.
PRESGROVE, JOHN
PETTY, FANNIE DUANNA
PARKS, AMBROSE L.
PHILLIPS, G.W.
PROBY, SARAH ANN
PATTERSON, BARNEY
PATTERSON, CALADONIA
PHILPOT, CHARLES T.

REEVES, ISHAM
RUSSELL, JOSEPH C.
REED, ROBERT
RIPPY, JAMES
RUSHING, THOMAS M.
RUSHING, ELIZABETH
RANSOM, ALFRED
RIGGS, ADAM S.
RIPPY, W.M.
REAGOR, WILLIAM J.
ROBINSON, HARRIET
REEVES, ABSALOM
RUSSELL, WILLIAM
ROBINSON, WILLIAM H.
RICHE, MALINDA C.
REAGOR, JOHN W.
REAVES, WILLIAM
ROANE, THOMAS J.
RUSSELL, JAMES L.
RUCKER, JORDAN
RIGGS, KELLEY
REAGOR, ELIZABETH
RAINWATER, J.W.
RANSOM, WILLIAM K.

STOKES, KINCHEON
SCOTT, JOHN
SMITH, MARTIN
SIMPSON, REBECCA
SUGG, NEHEMIAH
STEPHENSON, EDWARD
SHAW, ROBERT G.
SIMPSON, JOHN W.
SUTTON, CHARLES F.
SNELLING, SALLIE
SCRUGGS, E.F.
SHOFFNER, JOHN
SCOTT, THOMAS
STEELE, JNO. P.

STEM, J.R.
SIMS, MARTIN
SANDRIDGE, DR. JAMES S.
SHOFNER, JOHN
STEM, WILLIAM N.
SCRUGGS, JAMES
STEPHENSON, MARTHA J.
SMITH, TABITHA
SCUDDER, JAMES L.
SHUMARD, ELIZABETH M.
SUTTON, CATHERINE
STENNETT, WILLIAM E.
SHEARIN, MATHEW
STEPHENS, HENRY
SHAW, W.M.
SHOFNER, PLUMMER L.
STORY, JAS.
SHELTON, W.H.
STEWART, DANIEL B.
SINGLETON, MISS KATE
STEM, RICHARD H.
SUTTON, JOHN
STEWART, SYNTHA
STEED, KIZZIAH
SANDERS, MRS. MINTORIA A.
SUTTON, JANE

TUCKER, MARTHA E.
TEMPLE, WILLIAM P.
THRONEBERRY, DAVID
TUNE, WILLIAM T.
TIMMONS, EFFIE
TAYLOR, B.H.
TARPLEY, EDWARD
THOMAS, MRS. MARTHA F.
TATUM, MISS CLEMENZA T.
THOMPSON, NEWCOMB, 2ND
TALLEY, CLARK (COL)
TILLMAN, LEWIS
TURRENTINE, ELIZABETH
TROXLER, MARY
THOMAS, ASA
TAYLOR, ARMSTRONG B.
TILLMAN, ELIZABETH F.
TAYLOR, ELVIRA
TROXLER, HENRY C.
TURRENTINE, FELIX
TAYLOR, ELEANOR
TAYLOR, THERESSA
TROXLER, A.J.
THOMPSON, MINOS F.

VANCE, CHRISTINA
VINCENT, P.S.
VICKERY, ISAAC
VANNOY, MARY L.P.

WINSETT, ELIJAH D.
WILSON, REBECCA
WINN, E.P.
WOODWARD, GEORGE
WOOD, JNO.
WOMACK, SOLOMON

BOOK 11

WALLIS, ALLEN
WHEELHOUSE, DENNIS
WAITE, SQUIRE (COL)
WILLIAMS, WYNN D.
WHITSELL, JOHN
WHITE, ROBERT C.
WILSON, FORDYCE
WATKINS, WILLIAM S.
WHITTHORN, WILLIAM J.
WILLIAMS, ENOCH
WOODBERRY, SILAS
WINSETT, MARGARET
WOODS, STEPHEN
WOOD, WILLIAM
WOODFIN, JAMES H.
WAITE, JULIA P.
WARDLOW, THOMAS D.
WHITTAKER, THOMAS
WALKER, ELIZABETH
WALLIS, JACKSON
WORKE, W.C.
WISEMAN, W.R.
WEAVER, ZEPHENIAH
WILHOITE, MRS. ISABELLA C.
WILLIAMS, DAVID
WEST, L.D.
WILLIAMS, JAMES T.
WHEELER, MRS. MARY E.
WEBB, AMANDA
WOMACK, C.W.
WHEELER, WILLIAM B.
WIGGINS, JOHN W.
WEBB, M.H. 55
WORD, EDMOND
WHEELER, MARY A.
WILHOITE, W.W.
WRIGHT, C.H.
WILHOITE, JOHN R.
WALKER, MATT
WHEELER, N.M.
WELLS, JOHN W.
WORD, T.S.
WILLIAMS, P.W.
WALKER, SARAH A.
WAITE, WARREN

YOUNG, WILLIAM
YELL, F.M.
YOUNG, ELIZABETH S.

ATWELL, A.H.
ANTHONY, L.M. (ELIZA)
ALLEN, J.H.
AKIN, JOHN C.
ANDERSON, J.M.
ANTHONY, ANNIE MAY
ARNOLD, MALINDA
ANTHONY, E.M.
ALDERMAN, JOHN H.
ADAMS, ARABELLA T.
ARNOLD, L.K.
AYERS, THOMAS H.

BLACKMAN, BURRELL
BROADAWAY, SARAH E.
BLACKBURN, E.P.
BUTLER, J.S.
BRINKLEY, JOHN
BIGHAM, ROBERT B.
BATY, BETTIE
BLANTON, B.M.
BEARDEN, WYNN
BROWN, H.L.
BLESSING, SAMUEL A.
BUCKALOO, AMANDA F.
BOONE, MRS. LIZZIE S.
BELL, MRS. EVALINE
BLACKMAN, FRANCES
BURT, JOHN L.
BISHOP, EDWARD
BARNES, BENJAMIN L.
BARBER, WILLIAM D.
BIRDWELL, SARAH JANE
BUTLER, MRS. MARY A.
BAXTER, THOMAS
BIVINS, SUSAN S.
BARNES, D.W.
BRAME, MRS. MARY E.
BROOKSHIRE, ANCEL

CANNON, ALMON
CANNON, CHARLES L.
CAMPBELL, LETHEA B.
CANNON, ELEANOR (NELLIE)
CANNON, MARY ANN
CARMACK, CELIA
CRICK, ELIZABETH
COOK, GEORGE W.
CANNON, LIZZIE
COWAN, ALEXANDER
COFFEY, RICE A.
CULLEY, MARY A.
COFFEY, MARY A.
CROWELL, SARAH R.
CANNON, EMMA 88
CARLTON, MARGRETT E.
CASTEEL, SALLIE
COOPER, J.T.
CAROTHERS, JOHN
CARTWRIGHT, PHILLIP F.
CLAXTON, J.C.

CUNNINGHAM, DR. J.M.
CANNON, LOUISE (LOU)
CLARY, DR. W.F.
CARNEY, E.W.
CLAY, WILLIAM M.
COUCH, R.W.
COWAN, LEAH
CORTNER, G.A.
COVINGTON, MRS. E.G.
COOPER, EDMUND
COOPER, A.M.
CLAY, JAMES H.

DUGGAN, BENJAMIN F.
DYER, MARTHA
DAVIS, C.F.
DYSART, G.D.
DAVIS, W.G.
DAVIDSON, ROBERT H.
DICKENS, SARAH C.
DAMRON, J.T.
DOZIER, MARY ANN
DARNELL, JAMES
DURHAM, SARAH E.

EULESS, MARTIN
ENGLAND, REZIN
EARNHART, MICHAEL F.
EVANS, MARY C.
EULESS, CASSANDRA C.

FROST, AILSEY D.
FUGITT, ANN
FRAZER, MARY E.
FLEMMING, SALLIE D.
FREEMAN, W.R.
FOREMAN, RICHARD
FROST, JOHN E.
FINLEY, M.J.
FUGITT, REBECKER
FISHER, J.T.
FLOYD, JAMES W.
FALK, J.H.
FARRAR, L.A.
FARRAR, TENNIE V.

GREER, CARRIE
GLASSCOCK, HENRY D.
GEORGE, BETTIE
GAMBILL, N.C.
GILL, WINSTON W.
GREGORY, JAMES
GENTRY, MINUS B.
GREEN, B.G.
GALBREATH, SARAH F.
GIBSON, GEORGE W.
GENTRY, JOHN P.

HOLT, E.C.
HIMES, GRAFTON
HARRIS, MALISSA E.
HILL, NANCY C.
HIX, C.D.

HIME, JOHN ANDREW
HOLDER, JOHN H.
HALL, SUSANNAH L.
HART, CLARA
HAYNES, JOHN
HEAD, N.M.
HIX, NETTIE
HIX, C.C.
HIME, JOHN
HOLLAND, WILLIAM
HUNTER, J.B.
HASKINS, JOSEPH F.
HUFFMAN, JOSHUA
HAYNES, HENRY H.
HOOVER, W.J.
HUFFMAN, J.P.
HIX, MRS. SALLIE BOOTH
HUFFMAN, FANNIE
HOOVER, W.C.
HIX, A.B.
HALE, JORDAN R.
HASTINGS, MARY ANN

IVIE, LAURA R.
IVIE, THOMPSON B.

JONES, SAM
JONES, LAWRENCE E.
JONES, MARY
JONES, H.P.
JARRELL, A.J.
JONES, THOMAS G.
JONES, LAURANA J.
JOHNSON, MARY E.

KIMMONS, JULIA A.
KINNARD, FANNIE B.
KINGREE, ELIZABETH P.
KEY, DR. WILLIAM
KIMMONS, MRS. T.B.
KINGSTON, MRS. MALINDA
KAHL, EWALD H.

LOWE, A.
LEMING, JAMES C.
LYNN, JACOB
LEMING, W.H.
LOYD, W.J., SR.
LENTZ, SAMUEL J.

MOORE, NANNIE F.
MAXWELL, J.W.
MADISON, LEE & NANCY J.
MURPHY, P.A.
MOON, G.B.
MERRY, L.N.
MORRIS, F.M.
MORTON, M.J.
MELTON, A.
MORTON, CHARLES S.
MURPHREE, WILLIAM D.
MARTIN, JOHN T.
MORTON, SARAH JANE

MORTON, JOHN J.
MYERS, ALICE 93
MOSELEY, MATT W.

McGILL, PRISCILLA
McGILL, ANNIE
McCLELLAND, JOHN
McLAIN, JOHN A.
McGILL, WILLIAM
McKAIG, MILLEY H.

NORTH, ELIZABETH C.
NOWLIN, HULDY E.
NEELEY, JOSEPH N.

O'NEAL, W.M.
ORR, J.R.
OVERCAST, J.M.
ORR, JOHN H. & JANE BELL

PARKER, SYRENA
PHILPOTT, M.R.A.
PICKLE, THOMAS
PARSONS, JOHN W.
PAYNE, W.W.
PYLANT, G.J.
PARKER, ISAIAH
PRUETT, WILLIS K.
POWELL, SAMUEL T., JR.
PARKER, MISS MARGARET L.
PRINCE, H.U.
PEARSON, KINDRED JACKS

RIGGS, W.H.
ROBINSON, HENRY T.
RUSSELL, NANCY
RUSHING, MATTIE M.
REESE, F.S.
RANEY, G.R.
RIGGS, SARAH M.
RANKIN, I.G.
REED, ELZIRA
RUTH, JOHN W.
RUSSELL, W.J.
RIPPY, JOHN F.
RYALL, A.P.
RUSSELL, MRS. M.E.
RAMSEY, ASA
ROBERTS, E.
REED, GEORGE W.
RUTLEDGE, JOHN W.

SHRIVER, JOHN W.
STRONG, HARRY E.
SHOFNER, LOTON
SAUNDERS, ALEXANDER
STAMP, MRS. M.A.
SHORT, EMILY
SANDERS, R.C.
SHOFFNER, R.W.
SMITH, LEVI
STONER, BESSIE IRENE
SHOFNER, CAROLINE R.

SNELL, W.T.
SHOFNER, REBECCA A.
SMITH, MRS. RUTH
SHEARIN, ROSS
SMITH, W.L.
SHADDIE, MARTHIA
STEPHENS, HARRIETTE F.
STEPHENS, ED
SCUDDER, JENNIE D.
SNELL, JOHN W.
SHOFNER, WILLIAM J.
SUTTON, SARAH R.
SMITH, BESSIE W.
SWINNEY, L.J.
SIMS, W.R.
STEPHENS, T.J.
SANDERS, STEPHEN S.
STEWART, MARY A.
STEPHENS, JOHN T.
SOLOMON, W.T.
SHOFNER, JAS. B.
STORY, FRANK M.
SANDUSKY, GRANVILLE C.
SANDUSKY, SARAH F.

TALLY, SQUIRE
TRICE, NANCY
THOMAS, SALLIE
TURNER, JAMES L.
TAYLOR, SALLIE
THOMPSON, CALVIN J.
TUCKER, MAGGIE C.
TUNE, JOHN B.
THOMPSON, R.E.
TILLETT, J.M.
TAYLOR, C.P.

WHITTEMORE, W.H.
WALKER, JOSEPH
WILLIAMS, M.M.
WADE, P.H.
WHITE, THOMAS A.
WHILHOUSE, SARAH S.
WILLIAMS, W. FOUNT
WILSON, MILLEY
WOODS, WILLIAM G.
WHITAKER, L.J.
WHITESIDE, J.J.
WHITE, B.N.
WIGGINS, HARBERT
WILLIAMS, ELIZA JANE
WEAVER, WILLIAM L.
WHITE, DR. JOHN H.
WHEELER, MARGARET M.
WORD, THOMAS C.
WOOSLEY, WILLIAM C.
WOODFIN, M.
WILLIAMS, S.D.
WEBB, EDMOND
WOOSLEY, JOHN C.
WILLIAMS, MARY
WOODFIN, EVALINE
WOOSLEY, W.E.

WAITE, MRS. MACKIE
WILLIAMS, MRS. SALLIE
WILLIAMS, ROBERT H.

YOUNG, MRS. E.C.
YELL, J.C.
YANCY, W.L.
YOUNG, MRS. AMERICA A.
YOUNG, ROBERT H.

The Wills, Probate and Settlement Records of Bedford County, Tennessee suffered severe losses in the Court House fire that occurred in the Spring of 1863. With the exception of about six Wills that were recorded in the early 1860's, all Wills were destroyed in the fire.

****

CEMETERY INDEX OF BEDFORD COUNTY, TENNESSEE

From

Cemetery Records of Bedford County

By

Marsh

ALPHABETICAL ORDER

NAME	NUMBER	QUADRANGLE
Adams	5	Belfast
Adcock-Green	18	Unionville
Allen	20	Rover
Allison	11	Unionville
Allison	3	Unionville
Anthony	31	Normandy
Armstrong	48	Bedford
Arnold	33	Wartrace
Arnold	29	Deason
Arnold-King	40	Wartrace
Ault	26	Deason
Ault	44	Wartrace
Austin	15	Normandy
Barnes	4	Fosterville
Barrett	39	Bedford
Barrett	30	Bedford
Bates-Finch-Muse	10	Wartrace
Batt	67	Rover
Beachboard	2	Wartrace
Bell	12	Deason
Bell	35	Deason
Bell	2	Shelbyville
Bellenfant	14	Rover
Bethlehem	34	Unionville
Bethsalem	28	Wartrace
Bigham	16	Deason
Bigham	2	Webb Jungle
Bingham	1	Webb Jungle
Bivins	15	Webb Jungle
Blankenship	6	Fosterville
Blessing-Coats	12	Shelbyville
Bomar	39	Normandy

Boone	8	Booneville
Bounds	2	Unionville
Bradshaw	33	Bedford
Brame	15	Bedford
Brown	43	Deason
Brown	30	Deason
Brown	49	Bedford
Brown	6	Bedford
Brown-Little	53	Rover
Bryant	1	Cumberland Springs
Burton	17	Unionville
Burns	40	Deason
Byler-Marchant	45	Rover
Byler	48	Rover
Cannon	6	Shelbyville
Cannon	41	Wartrace
Card	40	Unionville
Carlton	6	Rover
Cawthron	20	Wartrace
Cedar Grove	59	Rover
Center Church	38	Shelbyville
Chambers	34	Wartrace
Clark	32	Unionville
Clark	4	Webb Jungle
Clark	72	Rover
Cleveland	27	Wartrace
Coffee	38	Wartrace
Coleman	8	Bedford
Collier	16	Bedford
Collier-Jones	50	Unionville
Cook	17	Rover
Cook	48	Unionville
Cooper	70	Rover
Cooper	22	Deason
Cooper	21	Rover
Cooper	60	Rover
Cooper	2	Deason
Cooper	5	Fosterville
Cortner	14	Cumberland Springs
Cothron	8	Rover
Couch	25	Wartrace
Cowan	10	Shelbyville
Crane	24	Shelbyville
Cross Road Church	18	Deason
Crowell	37	Unionville

Name	Number	Location
Crowell	49	Unionville
Crowell Chapel (Old)	62	Unionville
Crowell Chapel (New)	61	Unionville
Crowell Chapel	60	Unionville
Culley-Holt	20	Normandy
Cunningham	41	Bedford
Damron	32	Deason
Daniel	29	Normandy
Darnell	7	Farmington
Darnell	10	Farmington
Davis	1	Wartrace
Davis	10	Rover
Davis	47	Bedford
Davis	1	Fosterville
Davis-Redd	11	Bedford
Dial	17	Deason
Dickerson	2	Normandy
Dougan	14	Bedford
Dyer-Big Spring	28	Bedford
Eason	9	Normandy
Edmonson	48	Normandy
Elkins	41	Normandy
Elmore	3	Rover
Elmore	5	Rover
Enon	61	Rover
Erwin	29	Wartrace
Evans	31	Bedford
Fergurson	35	Normandy
Finney	12	Unionville
Flat Creek (Old)	25	Shelbyville
Floyd	7	Booneville
Frizzell	14	Webb Jungle
Frost	37	Shelbyville
Gabbert	29	Bedford
Gammill	4	Shelbyville
Gant	35	Bedford
Garrett	5	Chapel Hill
Garrett	1	Chapel Hill
Garrett	37	Rover
Gaunt	1	Bedford
Gentry	44	Rover
George	16	Normandy

Gill	39	Shelbyville
Glasscock	8	Farmington
Gray	15	Shelbyville
Green	21	Normandy
Green	24	Normandy
Greer	25	Bedford
Gregory	56	Unionville
Guy	8	Fosterville
Hailey	6	Normandy
Hall	55	Rover
Hall	37	Deason
Hall-Thompson	11	Normandy
Harper	45	Bedford
Harris	41	Unionville
Harris	68	Rover
Harrison	44	Bedford
Harrison	46	Unionville
Hart Chapel	34	Deason
Haskins	41	Rover
Haskins	14	Farmington
Hastings	36	Shelbyville
Hastings Camp Ground	21	Shelbyville
Hatchett	5	Webb Jungle
Haynes	13	Rover
Hazel	7	Wartrace
Helton	46	Bedford
Hendrix	43	Rover
Henry-Jarman	32	Wartrace
Hickory Hill Church	26	Unionville
Hill	11	Farmington
Hill	15	Rover
Hix	23	Shelbyville
Hix	2	Cumberland Springs
Hix	34	Shelbyville
Holland	13	Shelbyville
Hollywood	31	Wartrace
Holt	10	Normandy
Holt	37	Wartrace
Holt-Mitchell	33	Normandy
Hooser	4	Normandy
Hoover	58	Rover
Hoover	9	Webb Jungle
Hord (Color)	23	Wartrace
Hornaday-Miles	44	Normandy
Hornaday-Proby	37	Normandy

Name	Number	Location
Horse Mountain Church (Old)	27	Deason
Hoskins	31	Rover
Houston-Whitworth	7	Deason
Huffman	17	Normandy
Hurricane Grove Church	23	Deason
Ingle	36	Bedford
Jackson	35	Rover
Jarrell	3	Chapel Hill
Jarrett (Color)	29	Rover
Jenkins Chapel Church	17	Shelbyville
Jennings	42	Deason
Jernigan	8	Webb Jungle
Johnson	47	Rover
Jones	54	Unionville
Jones	9	Farmington
Jones	31	Unionville
Jones	33	Rover
Jones-Haynes	25	Rover
Joyce	6	Chapel Hill
Keeling	21	Wartrace
Keller	24	Wartrace
Kelly	12	Webb Jungle
Key	45	Normandy
Kimbro	3	Normandy
Kimmons	36	Rover
Kimzey	42	Normandy
King	12	Rover
Knight	17	Bedford
Lamb	46	Rover
Landers	51	Unionville
Landis	5	Unionville
Landis	30	Normandy
Lee-Stokes	39	Wartrace
Leming	22	Normandy
Lentz	38	Unionville
Lentz	63	Unionville
Lentz-Williams	47	Unionville
Little	2	Chapel Hill
Locke	9	Unionville
Lowell	64	Unionville
Loyd	21	Unionville

Lucas	42	Unionville
Lynch	10	Webb Jungle
Lynch-Frizzell	11	Webb Jungle
Lyon	6	Booneville
McAdams	31	Deason
McBride	23	Rover
McCuistion	40	Shelbyville
McCuiston	45	Deason
McElroy	9	Fosterville
McLean	3	Fosterville
McMahan	12	Wartrace
McQuiddy	19	Normandy
Madison	13	Bedford
Manley	3	Wartrace
Marsh	12	Bedford
Martin	14	Wartrace
Maupin	8	Normandy
Maupin	7	Normandy
Maxwell	52	Rover
Maxwell	42	Rover
Miller	1	Normandy
Miller	3	Webb Jungle
Molder	45	Unionville
Moon	33	Unionville
Moon	7	Unionville
Moore	8	Unionville
Moore Chapel	32	Bedford
Morgan	18	Shelbyville
Morris	10	Booneville
Morris	9	Booneville
Morton	75	Rover
Morton	71	Rover
Mount Moriah	25	Deason
Mt. Herman (New)	2	Booneville
Mt. Herman (Old)	1	Booneville
Mt. Lebanon	44	Unionville
Mt. View	28	Deason
Muse	18	Bedford
Muse	9	Wartrace
Nance	56	Rover
Neal	63	Rover
New Bethel	10	Bedford
New Herman	5	Booneville

New Hope Church	11	Wartrace
Norman	29	Shelbyville
Norvell	5	Wartrace
Norvell	64	Rover
Nowlin	1	Belfast
Nutt	28	Normandy
Ogilvie	13	Deason
Old City	11	Shelbyville
Old Salem	6	Wartrace
O'Neal	2	Bedford
Orr	39	Deason
Osborn	53	Unionville
Osteen	1	Farmington
Owens	20	Bedford
Parker	21	Deason
Parker	36	Normandy
Parker	14	Deason
Parker	4	Booneville
Parker	28	Shelbyville
Parsons	23	Unionville
Peacock	4	Wartrace
Pearson	11	Booneville
Phillips	24	Rover
Phillips	43	Wartrace
Phillips	44	Deason
Philpott	15	Deason
Pisgah	3	Bedford
Pisgah	20	Shelbyville
Pisgah	24	Unionville
Pleasant Garden	31	Shelbyville
Pleasant Valley	36	Unionville
Pope	9	Rover
Poplin	27	Rover
Porter-Cortner	42	Bedford
Potiller	1	Rover
Potts	28	Unionville
Powell	36	Normandy
Pratt	22	Shelbyville
Pressgrove	13	Unionville
Pruitt	35	Wartrace
Purvis	38	Deason
Putman	19	Rover
Putman	26	Rover

Rainwater	19	Deason
Ransom	8	Deason
Ray	4	Farmington
Ray's Corner	1	Unionville
Reaves	19	Shelbyville
Reaves	32	Shelbyville
Reed	5	Shelbyville
Reeves-Wheeler	25	Unionville
Reid	11	Rover
Renegar	25	Normandy
Richmond	37	Bedford
Roberts	38	Normandy
Robinson	24	Bedford
Robinson	16	Webb Jungle
Rogers	7	Chapel Hill
Rosebank	26	Shelbyville
Routon	16	Wartrace
Rucker	62	Rover
Russell	40	Bedford
Russell	3	Cumberland Springs
Russell	12	Normandy
Sanders	14	Unionville
Shaw	15	Wartrace
Shearin	5	Farmington
Shearin	34	Bedford
Shearin-Smith	39	Unionville
Shelton	18	Wartrace
Shiloh	19	Wartrace
Shofner	46	Normandy
Shofner Lutheran Church	47	Normandy
Shook	27	Shelbyville
Simpson	50	Rover
Sims	21	Bedford
Smith	22	Rover
Smith	1	Deason
Smotherman	51	Rover
Springer	3	Deason
Stacy	3	Booneville
Stallings	13	Farmington
Steele	5	Deason
Steele	4	Deason
Stem	57	Rover
Stephens	9	Bedford
Stephens	29	Unionville
Stephenson	4	Bedford

Name	Age	Cemetery
Stephenson	13	Webb Jungle
Stewart	41	Deason
Stinnett	7	Webb Jungle
Stone	26	Normandy
Stone	32	Normandy
Story	43	Unionville
St. Paul Methodist Church	49	Rover
Streater	59	Unionville
Streeter	58	Unionville
Sudberry	30	Rover
Sutton	20	Rover
Talley	23	Bedford
Tarpley	32	Rover
Tarpley	64	Rover
Tarpley	73	Rover
Taylor	40	Rover
Taylor	39	Rover
Taylor	38	Rover
Taylor	28	Rover
Terry	40	Normandy
Terry	19	Unionville
Thomason	4	Chapel Hill
Thompson	3	Shelbyville
Thompson	9	Belfast
Thompson	19	Bedford
Three Forks Church	5	Normandy
Troup	7	Shelbyville
Troxler	13	Normandy
Tucker	74	Rover
Tucker-Hopkins	6	Farmington
Tune	36	Deason
Turner	18	Rover
Unionville	4	Unionville
Unknown	7	Bedford
Unknown	3	Belfast
Unknown	30	Shelbyville
Unknown	6	Unionville
Unknown	6	Deason
Unknown	17	Wartrace
Unknown	8	Wartrace
Unknown	6	Webb Jungle
Unknown	50	Bedford
Unknown	14	Shelbyville
Unknown	26	Wartrace

Unknown	13	Wartrace
Unknown	66	Rover
Unknown	10	Deason
Unknown	9	Deason
Unknown	33	Shelbyville
Unknown	38	Bedford
Unknown	33	Deason
Unknown	16	Rover
Unknown	43	Bedford
Vance	27	Normandy
Vance	22	Wartrace
Waite-Friendship Church	30	Wartrace
Waite	18	Normandy
Wallis	36	Wartrace
Ward	7	Rover
Warner	57	Unionville
Weaver	23	Normandy
Webb	2	Fosterville
Webb	46	Deason
West	42	Wartrace
Wheel	2	Belfast
Wheeler	22	Unionville
Wheeler	11	Deason
Wheeler	2	Farmington
Wheelhouse	16	Unionville
Whitesell-Wilhoite	22	Bedford
Whitman-Gregory	55	Unionville
Williams	24	Rover
Williams	52	Unionville
Williams	20	Unionville
Williams	27	Unionville
Williams	15	Unionville
Willow Mount	1	Shelbyville
Willson	35	Unionville
Wilson	5	Bedford
Winn	54	Rover
Winsett	10	Unionville
Wood	2	Rover
Woodfin	2	Fosterville
Wood-Mayes	4	Belfast
Woodson	69	Rover
Word	26	Bedford
Word	35	Shelbyville
Wray	4	Rover

Yoes	3	Farmington
Young	16	Shelbyville
Young	43	Normandy
Zion Baptist Church	12	Farmington
Zion Hill Church	30	Unionville
Zivley	8	Shelbyville

Addendum

Hillcrest	40	Shelbyville
Dozier	10	Shelbyville

****

━━━━━━━━━━━━━━ TOPO MAP INDEX ━━━━━━━━━━━━━━

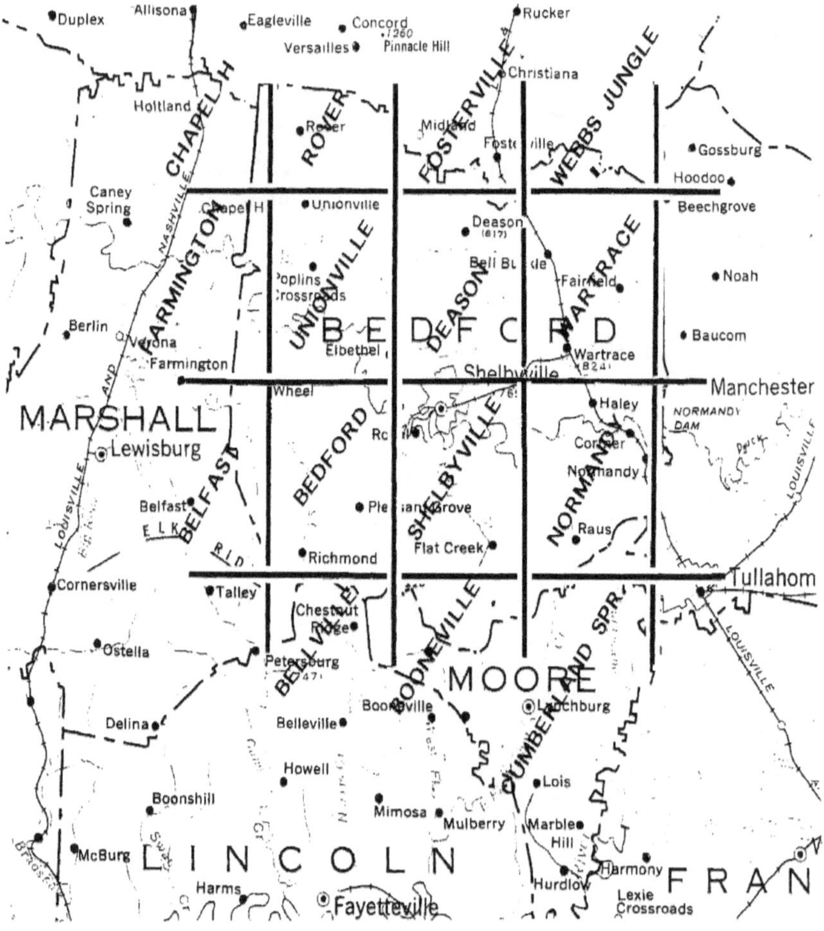

━━━━━━━━━━━━━ CEMETERY LOCATOR MAPS ━━━━━━━━━━━━━

These adapted locator maps are USGS, Tennessee Valley Authority, 12 1/2 minute Quadrangle Maps with cemetery locator numbers placed on the appropriate map, showing the location of each cemetery. For a detailed study, magnification may be desired.

These locator maps appear in the same order in which the cemeteries were located, visited and copied in 1975 and 1976 by the authors.

CHAPEL HILL QUADRANGLE

MAP 1

ROVER QUADRANGLE

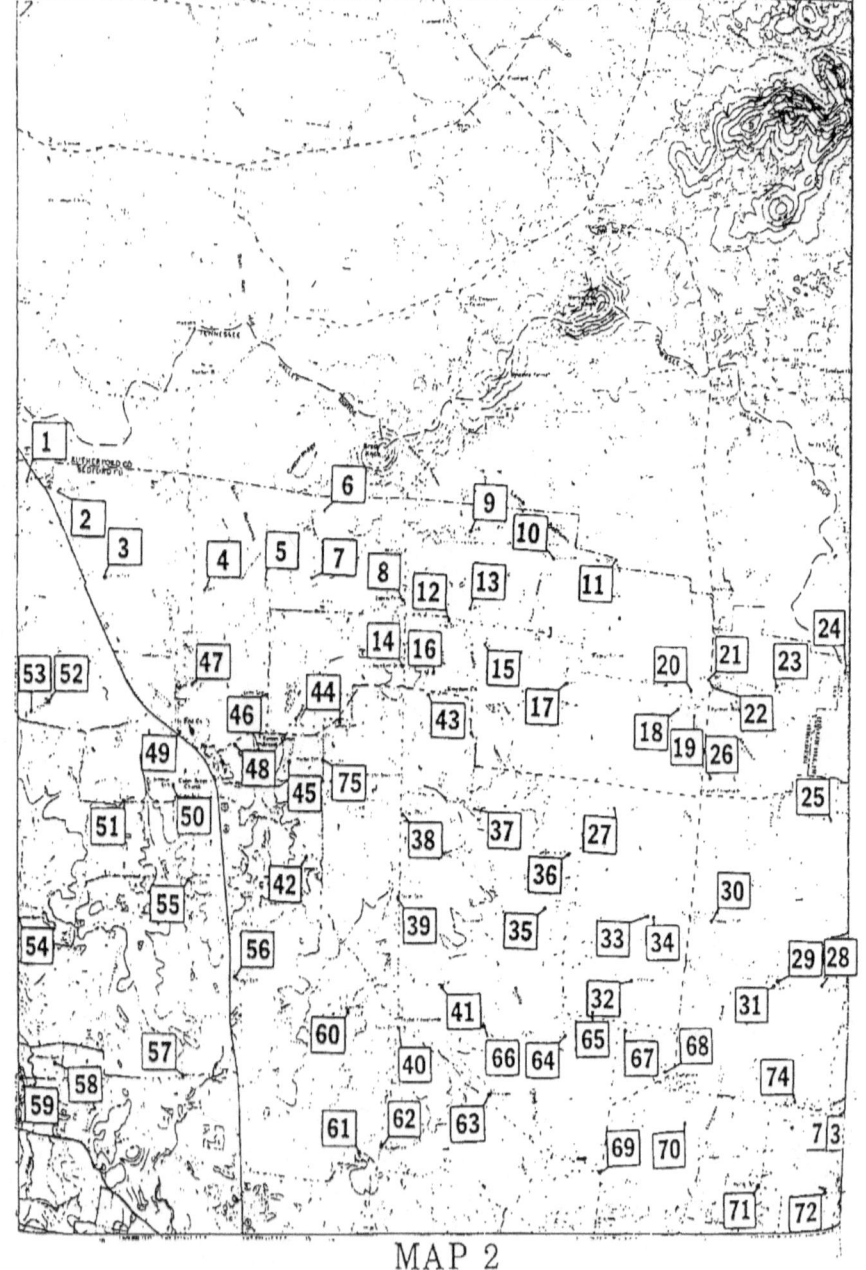

MAP 2

FOSTERVILLE QUADRANGLE

MAP 3

WEBBS JUNGLE QUADRANGLE

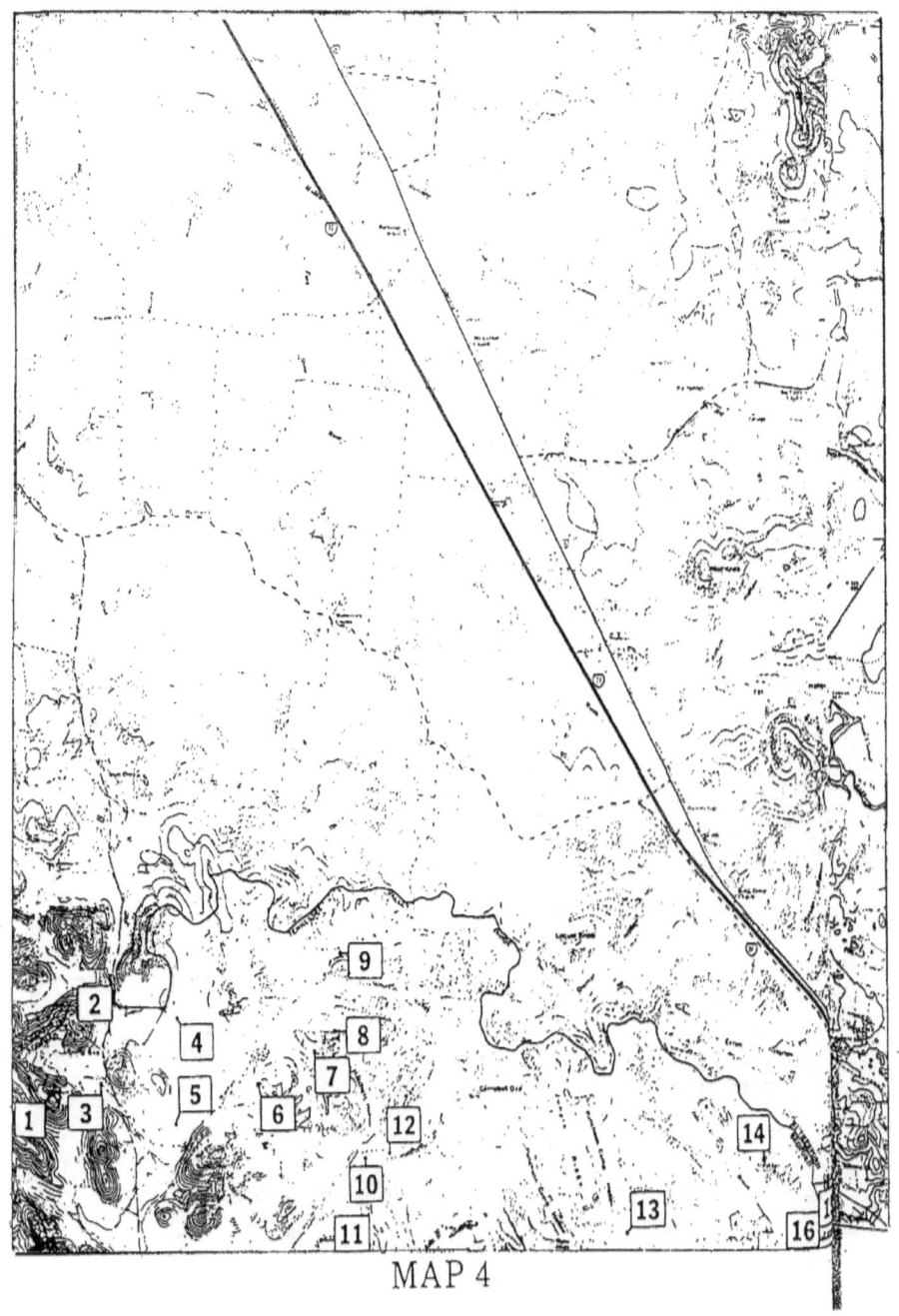

MAP 4

FARMINGTON QUADRANGLE

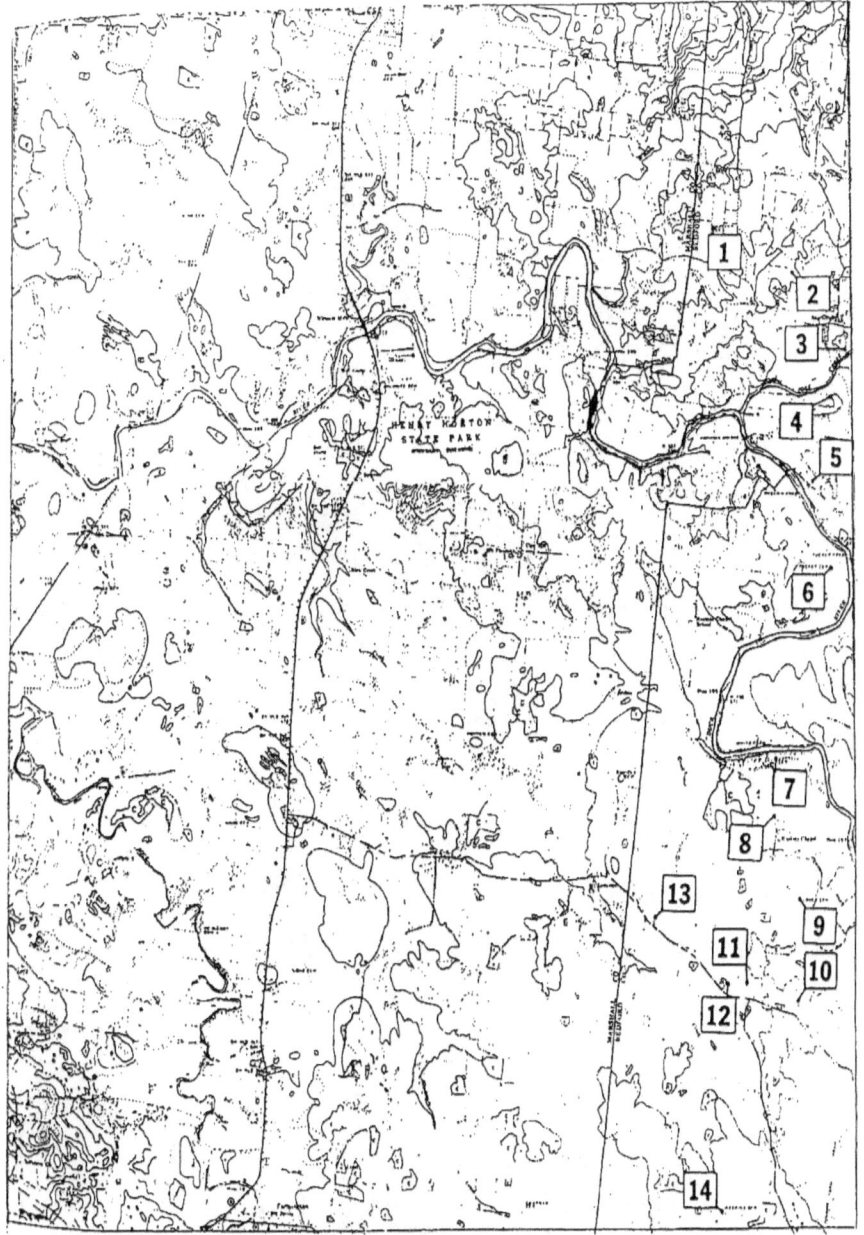

MAP 5

UNIONVILLE QUADRANGLE

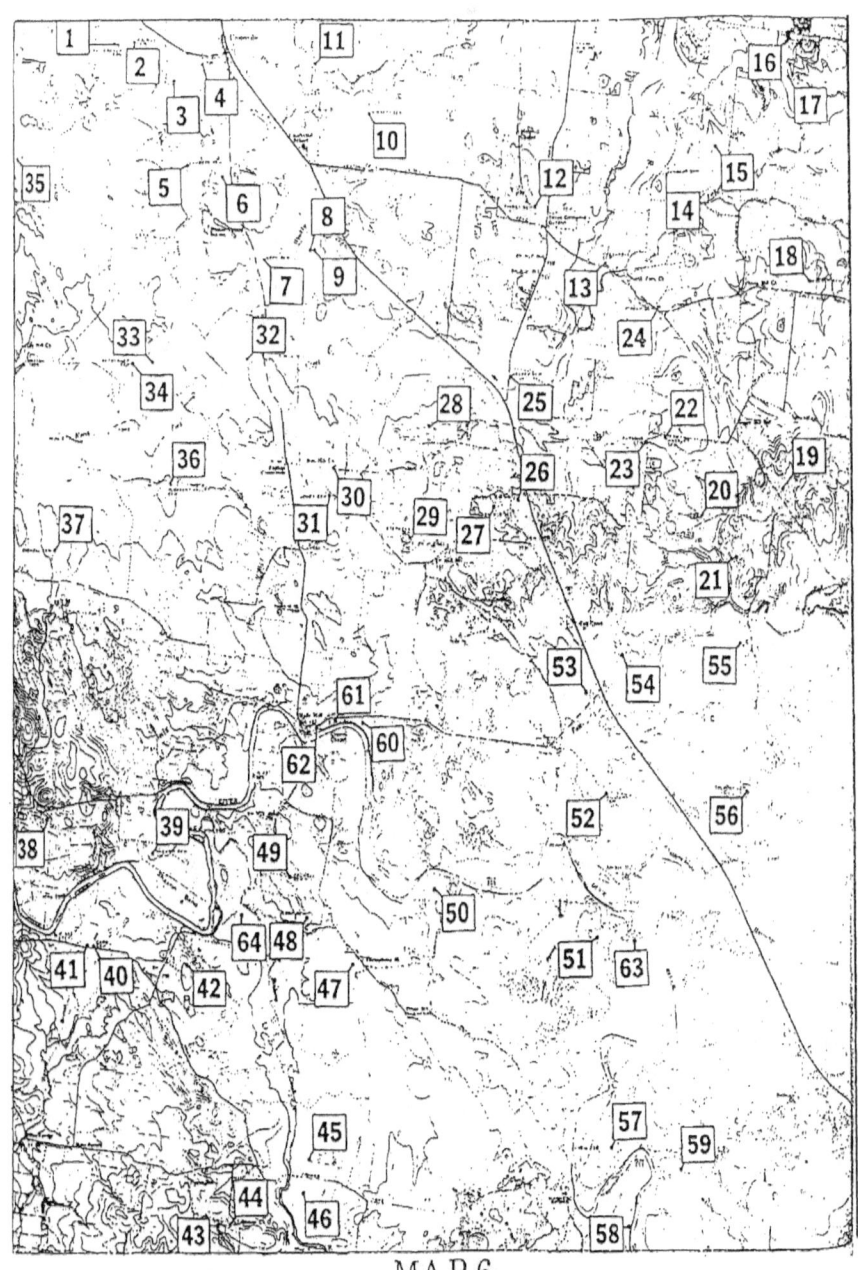

MAP 6

DEASON QUADRANGLE

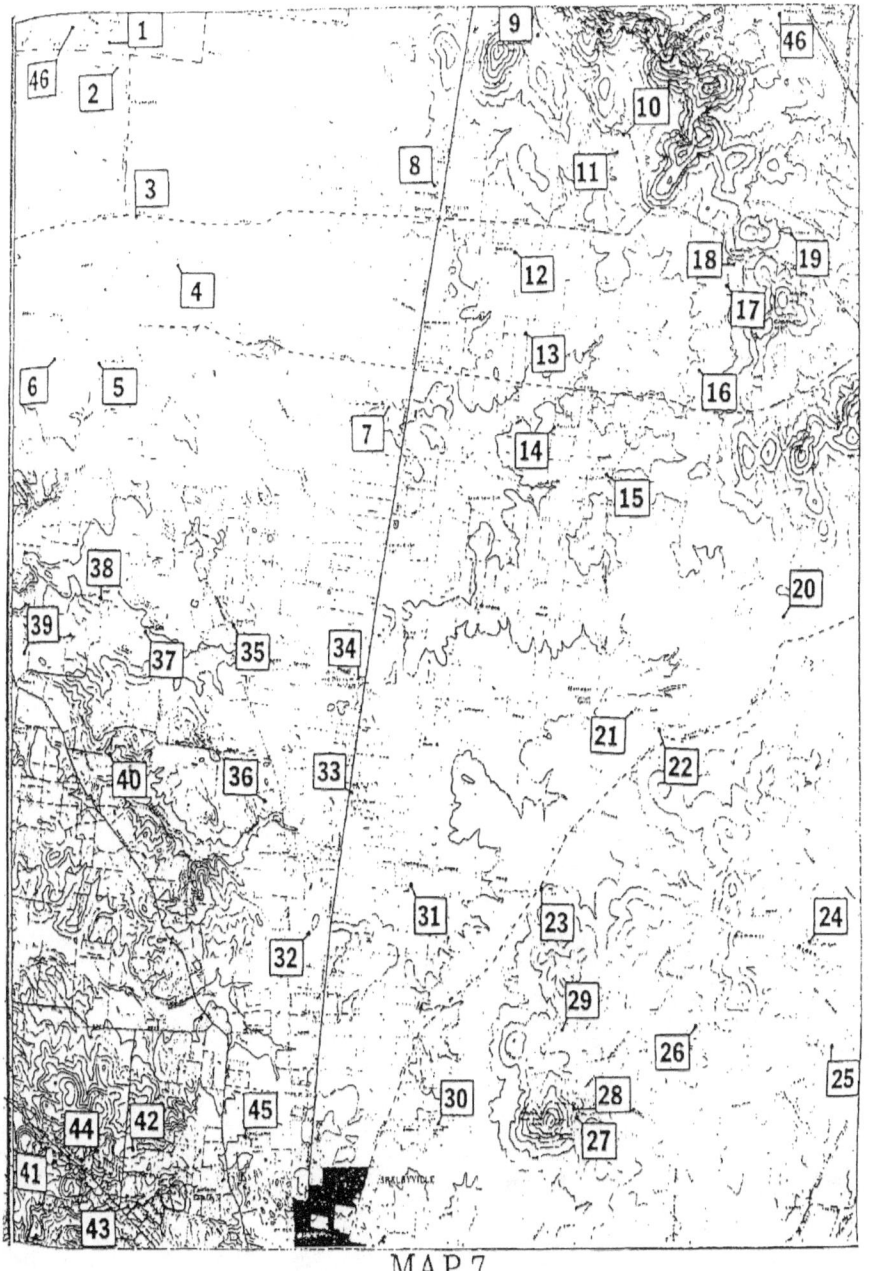

MAP 7

WARTRACE QUADRANGLE

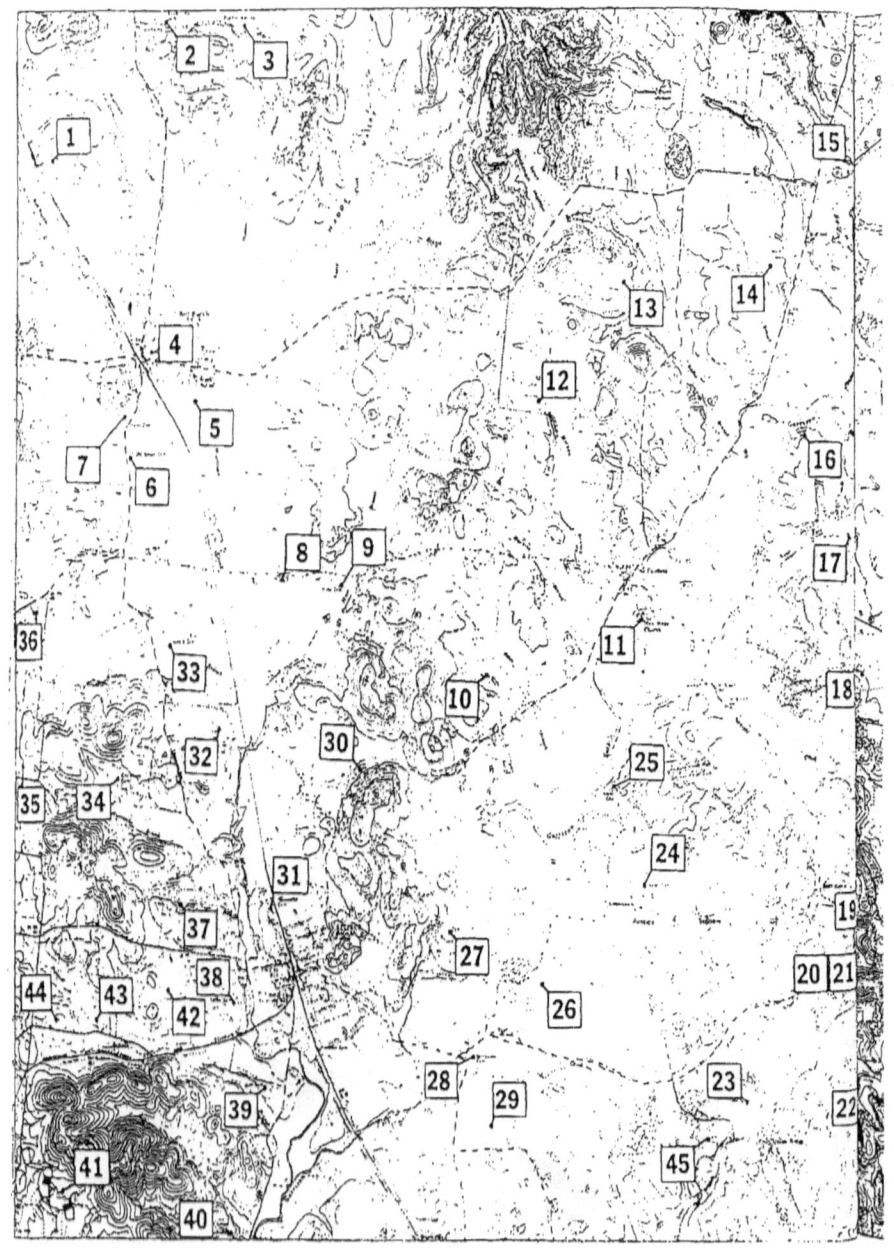

MAP 8

BELFAST QUADRANGLE

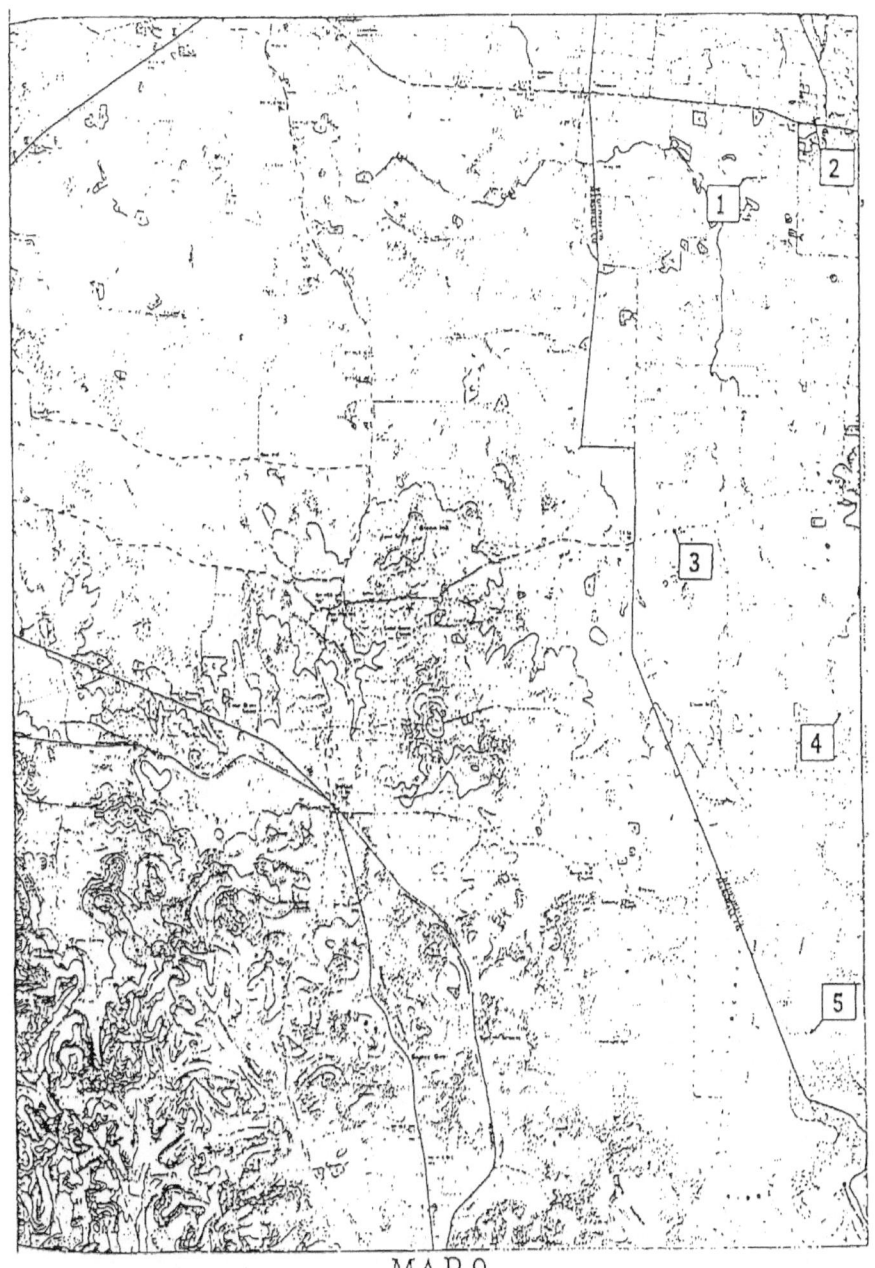

MAP 9

BEDFORD QUADRANGLE

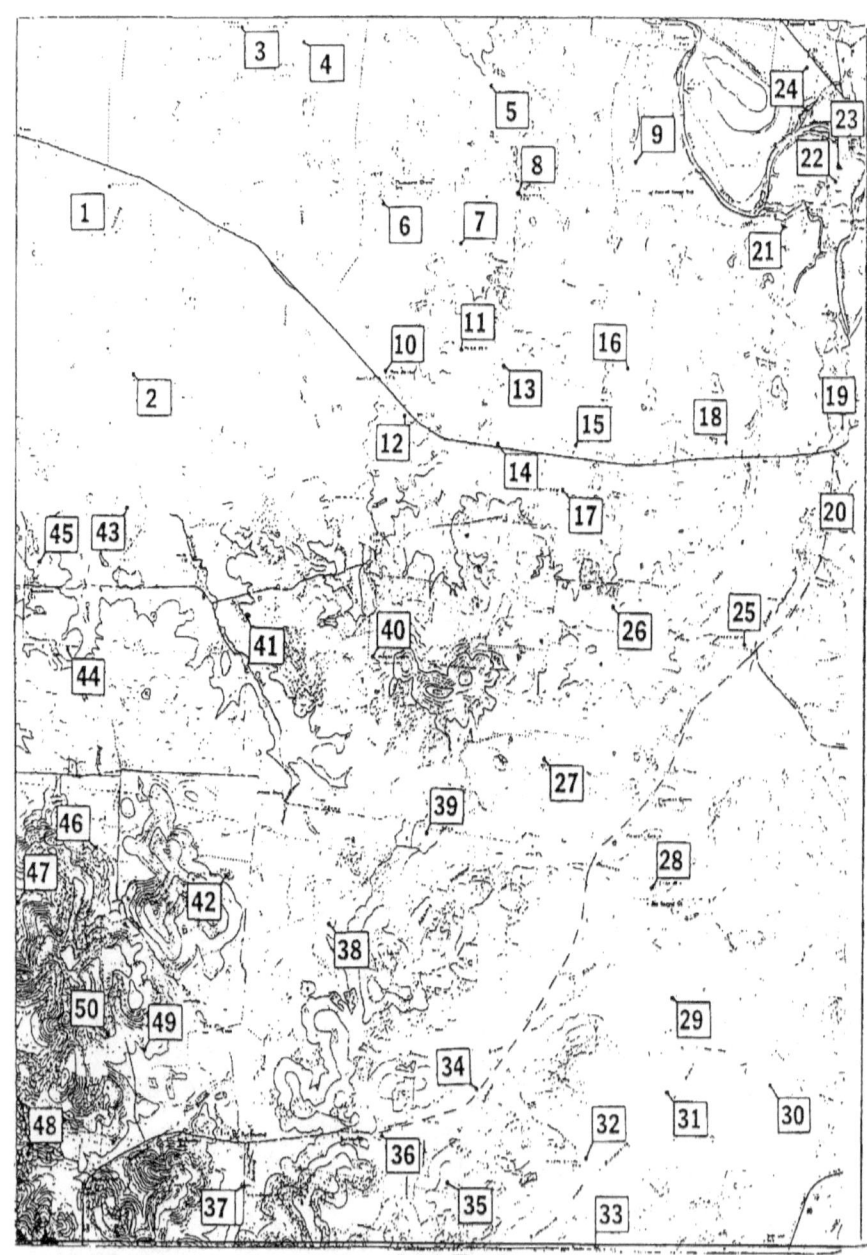

MAP 10

SHELBYVILLE QUADRANGLE

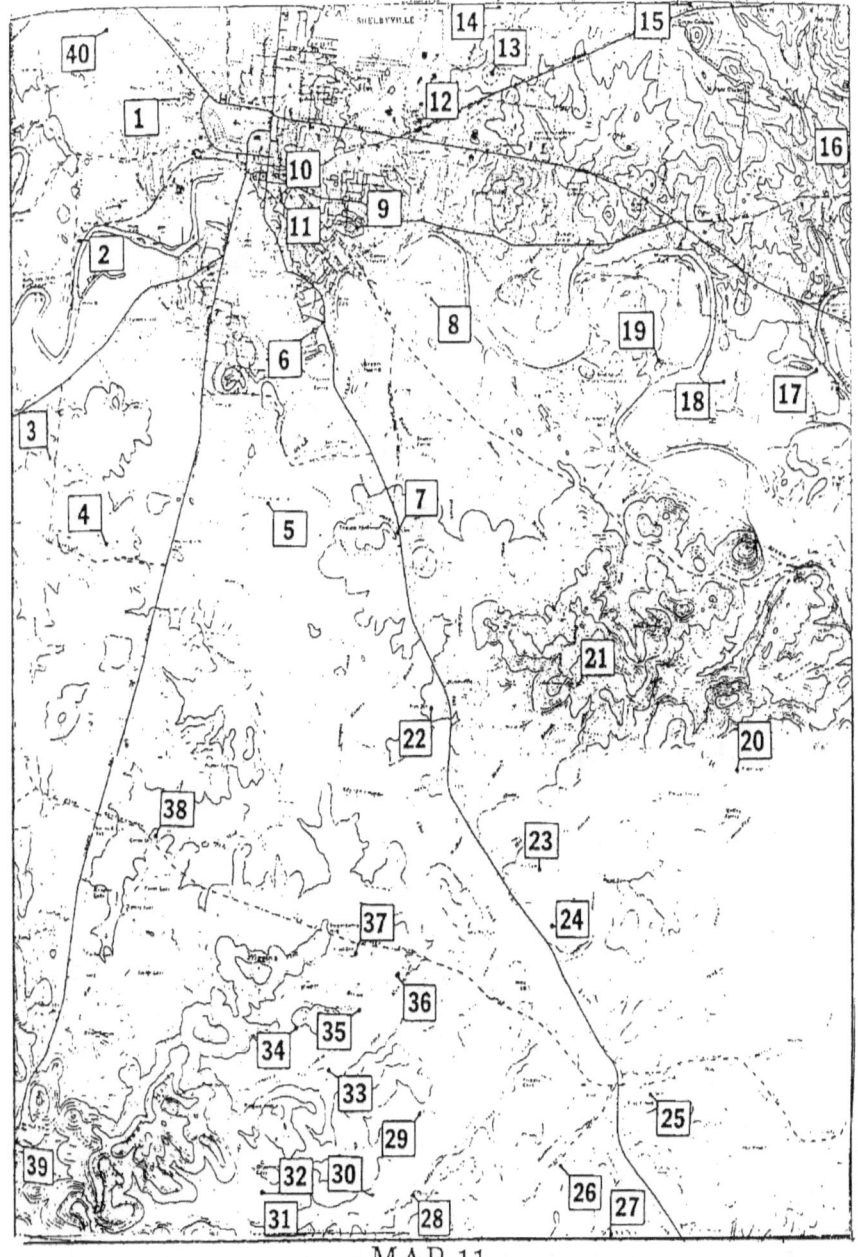

MAP 11

NORMANDY QUADRANGLE

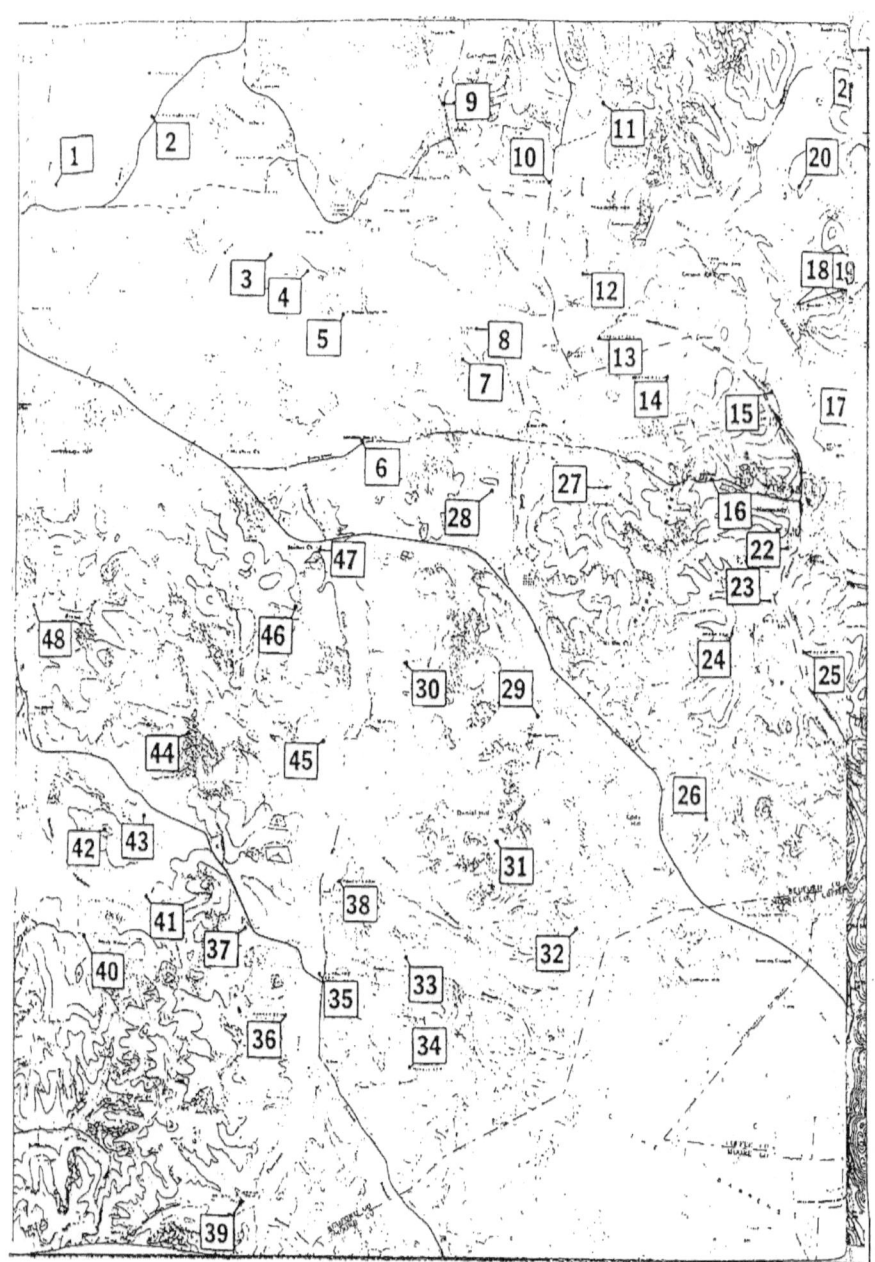

MAP 12

BOONEVILLE QUADRANGLE

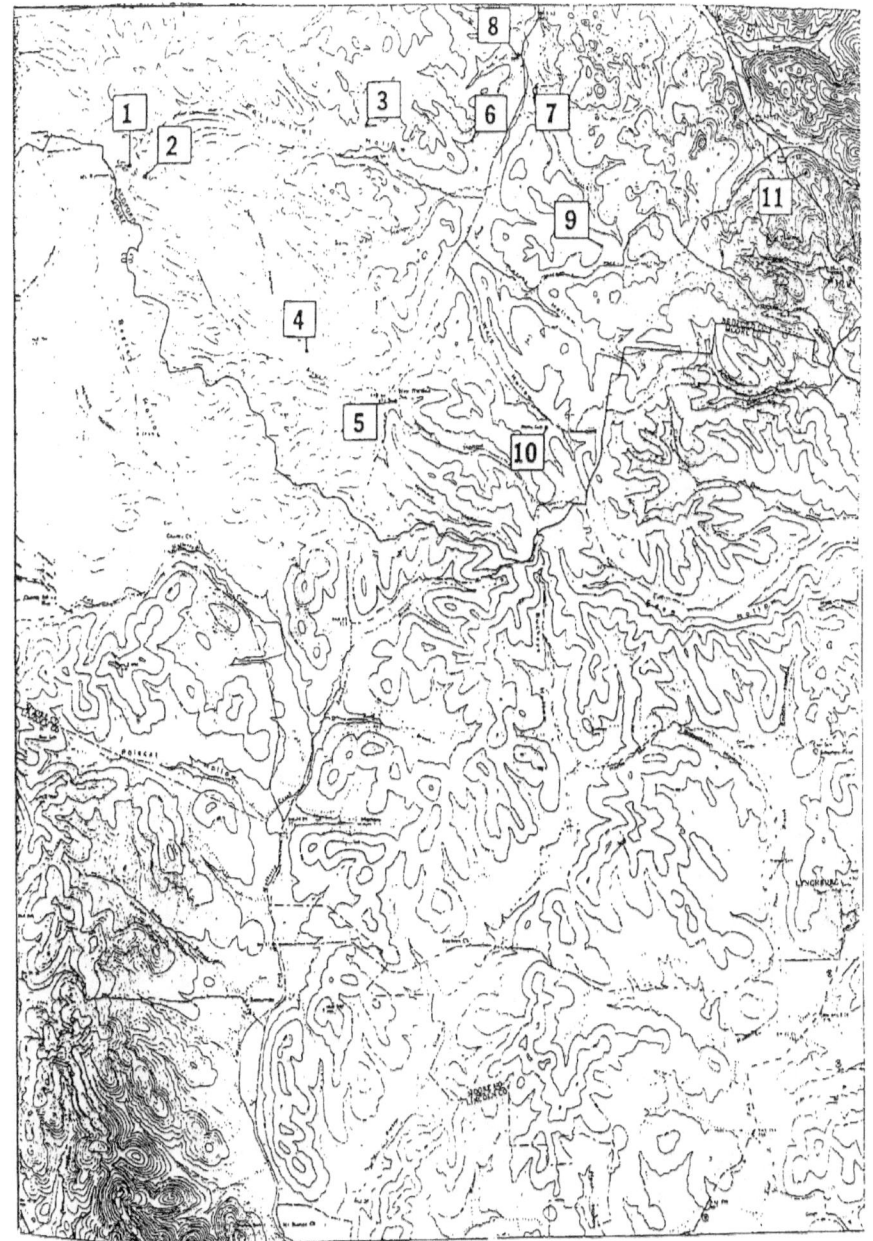

MAP 13

CUMBERLAND SPRINGS QUADRANGLE

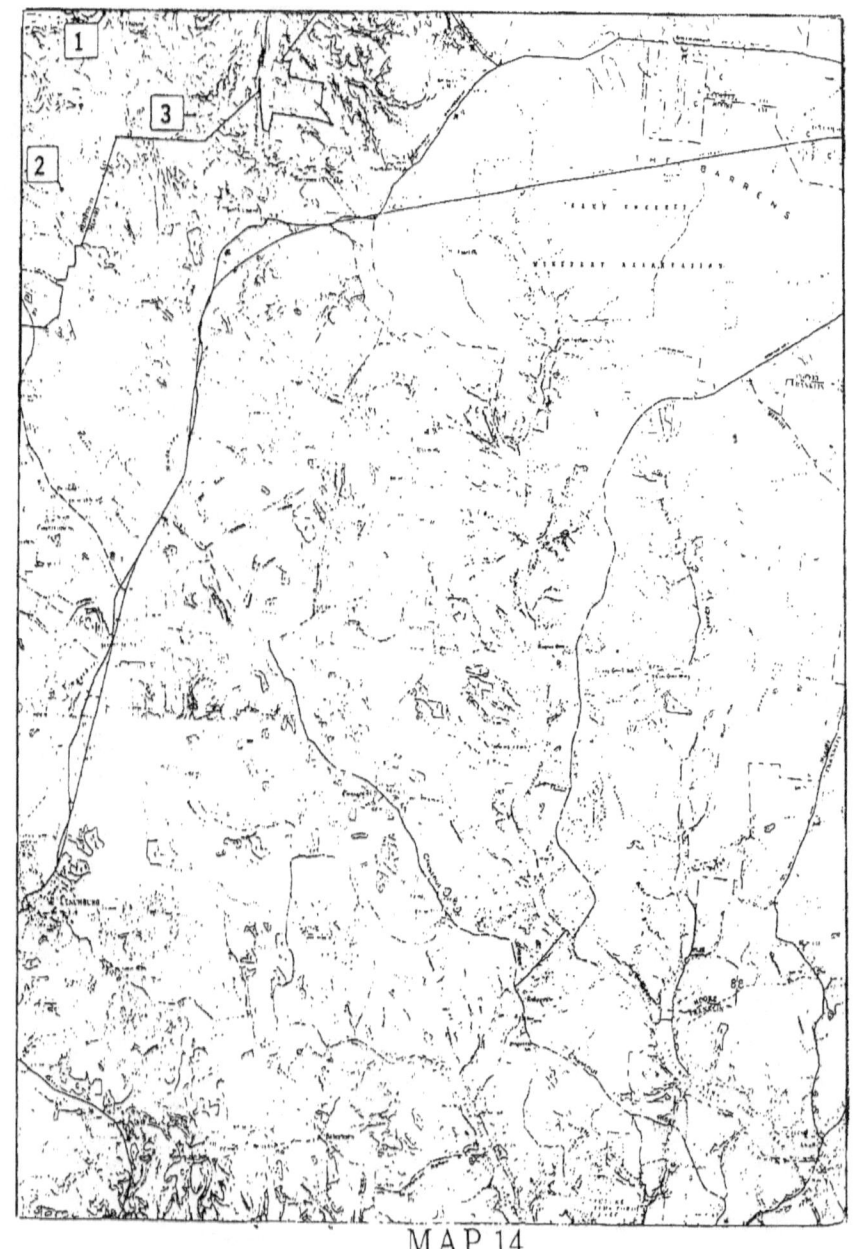

MAP 14

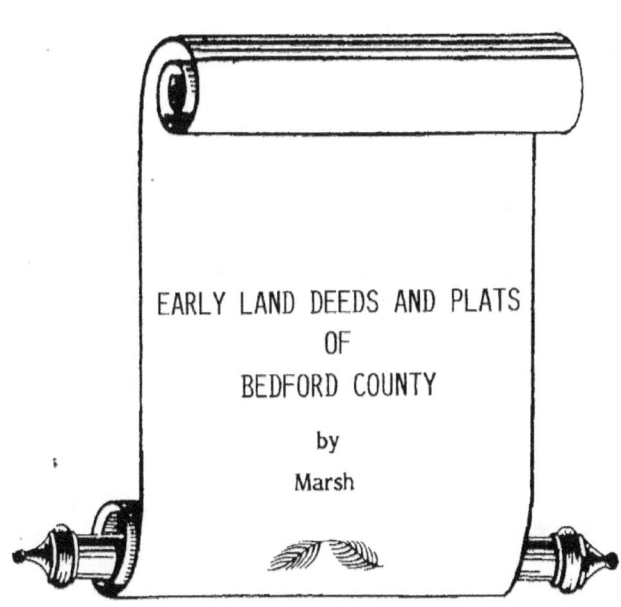

SELECTED PLATS IN BEDFORD COUNTY

1832 MAP... 400
231 SOUTH OF SHELBYVILLE... 363
ALEXANDER & THOMAS GREER LANDS............................ 355-356
ALEXANDER ROBERSON GRANT...................................... 372-373
BLOUNT GRANTS... 357
CLEMENT CANNON GRANT... 364-365
DOHERTY GRANT NEAR RICHMOND................................ 408
DUCK RIVER & FALL CREEK... 399
FIRST EXPLORER.. 353
FLAT CREEK AREA.. 384
GEORGE DOHERTY GRANT.. 375
GOOSE CREEK AREA.. 385
GRANT # 223.. 358
GRANT # 234.. 395
GRANTS AT FAIRFIELD... 393
GRANTS NORTH FORK... 387
GUARD RIGHT GRANT... 388
JAMES McKISICK GRANT.. 398
LANDERS GRANT... 368
LANDS OF BEDFORD COUNTY... 353
MATHEW LOCK GRANT & PLAT....................................... 379
MICHAEL ROBINSON GRANT... 374
NORTH WEST QUARTER... 405
OLD PISGAH AREA... 362
PHIFER GRANT S PLAT... 376-378
PLAT DEASON AREA.. 382
PLAT OF BEDFORD... 359
PLATS BELL BUCKLE AREA... 383
PLATS EAST OF HORSE MOUNTAIN................................. 381
PLATS GARRISON FORK & KNOB CREEK......................... 386
PLATS SOUTH EAST OF SHELBYVILLE............................. 380
RICHARD TROTTER GRANT... 389
RICHMOND AREA.. 370
ROBERT W. SMITH GRANT AT SHELBYVILLE................... 390-391
SCHOOL LAND GRANTS... 401
SHELBYVILLE TOWN LOTS... 392
SHIPMAN GRANTS... 366-367
SNELL-GABBERT PLAT... 396
SOUTH EAST QUARTER.. 406
SOUTH WEST QUARTER... 407
THE THREE FORKS... 397
THOMPSON CREEK SCHOOL LAND................................. 369
TRIBUTARIES OF DUCK RIVER, NORTH EAST QUARTER... 404
WARTRACE DEPOT PLAT.. 403
WARTRACE SCHOOL LAND GRANT................................. 402
WEST OF SHELBYVILLE.. 360-361
WHITESIDE & OVERTON DIVISION.................................. 394
WILDERNESS EXPLORERS MAPS..................................... 404-410

THE LANDS OF BEDFORD COUNTY

Vast Areas of the land lying within the present constituted boundaries of Bedford County, Tennessee were granted to early land speculators who were then living east of the Allegheny Mountains, at the close of the Revolution. Those presenting warrants were allowed to enter, locate, survey and file for grants to be issued out of John Armstrong's Land Office at Hillsborough, North Carolina, for ten pounds per hundred acres. There were over one hundred and thirty thousand acres granted to numerous grantees in various sizes up to five thousand acres each, in Bedford County.

The Blount brothers held grants for eighty five thousand acres of which about fifty thousand were located in the present bounds of Bedford County. Patton and Erwin, Alexander Outlaw and others later owned these grants that were all located on the Wartrace, Garrison and South or Barren Forks of Duck River, the major forks of said river. These grants were not issued for military service as many have assumed, the southern boundary line of the Military Reservation set aside for such purposes lay several miles to the north of Bedford County. Most of the land lying, in between the large grants in addition to un-appropriated lands were later issued as Tennessee Grants to holders of warrants that they had purchased from Soldiers of the North Carolina Line, these grantees were assignees of the soldiers. Other Tennessee Grants, generally for small acreages, called Waste Land, Penny, Twelve and One Half Cent, or School Grants, were issued for un-appropriated lands in the county.

In 1807, at the direction of the Legislature, the county was surveyed and sectioned off into townships divided by range and section lines, crossing at six-mile intervals. In early deeds, the section and range lines were often given, as was the surveyor's district, which was District Two (2) for Bedford County, not to be confused with Civil District No. Two. Within each section of six miles square, a tract of six hundred and forty acres was surveyed and set aside for benefit of the public schools, they were referred to as School Land tracts, so when deeds made reference to school land, it may mean one of the School Land Tracts, of which there were fifteen, not necessarily land upon which a schoolhouse was located. After 1846, these school tracts were auctioned off with approval of the Legislature and the local citizenry and grants issued to the purchasers by the State of Tennessee.

Editors

Timothy R. Marsh
County Historian

Helen C. Marsh
Deputy Historian

BEDFORD COUNTY, TENNESSEE

FIRST EXPLORER – FIRST SETTLER

The earliest documented North Carolina Land Patent or Grant located in Bedford County is the old Alexander and Thomas Greer's 5000 acre Grant. Located near Pleasant Grove, once called Rich Valley Post Office, it was North Carolina Grant No. 43 Warrant No. 1433, surveyed March 3, 1785, granted July 10, 17888. Surveyed by William Medlin.

In August of 1783, Alexander Greer, a Revolutionary Soldier, with Ambrose Mauldin, a woodsman, and Julius Saunders, acting as pilot, left French Lick, later Fort Nashborough, for the purpose of going through the wilderness to Elk River Country, near where Fayetteville now stands, to locate suitable large tracts of land for his family. He located two large tracts of several thousands acres each for each his father Andrew Greer and his sister Ruth Talbot, locating then just below Fayetteville on Elk River. They then turned north and located a large grant east of Petersburg, Tennessee for his brother Joseph Greer, also a Revolutionary Soldier, noted as "The King's Mountain Messenger." After making this location, they then crossed over Elk River Ridge, now called Chestnut Ridge near Bledsoe Gap, picked up a creek that they called Greer's Lick Creek, later Lick and still later Sugar Creek. They followed this creek to a Big Spring and Salt Lick near the creek east of Pleasant Grove and about three quarter mile south west of the old Peebles place, once Lot No. 2 of the division of the Alexander Greer Grant. They camped at the Lick which they named Greer's Lick, made the beginning corner location by chopping AG, AM and JS on a corner tree. The Grant was to run east then north. They then saddle up and made trek back to the French Lick crossing Duck River at Thompson Ford, now Halls Mill.

Alexander Greer, a first Justice of Bedford County was a Charter Member of the Bedford County Court that met at Widow Payne's cabin that was located about a half mile north of the community of County Line in now Moore County, on Christmas Day December 25, 1807. He died in 1810 while living on his grant. He is probably buried in the Old Dyer Burying Ground, which was located on Tract No. 1 or the widow's dower tract. In 1831, the widow Jane Greer having died, the twenty-five hundred acre half of the original 5000 acre granted to Alexander and half-brother Thomas Greer, who settled on the northern half, was divided off into lots as follows:

No. 1 – Dower Tract sold to Wiggins & Dyer. The Big Spring Baptist Church located on this tract.
No. 2 – Descended to James G. Whitney and wife Minerva, a daughter of said Greer. The 290 acres sold to Noah Scales, Scales sold to J.H.C. Scales, now home of Doctors Charles and Carol Stimpson.

5000 Acres- N.C. # 43

Surveyed March 3, 1785

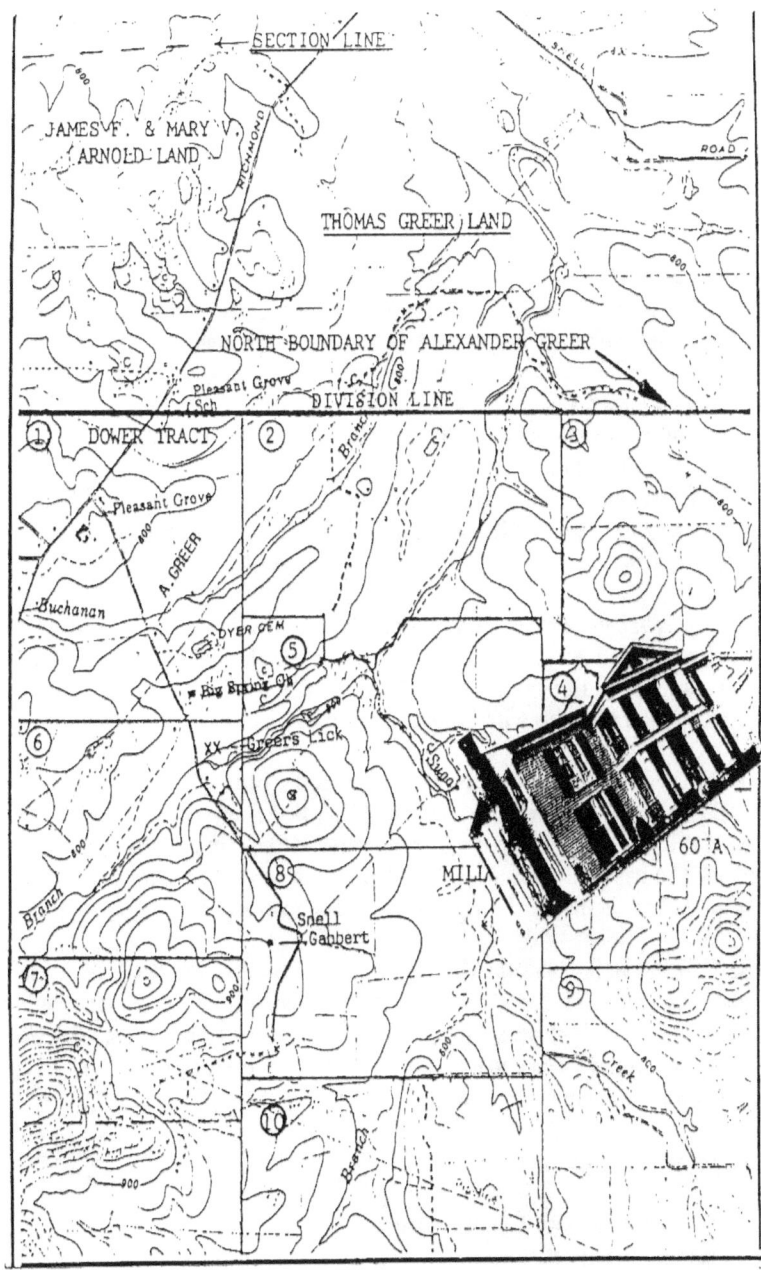

ALEXANDER & THOMAS GREER

No. 3 – To James R. White.
No. 4 – To Joseph A. Greer, now belongs to Nan White, Grassland Farms.
No. 5 – To James McKisick and wife Mary V. Greer McKisick.
No. 6 – Richard Williamson and wife Betsy.
No. 7 – Andrew Greer, then to Dyer.
No. 8 – Joseph KcKisick and Jane B., later to Roger Snell, to Gabbert, later to Dr. Burns, now Dr. Gary Jones.
No. 9 – Alexander Greer, Jr., now Mr. and Mrs. Donnie Thompson's place.
No. 10 – Nathan Evans and wife Louisa B. They are buried on this place in an old ancient graveyard.

Thomas Greer, half-brother of Alexander and Joint Grantee of the 5000 acre Grant, lived on Greer Road and is buried in the Greer family plot in the Old Greer or Sugar Creek Meeting House Graveyard located on Dixon Road at Sugar Creek. He was buried here in 1848, his wife Catherine in 1865.

If we can believe an inscription on a stone standing in the Greer Graveyard that reads, "Elizabeth Greer born December 6, 1803, died September 6, 1805," then we must except this burial as being the first recorded in the county. This Elizabeth was a child of Thomas and Catherine Greer and this area was part of Rutherford County in 1805 when the child was buried in this graveyard.

Thomas Greer gave the land for the Sugar Creek Primitive Baptist Meeting House that stood on the west bank of Sugar Creek between the graveyard and the Petersburg Road. A first preaching elder of this church was Brother Melchesdec Brame, a Virginian who settled on the Lewisburg Highway at Knight's Campground Road at an early date.

Researched and compiled by

Timothy R. Marsh, Bedford County Historian
Helen C. Marsh, Deputy Historian
1989

****** ORIGINAL BLOUNT GRANTS ******

By
Marsh

Bedford County
****

1792

GARRISON OR MIDDLE FORK

#232

T.D.
3000a   #219

WARTRACE
FORK

BELL BUCKLE

#217

SURVEY OVERLAPS

A.J.   J.D.
640a   640a

#222   #220

NOAH FORK

FAIRFIELD

J.D.
640a   S.D.

WARTRACE

#225

STRAIGHT CREEK

MAP BY T. MARSH
1986

A.J. = Andrew Jackson
J.D. = John Donelson
T.D. = Tillman Dixon

#234   #221

SOUTH OR BARRON FORK

#235   #223

#231   #229

#233

#230

DUCK RIVER
MAIN FORK

NORMANDY

THOMPSON CREEK

SHOFNER CH.

Surveyed in Aug. 1792
By
John Donelson Jr. DS

Note: Later surveys in 1807 & 1814
resulted in some shifting of lines
and corners.

357

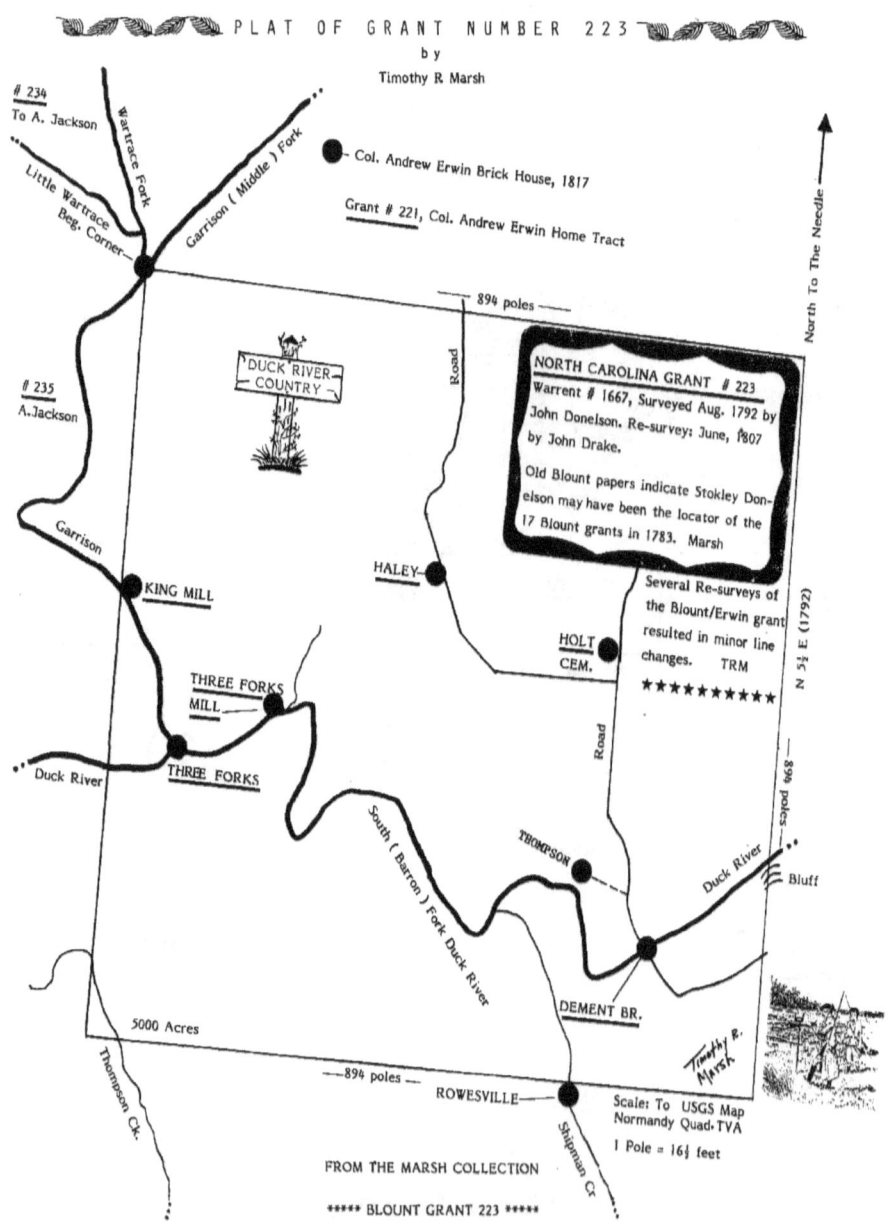

THIS PLAT IS ONE OF SEVENTEEN 5000 ACRE NORTH CAROLINA GRANTS ISSUED TO JOHN G. AND THOMAS BLOUNT IN 1793. ALL OF THE SEVENTEEN GRANTS REPRESENTING 85,000 ACRES OF VIRGIN UPPER DUCK RIVER LAND WAS RESEARCHED, PLOTTED AND PUBLISHED BY TIMOTHY R. AND HELEN C. MARSH.

***** EARLY LAND GRANTS AT BEDFORD *****

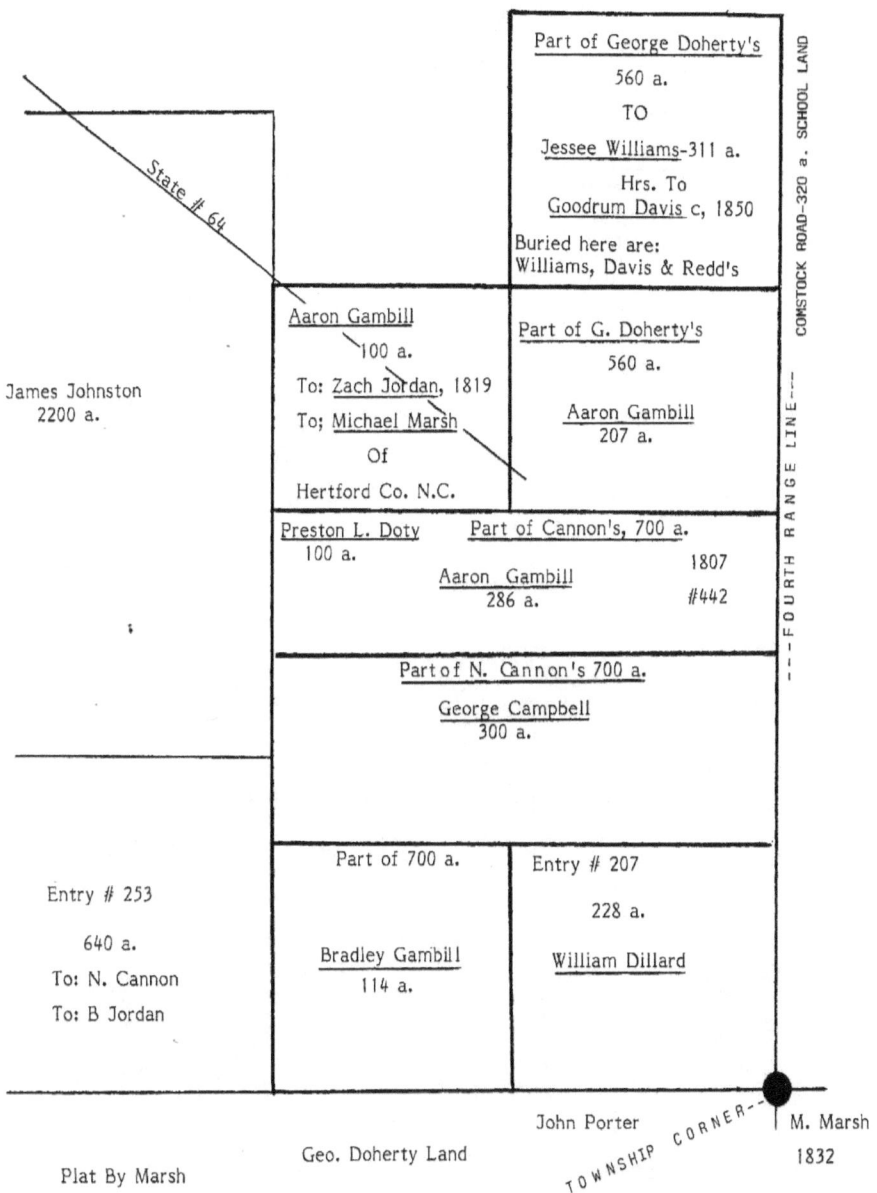

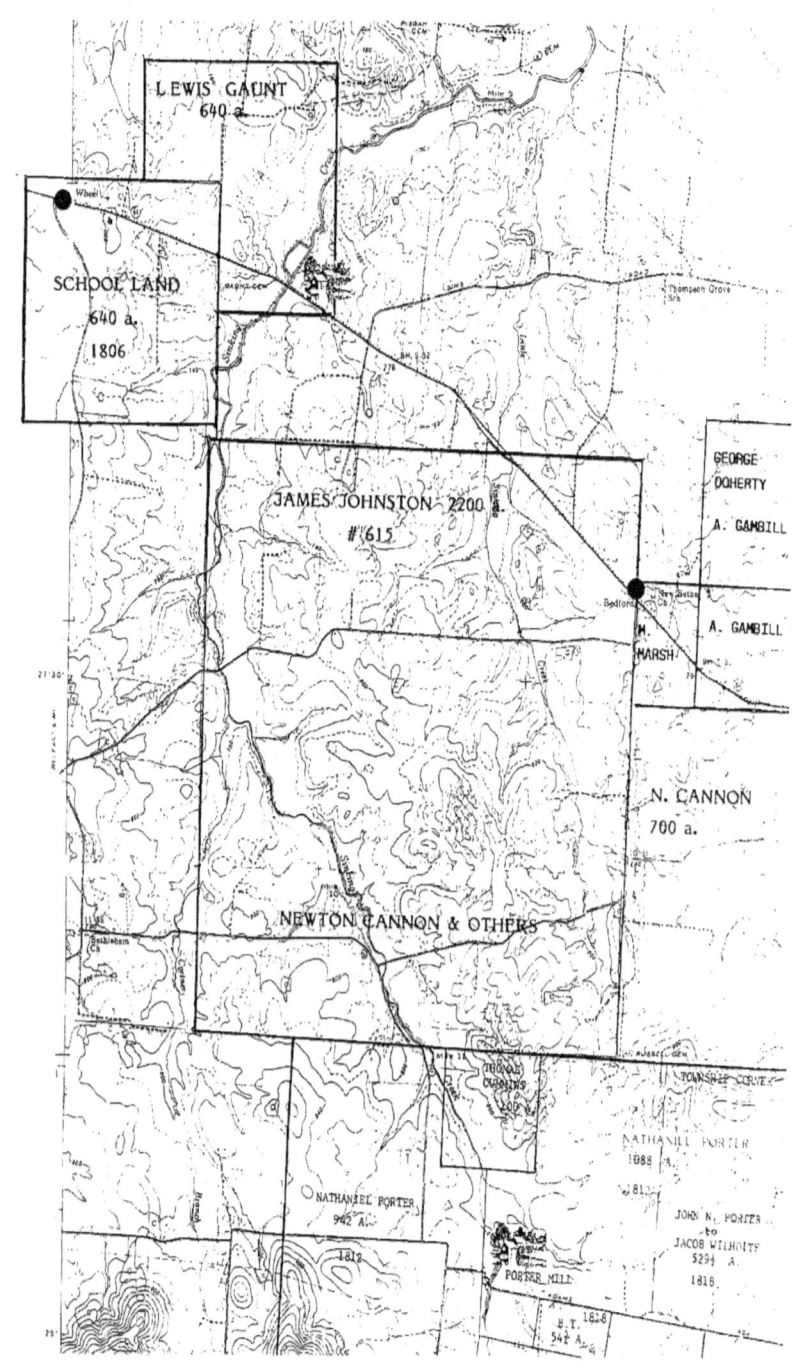

DIVISION OF JAMES JOHNSON GRANT NO. 615

Newton Cannon gets one third, 733 acres, for his locating services.
Wiley J. O'Neal, 201 acres.
Laben Ivey, 200 acres.
Lewis Gant to Janes O'Neal, 392 acres.
Logan Henderson
Jacob Bledsoe (sometime written Bletcher), 62 acres.
Thomas Moore, 50 acres.
Michael Moore, 244 acres.
David Dryden, 98 acres.
Samuel Harper, 98 acres.
____ Oliver

GRANTS ON THE SOUTH OF JOHNSTON

NEWTON CANNON
640 acres, No. 2199, 1810.
Division:
Hance Cunningham, 100 acres.
A. Hammel, 100 acres.
Thomas Cummins, 200 acres.
Samuel Harper, 240 acres.

AMOS JOHNSTON
638 acres, No. 253
Division:
John Ray
John H. Gambill
W. Patton
Hance Cunningham

****

***** OLD PISGAH AREA *****
18 Th. District

Much of the land in the lower 18th. district of Bedford County that had not been previously filed on by 1823, was then entered under the 12½ and Penny per acre law. These grants were frequently called waste land grants.

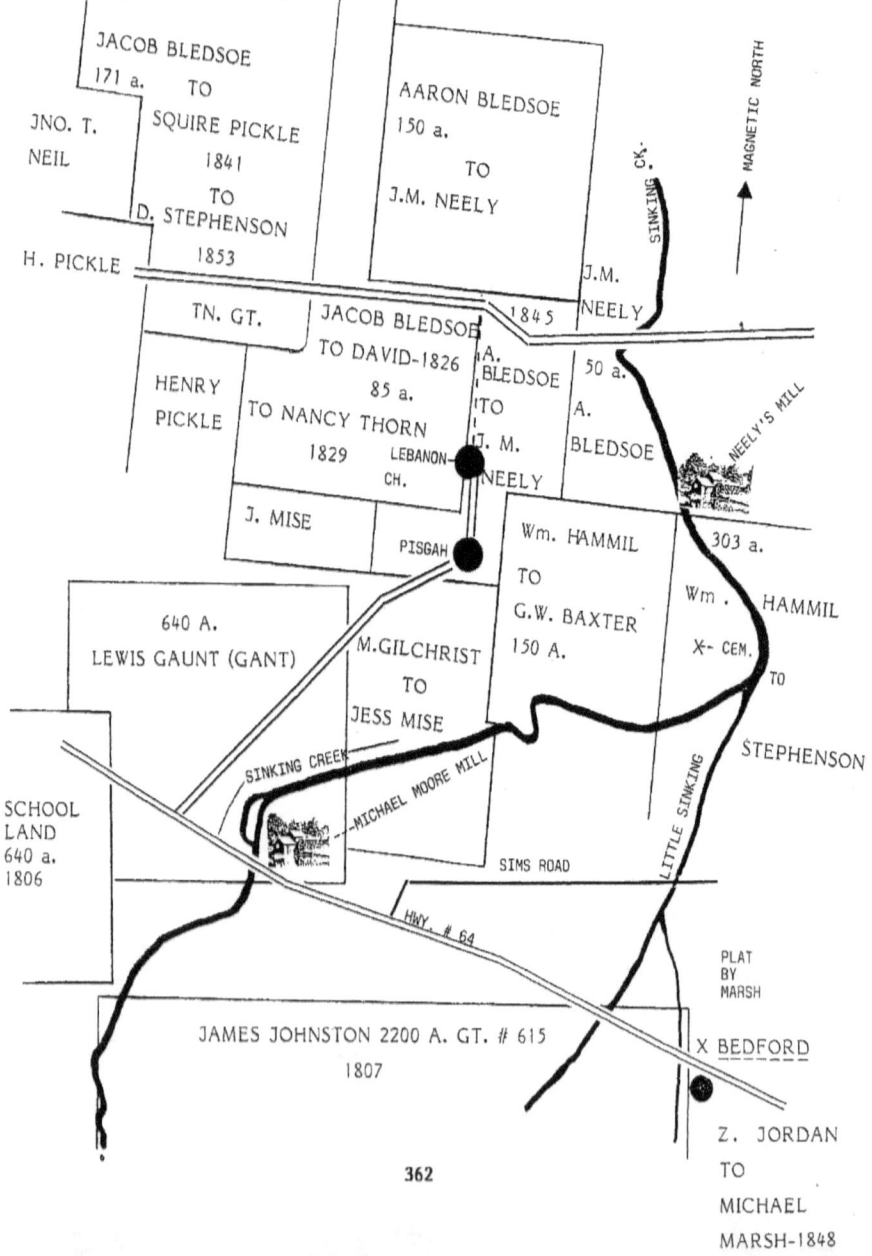

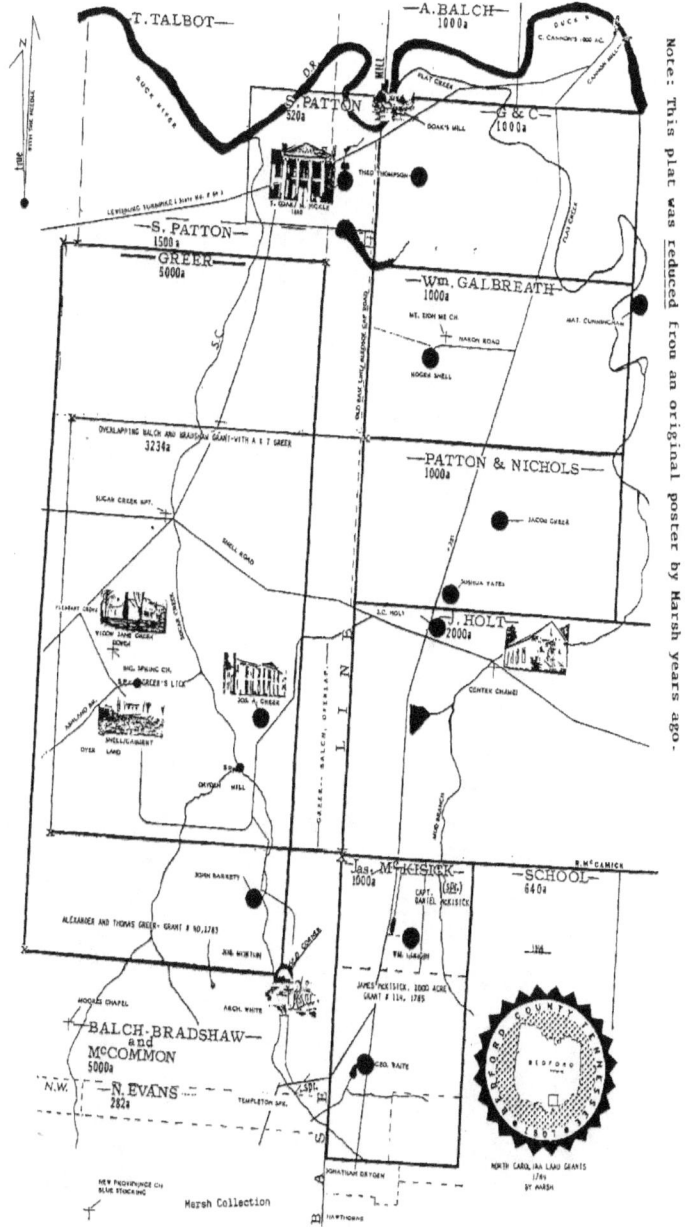

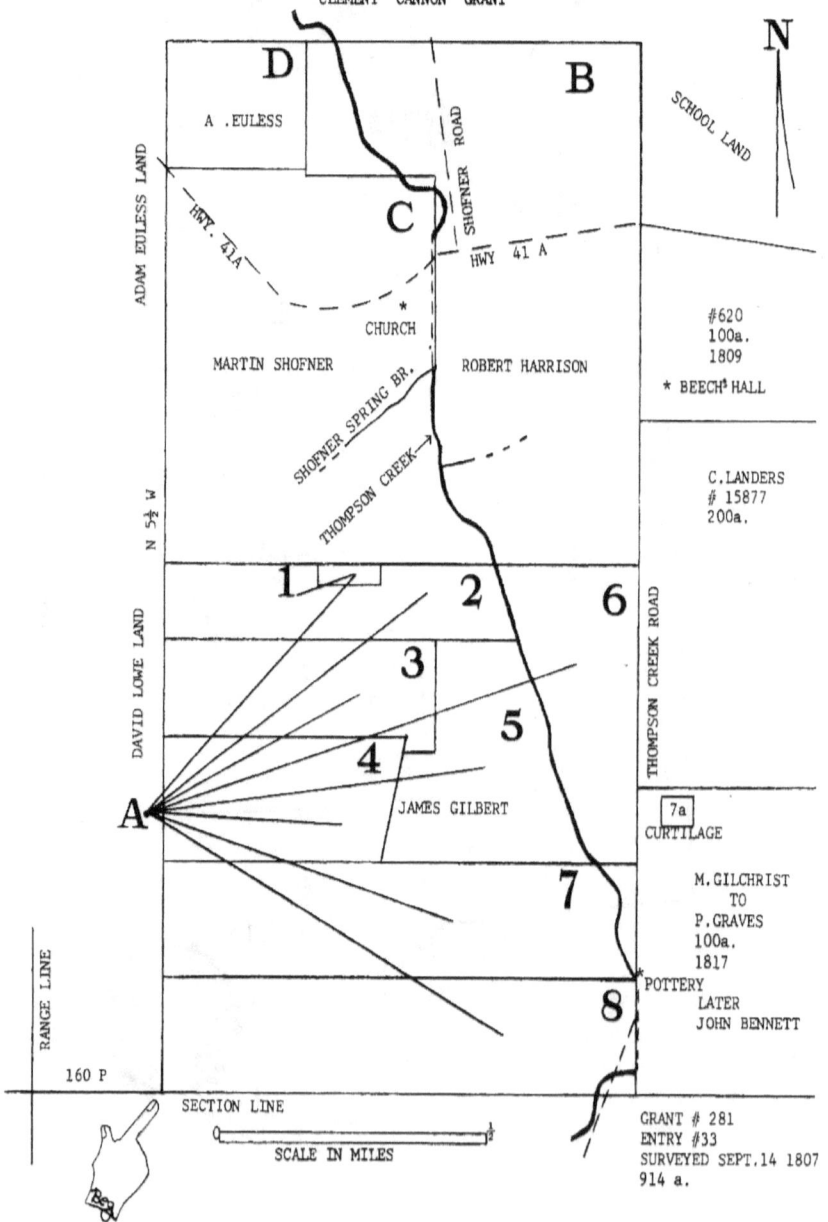

DIVISION OF CLEMENT CANNON GRANT # 281
By - Timothy R. Marsh

A - May 1809, Clement Cannon to James Gilbert containing 457 acres.

Subdivision of A

Tract No. 1, 1814, James Gilbert sold 1 acre to Martin Shofner and gave 1 acre, making a total of 2 acres, for a burying ground and Meeting house.

Tract No. 2, 1825, Edward W. Gilbert to Martin Shofner, 44 acres.

Tract No. 3, 1827, Lemuel A. Gilbert to David Lucas, 46 acres. In 1828, Lucas to John Smith. Smith to Absalom L. Landis.

Tract No. 4, 1819, William Gilbert to John Kimbro, 50 acres. Kimbro to Henderson Shofner.

Tract No. 5, 1825, Jeremiah Gilbert of Autauga County, Alabama, to John Landers (Landis), 60 acres. To William M. Smith. To Absalom L. Landis.

Tract No. 6, 1814, James Gilbert, Sr. to Heirs of Christopher Landers, 44 acres.

Tract No. 7, 1814, John Gilbert to Nicholas Anthony, 100 acres.

Tract No. 8, 1814, James Gilbert to Nicholas Anthony, 100 acres.

B - 1811, Clement Cannon to Robert Harrison, containing 212 acres. In 1857, John Harrison et. al., sold to R. L. and A. L. Landers.

C - 1812, Clement Cannon to Martin Shofner, 217 acres
Shofner had been renting the land and apparently was living on the land before the date of the Deed. In 1811, the Deed to Robert Harrison mentions Martin Shofner's Spring Branch.

D - 1812, Clement Cannon to Adam Euless, 20 acres. Euless, in 1824, acquired a 50 acre Tennessee Grant # 432, adjoining his 20 acres.

****

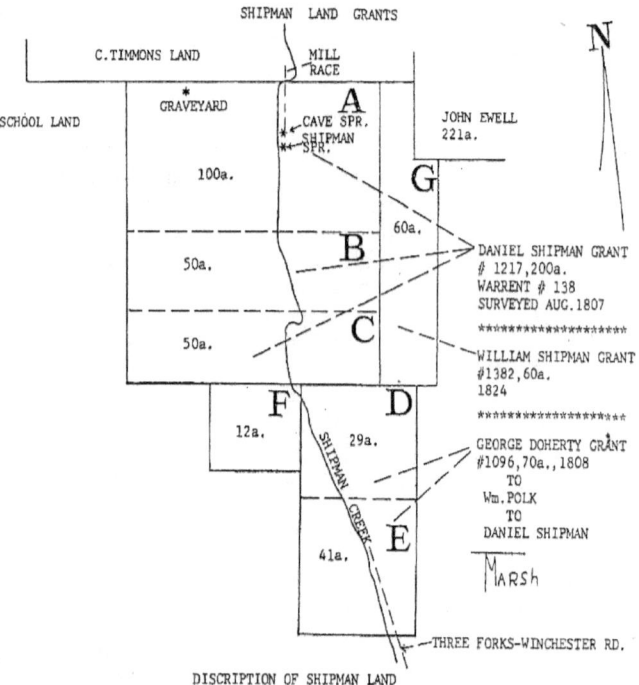

DISCRIPTION OF SHIPMAN LAND

A-1822- Daniel Shipman to William Shipman,100a.-In 1838 William Shipman sold 1a. to Timmons and Heard to be used as a mill race.William Shipman lived on this tract probably near one of the springs.An old graveyard is located on this tract with many unmarked graves that appear to date back to the earley days of the county. In 1841 just before making his move to Mo.Shipman sold this 100a. to George Cortner. This land is still in the Cortner family.

B-1825-Daniel Shipman to Charles Shipman,50a.

C-1825-Daniel Shipman to Jacob Shipman,50a.Both the 50a.tracts were sold with the agreement that Chas.and Jacob Maintain him for life.Daniel was living on one of the tracts at this time.In 1835 Chas.and Jacob sold the two tracts to John Stanfield. They soon made the moove to Mo.

D-1822-Daniel Shipman to James Shipman 29a.The top portion of his 70a. Grant that he purchased from Wm.Polk-James sold to Levi Turner in 1840.

E-1822-Daniel Shipman to Reuben Shipman,41a. The lower part of his 70a.Reuben sold to Abel Landers and Abel to Phoebe,provided Sallie A Nutt(wife of David) be allowed to occupy Said land.Levi Turner purchased land at Sheriffs sale in 1843.

SHIPMAN LAND GRANTS

F-1819- TENN.GRANT # 13119-To Daniel Shipman,12a.Daniel sold to Jacob Shipman. Jacob lived on the land and sold to john Stanfield in 1835.

G-1824-TENN.GRANT # 1382-To William Shipman,60a.William sold this 60a.to George Cortner in 1841. TRM.

****

MALCOM GILCHRIST GRANT # 446
200a.   1809
(ROWESVILLE)

```
                ERWINS OLD LINE
                               MILL
   D      C               o          A
                          |
                          |         63½a.
   34a. | 34a.   70a.    RACE
                          |     ← SHIPMAN CK.
                          |
   _____ROAD____|_____  SHELBYVILLE-POND SPR.RD.
                          |||
                          |||        B
                          |||
   WILLIAM SHIPMAN        | WINCHESTER      JOHN EWELL
        100a.             |  ROAD             221a.
                          |↙
                              W.S.
                              60a.          MARSh
```

DIVISION OF GILCHRIST GRANT

A-1809-Malcom Gilchrist sold this tract of 63½a. to James Walker who lived on this land for a number of years-In 1821 Walker sold to John McGee who the same year sold to Charles Timmons,who located the Mills and Gin on the N.W.Corner of the tract.In 1836 Timmons transferred the 63½a.to Jesse Holt.

B-1818-Gilchrist sold this 70a.to George Blair of Lincoln County Tennessee and in 1819 Blair sold to Charles Timmons and in 1833 Timmons conveyed part to Dr.Joseph Rowe.The major part of the town of ROWESVILLE was located on this 70a. In 1839 a strip of about 50a.that lay south of the Pond Spring Road was sold by Timmons to William Shipman,who two years later sold same to George Cortner.

C-1837-Dan!l.Gilchrist to Charles Timmons of Lincoln County Tenn.34a.

D-1837-Dan!l.Gilchrist to William Blanton 34a.

****

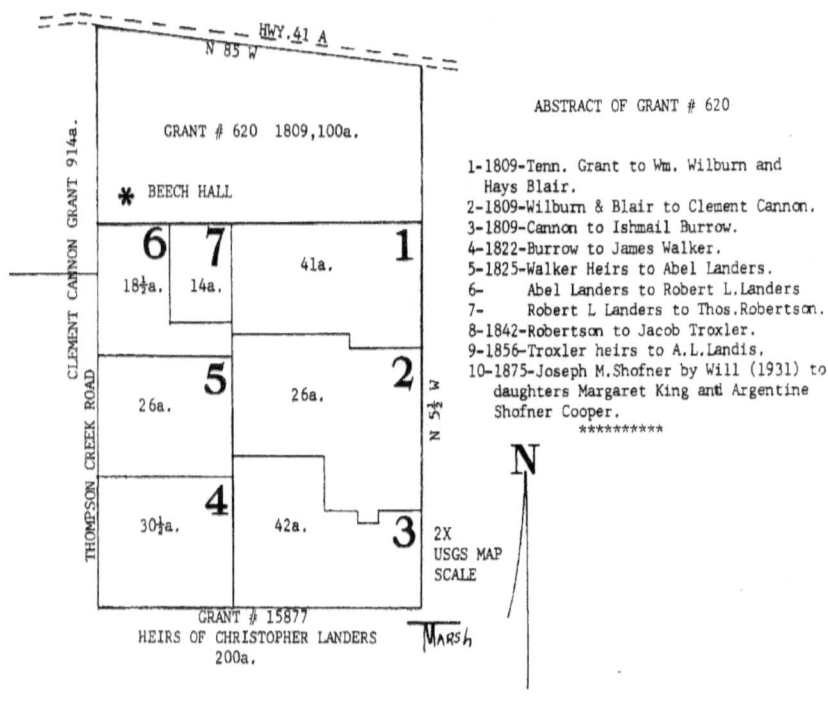

DIVISION OF LANDERS GRANT # 15877

1- 41a. To Abel Landers-to Robert Landers in 1837.
2- 26a. To Phoebe (Widow)-to Robert L. Landers in 1837.
3- 42a. To Henry Landers-to Abel and R.L. Landers after his death about 1835.
4- 30½a. To John Landers (Landess)-to Abel Landers-to Thomas Hill in 1831.
5- 26a. To Sally Ann and David Nutt- Abel Landers-to R.L. Landers in 1837.
6- 18½a. To Elizabeth Landers-to John and Abel Landers-to Thos. Hill.
7- 14a. To Joseph Landers-to Abel Landers -to Henry Landers in 1825.
8- 22a. To Robert L. Landers-This was part of a small tract Christopher Landers purchased of James Gilbert.

****

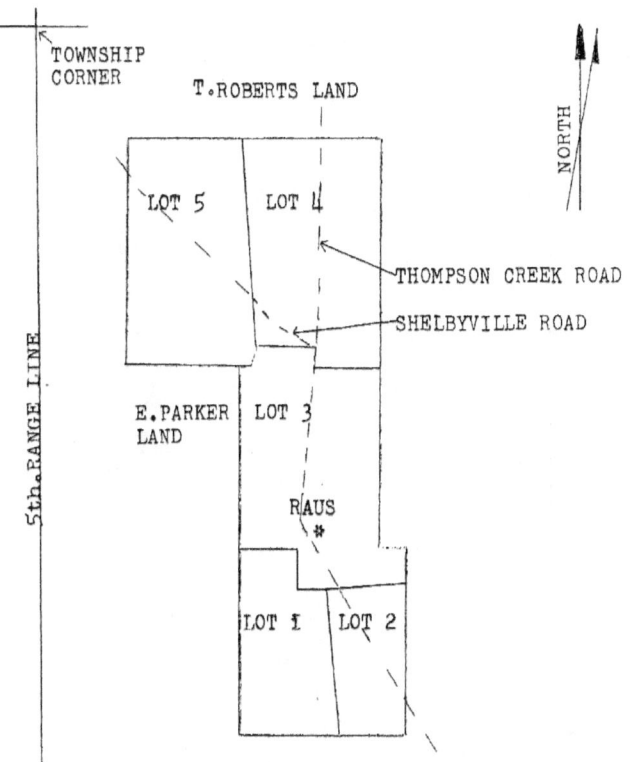

DIVISION OF 585 A SCHOOL LAND TRACT
1849-1855

LOT 1-81a Purchased by Presley Prince

LOT 2-60a Purchased by

LOT 3-160a Purchased by Wilkins Blanton

LOT 4-132a Purchased by H.C. Ferguson

LOT 5-152a Purchased by Willis Blanton

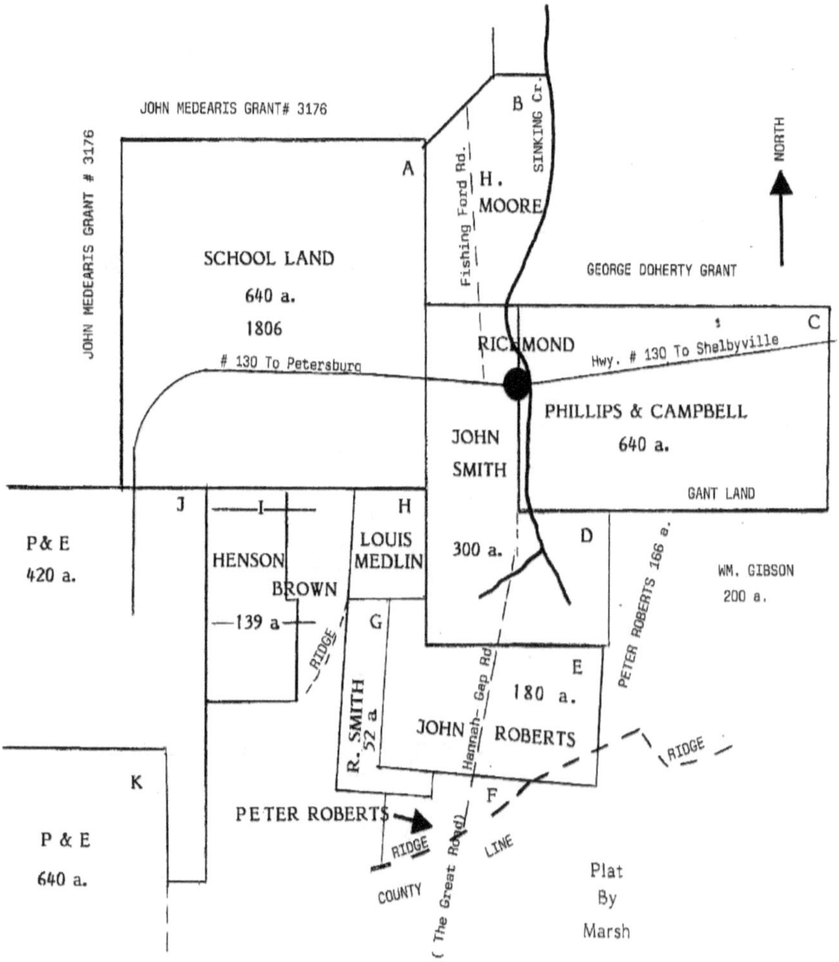

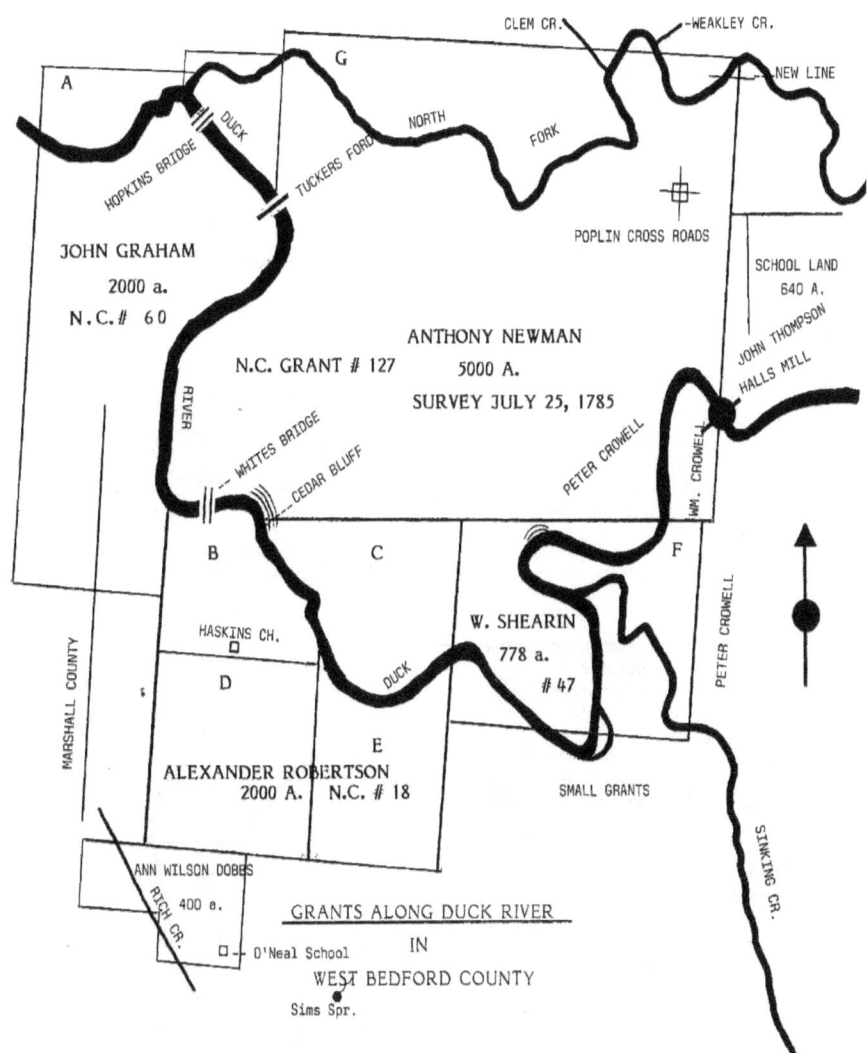

A- John Graham, 2000 a., part in Marshall County, on Rich creek
B- 1815- John Parker to Ezekial Reynolds, 400 a. Reynolds a Revolutionary Soldier, to Micheal Cleek, to Milton Birdwell.
C- 1811- John Parker to Abraham Mayfield
D- To Hugh Carothers, to John O'Neal, 1832
E- John Parker to Wm. S. Wilson, to Jas. M. Wilson, to Jas. Crow, to John Lentz, to James Harris, 389 a., 1840.
F- William Shearin (Shearin Bend). G- Anthony Newman Grant # 127.

****

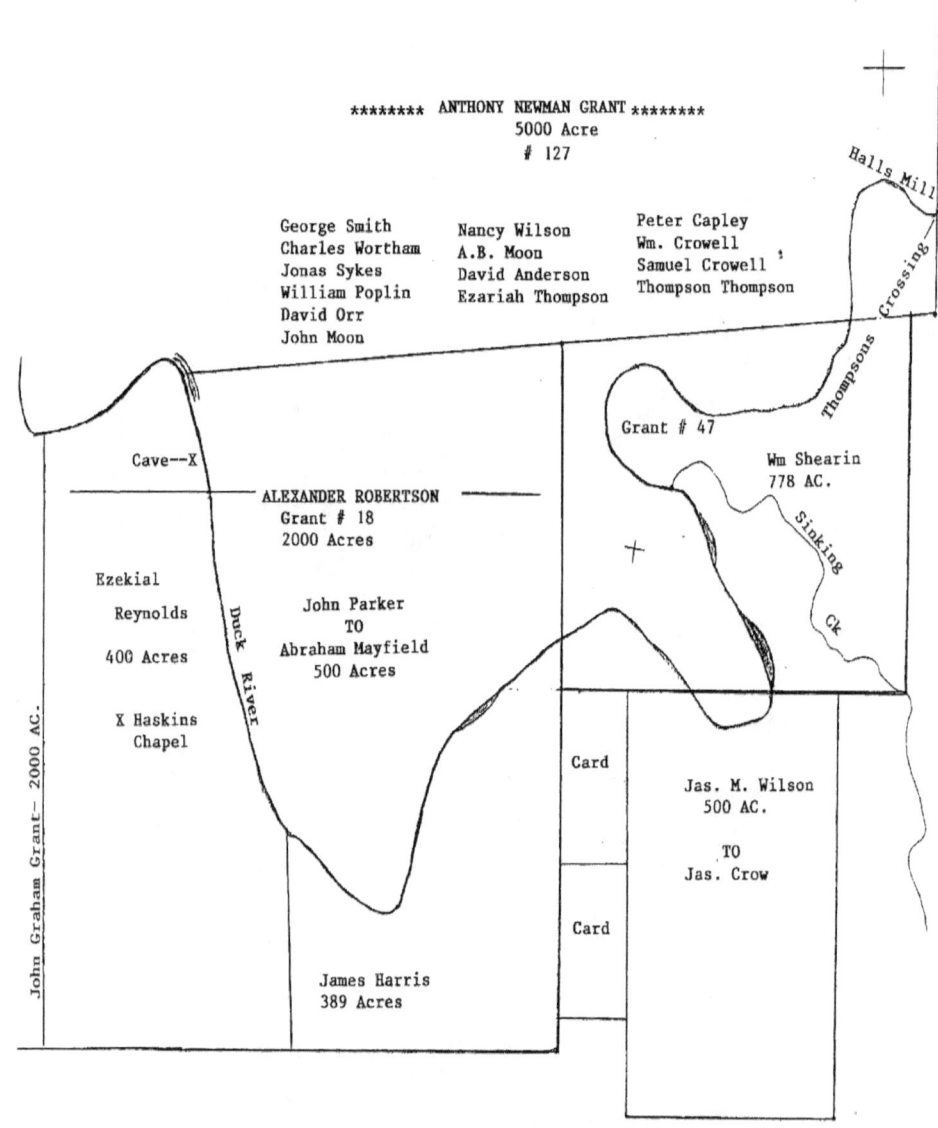

DIVISION OF A. NEWMAN 5000 ACRE GRANT NO. 127

Doctor John Newman of Davidson County, Tennessee, disposed of the A. Newman land in the following manner:

1810, John Newman to William Krowel (Crowell), 200 acres. Beginning south east corner of 5000 acre grant.

1812, John Newman to John Kepley, 125 acres. Beginning south west corner of William Krowel's 200 acres.

1812, John Newman to George Smith of Bedford County, Tennessee, 400 acres. Beginning east boundary line of Newman's 5000 acre grant.

1816, John Newman to George Smith, Sen., 300 acres. Beginning 160 poles south of the north east corner of the 5000 acre grant, west 260 poles, etc.

1818, John Newman to George Smith, Sen., 200 acres. Beginning the north west corner of Smith's 300 acre tract.

1812, John Newman to Thomas F. Thompson, 185 acres. Beginning on bank of Clem Creek on north boundary line of A. Newman's 5000 acre grant, on west side of Clems and North Fork Creeks.

1814, John Newman to James Wortham, 100 acres.

1814, John Newman to Elias Lovelace, 150 acres.

1820, John Newman to James F. Wortham, 212 acres. In same year Wortham sold 49 1/2 acres of his 212 acres to Azariah Thompson. Thompson erected a mill on the North Fork.

1819, John Newman to Isaac Wood, 100 acres. Beginning south east corner of David Anderson.

1822, DB-278, John Newman sold the balance of 5000 acre grant, amounting to 2721 acres, March 23, 1822.

1821, William Crowel to natural son, Samuel, 113 acres.

1822, September 20, Peter and Samuel Crowel, administrators of their deceased father William Crowel to John Capley, 38 1/2 acres, part of 200 acres.

1824, John Newman to Peter Capley, 150 acres.

1837, George Smith to Samuel Crowel, 1000 acres. Beginning north east corner of William Crowel.

Other owners were Baxter Ballard, Jonas Sykes, John Moon, David Orr, N. Harris, William B. Jones, Nancy Wilson, James Beavers, Jackson, Nichols, Volentine Lentz, and William Poplin.

* * * * * * * * * * *

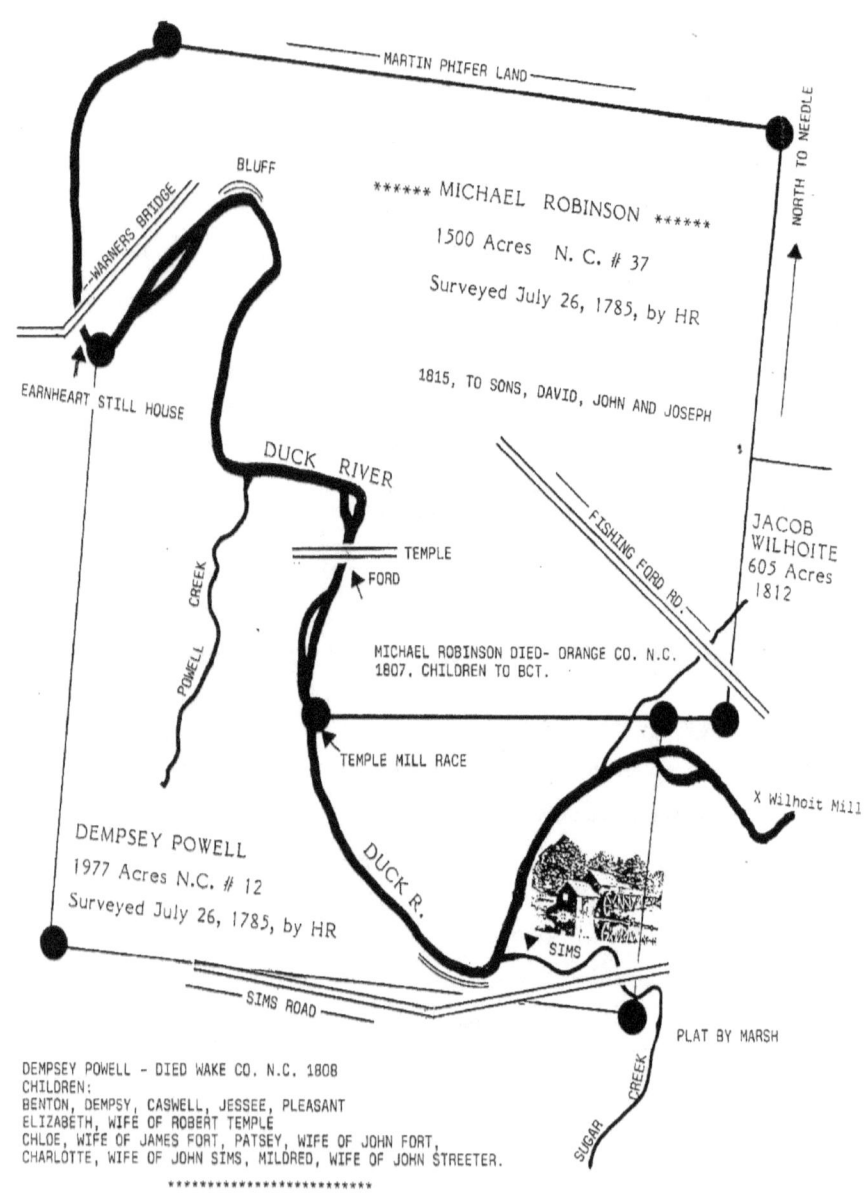

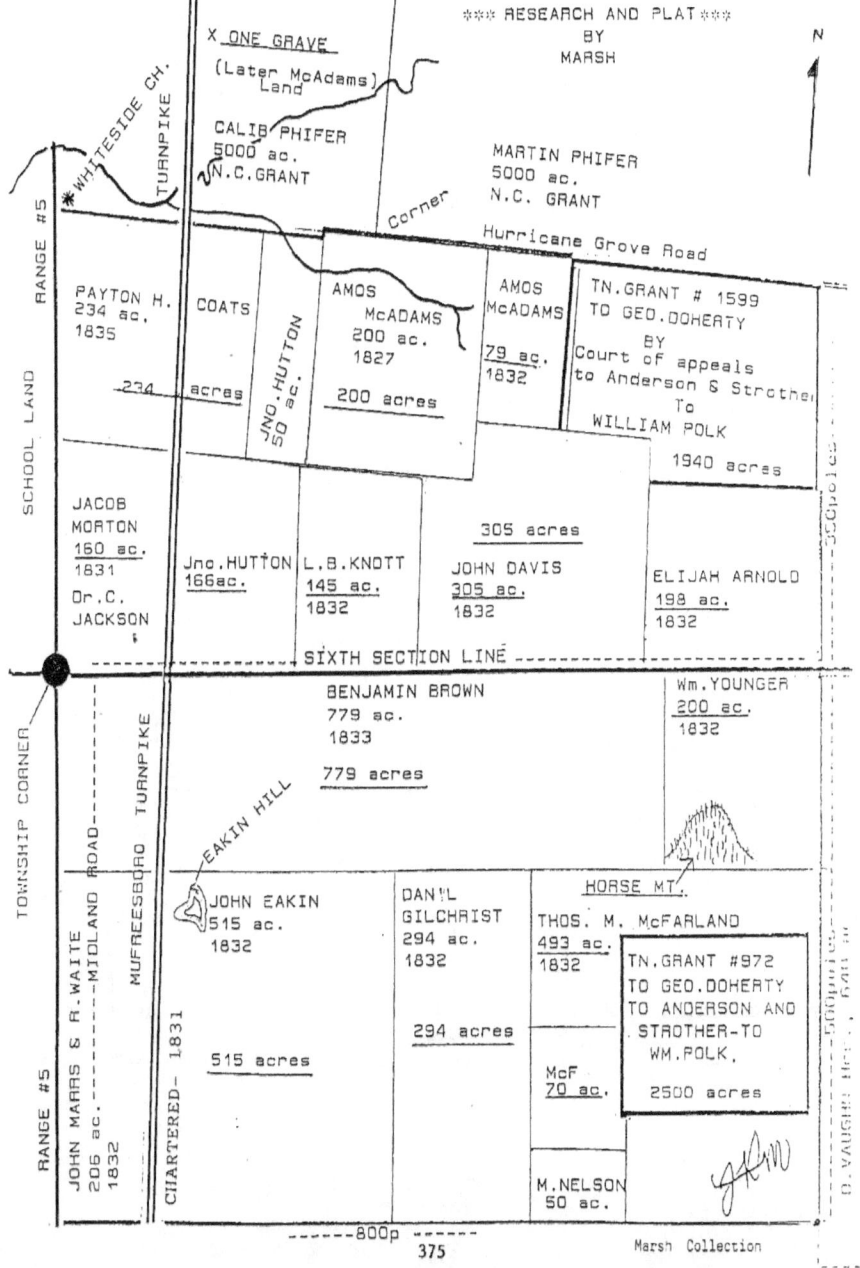

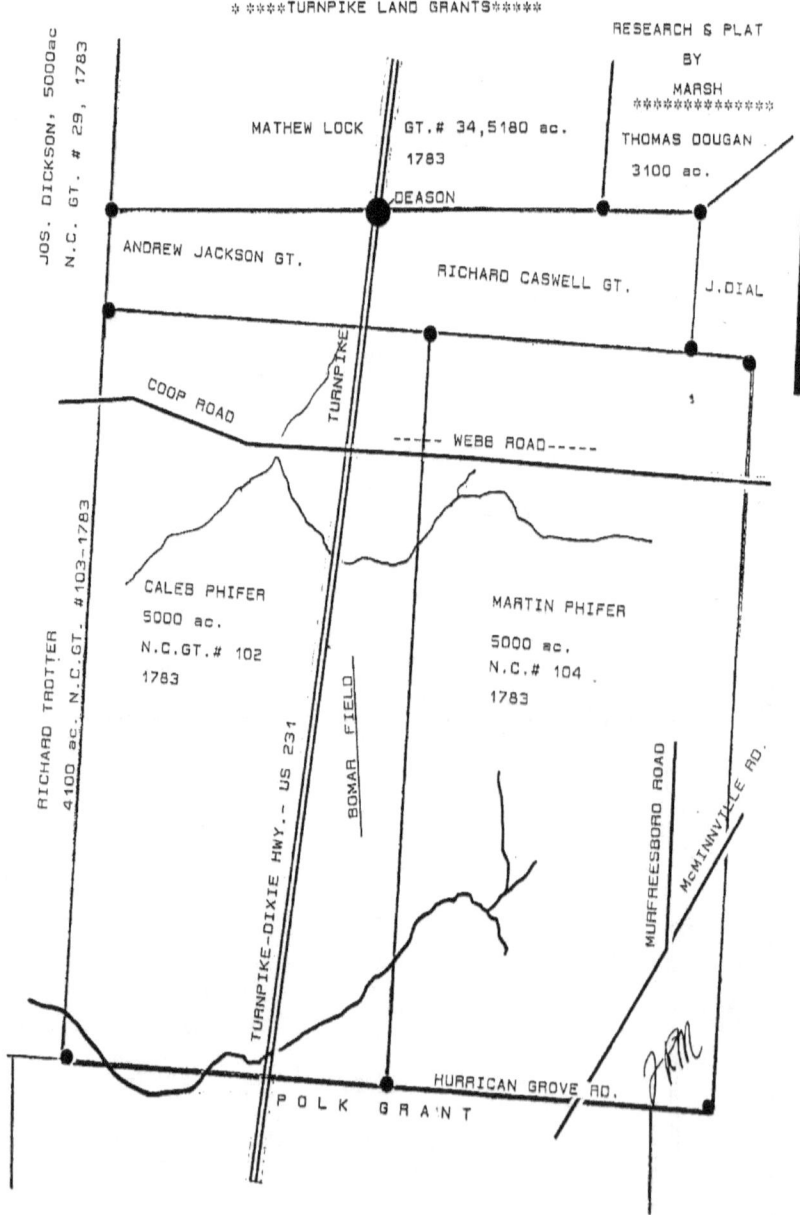

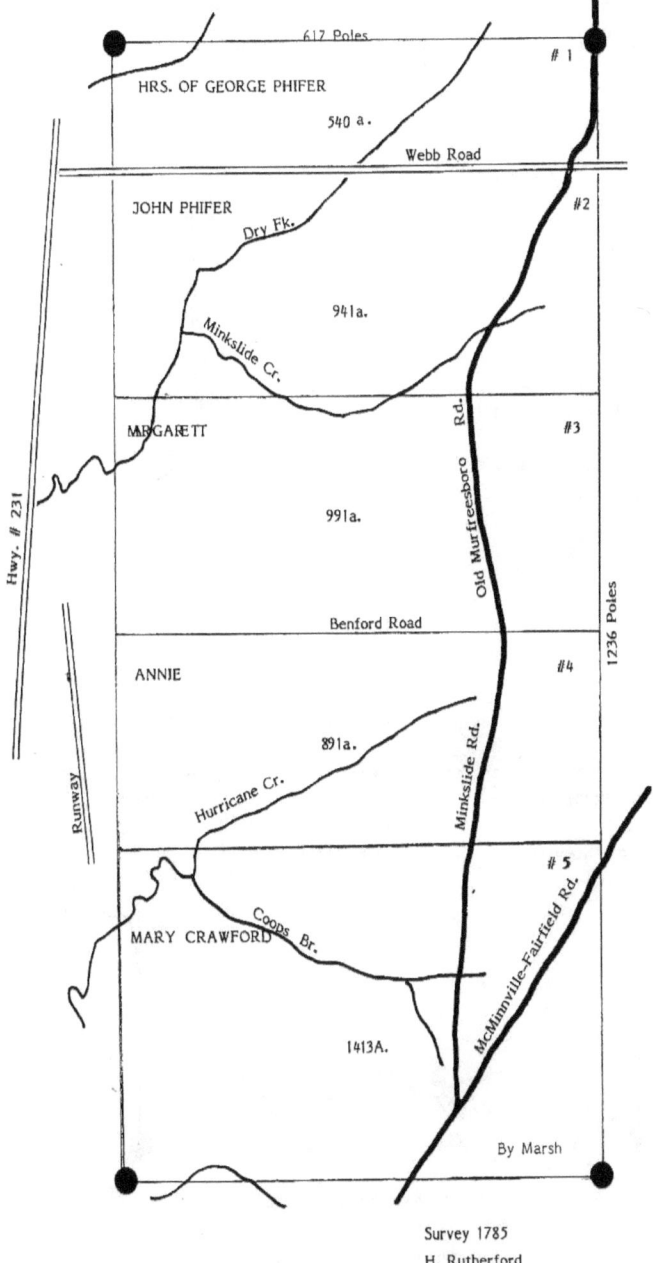

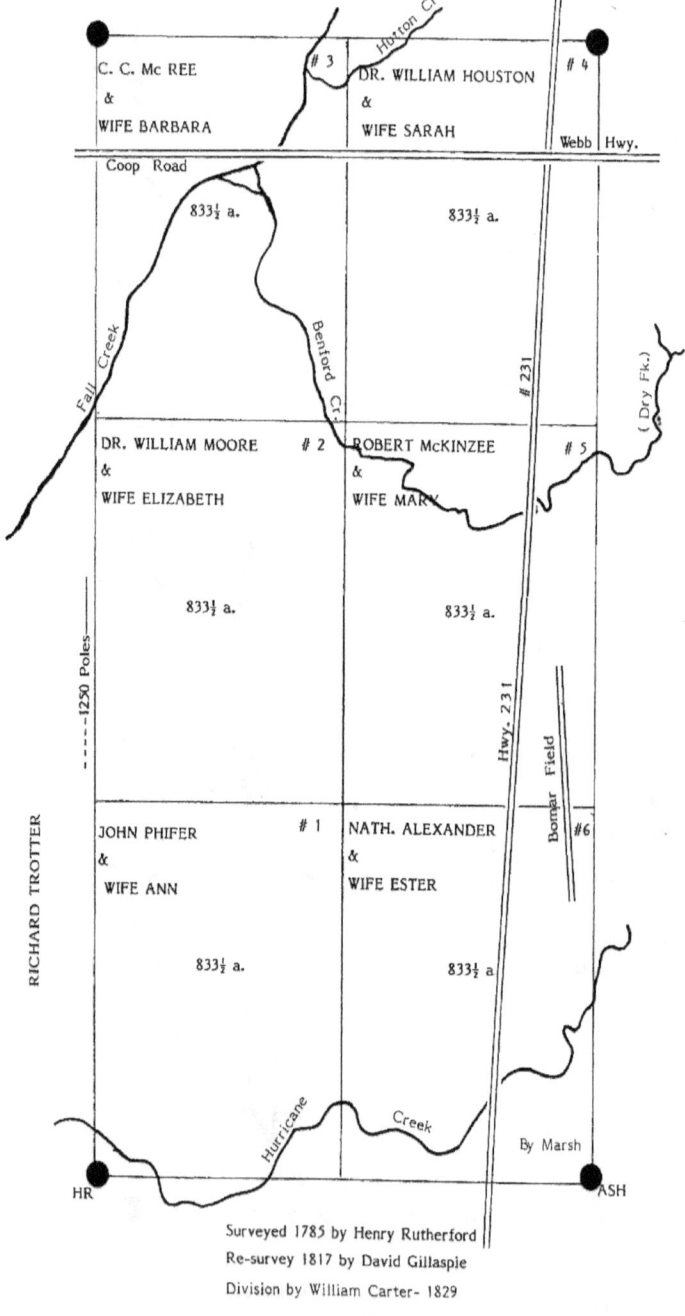

***** MATHEW LOCK GRANT *****

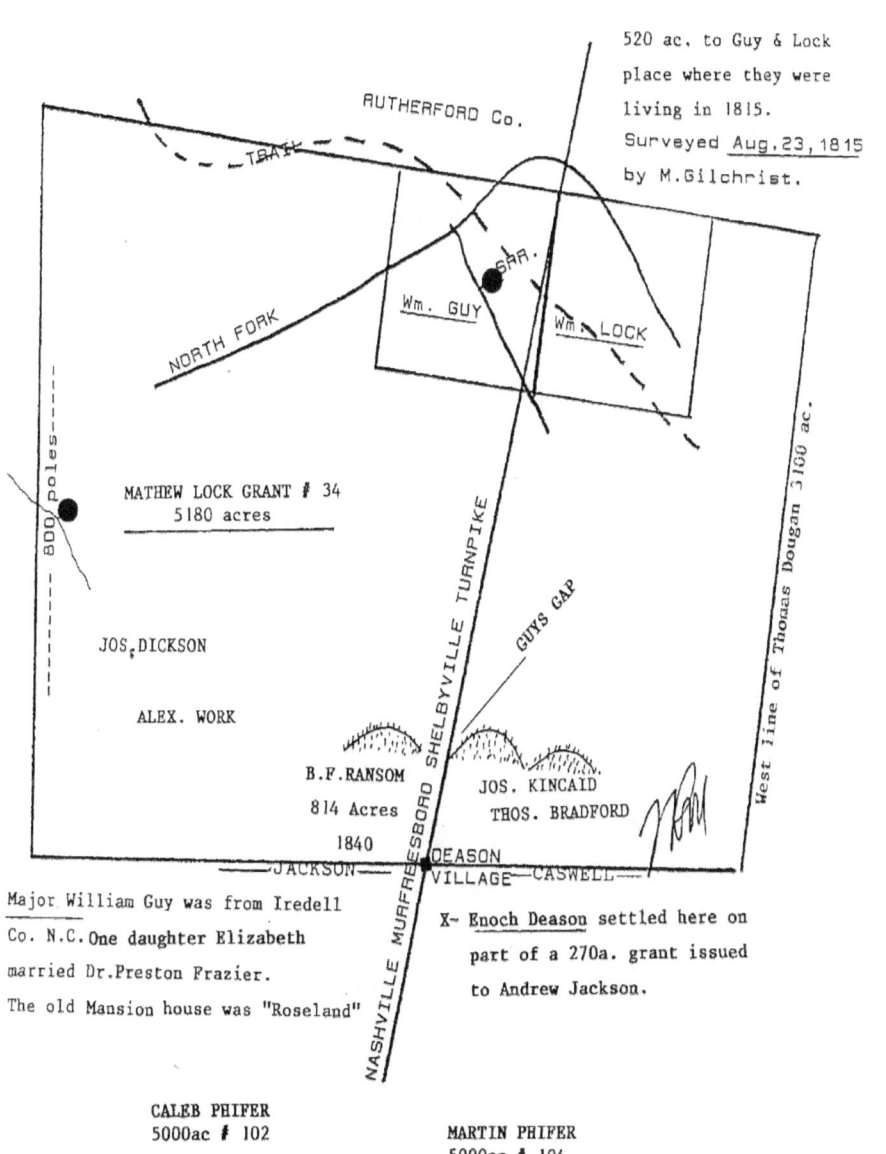

********* SOUTH EAST OF SHELBYVILLE *********

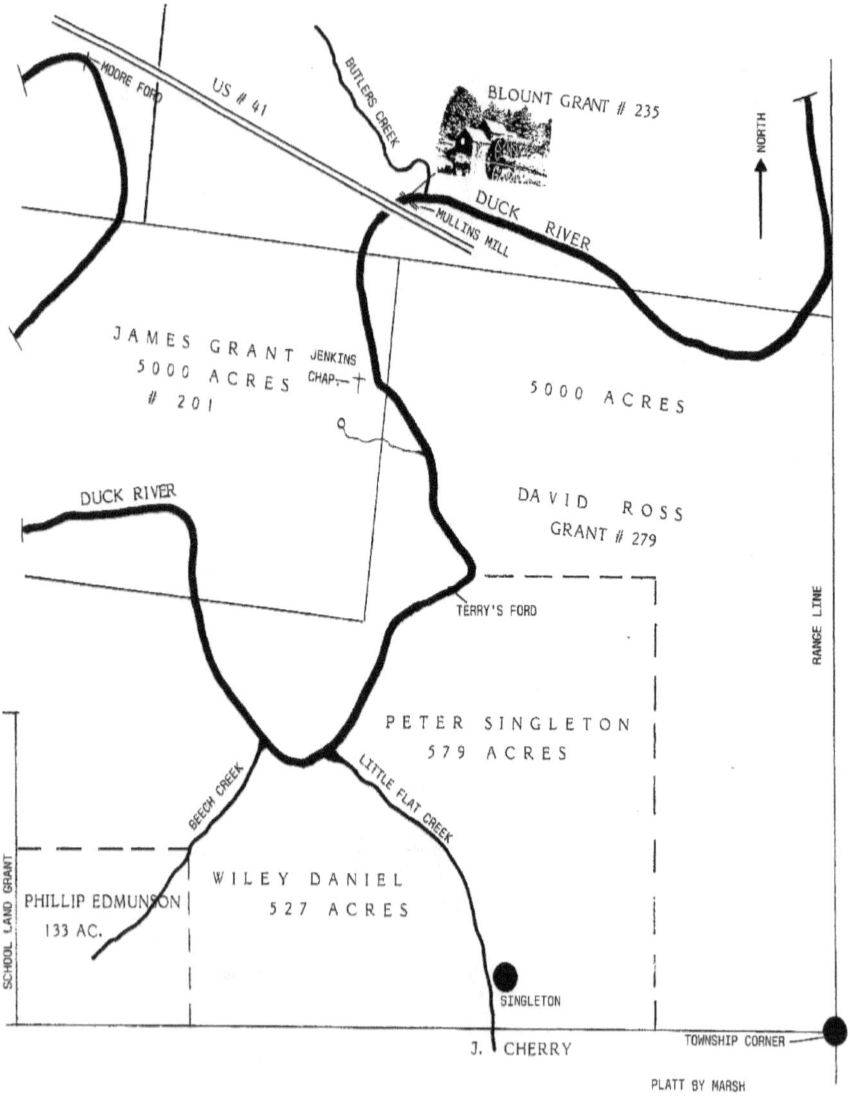

380

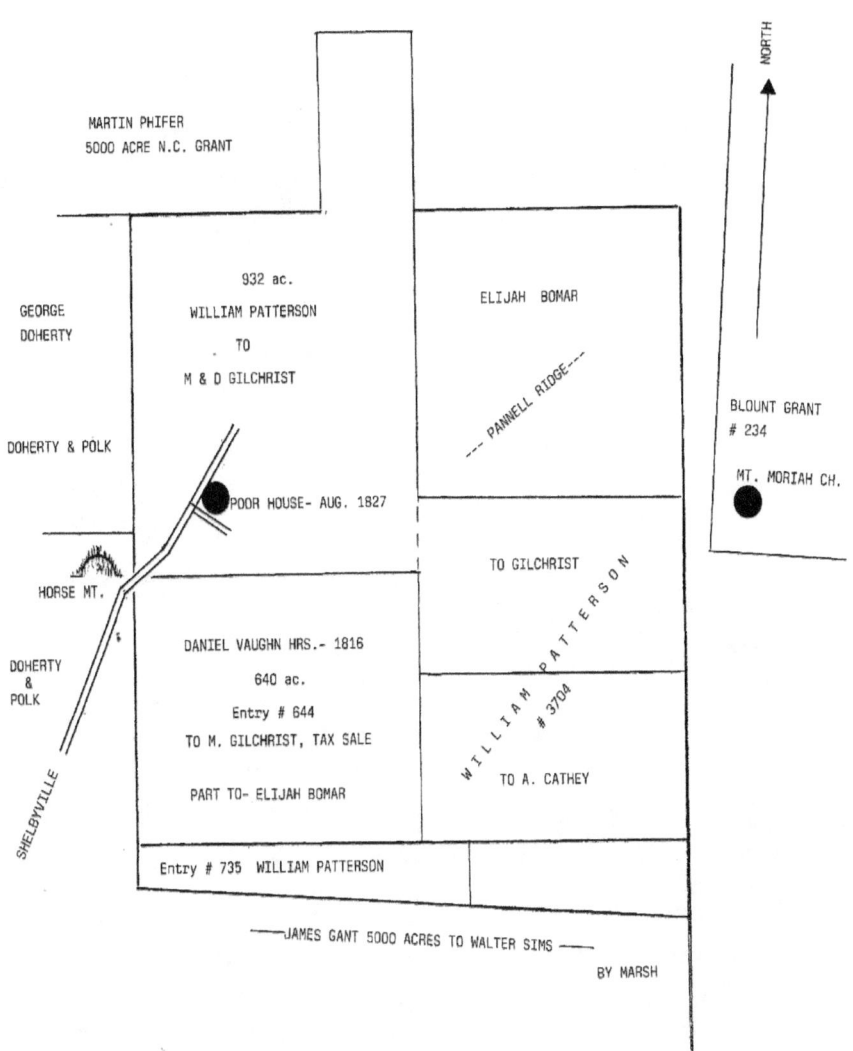

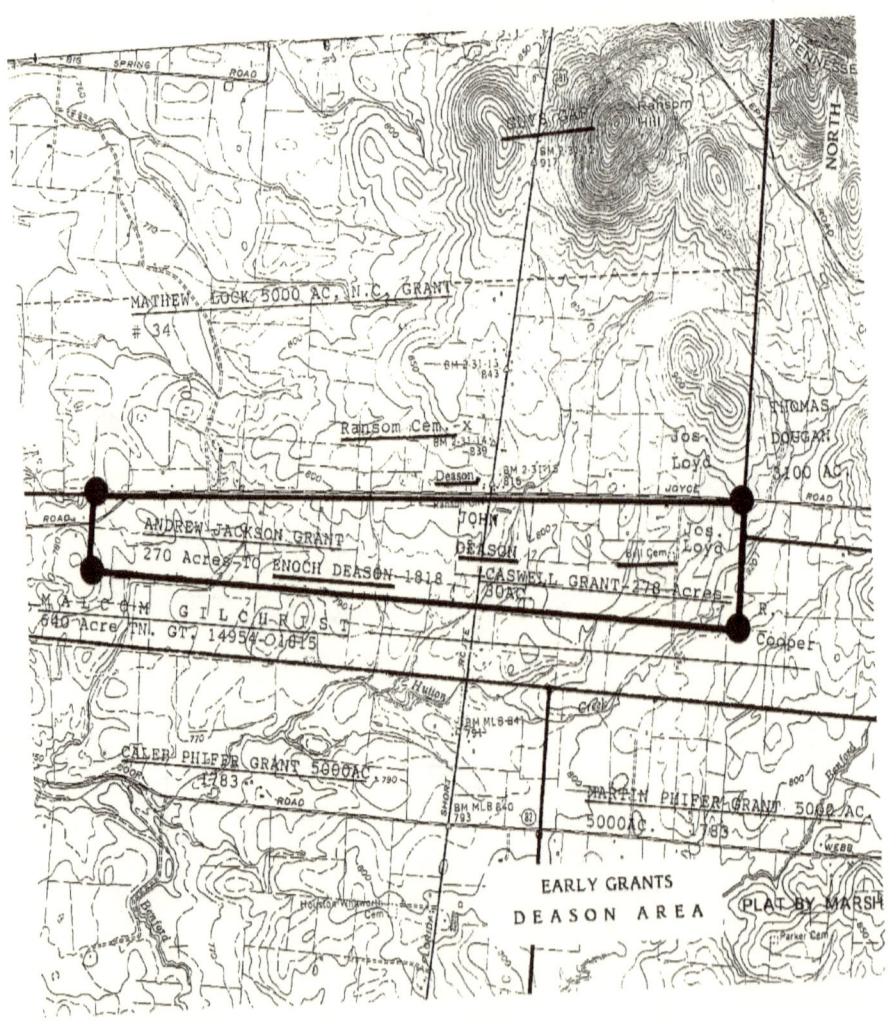

EARLY GRANTS
DEASON AREA
PLAT BY MARSH

★★★★★ BELL BUCKLE PLAT ★★★★★

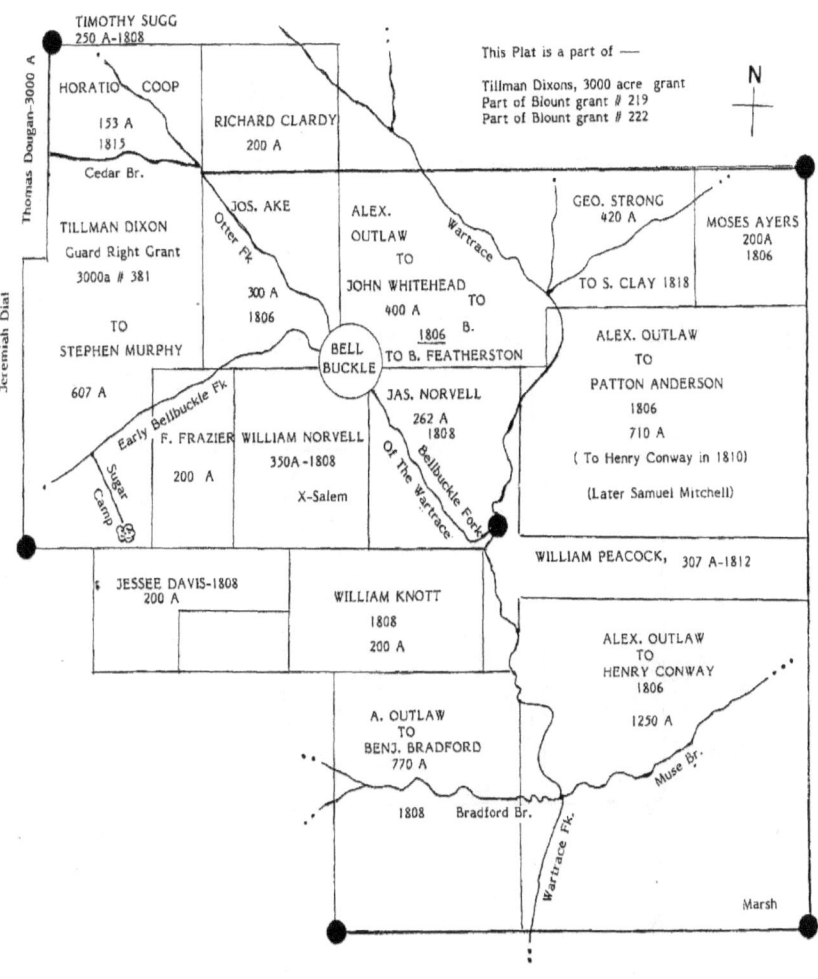

GEORGE DOHERTY 5000 ACRE GRANT

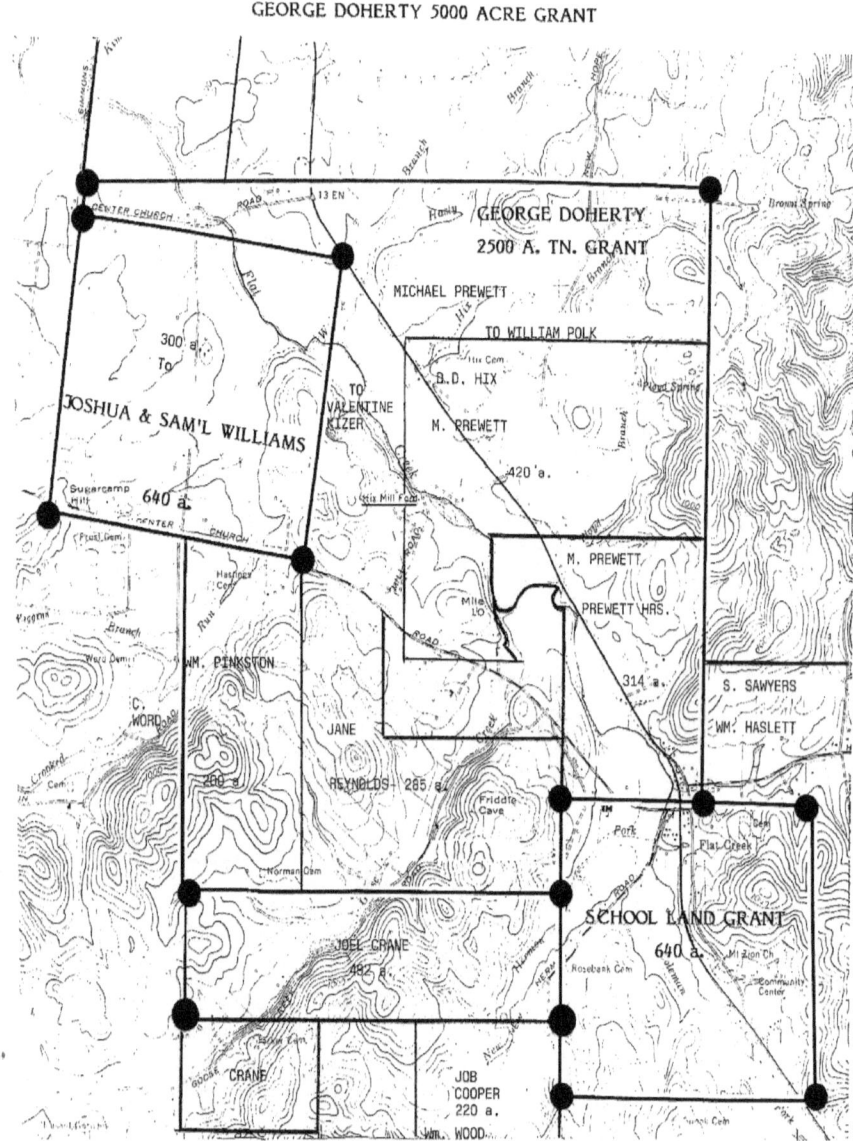

FLAT CREEK LAND GRANTS

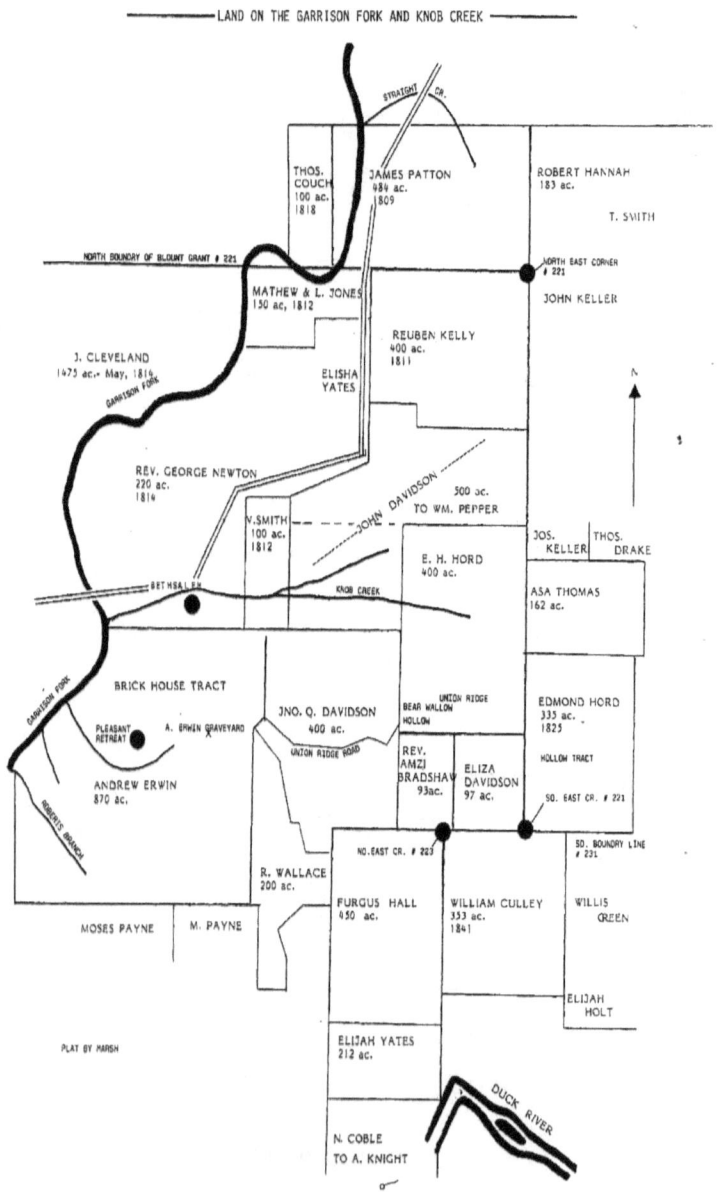

GRANTS ALONG THE NORTH FORK & ALEXANDER CREEK ******

The Marsh Collection

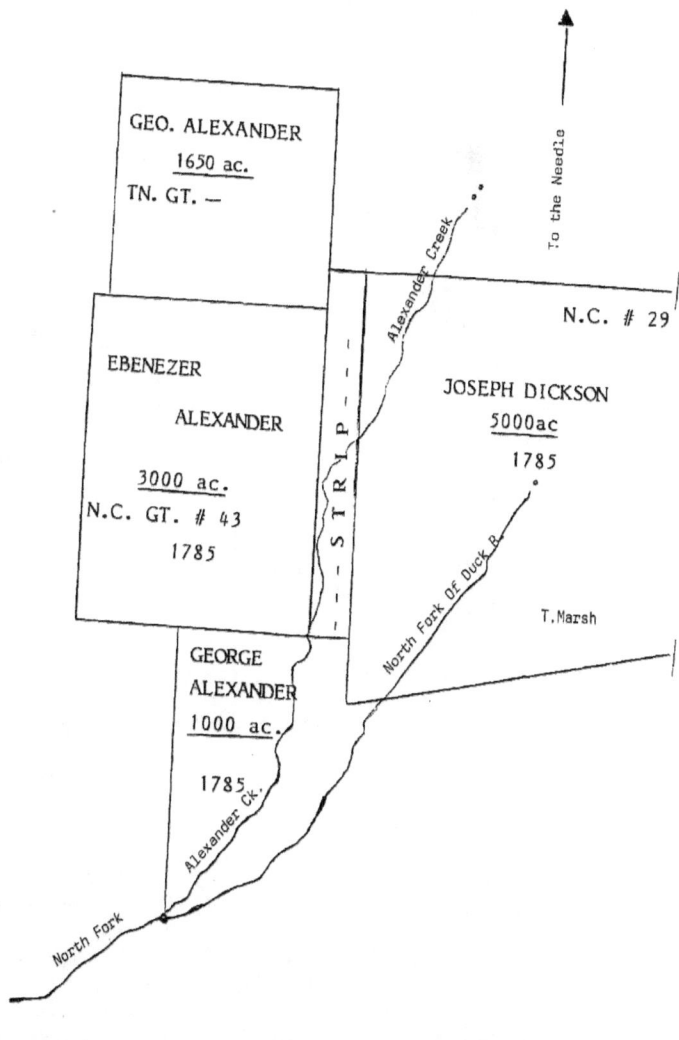

by
Timothy R. & Helen C. Marsh
1998

JOHN DONALSON TO STEPHAN MURPHY
Remainder of Tillman Dixon's 3000 Acre Guard Right Grant
Waters of Bell Buckle Creek
607 Acres

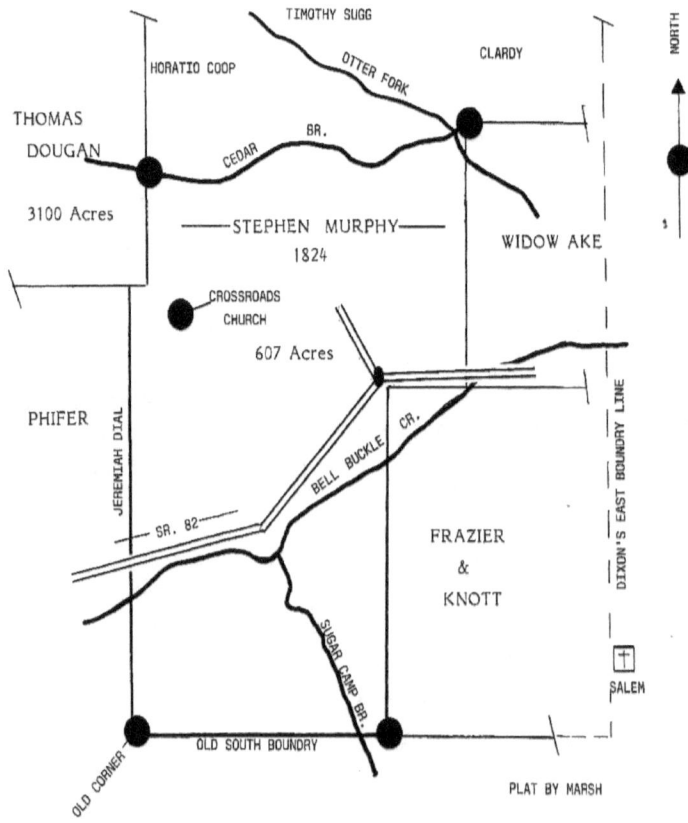

GUARD RIGHT GRANTS ******

The 3,000 acre tract that was issued to Tillman Dixon as shown in the above plat was granted him for his services in the North Carolina Commission Guard, a contingent of men appointed by the Legislature of the state of North Carolina in 1782, to set aside and survey a hugh tract of land located in north central Tennessee that had been appropriated to the officers and soldiers of the Continental line for their services to the state during the Revolutionary war. This tract was called the " Military Reservation " and was a fifty five mile wide strip that ran North & South from the Virginia, now Kentucky line, to a South line that ran immediately south of Murfreesboro,Tennessee. The East-West survey of the Reservation extended westward from the eastern boundry of the Reservation that ran North & South from where the Cumberland River crossed the Virginia line to near Rock Island, in White County, to the Tennessee River to the west.This contingent of surveyors were under the command of General Rutherford.

In February of 1783 another group of the Commissioners set out southward to Latitude Hill in Giles County, Elk River to ascertain the Thirty Fifth Parallel, or the southern boundry of the state of North Carolina, now Tennessee. Dickson settled in Smith County Tennessee. His grant was located in Bedford County because all the land in the Military Reservation had been appropriated by the time of his entry.

Marsh

******** DUCK RIVER-FALL CREEK-HURRICANE CREEK ********
LAND GRANTS

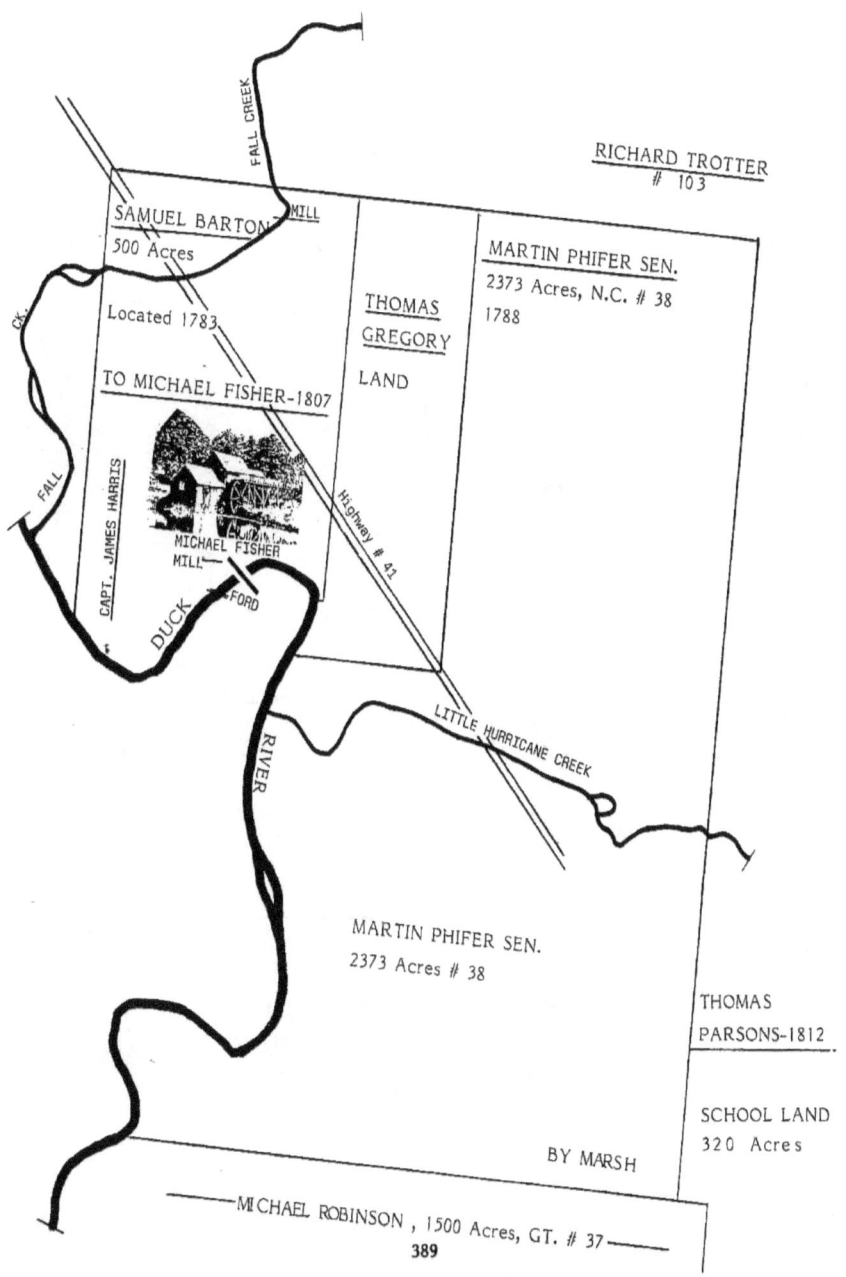

—LAND GRANTS—
AT
SHELBYVILLE

ROBERT W. SMITH AND JAMES GRANT
NORTH CAROLINA 5000 ACRE GRANTS
AT SHELBYVILLE, TENNESSEE

ROBERT W. SMITH and JAMES GRANT NORTH CAROLINA 5000 ACRE GRANTS

DESCRIPTION OF SMITH and GRANT

A - Robert W. Smith   Grant No. 15   5000 acres   Surveyed September 7, 1785 by Robert Weakley

Robert W. Smith lived in Cabarrus County, North Carolina. He never came to Tennessee. His grant was surveyed in September 1785 by Robert Weakley who surveyed thousands of acres in the Shelbyville area of Duck River. It should be noted here that it was later discovered by subsequent surveys that the adjoining James Grant 5000 acre No. 203, labeled E, was located and entered over much of the Robert W. Smith Grant No. 15. The James Grant land was not surveyed until 1792, seven years after the Weakley survey of the Smith grant, and the early land records were often vague and incomplete causing great confusion. This dispute with the James Grant land, later to be the Gideon Dennison land was in litigation for many years.

EARLY DIVISION OF THE SMITH GRANT NO. 15

B - Robert W. Smith to Clement Cannon of Williamson County, Tennessee   March 23, 1810   1000 acres

It has been said repeatedly that Cannon made the trip on horseback, with the purchase money in gold in his saddlebags, to Cabarrus County, North Carolina to purchase the thousand acres out of the Smith Grant. At this date, we have only tradition to confirm this statement.

The thousand acre tract was situated along the extreme western end of the Smith Grant and included the 100 acre tract later became Shelbyville.

C - Clement Cannon to the Commissioners   100 acres   May 2, 1810

The Town of Shelbyville was laid out on this tract in 1810. Sale of Lots began in May of said year.

D - Robert W. Smith to Clement Cannon   1552 acres   1811

This tract joined the above thousand acre tract on the west and the James Grant land on the east and was located on both sides of Duck River. Clement Cannon later settled on the southern part of this purchase and is buried in his family graveyard now located in the City of Shelbyville.

E - Clement Cannon to Wilson Coats   640 acres   1813

Beginning where Walter Sims' west boundary strikes the north bank of Duck River, north 321 poles to the north boundary of Robert W. Smith's 5000 acre grant, of which this is a part, west 269 poles, south 124 poles, east 2/3 pole, south 226 poles to the north side of the new road from Shelbyville to Winchester, now State Road No. 130, with said road South 49 degrees East, etc. etc., ... to bank of Duck River, thence up river to beginning. It was on this tract, on the river, at Coney Island, that James Sharp established the first grist mill east of the Town of Shelbyville. The mill changed hands numerous times down through the years. The old Coats graveyard is located in the north west section of this purchase.

F - James Grant   North Carolina Grant No. 203   5000 acres   Surveyed September 1, 1792 by John Donelson

As previously stated, this grant was entered and surveyed, overlapped much of the Robert W. Smith grant. The clear title remainder was transferred to G. Dennison and Dennison sold said remainder, amounting to 2448 acres to Walter Sims in 1816. Sim's mill was established up Duck River from Sharp's mill.

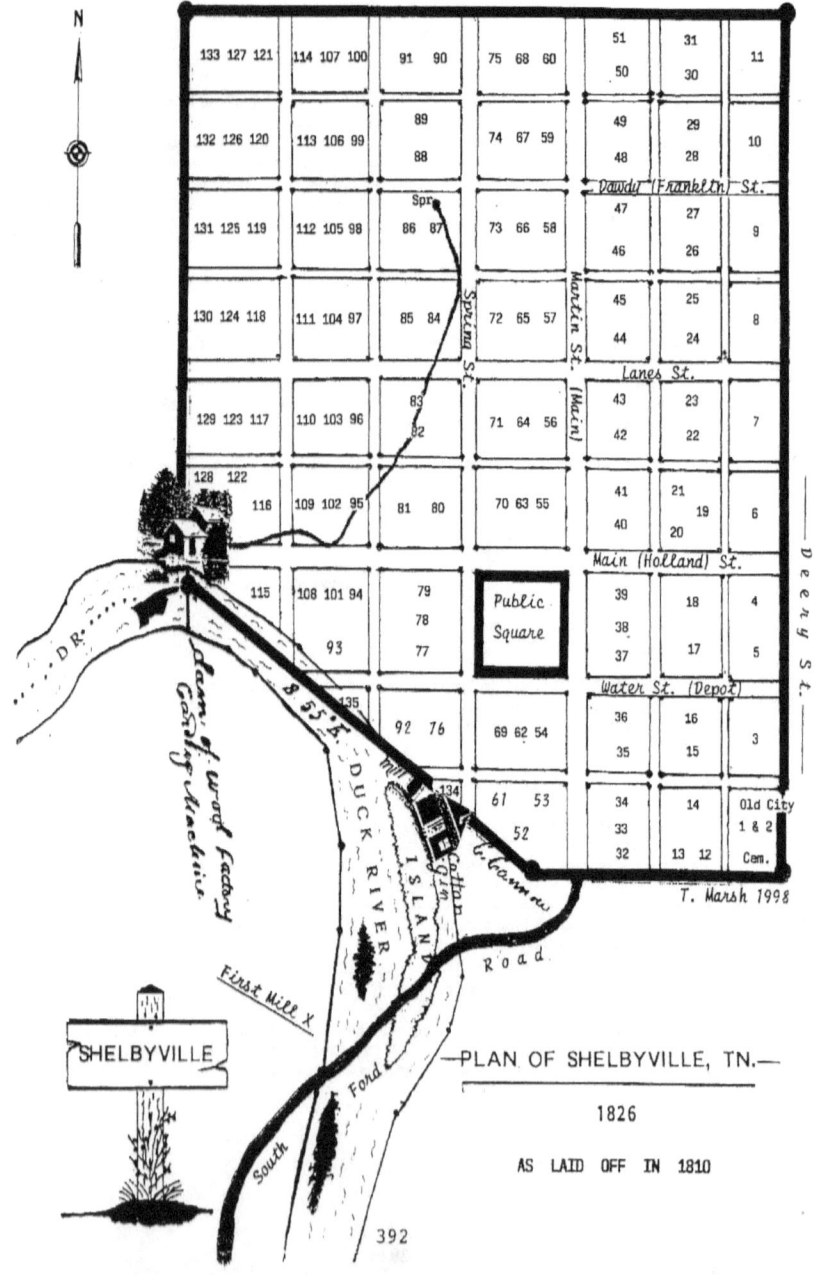

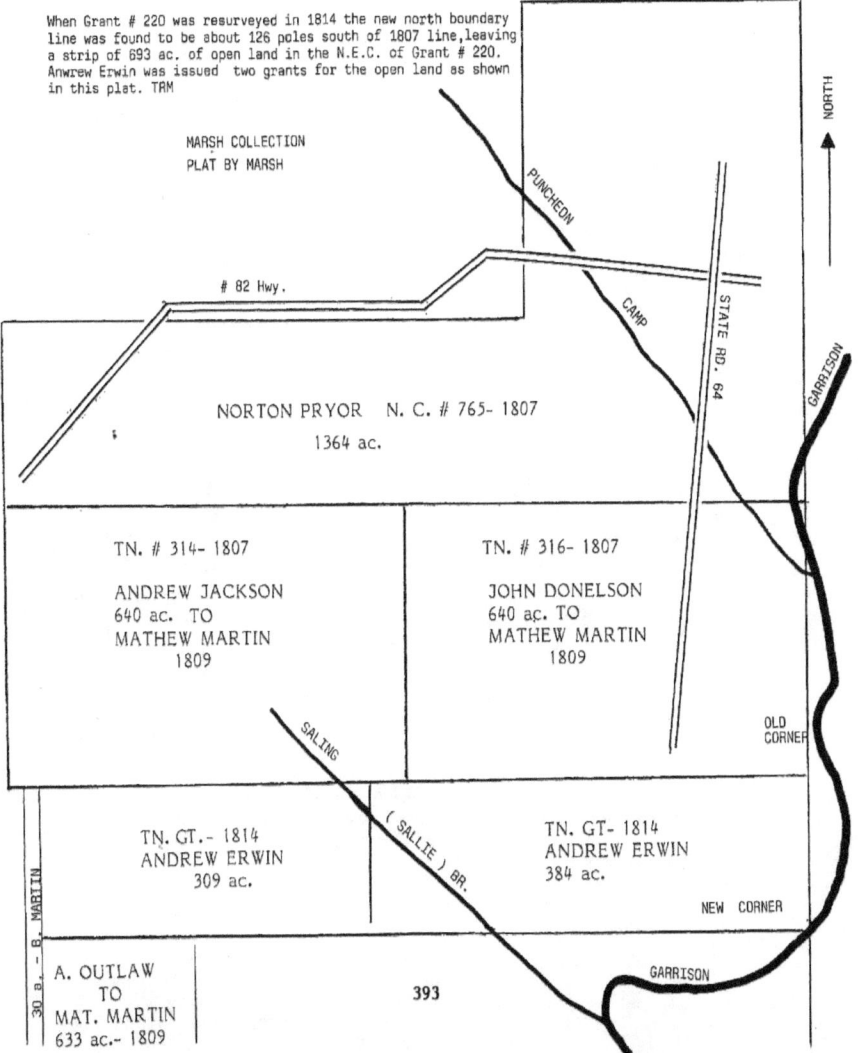

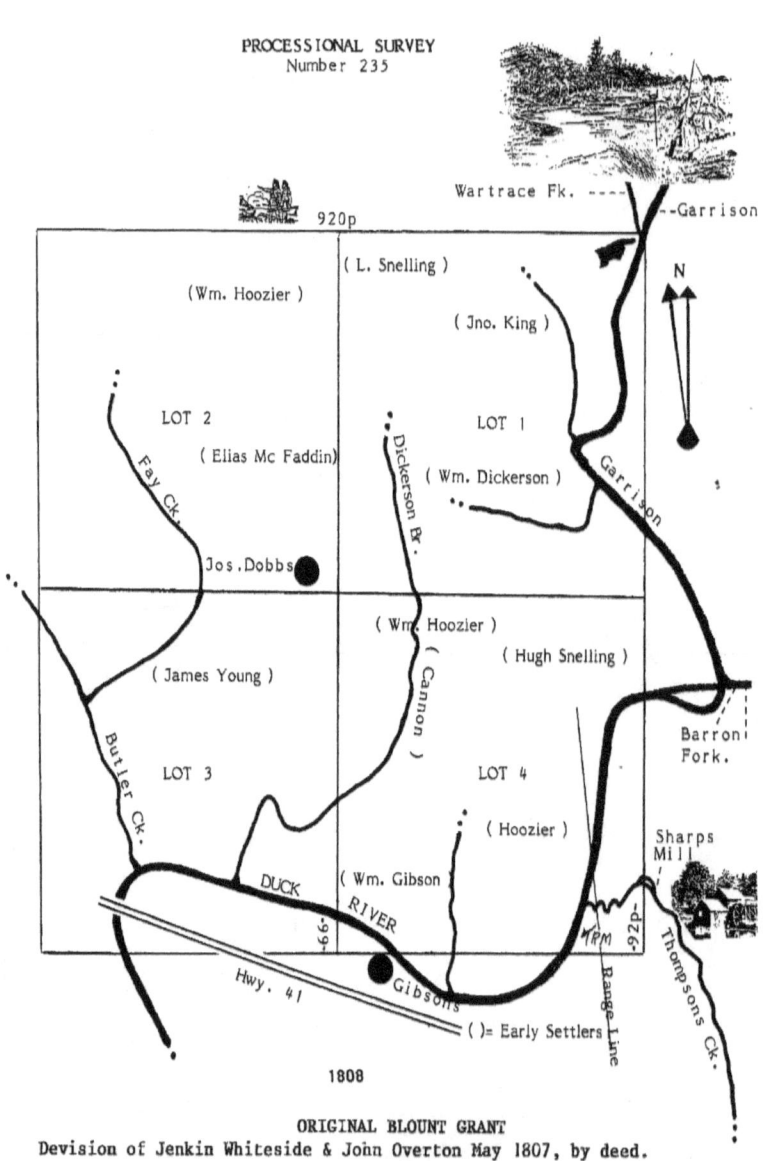

ORIGINAL BLOUNT GRANT
Devision of Jenkin Whiteside & John Overton May 1807, by deed.
Survey by William Gilchrist

Blount
Grant #234 --- 5000 a   *Granted 1793*

Grant purchased by Andrew Jackson at marshals sale
1802
Plat shows devision of grant

THE JACKSON CORNER

In 1806 Andrew Jackson, while attempting to locate the north east corner of his recently aquired grant number 234, mistakenly marked his corner on the wrong cherry tree, not finding the original forked cherry. This mistake generated confusion with overlapping of grants 234 & 222 untill 1814 when the original forked cherry corner was relocated.

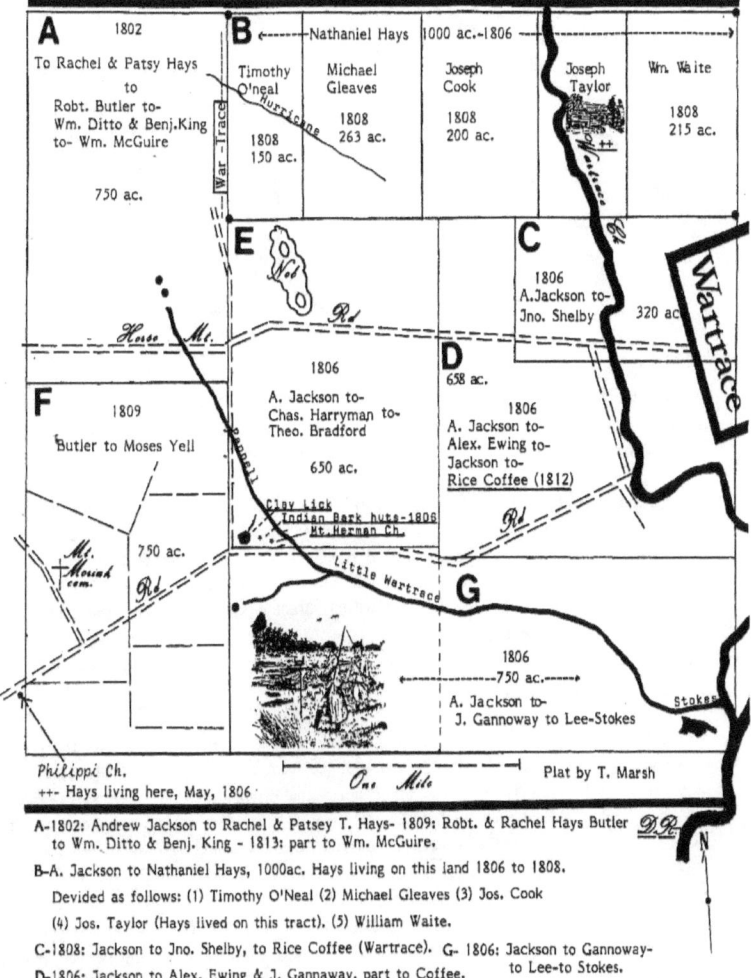

A-1802: Andrew Jackson to Rachel & Patsey T. Hays- 1809: Robt. & Rachel Hays Butler to Wm. Ditto & Benj. King - 1813: part to Wm. McGuire.

B-A. Jackson to Nathaniel Hays, 1000ac. Hays living on this land 1806 to 1808.
  Devided as follows: (1) Timothy O'Neal (2) Michael Gleaves (3) Jos. Cook
  (4) Jos. Taylor (Hays lived on this tract). (5) William Waite.

C-1808: Jackson to Jno. Shelby, to Rice Coffee (Wartrace).   G- 1806: Jackson to Gannoway-
D-1806: Jackson to Alex. Ewing & J. Gannaway, part to Coffee.   to Lee-to Stokes.
E-1806: Jackson to Chas. Harryman, to Theo. F. Bradford, 640 ac.
F-1809: Robt. Butler to Moses Yell, 750 ac., part to Sam'l. Phillips.

395

***** SNELL-GABBERT LAND *****

548 Acres

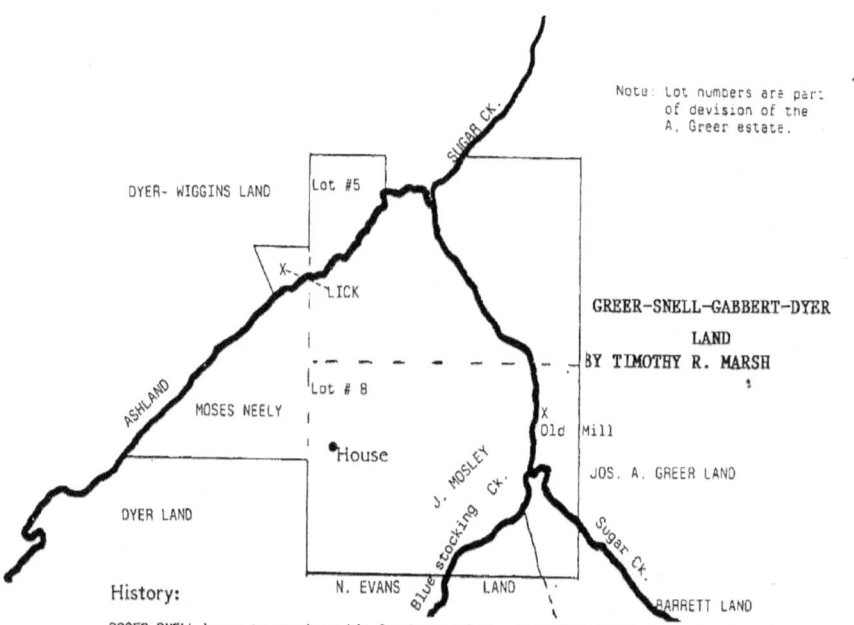

History:

ROGER SNELL began to purchase his land out of the ALEXANDER GREER North Carolina Grant as early as 1831. By 1845 he had accumulated 548 acres of the most valuable land of the old Greer grant, from the heirs of ALEXANDER & JANE GREER.

It appears that by 1845 SNELL had become "Land Poor" and in a desperate attempt to recover, mortgaged his 548 acres (main tract) that included the tract he lived on- to his son JAMES F. SNELL, then sold his personal property to help pay off debts before moving to Arkansas. That same year son James F., sold the 548 acres to WILLIAM GABBERT of Bartholomew Indiana for the amount of $5480.00. GABBERT then moved onto the land locating on Sandusky road where the HEFFNERS now live. The next year, in 1846, he purchased 150 acres adjoining his 548 acre tract from JOHN MOSLEY. This tract included the Swamp lands and joined DAVID DRYDEN 35 acre Mill tract.

GABBERTS wife died in Aug. 1849 and is buried in the family Graveyard across the road from the house. GABBERT remarried with-in the year to MARY ANN HOLLAND. GABBERT died in Jan. 1852 survived by wife Mary Ann and other heirs. The Widow Mary Ann later married JOHN T. HASTINGS son of a prominent Bedford County family. They were the G. Grandparents of Mr. Hart Hastings who with his wife Patricia live on the Lewisburg Hwy. at Knight Camp-Ground Road.

By the 1870's the house that stood (stands) in the turn of the road on Sandurky where GABBERT had lived was owned by W. H. DYER. At this time an old neighborhood road left Sanduskly and ran north, crossing the creek on to and past the old SCALES place, now (1995) the Doctors STIMPSON home. S.G. DYER lived the next house south, off Sandusky.

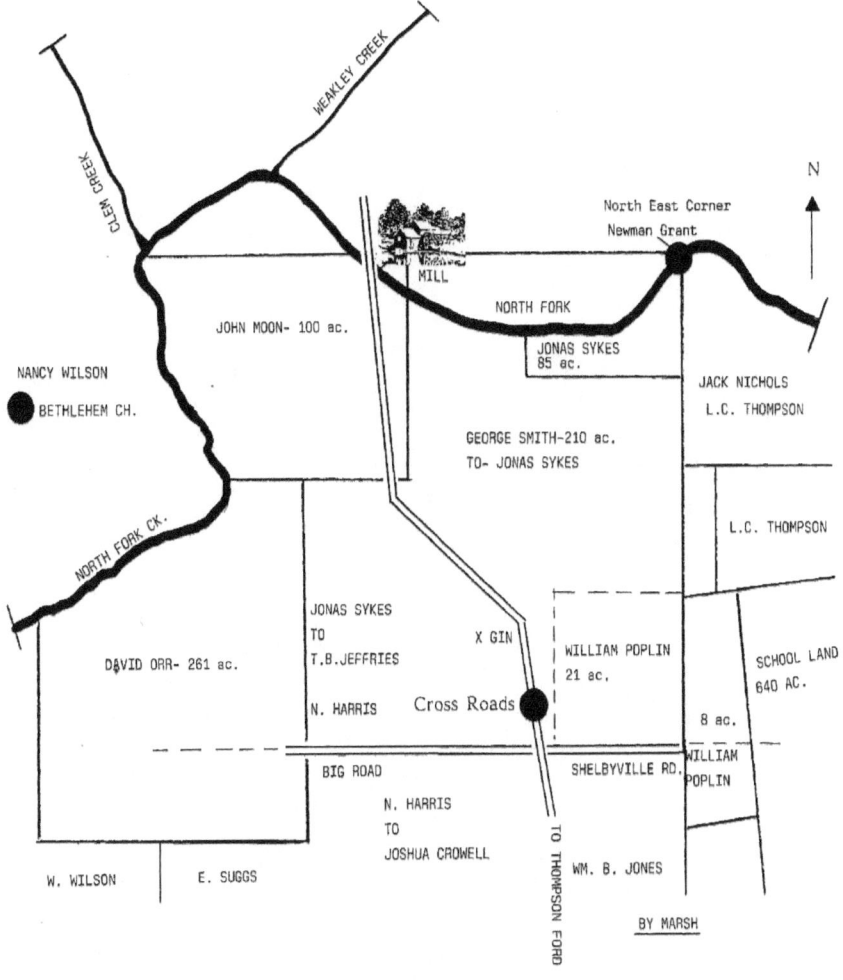

****** DEEDS ON THE NORTH FORK AT POPLINS CROSS ROADS ******
NORTH EAST CORNER OF NEWMAN GRANT

ARRENDUM PAGE

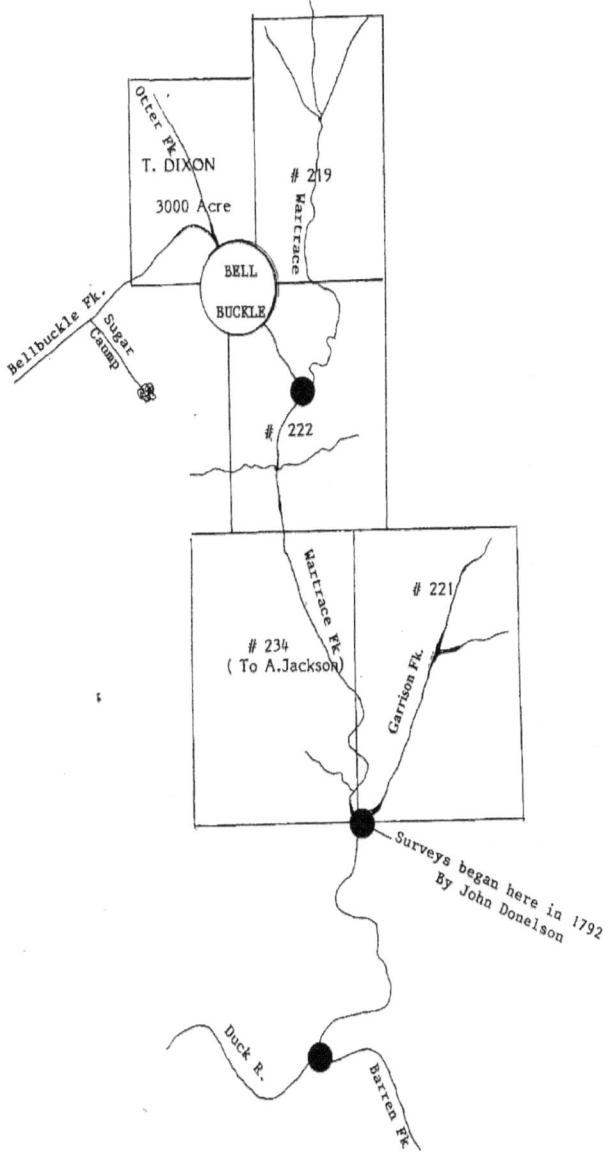

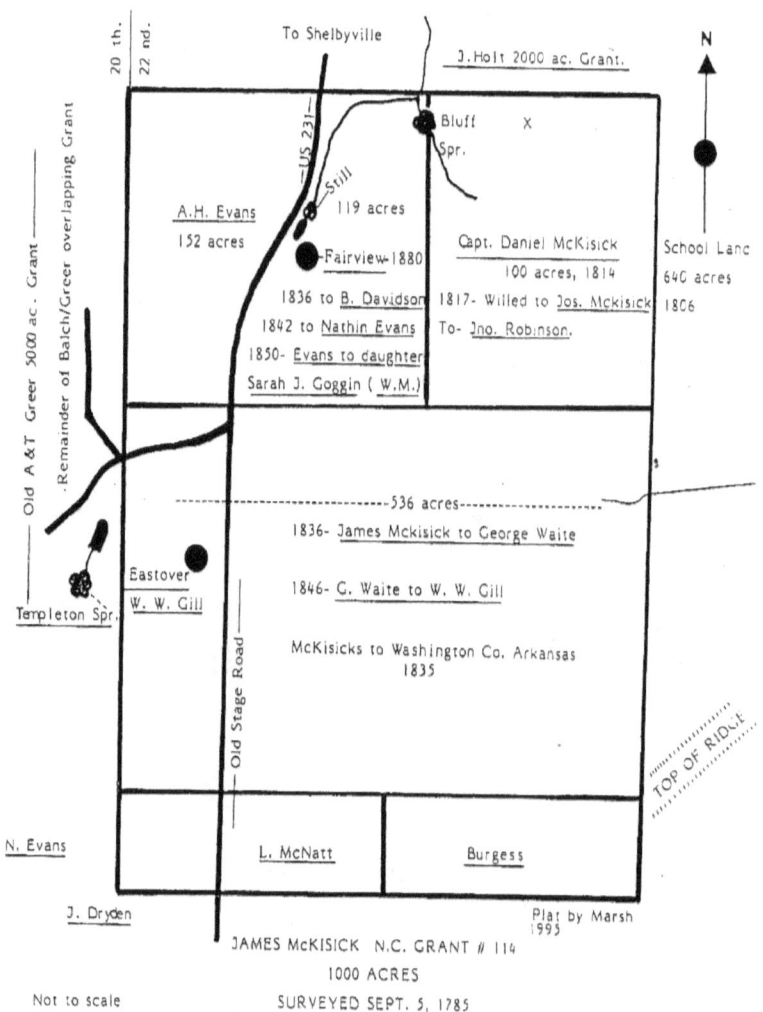

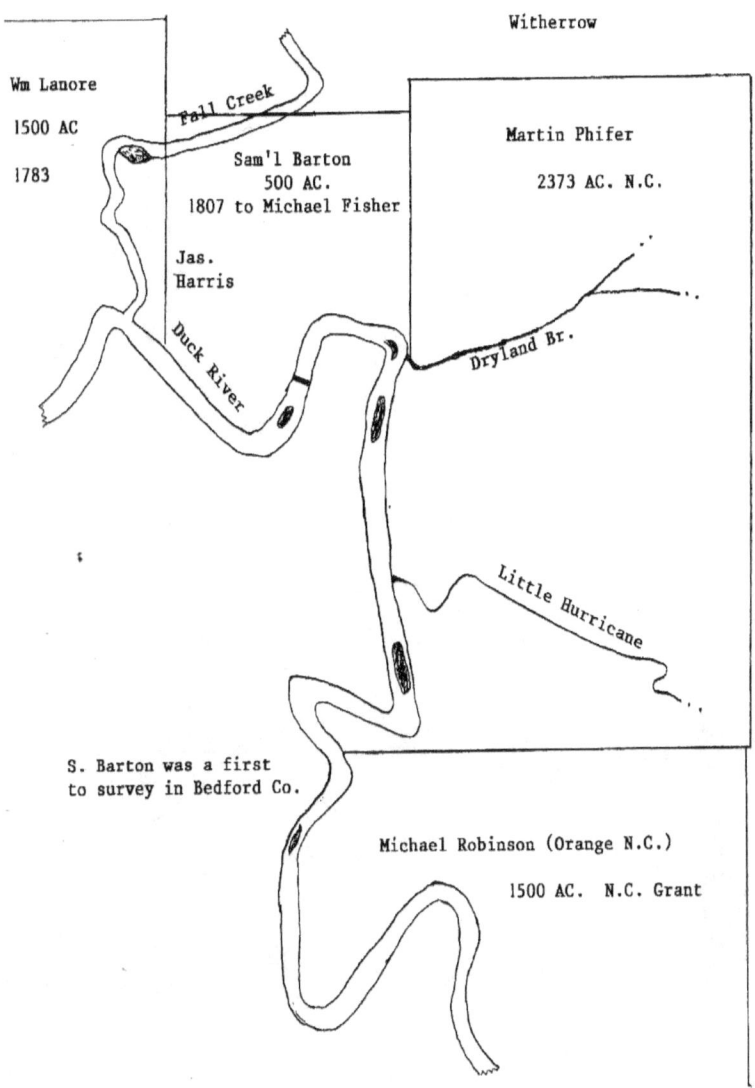

*********** BEDFORD COUNTY BEFORE THE REDUCTION ***********

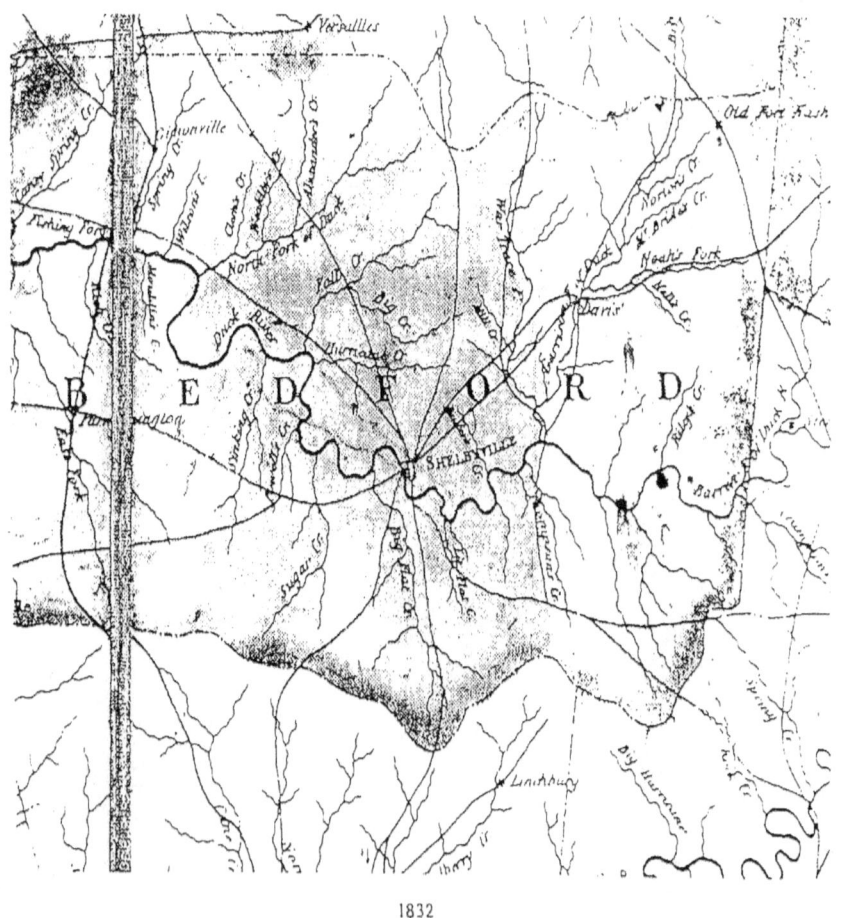

1832

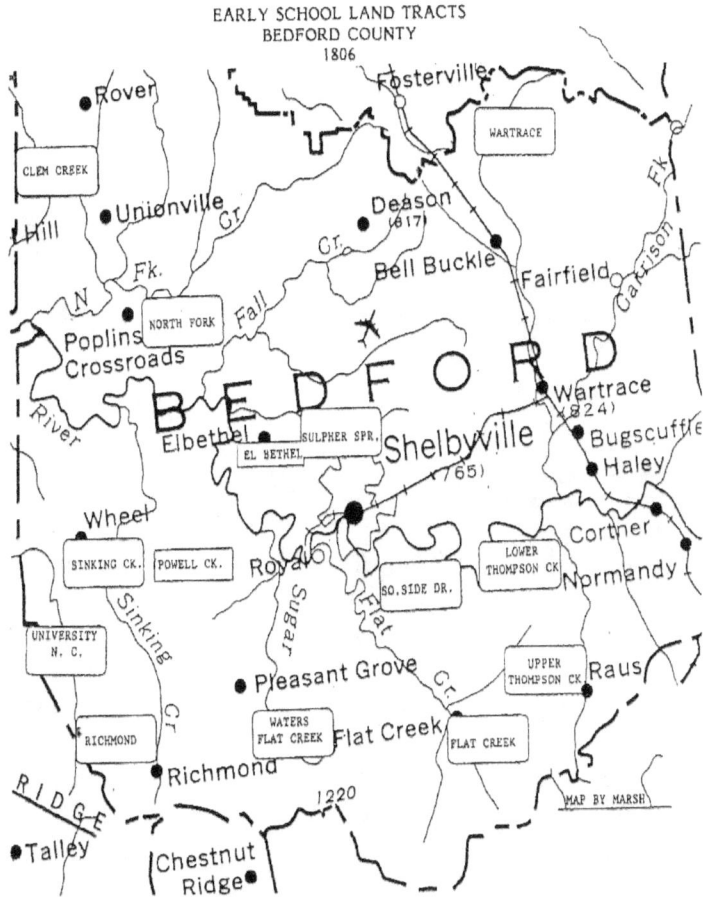

EARLY SCHOOL LAND TRACTS
BEDFORD COUNTY
1806

In 1806, the legislature directed the Surveyor General of the Second Surveyors District, including South Central Tennessee, south of the old Military Reservation, to section off that area into sections and townships of six miles square each and in each section to lay off as near the center of each section as pre-existing entries would permit, a tract of six hundred and fifty acres to be set aside for the purpose of the common schools. This land was known as school land and was mentioned in the calls of early land surveys. By about 1850, all these tracts were auctioned off to the highest bidder and Tennessee grants were issued. Marsh

WARTRACE SCHOOL SECTION
1806

717+ ACRES

```
                    — N. Chaffin Land —
                         300 poles
        78 poles              252 poles
        I.J.MILLER            RICHARD S. THOMAS
        63 A.                 208 A.
        # 24436               # 24435
        Ju. 1857              Apr. 1857
                                                 WARTRACE FORK    142 poles
                 107 poles
                              88 poles                88 poles
        ELNATHAN DAVIS
        108 A.                        JOHN NELSON
        # 24453                       145 A.
        Apr. 1857                     # 24434
                     166 poles        Apr. 1857
                                      LIBERTY PK.
                     JOSHUA MILLER                                 188 poles
                     193 A            (Later Beechboard)
                  BR # 24437
                     Ju. 1857         Graveyard
                                          X
        40p         199 poles             85 poles      William Sugg
        Plat: T. R. Marsh
                         — Brooks Mill —
                                X
```

N ↑

This plat of the old controversial <u>WARTRACE SCHOOL SECTION</u> was surveyed out at 717+ acres in 1806. It was rented out by the County Common School Commission until 1857, when it was divided into lots and sold to the highest bidder to those listed on the plat. A Tennessee Grant was then issued to each owner. It, appears that <u>JOHN NELSON</u> had lived on his 145 acre purchase long enough before the division in 1857. Nelson, his wife and daughter, were probably the first to be buried in the old graveyard. The first division and owners of the school land was finally un-covered by us in May 1997 in the Tennessee State Archives. Records could not be found locally.   Tim & Helen Marsh, 1997

———INCORPORATION OF THE TOWN OF WARTRACE DEPOT———
OCT 3, 1853

This day a petition of the citizens of the town of Wartrace Depot in Bedford County was filed in court which petition is in the words and figures following, to wit,

State of Tennessee
Bedford County

   To the Worshipful County Court of Bedford County.
"The undersigned petitioners of the town of Wartrace Depot in said county, petition your worship to grant us the privilege of incorporating said village, running one quarter of a mile in every direction from the center of said Depot ground so as to elect officers to carry into effect the laws provided in such cases, and for the benefit of the good citizens of said village for which your petitioners will ever pray. This the 3 day of October 1853.

Daniel Stephens	B. Z. Gannaway	J. D. Payne
Robert Buchanan	John R. Coffee	A. E. Mullins
John Stephens	W. T. Green	Joseph Sherwood
N. C. Harris	Willis Pruett	Robert Erwin
W. H. Clark	T. A. Prince	M. Payne
W. B. Norville	R. E. Coffee	A. T. Garrett
G. W. Martin	T. C. Mills	H. M. Keller
R. P. Gannaway	Wm. H. Sims	J. W. Tilford
T. P. Gannaway	C. M. Norville	

and on motion it war ordered by said court that said town be incorporated as the town of Wartrace Depot with all the privileges and liabilities prescribed by the General Assembly of the State of Tennessee Chapter No. 17 passed January 7th 1850 and that the corporation of said town extended one quarter of a mile in every direction from the center of the Depot grounds.

   And it was ordered by the court that said petition be spread upon the minutes and that a copy of this entry properly certified be given for registration and that the same be registered in the Registers office in Bedford County, twelve acting Justices being present and voting in the affirmative.

P. C. Steele
Jos. Hastings
Wm. Galbreath

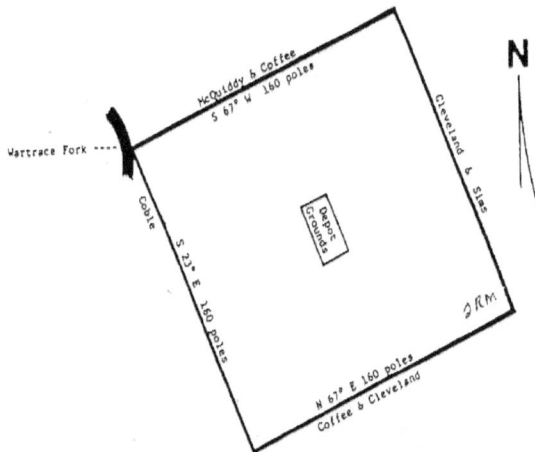

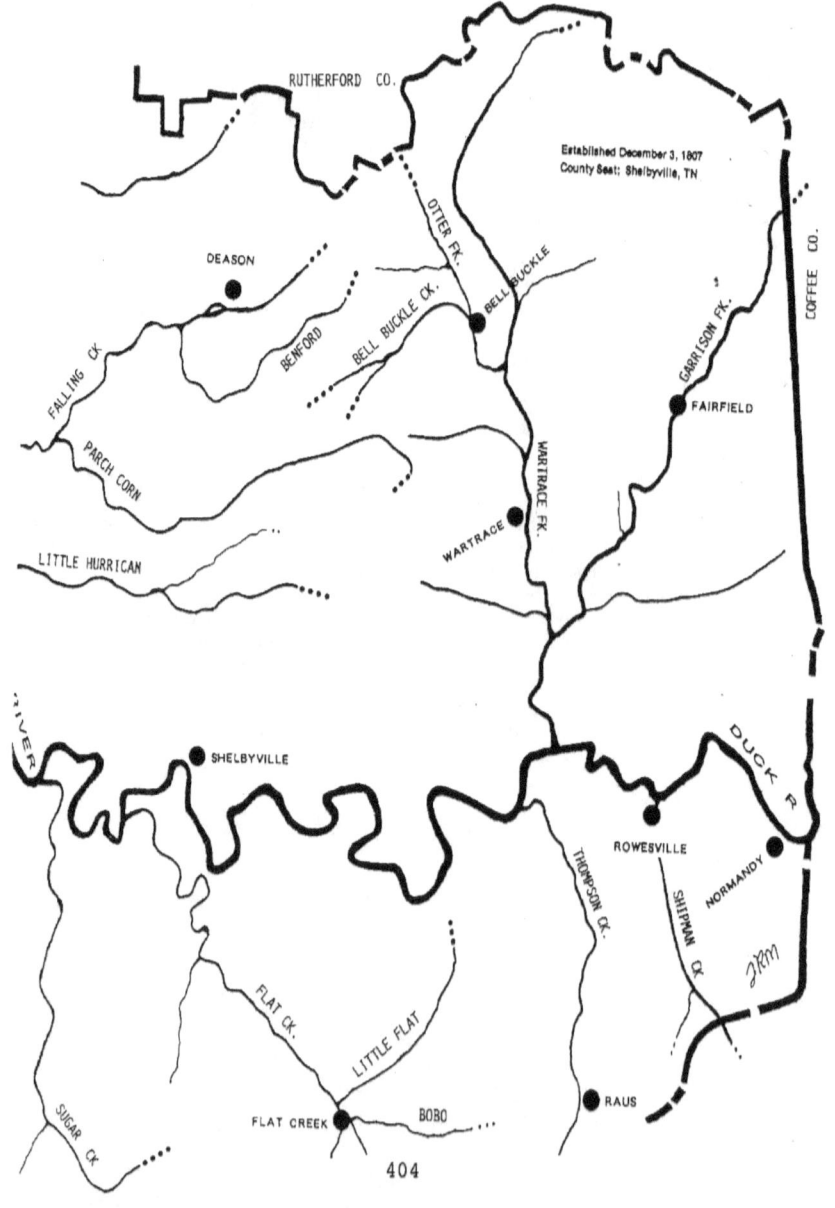

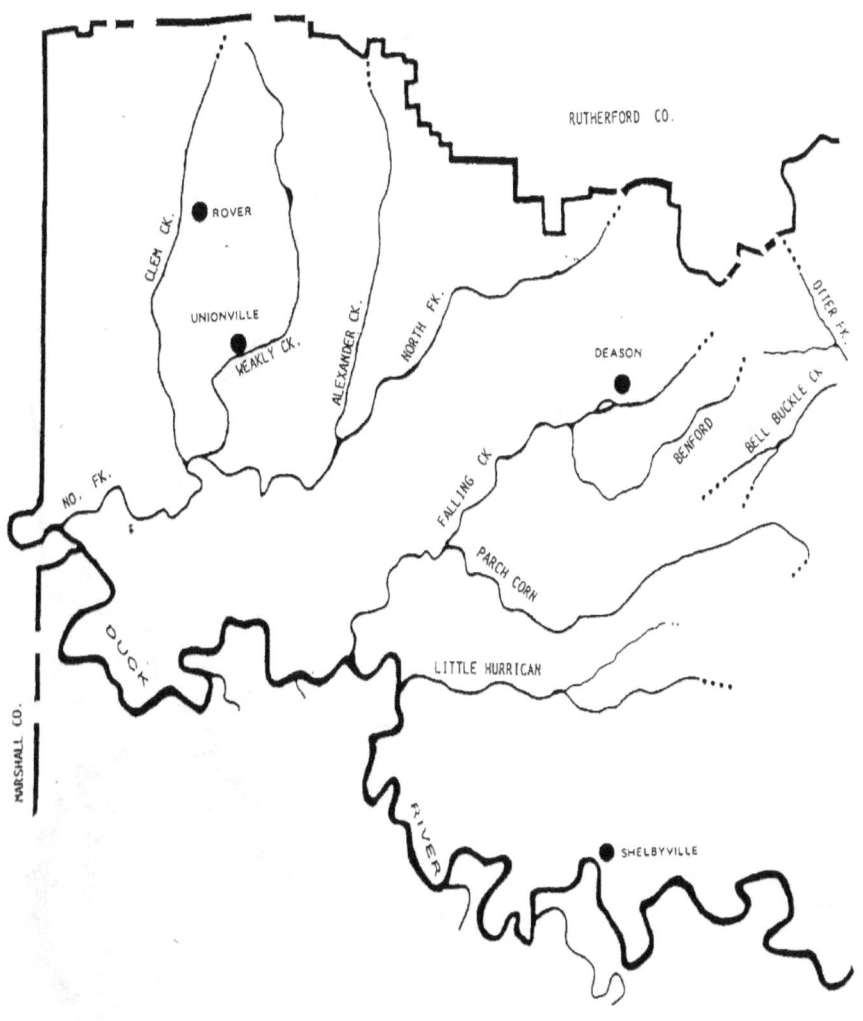

MAJOR STREAMS OF BEDFORD CO TN
NORTH WEST QUARTER

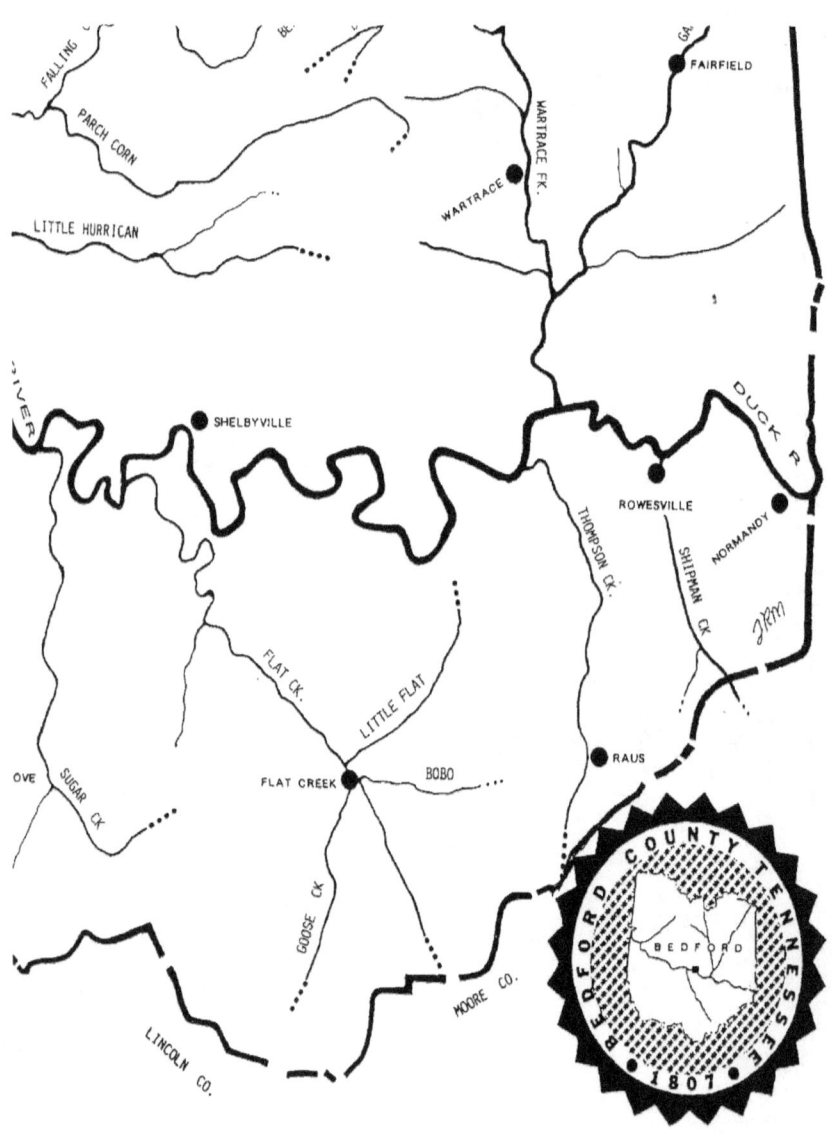

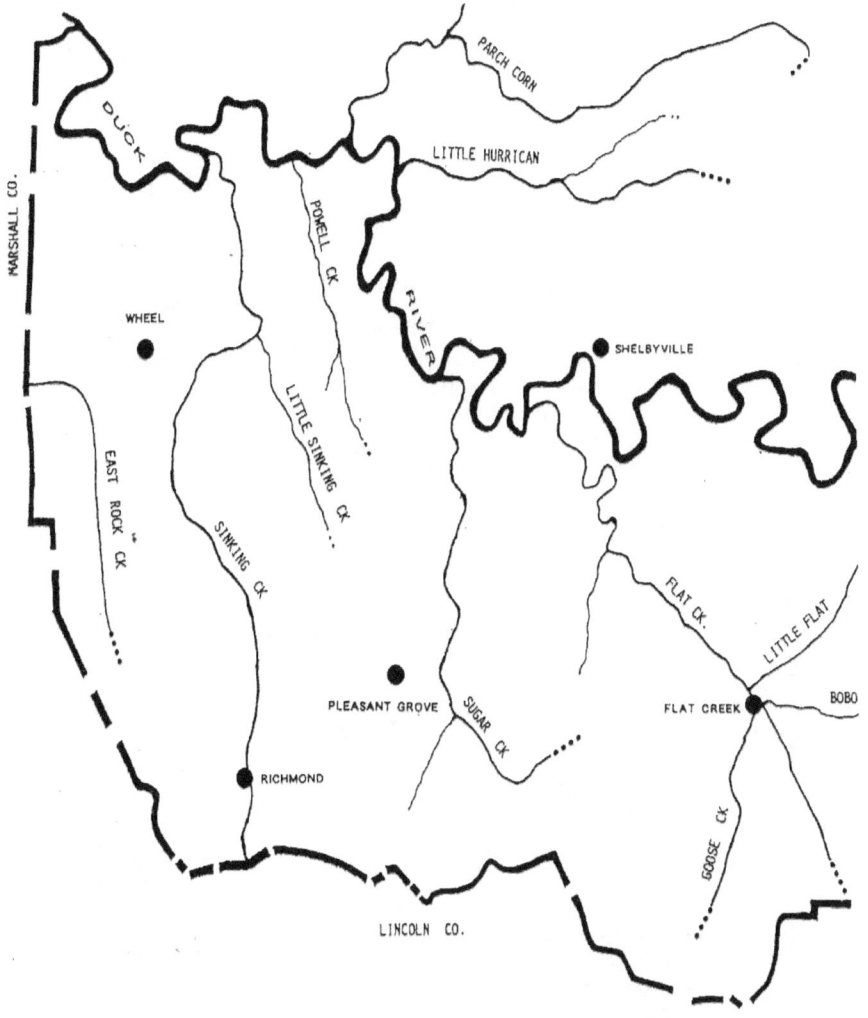

DOHERTY GRANTS NEAR RICHMOND

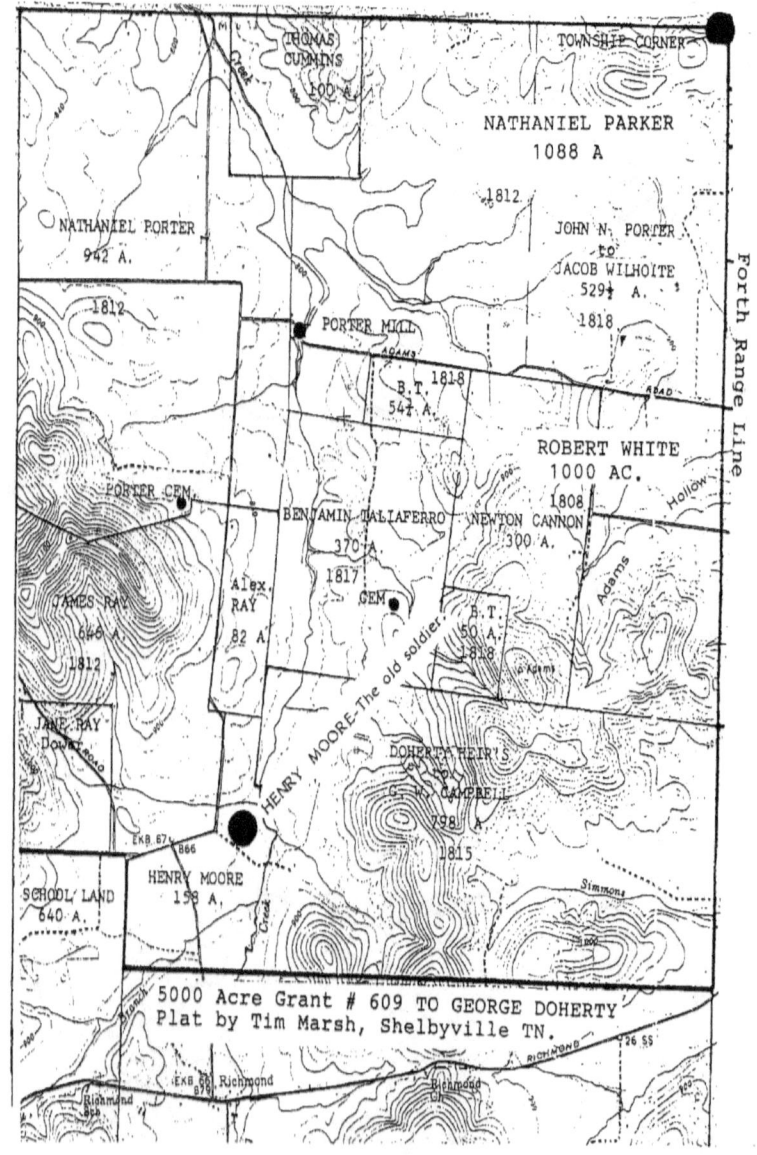

IN SEARCH OF THE STATE LINE

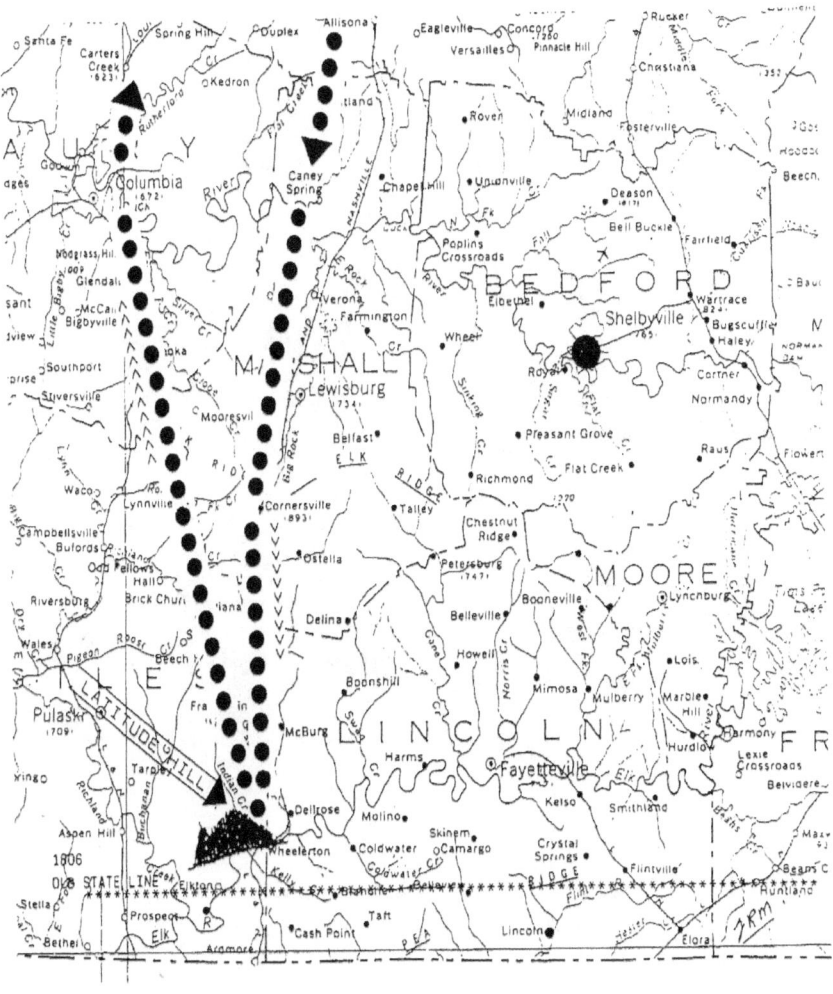

— MARSH MAP —
●●● ROUTE TAKEN BY THE COMMISSION GUARD IN SPRING OF 1783

THEY CAME THIS WAY

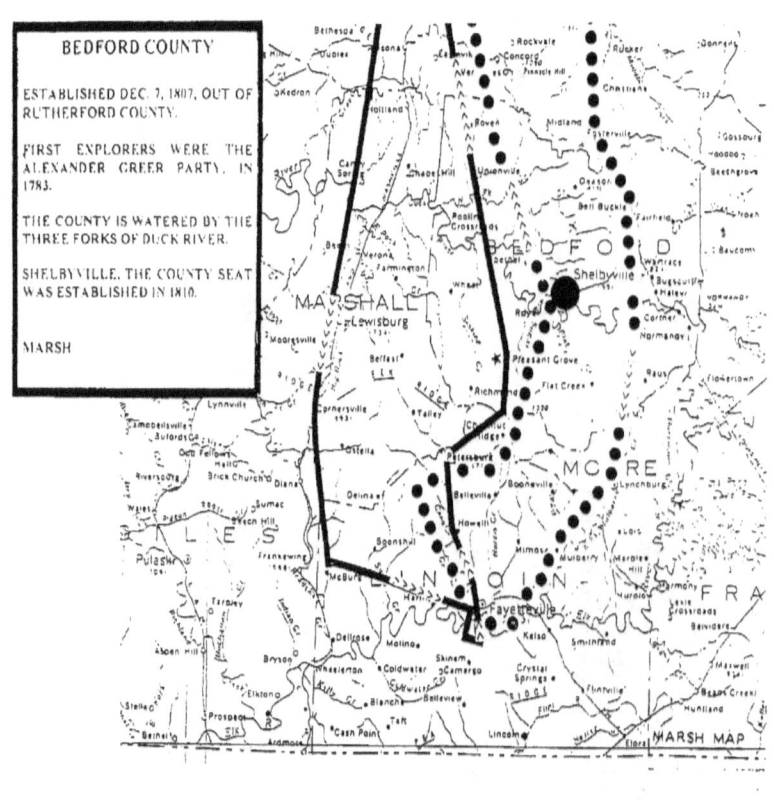

ROUTE OF ALEXANDER GREER LAND LOCATING PARTY IN AUG. 1783
● ● ● EDMISTON LAND LOCATING PARTY FEB. 1784
—Map by Marsh—

MASTER INDEX

Aaron, James	219
. Moses	219
. William	219
Abbott, Wilson	165
Adam, Thomas	245
Adams, A.C.	212, 215
. Alex. D.	212
. Archibald	224
. Benjamin	228
. Cophas	228
. Elizabeth	228
. James	224
. James Esq.	212
. James Jun.	212
. Joseph	228
. Martin	189, 192, 196
. Mary	224
. Robert W.	224
. William	189
. William W.	212
Adcock, Harmon	185
Henderson	183
Adkins, Margaret	241
Ake, Felix	72
. Joseph	23, 25, 73-75, 84, 86, 88
Aldridge, Flower	201
Alexander, Ebenezer	61
. Archibald	30, 35
. David	196
. Ebenezer	114, 137, 139
. Ezekiel	15
. George	15, 139
. James	185
. Joseph	231
. Memnon	205
. Nathl.	175
. Robert	114
. Wm.	196
Alford, John C.	185
Wm. H.	196
Allbright, Jacob	234
Allbritton, John	164
Allen, George H.	201
. John	208, 227
. John W.	161
. Josiah	227
. W.A.	107
. William R.	185
Allison, David	49-50, 53, 112
. James	224
. James P.	193
. Kimbro	137, 193
. Robert	137, 183
. Robt.	193
. Robt. J.	193
. Robt. Jun.	189
. Robt. Sen.	193
. Thomas	137, 189, 192-193
. Thomas H.	224
. William	137, 189
Alvis, Wm. C.	215
Amix, James	245
Anderson, Alfred	224
. Amzi D.	224
. David	193
. Elizabeth	219
. Jacob	161
. James	54
. James D.	224

Name	Page
. John	161
. John H.	38, 219
. Jon. H.	178
. Joseph	50-51, 73, 193
. Kenneth	54
. Livingston	219
. R.	219
. R.L.	178
. Richard	193, 219
. S.	219
. Saml.	219
. Samuel	171
. William	45, 193, 212
. William P.	45, 135
. Zachariah V.	164
Anderton, James Esq.	241
. John	241
. Mr.	241, 245
. Thomas	241
. Wm.	237
Andes, James	54
Andrews, B.G.	237
Benj.	228
Anglin, Adrain	165
. Adrain Jr.	164
. Adrain Sr.	164
. David W.	171
. Peyton	164
. Zephat	186
Anthony, Adam	245
. Alfred	234
. H.	237
. Henry	245
. Nicholas	245
Appleby, Saml.	234
Appleny, Benj.	205
. John Jun.	205
. John Sen.	205
. Samuel B.	205
. William	205
Armstrong, Dr.	127
. Dr. James	60, 66, 68
. Dr. James B.	25, 32
. Dr. James L.	143
. Geo. A.	212
. George C.	168
. Jas. L.	161
. John	224
. Nathan	224
. Robert	32
. Sophia Smith	32
. William	193
Arnold, Absalom	245
. Alsey	165
. Col.	164, 168
. D.D.	165
. Elijah	164, 175
. Elisha	189
. James	168
. Jesse	175
. John W.	189
. Joseph	189
. Joseph A.	189
. Joseph O.	30
. Mr.	98-99
. Nancy	237
. Richard	161
. Robert F.	245
. Smith	165
. Thomas	168
. Willie	165

Name	Page
. Wiseman	237
Arrington, R.S.	178
Ashby, W.D.	54
Atkins, Thomas	201
Atkinson, Isaiah	185, 189
. Isiah	192
. Jas. M.	189
. Jesse	189
. John	22, 26-28, 35-36, 84-85, 93-95, 97, 201
. Josiah	186
. Nancy	196, 201
. Squire	23-24
. Wm.	189
Atlinson, John	87
Ault, James H.	164
Margaret	164
Ausley, Wesley	208
Austin, Edmund	36
Ayers, Garland	245
. Moses	245
. Payne	161
Ayler, Anthony	245
Bailey, John	158
Bain, Andrew	228
Baird, John	39
Baired, John	133
Baker, James	158
. John	231
. Lewis	228
. William	197
Balch, Alfred	135, 178, 189
. Amos	13, 16-18, 28, 30, 32, 39, 54, 63, 82, 86, 89, 91, 95-96, 140
. Ann	29-30
. Ann Goodwin	17
. Ann Patton	63
. Geo. B.	34
. George	142
. George B.	91, 133
. Hezekiah	142
. Rev. James	17
. Saml. P.	228
Ballard, Baxter	197
. James	215
. Joel	215
. Thomas	215
Balls, Henry	189
Bandy, Richard	186
Bankston, Elliott	201
Barber, Ira	171
Thomas	171
Barkley, Mr.	193
Barksdale, J.G.	178
Wm. W.	224
Barnes, D.J.	186
Gabriel	186
Barnett, Isaac	245
John	245
Barnhill, Benj.	183
Barrett, John	228
Barringer, Genl. D.L.	189, 228
Bartlett, Joel	234
William	234
Barton, Samuel	11-12, 114
Bass, James Sen.	201
. John	201
. Lemuel	201
. Willis	201

Name	Page
Bateman, Thomas E.	245
. Tilman	241
. Wm.	234
Bates, John B.	161
. Matthew	161
. Randolph	161
Batt, James N.	205
Batte, Frederick	186
Robt. C.	186
Batton, James	215
Beard, George	78
Bearden, John	54
. Nancy	241
. Nimrod	241
. Willis	238
Beaty, John H.	205
Sherwood W.	205
Beck, A.H.	201
. Ebenezer	209
. Jeffrey	201
. John	208
Beckett, Susannah	205
Beckham, Willie	212
Bedford, Thomas	22, 59, 83
Thomas Jr.	22
Bedwell, Archibald	201
Mr.	201
Beidleman, Mr.	175
Bell, Feilding	219
. G.W.	131
. George	37
. James A.	193
. James W.	212, 219
. Mary	205
. S.A.	175
. Samuel	38, 137
Benford, Anderson A.	189
Bengarman, Benj.	212
Bennett, Hezekiah	241
. John	234
. Mary	234
. William	241
Berryman, William	186
Bethane, William	212
Bette, Rebecca	186
Bevins, Abraham	209
. Daniel	209
. Wm. S.	208
Bickett, John	208
Biedeman, Mr.	171
Bigger, Joseph Jr.	212
Biggers, Anderson	168
James	189
Bigham, H.B.	208
. Oliver H.	171
. Samuel	54
. William	208
Billington, Elias	197
. Ezekiel	201
. James	201
. Samuel	197
Bills, A.L.	212
. Amos L.	212
. Danl. B.	205
. G.	212
. Garsham	208
. John	209
. John H.	209
. Jonathan	205
. William	205
Bingarman, Benj.	212

Name	Page(s)
H.G.	212
Bingerman, Benjn.	208
Bingham, Robert	171
. Saml. M.	168
. William	133,168
. William G.	168
Bird, John	158
. Samuel	158
. Sharel	158
. Spirell	189
Birmingham, Elijah	209
. George W.	209
. John Sen.	209
Bishop, Henry	212
Black, C.W.	178
. George	234
. James M.	161
. Major Thomas	185,189
. Thomas	189
Blackburn, Elijah	189
. Leroy	189
. William	189
Blackman, Mr.	98
Blackwell, B.M.G.	224
. Elizabeth	224
. Gabriel	224
. J.W.H.	224
. James	224
. James G.	224
. John	231
. John Sen.	224
. Joseph	223
. Josiah	212,224
. Robert B.	107
. S.B.	224
Blagg, Jehu	228
Blair, Mr.	205,215
Blakeley, William	171
Blakemore, J.A.	178
Blankinship, Benj.	171
Jas.	241
Blanton, Meredith	193
. Sarah	245
. Wilkins	178
Bledsoe, Anthony	7,40
. David	126,157,219
. Isaac	147
. Jacob	54,219
Blendill, Henry	161
William	161
Blessing, David	178
John	178
Bletcher, Jacob	54
Blount, Gov. Willie	73
. John G.	73,110
. John Gray	4,49
. Thomas	4,49,73,110
. William	41
Blythe, Andrew	186
. Pheby	25
. Thomas	25,88
Bobo, Elijah	241
. Elisha	241
. Franklin D.	238
. Washington P.	241
. Welson W.	238
Bolton, Seth	205
Bomar, B.B.	165
. Elijah	165
. James	165
. Mary	241
. W.H.	71
. William	165
Bond, Mr.	198,240
Bonds, John	245
Boon, Jesse	245
William	234
Boone, Daniel	146-147
Booth, Benjerman	78
. J.B.	183
. John S.	183
. Lizney	77
. Stephen	78
Boren, James	215
Saml. H.	215
Bowden, Jas. M.	224
Bower, John	165
Bowles, Samuel B.	178
Bowling, James	169
Boyce, Jno.	189
Boyd, Aaron	104,201
. Eli	193
. J.B.	201
. John	201
. Lewis A.	231
. Rebecca	201
Boyt, Bethena	209
. Catharine	208
. Elizabeth	209
. James	208
. Jesse J.	209
. John F.	209
. Priscilla	209
Braden, James	189
. Saml.	197
. William	201
Bradford, Absalem	169
. Barkley	165
. Benj.	93
. Benjamin	28,35,84
	94-95
. Benjamin J.	112
. Henry C.	165
. James	165
. Jno.	165
. John	161,168
. Maj. John	158
. Theodrick F.	165
Bradley, Edward	209
. Jefferson C.	224
. Joel	224
Bradshaw, Benjamin	38
. Elijah	228
. James	17,19
. James E.	228
. Jas. N.	228
. Jno. W.	228
. O.W.	228
. Robt. E.	228
. Widow	234
Brame, John I.	231
. Melch.	231
. William C.	171
. Wm. B.M.	178
Bramlett, John	161
Branch, Anthony	28
Nicholas	38,133,143
Brandon, Charles	54,137
	189
. Elias	189
Brantley, Benjamin C.	215
Joseph A.	228
Brassfield, Isiah C.	178
Jas. H.	228
Braughton, Benjamin	219
Brecheen, Elizabeth	212
Josiah	212
Brechen, William Senr.	54
Brewer, Asa	205
. James	158
. Nathaniel	205
Briant, David O.	189
. David P.	189
. Frederick O.	189
. Jeremiah	197
. John P.	197
Bridges, George W.	245
Bright, James	44-45
. John M.	215
. Mr.	220
Brintle, Solomon	193
Britain, James	178
Brittain, Joseph	201
. Joseph H.	201
. S.B.	201
. Thomas	201
Britton, James	143
Broadway, Lemuel	234
Brook, Loyall	205
Brooks, Mr.	245
. Phillip	178
. Rev. John	245
. William	77
Brookshire, Benjamin	158
Josiah	158
Brothers, John	175
Brown, Archibald	224
. Benj.	175
. Benjamin	178
. Brazilla	212
. Caleb	212
. Daniel	241
. G.W.	175
. Harris C.	175
. Henry	175
. Hezekiah	234
. Hezekiah Jun.	234
. James	165,212
. Jesse	234
. Jesse Sen.	228
. Jesse W.	231
. John	234
. John M.	219
. John S.	228
. Jonathan	212
. Mary	228
. Miles	234
. N.M.	183
. Nathan'l	165
. Neal	220
. Paschal	238
. Philip	54
. S.S.	175
. Shad. S.	175
. Shadrick A.	178
. Shedrick	133
. Solomon	175,228
. Spencer	175
. Tho. E.	193
. Thomas	228
. Thomas S.	234
. Thos.	228
. William	175,178,224
. Willlliam	189
Bruce, Geo. W.	197
Bruco, William	165
Brunce, John P.	197
Brunfield, Anna	238
David	238
Bruton, Amilia	234
Bryam, Jesse	231
Joseph	231
Bryan, Nathl. C.	238
Bryant, Edward	219
. Elbert	219
. John	219,224
. Peter L.	219
. Russel	209
. Thomas	165
. Thos. W.	224
Buchanan, David	16-17,20
. George W.	107
. Jane C.	219
. Moses	16-17
. Robert	129
. Samuel	17
. Thomas	54
Buchannon, James	205
Buckingham, Nathaniel	178
Nathl.	238
Buffalow, W.E.	178
Bulling, Solomon	186
Wm.	193
Bullion, John	186
Bullock, John	215
. Leonard	201
. Nathan	215
. Olive	189
. William	189
Burdett, G.	37
Burditt, Giles	137
. Joel H.	178
. Patience	158
. Sarah	158
. Williamson R.	178
Burford, A.	222
Burgess, Richard	234
. Willie	212
. Wilsy	234
Burnett, Jas. M.	165
. John T.	231
. William	178
. Wm.	183
Burns, Cunningham	197
. John	201
. John Sr.	54
. Saml.	133
. Thos. P.	175
Burrow, Banks M.D.	234
. Duvaney W.	215
. E.	157
. Ephraim	205
. Eve	234
. F.	245
. Freeman	245
. Freeman H.	245
. Freeman Jr.	237
. Henry	205
. Ishmael	37
. Jacob C.	245
. James	234
. Jeffrey W.	215
. Jesse	234
. John	234

Name	Page(s)
. Joshua	245
. Mary	234
. Mr.	161
. Nimrod	245
. Numrod	238
. Phillip	234
. Phillip J.	245
. Widow Eve	234
. Wm.	183
Burt, Frederick	245
Burten, David	219
Burton, David	175
Nathl.	175
Bussey, Daniel	219
Butler, B.D.	201
. James S.	234
. John	238
. John G.	201
Byler, Abraham	22-23,62
	84,87,135
. Abraham Jr.	136
. Abraham Sr.	136
. Captain John	137
. James J.	189
. John	87,136-137,189
. Mr.	136
. Nancy	136,189
. Widow	130,157,189
Byram, Elijah	231
Cage, Alford	169
. Edward	78
. Wilson	169
Caid, Isaac	206
Calahan, Moses P.	245
Caldwell, Mr.	98
Samuel	242
Calhoun, George	201,220
. J.J.	201
. J.P.	190
Call, Daddy	54
Uriah	189
Callahan, Wm. S.	209
Callen, Thomas	186
Calton, Howard	201
Lewis	202
Campbell, Alfred	238
. Arthur	234
. Charles	228
. David S.	213
. General William	16
. George	219,227-228,231
. James	220
. John	228
. Major Charles	2
. Mr.	219,227
. Redmond	220
. Solomon	54
. William	234
. Wm. P.	158
Camples, Asa	220
Willis	220
Cannon, Almon	238
. C.	96,143
. Charles L.	178
. Clement	23,28,30,36-37
	59,65,94-96,133,142
	143,178
. Clement Sr.	58
. Elijah	238
. Elizabeth	212
. Gen. Robert	178
. General Robert	103,142
. Genl. Robt.	212
. Gov. Newton	238
. Henry	179
. Letitia	238
. Letitia Thompson	31
. Minos	30,37,100,133
	142,178-179
. Minos T.	100
. Minos Thompson	142
. Mr.	179
. Newton	29,31,36,38-39
	65,137,178
. R.T.	179
. Robert	36,65,143
Caple, Sarah	209
Capley, David	193
. George	193
. John	193
. Martin	193
. Peter Senr.	193
Caps, Daniel	201
Card, Samuel H.	220
Cardwell, Hosea G.	169
. John B.	165
. Richard	72
. Richard W.	169
Carliles, William	228
Carlton, Crawford	190
. James	228
. Thomas	190
. Thos. B.	189
. William	193
. Wm. C.	189
Carpenter, John	212
. John H.	241
. Peter	212
Carr, William	245
Carrington, C.D.	201
Carter, J. Carter	202
. John	23,84,88
. Landon	40
. William	238
Caruthers, A.	158,168
. Archibald	158
. Robert	54,197
. Stewart S.	238
Casteel, John	234
Castleman, John	47,114
Caswell, General	150
William	132
Cates, John	238
. John S.	232
. Jos. S.	238
. Timothy	242
. William	133
. William H.	238
Cathey, A.B.	212
. Charles	201
. George	197,215
. H.R.	179
. James	190,202
. John Jun.	202
. John Sen.	202
. Mr.	205,212,215
. Violet	212,215
Catowell, Robert	224
Cavin, Joseph	158
Chadwell, David	202
Chaffine, Nathan	169
Chamberlain, Wm. P.	245
Chamberland, Jeremiah	29
Chamberlin, Thos.	238
Chambers, Jno. A.	190
. Robert	165
. Wm. L.	165
Chandler, Allen	165
. Henry S.	241
. Joel	242
. John A.	165
. Mr.	215
. Wm. C.	165
Chapman, K.O.	215
. Robert	78,215,220
. William	215
Chappel, Abner	40
Robert	220
Chappell, Abner	54
Charlesville, Charles	2
Charlton, Elijah	209
Cheatham, Thomas	190
Cheek, Benjn. R.	209
. Edmund R.	215
. James	212
. Thomas D.	209
Cheeves, Calvin	220
. Jacob	220
. Mr.	220
Cherry, Jane	202
Cheshire, James	238
. Nathaniel	238
. William	238
. Zacheus	238
Chester, John	183
Chilcut, Peter	133
Chilcutt, Peter	36,142
Chilton, James Jun.	212
. James Sen.	212
. John	213
. Richard	212
. William	215
Christenberry, Thos.	212
Wm.	220
Christman, David	202
Christopher, John	208,212
Chumley, Jas. E.	173
Church, Robert	193
Clagett, Horatio	165
Claiborn, W. Coats	165
Clanton, Dudley	182,186
Clapp, Henry	205
John	245
Clardy, James	176
. Joseph	175
. Peter	165
. Richard	170
. Richardson	193
Clark, Anthony	54
. Elbert	183
. George	190
. George Rogers	149
. Henry	193
. James D.	183
. James H.	169
. James K.	186
. Joseph	197
. Moses B.	186
. Robert	169
. Stephen	36
. W.H.	129
. Walter	171
. William	137
Claunch, James H.	238
Jeremiah	238
Claxton, David	183
. George	183
. Hiram	171
. James	183
. Jeremiah	215
. John	133
. John Jr.	183
. John Sen.	183
. Jonathan H.	183
. Solomon	176
. Wesley	183
Clay, Henry	27
. Rachel	54
. Sallie	54
. Samuel	169
Cleek, Ezekiel	215
. Joseph	215
. William	215
Cleeks, M.	220
Clements, Willis	190
Cleveland, Jeremiah	161
Clift, James	220
John	220
Clinkingbeard, Robt.	171
Clinton, J.	190
Cloud, Joseph	209
Coalton, Thomas	158
Coats, Charles	190
. James	238
. John	36,133
. Mrs. S.	178
. Payton H.	175
. Wilson	133,179
Cobbett, Jesse	165
Cobbs, John W.	238
Coble, Jacob	245
. Neeley	165
. Nicholas	54
. Phillip	165
Cochrame, Jas. Sen.	209
Cochran, Willis	234
Cochrane, Cha.	178
. Ezra	209
. James Jun.	209
. Levi	209
. Silas M.	209
Cockrill, John	133
Coffee, Alex. H.	165
. General John	70
. Henry B.	165
. John	44
. John R.	129
. R.E.	129
. Rice	165
Coffey, Allen	212
. Benjamin	220
. James W.	225
. Jas. L.	224
. Rice	47,50
. Thomas	220
. Thos. Esq.	224-225
Coffman, Jacob	158
Cogswell, Dr.	33
Dr. Robert E.	90
Coldwell, Ballard	179
. J.C.	142-143,178
. John C.	78,175,178
. N.C.	142
. Nathaniel E.	39

Name	Page
. Nathl.	178
. Thomas H.	100
Cole, Levi	162
Colewell, Ballard	78
Collen, Thomas	36
Collier, William	197
Colline, Augustine	197
Collins, Adam	206
. Alex H.	224
. Henry	209,215
. Hollin	215
. Martin	234
. Thomas	36
Comb, John T.	228
Combs, John	228
Connel, John W.	171
Connelly, John	54
Conway, Henry	29,36,143
Conwell, Thomas	234
Cook, Elizabeth	225
. Elz.	241
. Grenville	178
. Henry	197,224,241
. Jefferson	193
. John	193,206
. Joseph	193
. Marcellus	201
. Stephen	158
. William	220
. William C.	190
Coop, George	171
. Horatio	54,169,173
. James	78,168,171,173
. John F.J.	171
. Richard	77
Cooper, Heirs	170
. Abraham	55,78
. Abram	178
. Belinda	186
. Charles	171,175
. Dayton	190
. Dr. Albert	137
. Dr. Herbert	101
. Edmond	100
. Elizabeth	171
. Herbert	141
. James	139
. Job	137,190
. Joel	190
. John	136-137,190
. John B.	175,234
. John L. Esq.	186,248
. Jonathan	171,183
. Mr.	190
. Mrs.	185
. Prentice	56
. Widow	164,175,182
. William	78,158
Coopes, Joseph H.	165
Corbett, William	190
Corbitt, Meredith	189
Needham	197
. Richard	190
Cortner, Daniel	161
Matthias	161
Cotes, James	235
Cothern, Jesse	165
John	165
Cotner, Daniel	228
. David	215
. George	189
. John	228
. Mr.	219
Couch, Isaac	161
. James	161
. Joseph	161
. Reuben	161
Coursey, James	55
William	186
Couser, Robert M.	245
Cousey, Charles	186
Covington, Lavisa	193
Cowan, William G.	179
Cowden, Joseph	206
. Robert Sen.	205
. Robt. Jun.	206
Cox, Caleb	190
. Martha	165
. Thomas	242
Craig, John	224
. Robert	225
. Widow	157,224
. Wm.	224
. Wm. H.	228
Crawford, Algernon	217
. John	215
. Thomas	242
Creicy, Calvin	169
Crews, Elisha	158
. George	238
. William	238
Crisco, Daniel	241
William	241
Criswell, Andrew	205
. David	206
. David C.	215
. Henry	205
Crockett, David	22,89
Samuel	197
Crolley, John	241
Cross, A.	240
. Joshua	238
. Sarah	238
. Uriah	165
. William	36
Crossland, Elijah	158
Crowel, Peter Sen.	220
. Samuel Jun.	220
. William	193
Crowell, Benjamin	193
. Henry	220
. Joshua	193
. Peter	126
. Saml.	193
. Samuel	193
Crutcher, Thomas	127
Crutchfield, Gideon	186
L.S.	183
Culberhouse, Jeremiah	186
. Jesse	186
. Moses	186
. Thomas	186
Culley, William	48
Cully, Bennett	162
. Thos. J.	162
. William	161
. Zachary	162
Culp, Adam	220
Henry	133
Culver, John	55,168-169
	171
Cumings, George Esq.	212
Cummings, A.E.	224
. Benjamin	213
. G.W.	225
. Hugh	224
. J.B.	178
. James F.	30
. John	212
. John B.	178,231
. Milton	212
. Newton	213
. Thos.	224
. Thos. A.	212
. Thos. E.B.	206
. Thos. Jr.	212
. Virgil	213
Cummins, Edward	178
Cunningham, William	55
. G.W.	228
. George	55
. Humphrey	228
. J.W.C.	228
. James T.	169
. Jeremiah	178
. John	209
. Mathew	29
. Matthew	55,238
. Sarah	24
. Thos. P.	224
. Wm.	224
. Wm. G.	238
Curtis, Jas. H.	224
Daisey, Jasper	190
Kinall	190
Dalby, Polly	165
Damorah, Sam'l T.	133
Damron, Edmond	173
. James	186
. Sion	183
. Tigney	55
Daniel, Drury	169
. Ezekiel	206
. Frances W.	238
. Hiram	242
. Martin C.	162
. Obadiah	183
. Plummer	242
. Robert	242
. Willie	238
. Z.	137
Darnaby, Edward	238
Darnell, Joel Jun.	220
. Joel Sen.	225
. Moses	225
Daughtry, George	23,41
Davidson, Andrew	55,228
. Andrew M.	162,248
. Bluford	28,235
. C	179
. Carlton	229
. G.	179
. Geo.	179
. George	143,176,248
. George N.	176
. H.M.	176
. Henry Brevard	57
. Hugh	48
. John	48,55,161-162
. John D.	197
. John P.	176
. John Q.	162
. McClain A.	176
. Mr.	105-106,179
. Robert B.	107
. Thomas	225
Davis, Daniel	133
. Elnathan	123,125,169
. Frederick	228
. Gabriel	225
. George	228
. H.L.	215
. Henry	32,133,142,158
.	165
. Hillard	197
. J.M.	190
. James	220,225
. Jesse	55,73-74
. John	169
. Jonah G.	193
. Mary	225
. Mary Ann	152
. Matthis	238
. Mr.	220
. Reuben J.	209
. Robert	209
. Saml.	197
. Samuel	209
. Thomas	33,127,133
.	142-143,179
. Timothy ?	225
. William	209,228,235
. Zachariah	225
Davour, Jackson C.	197
Dawdy, Alfred	39,133
. Daniel	38
. Danl.	133
. Howel	23,27,34,38-39
	55,84-85,87-88,93-94
	95,109
. Howell	133
. John Sen.	225
. John W.	225
. Phoebe	88
Dawson, Nelson	190
Dean, Henry	235
. Jeremiah	242
. John	162,242
. John Esq.	242
. Martin	242
. Payton S.	106
. Thomas	235
. William	242
Dearing, Wm. W.	173
Deason, Enoch	130
. Gilbert	183
. Jesse	173
. Joel	173
. Joel R.	183
. John	60,130-131,157
.	171,173
. Rebecca	130
. Widow Sarah Arnold	131
. William	190
Deery, James	36-37,133
.	142,179
. William	142,179
Deguerra, Lewis	101
Delk, Benjamin	228
. Geo. W.	229
. Jacob B.	232
. John	225
. William	229
Demet, Charley	190

Name	Page(s)
Demonbreum, Timothy	3
Dempsey, John B.	133
Demunbreun, Timothe	145
Denison, Robert	133
Denneston, Thos. L.	158
Denniston, Robert	158
Denny, Alexander	206
. John	205-206, 215
. Lucy	190
Deveraus, Thos. P.	215
Devin, Elizabeth	209
John	206
Dews, Solomon	98
Dial, Jeremiah	38, 55
Dickins, Daniel	193
Stephen	193
Dickinsin, Jas. W.	165
Letitia C.	165
Dickinson, Wm.	166
Dickson,	
. General Joseph	28
. James	137
. Joseph	22, 137
. Michael	176
Dillard, James	106, 225
Joel	173
Dillingham, Jackson	242
. Joshua	242
. William	242
Ditto, William	50, 165
Dixon, Colonel Tilman	8
. Harry	190
. James	232
. Jno.	190
. Joseph	22, 110
. Josiah	202
. Tillman	74-75, 78, 111
. Tilman	25
Doak, David	30
. Jane	30
. Rev. Samuel	148
. Samuel	29-30, 126, 232
Dobbs, Jeremiah	220
. John	225
. Lindsey	220
. William	220
Dobson, A.	178-179
. B.C.	179
. E.C.	248
Doddy, Howel	24
Dodson, A.C.	231, 237
Mr.	98
Doherty, George	136-137, 139, 150
Dollar, Reuben	193
Donaldson, A.	143
. Andrew	39
. Arthur	183
. John	5
. William A.	183
Donalson, Captain John	49
. John	111
. John Jr.	49
. Stokly	49
Donelson, John	51-52, 110, 150
. John Jr.	21, 47, 73
. Stokley	110, 150
Donnalson, Andrew	133
Donnelson, Captain	149
. John	114, 149
. M.	114
Dooley, Andrew J.	197
Doss, Phillip	202
Doty, Preston L.	220
Doud, Charles	193
Dougal, John	220
Dougan, Thomas	131
Doughtry, George	110
Dowdy, Howel	24
William	202
Dowson, Robert	190
Doxey, Daniel	202
Doyle, Edward	206
Drake, Catharine	162
. John	52, 143
. Jonathan	11, 15
. Thomas	55, 158
. Zachariah	134
Driver, Benjamin	242
. Jordan	235
. Noel	242
Drummond, William	238
Dryden, David	126, 220
. Jonathan B.	235
. Nathl.	218
. Robert M.	215
. Thomas	225, 228
. Widow	227, 234
Duckworth, Hezekiah	242
Dudley, C.S.	186
Christopher	136
Duncan, Landin	245
Dungan, Jacob	134
Dunham, Hardy	225
Dunlap, John C.	173, 186
Dunn, John	186
William	186
Dunnagin, Shad.	202
Dunnaway, John	238
Sam'l	165
Durrett, Solomon	225
Dwiggins, Daniel	186
Dwyer, Daniel	176
Dyer, Elijah	158, 168
. Gibson J.	228
. John	228
. Joseph G.	228
. Martha	228
. Samuel	228
. Thomas	168
Dysart, Alexander	213
. Andrew	212-213
. Cary A.	213
. E.B.	215
. F.	214
. Francis	206
. Gideon	213
. H.A.	215
. James P.	213
. Jno.	216
. John	212-213
. John Jn.	216
. Robert	213
. Robert C.	213
. Saml. D.	215
Eakin, Alexander	142, 179
. Ewell	216
. J.	179, 216
. James	216
. John	142, 179, 193
. John Esq.	176, 248
. S.	179, 216
. Spencer	179
. William	179
. William S.	143
. Willliam	55
Earnhart, Benj.	220
. Daniel	220
. George	175
. Henry	219-220, 231
Eaton, John	159
Edde, James	35, 134, 142
James S.	36
Edmiston, Col. William	74
. Colonel	20
. Colonel William	15-16
. G.W.C.	16
. Thomas	16
. William	16, 150
Edmonds, Bartlett	197
Edmondson, Phillip	238
. Robert	16
. Thomas	16
Edward, Amos	173
Edwards, James	165, 209
. Sterling	245
. Thomas	176
Elkins, Alexander	242
. David Jr.	246
. Harrison	245-246
. James	238
. Mr.	237, 241
. Richard	55
. Robert	169
. William	169
Elley, Josiah	173
Ellington, D.T.	202
Elliott, Cornelius A.	209
. Eli	209
. John	209
. L.B.	229
. Samuel J.	209
. Sarah	209
. Simon P.	169
. Thomas	169
. William	179
Ellis, B.F.	229
. George	229
. James	220
. John	134
. Michael	232
. Wm. M.	229
Ellison, James	216
. Jno.	216, 220
. John	216
. John Esq.	216
. Mr.	216
Elmore, William	190
Endsley, Bedford	213, 225
. Isaac N.	225
. Jno. M.	225
. Mary	212-213, 225
. Widow	223
England, John	225
Engram, Samuel	36
Eoff, John	159
William	158
Eperson, L.B.	190
William	190
Epps, Daniel	176
. Irby	179
. Joshua	225
Ervin, Adolphis	183
. Henry B.	213
. James	179
. James P.	216
. John R.	213
. Wm. P.	213
Erwin, Andrew	110, 142-143
. Andrew Jr.	53
. Colonel Andrew	49
.	51-52, 66
. James	162, 248
. Jane	52
. Mr.	162
. Robert	129
Escue, Samuel	179, 238
Euless, Adam	246
Eures, Mills	216
Evans, D.S.	164, 168
. Daniel	220
. David B.	220
. David S.	169
. Henry	186
. Jesse	37, 39, 134
. John	246
. Joseph	220
. Nathan	28, 229
. Sarah	235
. Theophilus	229
. William	220
. William M.	242
. Willie	220
. Zebellon	220
Ewell, John	48
Mary	245
Ewens, James P.	229
Robert	229
Ewing, Alexander	55
. George	206
. James D.	206
. James Esq.	206
. James V.	206
. Jas.	220
. Jas. L. Esq.	206
. Jas. P	206
. Lile A.	206, 216
. Mary	206, 248
. Saml. W.	216
. William D.	206
. Wm. A.D.	216
Ewings, Jas.	157
Ezell, Calvin	202
. Jepthah	202
. Joseph D.	197
Fain, David	78
. John	194
. Richd.	193
. William	194
Falwell, Elisha	197
. John	197
. Moses	197
. William	197
Fane, Charles	55
Fann, Charles	190
Farmer, Amos	183
. Benjamin	194
. John	194
. Margaret	194
Farrar, Jno. H.	229
. John	176
. Peter	206
Faver, Jas. E.	197

Name	Page	Name	Page	Name	Page	Name	Page
William B.	197	Frazer, Farwick	169	. John	179	. Daniel	133,166
Favour, Thos. B.	197	. Jane	166	. Kezia	232	. Malcolm	143
Featherston, Burrell	25	. John	166,175,183	. William	31,39,89	. Malcom	30,62,133,179
John	183	Frazier, Bryson	229	.	105-106,179	. Malcum	132,135,139,223
Featherstone, Burrell	169	. Dr.	130	. William Sr.	29	. William	38,143,179,248
Burrett	169	. Dr. Preston	66,143,152	. Wm.	129	. Wm.	223
Fergusen, John F.	202	. Elizabeth Guy	152	Gallagly, Stephen	162	Giles, Matthew H.	206
Ferguson, H.C.	162	. Granville	151	Gambell, John H.	219	. Milton Esq.	169
John A.	238	. Hugh	151	Gambill, Aaron	221	. Wesley A.	209
Ferrill, Richard	162	. James	143,151	. Alfred H.	232	Gill, George	159
Robert	159	. Jane	151	. Benjamin	38,229	Gilley, Simeon	183
Fields, Henry	229	. John	37	. Bradley K.	197	Gilliam, Harrison	202
. James	159	. John S.	151,179	. George	229	Gilly, John	246
. L.P.	125	. Mary	151	. James C.	221	Gilman, Hariah J.	202
Finch, Matt S.	159	. Mrs. Jane	143	. John	229	Gilmore, Elizabeth	169
. William	51	. Preston	151,179	. John H.	221	Heirs	169
. William P.	162	Freeman, A. Manier	235	. Newton C.	229	Glascock, Charnel	221
Finley, George	205,208	. Alexander	173	. Thomas	221	. George	221
John	209	. Christian	229	. William	229	. Richd.	216
Finney, James	242	. Ed	171	Gammill, James	30,232	Glascock, Peter N.	216
Norman	242	. Edward	168,173	Moses	202	Gleaves, Therman	133
Fisher, Frederick	206	. Hartwell	176,220	Ganeway, Burrel	133	Glenn, David	213
. George	206,221	. Joel	221	Gann, Iverson	246	. James	210
. George W.	206	. Nile	221	Gannaway, B.Z.	129	. Joseph	210
. Jacob	206	. Russell	220	. R.P.	129	. Wm. A.	210
. Jacob Esq.	183	. Stephen	229	. T.P.	129	Glidwell, Barrister	229
. James F.	206	. Wilson	220	Gardner, John W.	238	Glover, James	210
. James K.	206	Freymon, Jno. S.	190	Garmon, Charles	55	Gobble, John	242
. Joh.	206	Friddle, Martin	235	Garner, Brice	20	Gonan, Jacob	202
. John	183	Frierson, E.J.	143,179	. Hezekiah	186	Good, John	198
. Mary	225	Mr.	180	. John	194	Goode, Joel M.	78
. Michael	12,38,55,134	Frizel, Abraham	78	Garren, Peter	221	Goodman, Cynthia	183
.	221	. James	78	Garret, Darrington	197	Goodrum, A.J.	176
. Reuben	202	. Nathan	78	Garrett, A.T.	129	Goodwin, Geo. W.	225
. William D.	216	. Wm.	78	. Elijah	162,235	. Peter	221
Flack, Rufus K.	179	Frizele, John	183	. Elisha	208,210,212-213	Peter G.W.	210
Fleming, Henry	209	Frizer, John	183	. James	190	. W.P.	164,168-169
. Samuel	36	Frizle, Abram	169	. Stephen	166	Gordon, George	90,96
. Wm. A.	197	. David	169,183	. William	209	. Jonathan	166
Flenn, James	134	. James	169	. Wilson	242	. R.C.	29
Floyd, Anthony	242	. James M.	169	Garrin, Peter	225	. Sam'l B.	166
. David	242	. Nathan	186	Garrison, Samuel	229	Gore, Amos	242
. David Sr.	55	. Nathld.	183	Gaston, William	159	. Jno.	243
. Elijah	242	Frizzell, A.D.	166	Gault, Hugh M.	190	. Thomas	55,242
. John	162	Frost, Ebenezer	242	Renwick A.	190	. William	39,133
. Saml.	242	Fugate, Alfred D.	169	Gaunt, James Jun.	229	Gossage, Patten	235
. Samuel	242	. Benjamin	169	. James Sen.	229	. Walker	235
. William H.	238	. Townsend	169	. John	225	. Washington	235
Fogleman, G.W.	179	Fugett, Benjamin	221	. John Jun.	229	Gowan, Shadrick	183
Fonville, Asa	26,175	Nancy	221	. John Sen.	229	Wm. B.	180
.	178-179	Fugit, Moses	134	. Jon.	221	Gowen, James	89
. F.F.	107	Fulgram, John	235	. Lewis	221	. James B.	242
. Frederick	229	Fulkerson, James	242	. William A.	221	. Matthew P.	242
. William	232	Fuller, Isaac	134	Gentry, Meredith	64	Graham, David B.	197
Forbs, Jeremiah	220	. Jacob	134,242	Samuel	42,68	. J.H.	179
Ford, Simon T.	159	. William	235	George, Redding	166	. Richard	197
Forrest, Brittain H.	197	Fulmore, Andrew J.	190	Gibbs, E.F.	173	. William	210
. James N.	197	George	190	John	55	Grames, John	221
. Jonathan	197	Fulten, Grown	179	Gibby, John	55	Grammer, John Jun.	235
. Nathan	197	. James C.	197	Gibson, Asa	221	. Leonard	235
Foster, Jacob	176	. Shirly	179	. George B.	232	. Peterson	235
. James	166,186	Fulton, Edmond	216	. Jeremiah	133	. William	235
. Thomas	183	. H.F.	202	. Jesse	180	Graves, Aaron W.	197
Fowler, Harrison N.	246	. J.B.	202	. John	221	. Daniel	193
. Jacob B.	209	. James	216	. John Jun.	221	. James N.	197
. James	246	Fuqua, John J.	179	. John M.	225	. Jonathan	137
. John B.	209	Gabrille, Isaac	173	. Nathan	197	. Joseph D.	137
. P.W.	209	Gage, James	60,126	Gifford, William	210	. Peter	246
. William	77	John	61	Gilbert, Cynthia	246	. Samuel	197
Franklin, Jackson	162	Gaither, Reason	183	Gilberth, Robert	197	Gray, Jarman	210
Peter	165	Galbreath, Elizabeth	29	Gilchrist, Arch B.	223	. Joseph	232

Name	Page	Name	Page	Name	Page	Name	Page
. M.J.	179	Thos. B.	198	. George	166	Hawkins,John	243
. Samuel	55	Haggard,James	162	. Lewis	133	. Samuel	235
Greason,Henry	237	. Rector	162	. Lowe	232	Hay,John B.	216
Green,B. Green	159	. Richard	166	Harmon,Leonard	159	. Martha	216
. Daniel	133,238	. Samuel	162	Harp,Jefferson	169	. Samuel	30
. David	206	. Squire	162	Harper,Jno. M.	225	Hayes,Enoch	162
. Elijah	55,162	. W.	180	. Samuel	219,224-225,227	Haynes,Elizabeth	184
. Eph R.	206	. Wm.	186	. Thos. W.	225	Hays,Anderson S.	216
. Ephraim	206	Haile,Alexander	159	Harris,Andrew	198	. Henry	170
. Isaac	179	. James	169	. Ephraim	202	. Hezekiah	170
. James	162,179	. Joel	190	. Evan	137	. Hiram	170
. Jesse	238	. John	159	. Evan Esq.	192	. Jeremiah	216
. Joseph	176,180	. Meade	159	. George T.	183	. John M.	216
. Lewis	221	. Meade Jr.	159	. Hiram	184,187,216	. Nathaniel	50
. Littlebury	137	. Meshack	190	. J.	194	. Robert	112
. Robert	162	. Thomas	169	. J.W.	180	. Samuel B.	30
. T.C.	179	. William G.	159	. James	133,184,186,221	. Wm. T.	190
. Thomas	206	Hailey,Tauner	159	. Jno. S.	191	Haywood,G.W.	104
. U. Jr.	180	Haines,G.	220	. Jno. T.	191	Geo. W.	210
. U.M.	180	Hainey,Jno. P.	229	. Jo. M.	180	Hazlett,William	60
. W.D.	179	Haithcoat,Barney	246	. John	137,162,184	Head,Calvin H.	232
. W.T.	129	Halbrooks,Jno.	191	. John T.	216	. David W.	232
. Willis	162	Wm. C.	210	. L.B.	159	. Enoch	157,182,184
. Willliam	133	Hale,Green B.	173	. Lawson	216	. James W.	184
. Wm. Sr.	180	Haley,Barnaba	190	. Mosebey	133	. John A.	184
Greer,Alexander	11-14,17	. Barnaby	185,189	. Moseby	166	Headlee,David	206
.	19,22,27-28,30,55,61	. Charles	187	. N.C.	129	. Joseph	206
.	64,67,84,87,110,150	. Edward T.	176	. Newton	166	Heamiller,Thomas	225
.	229	. James	55,187,238	. Nicholas	221	Heard,George W.	246
. Andrew	12,148	. Wm. T.	176	. Ruth	216	Heaslett,E.H.	225
. Catharine	14	Hall,B.M.	229	. Samuel B.	38,137,143	. Henry E.	232
. David	229	. Fergus	162	Harrison,Barzilla	55	. William	238
. Edmund	202	. Hugh A.	225	. C.H.	225	. William Esq.	242
. Frances	229	. James	159,202	. Edward C.	187	. Wm. Esq.	180
. Henry Harmon	179	. Jno. G.	198	. Jacob	238	Heath,John	180
. Jacob	232	. John	180	. Jas. H.	106	Heathcoat,William	166
. Jane	15	. John Jr.	232	. John	221,229,246	Heathcock,Allen C.	243
. Joseph	13-14,148	. John Sen.	229,232	. Mary	225	Heathe,Rev. Lewis	190
. Robert J.	229	. L.W.	162	. R.P.	180,238	Height,John T.	246
. Thomas	14,17,19,61,67	. Thomas	202	. Robert	246	Helm,Moses W.	206
.	110,232	. Thomas A.	216	. Tyre	221	. Thomas	206
. Thomas Sen.	179,229	. Thomas J.	216	. William	55,225	. William	206
Gregerie,Heirs	169	. William	206	. Wm. H.	187	Helmich,John	206
Gregory,G.W.	106	Halsey,E.J.	106	Harryman,Charles	50	Helton,Abraham	55
. Henry	159	Ham,James	246	Harston,Robert	184	. James	225
. James	183	Hamilton,Frances	198	Hart,Calvin R.	198	Hemby,Dennis	246
. Thomas	159,183	. Mr.	205,215	. Henry	235	. Pherebe	246
Griggs,Ferrill	162	. Volney M.	173	. James	173	Henderson,Logan	221
Grininage,John R.	186	. Wm.	198	. John H.	235	. Rice	243
Wm. M.	186	Hamlin,Arthur	180	. John N.	225	. Wm. F.	133
Grooms,John	238	Hamm,Joshua	133	. Stephen	173	Hendricks,Elisha	191
Guest,David	221	Hammack,Willouby	242	. Thomas	173	Hendrix,John	246
. Moses	186	Hammil,William	221	Hartless,James	169	Henley,Elmore	173
. William	186	Hammond,Mary	221	Hartsfield,Andw.	232	. John	198
Gullett,We-tman	78	Hanby,George W.	221	Wm.	232	. John J.	194
Gunn,Judith	166	Harber,Christian	216	Hastie,Joseph	232	. Micjah	198
Gutteridge,Dawson	179	Henry	216	Hasting,Josiah Jun.	235	. William	198
Guy,Alexander	151	Harbour,George A.	216	. Josiah Sen.	235	Henly,Peter	213
. Ann	151,186	Hardin,Burgess	210	. Wm.	235	Henslee,Franklin	169
. Captain	130	. Henry	210	Hastings,Henry F.	238	Hester,James	176
. Elizabeth	151	. Jno. L.	210	. John	238	Hewitt,	
. John	151	. John L.	210	. John H.	166	Captain Benjamin	17
. Major William	66	. Mark	137	. Jos.	129,157	Hickman,Jos.	176
. Margaret	151-152	. Mary	210	. Joseph	35,55,237	William	127,143
. Margaret Ann	152	. Tho. H.	213	. Joseph Esq.	238	Higgs,Susannah	198
. Mr.	175	Harkness,Benjamin	216	. Susannah	238	Hightower,Joh. A.T.	206
. Sally	151	. Jas.	216	. Widow	231,237	Hill,George	169
. Samuel	151	. Jno. Sen.	216	. William	235	. Gillam	225
. William	151,173	. John Jr.	216	Hatchett,James	162	. Green	225
Hackney,Allen	210	. Samuel	216	Willis	202	. James	225
Haddock,John G.	198	Harman,Gedian	133	Hatehill,Thomas	169	. Lewis A.	242

Name	Page
. Spencer	187
. William	78,137,202
. William D.	190
Hime,Daniel K.	238
. J.	238
. John W.	238
. M.A.	238
. Mary Ann	238
. Nathaniel	238
. William	238
Himeman,Robt. A.	238
Hineman,Jonathan	194
Hite,Nancy	187
Hix,Demarcus D.	238
. James	221,235
. John	235
. John S.	232
. Joshua M.	232
. Sarah	235
. William	242
Hobbs,John	191
Hodge,Hugh R.	242
John	243
Hogg,J.F.	202
John B.	36,133
Hogge,Ezekiel	206
Holden,Dennis	184
Holder,Joseph	238
Thomas	166
Holland,James	38-39,166
. Nelson	229
. Thomas	133
. Thomas Jr.	248
. Thos. Jun.	180
. Thos. Sen.	166
Holly,William	221
Holt,Capt.	201
. Captain	196
. Elijah	162
. Eve	242
. H.F.	106,235
. H.H.	100
. Henry	166
. Hiram	232,242
. Jeremiah	243
. Jesse	162
. Jno. H.	202
. John	162
. John H.	202
. Jordan C.	227,232,234
. Joseph	162
. Joshua	56
. Joshua Jr.	235
. Joshua Sen.	235
. Larkin	162
. Lodwick	246
. Michael	50,166,232
. Shadrack	56
. William	162
Hooker,John	180
Joseph	180
Hooper,Elisha M.	187
. George	190
. James	191
. William	190
Hooser,Daniel	246
. Josiah	166
. William	162
. William Esq.	166
. Wm.	166
Hooten,John	206
Thomas	216
Hoover,Christopher	187
.	194
. Martin	78,169
. William	173
Hoozer,Mr.	215
Hopkins,Eli	216
. Thos.	238
. William	133
Hopper,Charles	216
. Jackson	206
. James	206
. Thomas	215-216
. Thos.	157
. Uriah	216
Hopwood,Clark	210
. Thomas	210
. Willis Sen.	210
Hord,Edmond	162
. Edmund	159
. Edwin	162
Born,Henry	38
Hornady,Christopher	243
Hornedy,Solomon	243
Horsley,William	180
William S.	166
Horton,Elijah	194
Hosking,John E.	186
Hoskins,Alfred	191
James	191
Houfman,Alfred	162
House,D.P.T.	246
Thomas	246
Housten,Wm.	186
Houston,Abner	104,210
. Christopher	210
. Dr.	130
. Hugh Esq.	205,208
. Hugh Jun.	210
. Hugh Sen.	210
. James G.	210
. Jno. W.	210
. John M.	210
. Robert	205
. William	173,202,248
. Wm.	174
Howard,Daniel	242
. Oliver	246
. William	202
Howe,John W.	246
Joseph M.	246
Howell,Joseph	38
Hubbard,Daniel	206
. John H.	232
. Sally	242
Hudgens,John	185
Hudgins,John	182-183
Hudlow,George	235
Hudson,Jessee	133
Huff,Ann	238
Huffman,George	246
. Jarrett B.	242
. Peter	48
Hugh,Houston Sen.	206
Hughes,Agnes	221
. John	221
. Madison R.	198
. Reuben	198
Hughs,Joseph	198
William L.	232
Hugle,Mary	170
Humphries,Larkin	166
Hunter,David	166
. E.W.	205,215
. Edwin C.	206,213
. Elihu W.	206
. Ephraim	216
. Robert	206,215
. Thomas O.	216
. Thomas Q.	248
. Thos. O.	198
Hurst,William	235
William Sen.	235
Hurt,John	166
Hutson,Cuthbert C.	242
William	184,243
Hutton,John	173,176
John W.	186
Hyde,Gray M.	229
Hyles,Joseph	238
I.J. Miller	123
Ingram,Samuel	133
Irvin,Samuel	221
Iseley,Benjamin	246
John	246
Isley,Benjamin	166
Ivey,James	243
Jackson,Andrew	4,47
.	50-51,67,73,111,132
. Avery	194
. Coleman	157
. Dr. Coleman	175
. General	21,25,35,50,70
. General Andrew	76,130
. Gilliam	191
. John	187
. John Sen.	194
. Saml.	191
Jacob,Solomon	202
Jacobs,John	180
Joseph	56
Jakes,John	159
James,Isaac	170
. John	170
. John P.	229
. Rylie	202
Jameson,John	246
Samuel	246
Jarrett,David	180
Jeanes,Thos. C.	226
Jeffress,Thos. B.	194
Jenkins,Rev. William	246
Jennings,John N.	206
Thomas	206
John,J.	191
. James A.	173
. John R.	206
. Levi C.	173
Johnson,Andrew	64,124
. Edward	226
. James M.	238
. John A.	229
. John B.	238,246
. Manchester	166
. Mr.	215
. Nathan	162
. Nathaniel	56
. Saml.	191
. Stephen	162
. Thomas	187
. William	162
Joice,James	198
Jolly,John	246
William	163
Jones,Aquilla	216
. Benjamin	159
. Elias	217
. Elizabeth	159
. Fanning M.	206
. George	187
. Hix	243
. James	226,235
. James B.	221
. James G.	216
. James W.	180
. John C.	206
. Jonathan	159
. Jonathan N.	243
. Joseph	159
. Lawrence E.	221
. Levi	162
. Lewis B.	216
. Luton	206
. Napoleon B.	221
. Presley	198
. Rebecca	243
. Robert Sen.	159
. Robert T.P.	187
. Samuel	159,162
. William¹B. Esq.	221
. William S.	198
. Willie B.	243
Jordan,Burton	137
. Jefferson	221
. Tabitha	221
. Wm. B.	187
Jordon,Benjamin	38
Josse,Michael C.	217
Keck,Isaac	246
John	246
Keek,John	163
Keele,David	194
. James	159
. William	159
Keener,William	194
Keith,John	170
Keller,Francis	163
. H.M.	129
. Jacob	163
. John M.	163
. Joseph	163
Kelley,Thomas	78
Kelly,Benjn. D.	246
. Nathan T.	246
. Nelson	56
Kelton,John	176
Kenier,John	210
Joseph	210
Kent,John	173
Thomas	166
Kerby,William	246
Keys,Hugh	198
Kidd,James Jun.	213
James Sen.	213
Killingsworth,H.	226
Henry	229
Kimbro,Allen	246
. Benjamin	246
. George	246
. James	246
. Jeremiah	163
. John	246
. Levi	243

Name	Page
. Powell	163
Kimery, Turley	238
Kimmery, Thomas	194
Kimmons, Esq.	196
Kimsey, Ham P.	246
Kincaid, Joseph	180
Kindell, John	180
William	180
Kindle, Thomas	159
King, Brother	48
. Charles	232
. Edward	56
. Franklin	238
. Henry A.	243
. Isaiah	232
. James	159
. John	159, 206, 221
. Nathaniel	229
. R.J.	166
. Samuel	47
. Wm. C.	232
Kirk, E.F.	202
Eli	232
Kirley, James	238
John	238
Kivet, Mr.	203
Kizer, David	238
. Enoch	238
. Jacob	232, 238
. Nancy	238
Knight, Allen	48, 163
. Charles	243
. Gab'l.	227
. Gabl.	231
. Gabriel	232
. Jim	88
. John	163
. Obadiah W.	232
. William	232
Knott, Blackman L.	176
. Jno.	78
. John	176
. Sarah	170
. Thomas	180
. William	73-74
. William S.	176
Knox, John	159
. Samuel	56
. William	159
Koonce, Blackman	238
. Jesse	238
. John Jun.	238
. John Sen.	238
Kortner, George	246
LANders, Alexander	187
. Anderson	187
. Elijah	187
. Frances	187
. George S.	187
. George T.	187
. Richard	187
. Rowland	187
. Thos. G.	187
Lacy, Ebenezer	166
. Elijah	235
. John	238
. Robert	166
Laird, Agnes	202
. John	202
. John H.	180
Lamb, Barram	187
Landers, F.S.	30
. Henry	194
. Robt. L.	106
Landis, A.	247
. Abel	247
. John	247
. R.L.	247
Lane, Drury	187
. H.G. Esq.	187
. Isham H.	187
. John	28, 94-95, 170, 215
	217
. John M.	217
. John R.	187
. Joseph	206
. Thos.	217
Lannders, Wm.	191
Lannons, William B.	173
Larimore, Hance	133
John	184
Larue, Isaac B.	226
. John	213, 226
. Squire	213
Latemor, Anderson	247
Lavender, B.B.	203
. Bird B.	198
. Charles	202
. John	203
Lawrance, Joseph	151
Margaret	151
Lawrence, James	191
Lawry, John	159
Laws, John	198
Leach, Elisha	222
Leah, Marcus H.	173
Leathers, William	187
Leavill, Benjn.	206
Ledbetter, Alfred	163
. Jesse M.	198
. Madison	198
. William	198
Lee, Alexander	159
. John	133, 198
. Peter	166
. William	166
Leeper, Allen	206, 248
Leggett, F.F.	206
. Holden W.	206
. James	206
Lenior, Thomas	68
. William	68
. Wm.	194
Lenoir,	
. General William	42
. Thomas	42
Lentz, Benj.	222
. Benjamin	56, 222
. Jacob	221
. John	222
. John J.	222
. John T.	194
. Thomas W.	221
. Valentine	222
Leverett, Jas. W.	184
Leverette, Johnson P.	173
Lewis, John	163
Liggett, Jonathan	221
Lile, Jackson	56, 187
. James	136
. James H.	191
. Mr.	194, 198, 240
Lillard, A.F.	194
Lincoln, Elijah	210
Lindley, James	176
. Mr.	247
. Thomas I.	247
Lingan, Archibald	159
Lingo, J.C.	173
Lipscomb, Dabney	180
Thomas	180
Little, Daniel	198
. Jackson	206
. John	198
. John L.	198
. William	30, 107, 198
Lively, James	184
Lock, John	15, 137
. Mathew	130, 151
. Susannah	31
. William	38
Locke, David	133
. James H.	194
. Martha A.	187
. Mathew	66
. Matthew	60
. Matthew P.	194
. Robt. W.	194
. Wm. H.	194
Lockhart, James	135
Logan, Jane	213
. Mary	213
. Robert	229
. Widow	212, 215
London, Thomas A.	210
William	210
Long, Andrew	235
. B.	217
. Benjamin	198
. John	243
. Mary	217
. Richard	217
. Rick	217
. Thomas	217
. William F.	180, 248
Looney, Hugh	226
. F.D.	226
. Wm. B.	226
Loranore, Thomas	36
Love, Martha	226
Thomas	29, 90, 96
Lovett, Enoch	226
Kitty	226
Lovins, P.H.	202
Lovorn, Edmund C.	187
Low, David	247
. Gabriel	187
. Iredell J.	247
Lowe, David	38
Lowrance, A.D.A.	173
. A.S.	173
. Alex	173
. Joseph A.	173
Lowrence, Merrett	194
Lowry, Jas. B.	226
Loyd, A.M.	226
. Anderson	170
. John	176
. Joseph	131, 173
. Lee	170
. Lemuel	238
. Nicholas	56
. Thos. J.	238
. William A.	238
. Wm. A.	238
Lucas, Charles	247
Lunn, Alfred	217
. Elbert J.	217
. Felix G.	217
. Nathan	217
. Nathaniel A.	217
Lurin, Henry	238
Lynch, Arden	170
. Gray	170
. William	170
Lytle, Abel	191
William	191
Mabin, Azariah	198
William	198
Madox, Charles S.	176
Notley	176
Magers, John	77
Noble	77
Major William Guy	151
Majors, Alexander	160
. Noble L.	160
. R.H.	170
. Robert	54, 158, 160, 168
. Robert H.	170
Malcom, John	206
Mallard, Alfred	176
Thornton	176
Malone, Murdock	210
Mangrum, James	199
Samuel	194
Manier, J.W.	203
. John A.	199
. Phillip	199
Mankins, James	191
Manly, Absalom	170
. James	170
. Nathan	170
. Reuben	77, 170
Manning, Mark	159
W.D.	167
Marbury, John	142
. Josiah H.	166
. L.W.	178, 180
. Mr.	179
Marchant, Willie	191
Marcum, W.B.M.	226
Marian, John F.	194
Marion, John F.	54
Marr, John	170, 226
. Nimrod	170
. Samuel	170
Marsh, Helen	123, 125
. John	168
. John W.	170
. Leslie	88
. Michael	59
. Tim	123, 125
Marshall, Capt.	201
. Captain	196
. Joseph	198
. Levan	35
. Levin	164, 178
. Moses	180
. Peter W.	199
. Robert E.	199
. Stephen	198
Martin, Mr.	160
. Andw. J.	247
. Asa	243

. Barclay	89,93
. Barkley	27-28,39,66,85
.	89,94-95
. Bartley	94-95
. Elizabeth	160
. G.W.	129
. George	16,54
. H.B.	160
. Henry	198
. Jas. C.	180
. Jas. K.	106
. John	243
. Josiah	54
. Lyttleton	240
. Mathew	89
. Matt	27,51,54,160
. Matt Jr.	160
. Matthew	66
. P.D.	203
. Rachel	170
. Richard	16,54
. Thomas	243
. Vincent B.	213
. William	213,243
Martindale,Thomas	194
Mash,John W.	170
Stires A.	170
Mason,John E.	159
. Michael	133
. Thomas W.	160
. William	217
Massey,John	243
Mathews,Robert	107,143
Matlock,William	77
Matthew,Robt.	180
Mauldin,Ambrose	11
Maupin,Blan	48,247
. Gabriel	48,247
. R.B.	60
. Robert B.	163
Maxwell,Anna	191
. Edward	238
. Mr.	136
. Thomas	23,135
May,George	203
Mayberry,Geo.	198
Joseph	198
Mayfield,Abraham	194
. Haram	194
. Jno. W.	194
. Q.T.	164,168,170
. Wm. S.	199
Mays,Lazarus	166
Willie	226
McAdams,Amos	133,176
. Ervin	213
. J.N.	180
. James	134,176
. John	214
. Joseph	226
. Thomas	176
McBride,John	37
McCall,Samuel	203
Thomas	191,203
McCarty,W.	180
McCarver,James	232
McCary,Hugh	54
McChristian,John	180
McCleary,John	206
W.D.	206
McClellan,Hugh	203
S.K.	203
McClelland,Samuel	217
Wm.	182
McClenson,Laban G.	78
McClintock,Geo.	180
. John	184
. Mrs. E.	180
McClung,Isham	176
McClure,A.E.	217
. Houston	230
. Jacob	163
. James	143
. Jno.	170
. John	170
. William	206,210,230
McCool,Benj.	226
McCord,Joseph	206
McCordy,Samuel	206
McCowan,William	170
McCoy,Daniel	39
McCrory,Hugh	54,170
. John	170
. Robt.	210
McCuestion,Benj.	134
. John	134
. Saml.	134
McCuistion, Robt.	191
. Benj. F.	176
. Benjamin	176
. Elizabeth	213
. James	54
. John C.	176
. S.B.	176
. Thos.	191
McCutchin,Patrick	16-17
McDaniel,Francis	210
Hiram	194
McDowell,Joseph C.	217
William K.	217
McElrath,Heirs	177
. Mrs.	182
. Widow	175
McElroy,Andr. M.	170
McElvaney,Robert	243
McFarland,N.P.	176
Thomas	176
McFarling,Robert	134
McFearson,Vincent	170
McFerrin,Dr. John	66
. J.B.	152
. Rev. Thomas S.	152
McGee,William	47
McGampsy,C.C.	179
Mr.	180
McGowan,James	187
. Jas.	187
. William	187
McGrew,Curry	164,168,170
William	170
McGuaioch,William	8
McGuire,John	167
. John B.	160
. Polly	160
. Thomas	50
. William	50,54,166
McKaimy,Francis	54
McKenzee,Mr.	174
McKinley,Mr.	174
McKisick,Col.	227
. Dan.	93
. Daniel	54,84-85,89
. Daniel Jr.	90
. James	28,89,134
. Joseph	28
McKissick,Daniel	27,95
. James	32,143
. Jas.	95
McKnight,Ezekiel	210
Thomas	210
McLain,George	54
McLaughlin,J.H.	226
. Samuel	236
. William	235
McLean,Andrew M.	206
. C.C.	163
. David V.	187
. Eph B.	187
. Ephraim H.	198
. Henry	213
. Jesse	213
. John	213
. Josiah T.	187
. Judiah A.	187
. Vance	191
McLemore,Amos	137
McLoy,William	184
McMahan,Abraham	160
. James	159-160
. Joel B.	160
. Mary S.	160
. William	78
McMamys,Mr.	233
McMillian,John	236
McMinn,Robert	173
McMorris,Alexander	217
McNatt,John	234,236
. Levin	236
. William	236
McNease,Washington	206
McNit,James	16-17
McQuistain,John	175,178
McQuistion,Benjamin	38
James	37,142
McRee,Margaret E.	174
Wm. C.	173
McRoberts,David	54
Mckissick,Daniel	94
Meadors,Daniel	54
Meadows,E. Jr.	184
. Henderson	166,184
. Jane	167
. John	167
. William	163,166
Means,Robert S.	174
Medearis,W.D.	226
Meek,Mary	217
Meeks,Jas. F.	219
William	137
Maigs,Colonel	45
Merrill,Jonathan	243
Merritt,Benjn.	170
. Mrs.	168
. Wm.	158
Miles,James H.	238
. John H.	238
. Wm. H.	238
Miller,Adam	194,198
. Andrew	213
. Arnold	167
. David H.	217
. Henry	38,134
. Isaac J.	125,170
. James	54,213
. James Jr.	166
. James Sen.	213
. John	213
. John H.	206
. Joshua	123,125
. Peter	54,167
. Thos. C.H.	198
Mills,T.C.	129
Minafee,Joseph	39
Minton,Zachariah	198
Mirchell,Sam'l	158
Mitchel,Saml.	170
Mitchell,Col.	168
. M.D.	142
. Marmaduke	134
. Mr.	243,245
. Richd.	194
Moffatt,Robert	182
Molder,Jacob	222
Montgomery,Esther	213
. John A.	198
. Robert	219,224
. Robt.	214
. Stewart	198
. Thomas	170
. Widow	219,224
. William ?	198
Moody,Alexander	84,87
William	23
Moon,Alex. B.	194
John P.	194
Moore,Carlos	166
. Charles R.	226
. David	230
. Green M.	166
. Harmon	163
. Henry	26,54,226
. J.A.	191
. James	54,222,230
. Jennings	191
. John	167
. John A.	167
. John Sr.	54
. Margaret	226
. Mary	230
. Michael	126,219,224
.	226
. Randolph	54
. Samuel H.	184
. Serad	180
. Thomas	32,40,84,134
.	222
. Widow	42
Moran,Samuel H.	174
Morgan,Andw.	236
. Benjamin B.	240
. Jacob	222
. James	134,167
. John	180,184
. M.A.	180
. Mrs. S.	180
. Ridley	184
. Robert G.	240
. William	222
Morphis,David	213
Morris,Allen	217
. Austin P.	184
. Daniel	168,171,173
. Henry	203,206
. James	174

Name	Page	Name	Page	Name	Page	Name	Page
. James B.	235	. Jacob	222	. John S.	160	. John T.	171
. Jesse	194	. Jesse	219,227	Neils,Col.	157	. Sefaney S.	171
. Jno.	191	. John	163	Nelson,Adam	243	. Thomas	164,167,175
. John	217	. John T.	232	. John	123-124,171	. W.B.	129
. Thomas	235	. Joseph C.	222	. Moses	167	. William	171
. Willis J.	199	. Orvill	163	. Robert	230	Nowlin,Armstead	217
. Zenor C.	191	. Richard	163	. William	243	. Benjamin	177
Morrison,A.W.	230	. Saml.	236	Newman,Anthony	110	. David	210
. Jane H.	230	. Thomas	230	William C.	90	. Eliz	210
. Jas. W.	187	Musgrave,Jas.	226	Newsom,Randolph	233	. Jabus	219,222,224
. John	54,137	. Joshua	63,222	. Sterling	180	. James R.	176
. Robert	137	. Samuel	32	. William	37,133,142	. John	224
. Ziza	232	. Thomas	222	Newsome,Sterling	38	. Thomas	177
Morrow,James	159	Musgraves,Samuel	23	Newson,Allen	230	Nunn,Thomas	191
Morten,Charles P.	206	Musgrove,Samuel	59,67,88	. Thomas	180	. Wm. R.	191
. John O.	206		94,109	Newton,Ebenezer	214	Nutt,David	247
. Joseph	206	Mustain,Shadrick	208,212	. John	243	. Jesse	247
Morton,A.B.	143,180	Shadrock	210	. Mr.	98	. Murphy	247
. Jacob	176,180	Myers,Abraham	163	. Nicholas	243	O'Meal,Wm. Sen.	222
. John	203	. John	163	. Rev. Geo.	37,180	O'Mahundro,Wm.	133
. Joseph	230	. Jonas	163	Nicholas,Arthur	247	O'Neal,Isham	217,222
. Josiah	217	. Mr.	162	. Jno. T.	222	. James H.	217
. William	232	Mysenhammer,Mr.	175	. John	243	. Jno.	217,222
Moseley,Isham	232	Mysenhemmer,Mr.	171	Nichols,Alfred	184	. Jno. P.	222
. Jas.	198	Nailor,John	174	. Coleman	171	. Moses	217
. John	232	Woodfin	174	. Isaac	174	. Timothy	50
. Jonathan	232	Nall,John	120	. Jackson	194	. Wiley J.	217
. William	232	Nance,Hon.	230	. Jacob	160	. William Jr.	222
Mosely,James	54	. Reuben	133	. Jeremmiah B.	184	. Willie Sen.	222
Moses,Phillip	203	. Richard	187	. Nathan	184	Oakley,M.W.	217
Mosley,E.A.	158,168	Narran,Francis E.	171	. Thomas	171	Stanford T.	199
. Ed. A.	170	Nash,Colonel Francis	2	Nickens,Andrew	199	Oaks,Hezekiah	133
. Edwd. A.	159	. George W.	210	. Calvin	199	Odum,Mr.	210
. Jonathan	30	. James C.	174	. Lamb	199	Ogilvie,William	137
. Mr.	160	. Travis C.	174,184	. Samuel	199	Oglevie,Archibald	203
. Thomas	159	Neadlett,Mr.	180	Nicks,Doak	77	. Elizabeth	203
. Thomas B.	159	Nease,Mr.	237,245	George	77	. Geo. W.	217
. Thos. B.	170	Neatherly,John	203	Nix,Thomas S.	210	. James	194
Moss,Eli	247	. Robert	203	William	206	. Jason W.	199
. Felix	247	. William	203	Noblett,Abraham	236	. William	194
. James	222	Neece,Sampson	236	. Isaac	236	Olive,Sarah	233
. Matthew	247	Neeley,Elias	217	. Sarah	236	Oliver,Wright	222
. Matthew Sen.	247	. Elijah	243	. Wm.	236	Omohundro,James Y.	184
. Samuel	222	. George	217	Noblin,Samuel J.	217	Orr,Alexr.	214
Moxfred,Hiram	184	. Green T.	222	Norman,David	180	. Col. John	217
Mullins,A.E.	129	. James G.	184	. John F.	236	. David	177
. David	236	. Moses	243	. Jonathan	236	. James	55
. James	167	. Samuel	180	. Robert	226	. Jno.	206
. Jordan	235	. Thomas	217	Norris,Ezekiel	16,19,137	. John	175,177,182,206
. Joseph	54	. William	243	Norsworthy,James	55	. John Sen.	214
. Matthew	167	Neese,Susannah	199	Norton,Dr.	158	. Joseph C.	214
. Richd.	235	William	247	William	160	. L.B.	177,180
. Thomas R.	243	Neil,C.R.	203	Norvell,Esq. James	78	. Mr.	210
. William	167	. Geo. C.	214	. George	74	. Robert Sen.	214
Murdock,Hiram	199	. J.H.S.	203	. James	75	. Robt. J.	214
. Thomas Jun.	203	. James H.	107,217	. James Sr.	75	. Robt. Jun	214
. Thomas Sen.	203	. Jno. L. Jun.	214	. John	72	. Samuel	214
Murkison,Murdock	134	. John C.	203	. Mary	75	. W.D.	206,208
Murphree,Cader	168,171	. John T.	180,222	. Mary Knott	75	. William	29-30
. Davis	238	. Joseph	222	. William	73-74,84,87	. William D.	214,233
. William	173,240	. Newton F.	222	Norvile,JohnH.	171	. Wm. D.	210
Murphry,Stephen	134	. W.L.	203	Norvill,Mary	24	. Wm. N.	177
Murphy,John	222	. William	203	William	23-25	Orrick,James	243
Neil	222	Neile,Nicholas	133	Norville,C.M.	129	Ortner,Jesse	236
Murray,Francis	133	Neill,A.	217	. David	171	Phebe	236
James Sr.	54	. Andrew	222	. David Jr.	167	Osburn,Abner	233
Murry,Francis	39,142	. Ann	217	. David Sr.	167	. Daniel	226
Henry	38	. Col. John L.	158	. E.M.B.	167	. G.G.	163
Muse,George	158,161,168	. George	217	. James	167,171	. John	206,210
. George P.	163	. James	222	. Jno. W.	171	. Mr.	205
. Isaac	163-164	. James D.	222	. John Sen.	171	. R.T.	163

Name	Page	Name	Page	Name	Page	Name	Page
. Willie W.	233	Patton, Colonel	2	. Samuel B.	90	. Presley	244
Osteen, Benjamin	191	. Ann	17,89	. Thomas	180	. Ranson	195
. David	55	. B.F.	226	. William	236	. Simeon	195
. Edward	191	. Daniel	51	. Wm.	233	. T.A.	129
. Samuel	226	. David	236	Philpot, C.T.	180	. Tazey	78
Outlaw, Alexander	24-25	. James	22,24,36,51-52	Pickens, Wm. M.	230	. Thomas	195,243
	28,50,73-74,127		55,67,84,87,110,133	Pickle, Henry	222	. William	243
Overcast, John	174	.	142	. James	222	Privit, Berys	226
Overton, John	50	. James W.	233	. John	222	Proby, James	180
Mr.	167	. Jane	4,51-52,203	. Major	222	Pruett, Willis	129
Owen, Ephraim	174	. Jane Shaw	51	. Murray	30	Pryor, Norton	50,110,112
Robert	206	. John	55,233	Pinkerton, Hugh	187	Puckett, Elam	188
Owens, David	133	. Joseph	236	. Wm.	191	William S.	188
Travis W.	194	. S.M.	180	. Wm. Sen.	191	Purdam, George	211
Pace, Richmond	167	. Samuel	18,24,30	Pinkston, Wm.	195	Purdy, Thomas J.	177
Pannell, L.D.	199	. Samuel Sr.	17,30,89	Pinson, Jno. B.	180	Puryear, Robert	247
Panton, John	211	. Thomas	51	John B.	39	Putman, Bazil	199
Pardee, Miles	218	Paulden, William	177	Pitts, Isaac	171	. Danl.	195
Parkason, Alfred	184	Paxton, Jno. F.	211	Knox	37,65	. Hiram	195
Joab	184	Payne, Ann	82	Poe, Terry	47,114	. James W.	199
Parker, Charles H.	243	. Harrison	226	Polk, John	236	. John	218
. Elijah	62,247	. J.D.	129	. Maj. Gen. Leonidas	57	. Michal	191
. Elijah Esq.	243	. M.	129	. William	110,150	. Sarah	226
. Elizabeth	184	. Moses	163	Pollock, Jno. M.	195	Pyland, Bennett	218
. James H.	243	. Mrs.	83	. William	244	. Bluford	218
. Jonathan	244	. Widow	14,22-24,26-27	. Zachariah	244	. Cullin	217
. Joseph	236	.	91	Pope, Hardy	191	. James	218
. Rev. J.C.	180	. Widow Ann	89	Quinn	191	. William	218
. Susan	223	Peacock, John Jun.	171	Poplin, Wm.	191	Quisenberry,	
. Timothy	171	. Mr.	175	Porter, John	36	. William A.	87
Parks, James P.	236	. Tho. A.	171	. John N.	142,230	. William M.	22,84
. Jefferson	233	. Thomas J.	171	. Nathaniel	64,126	Rackley, Jackson	184
. John	230	. Thos. A.	168,171	. Samuel	36,142	Radford, Henry	230
. Joshua	233	. William J.	171	. Stephen	226	. J.W.	203
. Robert	230	Pearson, James	222	Potter, Wm.	230	. Saml.	204
Parkson, Richd.	188	. John	222	Pounds, John	195	Rager, James	236
Parnell, Gideon	218	. Kindred Esq.	244	Wm.	191	Ragsdale, Baxter	55,171
. Henry	218	. Sarah	244	Powdille, Mr.	217	. D.M.	160
. Mr.	218	. William	55,243	Powdrill, Thomas	217	. David A.B.	167
. Reiley	218	Penland, Mr.	237,241	Powell, John	171,244	. Edward	133
Parr, Jonathan	127	Penn, John	218	. Robert	188	. Henry M.	167
Parrish, Abraham	226	Perry, Isaac	199	. Tho.	157	. John	204
Isaac	233	Willie Esq.	191	. Thomas	185,203	. John W.	160
Parson, George	133	Pettis, Garrison	211	. Thos. P.	187	Rainey, B.G.	204
. Thomas	133,175	Thomas	180	Pratt, Henry	240	. Capt.	201
. Thos.	182	Peyton, John	47,114	James	240	. Captain	196
Parsons, Abijah	184	Phelps, Amos	211	Presgrove, Jno. M.	187	. Isaac N.	203
. George W.	184	Phifer, C.	132	William	184	. Isaac Sen.	203
. Michael H.	184	. Caleb	60,110,130	Pressgrove, Andrew	184	. Jesse G.	204
Paschal, James	222	. M	132	Prewitt, Michael	60	. John	55
Patten, Elisha A.	199	. Martin	110,177,184	. Moses	35	. Stephen	203
. James	230	. Mr.	171	. P.H.	240	Rains, Captain John	5,147
. Joseph	230	Phillips, Allen	236	Price, Franklin B.	174	Rambow, Elias	211
Patterson, Andrew	199	. Benjamin	236	. James K.	226	. F.K.	211
. Elijah	167	. Calvin	230	. Jesse	226	. Samuel	214
. Fitzeller	199	. Charlott	191	. Jno. H.	199	Ramsey, David	214
. George	203	. Garrett	177	. Mathis	174	. Robert	199
. Housten	199	. Ivey	191	. Reece	133	. Samuel	214
. Isaac	167	. James	167,230	. Thomas	174	. Solomon	211
. James	201,203,214	. Jefferson	236	Primrose, Geo. W.	188	Ramsy, John	218
. James Sen.	203	. Jesse	177,230,236	. Thomas	187	Randall, Griffin	230
. Jas.	157	. John	62,226-227	. William	187	Raney, Bennett C.	244
. Jno.	203	. John Jun.	230	Prince, Asa	195,243	. Henry K.	236
. John	203,226	. John Sen.	230	. Cary	195	. John	240
. Robert Jun.	199	. Lemuel	236	. Elijah	199	. John W.	236
. Robert Sen.	199	. Matthew	133	. Hosea	195	. Peter	236
. Robt. A.	214	. Matthew Esq.	177	. Jeremiah	243	. Thomas	236
. Robt. S.	199	. Miles	230	. Joshua	199	Rankin, Richd. D.	214
. Thomas	211	. Mr.	219,224,227	. Lytleton	195	Thos. C.	188
. William W.	167	. Rich'd	105-106	. Miles	195	Rankins, Thomas C.	136
. Wm. L.	199	. Samuel	38,167	. Owen	199	Ransom, Alford	191

Name	Page
. Benjamin C.	130-131
. Benjamin F.	131
. W.K.	131
. William King	131
Raus, Frederick	62
Rawling, Hosey	133
Ray, Alexander	226
. Charles	222
. David	195
. George M.	227
. Hezekiah	244
. Hugh	218
. James	26,137
. James M.	230
. Jas.	226
. Jason	244
. Jennet	227
. John	189,191-192,227
. Mr.	241
. Robt.	195
. Sarah	195
. Thomas	195,244
. William	244
Rayburn, Jos. M.	163
Reach, Willie	177
Read, William	133
Reager, A.W.	236
Abraham	236
Reagor, Anthony	55
Reavis, David	55
Record, James C.	104,211
Reed, A.R.	215
. Alex. B.	212,218
. And.	237
. Andrew	231,240
. Esq.	208
. Hannah	203
. James Esq.	211
. John	55,212,215,218
. John H.	211
. Mathew Jr.	29
. Robert	29
. Samuel D.	203
. William	29
. Wilson C.	244
Reese, James R.	244
William	244
Reeves, Absalum	195
. Archibald	236
. Benjamin	240
. Isham	240
. John H.	233
. William	240
Reid, James	98
. Robert	240
. Thomas C.	171
Revis, David	227
Johnson	227
Reynolds, Ezekiel	55,195
. Jane	236
. John	195,199
. Michael	222
. Richd.	236
Rice, Claibourne	240
John	240
Richards, David	230
William	230
Ricketts, James H.	174
Rickman, Jno.	199
. John A.	199
. Lawson	199

Name	Page
. Len A.	199
Riddle, Samuel	214
Stephen	244
Rideout, Mr.	98
Rigg, Gideon	87
Riggins, Willie	247
Riggs, Adams	233
. Gideon	203
. James M.	199
. Widow	196,201
Rigs, C. Jacob	77
Riley, J.A.	203
. J.W.	203
. John	204
. Robert	230
Ring, Lewis	204
Ringstaff, Jno.	180
Rippy, John	167
Roane, Henry	206
. Levi	206
. William	174,177,233
Robenett, Alfred	160
. Jesse Jr.	160
. Jesse Sen.	160
Roberson, A.	157
. Alexander	227
. David	180
. James	178
. John	175,178
. Joseph	180
Robert, Alexander	171
Roberts, Bright	199
. George	78
. John	226
. John H.	199
. Levi C.	36,142
. Minton	222
. Nathanl.	236
. Peter	226
. Rezin	226
. Thomas	237,241,244
. William	163
. Zachariah	247
Robertson, Col.	149
. Col. James	148
. David	84,87
. General James	9
. James	5,147
. John	236
. Thomas	247
. William	226
Robeson, James Jr.	160
. John	204
. John Esq.	160
. John Sen.	160
. Margaret	167
. Michael	203
. Nancy	167
Robey, H.	174
Robinson, Alexr.	230
. David	23,26
. James	180,203
. John	26,55,180,204,230
. Joseph	26
. Michael	26
. William	204
Robison, John	55
Rodgers, Bedford	195
. David R.	195
. Dennis	240
. Drury	171

Name	Page
. Erwin	188
. George	199
. James	195,214
. John	195,218
. John M.	195
. Joseph	195
. Peter	199
. Saml.	195
. Thos. D.	192
. William	171
Rogers, Elijah	195
. Jesse	240
. John J.	240
. Joseph	55
. Mr.	240
. William	168,174
Rose, William	163
Ross, James	247
. John P.	236
. Thomas Esq.	211
. Thos.	104
Rosson, John	204
. Jos.	203
. Joseph	203
. Osburn	203
Rotrammel, Abraham	236
John	236
Routen, Abram	160
Rowe, Dr. Joseph	62
Rowland, A.	177
Harrison S.	174
Rozer, David	236
Rucker, Elliott	188
. James	192
. Jesse	188
. Saml. R.	160
. William	188
Rue, Jefferson	204
Rumsey, James	199
Rushiing, Elijah	177
Rushing, Abel	185,188,192
. Asa	195
. E.D.	192
. Jno.	188
. John	182,185
. Keziah	191
. Peter	78
. Thomas	77,171
. Wilson E.	171
Russell, Chas. B.	230
. James	39
. Jas. R.	230
. Jno. M.	227
. John	218
. Lewis	240
. Thomas	227
. William	227,244
. William B.	174
. Wm. M.	230
Ruston, Elijah	211
Ruth, G.W.	180
John W.	100
Rutherford, Henry	21,137
Rutledge, Elijah	137
Sack, John	55
Sample, W.P.	72
Sandford, Joseph	180
Sark, John	55
Thomas	133
Sarrett, Samuel	55
Saunders, Alex.	177

Name	Page
. Gabriel	218
. George	184
. John	185
. Julius	11-12
. Mr.	205,212
. Nathan	185
. Susannah	185
. Wm. J.	204
Saxon, Benjamin	195
Scales, Noah	230
Schooler, Nathan H.	177
.	180
. Nathaniel	35,39
Scott, Elias	200
. Elijah G.	163
. George R.	200
. James	200
. Jeremiah	174
. Jesse	174
. Jno.	200
. John Esq.	163
. John H.	247
. John W.	174
. Joshua P.	163
. William	163
Scraggs, Jas.	171
Matt	171
Scruggs, David	247
. John E.	163
. Mary	163
. Samuel	247
Scudder, Eliz. S.	240
. Elizabeth	199
. Elizabeth S.	199
. James S.	107
Searse, David	174
Seaton, Ryan	214
Sebastian, Saml.	133
Sent, John	236
Sexton, Jesse	244
Robert B.	244
Shaddy, Jacob Jun.	230
. Jacob Sen.	230
. Peter	230
Shanks, Charles	180
. John T.	38
. Jos. S.	180
Shapard, Booker	180
Mr.	180
Sharp, Andw. D.	211
. James	127
. John	167
. Joseph P.	223
. William	50,160
. William Esq.	167
. William Jun.	167
Sharpe, Alexander	174
Sharpr, Anderson	167
Shaw, C.G.W.B.	160
. Christopher	55
. James	218
. John	195
. Mary	160
. R.C.C.P.	160
. Richard L.	218
. William M.	195
Shearin, Matthew	195
. Thomas	223
. Wm.	195
Shelby, Evan	33,59,90
. Isaac	7,33,90

Name	Page
. John	50
Shepard, James	204
Sherrill, George	247
Sherwood, Hugh	192
Joseph	129
Ship, Elizabeth	240
Shipman, Daniel	48,62,127
. Danl.	247
. James	247
. Reuben	247
. Wm.	247
Shoddy, Robert	241
Shofner, Austin	167,244
. Frederick	247
. Gabriel	247
. John	167
. Loton	167
. Martin	55,244,247
. Mr.	241
. P.L.	247
. Peter	237,241,245
. William	247
Shook, Abram	244
. John	244
. Jonathan	244
. Levi	244
. William	244
Short, William	195
Shote, Arthur	133
Shuffield, Arthur	192,200
. Jason B.	200
. John	199
. John A.	200
Sides, Henry	214
Sikes, Thomas Aldridge	55
Siles, Mary	200
Simar, John	192
Simmons, Cyrus	227
Simpler, Andrew J.	247
Simpson, Jno. W.	192
. John W.	188
. Mr.	192
Sims, Briggs G.	218
. John	127,233
. Martin	223
. Mr.	196
. Richard H.	233
. Robert W.	218
. Swepson	188
. Walter	137,200
. William	223
. Wm. H.	129
Singleton, Allen	240
Peter	62,194,240
Skipper, Benjamin	135
Slaton, James	55
Martha	163
Smalling, Elizabeth	171
Smiley, Hugh B.	227
. Matt A.	240
. Matthew A.	233
. Willis H.	233
Smith, Alexander	233
. Allen J.	233
. Amon	195
. Andrew	200
. Barry	195
. Benjamin	200
. D.M.	233
. Daniel	2
. E.D.	204
. Edward	167
. George	163
. George Jun.	195
. George Sen.	195
. George Sr.	55
. Harbert	233
. Hardy S.	177
. Henry	204
. James	171,192
. James P.	192
. Jno. E.	195
. John	163,204,247
. John Sr.	62
. Major Daniel	8
. Meredith	174
. Morgan	177
. Mr.	215,219
. Reizen	227
. Robert	23,94,110
. Robert W.	31,96
. Robert Washington	94
. Samuel	204
. Thomas	77,160,171,204
	227
. William	11,55
. Work	206
Smitherman, Sarah	188
Thos.	188
Smithson, Benjamin W.	171
Smothers, James	188
Snell, Charles	133
. Curtis	137
. John A.	211
. Mr.	240
. R.	157
. Roger	230-231,233
. Willie B.	240
Snelling, Hugh	167
. John	36
. Lemuel	167
Snoddy, Mr.	241
Robert	234,237,244
Solomon, Willie	233
Spand, Robt. L.	244
Spears, James	247
. Nathan	247
. Saml. F.	200
. Saml. T.	200
. Samuel	55
Spence, Rancher	188
Spoffard, Mr.	180
Springer, Dennis	184
. Josiah	174
. Mr.	185
. N.W.	185
. Zadock	184
Spruce, Phillip	188
Sriver, Abraham	167
John J.	167
Stafford, Josiah J.	55
Staggs, James	230
Unity	230
Stallings, John	223
Wm.	223
Stallions, William	218
Stamps, Wm. D.	223
Stanfield, John	247
Stanley, John	200
Steel, Margaret	17
Volney H.	188
Steele, Carlos D.	184
. John P.	184
. Jos.	174
. Joseph	174,184
. P.C.	129
. Price C.	174,185
. Wilson	185
Stegall, Jesse	218
Ralph	200
Stem, Asa	192
Stephen, John	163
Thomas	163
Stephens, Augustine	180
. Dabs. G.	218
. Daniel	129,163
. James Jun.	204
. James Sen.	204
. Jeremiah	204
. John	129
. Martha	233
. Ransom	233
. Redding	200,223
. Richard	160
. William	160
. Willie	233
. Wilson	230
Stephenson, D.G.	223
. Edward	223
. Geo. W.	192,223
. John	223
. Jos.	206
. Richard P.	223
. Sarah	160
. William	233
. Wm. H.	223
Stevens, Ervin	240
John	248
Stewart, Chas. E.	244
. G.H.	180
. Grayson	177
. John	223,230
. Saml.	236
. William	214,240
Still, Joel H.	247
. Mr.	247
Stilwell, Eleazor	211
Elias	205-206,208,211
Stinson, William	233
Stockden, L.D.	214
Stokes, David	206
. John	167
. Kinchen	47,50,167
Stollard, Joseph P.	174
Stone, Billy	82
. James	244
. John	35-37,55,133,142
. Uriah	3,146-147
. William	133
. William S.	218
. Willie B.	177
Stong, Thomas	195
Story, James	180
Mr.	180
Stovall, J.A.	171
. Jackson W.	188
. Saml. Jr.	171
Strator, Adam	189,192,195
Stratten, William	192
Street, Mary	204
Streeter, John	233
Strickler, Benjamin	143
Stringer, James	133
Strong, George	74
Joseph C. Jun.	180
Strother, General John	45
John	135
Stroud, Bethel	163
Hodge	163
Stuart, Oth'l.	206
Stuckart, Absalom	192
Sugg, Aquilla	171
. Davidson	171
. Edmund	78,195
. Harbert	78
. James	171
. John H.	78
. Micajah	171
. Nehemiah	171
. Thomas	78
. Timothy	47,78
. William	123,157
. William Jun.	171
. William Sen.	171
. Wm.	78
Suggs, Thomas	163
William	168
Suiter, William	240
William E.	167
Sullivan, Alfred	227
Summer, Samuel	133
Suton, Charles F.	171
. John Jun.	171
. John Sen.	171
Sutten, Samuel	167
Sutton, James	160
. John	160,175,236,240
. John Jr.	164,168,171
. John Sen.	180
. M.B.	180
. Thomas	236
. Wm. B.	161
Swan, Alex. H.	211
Swanson, William C.	227
Swift, Flower	180
. Jacob	180
. Thomas W.	180
Sykes, Jonas	189,192,195
Tacke, John	55
Talbot, Mathew	11
. Ruth	12
. Thomas	30,55,143
. Thomas Rollins	55
Talleafairo, Charles	231
Tally, Abram	211
. Berry	211
. William	211
Tankersly, David	208
John	208
Tarpley, Edward	188
Tatum, Absolom	7
Taylor, Charles	55,177
. Frederick	204
. Henry	204
. James	200
. Jas. P.	106
. John	168
. Lewis	218
. N.	139
. Nathaniel	23,135-136
. Robert	188
. Stephen	192
. William	192
. Winston	160

Name	Page
Wm. G.	188
Tedrow, John C.	160
Temple, Anne	152
. Anne Elizabeth	152
. D.P.	180,223
. Dempsey P.	151
. Dr. William P.	152
. Eliza	180
. L.C.	180,233
. Mary	151
. Robert	134,180
. William	151
. William A.	152
Templeton, Mr.	227,234
Terry, Dorothy M.	180
. Henry	230
. Henry B.	200
. James R.	36
. Jas. R.	180
. Keeble	36-37
. Kibble	240
. Vincent	192
. Vincent S.	200
Thomas, Anthony	158,160
.	168
. David	171
. James	231
. Jonathan	218
. Mark	231
. R.S.	171
. Richard S.	123,125
. William	160,171
. Winne	171
Thomason, Wm. T.	192
Thomborough, Allen	200
Thompson, Abraham	38,211
. Balaim	223
. Benjamin	211
. Calvin	195
. Christiana	185
. Elizabeth	196
. H.L.	180
. Henry	211
. Hugh	211
. James	154,192,204
. Jas. Esq.	196
. Jas. P.	196
. Jno. A.	196
. Joe	205
. John	164,185,223,233
. John F.	223
. John Sen.	196
. John Theophillis	55
. Jos.	100,196
. Joseph	16,39
. Joseph H.	100,107
. Joseph M.	107
. Joseph P.	218
. L.C.	188
. Martha	196
. Moses	211
. Mr.	196
. N. Sen.	180
. Newcome	30
. Newcum	42,231
. Pinckney H.	196
. Saml.	180
. Samuel	29,230
. Squire	37
. Theophilus	18
. Thomas	56,136
Thorn, Harbert	223
. Wm.	231
. James	168
. William Jr.	223
. William Sen.	223
Throgmorton, B.	164
. Wm.	164
Thronberry, Levi	168
. Lewis	168
Throneberry, Benjamin	164
Mr.	196
Tilford, David	195
J.W.	129
Tillamon, Mr.	180
Tilman, John	160
Saml. T.	208
Timmons, Ambrose	248
Charles	248
Tindall, James	164
Tipper, William	56
Tolbot, Thomas	38
Tolliver, Charles	160
William	160
Towell, Jesse F.	227
Townsend, Joshua	240
Towson, John	56
Trammell, W.T.	168
Trammill, David	164
Tribble, James C.	244
. Melches.	240
. Michael	233
. William	233
Trice, John	231
Mr.	227,231
Trollinger, Jacob	223
. John	240
. Joseph	223
Trot, Enoch	240
Troxler, Anthony	248
. Isaac	248
. Jacob	48,240,248
. Nicholas	248
Truman, William	248
Truslove, Zepaniah	164
Tucker, David	56,174
. George W.	218
. James	134
. Jesse P.	174
. John W.	218
. Kinchen	188
. Mr.	175
. William	218
. Wm. E.	196
Tull, Josiah B.	204
Tullop, Mr.	177
Tune, Demarcus	177
. John	177
. Thomas	177
Turman, John C.	244
Turnage, Mr.	220
Turner, Henry	244,248
. James	211
. John	248
. Joseph R.	204
. Littleberry	188
. Rebecca	244
. Wesley	244
. William	200,211
Turpin, Henry	231
Matthew	177
Turrentine, Alexander	137
. Archelaus	196
. Charles	185
. Daniel	142
. Felix	195
. James	182,192
. James Jun.	196
. James Sen.	195
. Major Samuel	137
. Mr.	99
. Samuel	137
. Samuel A.	56
. Wilson	185
Twitty, Leonard	211
Whitfield	214
Vance, David	21,208
Vancleave, Thomas	171
Vanderow, Francis	161
Vannoy, Andrew	164
Vanwee, Isaac	182
Vaugh, Willis	171
Venable, Andw.	204
. John	204
. Larkin	204
. Richard	204
. Simeon	204
. Thomas	227
Verner, Ezl. E.	208
Vernon, E.E.	205
Ezl.	205
Vernor, E.E.	208,212
Vest, Sabrel	157
Samuel	196,200
Victory, Andw.	192
Jonathan	192
Vincent, Jacob	196
. Susannah	208
. William	208
Wade, Charles E.	196
. Edw. Jr.	134
. Edward	39,90
. Martin F.	182
. Maslin	188
. Nathan	182
. William	188,196
. Willliam	182
Wadley, Geo. W.	196
Waite, G.	165
. George	28,237
. Magdalena	168
. William	50,171
Waits, Mrs.	161
Walbanks, Bazel	185
Walker, Callaway	240
. Dr. Thomas	2,146
. Edward	204
. Isaac W.	212,218
. J.W.	215
. James	39,164,196,200
.	215,244
. James T.	218
. Jas.	212
. John	204,237
. John G.	161
. Jos.	39
. Joseph	23,25,37,56,84
.	88,127
. L.D.	240
. P.M.	161
. Robert	182
. William	164,174,237
Wall, David	200
John	134
Wallace, Evan	188
. John	240
. Joseph	137
. Matthew	204
. William	204
Wallis, Allen	171
. John	205
. Matthew	56
Walls, Anderson	188
. Benjamin	188
. John	192
. William	164
Walsh, Elizabeth	241,244
Walter, Robt. W.	219
Ward, Burwell	192
. Ezekiel	192
. Spias	192
. Wyatt	248
Wardlow, Hugh	182
Warner, Eunice	233
. John	26,38
. John Sen.	223
. Mrs.	178
. Mrs. Eunice	182
. Richard	218-219
. Widow	175
Warren, Benjamin	237
. Charles A.	107
. John	171
. Montgomery	233
. Rebecca	168
. William	171,200,218
Warrener, Joseph	200
Watkins, John M.	188
. Thos. G.	177
. William A.	248
. Willis B.	182
Watson, D.	174
. Jesse	174
. John	237
. Mr.	234,241
. Nathan	177
. Saml. M.	208
. Walter	244
. William	177
Watterson, Wm. L.	182
Watts, Mr.	180
Waxter, David	164
Weakley, Robert	15,21,64
Weaver, David	248
. Jno. S.	211
. Sarah	248
. William	77,175
. Zephaniah	248
Webb, Bushrod	188
. Isiah	174
. Jesse	218
. John	227
. John A.	188
. John M.	57
. William	174
. William R.	57
Webster, Henry	248
. Jonathan	35
. Mr.	219
Welch, Charles	211
. H.B.	211
. John James B.	164
. Mr.	243
. William	211

Name	Page	Name	Page	Name	Page	Name	Page
Weldon, William	204	Wilhoit, Jacob	56	. Jonathan	204	. Edmund	237
Wells, J.B.	204	Wilhoite, John	233	. Joseph	192	. Thomas	237
. Mary	204	. Joseph D.	143	. Joseph W.	200	. William	237,244
. W.R.	204	. Mary	237	. Josiah	200,204	Work, Alex.	175
West, Isaac	168	. Mr.	182	. Josiah Jun.	204	. Alexander	188
. Joshua F.	171	. Pearce	200,237	. Marcus	204	. May	174
. William	142	. William	182,233	. Mary	185	Worke, Alexander	151
Westerman, Clifford	223	. Willie	237	. Moses	200	Worley, Moses	214
William	223	. Willis W.	182	. Nancy	196	Wortham, Edward	196
Westmoreland, Robt.	200	Wilkerson, Debarry	218	. Robert	200	. James	182
Vincent	134	. Mr.	217	. Robt.	200,214	. William	196
Wheat, Josiah	223	Wilkes, Jesse M.	237	. Saml.	200	Wrught, John O.	214
Wheeler, America	188	Miner	174	. Samuel	200,223,237	Wynn, Kibble T.	240
. Jesse	192	Wilkinson, Mr.	152	. Thomas	192	Wynne, Ridley B.	177
. Martin	185	Wilkorison, John	208	. Thos.	205	Yancy, A.W.	182
. Mr.	185	Willes, William N.	185	. Widow	157,193	. David	227
. Nathan	188	Williams, Alfred	192	. William	196	. Henry	100
. Samuel	192	. Bayer	211	. William W.	240	. Kavanaugh	182
. Thomas	185	. Charles	244	Windrow, Henry	37	Yarboro, George	219
. William	137,185	. D. Wm.	205	Winsett, Elijah D.	192	Yarborough, H.D.	208
Wheelhouse, Dennis	188	. D.M.	182	. Jarman	177	. Reuben	208
Whelman, Edward	185	. Edmond	40	. Robert	177	. Samuel	208
Whinning, Joshua	237	. Elijah	175	Winstead, Samuel	218	Yates, Elias	164
White, Aden	223	. Elisha	134	Winston, Wm. D.	200	Samuel	164
. Augustus H.	171	. Isaac	134,237	Winters, Joh. W.	192	Yeates, Joshua	233
. B.G.	171	. James	137,200,205,208	Wisener, Martin	214	William	231
. James G.	219	. Jesse E.	223	Wisner, W.H.	182	Yeatman, Thomas	143
. John R.	182	. John	56,78,164,248	Wommack, Hawkins	237	Yell, Alex tC.	168
. Joshua	137	. John Jr.	231	Michael	237,240	. Archibald	130
. Moses	177	. Joseph	196	Wood, Abslom	161	. Moses	37,50
. Mr.	200	. Moses	177	. Andrew C.	244	. Pearcy	157,164,168
. Nathaniel	231	. Nathl.	134	. Hugh	219	Young, Abijah	241
. Sion	223	. Patrick	248	. James	77,219	. Acton	168
. Sorrell	218	. Patrick W.	164	. Jas. B.	196	. Alexr.	182
. Thomas	196	. Phillip	174	. Jno. P.	196	. Asa	241
. William	244	. Richard	218	. John	56,185	. Edward	134
. Wm. S.	231	. Robt.	214	. Jonathan	196	. J.	167
Whitehead, John	73-74	. Stephens	241	. Peter	218	. James Esq.	168
Mansfield	192	. T.T.	182	. R.W.	168	. William A.	39
Whiteside, Jenkin	50	. Wallis	177	. W.D.	30	. Wm. A.	182
. Lewis	233	. William	104,171,188	. William	27,78,85,88	Younger, John B.	168
. Mr.	233		211,214		106,161,208	Yowell, Joel	104
. T.C.	168	. William F.	204	. William G.	168		
. Thomas C.	107,143	. Wm.	241	. William H.	208		
. Thos.	168	Williamson, Jno.	218	. Wm.	93		
. Thos. C.	182	Mary	218	. Zadoc	56		
Whitfield, F.M.	248	Willis, D.	157	. Zadock	168		
Travis	227	. David	208	Woodard, Garman	227		
Whitman, Robert	241	. Davis	211	. George	237		
Whitney, James G.	182	. Phillip	237	. John	227,237		
Whitsell, G.W.	231	Wills, James M.	204	Woodfin, Hannah	175		Index By
. Jno. Jr.	231	Wilson, Aaron C.	205	Nicholas	56		Timothy J. Edwards
. John Sen.	231	. Archibald	237	Woods, Allen N.	219		
Whitson, David	98	. Augustine	196	. Edmond	188		
Whitthorne,		. Capt.	201	. F.H.	214		
. William J.	142	. Captain	196	. Francis B.	214		
. Wm. J.	218	. David	15,114,137	. Francis H.	214		
Whitworth, B.F.	200	. Ebenezer	185	. James	185		
. Edw.	200	. Elizabeth	237	. James L.	214		
. Jacob	134	. Fordic	185	. James Sen.	214		
. Samuel	171	. H.S.	185	. Joseph	39		
Whorley, Joel	233	. Hiram	204	. Peter	205,208		
Wiggins, Harrell	231	. James	185,200,237	. Saml. W.	214		
. Hundley	233	. Jane	28,89	. Samuel	214		
. Jno. W.	231	. Jas. C.	200	. Thomas	218		
Wiggs, Needham	208	. Jas. S.	185	. William	27,88,94-95		
Wilbourn, William	23,84	. Jno. H.	200	Woosley, Aaron	56		
	88	. John	15,114,137,139	. Elijah	240		
Wilburn, William	26		200,218,231	. Joshua	240		
Wilcox, J.R.	182	. John C.	196	. William	240		
Wilder, David W.	211	. John H.	205	Word, Ann	174		

www.ingramcontent.com/pod-product-compliance
Lightning Source LLC
Chambersburg PA
CBHW020636300426
44112CB00007B/129